TEXAS
LOUISIANA
MISSISSIPPI
ALABAMA
Sabine R.
New Orleans
Galveston
N
Río Grande
Nueva Laredo
Brownsville
Matamoros
NUEVO LEON
Carmen
Monterrey
Saltillo
TAMAULIPAS
Ciudad Victoria
Sierra Madre Oriental
Tampico
San Luis Potosí
QUERÉTARO
Guanajuato
HIDALGO
Pachuca
VERACRUZ
Jalapa
Mexico City
MEXICO
TLAXCALA
Tlaxcala
FED. DIST.
Toluca
Puebla
Mt. Orizaba
Fortín
Cuernavaca
PUEBLA
MORELOS
Taxco
Veracruz
Gulf of Mexico
GUERRERO
Chilpancingo
Sierra Madre del Sur
Acapulco
OAXACA
Oaxaca
R. Atoyac
R. Verde
Puerto Angel
Salina Cruz
Gulf of Tehuantepec
L. Catemaco
Coatzalcoalcos
Coatzalcoalcos R.
ISTHMUS OF TEHUANTEPEC
Tuxtla Gutiérrez
EL SUMIDERO
TABASCO
Villahermosa
R. Grijalva
Bay of Campeche
CHIAPAS
San Cristobal de las Casas
Usumacinta R.
L. de Montebello
GUATEMALA
Progreso
Mérida
Yucatán Peninsula
YUCATÁN
Campeche
CAMPECHE
QUINTANA ROO (TERR.)
Chetumal
Belize
BR. HONDURAS
Caribbean Sea
HONDURAS
Don Pitcher

TERRY'S GUIDE TO MEXICO

by

James

Norman, pseud.

TERRY'S GUIDE TO MEXICO

A completely revised edition

of T. Philip Terry's

standard guidebook

to Mexico

DOUBLEDAY & COMPANY, INC.

GARDEN CITY, NEW YORK

Cartography by Donald T. Pitcher
Designed by Alma Reese Cardi

Printed in the United States of America

For my son, Paul, who helped research much of this

FOREWORD

Although Mexico lies contiguous to the United States and its heart-land is but five hours air travel from most U.S. cities, Mexico is more of a foreign land to us, indeed, than are most of the countries of Europe. Her people, their ways and background, are a curious blend of both the Orient and Europe. Those who visit Mexico find it an extraordinary land, rich in vivid contrasts, physical beauty and charming customs. Mexico offers something for almost every taste: spas equal to any in Europe, beach resorts of breath-taking beauty, picturesque villages and colonial monuments, an archaeology richer than that of Egypt and markets that are like the bazaars of Persia. Mexico is so different from anything most American travelers are familiar with and the country's attractions are so varied, to travel there without first knowing something of the country would be like trying to make one's way through a maze blindfolded. A travel guidebook is essential.

For fifty years *Terry's Guide to Mexico* has fulfilled this need. It has stood out as a major institution in Mexican tourism. The original Terry's was both a guide and handbook in the old tradition of Europe's Baedecker and Muirhead. It was also something more than these. In addition to being a miniature encyclopedia about our colorful neighboring republic, it was also full of amazing scholarship and delightful old-fashioned wit.

Its creator, T. Philip Terry, was one of those untiring travelers, blessed with a relentless curiosity. Around the turn of the century, and for many years to follow, when travel in Mexico was fantastically difficult, he shuttled back and forth by train, carriage and by burro, peeking into the vivid nooks and crannies of Mexico. It is an unusual tribute to Mr. Terry that, years after his death in 1945, and despite the vast changes that have occurred in Mexico, the early editions of his work (1909 and 1922) are now avidly sought-after collectors' items. They are worth more than their original list price.

Unfortunately, such unique literary monuments are not especially useful when it comes to locating hotels, resorts, and places of interest which did not exist a dozen or more years ago — hence, this completely new edition of *Terry's Guide to Mexico.*

Our travel habits have changed radically in a generation. The era of leisurely three- or four-month grand tours has vanished. The scholarly gadabout who spent weeks with a Terry or Baedecker in hand, conscientiously "taking in" all the riches in a museum or church, is now an almost extinct breed. Today's travelers are vacationists. They pop into Mexico by plane or automobile and they have at most a week or a month to look around. Although they may peek into a museum or spend a fascinating morning at an archaeological ruin, their main reason for traveling is to relax, see new places and have fun.

This new *Terry's Guide* is designed for the modern traveler. It is not a hasty revision or updating of the older editions. Although it is based on them, it is a brand-new book, completely rewritten for present-day travel in Mexico. At the same time, though we have shifted the focus from the minute scrutiny of church and museum interiors and from the quaint preoccupation with insect life in foreign places, which was the fashion in older guidebooks, we do not ape some of the newer guides which conceive of travel as a matter of hotels and night clubs and totally ignore the physical and cultural riches of a country. The objective of *Terry's Guide to Mexico* is to provide the most thorough and up-to-date information about everything in Mexico that might interest the casual vacationist, as well as the sportsman, student, amateur explorer and even the orchid hunter.

In order that you may pinpoint information quickly and easily, this book is thoroughly indexed. In addition, it is divided into handy departments covering Mexican travel information and background.

There is a unique, preliminary Where to Go section, suggesting different types of vacations in Mexico — for the one-week tourist, to the traveler with a month to spend; for the budget traveler, for the newlyweds, for the hunter, the fisherman, the off-trail explorer and even a vacation plan for elderly folks seeking a quiet place in the sun.

Part One, General Travel Information, covers everything that you need to know regarding preparations for travel south of the border — visas, custom regulations, tips on health, travel costs, motoring and air-travel advice, shopping and shipping, study in Mexico, etc.

Part Two, Physiography, History, and Culture, includes a series of short sketches to acquaint you with Mexican history, geography, government, art and literature, fiestas, regional food and drink, as well as a bit about the personality of the Mexican.

Part Three, Routes, covers the major highways, air and railway routes. It includes a log of each route and strip-maps. It is especially designed for quick reference during motor trips.

Part Four, The Regions of Mexico, explores in detail all the fascinating regions of the country and includes brief descriptions of each area, the physiography, history, roads, places of interest, as well as a thorough report on hotels, restaurants, shops, etc.

At present, Mexico is changing so rapidly it is difficult to ensure abiding accuracy in such details as travel costs, hotel prices and road conditions. The quality of service in restaurants and hotels often varies from week to week, depending on changes of ownership and even the day to day moods of the help. We include an extensive list of hotels because during the height of the two travel seasons (June to September and December to April) one is sometimes forced to take second-best. Those hotels and restaurants especially recommended in the guide have been visited and checked by us.

Both the publishers and the present author of this volume will genuinely appreciate any criticism, corrections or suggestions visitors to Mexico may offer, especially those that will help inform future travelers and make their stay in Mexico more pleasant. Such communications should be addressed to the publishers, Doubleday & Company, 575 Madison Avenue, New York 22, N.Y., or to James Norman, San Miguel de Allende, Gto., Mexico.

WHERE TO GO IN MEXICO

First-time visitors south of the border are often at a loss as to what they should see in Mexico and how they should parcel out their vacation time. Here are 12 vacation-plan groupings designed for various seasons, a variety of tastes and covering the most interesting of Mexico's attractions.

Where it is advantageous to do your sightseeing with a guide or guided tour, it is so indicated. All of the suggested trips begin in Mexico City. Detailed descriptions of the places are included in the body of the Guide and may be located throughout the Index.

For your first trip to Mexico we suggest you follow the well-worn tourist routes. Regard your first visit as a sampler. The colors and contrasts will be so vivid you won't have enough time really to peek under the skin of Mexico, but you'll see enough to whet your appetite for more. If your trip is to be a short one and you are traveling alone, your best bet is to go with a guided tour, or hire a guide and car to spin you about. (See Index: Mexican Travel Agencies.)

One-week trip

Begin with *Mexico City and Environs* (2 days). Guide or conducted tour recommended. See — the National Palace, the Cathedral and its museum, Chapultepec Palace and park, University City and the handsome nearby Jardines de Pedregal residential area, Palace of Fine Arts. The city tour can be done in a morning and an afternoon, but it is best to spread it and allow yourself time to browse through some of the city's fabulous markets and shops. For a relaxing evening, dine and listen to the music at a good restaurant.

Teotihuacán (1 day) Tour or guide. Start in the morning with a visit to the famed Museum of Anthropology near the Cathedral, then drive to the archaeological zone at Teotihuacán. See — the huge pyramids of the Sun and of the Moon, the Citadel. On the drive back pause at Acolmán to view the noteworthy monastery-church. The Shrine of Guadalupe can be visited on the same trip.

Cuernavaca and Taxco (2 days). Guide optional. This is tourist-belt country, but the gardens and climate of Cuernavaca, the picturesqueness of Taxco and its silver crafts make it worthwhile.

Xochimilco (1 day). Sunday is best. Guide optional. This trip out of Mexico City usually includes a stop at the gem-like convent and church of Santa María de los Angeles at Churubusco, the "floating gardens" at Xochimilco and a late afternoon session at the bullfights.

Last day. Allow yourself an unescorted day for shopping, strolling along the Reforma in Mexico City, etc.

Two-week trip

Begin in Mexico City and enjoy the usual city tours, including *Teotihuacán, Xochimilco* (see above). Then take the Colonial circuit into the country toward the baroque sanctuary at *Tepotzotlán* (hour stop), *San Juán del Río* (en route) for basketry, *Querétaro* (½ day), *San Miguel de Allende* (½ day), *Guanajuato* (1 day), *Morelia* and the *Lake Pátzcutaro* district (2 days) and *San José Purua.* Including driving time and some dawdling you'll need five days to a week to enjoy the colonial cities. The best overnight stopovers are at San Miguel de Allende, Querétaro, Morelia. (Take a tour or pick up local guides.)

To finish off your two-weeker, either drive via *Cuernavaca* and *Taxco* to the magnificent beach resorts of *Acapulco.* (Allow four days, or, fly and have more beach-time.)

Three- or four-week trip

Mexico City and Environs (4 days). Guided tours of the city, *Xochimilco, Teotihuacán.*

Oaxaca region: a spectacular drive by car or bus via *Puebla* (1 day), to Oaxaca City. Using the city as your base, range out to nearby pottery-making villages, *Coyotepec* and *Ocotlán* (½ day), the archaeological ruins at *Monte Albán* (½day), the temples at *Mitla* (½ day). Allow at least 2 days in Oaxaca City itself, and be sure one of them is a

Saturday. The street market on that day is one of the fabulous market gatherings in this hemisphere.

Yucatán (7 days). Fly from *Mexico City* to *Mérida.* See — the Mayan ruins at Chichén Itzá, Uxmal, Labná and Sayil. Side trips to Campeche and to the Island of Cozumel. For these latter add a few days to your tour. Season: best time of the year for travel in Yucatán is from November to April. The heat is excessive during the summer.

Extended Colonial route (5 days). Including *Querétaro, Guanajuato, Guadalajara & Lake Chapala, Pátzcuaro* and *Morelia.*

Spa vacation

For the gadabout suffering from twinges of lumbago, rheumatism or other of the classic disorders which for centuries have sent people seeking curative waters, Mexico has countless spas with sulphuric, radioactive or mineral loaded waters claimed to be effective in relieving odds and ends of discomforts. (See Index: Hot Springs and the ailments they are recommended for.)

If you're seeking a vacation packed with non-strenuous loafing and dips into curative waters and mud baths, even though there is nothing wrong with you, we suggest a day or two sightseeing in Mexico City, then a few days to a week at one or more of the following hot spring resorts.

DE LUXE AND FAIRLY EXPENSIVE: *San José Purua,* thermal waters, mud baths, fine swimming pools, beautiful hotel and grounds; *Fortín de las Flores,* tropic sunshine, fine accommodations and swimming in a pool covered with a blanket of exotic flowers; *San Miguel Regla,* a beautiful, restful stay in an old hacienda.

MODERATELY PRICED: *Agua Azul* (near Puebla), thermal sulphurous waters said to be beneficial in the treatment of arthritis, rheumatism and nervous disorders; *Ixtapan de la Sal,* with radioactive waters, mud baths and numerous good hotels.

BUDGET SPAS: In the following the facilities are not so luxurious, but the surroundings are restful and the accommodations are surprisingly good: *Comanjilla* in the State of Guanajuato; very hot thermal waters and a Russian bath; *Lourdes,* modest hotel, beautiful country, mineral waters said to be good for the kidneys, liver and stomach; *Tequisquiapan,* thermal waters in a pleasant village blessed with numerous small hotels.

Student vacation

For vacationers interested in combining a stay in Mexico along with summer schooling, Mexico offers ample opportunities for book-cracking and planned cultural field trips. Serious students working for credits, primarily in languages, literature, Latin American affairs, and archaeology, will find the summer session at the National University and the year-round courses at University of the Americas most promising. Other schools offer non-credit courses ranging from folklore, guitar-playing to skin-diving for the traveler out to have fun. (See Index for directory of schools and courses offered in Mexico.)

Photographer and painter tours

Camera tours and painting tours have become more and more popular in Mexico. Several schools: University of the Americas, the Instituto Allende in San Miguel de Allende and the Escuela de las Bellas Artes of the University of Michoacán offer art and photography courses and combine these with field trips.

The independent photographer or painter anxious to do his own exploring with camera or easel will find the following localities most satisfying, both for capturing the scenic charms of the country and for doing studies of the people:

Skip Mexico City and concentrate on the colonial towns and villages — *Guanajuato, San Miguel de Allende, Morelia, Taxco,* and *Pátzcuaro.* You can also spend pleasant hours working in two picturesque abandoned mining towns that are full of interesting architecture and vistas. There are *Marfil* (near Guanajuato), and *Los Pozos* (near Querétaro). Tourist agencies don't know about them.

For pictures of village life, and for "the faces of Mexico," include the colorful market-days in Oaxaca City and Pátzcuaro. (See Index: Photography in Mexico.)

Sportsmen's vacations

FISHERMEN: The finest, and least known, fishing grounds for deepsea and lagoon fishing in Mexico are around the islands of El Carmen and Aguada along the edge of the Bay of Campeche. You can drive there. The best seasons are fall, winter and early spring. Best fishing months, July and August.

La Paz (Lower California) and the west coast ports — *Guaymas, Los Mochis, San Blas, Puerto Vallarte, Mazatlán, Manzanillo* and *Acapulco* are fishermen's paradises. (See Index: Sports, for fishing and hunting regulations, seasons, etc.)

HUNTERS: The best hunting, particularly for big game — jaguar, deer, wild pig, turkey, etc., occurs in the southern states, especially Chiapas, Campeche and Tabasco. Best season is winter. It is recommended that you arrange such a vacation through a professional outfitter (see Index) or contact the hunting guides recommended in the regional sections of this volume.

SKIN-DIVING: Fly to the island of *Cozumel* off of the Peninsula of Yucatán for a try in the most magnificent skin-diving waters in this hemisphere.

Cactus and orchid hunting

For orchid fanciers and cactus collectors Mexico is filled with inviting places to tour. Any trip involving a hunt for either cactus or orchids should begin in Mexico City with a visit to the Botany Department of the Institute of Biology in Chapultepec Park, where you can oh and ah over the plant collections there.

If you can afford guides and have plenty of time, the best orchid hunting state is remote Chiapas, a veritable orchid paradise. Next best is the State of Veracruz. Follow what is called the Vanilla Route from Mexico City to *Pachuca,* then to *Huauchinango, Villa Juárez, Papantla, Tecolutla, Nautla* and around up through *Teziutlán* to *Puebla.* At Villa Juárez, Papantla, Teziutlán and other towns stop in the market and ask the flower sellers to find you a guide to take you out orchid hunting.

Mexico's countless variety of cactus are less elusive. You'll find them along all the highways leading toward Mexico City. For the greatest concentration of certain types of cacti here are the best areas:

1. Giant organ cacti — the mountain region between Tehuacán and Zapotitlán.

2. Cardonal or huge candelabra cacti — the Cañon de Tomellín in Oaxaca.

3. Biznaga or barrel cacti — the plains around Ixmiquilpan (State of Hidalgo).

4. Bearded *viejito* or *cephalocereus senilis* — the Canyon of the Deers in Meztitlán (State of Hidalgo).

5. Nopal cacti — the plains of Zacatecas and in San Luis Potosí.

6. Peyote, Giant Saguaros, etc. — the northern desert states.

Off-trail vacations

With new roads lancing through remote parts of Mexico more and more travelers are slipping away from the well polished tourist track to peek at parts of the country where folks arts, picturesque customs still can be observed and of course, where prices remain low and accommodations are somewhat primitive. Here are a number of off-the-highway vacation spots that remain unique.

1. *Tlacotalpan and Lake Catemaco:* not far south of Veracruz. You take a launch from Alvarado, up the River of Butterflies (Papaloapan) to the quaint river town of Tlacotalpan. It was once an important port and pirate hangout. The fiestas are wonderful, the river fishing excellent and there are several small hotels. From Tlacotalpan or Alvarado you ferry across the river and continue down the coast to Lake Catemaco, one of Mexico's loveliest and least visited lakes.

2. *The Montebello Lakes:* recommended only for people willing to rough it during the three best months — January to March. A series of spectacularly beautiful lakes in the Lacandón Forest Country of Chiapas. Rough road, you pack in food and stay at a hacienda.

3. *Usumacinta Boat Trip:* By power-boat up the Usumacinta River, through virgin jungle region to Tenosique, then out by railway. Or, you can continue on by boat to within easy reach of the most interesting of Mayan jungle-ruins and temples at Yaxchilán.

4. *Puerto Angel and Puerto Escondido:* Two delightful, rarely visited South Sea Island style ports far south of Acapulco. Good fishing, beaches, seafood and simple accommodations. You can fly in, or (during January, February and March) drive in if your car isn't too low-slung.

5. *Barra de Navidad and Tenacatita:* two somewhat primitive beach areas on the West Coast just north of Manzanillo. A good paved road connects Barra de Navidad with Manzanillo and Guadalajara. Tenacatita is harder to reach. You must go by boat or small plane and take your own camping equipment.

6. *Las Grandes Barrancas de la Tarahumara:* Popularly called *Barranca del Cobre* (after one of the canyons). These gigantic canyons in southwestern Chihuahua compare in beauty, complexity and impressive size with the Grand Canyon of Arizona. Trails in are still rough, but a road is being planned. It is camping country.

7. *Las Tres Marías:* three islands off the West Coast that house Mexico's penal colony. Deep-sea fishing and the beaches are among the finest in the world. Arrangements to visit there can be made in Tepic, Nayarit.

Honeymoon tour

A tour for newlyweds or people just looking for romantic settings.

Begin in Mexico City. Spend an afternoon in *Chapultepec Palace* and *Park* (without a guide, of course), perhaps a trip to the *Desierto de los Leones,* have cocktails on the roof terrace of the *Hilton Hotel,* then supper and an evening at a good restaurant. Then, if you like beaches, fly to *Puerto Vallarta* or to *Zihuatanejo* and try to be there when the moon is full.

If you are a well-heeled honeymooner and have time and the event has occurred during the winter season, fly to Yucatán. Book yourself for the full Barbachano Tour treatment: three or four days at Chichén Itzá and another couple at Uxmal (use a guide one day, and moon about the rest), then fly down to the beaches of Cozumel.

CONTENTS

Part One — General Travel Information

Part Two – Physiography, History, and Culture

Part Three — Routes

Part Four — The Regions of Mexico

MAPS

ABBREVIATIONS

Alt. — Altitude above sea level
AP — American Plan
EP — European Plan
a/c — air conditioned
E. — East, eastern
CN- — *Carreterra Nacional,* Federal Highway
CE- — *Carreterra del Estado,* State road or highway
dlls. — Dollars
Ft. — Feet
Km. — Kilometer (⅝th of a mile)
l. — left
mi. — mile or miles
Mex. — Mexico or Mexican
MN — *Moneda Nacional* (Mexican currency). Most prices in the guide are in Mexican money, indicated by the MN. When not followed by this symbol, the price quoted is in dollars. In Mexico the dollar mark ($) is often used to indicate both the Mexican *peso* or the dollar.
N. — North
P. — *Plaza* (A park or square)
p. — page
Pop. — Population
r. — right
S. — South
Sp. — Spanish
Telg. — Telegram
Tel. — Telephone
W. — West
Av. — Avenue
C. — *Ciudad* (city) or *Calle* (street)
Calz. — *Calzada* (A street or thoroughfare, originally a causeway
Ote. — *Oriente* (East) Used with Mexican street names
Nte. — *Norte* (North) Used with Mexican street names
Pte. — *Poniente* (West) Used with Mexican street names
Sur. — *Sur* (South) Used with Mexican street names

TERRY'S GUIDE TO MEXICO

PART ONE

General Travel Information

1. Travel Costs, Banks, Money Exchange, Tipping, Mexican Money

TRAVEL COSTS

The cost of your vacation in Mexico depends on how much you want to do, the comforts you demand and your mode of travel. During the last decade the cost of living in Mexico has scaled upward alarmingly. Residents living in Mexico City and some tourist-favored centers find that living costs are about equal to those in the larger U.S. cities. In the areas beyond the capital and away from the well-visited tourist centers prices are much lower. Your dollar can go a long way.

Transportation expenses within Mexico (bus, train, air, or even hired car) are much lower than in the U.S. One should note that anything involving manufacture, such as appliances, auto parts, canned food and most clothing, runs as high or higher than in shops north of the border. Anything involving pure service or labor remains ridiculously low. The minimum wage for unskilled labor in urban centers is around a dollar a day rather than a dollar an hour. A maid, gardener, or bellhop works for $10 to $16 a month, and food.

If you wish to travel in Mexico in comfort — though not lavishly — allow yourself about $15 a day, including transportation. For a stay in Mexico City, add around 50 per cent.

Budget-minded and skillful travelers can manage on far less. You can actually travel below the border, eat well, enjoy comfortable accommodations and see everything for about $6 to $7 a day.

In general, hotel, restaurant and other rates in this guide are listed in Mexican money, appearing thus — $100.00 MN, (meaning, 100 pesos in national currency).

You can shave down your Mexican vacation expenses in the following ways:

1. *Off-season travel.* You take advantage of the lower rates offered by hotels, etc., during the nontourist seasons, which are, throughout most of the country, from September to November, and from April to June. Along the northwest coast and the Gulf coast (Mazatlán to Guaymas; Veracruz and Tampico) the off-season occurs during the very hot months of July, August, and September. Sometimes you must remind the hotel staff of the off-season and lower rates. If you don't ask, they conveniently forget.

2. *Bus travel.* Mexican first-class buses are often cleaner and more comfortable than those in the U.S. They are safe, maintain frequent and good schedules, and their rates are fantastically low.

3. There are numerous *restaurants* in Mexico where tasty and good fare is served at half the price tag one finds in the obvious tourist places. Many are listed in this guidebook.

4. You can also save by *tipping properly* as well as *exchanging money* in the right places. See below.

5. Don't do your *shopping* with a guide in tow, or in places he takes you. Guides get 15 to 20 per cent of your purchase price as a kickback. Shop alone. You have a better chance at bargaining.

6. In *all* negotiations where there is an exchange of money for goods to be delivered or made, or for services (car repairs, etc.), *always* get an *estimate of costs* and come to a clear understanding on price beforehand. This applies likewise to hotel rates and restaurant prices where the rates are not posted or listed. When you do this you're not being a miserly American. It is the accepted custom and all Mexicans do it.

TIPPING

Tipping can be a normal part of your travel expense, or it can become an excessive addition. When it comes to tipping a waiter or a porter many Americans become curiously flustered. They seem to forget all the arithmetic they learned and they act like guilty children making a first confession.

Tipping in Mexico is simple. Learn what the Mexican monetary units are and don't tip like a Croesus; it annoys both your fellow travelers and Mexicans. It makes it appear as if you're flaunting your wealth and rubbing it in that Mexico is poor. On the other hand, don't undertip. Here are a few handy "tips" for the "complete tipper."

1. *Hotels.* Give approximately 15 to 20 per cent of the bill in cities, at resorts and along major highways for normal size accounts. Elsewhere, especially in small towns and off-trail areas, 10 to 15 per cent. Never give a lump sum to one person (even a hotel owner) hoping he will distribute it to the other help. They may never get their share.

2. *Restaurants, cafés, cocktail lounges.* If your bill is a small one, perhaps a few pesos for coffee or beer, then, of course, a 10 or 20 centavo tip (two American cents) would be ridiculous. In such instances you tip higher, figuring the time and service involved rather than the bill itself.

3. *Baggage.* For handling baggage, a peso to a peso fifty per bag is sufficient, except in the more plush establishments.

4. *To tip or not to tip:*

— Tip washroom attendants.

— Do not tip cab drivers. It is not done, unless the cabbie has tendered special services such as helping you in and out of a building with your luggage.

— Give museum attendants 50 centavos to a peso. This is apart from the infinitesimal admission fee charged and for which you get a receipt or ticket.

— On airlines, don't tip. Compliment them.

— When you have trouble along Mexican highways, truck drivers and ranchers will stop at the drop of a hat to help you. Most of them are born mechanics. They may spend a good deal of time cleaning your fuel pump or towing you into town. You can graciously offer them something, but don't make it look like a tip. Say that it's for a beer, or a toy for their children. *("Tómelo, señor, para unas cervezas.")* Usually they'll refuse. They just like to help out.

BANKS AND MONEY EXCHANGE

With the exception of towns along the U.S.-Mexican border and the northern half of Lower California, American money is not current in Mexico. You must visit a bank or money exchange and convert your dollars into pesos. In almost all towns there are excellent banks where you can make exchanges. Banking hours throughout the republic are from 9 A.M. to noon or 1 P.M., Monday through Saturday. Federally chartered banks are closed during the official government holidays and for some important religious fiestas such as Christmas, Easter, and Day of the Dead. If a major holiday falls on a Friday the bank may follow the happy Mexican custom of making a *puente* (bridge), stretching the holiday over several days. In small towns and villages there are also "bean banks," a grass-roots bank run by a local grocer or dealer in produce such as corn and beans. Although not controlled or supervised by federal or state bank examiners, these institutions lend money and cash checks. They are useful to know about because they are usually open all day long, including Sundays. They are often very accommodating in cashing small checks. One such bank once cashed a California driver's license.

At present the official exchange rate is 12.50 pesos for a dollar. However, almost no bank or money exchange gives exactly this. In big banks you get 12.49 pesos to the dollar. In smaller, country banks you may only receive 12.47. Hotels and money exchanges not connected with banks offer as low as 11.60 to 12.25 pesos for a dollar. The wise traveler should arrange his time and money negotiations so as to do the bulk of his or her money exchanging at recognized large banks in order to get the best exchange rate. The Banco Nacional de México which has branches all over the republic is by far the best bank to deal with. It gives the best rates and it offers courteous service. There is usually someone who speaks English in each of its branches.

It takes ten to fourteen days to cash a personal check in Mexico. You must wait until it goes through both the Mexican and the American clearinghouses before you can draw on it. The traveler's checks issued by the Bank of America, the American Express Company, Thomas Cook & Son, Inc., and the First National City Bank of New York are the safest and best method for carrying travel funds. These checks are accepted everywhere in Mexico; are cashable on sight and are insured against loss or theft. *Note:* When you exchange dollars for pesos in Mexico, banks give you a slightly better exchange rate for traveler's checks than for dollars in cash.

MONEY

(dinero or *moneda).* Mexico employs the decimal system and the silver standard. Money is issued in paper bills *(billetes de banco)* and in coins of copper, silver and nickel alloys *(moneda acuñada).* The peso is the basic monetary unit. There are 100 centavos (cents) to a peso. The peso is issued in paper bills as well as in silver coin.

The one peso paper note has on one side a reproduction of the Aztec calendar stone, on the other a picture of the Independence Monument in Mexico City. The five peso note has a picture of a Mexican girl with a chain of gold coins looped around her neck, and on the reverse side, the Independence Monument. The ten peso bill displays a picture of a proud Tehuana woman in traditional costume, and a view of the colonial city of Guanajuato. The twenty peso note has a portrait of La Corregidora, Josefa

Ortiz de Domínguez, heroine of the struggle for independence from Spain; on the reverse side, a picture of the building in Querétaro where she lived. The revolutionary hero, Ignacio Allende (wearing a cocked hat), graces the 50 peso bill; the Independence Monument, affectionately known as "The Angel," is on the reverse side. The 100 peso note bears a likeness of Padre Hidalgo de Costilla, Mexico's George Washington. Although bills are issued in larger denominations they are rarely seen or used — no one has change for them.

Coins change frequently in design. The government mint has been issuing silver coins in denominations of one, five and, a few years back, 10 and 20 peso cartwheels. The most common are the copper coins: 5 centavos, 10, 20, and 50 centavo pieces. The brass one centavo is so tiny in size and weight it is scarcely used. Small alloy coins, nickel and/or silver are also issued in 5, 10, 25, and 50 centavo denominations.

Slang terms for paper and coin are used as often as the formal nomenclature and it is useful to know some of them. *Lana* (wool) is a general slang term for money or cash. The 50 centavo piece is called a *tostón* (from the Portuguese *testón*). A 25 centavo coin is a peseta. The 5 centavo coins are referred to as *níquel, quinto,* or *Josefina* (this latter after Doña Josefa, the revolutionary heroine whose profile graces the coin). A 20 centavo piece may be called *dos décimos.* Metal coins and small change are also referred to as *tecolines* and *fierros* (iron pieces), as *menudo* (small money), *moneda suelta* (loose change), as *moralla* (chicken feed) and *feria* (bartering stuff).

For useful phrases and vocabulary related to banking and money exchange, see glossary.

EXCHANGE TABLE AT THE RATE OF $12.50 MN FOR THE DOLLAR

PESOS	DOLLARS	PESOS	DOLLARS
$ 1.00	$ 0.08	$18.00	$ 1.44
2.00	0.16	19.00	1.52
3.00	0.25	20.00	1.60
4.00	0.33	25.00	2.00
5.00	0.40	30.00	2.40
6.00	0.48	40.00	3.20
7.00	0.56	50.00	4.00
8.00	0.64	60.00	4.80
9.00	0.72	70.00	5.60
10.00	0.80	75.00	6.00
11.00	0.88	80.00	6.40
12.00	0.96	90.00	7.20
13.00	1.04	100.00	8.00
14.00	1.12	200.00	16.00
15.00	1.20	300.00	24.00
16.00	1.28	400.00	32.00
17.00	1.36	500.00	40.00

Note well: If you are registered at a hotel, traveler's checks are readily cashed there. To cash them in shops and at banks you will have to show positive personal identification. A passport, driver's license, or bank identification is best. A tourist card is not always acceptable.

2. *Border Regulations. Passports, Visas, and Tourist Cards; Renewing Permits within Mexico; Health Requirements; Mexican Customs Regulations and Inspections; U. S. Customs; Automobile Permits; Permits for Private Planes and Yachts*

Formalities for entering and leaving Mexico as a tourist are extremely simple. Mexican immigration and customs officials are instructed to help make your border crossing as painless as possible. No passport is required of U.S. citizens. However, you will need: some proof of citizenship, a Mexican tourist card, and a smallpox vaccination certificate.

PROOF OF CITIZENSHIP

This can be a birth certificate, passport, voter registration card, or affidavit. Mexican consular officials have at times even accepted U. S. Army discharge certificates and driver's licenses as sufficient identification. *Naturalization papers or a passport must be carried by naturalized citizens.*

TOURIST CARD

A *tarjeta de turista* (tourist card) is required of all persons fifteen years of age or older who plan to visit the interior of the country. Several types of cards are being issued by the Mexican government at present: one is good for a single visit or border crossing; the second is valid for multiple visits. Each is valid for 180 days.

The single-visit card costs $37.50 MN or about $3.00. It must be surrendered to immigration authorities for cancellation upon leaving the country. Two front-view, passport-size photographs are required for the multiple-entry card. The cost of this card is $5.00. A new, 29-day free visit permit has just been introduced.

Minors (under fifteen years of age) are included

on the tourist card of their parents at no extra charge. Children under fifteen years of age, traveling in groups sponsored by educational or cultural institutions and accompanied by an authorized person from the institution, are not required to pay a tourist card fee. They may remain in Mexico up to 60 days. Minors traveling alone, or with friends or relatives, must present notarized authorization from their parents or legal guardians.

Tourist cards can be procured from any Mexican consulate or from the Mexican immigration office at whichever port of entry you go through. (See Index: Mexican Consulates in the U.S.)

Requirements for other than U. S. Tourists. Citizens and residents of Great Britain, North Ireland, Australia, South Africa, New Zealand, France, Holland, Norway, Italy, Portugal, Sweden, Switzerland, Denmark, and Belgium must have: a visaed passport, a tourist card, and a certificate of smallpox vaccination. Canadians must have a valid passport and a tourist card. Their passports need not be visaed.

Other nationals are subject to special requirements and should confer with their nearest Mexican Consulate before any proposed trip to Mexico.

Military and U. S. Government Employee Courtesy. U.S. military personnel and employees of the U. S. Government, on presentation of proper identification, are permitted into Mexico (with their immediate family) free of charge for a period of 29 days or less.

Tourists flying into Mexico via a nonstop commercial airline can get their tourist cards at the airport of entry, usually the Mexico City airport. Tourists arriving by train can also get their cards at the point of entry.

Tourist Card Renewals. If due to accident, illness, or other valid causes you find that you cannot leave Mexico within the required 180 days, you can procure a temporary extension of your tourist card by applying within the 30 days before the time on your card is up (but not before 30 days), at the offices of Gobernación in Mexico City. There is usually no charge for the extension. If you have any trouble, get in touch with the Departmento Autónomo de Turismo (Federal Tourist Bureau) at Av. Reforma 35, Mexico City. This office does not issue tourist card extensions but they will assist and advise you and see that you are treated fairly.

Warning: It is rigidly prohibited for a visitor to engage in business, work or conduct business negotiations in Mexico while traveling on a tourist permit. One is liable to arrest, expulsion, heavy fines and/or imprisonment.

Student Visas. A U.S. student intending to study in Mexico for 180 days or less, can enter the country on a tourist card. If the student's study courses extend beyond 180 days a student immigration visa is required. *It should be secured from a Mexican Consulate before entering Mexico.* The following is required: a passport, completion of Student Immigration Form F.M.-2, twelve passport-size pictures (six front, six profile), a letter from the school indicating that the student is registered or accepted for enrollment, and finally proof of financial solvency or support. These should be submitted to your nearest Mexican Consulate. In time, the student will be issued a student immigration book, permitting him or her to enter Mexico to study. There is no fee for this. However, within a month after entering the country the student book must be presented at the offices of Gobernación in Mexico City for registry. There is a fee of $50.00 peso. Thereafter, each year (during the final thirty days of the student's year-period) the book must again be presented at Gobernación for renewal *(refrendo).* There is a $50.00 MN charge each time. While studying in Mexico a student is not permitted to work.

Special Entry Permits. There are several other types of entry permits, some for people planning to work in Mexico, others for U.S. citizens intending to set up residence in Mexico, but not to work. (See Index: *Residence in Mexico.*)

SMALLPOX VACCINATION CERTIFICATE

To enter Mexico one must show a certificate or proof of a valid vaccination against smallpox. Often the Mexican authorities do not trouble you for this. It is required also for re-entry to the United States. The information regarding your vaccination should be recorded on an International Certificate of Inoculation and Vaccination, available at any U. S. Public Health Service office. On returning to the U.S., if you lack such a certificate or other valid proof you may have to submit to vaccination by the U.S. quarantine officer. Usually such a procedure is not too troublesome. The quarantine officers are both courteous and efficient.

If vaccination is detrimental to a person's health because of infancy, old age, or illness, the requirement may be waived — judgment on this is left to the quarantine officer. It is advisable in such cases to have a doctor's certificate concerning the case.

BORDER-TOWN VISITS

You are permitted to cross into Mexican towns along the border for periods not to exceed 72 hours, no tourist card being required. It is best, however, to carry some personal identification.

AUTOMOBILE PERMITS

Visitors entering Mexico on tourist cards may bring their cars on fulfilling the following requirements: At the port of entry you must show proof of ownership of the car. A clear title, registration slip, or notarized bill of sale are all acceptable. You'll encounter less trouble if you show the title. If the car is not fully paid for a notarized statement from the lien holder, giving you permission to take the car out of the United States, is necessary. Likewise, if the car is registered in another person's name, or in the name of a company, you must show the same sort of notarized authorization to take the car across the border. Along with these, you should have the car ownership papers.

American drivers' licenses are honored in Mexico. The temporary import permit for a car is issued at the port of entry. It is valid for 180 days. There is no charge for it. If you enter Mexico with a car the phrase *con automóvil* (with car) is stamped upon your tourist card. You may not leave Mexico without the car unless proper arrangements are made with the Mexican Customs.

If you have to leave the country without your car you can either put up a bond for the car, or leave it in the care of the customs authorities at the Mexico City airport. The bonding method is difficult and unsatisfactory for it calls for depositing cash or a valid bond (minimum $10,000 MN) with the customs office in Mexico City. Mexican bonding companies charge exorbitant rates. The second way is easier. You simply leave your car with the customs people at the airport. You are given a certificate which is canceled when the car is reclaimed. There is usually no charge for the first ten days that the car is in official custody. Thereafter there is a daily nominal charge.

A new government regulation designed to curb illegal importation of cars into Mexico, and to curb so-called tourists who actually reside in Mexico and make regular six-month trips to the border, turn around and come back immediately, specifies that if a car has been driven in Mexico on a temporary tourist import permit for six months it cannot be brought back into Mexico for another six months. Although apparently still on the books, this regulation is rarely enforced.

You must apply for extensions of car permits not more than 15 days nor less than 10 days before the expiration date of your old permit.

Car permits can also be extended by applying at the branch offices of the Secretaría de Hacienda in towns outside of Mexico City. However, in such cases you may run into trouble and delays. In many of the towns they are not accustomed to such requests. It is wise to go armed with a petition for *prórroga* (extension of time). It should be written up in the following form.

Dirreción de Registro Federal de Automóviles: Yo, (your name), *con domicilio en este país en la calle* (insert your address in Mexico, the city and the state), *solicito se me amplié por tres meses el plazo para el retorno del vehículo de mi propriedad importado temporalmente conforme con los siguientes datos:*

Calidad migratoría Turista.
Tarjeta de turista # (insert tourist card number)
Permiso del coche número (insert number listed on your present car permit)
Fecha del Permiso (insert date it was issued)
Fecha del vencimiento (its expiration date)
Aduana de entrada (where you crossed the border)

CARACTERISTICAS DE VEHICULO

Marca (make of car)
Tipo (type or model, station wagon, etc.)
Modelo (the year)
Número de motor (motor number)
Número de Série (body number)
Placas (your license plate data)

Yo protesto en (Insert the name of the town where you are filing the petition), *el* (date) *de* (month) *de* (year)
(here add your signature)

If your license plates expire during your stay in Mexico you should arrange to get new plates from your home state and have them sent to: U. S. Customs, Borderline Office, at your point of exit, or to the American Automobile Association offices in Laredo, Brownsville, or El Paso (Texas), or Nogales (Arizona). If you receive your plates directly in Mexico there is no need to put them on the car. Mexican customs officials expect you to leave the country with the same plates you had coming in. If you don't have those old plates there can be trouble.

Regulations regarding bringing camping or house-trailers into Mexico are the same as automobile regulations. (See Index: motoring tips, road regulations, insurance.)

PERMITS FOR PRIVATE PLANES

To fly your own plane into Mexico, the only requirements are: a tourist card; that you file your flight plan with the Mexican Consul nearest your home; and that you notify by telegram, sufficiently in advance, the commander of the international airport where you expect to land first. For any other information write: Dirección General de Aeronáutica Civil, Calles Niño Perdido y Xola, Mexico D.F.

CUSTOMS REGULATIONS ON ENTERING MEXICO

Although the official policy of the Mexican Government is to make border crossings for tourists as trouble-free as possible, occasionally an overofficious border officer may destroy a lot of good will. If you have trouble, report it in writing to the Federal Tourist Bureau. It will help others. For ordinary tourists no written declarations are required, the paper work and baggage inspection are kept at minimum.

You are allowed to bring clothing, articles of personal use, and jewelry in quantity up to 50 kilograms (about 110 lbs.). If you bring in 50 kilos of all one kind of article (all jewelry or all dresses) they are subject to an import tax. According to Articles 294, 298, 300, 302, and 307 of the Mexican Customs Code, here is the official list of what a tourist can bring in duty-free:

Women — 12 changes of underclothing, 3 nightgowns or pajamas, 6 pair of hose, 12 handkerchiefs, 1 pair of bath slippers, 1 pair house slippers, 1 bathing cap, 1 bathrobe, 2 swimming suits, 6 pair shoes, 1 pair of riding boots, 1 pair tennis shoes, 1 house or lounging robe, 1 overcoat, 1 raincoat, 3 sweaters, 3 scarves, 6 pair gloves, 2 belts, 8 dresses, 3 skirts, 3 blouses, 2 crinolines, 1 parasol, 5 hats, 4 handbags, 2 pair of fine earrings and 6 of costume jewelry, 1 fine brooch or pin and 6 of costume jewelry, 1 fine necklace and 3 of costume jewelry, 2 fine bracelets and 3 of costume jewelry, 2 watches for personal use.

Men — 12 changes of underwear, 6 shirts, 6 pair of socks, 3 pajamas, 6 pair of shoes, 1 pair riding boots, 1 pair tennis shoes, 1 pair bath slippers, 1 pair lounging slippers, 1 bathrobe, 2 swim suits or trunks, 1 lounging robe, 24 handkerchiefs, 2 scarfs, 6 ties, 2 mufflers, 3 sweaters, 2 pair of braces, 3 pair of gloves, 2 belts, 3 pair of slacks, 2 hats, 1 umbrella, 6 suits, 1 dress suit and accessories, 1 sport jacket, 1 overcoat, 1 raincoat, 2 pair jeweled cuff links and 3 ordinary, 2 fine tie clips and two ordinary, 3 fine rings and 3 ordinary, 2 watches for personal use.

Extras — In addition to the articles of personal wear listed above you can bring in up to 12 toilet articles, 5 cartons of cigarettes and 50 cigars (adults only), 1 kilo (2¼ lbs.) of tobacco, up to 50 books, scientific instruments or tools pertaining to the traveler's profession, providing they are not intended to equip a workshop, 1 still camera and 1 motion picture camera, 6 rolls of film for each camera. Sports equipment for the traveler's personal use, sports firearms and ammunition, provided the requisites specified by the Departamento de la Industria Militar have been fulfilled (See Index: *Hunting and Fishing*). You may also bring in used toys for children accompanying adults, 1 pair binoculars, medicine for personal use, luggage, up to 3 bottles of wine or spirits, up to 3 bottles of perfume or toilet water. You can also bring in tents, camping beds, folding chairs, tables, table linen, kitchen utensils, and 1 portable radio or 1 TV set.

Note: According to the law the above listed personal belongings can neither be sold nor given away while you are in Mexico. They must be taken out with you. At times the customs officials will list certain articles on your tourist card (typewriters, radios) just to make sure they recross the border.

DOGS AND PETS

You can bring your pets into Mexico. If you come by car there is rarely any fuss made about them or the papers required for them. However, according to Mexican regulations, a veterinarian's certificate stating that the animals are in good health, plus a certificate of inoculation against rabies (given within the past six months), should accompany the animals. To be doubly secure, it is a good idea to have these certificates notarized by the Mexican Consulate nearest your home.

THE BORDER CROSSING

When making a border crossing many travelers get unduly nervous. There is no need for it. Here, briefly, is all that happens. If you are entering Mexico by car, at the port of entry you will be asked to park your car near the customs and immigration building. Someone connected with the offices will show you where to park and will guide you about. You can leave your car unlocked. It is safe. First you go to the immigration department office where you secure your tourist card. If you already have one, you hand it over to the clerk to be registered and stamped. Next, you go to the office that handles motor vehicle affairs, (usually right next door), where you present your tourist card and the ownership title for the car. You will be issued a temporary import permit for the car, which you sign there. At the same time a man connected with this department checks the serial numbers of your car and its motor. Lastly, there is a customs inspection, normally very informal; the inspector may ask what you have in the car, may ask you to open a single suitcase. If traffic is light the entire routine of immigration, car and customs will take from fifteen minutes to half an hour. Tips are expected; anything from a quarter to a half dollar to the man who guides you around and to the man who helps with your baggage.

For many years a serious border problem was the *mordida* (the bite), where border officials tried to take advantage of the tourist's uncertainty concerning regulations and would cause trouble in order to exact exorbitant fees to smooth the way. The Mexican Government is anxious to discourage such veniality. If you run into such a situation you can help by noting the hour, the day, the port of entry and the situation and reporting it by letter to the Federal Tourist Bureau in Mexico City.

After you have crossed the border by car, there are generally two check points farther along the road where the car papers are inspected. Your baggage is not usually inspected at these points. At the Nogales port of entry the customs inspection occurs at the first check point some distance out of town.

If you enter Mexico by train your papers are checked and baggage inspected right aboard the train at the port of entry. If you come in via international airlines the immigration inspection and baggage check are made at the airport of entry.

ON LEAVING MEXICO

If flying out or leaving by train, your tourist card is picked up at the airport or aboard the train. There is usually no baggage inspection. If you are driving out, stop at the Mexican immigration office at the border to surrender your tourist card and the temporary import permit for your car. In some cases these are collected at inspection points somewhat south of the port of entry.

U. S. IMMIGRATION REQUIREMENTS

On re-entering the United States, American tourists must show proof of citizenship. The U.S. immigration officials are courteous, efficient and can often spot whether you are a citizen without having to check your papers. You will need proof of recent smallpox vaccination.

U. S. CUSTOMS — WHAT YOU CAN BRING HOME

Baggage examination by U. S. Customs officers is often stiffer than what you encounter going into Mexico.

As a returning resident of the United States you may bring back free of duty up to 100 dollars' worth of merchandise for personal use or gifts every 31 days, if the purchases are acquired merely as an incident of the trip. A new ruling by U. S. Customs gives tourists a slight break by figuring the *value* at 40% of the retail price, thus you can bring home merchandise on which the sales slips total $166.66 — 40% of this equaling $100. There is one exception — made to order clothing continues to be valued at full retail price. To claim this extra bonus you must show all the sales slips or invoices for purchases made in Mexico.

At Mexican border ports you may make your declaration orally *if: the total value of all articles you bought is not more than $100* (this includes alterations and dutiable repairs to articles you took abroad), the articles are for your personal or household use, and you have the articles with you. If your load of loot cost you more than $100 you may be required to turn in a written declaration.

It is wise to get receipt slips for everything of value that you've purchased so you can show them at the border. Don't try to tell the customs officer that you paid less than you did for something. He knows the market value of almost everything made or sold in Mexico.

If you plan to ship merchandise home from Mexico be sure to secure an itemized bill for all your purchases. Make out duplicate customs declarations and list the shipped articles under the heading "Goods to Follow." Have your customs officer stamp the duplicate declaration. Send this declaration to your customs broker whose job it is to escort your shipment through both Mexican and American customs, then send it on to your home.

If you intend to sell, or even give away your purchases as business gifts, that is to say for promotion, good will, etc., your exemptions do not apply and the articles are subject to import duty.

While in Mexico you can send small "unsolicited gifts" to friends in the United States — duty free. The gift must be valued at less than $10.

LIQUORS AND CIGARS: You can include up to one gallon of alcoholic beverages and 100 cigars in your exemption. Adults only. *However,* the U. S. Customs officers will not release liquors destined to any state for use in violation of its laws.

If you re-enter the U.S. at ports along the California border you may not import any liquor unless you possess a California liquor importer's license. Texas specifies a minimum amount, 8 ounces, thus forbidding the import of miniature bottles. Texas charges a state tax per quart (36 cents on liquor, 6 cents on wines). Residents of states prohibiting or restricting the importation of liquor may bring one quart into Texas or one gallon into Arizona, provided it is their intention to consume the same within the state of entry. *Note:* state restrictions on liquor imports, below.

STATE	GALS. LIQUOR PERMITTED	SPECIAL NOTE
Alabama	none	
Connecticut	1	permit for larger amounts
Iowa	1	
Massachusetts	1	
Nebraska	1	
Wyoming	1	
California	none	holders of state liquor licenses may import
Colorado	none	holders of state liquor licenses may import
Nevada	none	holders of state liquor licenses may import

STATE	GALS. LIQUOR PERMITTED	SPECIAL NOTE
South Carolina	none	
Kentucky	no restrictions	
Louisiana	no restrictions	
New Mexico	no restrictions	
North Dakota	no restrictions	
Missouri	5	
Rhode Island	3	
Vermont	2	
Arizona	1	
Florida	1	
Minnesota	1	
Illinois	1	
New Jersey	1	
New York	1	
North Carolina	1	
Ohio	1	
Virginia	1	
Washington	1	
West Virginia	1	
District of Columbia	1	
Maine	¾ gal.	
New Hampshire	¾ gal.	
Idaho	2 qts.	
Kansas	2 qts.	
Indiana	1 qt.	
Maryland	1 qt.	
Montana	1 qt.	
Oregon	1 qt.	
Texas	1 qt.	
Michigan	1/5 gal.	

The remainder of the states prohibit importation.

PROHIBITED AND RESTRICTED ARTICLES: You are not permitted to bring certain plants, fruits, vegetables, cuttings, and seeds into the U.S. Others must be inspected and treated before they can be brought in. If you plan to bring plants home make arrangements in advance by applying to the Import Permit Unit, Plant Quarantine Branch, 209 River Street, Hoboken, New Jersey, for information as well as applications for import permits.

The U.S. requirements for importing fresh, frozen, cured, and smoked meats and meat products are so specialized the average tourist cannot conform with them. For all practical purposes you can consider such imports prohibited.

The entry of pets (cats, dogs, monkeys, and psittacean birds such as parakeets and parrots) is subject to the regulations of the Public Health Service. At present, here are the steps you must take in order to bring pets into the United States. Ten days before your arrival at a port of entry: (1) have the animal immunized with an approved rabies vaccine, if that has not been done within six months of the anticipated date of arrival in the U.S., and obtain a certificate of immunization, (2) have the animal physically examined by a registered veterinarian from whom a statement should be obtained regarding the presence of demonstrable diseases involving emaciation, lesions of the skin, nervous system disturbances, jaundice, diarrhea, (3) present the certificate of rabies immunization and the vet's report at the offices of the Aftosa at 116 Avenida de los Maestros, Colonia Jacinto, Mexico City. They will give you a permit to transport the animal through Mexico to a port of exit, (4) you can stop at the U. S. Embassy in Mexico City and make out a sworn statement for presentation to the U. S. Public Health Inspector.

Note: Although this elaborate procedure is on the books, for personal pets such as dogs, obviously in good health, and accompanied by a certificate of rabies immunization and a clearance from a registered veterinarian, in most instances you do not have to take steps three and four.

Certain foreign-made articles (watches, cameras, perfumes, etc.) having a trade-mark registered with the U. S. Treasury Department, cannot be brought into the U.S. without consent of the trade-mark owner. The law, however, is given a lenient interpretation and most such firms have extended a blanket permission allowing one "sample" of such articles to be brought in as a souvenir. Usually, the label must be removed or destroyed.

Note: If you take valuable foreign-made articles (guns, cameras, binoculars, furs) into Mexico from the U.S. it is advisable to stop at the U. S. Customs office, and have them registered before you leave the United States.

MEXICAN CONSULATES IN THE U.S. AND CANADA

IN THE U.S.

Albuquerque, N.M.	1306 W. Central Ave.	Tel. 2-23-20
Amarillo, Tex.	306 Blackburn Bldg.	7789
Atlanta, Ga.	917 Grant Bldg.	
Austin, Texas	330 Perry Brooks Bldg. 706 Brazos St.	Tel. Gr 8-28-66
Boston, Mass.	40 Central St. Room 612	Tel. Lafayette 3-80-91
Brownsville, Tex.	1055 E. Elizabeth St.	Lincoln 2-4431
Buffalo, N.Y.	610 Chamber of Commerce Bldg.	
Calexico, Calif.	307 Sherman Ave.	Elliot 7-2614
Chicago, Ill.	201 N. Wells St., #842	State 2-5888
Cincinnati, Ohio	Provident Bank Bldg. 7th & Vine St.	Tel. Ga 1-04-04
Corpus Christi, Tex.	601 Jones Bldg. Chaparral & People	2-3375
Dallas, Tex.	527 Southland Center	Riverside 8-6437

Del Rio, Tex.	Graham Inc. Bldg. W. Greenwood & Main	775-2352
Denver, Col.	410 Cochrane Bldg. 131 15th St.	Tabor 5-8042
Detroit, Mich.	1016 Fox Theater Bldg.	Woodward 5-1868
Douglas, Ariz.	Brophy Bldg.	Em 4-2711
Eagle Pass, Tex.	455 Main St.	Prospect 3-2126
El Paso, Tex.	International Merchandise Mart Suites 212-222	
Fort Worth, Tex.	Wagner Bldg. 810 Houston St.	61023
Fresno, Calif.	Bank of America Bldg. Fulton & Tulare St.	Adams 3-8714
Honolulu, Hawaii	P.O. Box 9098	
Houston, Tex.	World Trades Center Bldg. 1520 Texas Ave.	
Kansas City, Mo.	706 Watchtower Bldg. 9th St. & Walnut	Harrison 59-59
Laredo, Tex.	1612 Farregut St.	Randolph 3-6360
Los Angeles, Calif.	354 S. Spring St.	Michigan 0604 & Madison 5-88-43
Marfa, Tex.	P.O. Drawer M Paisano Hotel	
McAllen, Tex.	519 S. Main St.	
Memphis, Tenn.	410 N. Waldran	Broadway 6-8621
Miami, Fla.	1508-9 Congress Bldg. 111 N.W. Second Ave.	Franklin 9-5085
Milwaukee, Wis.	228 E. Wisconsin Ave.	
Mobile, Ala.	59 N. Water St.	
Newark, N.J.	48 Commerce St.	
New Orleans, La.	533 Whitney Bldg. St. Charles & Graves Sts.	523-3733
New York, N.Y.	8 E. 41st St.	Murray Hill 9-0456
Nogales, Ariz.	135 Terrace Ave.	Atwater 7-2521
Norfolk, Va.	404 Western Union Bldg.	
Oklahoma City, Okla.	1120 Haler Bldg. 107 N. Robinson St.	Central 2-8433
Philadelphia, Pa.	12 S. 12th St.	Walnut 2-4262
Phoenix, Ariz.	Goodrich Bldg. Central Ave. & Washington St.	Alpine 8-3721
Sacramento, Calif.	1009 South St.	6-46-96
St. Louis, Mo.	Lauderman Bldg., #510-512 317 N. 11th St.	Tel. Main 1-4032
Salt Lake City, Utah	122½ South Main	El 5-2251
San Antonio, Tex.	127 Navarro St.	Ca 7-9145
San Bernardino, Calif.	392 Court St.	
San Diego, Calif.	901 Bank of America Bldg.	Belmont 9-9483
San Francisco, Calif.	870 Market St.	Exbrook 2-5554
Seattle, Wash.	618 Securities Bldg. 1904 3rd Ave.	Mutual 3634
Tucson, Ariz.	553 S. Stone St.	Main 2-3031
Washington, D.C.	2829 16th St. N.W.	Adams 4-6000 & Columbia 5-5112
IN CANADA		
Montreal, Que.	1245 Sherbrook West	288-2502
Ottawa, Que.	88 Metcalfe St.	3-8988
Quebec, Que.	51 Desjardines St.	
Toronto, Ont.	20 Carlton St.	Central 38988
Vancouver, B.C.	Burard Bldg. 1030 W. Georgia St.	Mu 4-3547

Tourist cards as well as tourist information can be obtained at the above listed Mexican Consulates, and also at the following offices of the Departmento Autónomo de Turismo (Mexican Government Tourist Bureau):

New York City 630 Fifth Ave., #3508
Chicago, Ill. 210 North Michigan Ave.
San Antonio, Tex. 209 E. Travis
Los Angeles, Calif. 3106 Wilshire Blvd.
New Orleans, La. 203 Charles St.
Miami, Fla. First National Bank Bldg., Arcade #20
Tucson, Ariz. 80 N. Stone St.
San Diego, Calif. 1301 Fifth Ave.
Dallas, Tex. 1905 Commerce St.
Houston, Tex. 809 Walker Ave.
Toronto, Ont., Can. 13 Bloor St., West
Montreal, Que., Can. 700 Dorchester Blvd., West
Washington, D.C. 1302 Connecticut Ave., N.W.

3. *What to Take: Travel Clothing, Luggage, Travel Aids*

Your travel wardrobe should be dictated not only by your personal fancy in dress, but also by your mode of travel (air, auto, train, or bus) and by Mexico's climate as well as certain Mexican customs.

Although much of Mexico is within the tropic zone, in many areas the weather is never torrid (See Index: *Climate of Mexico*). In Mexico City and most of the Central Plateau you will find that lightweight woollen clothes are suitable at all times and for the few weeks of nippy winter weather all you need add is a light topcoat or a warm sweater. During the summer rainy season you'll need a lightweight raincoat.

If you plan to visit subtropical areas such as Cuernavaca, Taxco, the coastal resorts, you should take along summerweight garments for daytime wear and light woollens for evening wear. Even in the tropics the nights can be chilly except during the month of May.

Ordinarily Mexicans dress in a conservative fashion. In the larger cities the women are among the most smartly dressed in the world. Men do not normally go about in sport clothes. Well-cut gabardines are almost *de rigeur* in Mexico City, Guadalajara, and other large cities. Casual wear and sport clothing are reserved for outings, resort areas, and the beach towns. Both male and female tourists should dress comfortably, but reserve those wild California and Hawaiian shirts, hand-painted skirts, and vivid blouses for resort areas.

Evening clothes are not necessary except for diplomatic functions.

The era of heavy steamer trunks is gone. Modern garments, lightweight fabrics and slim luggage have made it so you can travel for a month or more out of a single suitcase. Whether you travel by air, by train, or by bus we suggest that you take along no more than you can pick up and carry yourself—preferably in one hand!

LUGGAGE

Equip yourself with lightweight but strong airplane-type luggage with good locks. Either the Samsonite Silhouette three-suiter and companion case made by Shawayder Brothers, or the Hartmann Luggage Company's Asymate Aerobe two-suiter, are recommended. (Ladies' model is called the Mayfair.)

CLOTHING FOR MEN

Here is a minimum wardrobe that should cover all your needs while traveling in Mexico in any season and altitude:

—lightweight suit, wool or combined wool and silk.
—2 pair shoes (1 for dress, the other casuals). The ankle-high crepe-soled desert boots are fine for climbing pyramids and navigating cobbled streets.
—summer suit, Dacron-nylon wash and wear type, such as those made by Haspel Co., New Orleans.
—6 shirts (at least two of them wash and wears).
—underwear.
—9 pair sox, some wool, some lisle.
—lightweight slippers.
—handkerchiefs (or buy Kleenex anywhere in Mexico).
—lightweight bathrobe.
—(for winter, high altitudes), a gabardine raincoat. During the summer carry a featherweight, fold-up raincoat such as the Nylonair made by Rainfair, Racine, Wis. Carry it in a tuckaway pouch. The plastic types are impractical; they harden and crack and burn too easily.
—belt, garters, and braces.
—lightweight hat.
—a cashmere sweater.
—2 pair slacks and a sport jacket.
—2 pair pajamas.
—2 neckties.

If you have a hankering for rich solid colored or striped hand-loomed cambric shirts, then leave a few shirts at home and do some shirt buying in Mexico. There are real bargains.

—toilet articles, including a small can of pressurized shave cream for Mexico's hard water.
—bathing trunks.

For hunters, jungle explorers, orchid seekers, and archaeologists, see Index: recommended camping outfits.

CLOTHING FOR WOMEN

—2 suits.
—2 crepe dresses.
—3 scarves.
—1 nylon or Dacron dress.
—1 woollen dress.
—3 blouses (or, you can wait and buy the finely hand-embroidered batiste blouses Mexico is famous for).
—several bras and panties.
—bedroom slippers.
—lightweight robe.
—3 pair shoes (at least one pair of low-heeled shoes for walking on cobbles). If you have small feet you can purchase beautifully styled high-heeled shoes in Mexico.
—1 purse (if you need more buy them in Mexico).
—2 nightgowns.
—9 to 12 pair hose.
—stoles, but wait and buy them in Mexico.
—panty girdles.
—(for winter travel) 1 pair long woollen stockings. Hotel rooms are often chilly.
—1 swim suit, bathing cap.
—jewelry (or, wait and buy it in Mexico).
—toilet articles.

Beauty preparations are cheaper in Mexico, there being no tax on them. You can find most of the standard brands you are accustomed to at home.

Take plastic bags to pack your shoes, scarves, bras, and hose in.

You need take no hat to Mexico unless you plan to attend a fashionable wedding or sit in a box at the race track. While visiting churches *you must* wear a head covering. It can be an easily carried scarf or stole. If you wear a Mexican *rebozo* (stole) on your head in church, be respectful of Mexican customs. Women don't wear loud or garish ones into church. If you are a young girl it can be a white or light colored one; older women should wear one of a more conservative (darker) color.

Don't bring shorts or slacks to Mexico unless you are going to a beach resort such as Acapulco. Women in Mexico do not wear slacks or shorts in public. This also applies to men wearing Bermuda shorts.

TRAVEL AIDS

Here are a few items you might add to your list which will make travel in Mexico much more comfortable.

Sunglasses. The brilliance of the Mexican sky makes sunglasses almost mandatory. Take along a pair of Calobar, Rayban, or Soft-lite glasses, either number 3's or 4's.

Cigarette Lighter. Except in swanky restaurants and hotels, book matches are not given away in Mexico. The matches you must buy come in boxes the size of a cigarette lighter. Usually you run out of them at a moment when there are no stores open. We find that a good-grade lighter (Ronson, Evans, or Zippo) with a wind-guard are ideal for Mexico. Cheaper lighters have a tendency to leak at high altitudes. Standard lighter fuels and flints are available in most towns.

Janie Spot Cleaner. A handy lipstick type chalk stick and tiny brush that does the job of a drycleaner. You rub it on the spot, then brush the spot away. It is sold at notion counters in the U.S. Made by the R. S. Cowen Company, 9 E. 38th St., New York, N.Y.

Flashlight. You'll find a pen-style or keyring flashlight just the thing.

Soaps and Detergents. Mexican rest rooms are rarely equipped with soaps and towels. Take along a pack of Wash 'n Dri towelettes, those ever-useful, individually packed moist paper towels that are no larger than a folded Kleenex. You'll find them in most drugstores at home. They're made by R. R. Williams, Inc., Canaan, Conn. Add to this one of those book-match type packs of soap leaves made by Dorin and distributed by Mauvel, Ltd., 13 W. 57th St., New York, N.Y. They're lifesavers. Also, pack along a good detergent in a plastic container, for washbowl laundering and nylons. Never trust your fine silks and synthetic fabrics to Mexican laundresses. As a rule they beat and rub the devil out of clothes and press them with too hot an iron. The same applies to men's woollen and nylon socks.

Insect Repellents. A good repellent is a "must" below the border the year around. *6-12*, marketed by the Union Carbide Corporation, in liquid form as well as in a lipstick tube is an effective all-around repellent. Hunters have reported that for the tropics the most effective repellent is a spray-type repellent named Off. It contains Meta Delphene, a most effective bug chaser developed for the U. S. Navy. When you are bitten by mosquitoes and other insects the quickest and best relief is gained by rubbing the bite with the juice of a lemon or lime.

Electric Razors. Most parts of Mexico are now on 60 cycle, AC 110 volt power, so electric razors are usable. It is wise to have a safety razor in reserve, however, for in many towns and cities the current goes off for long stretches.

Clip-on Reading Lamp. Due to the bad lighting and inadequate fixtures in the average Mexican hotel a most useful item to pack along is a small clip-on reading lamp and a rather long extension cord. You might also carry one of those handy plugs which fit various type sockets. Mexican electrical connections are far from standardized.

Coffee Comforts. If you are a tea or coffee fan, and are motoring in Mexico, add a small electric hot plate or a spirit stove, a one or two cup aluminum pot, plastic cups, powdered coffee, teabags, etc., to your travel kit. In small towns and roadside hotels you'll encounter difficulties getting coffee early in the morning and after 9 P.M.

Medical Needs. For suggested items to include in your traveling medical kit see the following section.

4. Health Hints: Inoculations, Precautions with Food and Water, Cheeses, Seafood, Your Traveling Medical Kit

Along Mexico's well-traveled tourist routes one is not likely to run into health problems any more serious than one encounters on a trip from Illinois to Louisiana.

INOCULATIONS

For a normal vacation trip involving no off-trail travel certain minimum inoculations are recommended. You should at least have a recent smallpox vaccination, (it is required for re-entry into the U.S.), and the series of three anti-typhoid inoculations. If you plan an extended stay and intend to visit around in rural villages or the tropics, you should also be inoculated against tetanus, typhus, and possible cholera. Before heading for Mexico you should allow yourself from four to six weeks for the series of shots. You can go to any U. S. Public Health Service office and get all your shots free of charge.

Children and young adults coming to Mexico should have had their Salk polio shots.

FOOD PRECAUTIONS

Along the most traveled routes hotels and restaurants are equipped to serve well-prepared, good food. Usually the sanitary conditions are good, yet certain precautions should be taken.

The most common complaint suffered by visitors in Mexico is an upset stomach and a mild diarrhea, popularly called "The Aztec Two-Step" or "Montezuma's Revenge." In most instances the ailment is usually no more serious in nature than the names imply. The cause is generally due to: (1) tension and overfatigue resulting from trying to do too much and see too much in a strange country and at high altitudes; (2) a change in your normal eating habits. The big Mexican meal is at mid-day rather than in the evening. Tourists often overstuff themselves; (3) a change in the mineral content of the water you drink; (4) eating heavily of certain foods we are not accustomed to (a great deal of oil and mountains of tomatoes are used in most Mexican cookery) and; (5) bacteria or amoebic infection. This last is least likely to occur if you are sensibly cautious.

There are a number of medical remedies and some folk remedies which will usually give relief to upsets due to the first four causes. For simple stomach upset due to rich and unfamiliar foods try Tums or a teaspoon of ordinary baking soda in warm water. For mild cases of dysentery the two Mexican pharmaceutical products Enterovioforma and Viotaladina are old standbys and can be purchased in any pharmacy. For severe cases of dysentery Polmagma, made by Wyeth-Valles S.A., and available in most Mexican drugstores, is most efficacious. It contains antibiotics. Polmagma may not relieve the severe cramps that accompany dysentery. Bellafolina tablets (one about every six hours) should relieve the cramps. If dysentery and cramps persist it is advisable to see a doctor. Mexico has excellent private clinics and doctors noted for their valuable research and work in tropical diseases.

In the regional sections of this guidebook doctors are listed for most of the major cities and towns.

Rural Mexicans also have their own home remedies for mild cases of dysentery and some seem to give relief. One is to let slices of a peeled apple become brown, then eat them. Another is a tea brewed with a few leaves of the Seville or bitter orange tree. Teas or decoctions made of the crushed flowers of both the angel's-hair plant and also the acacia are said to give relief.

While traveling in Mexico, take it easy during your first few days at high altitudes. Eat moderately and do not overimbibe, especially hard liquors.

One should be cautious of water. Although the drinking water in many large cities is purified, nevertheless, avoid taking it directly from the tap. Frequently the plumbing system in buildings and city waterworks is antiquated and the water is contaminated en route to you. The larger and better hotels and restaurants make an effort to provide purified bottled water for guests. However, due to lack of supervision, occasionally a chambermaid may fill your pitcher with water drawn from the tap. To put your mind at rest, carry a small bottle of water purifying tablets. It only takes a second when you walk into a hotel room to drop a tablet into the water jar. In a half hour to an hour your drinking water will be safe. The U. S. Army's halazone tablets (Abbott) can be bought in any stateside drugstore. In Mexico a similar Swiss product, hydroclonazone, is available in all pharmacies.

In restaurants, if you have doubts about the water, order bottled purified or bottled mineral water *(agua purificada* or *agua mineral).* In tropical regions *always* purify your water. It may be contaminated with organisms causing typhoid, paratyphoid, cholera as well as bacillary and amoebic dysentery.

Although Mexico now produces some wonderful cheeses, unless you know cheeses and their background, it is best to skip eating them, especially in outlying villages and small off-beat restaurants. Sometimes cheeses are produced under unsanitary conditions, are improperly handled, and may be made of contaminated milk. The goat's milk cheese in some regions is a potent source of Malta fever.

Milk should be drunk only when properly boiled or pasteurized. Many Mexican doctors do not recommend commercially pasteurized milks and even the irradiated canned milks for children unless the milks are boiled. Both pure food controls and sanitary inspections in many parts of the country are almost nonexistent.

If you are a seafood fan, limit your dining on fish and crustaceans to coastal areas where the products are fresh-caught, or to a restaurant you can trust. Bad fish and oysters can usually be spotted by smell and taste, unless they are smothered in a garlic sauce as is done. With lobsters, the meat in the tail should be tight and not flabby; when cooked, if the meat is at all grayish, instead of snowy white, the lobster is on its way to perdition. Don't be afraid to send a dish back if it doesn't look, smell, or taste right.

MOSQUITOES

While visiting in tropical areas see that the hotel management furnishes you with mosquito bars or nettings for your beds. Resorts like Acapulco are just about malaria-free, but occasionally an anopheles mosquito lurks around. Do not be afraid to put on a good insect repellent when planning to spend time in a village market or even a village movie theater.

TRAVELING MEDICAL KIT

You can purchase most modern medicines and prescription medicines in the larger Mexican pharmacies. There is no need to load up on a variety of medicines. In many instances you can buy them for less in Mexico. Most medicines that require a prescription in the U.S. can be bought directly over-the-counter in Mexico.

The following is a suggested minimum medical and first-aid kit for travel in Mexico. The asterisked (*) items can be purchased in Mexico.

—Halazone or hydroclonazone* for purifying water.
—Band-Aids* treated with metaphen, tirotricina, etc. (In Mexico they are called *Band-itas.*)
—Polmagma* for dysentery.
—A medical thermometer. Mexican thermometers are in centigrade.
—Tums or other antacid*.
—Aspirin* *(Bayeraspirina, Cafeaspirina, etc.).*
—Insect repellent*.
—An antihistamine for relief of insect bites*.
—Syringe and hypodermic needles*. (Doctors in Mexico rarely give injections. If you have to have an injection for anything a nurse gives it, or usually you go to the pharmacy for it. It is best to have your own needle and syringe because the local ones are not always properly disinfected and they are used repeatedly.)

PHARMACIES

Except for the Sanborn establishments in Mexico City and Monterrey and a few spots in Baja California, Mexico has no catch-all drugstores where you can buy anything from Amphojel to swim suits. In Mexico medicines and drugs are sold in pharmacies which handle nothing else. There are three types: first-, second-, and third-class pharmacies. A first-class drugstore usually has an extensive stock of medicines and drugs plus the services of a registered pharmacist who can compound prescriptions. The other grade shops can only sell bottled or patent medicines.

5. *Transportation. To Mexico via Air, Railroad, Boat, Bus. Motoring, Highway Regulations, Insurance, Road Signs, Auto Repairs, Motor Travel Tips. Renting Cars. Trailer Facilities. Camping. Taxis. Maps of Mexico*

Less than twenty years ago the only safe and comfortable way one could get into Mexico was by boat or railroad. There was practically no air service and but a few hundred miles of passable roads. Today the only limit on where you can go in the country is your budget and your time. The republic has made incredible progress during the last two decades in solving its transportation problems. The country is serviced by a dozen international airlines as well as local airlines; a vast network of highways and secondary roads crisscross the nation; service stations, hotels, and resorts are sprouting all over.

To get maximum enjoyment out of a trip south of the Rio Grande you should select your mode of transportation carefully. Air travel is the fastest and most comfortable. You can hop from New York, Chicago, or Los Angeles to Mexico City in an afternoon. Naturally, you'll miss much of the scenery, the intimate color, and impressions you can only get via automobile or bus travel. Your best bet if you are a one- or two-week vacationer and do not live near the Mexican border is to fly in, then rent cars or use bus transportation to soak up the local color. If you have more leisure or are traveling with family, motoring is more comfortable, cheaper, and more fun. Here is a rundown on various transportation services and routes into Mexico.

AIR TRAVEL

Over a dozen international airlines have direct flights to Mexico, using the newest equipment — jets, turbo-props, radar-equipped Super Star Constellations, DC-7s, etc. Service includes regular first-class and tourist class. Most flights arrive in Mexico City in the evening, giving you a spectacular view of the illuminated city.

Flight rates from New York to Mexico City (at time of publication) are about $153 first class and about $105 tourist. From Los Angeles, $98 first class and $79 tourist. Lower rates are offered by several Mexican airlines whose flights begin at the border and make several stops before reaching the capital. You can fly from Brownsville, Texas, (Matamoros) to Mexico City for as little as $34 round trip.

The Mexico City airport is a delight to come into. Located on the eastern edge of the city, on the dry bed of Lake Texcoco, its approaches are long and uncluttered. The new airport building is one of the finest in the world. There are comfortable lounges, restaurants, cafeteria, bar, drugstore, souvenir shops, and money exchange booths that give the same exchange rate as the best banks. The immigration and customs officials are courteous and efficient. The airport is about a ten-minute taxi ride, via a new boulevard, into the heart of the city.

During the height of the two travel seasons, when airlines are crowded, you can sometimes get passage to Mexico by signing up for Go Show. This means, you are ready to take off at a moment's notice. Aircraft loads are made up 30 and 10 hours before flight time on a basis of maximum bad weather. If the sun is out at take-off time there is room for extra cargo or a few extra passengers. On the Mexican side there is no Go Show service.

Before your return flight home it is necessary to reconfirm your reservation within 24 hours before the flight. On this, be absolutely sure the reservation clerk has understood you. There is a certain amount of inefficiency in local office procedures and many tourists have arrived at the airport only to find that no one really bothered to note down their reconfirmation.

The international lines do not offer service to points of interest within Mexico. For travel within the country you shift to local airlines. In some instances the airlines are the only means of comfortable transportation to certain resorts, such as Puerto Vallarta, Zihuatanejo, Puerto Angel, Cozumel, and some of the archaeological sites.

The local airlines have improved considerably in equipment and the extent of their service, as well as safety. However, they have not achieved the timetable efficiency of flights in Europe and the U.S. It is not unusual to wait for hours for a plane to be made up. Flights are canceled, or your reservation is canceled, without your being advised.

Flight rates are very inexpensive on the national and local lines. There are no tourist-class flights; everything is first class. One line, Aeronaves de Mexico, has recently instituted an air-coach service linking various cities.

On most flights, international and local, you are allowed six-month stopovers. You can carry approximately 65 lbs. luggage free of charge on first-class international flights, 44 lbs. on tourist flights, 55 lbs. (25 kilos) on all domestic flights.

Domestic and International Airlines Serving Mexico (Addresses and telephone numbers are for the offices and reservation centers in Mexico City, unless otherwise indicated.)

AERONAVES DE MEXICO S.A. Av. Reforma 64. Tel. 34-49-00. International and domestic. Daily flights New York–Mexico City; Mexico City to Guadalajara, Acapulco, La Paz, Tijuana, Nogales, Torreón, Monterrey, Cuidad Juárez, Equip.: Britannia turbo-prop, DC-6, DC-3, Convair.

AIR FRANCE. Av. Reforma 76. Tel. 46-91-40 and 35-16-05. The French line with direct flights from Paris, Montreal, New York, Chicago to Mexico City. First class and tourist. Equip. Super Star Constellations. Daily flights.

AMERICAN AIRLINES. Av. Juárez 117. Tel. 35-94-70. International flights between Boston, New York, Chicago, Cleveland, Memphis, Fort Worth, Dallas, San Antonio, and Mexico City. Equip. DC-6, DC-7, Convairs.

CANADIAN PACIFIC AIRLINES. Av. Reforma 60. Tel. 46-95-40 International flights daily linking Mexico, Canada and South America. Equip. Super DC-6 and Britannia.

CUBANA AIRLINES. Av. Reforma 56. Tel. 35-79-00 and 46-75-04. The Cuban airline. International flights linking Mexico City to Cuba, Miami, Nassau, New York, and Haiti. Equip. Viscount, Super G Constellation with radar, DC-3.

EASTERN AIRLINES. Av. Reforma and Morelos. Tel. 35-78-50 and 46-29-00. International flights between Mexico City, Boston, New York and Montreal, and New Orleans. (Connections with most southern and eastern seaboard cities in the U.S.) Equip. DC-7B with radar.

IBERIA (LINEAS AÉREAS DE ESPAÑA). Av. Reforma 24. Tel. 21-56-19. The Spanish airlines running direct flights between Madrid, New York, Cuba, Mexico. Equip. Super G Constellations. Offers first class, tourist, and economy class.

KLM (ROYAL DUTCH AIRLINES). Av. Reforma 87. Tel. 35-10-00. International flights between Mexico City, Houston, Montreal, and Amsterdam (Holland). Also, flights from Mexico City to Guatemala, San Salvador, Costa Rica, Panama, Barranquilla, and Curaçao. Equip. DC-7, DC-6.

MEXICANA DE AVIACIÓN (CMA). Av. Reforma y Balderas. Tel. 18-08-70. International and domestic flights. Service (direct and local flights) between Mexico City, Los Angeles, Acapulco, Guadalajara, Puerto Vallarta, Mazatlán, Hermosillo, Mexicali, Tijuana, Tuxpan, Tampico, Monterrey, N. Laredo, Matamoros, San Antonio, and Chicago. Equip. DC-3, DC-4, DC-6, Britannia, and a new jet service to Los Angeles.

LACSA (LINEAS AÉREAS COSTARRICENSES). Independencia 66. Tel. 21-81-60. The Costa Rican airline offering international flights between Mexico City, Cuba, the Cayman Islands, San Salvador, and Panama.

PAA (PAN AMERICAN WORLD AIRWAYS SYSTEM). Av. Reforma 35. Tel. 46-46-60. International flights between Mexico, the United States, South America, and Europe. Equip. DC-6, Douglas Super Clipper, DC-7B and jets. First and tourist class.

TACA INTERNATIONAL AIRLINES. Av. Reforma 52. International flights connecting Mexico with Central America — Guatemala, Panama, El Salvador, Honduras, Costa Rica, and Nicaragua. Equip. Jet prop Viscount, DC-4.

WESTERN AIRLINES. Av. Reforma 51. Tel. 46-90-40 and 35-17-87. International daily flights connecting Seattle, Portland, San Francisco, Los Angeles, Salt Lake City, Las Vegas, Phoenix, San Diego with Mexico City. Equip. DC-6B, Convair. Offers tourist class and "champagne flights."

AEROLINEAS VEGA. Av. Reforma 34, Mexico D.F. Tel. 46-57-50. Small, well-equipped line making local flights between Acapulco, Oaxaca, and Puebla. (Local offices listed under those cities.)

AEROVIAS ROJAS. 5 de Mayo y Morelos, Oaxaca City, Oax. Small local line making the run of coffee ports and interior towns in the States of Oaxaca.

CIA, IMPULSORA DE AVIACIÓN, S.A. 1 Avenida Sur 94, Tuxtla Gutierrez, Chiapas. Small line serving isolated Chiapas, with special flights to Bonampak, Palenque, etc.

COMPANIA TABASQUEÑA DE AVIACIÓN, S.A. Juárez 64, Villa Hermosa, Tabs. Small line serving Tabasco and making special flights to Palenque, Tenosique, and Bonampak.

RAILWAY TRAVEL

Two of the principal U.S. railway lines make direct connections with the Mexican railway lines at the border cities of Nogales, Cuidad Juárez (El Paso, Tex.), and Nuevo Laredo (Laredo, Tex.). The Southern Pacific Railway network links the American Southwest with the Mexican west coast lines at Nogales and with the central lines at Cuidad Juárez. The Missouri Pacific system joins with the Nuevo Laredo-Mexico City line at Laredo.

The Mexican railways (*ferrocarriles*) are an extensive network, now largely nationalized and unified under the name of Ferrocarriles Nacionales de México. A few lines remain separate from this central organization: the Ferrocarril del Pacifico, S.A. de C.V., which goes from Nogales to Guadalajara and there connects with the National Railways; the Ferrocarril del Sureste, which traverses the Gulf Coast southeast of Veracruz and links the body of the republic with Yucatán.

Many of the Mexican lines cross areas of exceptional beauty and interest that still can not be reached by auto or plane. For comfortable travel, however, most such trips cannot be recommended. Only on the major lines are the first class Pullmans fairly comfortable at the present moment. Generally the train schedules are slow, there are frequently meaningless stops, the air-conditioning or heating in the cars inoperative.

Mexico's best train at present is the *Aguila Azteca* (Aztec Eagle), daily between Laredo and Mexico City. The coaches and Pullmans are of Swiss manufacture. It has a comfortable lounge car, bar, dining service, and de luxe compartments.

Railway fares (*precios de pasaje*) are much lower than those in the U.S. Ticket offices at the stations are opened a half hour before train departure and they close three minutes before the train leaves. Since the ticket office is often crowded, it is best to secure reservations and tickets through your hotel or a travel agency. Half-price rates are in effect for children from the age of five to twelve.

On international tickets you are allowed 68 kilos of baggage without charge. On domestic first-class tickets, 50 kilos; second-class tickets, 25 kilos. You can take 25 kilos of baggage into the car with you.

No animals are permitted in passenger cars. Animals may be transported in cages or proper containers in the baggage car. A fee of $2.50 MN is charged for transporting animals a distance of less than 250 kilometers; $4.00 MN for distances 250 to 500 kms.; $6.00 MN for distances above 500 kms.

When crossing international borders, both immigration and customs inspection is made on the train.

In small towns along the railway lines Pullman reservations cannot be made on the spot. The ticket agent must telephone to Mexico City or the nearest large city office. You have to pay for this call. During off-seasons you can gamble on getting a Pullman by just buying a first-class ticket, then paying for your Pullman after you board the train.

Information regarding railway service between

tourist points of interest is given in the regional sections of the guidebook.

AUTOBUS TRAVEL

In the past few years bus travel has become one of the most convenient, low-budget methods of getting around Mexico. You can travel first-class from one end of the country to the other for less than $40. Most buses run every hour or two. There are convenient stops along the road and you can have stopover privileges. The network of first- and second-class buses is now incredible. They poke into some of the most remote corners of the republic. There is a popular saying in Mexico that buses will go places that even a donkey would think twice about.

The major bus lines, running regular schedules from U.S. border cities to Mexico City and other lines extending to Cuernavaca, Veracruz, Manzanillo, Oaxaca, etc., are first class, air conditioned and often so gadget-equipped they are more de luxe than buses in the United States.

In small towns you will find that the buses start from the central plaza. Ninety per cent of the time their headquarters are at a restaurant or lunchroom which serves as their ticket office. In larger towns and cities there are regular bus terminals. In Mexico City there is a central bus travel agency at Paseo de la Reforma 34 (Tel. 46-67-99) where they will work out schedules for bus trips and make reservations for you on any bus line in Mexico. Also, *Guia de Transportes Aereos y Autotransportes de México,* is the schedule book for air and bus travelers, listing all the bus lines, routes, timetables, and rates. It is revised each month and sells for $1 MN in Mexico. The editor, Sr. E. de la Rosa, at Apartado Postal 8929, Mexico, 7, D.F., will mail it to you. Subscription abroad is $1 a year.

As a rule, restaurant and comfort stations along the road are not de luxe. Often you can get adequate meals for a half to a third of what you would pay in the usual tourist havens.

Rest rooms leave a great deal to desire. If your road stops are long enough, it is best to go in search of a good hotel for such conveniences. For your comfort you should also carry a small kit containing toilet articles, soap leaves, a small hand towel, and Wash 'n Dris.

Regional terminals and lines are included in Part Four of the guidebook.

MOTORING IN MEXICO

Driving your own car — or a car rented in Mexico — is one of the most satisfactory ways of seeing the republic. The skein of roads covering the country is now enormous; service stations, hotels and motels are so spaced that your driving day is now hardly ever dictated by these factors. The red tape involved in bringing your car into the country is negligible. (See Index: Automobile Permits.)

Insurance. Normally American and Canadian auto insurance policies *(póliza de seguros para automóviles)* are not in effect in Mexico except along the border, within a radius of 25 miles of the international boundary. Your local insurance agent can arrange for coverage in Mexico, which is done in conjunction with a Mexican company, or you can purchase an insurance policy at any of the Mexican-United States border towns. The American Automobile Association (AAA) representatives in any of these towns will arrange Mexican insurance for you whether you are a member of the AAA or not.

You are strongly advised to carry adequate insurance for any trip into Mexico. In case of an accident you and your car can be held, *whether you are guilty or not,* until the accident has been thoroughly investigated and payment of damages or claims has been settled. If, for example, you fell asleep and drove off the road, though you injured no one and only damaged your car, you could still be held by the authorities, and even fined. A Mexican insurance policy can help considerably in such situations. The authorities recognize it as a guarantee of proper payment of damages. Presenting such a policy will assist in your early release. The larger Mexican firms have representatives and adjusters in towns all along the major highways. Many of these men speak English and can be of great assistance.

Your minimum auto insurance coverage should include: public liability *(daños a terceros en sus personas)* $20,000 MN, property damage *(daños a bienes de terceros)* $10,000 MN, theft, fire, etc., *(robo de vehículo, incendio, etc.).* Mexican insurance only covers theft of the car itself, not extras on the car or valuables within the car. Before leaving home it is wise to get a personal property policy covering cameras, luggage, and other valuables. Other coverage most Americans also take out are: collision and upset *(colisiones y vuelcos),* glass breakage *(rotura de cristales)* which is almost a must because windows are often smashed by thieves breaking into cars.

The minimum premium that can be written on a car is $3.07, (including policy fee and government tax). You can secure policies covering you for a specific number of days, months, or by the year. Long-term policies are less expensive.

The very efficient Sanborn's Tourist Service will handle your Mexican insurance, and they toss in an extra convenience — they give you an immediate refund for the days you have not used up. There are

MEXICAN ROAD SIGNS

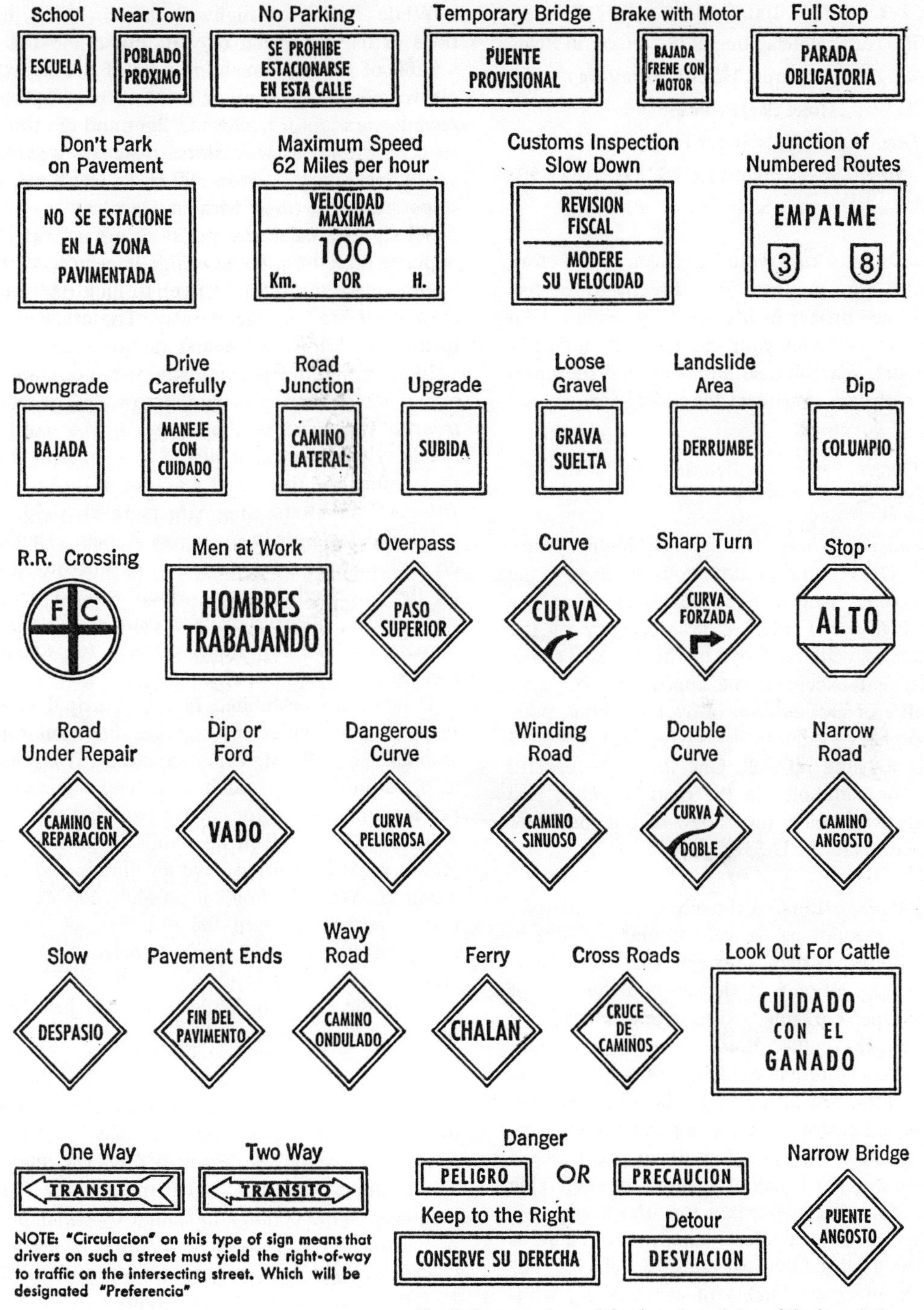

NOTE: "Circulacion" on this type of sign means that drivers on such a street must yield the right-of-way to traffic on the intersecting street. Which will be designated "Preferencia"

Road signs courtesy of the American Automobile Association

no tedious negotiations and red tape. This applies, of course, only on policies they write out for you.

(Sanborn's Tourist Service offices as follows:)

San Antonio, Tex. 203 E. Travis St. Ca 3-1201

Laredo, Tex. 2319 San Bernardo (U.S. 81-83-59) Ra 3-7419

McAllen, Tex. 2015 S. 10th St. Mu 6-4982

Brownsville, Tex. Holiday Inn, 2617 N. Central Blvd.

Brownsville, Tex. El Jardín Hotel (Downtown)

Eagle Pass, Tex. Hotel Eagle Pr 3-3806

El Paso, Tex. Desert Hills Motor Hotel, 4501 N. Mesa

Nogales, Ariz. Tucson Highway (U.S. 89) At 7-3903

El Centro, Calif. 444 S. 4th St. El 2-4647

If you wish to secure your car insurance before reaching the border you can write directly to the following insurance broker in Mexico City, giving them the pertinent data about your car (motor and body number, model, year, license number) and the dates and number of days you want the policy for, as well as the type of coverage.

Agencia Técnica, Paseo de la Reforma 134, Mexico, 6, D.F. Tel. 35-79-04 and 46-03-30.

Roads and Highways. The Mexican highways are fairly good. Due to the mountainous nature of the country the roads wind a good deal and cannot be considered high-speed arteries. Scarcely any of the highways are as wide as those in the U. S. Traffic, however, is light except at the approaches of large cities. Because of lack of control over trucking, poor maintenance, heavy rains and excessive heat, the road surfaces do not hold up well. One should be careful and watch for bad holes in the road *(baches)*, and for washouts after heavy rains. Few of the roads are as well marked as in the U.S. or Europe.

Driving Precautions. Although rules-of-the-road and motoring regulations are very similar to those in the United States, certain Mexican road conditions demand greater caution and alertness on the part of the driver. Open grazing exists along almost all routes. Livestock, cattle, horses, burros, and pigs constitute an ever-present road hazard, especially at night when cattle are attracted to the highways because of the heat stored in the asphalt. When you see an animal near the road slow down and proceed with caution. Animal behavior is most unpredictable and a small donkey can wreck a four-ton truck.

Night driving is particularly dangerous. There is no federal or local safety inspection of vehicles, nor is there very effective policing of cars driving without proper equipment. Vehicles are frequently met which are operated without taillights, with only bright lights which cannot be dimmed, or they may be operated without lights at all.

Bridges and culverts on many highways are very narrow and the approaches to them are bumpy. Drive slowly at these points. Often, at the entrance to towns and villages, the federal pavement ends. The route through the town may be in very poor condition, so go slow. Do not park on curves. Whenever you stop, pull entirely off the road if possible.

While driving on highways and in cities, be cautious of the car ahead of you. Buses and taxis have a habit of stopping in the middle of the street, without warning, to pick up or leave off passengers. Until recent years motor traffic was light and the traditional road courtesies as well as hand-signals were considered unnecessary. Drivers still make left turns, abrupt stops and right turns without signaling.

When two cars are approaching a bridge from opposite directions, if the bridge is narrow or marked *puente angosto,* the first driver to flick his headlights on and off has the right-of-way. The other must pull to the side, allowing the first car to cross the bridge.

In cities and towns many streets are one-way. They are marked with a white arrow, with the word *tránsito* (passage) in the arrow. If the word *preferencia* (right of way) is placed in the arrow it means that traffic on the street has the right-of-way and cars on the intersecting streets must yield. If the word *circulación* is in the arrow it means that drivers on such a street must yield the right-of-way to traffic on the intersecting street, which will be designated *preferencia.* These signs are usually posted at the corners, on building walls, at least ten to fourteen feet up.

U-turns are prohibited in the principal thoroughfares of large cities. Most cities have international stop-and-go traffic signals at crossings. If a policeman is directing traffic, watch for these signals: If the policeman is facing you, or his back is turned to you, it means *STOP.* When he stands in profile, you can go. At night he'll often have an illuminated baton or a lantern. When he holds it up high, *STOP.* To move traffic, he swings it in the direction of preference. Many cities have large circles *(glorietas)* where traffic from as many as a half-dozen streets pour in. If there is no traffic signal or policeman, you just grit your teeth and hope for the best.

Police Uniforms. The Mexican civil police wear dark blue uniforms and Sam Browne belts. If there is a small flag (U.S., French, German, etc.) sewn above the left breast pocket it means they speak the language of the country indicated by the flag. Traffic police in the larger cities are dressed in natty brown coats and light tan trousers, Sam Browne belt, etc. Federal highway patrolmen (auto and motorcycle) wear the same smart uniforms. In the larger cities, automobile and block watchers *(veladores* and *vigilantes)* wear not too well-fitting suntans and a badge indicating that they are auxiliary police. If they watch your car you tip them anywhere from 30 centavos to a peso. They are not regular salaried police.

The principal highways are patrolled by federal highway police. They use motorcycles, jeeps, and standard cars, painted black and white, and with SOP written on them (Secretaría de Obras Públicas, Sec. Public Works). They carry fire extinguishers, first-aid kits and they are trained in the fundamentals of first aid.

Service Stations and Garages. Service stations *(gasolineras)* in Mexico are privately owned, but the gasoline concession is leased from the government fuel monopoly, PEMEX. These stations sell only PEMEX gasolines and lubricants. In northern Baja California and some border towns service stations are permitted to sell U.S. brands of gasoline.

At present there are two grades of gasoline: Supermex, an 80-octane gas equivalent to what is called "regular" in the U.S. and Canada, and Gasolmex, a new high-octane, ethyl gas (approximately 90 octane). Gasoline prices are government controlled, but vary from one area to another due to shipping and handling costs. Roughly they average out as: 25 cents a gallon for Supermex and 32 cents for Gasolmex. Gasoline and oils are sold by the liter *(litro)*, one gal. equal to 3.79 liters.

Service stations are only authorized to sell Pemex oils, lubricants, and additives. Oil comes in liter bottles and cans instead of quarts, so you get slightly more for your money. The Pemex oils are good: Pemex-sol is the best grade multipurpose motor oil. It comes only in cans. Mexolub is the less expensive motor oil. The oils are rated the same as in the U.S. If you have a preference for U.S. name-brand oils, watch for the independent service stations along the highways. They handle Shell, Mobiloil, Quaker State, etc.

While gas and oil are measured out in the metric system, service stations use pounds *(libras)* on the air gauges.

Practically no 4-ply tires are sold or used in Mexico. The 6-plys are equivalent in quality and about the same price as tires in the U.S.

Finding a clean, well-equipped comfort station or rest room in any of Mexico's countless service stations is as difficult as finding a needle in a haystack. Such conveniences hardly exist. If you can't hold out between hotels, you may be in for some grim experiences. When motoring, always carry a supply of toilet paper, soap leaves, and a hand towel.

Although you will usually be treated honestly and with courtesy, there are times — due to poor managerial supervision and the help being underpaid — when attempts will be made to cheat you. It occurs enough to warrant comment. Gas-station attendants take advantage of tourists most unfamiliar with the language and money. *Watch for these:* (1) Make certain that the previous customer's total has been wiped off the gasoline vending machine or pump before gas goes into your tank. A favorite trick is to add your bill to someone else's, and you pay for gas you never got. (2) Watch the oil being poured. Sometimes the can isn't fully emptied. Anywhere from a few ounces to a half-quart can be held out on you. (3) Check your own oil. Some attendants are clever at measuring your oil, or will blandly tell you you need a liter when you don't. (4) Count your change. The decimal system isn't difficult, the national coins can be easily learned. Station attendants often short-change you, either accidentally or on purpose — whichever way, it is done most adroitly.

The cost of changing and repairing a tire, simple patch or plug, varies greatly by region. In Baja California and the northern border states prices are high. In central Mexico and the south the charge will be anywhere from four pesos to 12 pesos. A newcomer will sometimes be asked 20 to 30 pesos for a simple patch. If you feel you are being overcharged and you mind it, demand a receipt for the work, pay for it, note down the number of the service station (they are all licensed by Pemex) and send a complaint both to the Pemex Tourist Bureau (Av. Juárez 89) and the Government Tourist Office (Paseo de la Reforma 35), both in Mexico City. Usually when an attendant sees you noting down the information and demanding a receipt the overcharge is dropped to a normal one.

Mexican service station attendants do not as a rule clean windshields, check tires or the battery unless you specifically request them to do so. A small tip, 50 centavos to one peso, is in order for such services.

If you should have mechanical troubles, don't let it worry you too much. Most filling stations have good mechanics, or will recommend one. For major repairs, if possible, go to a garage in a town. (Garages are listed in the regional section of this guidebook.)

Replacement parts for cars cost a great deal more than they do in the United States. There is a hefty import tax. Labor costs, on the other hand, are modest and more than make up for this difference.

Spare Parts Kit. If you plan to do much motoring it is a comfort to carry a few spare parts for highway trouble-shooting. The following are recommended: one extra fan belt and one generator belt, one set of distributor points, one tube patch kit or tire plugs, one spare fuel pump (or fuel pump replacement kit including diaphragm, filters, etc). Sludge and water accumulates in the reservoir tanks at service stations and the gasoline is not always clean, hence the need for fuel pump replacements: one bumper jack, lug wrench or cross, a few tools such as screwdriver, wrenches, etc. A container for extra water and gasoline. Water boils at a lower temperature in high altitudes. The canvas water bags are not very useful.

If you have motor trouble on the road, wait for a truck driver to stop. The Mexican truck drivers are gallant, and most of them are expert mechanics. They have a considerable reputation for going out of their way to help stranded motorists and they do it well.

Mexico's newest motor-tourist aid is a fleet of patrol cars equipped with two-way radios, spare-parts and gasoline. The crews of these green and yellow patrol cars include a trained mechanic and an English-speaking driver. They cruise the major highways from the U.S. border to Acapulco. Each car patrols a given section of the road four times a day. Their services are free. You pay only for spare-parts or gas furnished by them.

Your car may act up in Mexico City's high, 7400-ft. altitude. It's the carburetor admitting too much gas in relationship to the thinner air. If you intend to be at such altitudes for a while a mechanic can adjust the carburetor in a few minutes. If you want to go whole-hog, you can have high-altitude jets installed.

Gasoline credit cards are neither valid nor honored in Mexico.

Trailers. The requirements for bringing a trailer into Mexico are the same as for automobiles. (See Index: trailers). Good trailer facilities in the republic are still limited. Often motels, though they may have no regular trailer facilities, will rent trailer space.

Because of Mexico's mountains and narrow roads it is advisable to do your trailer traveling along the major highways. Unusually high centers, narrow bridges, and sharp turns are often encountered on secondary roads. The best trailer highways are the route from Eagle Pass or Laredo, through Saltillo to Mexico City, then on to Acapulco; also, the route from El Paso to Mexico City. The old Pan American Highway (Laredo, Tamazunchale to Mexico City) can be driven by experienced trailerites; however, the 120 miles of rugged mountains south of Tomazunchale have a six per cent plus grade.

Camping. There are very few campsites along the highways and none with the usual facilities found in the state and national parks in the U.S. Overnight camping along the road is not advisable. (See Index: information and equipment related to in-country camping and hunting.)

Renting Cars. One of the pleasanter methods of touring Mexico is to come in by railway or plane, then rent a car and motor to the regional points of interest. There are a number of rent-a-car services in Mexico, several of them international in operation. Most of the companies will deliver a car to your hotel, airport, or bus terminal. They provide tourist information, road maps, make hotel reservations, offer bonded bilingual guides. With several of the companies you can pick up a car in one city and drop it off in another.

The rates vary with the type of cars (Pontiacs, Buicks, Fords, Chevrolets, and smaller European cars). Full insurance coverage (some have $100 deductible on collision) is included in the rental charge, as well as gas, oil, and maintenance. Rates range from $35 per week plus .05 cents a mile (without gas) on small cars ($7 per day), to $58 a week ($10 per day) plus mileage.

The principal car rental agencies are:

Aviz de Mexico (Aviz-Rent-a-Car) Del Prado Hotel Arcade, Mexico, 1, D.F. Tel. 18-65-85 and 12-06-59. *Hertz Driv-Ur-Self System,* Versailles 6, and International Airport, Mexico City. Tel. 46-76-53 and 46-76-58. *Mexi-Car Rent,* Av. Juárez 30, Mexico, 1, D.F. Tel. 18-58-03. *Volkswagen Rents,* Balderos 24. Tel. 10-21-78 and 18-08-00.

TAXIS

The vast broods of Mexican taxicabs range from relics of the 1920s through Monterrey's unique fleet of trim Model A Fords to the de luxe crocodiles *(cocodriles)* of Mexico City. The latter are painted black and green and have white teeth designs to resemble crocodiles. In most towns and cities the fares are so reasonable that people garage their cars and use taxis for in-city sightseeing. The name for cabs are *libres,* but more and more Mexicans are beginning to call them *taxi.*

In Mexico City cabs are required to have meters. At present, the rate you pay is what the meter reads plus 50 centavos if the cab is picked up on the street, or the meter reading plus one peso if the cab is summoned from a stand *(sitio de libres).* The hourly rate is 15 pesos. In front of big hotels you'll find cabs marked *Turismo.* These are licensed for sightseeing and come equipped with English-speaking chauffeurs. Their rates are higher than regular cabs. Before taking one you should come to a clear understanding about price.

Throughout the rest of Mexico, though cab fares are set by local town administrations, you must bargain stiffly. No driver is going to let you know what the official rate is.

BOAT TRANSPORTATION

At the turn of the century the most comfortable way of reaching Mexico was by boat. Today, with few exceptions, there is no dependable water transportation to Mexican ports.

The Cuba, Mexico & West Indies Steamship Company runs a more-or-less weekly cargo ship service between New York and Veracruz. There are accommodations for up to four people. Ships are comfortable and the trip takes about eight days. Other freighters plying irregularly between U.S. and Mexican ports offer comfortable, though somewhat haphazard passage. For information consult *Ford's Official Freighter Guide* which lists most sailings from the U.S., as well as the offices of the various lines.

Each year the Matson Line's *Lurline* plays truant from its regular Honolulu run and makes one vacation cruise from California to Acapulco. This mid-December holiday trip takes two weeks (four days in Acapulco), and costs $355 and up.

Mexico has a new de luxe cruise ship, the S.S. *Acapulco,* making regular runs between Acapulco and Los Angeles, Calif. Reservations available through travel agencies or Naviera Turistica Mexicana S.A., Av. Reforma 46, Mexico D.F.

Small packet boats make regular runs along the East or Gulf Coast from Veracruz to Yucatán. Although all of them are fairly uncomfortable, the best is the *S.S. Emancipación.* Fare is about $20.

If you are young and adventurous and do not mind sleeping upon an open deck, surrounded by pigs, coconuts, beer cases, and filthy gear, you go *cabotage* along the Mexican coasts, riding tiny cargo vessels that pull into those rarely visited tropical ports that the world seems to have forgotten. No travel agent can help you here. You just go down to the ports and make your own arrangements with the ship captains.

MAPS OF MEXICO

The road maps and city plans included in this book are based on the latest available information and have been personally checked by the author. For the motorist, off-trail explorer, and those desiring more ample coverage of Mexico the following maps are recommended:

Caminos de Mexico — a handy indexed, pocket-size book containing 40 gatefold maps of the various regions of Mexico. Fairly good detail regarding principal highways and secondary roads. Published by the Goodrich-Euzkadi Tire Company. On sale at all bookstores in Mexico. $20 MN.

The best and most detailed maps of Mexico, based on aerial surveys, are multi-sheet maps published by the U. S. Geodetic Survey, Department of Commerce, Washington, D.C. are a "must" for hunters, explorers, and orchid hunters. The sheets covering Mexico, of this series are: numbers 470, 471, 520, 521, 522, 587, 588, 589, 590, 642, 643, 644, 645. Less expensive overlays of these sheets can be procured through the USAF.

Tourists planning to fly into Mexico in their private planes can procure a simplified flight map from the Mexican Tourist Bureau. It contains airport maps indicating the layout of landing strips, altitudes, visibility, airport radio frequencies, etc.

TRAILER FACILITIES IN MEXICO

ACAPULCO *Playa Suave Trailer Park,* 1 m. E. on Av. Presidente Alemán. 43 spaces. Tel. 11-63.

AGUASCALIENTES *San Marcos Motor Hotel Trailer Park,* ½ m. S. on CN-45. Ten spaces. Tel. 13-08.

CHIHUAHUA *Santa Rita Motel,* N. end of town on CN-45. Few spaces.

CULIACÁN *Tres Ríos,* 2 m. N. on CN-15. Tel. 15-35.

DURANGO *Campo México,* NE. end of Av. 20 de Noviembre, off CN-45, 20 spaces. Tel. 30-05.

ENSENADA *King's Coronita Trailer Park,* N. end of town. APO 133.

Estero Beach Resort, 6 m. S. off CN-1. 30 spaces. Tel. 13-80.

GUAYMAS *Escalantes Trailer Park,* 2½ m. W. on CN-15, at Bocochibampo Bay. 125 spaces. Tel. 7-19.

GUADALAJARA *Del Valle,* 4⅓ m. S. on CN-15. 70 spaces. Tel. 5-96-66.

Paradise, 3¼ m. S. on CN-15. 57 spaces. Tel. 5-91-52.

HERMOSILLO *El Capitán Trailer Park,* 2 m. NE. on CN-15. 50 spaces. Tel. 3-61-27.

LINARES *Escondido Court,* 1 m. N. on CN-85. 5 spaces. Tel. 5-55.

MONTERREY *Regina Courts,* N. edge of town, CN-85.

Royal Courts, N. end of town, CN-85.

MEXICO CITY *Cabello Trailer Park,* Hortensias 235, San Angel, just off Av. Universidad. 40 spaces. Tel. 24-29-20.

MATEHUALA *Las Palmas,* on CN-57. 22 spaces. Tel. 2.

MAZATLAN *El Palmar,* 3½ m. NW. on Av. Del Mar. 63 spaces.

Las Palmas, 4 m. NW. on Sábalo Beach Road. 80 spaces.

MANZANILLO *Audiencia Cove,* 6¾ m. NW. on Playa de Audiencia. 18 spaces. Tel. 16.

NAVAJOA *Navajoa Trailer Park,* 1 m. S. on CN-15. 22 spaces. Tel. 5-42.

CIUDAD OBREGÓN *El Yaqui Trailer Park,* 1 m. W. off CN-15. 20 spaces.

San Jorge Trailer Park, N. end of town.

OAXACA *Motel Margarita,* ¼ m. S. of W. turnoff into town. 15 spaces. Tel. 506-A.

PARRAL *"Y" Inn,* near junction. Room for a few.

QUERÉTARO *El Jacal,* 1 m. W. of town on CN-45.

SAN LUIS POTOSÍ *Cactus Courts,* at Monument at by-pass.

TAMAZUNCHALE *Quinta Chilla,* S. end of town. Few trailers.

TAMPICO *San Antonio,* in town on CN-100. Room for a few.

TEPIC *Motel San Juan Trailer Parks,* NW. edge of town, ½ block off of CN-15. 18 spaces.

C. VALLES *Palma Courts,* N. end of town.

El Bañito, 6 m. S. on CN-85.

C. VICTORIA *Jardín Courts,* N. end of town. Room for a few.

NOTE: In addition to the trailer parks and courts with some trailer facilities, most Mexican motels can usually offer spaces and some facilities.

6. *Travel Agents and Guides. Travel Agencies at Home and in Mexico. Guides and Chauffeur-Guides. Information Services about Mexico*

TRAVEL AGENTS

When you go to Mexico, particularly on a first trip, the services of a travel agent can be so invaluable we feel he is as important to the tourist as a toothbrush. He performs as your silent social secretary, your map, your advance ambassador and your trip manager. He helps plan your routes and timetable, secures your tickets and reservations for transportation, hotels and night clubs. He performs a thousand time-saving services which for you would be annoying and difficult because of problems of language and other circumstances. He does it all, seemingly without charging you a penny. Of course he gets paid — a percentage out of airline, railway, and bus tickets, hotel charges, etc. But usually, as far as you are concerned, his services don't cost you any more than if you tried to do it all yourself.

Most travel agencies and agents in the U.S. have some sort of affiliation or tie-up with agencies in Mexico. In the U.S., they simply take your orders and transfer them to their Mexican associate who handles the details below the border. Some agencies have their own branches in Mexico. When you pick a travel agent or agency, be sure that you pick one you can have confidence in and who can serve *your* particular needs. For your own security it is advisable that the agent be a member of ASTA (American Society of Travel Agents), an organization having a 24,000 member roster, a basic code of professional ethics and self-policing set-up. The agency, or its affiliate in Mexico, should also be a member of AMAV (La Asociación Mexicana de Agencias de Viaje).

Even among such seal-of-approval agencies there are great differences. Some are simply booking agencies for cut-and-dried tours. Others offer more individualized services such as mail pickup and forwarding, money exchange, shopping help, etc. Still others, often run by enthusiastic and dedicated travelers, really dig information for you and give so much help you almost feel as if they are in business to help you alone.

It has been our experience that most travel agencies are completely efficient in setting up standard tours, making reservations and bookings for transportation and the better hotels, *as long as you stay on the beaten path.* But frequently the agents and office help know little else of the country they book you into. This is true also of many agencies in Mexico. The author has been flattered by Mexican agents coming to him for information about parts of Mexico they are unfamiliar with. Here and there you can find small agencies run by someone who makes a specialty of Mexico and who has gone to some trouble personally exploring the country. One such agency is Sanborn's. Its staff personally checks restaurants, hotels, resorts, and places off the beaten track, and they try to keep up to the minute. Another is the McKee Travel Inc., organization at 202 Gateway Center #2, Pittsburgh, Pennsylvania, which has a novel way of tailoring Mexican trips for you. They have a technique of making personal interviews with you, discovering your likes and dislikes so that they can pick out of Mexico just the things you might most enjoy. You get similar individualized attention from Holiday House at 22 E. 60th Street, New York, N.Y., and from Edith L. Turner Hotel Representative, Inc., 125 Park Avenue, New York, N.Y.

Among the many excellent agencies in Mexico, here are a few we can personally speak for.

IN MEXICO CITY

Continental Tours. Av. Sullivan 166, Tel. 46-20-40.

Del Prado Travel Bureau. Av. Juárez 70. Tel. 13-80-53.

Garza Travel Service, S.A. Londres 106. Tel. 25-77-05.

Mexico Ramírez Tours. Marsella 48, Tel. 11-26-77, Local 34. Tel. 35-14-15.

Patricia Ann Tours. Sonora 208, Tel. 11-77-34. A small agency giving excellent individual attention.

Wagon-Lits Cook. Av. Juárez 88. Tel. 18-11-80. This is the big, international Thomas Cook travel agency.

Wells Fargo Co. Express, S.A. Niza 22, Tel. 11-17-77. Better known to U.S. travelers as the "American Express." All sorts of services, mail, money exchange, etc.

Sr. Max Kahn. Viajes Azteca, S.A. Balderas 36. Tel. 21-71-77. Mr. Kahn is one of the most efficient agents we have encountered in Mexico.

IN GUADALAJARA

Hecht Travel Service. Hotel Fenix. Tel. 44-73-69.

IN MÉRIDA, YUC.

Barbachano's Travel Service, S.A. Calle 60 #44. Tel. 46-67.

Yucatan Trails. Calle 62 #482. The Mayan ruins and individually tailored trips.

IN ACAPULCO

Caleta Travel Bureau. Hotel Caleta, Tel. 2-85.
Viajes Ortiz. Av. Miguel Alemán 100.

U. S. BORDER

See Sanborn's Travel Service, Index.

GUIDES IN MEXICO

In Mexico travel agencies, your hotel or you yourself can arrange for bilingual guides to show you around, to travel with you, or to chauffeur your car. Most of the guides are very pleasant, are courteous and have a wonderful sense of humor and, above all, they are easy to travel with. *Warning:* If you arrange for a guide yourself, make certain that he has proper credentials. If he is to drive your car, be sure he has a chauffeur's license. If you get your guide through a responsible agency or a big hotel you need not worry about this.

The Mexican Government requires that tourist guides be bonded for $2500 MN. They belong to a union called Union de Chofers, Intérpretes y Guías de la República Mexicana. Each guide must carry a credential or identity card issued by the government Tourist Department. No credential issued by any other organization is valid. Guides are not required to wear any special uniform. Also, according to the law, travel agencies and hotels are strictly forbidden to use or recommend unauthorized guides. The official rate of pay set by the government for guides is $8 per day in Mexico City, and $10 per day if the guide accompanies you outside the city.

It is suggested that when you do any shopping, either in Mexico City or throughout the republic, you do it without your guide. They generally lead you to shops that kickback 15 to 20 per cent of your purchase money.

LIST OF GOVERNMENT AUTHORIZED AND BONDED GUIDES

Luis Benavides, José. Ceballos 45, or Hotel Presidente. Tel. 15-75-27.
Manuel N. Benitez. Costa Rica 9-4 and Paraguay 55-4.
Angel Dorantes. Pte. de Alvarado 6-12. Tel. 47-39-98.
Alfonzo Escandón E. Puebla 14.
José Mariscal Flores. Ignacio Mariscal 31 bis. Tel. 46-76-69.
Pedro Jaimes Gama. Calle Lirio 14. Tel. 47-49-98.
Sergio A. Mendez. Calle Norte 54-374. Tel. 17-65-03.
Miguel Ramírez Morales. Oriente 168, 441. Tel. 47-39-98.
Luis Delgado Ramos. Arcos de Belém 62-303. Tel. 13-70-14.
Jorge "Morelia" Guzmán. Rosas Moreno 51-105. Tel. 46-85-77.
Alejandro E. Vite. Soto 68-13. Tel. 26-80-23.
F. J. Reyes. Rafael Angel de la Peña 64. Tel. 18-38-73.
Ladislao Paray Polnik, Melchor Ocampo 454-7.
Enrique Mora Ferrer, Rhin 84-203.

NOTE: All above addresses are in Mexico City.

Present Government rates for guides with cars are: 5 passenger car per hour in city (Mexico, D.F.) $25.00 MN; 7 passenger car, $37.50 MN.

Car per day in city, $175.00 MN, 5 passenger car.

For trips out of the city, $187.50 for a 5 passenger car. $281.25 for 7 passenger car.

The above rates are just for the car. The guide receives in addition: trips in the city, 8 hours, $87.50. For trips outside of the city, 8 hours, $106.25.

The government also has set rates for different tours via hired car and guide. The Mexican Government Travel Bureau, travel agents and hotels can give you the price schedules. For example, a trip to Querétaro and Guanajuato, three days, 5 passenger car, costs $687.50 MN, apart from the guide's daily fee.

7. Hotels and Restaurants. Hotel Reservations. Seasons. Discounts. Spas and Hot Springs

HOTELS

Motel and hotel accommodations have increased enormously in Mexico during the past few years, both along the traveled tourist belts as well as in off-trail places. The variety is extensive, ranging from the very primitive inns *(posadas)* in small towns where both you and your burro can put up, the modest *casas de asistencias* and *casa de huéspedes* (types of boardinghouses, the latter more like the French *pension*), up to the lavish hotels and de luxe resort establishments. In these you can pay anywhere from 60 cents a day to $100 a day without food.

As a rule hotel and motel accommodations along the principal highways are good. However, due to inflation in Mexico, lack of managerial know-how or indifference and because American tourist behavior has sometimes led some Mexicans to believe tourists from the north are gold-plated and fair game, in most cases you do not get the same quality of attention, service and conveniences for your money that you would receive in similar establishments above the Rio Grande. The very low-price hotels offer no service to speak of and the comforts are rather Spartan, that is, insufficient lighting in rooms, hot water that isn't hot, toilet equipment that doesn't work, and service that is careless. Some of this carries on into the medium-priced hotels and also into a number of first-class establishments. It is only when you favor the de luxe hotels, where money is not supposed to matter, that you usually get the same or better refinements and service you receive in top European and American hotels.

When you check into a hotel, especially the medium-priced ones and those in smaller cities, always ask to see the room before you move in. For your own comfort check on these items: that hot water comes from the taps, that the toilet works, that the key will properly lock the door, that the linen is adequate and clean, that there are screens or that the windows can be shut so you can protect yourself against mosquitoes, and, finally, that somewhere in the room the official prices for the room are posted. The government sets room prices and requires hotels to post these in each room in a visible place. Sometimes hotels hide them in the closet.

When absent from your room carry your valuables with you or deposit them with the hotel manager and get a receipt for them. Always lock your suitcases when you go out.

When you mail letters, don't just give the bellhop your envelope and money for stamps. Buy the stamps yourself and mail the letter yourself if it is important to you that it gets out. These may seem like the warnings of an oversuspicious soul, but they are based on years of living and travel in Mexico and on the fact that Mexican tourists themselves follow such procedures.

When you take a room try to get one with south or southeast exposure and, best of all, on the upper floors to avoid the street noises. However, during the summer months in tropical areas, skip the south and southeast rooms. Too hot.

See Index: Tipping.

Hotel Reservations. In most instances you come out ahead if you let a travel agent make your hotel reservations. If you don't — and even though you've sent wires or telephoned long distance — the reservation may not be there. Hotel help has a penchant for forgetting to note them down. They rarely ever confirm a reservation written or wired for. This is pointedly true during the two heavy-traffic tourist seasons. If you are motoring and don't know exactly where you want to light for the night, it is best to try to check into a hotel or motel during the late afternoon. If you wait until evening you may find no habitable hotel rooms in the town.

Seasons, Rates, and Discounts. Although the government sets the maximum rate for a hotel room, there is no objection if a hotel wishes to give a discount. During the maximum travel seasons (July, August, January, February, March) you'll usually pay full price. During the off-season months, particularly in resort areas (Acapulco, Mazatlán, Guaymas, etc.) hotels will give you a 10 per cent discount. It is not automatic. You have to remind them. Many hotels in the republic also give 10 per cent discounts to members of the AMA, the Mexican automobile association. This is often also extended to U.S. (AAA) motor club members. You must carry your membership card, or get a temporary courtesy membership card from the AMA office in Mexico City.

RESTAURANTS

Along the principal highways and in most cities there are good restaurants. In the first-class hotel dining rooms and restaurants you can safely eat everything and drink their water. Away from these spots stick to cooked foods and bottled water (See Index: *Health Hints*). The quality of cooking in Mexico varies tremendously. If you are a gourmet, accustomed to trying dishes that are different and richly flavored, you'll have no trouble finding something to your taste everywhere in Mexico (See Index: Mexican Food and Drink). If you must have so-called American food you'll find hundreds of restaurants catering to your desire. Although adequate, what they serve you may sometimes be a travesty on what you are used to. Mexican cooks haven't altogether mastered the style of American cooking.

You will also be pleasantly surprised by many restaurants in Mexico City and some other cities. The prices are generally lower than up north and there are some matchless restaurants specializing in French, Mexican and American cuisines.

In smaller cities and towns the eating hours are: breakfast, 7 A.M. to 10 A.M.; dinner, 1:30 to 4 P.M.; supper, 7 to 10 P.M. This applies particularly to hotel dining rooms. In Mexico City, Guadalajara, and Monterrey there are restaurants open round-the-clock. For a list of handy restaurant phrases, dishes, and food vocabulary, see glossary. In larger cities and tourist areas, menus are generally printed in both Spanish and English. Prices are normally in pesos.

SPAS AND HOT SPRINGS RESORTS

Mexico is noted for its many mineral and thermal baths and resorts. Whether the claims made concerning the curative powers of the waters are justifiable, nevertheless many of the resorts themselves are delightful and restful vacation spots. Here is a list of the better-known spas, accommodations, and curative claims.

THERMAL SPRING AND RESORTS

Peñon de los Baños — east outskirts of Mexico City. No hotel. Swimming pools *(Cascada, Elba* and *Deportivo Peñon)* and private baths fed by radioactive mineral springs. Claimed to be helpful for skin disorders, rheumatism, and sterility.

Agua Azul — on the outskirts of Puebla. Hotel, restaurant, and bar. Thermal sulphurous waters for arthritis, rheumatism, nervous disorders, and skin ailments.

El Riego — at Tehuacán, Pue. A seventeenth-century hacienda turned into a spa. Thermal mineral waters for disorders of the liver, kidneys, and digestive organs. Other hotels and baths in nearby Tehuacán. Also, *Hotel Spa Peñafiel.*

Fortín de las Flores — Fortín, Ver. An excellent resort noted principally for its relaxing atmosphere, flowers and flower-filled swimming pools.

Lourdes — 30 miles south of San Luis Potosí, off of CN-45. Modest hotel, pool, and mineral baths. Waters recommended for stomach, liver and kidney troubles.

Comanjilla — in the State of Guanajuato, near León. An inexpensive, well-run little spa. Extremely hot spring, Russian bath, etc. For circulation, nerves, rheumatism, etc.

Ixtapan de la Sal — south of Toluca, Mex. Several good hotels, pools, and baths. Radioactive waters for rheumatism, etc.

San José Purua — on CN-15, near Zitácuaro, Mich. Excellent hotels. Thermal waters, mud baths said to be good for circulation, heart, liver, and skin.

Tequisquiapan — Tequisquiapan, Qro. Picturesque town, only fair hotels, thermal mineral waters.

Taboada — on outskirts of San Miguel de Allende, Gto. Hot mineral waters said to help circulation, skin, nerves, and rheumatism. Good hotels in San Miguel.

Cointzio — 30 miles NE of Morelia, Mich., near village of Atzimba. Accommodations not good. Waters claimed to help circulation, stomach, and liver.

Cuautla — Cuautla, Mor. Fair hotels. Waters said to help rheumatism, nerves, skin, and stomach disorders.

Ojo Caliente — at Ojo Caliente, Ags. A popular spa with fair accommodations, 70 miles from Aguascalientes. Thermal waters for disorders of stomach, kidneys, and circulation.

Topo Chico — 5 miles north of Monterrey, N.L. Good hotel. Waters claimed to be good for rheumatism and skin ailments. Salts in the waters are said to destroy fatty tissues and help reduce.

8. Useful Information. Postal Service. Telegraph. Telephones. Time. Weights and Measures. Street Addresses. Those Mexican Abbreviations. Sounds and Gestures. Personal Names and Forms of Address. Newspapers

POSTAL SERVICE

Despite the complaints of some residents, the Mexican postal service is both efficient and remarkably logical. By the way of illustration, once when the author of this guide sent a package to Honduras, for some weeks the package seemed to have been lost. However, it finally reached its destination, somewhat battered and covered with postmarks indicating that it had first gone to the United States, then Guatemala, and finally Honduras. When I complained about the circuitous route our local postal clerk logically replied, "*Sí Señor,* Honduras borders Mexico on the south, but in this case the United States was closer. The important thing was to get your package out of the country so it could start on its journey."

There is a post office *(oficina de correo)* in almost every Mexican town. The hours are from 9 A.M. to 1 P.M. and from 3 to 6 P.M. Post offices are also open on Sunday mornings from 9 to noon. There are two mail deliveries a day on weekdays, one on Sundays.

Postal rates at the present writing are: domestic postcards, 15 centavos; letters and letter-postcards (20 grams or less), 40 centavos anywhere in the republic and to the U. S. Airmail letters (20 grams or less), 60 centavos within the republic. Airmail to the U.S. (10 grams or less, which means one thin sheet of paper), 80 centavos. Special delivery *(entrega inmediata),* 35 centavos extra. Registered mail *(certificado or registrado),* 40 centavos extra. Stamps are *timbres, estampillas, portes.*

When mailing documents, important letters or anything that requires more than a few pesos' worth of stamps, always have the packet registered or certified. The stamps are usually canceled before you and you are given a receipt. The Mexican postal service watches over its registered mail like a hawk. If you don't do this, someone may steam or tear your stamps off the package, take the stamps and throw the package away.

There are not many street post boxes in Mexico *(buzones).* You can have mail addressed to you, care of a post office. The letters should be addressed as follows: *your name, a/c Lista de correos, name of the town, name of the state.* The sign *a/c* stands for *al cuidado de* (care of).

TELEGRAPH

The Mexican telegraph service, a government monopoly, is under the control of SC (Ministry of Communications, a cabinet department). Its offices are recognizable by the words *Telégrafos* and *SC* on the front of the building. Rates are based on a ten-word message and distance, with a small extra charge for additional words. Services include regular messages, night letters *(mensajes nocturnales)* and rush messages *(urgentes)*. Messages are accepted in English, Spanish, French, and other languages using the Roman alphabet. The rates within the republic are amazingly low.

TELEPHONES (*TELÉFONOS*)

Until a decade ago Mexico had two major telephone systems. If you had friends subscribing to one system and friends on another, you had to have two telephones in order to communicate. Eventually the two systems were joined and now the two previously foreign owned companies (Ericsson Company and the Mexican Telephone and Telegraph Company) have been taken over by national interests and are combined under Teléfonos de Mexico.

The system has been vastly modernized. Dial phones are used in all the larger cities and there is even automobile radio phone service.

To telephone long distance (domestic) you either dial 02 or ask for *larga distancia.* For international calls, dial 09 or ask for *larga distancia, internacional.* The international operators all speak English. *For telephone vocabulary and phrases see glossary.*

You can now place "collect" phone calls to the United States.

TIME

All of Mexico is on Central Standard Time, except Baja California and a stretch along the west coast as far south as Mazatlán. These latter are on Mountain Time.

Transportation systems in Mexico (trains, airlines, buses, some theaters, etc.) use the 24-hour timetable. Midnight is 24:00. 1 P.M. is 13:00; 6 P.M. is 18:00, etc.

WEIGHTS AND MEASURES

Although the metric system was introduced into Mexico in 1856, and in 1895 was declared by law the only legal weights and measures in the republic, the old Spanish system and the English system are used in some instances. Gasoline stations measure air in pounds. In rural areas the Indians often use the Spanish terminology: *varas,* the Spanish yard, etc.

LINEAL MEASURE

1 meter *(metro)*	= 1.09361 yards
1 meter	= 39.37 inches
1 meter	= 3.28 feet
1 centimeter *(centímetro)*	= 0.39376 inches
1 yard	= 0.9144 meters
1 foot	= 0.3048 meters
1 inch	= 2.5400 centimeters
1 mile	= 1,509.35 meters

For practical purposes a kilometer *(kilómetro)* equals ⅝ mile *(milla)*. A *legua* (league) 2.6043 miles. A *vara* (rod), 2.749 feet.

SURFACE MEASURE

1 hectare *(hectárea)*	— 2.47104 acres
1 sq. meter *(metro cuadrado)*	— 1.19598 sq. yards
1 sq. foot	— 0.09290 sq. meters
1 acre	— 4,046.9 sq. meters
1 *palmo* (Spanish)	— 68.03 inches

WEIGHTS

1 kilogram *(kilo or kilogramo)*	— 2.2046 pounds
1 gram *(gramo)*	— 0.0353 ounces
1 ounce *(onza)*	— 0.0283 kilograms
1 pound *(libra)*	— 0.4335 kilograms
1 metric ton *(tonelada mét.)*	— 1000 kilograms
1 *carga* (load)	equals 2 *fanegas* or 5.1543 bushels
1 *almud*	equals 4 *cuartillos* (dry quarts) or 0.8591 pecks
1 *cuartillo*	equals 1.7181 dry quarts

VOLUME

1 liter *(litro)*	— 1.0566 quarts, or 0.2641 gallons
1 quart *(cuartillo)*	— 0.9483 liters
1 gallon *(galón)*	— 3.7884 liters
1 pint *(pinta)*	— 0.47 liters

A dozen is *una docena.* Eggs, rolls, etc., are also sold by the *decena,* here meaning ten.

The Centigrade, rather than the Fahrenheit, thermometer is used in Mexico. Freezing on Centigrade is 0; on Fahrenheit, 32°. Body temperature (normal) is 37° on Centigrade and 98.6° on Fahrenheit. For reducing Fahrenheit to Centigrade (if above zero) multiply the difference between number of degrees and 32 by 5, and divide product by 9. Thus: 212° −32° × 5÷9 = 180° × 5 ÷ 9 = 100°.

For converting Centigrade to Fahrenheit (if above freezing point) multiply number of degrees by 9, divide product by 5 and add 32 to quotient. Thus, 100° × 9 ÷ 5 = 180° + 32 = 212°.

THOSE MEXICAN ABBREVIATIONS

On street signs, letterheads, in elevators, etc., you will see puzzling abbreviations. Here are the solutions to the more common ones.

D.F. — *Distrito Federal,* the Federal District, like our D.C. after Washington.

S.A. — After the name of a business or firm, means, *Sociedad Anónima,* i.e., incorporated or limited. If *C.V.*, follows it, this means, *capital variable* (variable capitalization).

P.B. — The lowest button on an elevator. It means *planta baja* or ground floor. The first floor is our 2nd floor.

Cd. — Before the name of a city or town, means, *ciudad* (city).

Av. — Is the abbreviation for *avenida* or avenue.

Calz. — Means *calzada,* a bigger avenue. Originally it meant causeway.

C and F — In bathrooms the *C* on a faucet means *caliente,* for hot water. The *F* stands for *frio* (cold). If

confused, remember that the left tap as you face it should be the hot. Sometimes they're both cold.
Depto. — Means *departamento* (apartment)
Aptdo. — Means *apartado postal*, P. O. Box.

See Index: abbreviations for Mexican States.

SOUNDS AND GESTURES

Mexicans are both a very vocal people and also articulate in gestures. Although many sounds and gestures are purely personal, there are also a large number that are national. To be familiar with some of them may be both useful and they can enrich your visit below the border. Some of the most common sounds, signs and gestures are:

A single hand clap accompanied by "Psssst," is used to attract someone's attention — a waiter, porter, or a taxi driver. In a restaurant you might also tap your glass and give a gentle "Psssst."

At concerts and bullfights, a sound very similar to the "Psssst," but actually a hiss, is given to express disapproval.

When you are backing your car and someone begins slapping the car body or fender, he is just trying to help. Two quick slaps or knocks means "Come ahead or continue backing." One quick knock is a signal to stop.

When you see two Mexicans meet and go into a clinch, first on the left side, then on the right and giving each other slaps on the back, they are performing the traditional Mexican greeting or *abrazo* (embrace). In ancient times it was a handy way of keeping your opposite from drawing his sword or pistol.

The thumb and little finger upraised, while the fingers between swiftly wiggle inward toward the outturned palm, is the common way of waving a salute to a passing acquaintance.

Waving the slightly cupped hand at someone, with a slight downward motion as if you were doing the dog-paddle with one hand, means for the person to come to you, or come closer.

Clapping the hand against the hip means, "I give up. It can't be helped."

The hand raised in salute with the palm toward one's face means you are saying "good-by."

The wide-open and trembling hand held transversely to the body means "disgust, indignation, or a plea for fairness."

The extended hand, fingers spread outward, palm down, indicates "What's the use?"

Rubbing the thumb on the upturned forefinger, as if testing the fineness of some powder, indicates "money is involved."

The thumb and forefinger touching at the tips so as to form an oval and with the three fingers flaring upward signifies something very tiny, a very short wait, or "Just a moment!"

Patting an elbow with the palm of the other hand is an indication that whoever you're talking about is *codo* (stingy). It also describes natives of Monterrey who pride themselves as being the industrious and canny Scots of Mexico.

To put a finger to an eye means "Watch this for me, please."

The hand shaken downward loosely and with vigor, just once, with an air of vexation, indicates that the gesticulator has "forgotten something."

Wagging the first finger of your hand toward someone signifies a polite "No."

All the fingers pinched together and jerked up toward the mouth means "an invitation to dine," or that the person making the gesture is going to eat something.

The little finger held stiffly erect, the middle fingers curled against the palm and the thumb jerked toward the mouth means "an invitation to drink," or "someone has taken too much to drink."

The palm facing up, fingers together and somewhat cupped, with the thumb and forefinger touching and the whole hand indicating height tells "how tall a child or person is." If the palm is faced down, it is used to indicate the height of an animal.

Indifference is usually expressed by a shrug of the shoulders and a questioning pucker of the lips.

When a Spanish-speaking person hears a noise he often inquires about it without speaking — simply by wrinkling his nose in a questioning way.

PERSONAL NAMES AND FORMS OF ADDRESS

Titles of respect and of professions are used much more in Mexico than in the United States, both in correspondence and direct address. Some of the more common titles and their abbreviations are:

Sr. for *Señor* (Mr.); *Sra.* for *Señora* (Mrs.); *Srita.* for *Señorita* (Miss). *Don* and *Doña* (like the English title sir) is only used before a Christian name. When a Spanish-speaking woman marries, her family name is often kept alive by being added to that of her husband, as, *Doña Guadalupe Cuervo* (her name) *de Mengano* (husband's name). Children may use this combined form until they marry, then daughters add their husbands' name to their family name when they marry. Sons may add their maternal name to their paternal name, as, *José Ortega y Gasset.* If the husband dies the widow *(viuda)* calls herself, *Señora Guadalupe Cuervo Viuda (or Vda.) de Mengano.*

Lic. for *Licenciado* (attorney); *Ing.* for *Ingeniero* (engineer: civil, chemical, electrical, etc.); *Dr.* for *Doctor* (doctor, both medical as well as the academic doctors of law, philosophy, etc.).

NEWSPAPERS

While in Mexico you can keep in touch with new events through several daily papers having an English-language page and through *The News,* a daily paper published in English which carries the U.S. wire services bulletins, cartoons, U.S. columnists, and stock market reports. *The News* is distributed throughout the republic. Papers carrying English language pages are *Excelsior* and *Universal.*

The English-language magazine *Mexico: This Month* (published in Mexico City) is a lively, colorful travel magazine carrying interesting articles about Mexican travel, folklore and some very useful departments covering fiestas.

9. Entertainment and Sports. Tickets for Theater, Bullfights, Frontón, Horse Racing, Golf. Hunting and Fishing Regulations. Outdoor Equipment and Tips

SPECTATOR ENTERTAINMENTS

With the exception of bullfights, *jai alai, futbol* (which can be seen in various cities) most Mexican spectator entertainments center in Mexico City.

Theaters are small and most productions have a very short run. The quality of the production in Mexican legitimate theaters is not very good. Usually there are two evening performances, one about 7:30 and the other about 9:30 P.M. Tickets should be gotten a day or so in advance, either through your hotel desk or at the box office. (See Index: Mexico City.)

For major bullfights featuring top toreros it is almost imperative to get tickets well in advance, both in Mexico City and in smaller cities. In Mexico City bullfight tickets can be gotten through your hotel or at the main ticket office of the bullring impresario on Calle Edison, five doors west of Calle Ponciana Arriaga. Tickets go on sale the Thursday before the fight. For less important fights you can buy tickets at the bullring ticket offices where you see a sign saying TAQUILLA or BOLETOS. Scalpers outside of the ring offer tickets. According to the law they are permitted to add 10 per cent to the box office price. Frequently this is violated.

Tickets for other sporting events: football (except for publicized international and championship matches), for *frontón,* baseball, or horse racing can usually be bought without trouble at the stadium or track ticket office just before the event. For information regarding golf, green fees, and a list of country clubs in Mexico, see Index.

HUNTING

For the modern hunter present-day Mexico is very much like the American West of a century ago — a scarcely tapped, fabulous game paradise. Its wetlands and ponds are the winter resort for northern ducks and geese. Its highlands abound with deer, bear, and small game. Its tropic forests are alive with wild boar, wild turkey, alligators, royal pheasants, chattering monkeys, and big cats — the most prized, the big-game hunter's spotted jaguar *(tigre).*

Very little has been done properly to exploit the country's hunting potential or to attract tourist hunters. Actually, very little is known about Mexican hunting. The government gives out little information because it actually doesn't know much about game resources in the republic. Up until recently sport hunting was limited to the wealthy; however, with the increase of a substantial middle-class in Mexico, it is gradually becoming more popular. The number of Mexican sport hunters remains small. According to the last available figures approximately three hunting licenses were issued per 10,000 people in Mexico compared to 912 licenses per 10,000 people in the U.S. This figure, admittedly, is not an exact comparison, for in Mexico the shortage of law-enforcement officers makes apprehension of unlicensed hunters most unlikely. There are countless hunters, usually farmers after food, who never think of applying for a license.

For the tourist-sportsman interested in a Mexican hunt, there are three ways to go about it: be a guest or member of a local hunting club that is registered with the Mexican Department of Agriculture; go on a hunt arranged and conducted by a reputable hunt outfitter; and know someone, either a rancher or man of influence, who'll invite you to shoot on his spread. Also, in various localities you can arrange a hunt yourself with local guides.

If you are an *inviteé* of a club or go with an outfitter, they can arrange for your hunting license. There are no state licenses; everything is federal. According to presidential decree dated December 30, 1944, the nonresident hunting license rates were set as: Six-month permit for sportsmen affiliated with a recognized club and valid throughout the republic — $300 MN. License for a specific region — $180 MN. License for a hunter not affiliated with a club — $420 MN.

Licenses are issued by the Departmento de Forestal y Caza (Forestry and Hunting, a division of Ministry of Agriculture). You can do it in person, but there is a good deal of red tape involved. Better to get it through a club or have a travel agent help you.

In order to hunt you need a gun — but there's a catch. In addition to your hunting license, you will need a permit from the Defense Department letting you transport a gun. You can bring your own guns to Mexico if you take the following steps:

1. Secure a certificate of good conduct from your local sheriff or police department. It should have the city seal affixed.

2. Present this document along with a description of the guns you wish to take into Mexico (including serial numbers, etc.) to the Mexican consul nearest your home.

3. The consul issues a permit for the guns. You must present this permit to the military authorities at the port of entry who will endorse it and grant entry. The license fee payable here is 240 pesos or $19.50 U.S.

If you enter via the Mexico City airport your guns are impounded by the customs, pending issue of a special license by the Department of Military Industry. This normally requires from 36–48 hours.

Each hunter is permitted to bring four portable firearms for hunting in Mexico. Each caliber must be different. Being considered as military weapons, 7-mm and 45-caliber guns are prohibited. You may bring in one hundred rounds of ammunition for each caliber gun listed on your permit.

Hunting Regions. The richest hunting areas are the following:

DEER *(venado):* White tail in all parts of the country except Baja California. Mule deer in the northern border states, except Tamulipas. *Temazate* (a dwarf jungle deer) — Tabasco, Campeche, Yucatán.

QUAIL, CURASSOW, DOVE *(cordoniz, faisán, palomas):* Throughout most of Mexico. White wings especially along the northeast border.

DUCKS AND GEESE *(patos y gansos):* Teel, pintails, some mallards, shovelers, etc. Along the west coast, central plateau and Yucatán. Several of the flyways converge in Mexico.

BIG GAME: Grizzly and black bears in the sierras of Sonora and Chihuahua. Cats, jaguars, etc., — Nayarit, Campeche, Chiapas, Yucatán, Quintana Roo.

Mexican game seasons and bag limits

SPECIES	REGION	SEASON	LIMIT*
CATS (Family *felidae*) jaguar, wild cats, ocelot, jaguarondi, etc.	All Mexico	All year	No limit
BEARS *(Ursidae)* Black, grizzly and cinnamon	All Mexico	Hunting temporarily suspended	2 adults per season
(Myrmecophagidae) Honey bear or anteater	All Mexico	Dec. only	2 per person
DEER *(cervidae)* White-tail	In cold zones of Veracruz, Oaxaca, Chiapas, Guerrero, Michoacán and in the rest of Republic	Oct. 16 to Dec. 31	2 adult males per season
"	In Colima, Tabasco, Campeche, Yucatán, Quintana Roo and warm zones of Veracruz, Chiapas, Oaxaca, Guerrero, Michoacán	Sept. 1 to Oct. 15	"
"	In Valley of Mexico, Querétaro, México, Morelos, Tlaxcala and Puebla	Prohibited	Prohibited
Mule deer	All Mexico	December	1 adult male per season
Temazate (Brocket or red deer)	All Mexico	Oct. 15 to Dec. 30	2 adult males per season
JAVELINA *(Tayassuidae)* Peccaries, wild pig, *jabalí*	Nuevo León, Tamaulipas	Oct. 1 to Jan. 31	3 specimen per season
"	In Morelos, Sonora, Chihuahua	Prohibited	Prohibited
"	Rest of Mexico	Nov. 1 to Feb. 15	3 specimen per season
WOLF, fox, coyotes	All Mexico	All year	No limit
BIGHORN SHEEP	All Mexico	Prohibited	Prohibited
ANTELOPE	"	"	"
TAPIER	"	"	"
MOUNTAIN GOAT	"	"	"
BEAVER	"	"	"
MONKEY *(cevidae)* Howlers, spider, etc.	All Mexico	Nov. 1 to Feb. 28	2 adult males per day or in possession
ARMADILLOS *(Dasypodidae)*	All Mexico	Aug. 1 to Sept. 30	2 per day or in possession
HARES *(leporidae)* Rabbits, etc.	In Valley of Mexico, States of Morelos and Puebla	Prohibited	Prohibited
"	Rest of Mexico	Nov. 1 to Feb. 28	5 per day or in possession

* Bag limits subject to change from year to year, depending on wildlife count and conditions.

SQUIRRELS *(Sciuridae)*	All Mexico (except the Valley of Mexico)	All year	No limit
GEESE, DUCKS, SWANS *(Anatidae)*	All Mexico	Nov. 1 to Mar. 1	15 per day or in possession
DOVES *(columbidae)*	In Baja California, Chihuahua, Sonora, Sinaloa, Nuevo León and Tamaulipas	Dec. 1 to Mar. 31	20 per day
"	In rest of Mexico	Nov. 16 to Mar. 15	15 per day or in possession
WILD TURKEY *(meleagrididae)*	All Mexico	Nov. 1 to Feb. 1	2 per day or in possession
CHACHALACAS, CURASSOW, GUAN, etc. *(cracidae)*	All Mexico	Oct. 1 to Mar. 15	5 per day or in possession for entire season
PHEASANT *(Phasianidae)* Ring-necked	In Mexicali Valley (Baja California)	Nov. 1 to 30th	2 males per day or in possession
"	Rest of Mexico	Prohibited	Prohibited
MOUNTAIN QUAIL	All Mexico	Nov. 1 to Jan. 31	15 per day or in possession
MONTEZUMA QUAIL	Valley of Mexico	Jan. 1 to Mar. 1	"
PARROTS *(Psittacidae)*	All Mexico	All year	No limit
REPTILES Iguanas	All Mexico	Nov. 1 to April 30	10 per day or in possession

Other reptiles — Season, limit and bag according to judgment of the Ministry of Agriculture.

The hunting of wild animals and birds is prohibited in national parks and game reserves. The shooting of migratory and nonmigratory birds which are not classed as game birds is prohibited.

In the Index and various regional sections of the guidebook, Part Four, addresses of local hunting guides are listed. In addition to these, for information regarding both hunting and fishing in Mexico, inquiries can be made to: Dirreción General de Caza, Serdán 28. At present there are several organizations equipped to take you on a big game hunt in Mexico. The best is: Central de Caza y Pesca, S.A. de C.V., Hamburgo 64, Mexico, 6 D.F. Tel. 25-84-39. The cost of a tiger (jaguar) hunt doesn't run low. Including supplies, flying into the camps maintained by this organization, guides, etc., a hunt runs from $500 to $600 per person a week.

FISHING

Mexico, with almost 6000 miles of rugged and sandy coastlines, is world famous for its sport fishing waters which abound with marlin, sailfish, tarpon, tuna, corbina, and others. Few restrictions are imposed upon fishermen in Mexico — compared to hunting restrictions and red tape.

The only requirement for fishing is a license obtainable from border authorities, at the larger seaports and resorts and from local Federal Tax Offices, Oficina de Hacienda. All fishing regulations are controlled by the government, the individual states having no rights to impose local ordinances. A license covers all types of fishing and is valid throughout Mexico.

In interior waters (rivers, lakes, and dams) fishing concessions are often granted to sport-fishing clubs. If you wish to fish in such areas you must obtain your permit or license through these clubs.

Fishing license fees for nonresidents are: $6 MN for three days; $10 MN for one month; $25 MN for three months; $50 for one year. Owners of foreign boats, desirous of fishing *for sport* in Mexican coastal waters, must pay a $25 MN fee for a 30-day fishing license. For small fishing craft the fee is $4 MN.

Members of scientific societies, museums, university faculties, and students collecting specimens of fish for scientific purposes will be issued a special permit at no cost by presenting their credentials to the Federal Fisheries Bureau at Avenida Cuauhtémoc 80, 6th floor, Mexico D.F.

For game fish there are few closed seasons and restrictions. The most important closed seasons are: *Catfish* — July 1 to August 15 in Lake Chapala and ponds and rivers of Jalisco. Elsewhere no closed season. *Robalo* (snook) — from mid-April to the end of May along the Gulf Coast between Soto Marina, Tamps. and Tonalá, Tab. *Trout* (rainbow and brook) — closed season throughout the republic during November, December, January, and February.

You are permitted to bring your own fishing tackle into Mexico, duty-free, as long as the amount is considered reasonable.

At most Mexican ports and fishing resorts boats and launches can be rented at moderate prices. Rates depend on length of trip, size of boat and crew and the season. Deep-sea fishing launches usually provide tackle and bait. Many of the boats are equipped with ship-to-shore radios. *Lists of fishing fleets, boat owners and other coastal fishing data is provided in Part Four of the guidebook under coastal ports and resorts such as Guymas, La Paz, Mazatlán, Acapulco, Tampico, etc.*

Deep Sea Fishing Rodeos sponsored by the Rodeo

Clubs (affiliated with the International Game Fish Association) hold annual fishing competitions or rodeos at the principal Mexican game fish resorts. For information concerning the various rodeos, address Sarah Bright, Room 404, 509 S. Wabash Ave., Chicago 5, Illinois. For information and entry applications to the International Tampico Tarpon Rodeo, address Sr. Félix Florencia, Aptdo. Postal 439, Tampico, Tamps; for the International Acapulco Sailfish Rodeo, Sr. Carlos Barnard, Hotel Mirador, Acapulco, Gro.; for the International Guaymas Deepsea Fishing Rodeo, Sr. Ernesto Zaragoza, Guaymas, Son.; for the La Paz Deepsea Rodeo, Sr. Luis Troy Elias, Hotel La Perla, La Paz, B.C.; and for the Mazatlán Deepsea Fishing Rodeo, Sr. Roberto Gorostiza, Aptdo. Postal 199, Mazatlán, Sin.

If you want that marlin or sailfish mounted and sent home so it will look right above the mantel, have the captain of your fishing launch skin and send your prize to Montadura de Peces Lomeli, Leon Cavallo 278, Mexico, 14, D. F. Most deep-sea fishermen in Mexico know the address. Montadura is a family enterprise run by Sr. Carlos Lomeli and his daughter Cecilia Lomeli. They speak English and do beautiful mounting. Their present prices, F.O.B., Laredo, Tex.: Sailfish, $185. Marlin, $4 per pound. Delivery is guaranteed within 30 days. Each mounted fish is accompanied with a gold seal certificate of the catch.

Freshwater Fishing. Inland sport fishing, especially for trout and bass, is just beginning to attract attention in Mexico. The government has almost no statistics on fishing streams. What little there is known is harbored by members of fishing clubs (see list below). Several attractive fishing areas are described in Part Four of the guidebook, under States of Chihuahua, Sonora and Baja California. Also, under Real del Oro, Mex.

FISHING CLUBS

Club Deportivo Don Martín, S.C. Don Martín, Coah.
Club Deportivo de Pesca Lago Toronto, La Boquilla, Chih.
Club Regiomontano Deportivo S.C. Monterrey, N.L.
Club de Caza y Pesca Monterrey, S.A. Comales, Tamps.
Club de Caza y Pesca Sanalona, S.A. Culiacán, Sin.
Club de Caza y Pesca Rodriguez, S.C. Tijuana, Dto. Norte. B.C.

AMERICAN CLUBS WITH AUTHORITY TO FISH IN MEXICO

San Diego Sport Fishing Association, Inc. 1050 Harbor St., San Diego, Calif.
Point Loma Sport Fishing Association. San Diego, Calif.
Pularto Sport Fishing Assn. San Diego, Calif.

CLUBS WITHOUT WATER CONCESSIONS, BUT WITH RIGHTS TO FISH FOR SPORT IN INTERIOR WATERS

Centro Nacional de Caza y Pezca Deportiva, A.C. Aptdo. Postal 40, Piedras Negras, Coah.
Club Deportivo Corsarios, S.C. Calle Hidalgo y Matamoros 649, Cuidad Reynosa, Tamps.

GLOSSARY OF FISH NAMES

As Spanish and, often, purely Indian names are used in all localities of Mexico, it is advisable that visitors familiarize themselves with these names. Frequently Mexicans call any white-meat fish *pez blanco* or *pescado blanco,* no matter what the species. In certain areas small bass and other fish are called *truchas* or trout.

Tuna	Atún
Yellowfin	Atún de aleta amarilla
Albacore	Albacora
Bonito	Bonito
Sailfish	Pez Vela
Marlin	Pez Marlin
Dolphin	Dorado
Shark	Tiburón
Sea trout	Trucha del mar.
Swordfish	Pez espada.
Pacific mackerel	Macarela
Mexican sea bass	Totoaba
Rock bass	Cabrillas
Black bass	Lobina negra
Whitefish	Pescado blanco.
Bluegill sunfish	Mojarra de agalla azul
Catfish	Bagre
Tarpon	Sábalo
Mullet	Lisa
Barracuda	Picuda
Spanish mackerel	Sierra
Jackfish	Jureles
Pómpano	Pompano
Snook	Robalo
Grouper	Mero
Red snapper	Huachinango
(other snappers)	Pargos
Yellowtail	Jurel
Corbina	Corvina
Flounders	Lenguados
Rainbow trout	Trucha arco iris
Brook trout	Trucha de arroyo

OUTDOOR EQUIPMENT

One should not attempt camping in Mexico without some knowledge of the language and country, or a good guide and, of course, experience in camping. For hunting or trout fishing in the northern Sierras you should use about the same equipment as you would take for a similar trip in the Rockies.

Jungle camping (either tiger hunting, orchid seeking, or archaeological expeditions) calls for entirely different gear. Here is a basic list needed in the southern tropics and lowlands:

Hammocks with mosquito nets and ropes. A thin blanket per person for the tropic nights get cold. Head-veils. Medium-weight cotton twill shirts and pants that have been mosquito-proofed. A heavy overshirt or waterproof jacket. Medium high-top boots for tucking in trousers. Tennis shoes for wading in lagoons and marshes. Comfortable camp shoes. Pajamas, sox, cotton underwear, lightweight waterproof poncho.

Also take scissors, nippers, a *machete*, and a hunting knife. Things affected by rain or humidity such as matches, cameras, and film should be packed in plastic bags.

Cooking equipment should be minimum: aluminum frying pans and pots because they do not rust; plastic plates and cups (these should either be yellow or red, the greens and blues get lost too easily in jungle terrain). Plastic containers for sugar, salt and coffee, rice, etc. Plastic or aluminum canteens.

In the southern regions (Chiapas, Oaxaca, Campeche, and Yucatán) it is advisable *not to carry a pistol*. The Indians are suspicious of people with pistols. It is considered an offensive weapon. They look upon shotguns in another light, as tools for hunting food. Most jungle hunting can be done without a rifle. You are usually too hedged in by verdure to get a long shot. Old jungle-hands recommend: for jaguar — a 16-gauge double-barrel shotgun with a slug in one barrel and 0 gauge in the other. For deer and javelina (wild pig) — No. 1 or 0 gauge. No. 4 shells for wild turkey and other birds.

As important as your compass is your first-aid kit and insect repellants. You should carry a plentiful supply of the latter. *OFF* and *6-12* or other repellants containing diethyl toluamide are the most effective against mosquitoes. Vitamin B_1 is also said to make you smell like a circus lion but it drives away mosquitoes. If you try it, check with your doctor on how much you can safely take. To reduce the irritation caused by insect bites rub with lemon or lime juice and/or take an antihistamine tablet (See Index: *Health Hints*).

10. *Study in Mexico. Postgraduate Courses and Special Courses for Foreigners. Directory of Mexican Summer Schools. Directory of American Colleges and Universities Conducting Summer Sessions in Mexico*

STUDENT SUMMER

Each year vastly increasing numbers of Canadian and U.S. students trek south to study in Mexico. Some come to pursue a regular curriculum leading to a postgraduate degree, others merely fill in some needed credits and still others pursue noncredit studies as a way of enjoying their vacation. There are at present some 15 institutions in Mexico ranging from the National University, the state universities to specialized schools which open their doors to foreign students. In addition a number of United States universities annually conduct seminars in Mexico.

A student planning year-round studies must secure a student visa before entering Mexico. (See Index.) For one term studies or summer sessions you can come in on a tourist visa.

Most Mexican schools list their courses as being accredited in the U.S. This is not entirely true. Some U.S. schools accept Mexican credits, others do not. The same applies to U.S. credits transferred to Mexican universities. If you plan to receive credit for a Mexican term it is advisable to check with your own school to find what courses offered by Mexican schools are recognized.

With the exception of the National University's School for Foreigners, the summer sessions at state universities and courses at specialized schools, the regular Mexican university curriculum is not tailored for American undergraduates. Mexican universities are in a sense graduate schools offering studies leading to a Master's or Doctor's degree. To enter them you must have a Bachelor's degree or credits equivalent to a Mexican *bachillerato*.

For most American students contemplating a visit to a Mexican campus, your best advice is to dovetail one term of study in Mexico with your regular U.S. curriculum.

Mexican schools do not have campus dormitories. Most of the schools make an effort to find housing for students in either private homes, small apartments, or at boardinghouses. At present the average expense for a student studying in Mexico — excluding tuition and books — ranges from $80 to $150 a month. Rates listed below — in U.S. currency.

MEXICAN UNIVERSITIES AND SCHOOLS

The National University of Mexico *(Cuidad Universitaria)*. The nation's top university. Its *escuela de verano* (summer school) has been renamed School for Foreigners and has been extended to a year-round basis. There are fall, winter, and spring terms of three months each. The summer session remains a concentrated five-day-per-week, six-week session.

The School for Foreigners offers studies leading to a Master of Arts degree in Hispanic Languages, Spanish or Latin American Literature and History. The school also gives courses in Anthropology (Mexican Archaeology and Ethnography), Latin American Economics, Art, Art History, and various courses on

Mexican culture with credits to be applied toward degrees at other institutions. No B.A. is offered, but U.S. undergraduates can take courses here and have them applied toward their degrees at their home universities.

Tuition is $90 per term. Students have the facilities of the university libraries as well as all the campus sports facilities. On campus there are lunch rooms, bookstores, theater, bank, telegraph office, etc. On weekends during the summer session there are teacher-guided excursions to points of interest throughout the country. The summer classes usually draw about a thousand students.

For additional information write to: Miss Rosa María Stephenson, Cursos Temporales, Cuidad Universitaria, Mexico, 20, D.F.

University of the Americas. This institution is on the outskirts of Mexico City. Founded in 1940, it is the only American-type college in Mexico offering undergraduate courses leading to a degree of Bachelor of Arts. Majors are offered in Anthropology, Business Administration, Creative Writing, Economics, Education, English, Fine Arts, History, Latin American Studies, Philosophy, Spanish Language and Literature. In addition to the regular four terms there is a special six-week summer session for students unable to attend the full summer term.

Tuition for the regular ten-week terms is $185; for the six-week session, $110.

For students interested in archaeology University of the Americas has a program for field work in Meso-American archaeology which divides its study time between the college campus in Mexico City and the college operated Centro de Estudios Regionales in Oaxaca.

For information: University of the Americas, Kilometer 16, Carretera Mexico-Toluca, Mexico, 10, D.F.

The Mexican-Northamerican Institute of Cultural Relations, Hamburgo 115, Mexico D.F. gives year-round, noncredit courses in Spanish and intensive three-week, three-hour-a-day courses during the summer. Tuition is $36 or $450 MN.

Centro de Escritores Mexicanos is a bilingual writing center which conducts year-round sessions and workshop courses as well as special summer sessions. A number of leading Mexican authors are involved in this group. Fees, $75 for full six-week summer session, or $35 for two-week participation. Address: Valle-Arispe 23, Mexico, D.F.

Universidad Iberoamericana in Mexico City has two summer courses, including studies in Ethnology, Fine Arts, Economics, Folk Arts and Crafts, History, Literature, Sociology. Registration and tuition is $110. For further information: Escuela de Verano, Universidad Iberoamericana, Mexico, 21, D.F.

Acapulco Summer School, located in Mexico's most glamorous resort area, is a rather lighthearted enterprise. Courses include Spanish Language and Literature, Italian, Fine Arts, guitar playing, water skiing, and bullfighting. Tuition is $80. Direct inquiries to: Escuela de Verano, Colegio del Estado de Guerrero, Calle de Juárez, Chilpancingo, Gro.

University of Guadalajara, in Guadalajara, Jalisco, has a summer school offering credit courses in Spanish Language and Literature, History, Art History, Mexican Folklore. For further information write to: Escuela de Letras y Artes, Belém 120, Guadalajara, Jalisco.

University of Guanajuato, located in Guanajuato, one of the most picturesque cities in Latin America has summer-session classes in Spanish Language, Spanish, Mexican and Latin American Literature, Mexican History, Fine Arts, Mexican Folklore. Tuition is $60. Address inquiries to: Director of La Escuela de Verano, Universidad de Guanajuato, Guanajuato, Mexico.

University of Veracruz, situated at Jalapa, capital of the State of Veracruz, has an excellent, well-staffed summer school giving credit courses in Archaeology, Spanish and Spanish Literature, Philosophy, Theater, Public Health, etc. Tuition: $60 for six-week session. For additional information write to: Director of La Escuela de Verano, Universidad Veracruzana, Juárez, 23, Jalapa, Veracruz, Mexico.

Instituto Tecnologico y de Estudios Superiores de Monterrey, situated outside of Mexico's busy industrial city, Monterrey, is primarily a technical school. It is a member of the Southern Association of Colleges, the Association of Texas Colleges and is also accredited by the Texas Education Society. Its summer school offers credit courses in Art, Folklore, English Composition, Economics, Languages, Geography, History, etc. The fee is $260 (includes tuition, room, meals, medical attention, extra curricular activities. For additional information: Ing. Fernando Macías Rendón, Summer School and Extension Division, Sucursal de Correos "J," Monterrey, N.L. Mexico.

Universidad Interamericana in the mile-high city of Saltillo is one of the oldest of Mexican summer schools. It utilizes the facilities of the University of Saltillo. There are several summer sessions and credit courses leading to degrees of B.A., M.A., and Ph.D. are offered. The six-week summer session fee, including room and board, tuition, books, university activities is $270. For further information query: Profa. María del Refugio Galindo de P. Parque Azteca, Apartado Postal 255, Saltillo, Coahuila. Mexico.

Instituto Allende, one of Mexico's largest art schools, is situated in colonial San Miguel de Allende, one of the few towns in the country to have been declared a national monument. The school offers year-round courses in Fine and Craft Arts, Photography, Creative Writing, and Spanish. Most classes are conducted in English. Tuition is $45 a month. For additional information query: Mr. Stirling Dickinson, Instituto Allende, San Miguel de Allende, Gto. Mexico.

Academía Hispano-Americano is also in San Miguel de Allende. An unusually fine language school offering year-round, intensive courses in Spanish, Mexican and Spanish Literature and Culture. Through the fall, winter, and spring there are regular three-month terms. During the summer special six-week courses are offered. The summer session fee, $75; for the regular three-month semesters, $110. For further information address: Sra. Carmen Masip de Hawkins, Academía Hispano-Americano, Insurgentes 7, San Miguel de Allende, Gto. Mexico.

Universidad Michoacana in Morelia, one of Mexico's most beautiful cities, has just begun summer courses in Spanish, Mexican Literature and History, Folklore and has opened its School of Fine Arts to foreign students. Tuition is $70 for the summer session. Address: Director de Cursos de Verano, Universidad Michoacana, Morelia, Michoacán, Mexico.

University of the State of Mexico, in the state capital, Toluca, has one six-week summer session offering credit courses in Spanish Language, Art History, Mexican Literature, Painting, Folklore. Tuition is $80. For information address inquiries to: Mrs. Martha B. de Guzman, Escuela de Verano, Universidad de Mexico, Constituyentes 39, Toluca, Mexico.

AMERICAN UNIVERSITIES AND COLLEGES CONDUCTING SEMINARS IN MEXICO

Arizona State University. A one-month residence study program in Mexico City. Query: Arizona State University, Tempe, Arizona.

Bradford Junior College. A summer seminar, conducted by Bradford Junior College at Bradford, Massachusetts, limited to young ladies. It makes the Instituto Allende its headquarters.

Florida State University. Summer workshop at Instituto Tecnológico de Monterrey. Query: Dr. Herberto Lacayo, Department of Modern Languages, Florida State University, Tallahassee, Florida.

Indiana University. Intercollegiate study projects in Mexico. Write: Dr. Harvey L. Johnson, Department of Spanish and Portuguese, Indiana University, Bloomington, Indiana.

Sacramento State College. Summer session based at the National University in Mexico City. Group Leader, Dr. William Thompson, Sacramento State College, Sacramento, California.

University of Kentucky. Language workshop in Puebla. Query: Summer Sessions in Mexico, University of Kentucky, Lexington, Kentucky.

University of Miami. Special summer workshop in Anthropology, Archaeology, Art, History, and Spanish. Headquarters are in Oaxaca. Limited to 25 students. Query: Box 8556, University of Miami, Coral Gables, Florida.

University of San Francisco. Summer sessions utilizing the facilities of the University of Guadalajara. Address: Dr. Carlos Sánchez, Summer Sessions Abroad, University of San Francisco, San Francisco 17, California.

Associated Colleges of Claremont (Pomona, Claremont, and Scripps Colleges). Mexico Study Tour. Dr. Leonard C. Pronke, Pomona College, Claremont, California.

Brigham Young University. The university's Spanish Department conducts a summer seminar at the Mexican-Northamerican Institute of Cultural Relations for students willing to co-operate with the Mormon standards, including non-use of alcohol and tobacco. Query: Dr. H. Darrel Taylor, Brigham Young University, Provo, Utah.

Louisiana State University. Mexico-Spanish study tour from June to August. Write: Chairman, Department of Foreign Languages, Louisiana State University, Baton Rouge, Louisiana.

Southern Illinois University. Conducts a summer biennial study tour of Mexico in co-operation with the Director of Regional Museums of the Mexican Government. Write: Department of Foreign Languages, Southern Illinois University, Carbondale, Illinois.

University of Arizona conducts a history study tour in Mexico. Query: Dr. Russel C. Ewing, Department of History, University of Arizona, Tucson, Arizona.

University of Chicago has initiated a graduate student study program in San Cristobal de las Casas, Chiapas, to investigate existing social conditions, nutrition, etc. For additional information query: Dr. Sol Tax, University of Chicago, Chicago, Illinois.

Antioch College. For students enrolled at Antioch, the college has established a Mexican branch utilizing the facilities and faculty of the University of Guanajuato. Fall, winter, and spring terms. Query: Ester Oldt, Director of Antioch Education Abroad, Antioch College, Yellow Springs, Ohio.

11. Residence in Mexico. Requirements and Legal Status. Owning Property. Rents. Servants. Cost of Living. U. S. Tax Situation for Residents.

RESIDENCE

Mexico's charming villages and resort areas, the climate, the somewhat lower cost of living as well as the business opportunities are a powerful magnet attracting aliens to settle below the border. Perhaps because the magnet is so strong, the Mexican Government has set up rather stiff requirements for the alien who wishes to engage in business or employment or retire. In addition a great deal of confusing red tape has been tossed in to discourage all but the most persistent. As a tourist you may enter Mexico on a six-month (180 day) nonrenewable permit, but you may not engage in business or work. A U.S. businessman may also enter Mexico on a special six-month, renewable, permit to engage in nonremunerative activities such as inspecting shipments for export or negotiating contracts. If you wish to engage in business, work, or retire in Mexico, you must apply for resident status which, with the exception of student resident status (see Index), requires the service of a lawyer specializing in immigration matters.

In Mexico resident status is either provisional *(inmigrante)* or permanent *(inmigrado)*. After going through the hoops of provisional residence which must be renewed annually for five years, one's status becomes permanent. During the five-year *inmigrante* period gainful activity is limited to the job or work authorized by the Ministry of Interior. In other words, if you are employed as a chemist at a particular plant you have to stick there unless you receive authorization from the Ministry to change employment during this period. Student *inmigrante* and persons whose provisional residence is based on retirement are not permitted to work or engage in business during the five-year period. When residence becomes permanent (after five years) you are permitted to engage in almost any legitimate employment or business.

Work and Business Residence Status. You can establish provisional resident status in order to occupy a technical, managerial, or other responsible position with a business organization operating in Mexico. In such instances the firm must request your service and also prove that similarly qualified personnel are unavailable in Mexico.

Or you can engage in industrial, export, or agricultural business on your own provided that you invest a minimum sum of 400,000 pesos if your business is established in the area directly around Mexico City, or 200,000 pesos in other parts of the country.

Resident Status for Those Retiring on a Pension or Fixed Income. At present the Mexican government offers two categories for people interested in settling in the country on fixed incomes. You may come in as an *inmigrante rentista* if you can show you have a fixed monthly income of $240 U.S. for yourself, and $80 U.S. for each dependent over fifteen years of age. At the end of five years provisional residence you can obtain permanent or *inmigrado* status and can pursue any economic activity within the wide margin which Mexican laws provide. The government fee for obtaining this provisional status is $1286 MN, plus an annual $50 MN., for renewal of residence each year, and a final fee of $200 MN, at the end of the fifth year. During the provisional period you cannot be gainfully employed.

The other category is as a *visitante rentista*. For this status you must prove a regular minimum income of $160 U.S., per month, plus an additional $80 U.S. per month for each dependent over fifteen years of age. Though less expensive, people in this category *never* acquire permanent (*inmigrado*) at the end of five years.

People entering as *visitante rentistas* may bring in their own car under bond. The car permit is renewable for a period of up to two years.

The former student *inmigrante* category, which,

after five years entitled one to permanent residence status, has been abolished. Students entering for short periods should use regular tourist permits.

For additional information regarding retirement regulations and arrangements it is advisable to confer with a Mexican consul as well as a Mexican immigration lawyer.

OWNING PROPERTY IN MEXICO

You may own land or a home in Mexico even though you are a foreigner. The one exception to this is that no alien or corporation with foreign shareholders may acquire direct ownership of land within 50 kilometers of a Mexican seacoast or 100 kilometers of a land frontier. In almost all other regions ownership of land will normally be granted if you accept the legal position of Mexican citizens in regards to this and waive the right to appeal to your government in matters affecting your property.

In some popular resort areas (Acapulco, Cuernavaca, San Miguel de Allende) where aliens have tended to concentrate, government officials may make it difficult to purchase property. Legally, at the moment, there is no prohibition regarding ownership of land in the inland areas, but red tape can thoroughly discourage the would-be purchaser.

Permit to Enter Mexico to Purchase Property. In the past years a special nonresident short-term entry permit was available to U.S. citizens to enter Mexico for the specific purpose of purchasing property or a home. Such permits could be obtained at a nominal fee on the sole authority of your nearest Mexican consul. After property had been purchased you could return to the United States and re-enter Mexico on a tourist card, utilizing the home in Mexico as a temporary summer or winter home without having to establish residence. Although the existence of this special permit has not been officially abolished, recent applicants report that consular offices have almost completely discouraged them from applying.

RENTS

For an alien setting up temporary or permanent residence in Mexico, the least complicated housing arrangement is to rent an apartment or home, rather than think in terms of purchase. There are few real estate agents in Mexico. Most rentals are handled through the classified section of local newspapers or by simply putting a FOR RENT sign (SE RENTA, or SE AQUILA) outside the house. Often houses or apartments for rent are marked by old newspapers tied to a window grill. When you find something you like stop, ring the bell and look the place over then and there.

Leases usually run from one to three years. Most landlords (in the larger cities) require surety from their tenants. The surety may be the signature of a *fijador* (a signer or person established in the community), or you may be required to make an advance deposit of the first and last months' rent. When you rent, make certain that the utilities have been paid up to date by the former tenants. Utility bills often run several months behind.

Rents for modern dwellings in Mexico City and the more popular tourist centers are (convenience for convenience) about the same or a little higher than rents in Los Angeles or Chicago. In a good residential district of Mexico City a two-bedroom unfurnished apartment at present runs from $90 to $300. In Guadalajara average rents run between $50 and $100. In small towns unfurnished houses may be found for as low as $20 to $50, but in the latter most of the conveniences (adequate kitchen, lavatory and electrical wire) Americans are accustomed to, are missing.

SERVANTS

Residence in Mexico is almost impossible without servants. Lack of low-cost electrical appliances, adequate refuse and garbage disposal and delivery services make domestics a necessity. Most houses and apartments have servants' quarters.

Although the average person doing domestic work in Mexico may be very hard-working and charming, don't expect the same degree of service, training or responsibility that you get from domestic help in Europe or the U. S. Mexican servants often have had little schooling; few can read and write. Also, job and money are not always really important to them. They may leave you without notice to go on a pilgrimage, to spend a day with a boy friend or just to go back to their home village.

When you hire domestic help be sure it is understood that you are hiring them for a trial period up to 30 days. If you find it necessary to discharge a servant after the trial period has ended, be sure the settlement is satisfactory to all sides. It is advisable to have him or her sign a statement to the effect that the amount you have given is satisfactory severance pay and nothing is owed. Under Mexican Labor Laws an employee dismissed for other than just cause is entitled to three-months' salary plus 20 days' pay for each year he has been employed. The phrase *"Voy a darle gracias"* is the usual and most satisfactory formula for telling a person you're terminating his service.

At present, in small cities and towns, a general maid or *criada* earns about 60 to 125 pesos a month, plus room and food. A *mozo* (handyman) about 80 to 160 per month. A cook *(cocinera)* will receive from 100 to 200 pesos per month. In Mexico City and resort areas the division of labor is more complex and the pay scale higher. At present a cook gets from 250 to 400 pesos a month, plus board and room and, being a specialist, she usually will not help in other parts of the house. A cook-maid *(galopina)* who does some cooking but will help elsewhere in the house now gets from 150 to 250 pesos a month. A chambermaid *(recamarera)* who does the bedrooms, the washing and ironing, gets 150 to 200 pesos a month. A nursemaid *(nana)* who cares for the children, their food and clothing and who may do some housework receives from 200 to 300 pesos a month. The laundress or *lavandera,* who comes in by the day, receives 12 to 18 pesos a day, plus breakfast and lunch. A gardener *(jardinero),* if not living in as a *mozo,* receives from 15 to 20 pesos a day. A houseman *(mozo)* gets around 250 to 300 pesos a month if living in.

In larger towns and cities residential districts have night watchmen *(veladores).* They make the rounds on foot or bicycle, blowing a whistle. They are usually affiliated with the local police. They expect payment, from 5 to 25 pesos a month. Check with your neighbors.

COST OF LIVING

In Mexico City the cost of living has spiraled upward in a decade and closely parallels that of most large American cities. Basic costs — rent, utilities, clothing, auto insurance, etc. — are as high and at times higher than north of the border. Even in the smaller outlying communities where rents are lower, food costs are somewhat less and domestic servants do not tax the budget, these various savings are offset by the high cost of utilities and household appliances. A seven-cubic-foot refrigerator in Mexico costs about $400. A new Ford or Chevrolet, more than double the U.S. list price. All cooking and water heating is done by bottled gas, expensive in itself, plus the cost of tanks which you have to purchase. Electric rates are equally high, the basic rate being determined by the number of outlets and light sockets in your house. The more power you are liable to use, the higher your basic rate. To secure a telephone (in short supply) you must invest in the telephone company, purchasing anywhere from $100 to $300 in stock, plus an installation charge ranging from $12 to $20.

For most foreigners residing in Mexico now, the deciding factor is no longer the appeal of low-cost living. In some cases the incentive is a more favorable tax situation, but for the majority it is simply the Mexican way of life that charms them. This includes benign climate, a easier, slower living pace, roomy old houses, and the pleasure of being able to afford servants.

TAX SITUATION

U.S. citizens who are bona fide residents in Mexico are exempt from U.S. income taxation on earned income received from sources outside the United States. The word "source" is interpreted as the place where the work or personal service which produces earned income is performed. In short, if you perform work in Mexico for an American company located in Chicago, and even though your check comes from Chicago, the first $20,000 of annual earned income is exempt from U. S. Federal Tax. Income received by U.S. citizens resident in Mexico from sources other than wages, salaries (from dividends, rents, annuities, royalties) do not come under this category and are taxable as usual.

In Mexico capital gains on the sale of stocks escape Mexican income tax simply because there is no register of stock transactions by the companies and because all Mexican securities are payable to the bearer. The Mexican treasury finds it impossible to collect such taxes. U.S. citizens are, of course, responsible for reporting such capital gains to the U. S. Bureau of Internal Revenue.

For additional details regarding the tax situation for U.S. citizens in Mexico see: *Tax Guide for U. S. Citizens Abroad,* publication #54, issued by the U. S. Treasury Department, Washington, D.C.

12. *Investing in Mexico. Sources of Investment and Business Information*

The steady economic growth of Mexico (See Index: *Mexican Economy, Industry and Mining*), the lack of exchange restrictions, the potentially vast market and the apparent economic and political stability of the nation are presently interesting U.S. firms and private investors. On the surface the investment and business climate in Mexico appears very attractive. However, because the country is still a nation-in-process-of-formation, with its social and economic and legal structure still being tested, only investors and businessmen who can afford expensive legal advice and make intensive economic studies should attempt to establish themselves in the Mexican economy. The small operator, businessman, or investor is often liable to be caught in a contradictory situation which may require extensive capital or even political influence to weather out.

At the moment the Mexican administration looks favorably upon private initiative and foreign capital investments which serve to assist Mexico's industrialization and raise the standard of living. This outlook, however, generally applies to large capital investments and not shoestring operations.

For visitors in Mexico interested in the business or

investment picture it is suggested that he read *How To Invest in Mexico* by Daniel James (Carl Ross, Publications), Reforma 366, Mexico, D.F.

For additional information regarding Mexican corporations, the stock market, industry:

Bolsa de Valores de México (Mexican stock exchange) publishes a monthly bulletin summarizing price, balance sheet and income data on listed securities. Write to: Estudios Especiales, Bolsa de Valores de México, S.A. Uruguay 68, Mexico, 1, D.F.

El Mercado de Valores is a weekly economic publication issued free of charge by the Nacional Financiera, Venustiano Carranza 25, Mexico, 1, D.F. In Spanish only.

Boletín Financiero y Minero is Mexico's sole financial daily. Printed in Spanish. Address: Venustiano Carranza 69, Mexico 1, D.F.

Comercio Exterior, English, French, and Spanish editions published monthly by the Banco Nacional de Comercio Exterior, S.A. Venustiano Carranza 32, Mexico, 1, D.F. This is considered the best general economic review in Mexico. Copies are free.

13. Tips for Photographers in Mexico. Supplies. Photo Labs

Mexico, land of spectacular scenery, quaint villages, storybook architecture and picturesque contrasts is, indeed, a camera-bug's paradise. For successful shooting results below the border here are some useful tips on light, films, camera treatment, and shooting procedure.

LIGHT

The quality of Mexican light is not as treacherous as some people imagine. According to the technical chief of Kodak Mexicana, the Eastman Company's Central American headquarters in Mexico City, "the most important thing to remember about the light in Mexico is its uniformity throughout the year. It is equivalent to the light you get on a bright spring day in Washington, D.C."

However, since much of Mexico is very dry during some ten months of the year and because of the intensity of the tropic sun and lack of haze, the use of filters is very important. For black and white shooting use *red filters* to lighten red subjects (including suntans) and to darken blues and greens, as well as to create dramatic sky and foliage effects. Use *green filters* to lighten greens and make reds and blues darker. A *light green XI filter* accomplished the same ends as a yellow filter with better rendering of green foliage. Use *yellow filters* for beach shooting and to intensify skies.

CONTRAST

With the exception of a few winter months the Mexican midday sun is an intense vertical one creating dense shadows beneath any overhang. Most buildings are plastered and whitewashed, thus producing further alarming contrasts. Also, the Mexican Indian's facial complexion is dark and nonreflective, his dress is usually pure white; add to this the excessive shadows made by his cartwheel sombrero and you have contrast problems.

For the visitor with a simple camera the best advice is to shoot in the morning hours or late afternoon when the side lighting is stronger. For camera fans able to control exposure and do their own processing, the simplest procedure for general shooting under such conditions is to overexpose (black and white only) one full stop or more, then reduce development time 25 to 30 per cent. It will give a softer negative, but with fuller definition at each end of the gray scale. The following contrast guide is most helpful for successful shooting in Mexico.

EXISTING SUBJECT CONTRAST	DESIRED PICTURE CONTRAST LOW	MEDIUM	HIGH
HIGH	Overexpose greatly Extreme overdevelopment	Overexpose slightly Underdevelop	Expose normally Normal development
MEDIUM	Overexpose Underdevelop	Normal exposure Normal development	Underexpose Overdevelop
LOW	Normal Normal development	Underexpose Overdevelop	Normal Extreme overdevelopment.

TRAVELER'S DO AND DON'T

Keep your cameras, meter and film out of your glove compartment. The ovenlike heat there will ruin them.

Summer heat, humidity, and fungus are major troublemakers in Mexico's tropic regions. Fungus thrives on the gelatinous surface of film. Keep your film in tropic packs, aluminum screw-top cans or wrap them in aluminum foil. Develop as soon as possible. In tropic areas make a daily inspection of your equipment, inside and out. When not being used, your cameras, meter, and lenses should be kept in a zippered bag (plastic is best) in which you have stowed a small sack of dehydrant, Sterling Gel, or a similar silicate.

During the dry months the Mexican dust is as dangerous to cameras as moisture in the tropics. It is as fine as talc. When traveling along unpaved roads keep cameras well protected. Carry two camel-hair brushes in airtight containers, one for cleaning lenses, the other for cleaning your camera body.

If your camera is damaged or needs cleaning (and you have time), have it repaired in Mexico City. There are excellent repair shops specializing in precision work at far less than it would cost at home. Recommended are the repair services of Casa Calpini, Avenida Madero 34; Foto Regis, Avenida Juárez 80; and Sr. Mariano Flores, Bucareli 107, Suite 309.

When taking your camera to the beach keep it wrapped in a heavy towel to protect it from heat, and keep a filter or lens guard over the lens.

Before leaving home get a camera insurance or floater policy covering your camera equipment. If your American policy does not serve south of the border the American Photo Supply Company, Madero 21, or Foto Regis, Juárez 80, both in Mexico City will recommend a responsible Mexican camera insurance underwriter.

Keep your camera with you or properly locked up when traveling. In Mexico, as in Europe, cameras are sought-after items. If you lock your camera in your car, make certain it is covered or out of sight. In sight it tempts people to break in.

If your camera gets wet or is dunked in fresh water simply wipe off carefully and send to a repair shop as soon as possible. If dunked in salt water or affected by salt spray, which causes corrosion, wipe down sparingly with clear tap water and dry. If it has had a severe sea-water bath, wet it down with clear tap water and dry. If after several hours of standing, white salt deposits begin to show, repeat the process. Get the camera to a repair shop.

Your most important camera equipment needs while traveling are: a daylight changing bag, camelhair lens brush, tripod, filters, tropic pack film. For extended travel, Spiratone Inc., 369 Seventh Ave., New York, N.Y., puts up a handy portable darkroom kit including a daylight loading tank, developer, and fixers in a plastic case.

SHOOTING TIPS

Mexico's exciting markets, plazas full of colorful people and exceptional scenes are a cameraman's delight. At times these are difficult to memorialize on film. In villages people are sometimes resentful, suspicious, or frankly afraid of having their picture snapped. In Mexico, more than in the U.S. or Europe, you have to shoot unobtrusively or make courteous arrangements to shoot. Nothing is more irritating to a Mexican than a foreigner importantly poking about with a camera, snapping pictures as though the subjects were on exhibition in a cage. Here are a few simple ground rules for picture snapping.

Be courteous. Before taking a closeup of a Mexican or barging into his patio to snap a picture, always ask for permission.

When sallying out into villages and rural areas don't dress loudly, or overdress. You can't hide the fact that you are a foreigner, but you needn't flaunt it.

A pocketful of hard candies for children or cigarettes for men will do more toward winning friends than all the Point 4 largesse you might muster. To get significant pictures of Mexican life don't just hop out of a car and snap away. Best — select a town or village that has a pleasant plaza and marketplace and spend a few days there. On the first day carry your camera, explore the town, but don't shoot much. Let the people feel you're honestly interested in their town and not just rushing through. By the second or third day the people are used to you, are much more relaxed and your shooting prospects are better. A local schoolteacher or student will often prove to be a better guide than a hotel guide and they'll open picture prospects for you.

For those "candid" closeups and magnificent shots of village life no amount of posing will help. These have to be shot unobtrusively otherwise your subjects will freeze up if they suspect you're taking pictures. Learn to shoot from the hip, or with a reflex camera, sidewise or backward. With medium speed film preset your camera at f/8 and 1/250 or f/11 and 1/100 with focus set at 8 or 16 feet you can cover a lot of candid subjects without fumbling with your camera and giving away the fact that you're snapping pictures.

PHOTO TERMINOLOGY

Cámera (camera), *película* (film), *rolla de película* (a roll of film), *obturador* (shutter), *exposición* (exposure), *indice de exposición* (exposure index), *revelar* (to develop), *amplificar* (to enlarge), *copias de contacto* (contact prints), *tripié* (tripod), *diafragma* (diaphragm), *filtrarayos* (filters), *lentes* (lenses), *luz diurna* (daylight film), and *foto* (photo).

SUPPLIES AND PHOTO LABS

Most of the standard American and European makes of films and camera supplies can be purchased in Mexico. Prices of film are somewhat higher than in the U.S. Camera supply shops and photo labs are listed in this guide under the principal cities.

It is not advisable to leave color film to be developed in small-town camera shops where lab controls and techniques are inadequate. For color film processing the following laboratories are recommended.

For Kodachrome and special handling of color work, Kodak Mexicana, Londres 16, Mexico, D.F.

Laboratorio Mexicolor, Calles Gabriel Mancera y Miguel Laurent, Mexico, D.F., for excellent quality color processing.

14. Emergencies. U. S. Embassy Protection Officer. Telephone and Telegraph. Hospital and Doctors. Benevolent Society. List of U. S. Consulates in Mexico

The U. S. Embassy in Mexico City, at the corner of Danubio and Paseo de la Reforma, has a protection officer on duty day and night. In cases of serious trouble or death he can be most helpful. It must be remembered, however, that officially he cannot demand things for you. You are subject to Mexican law when traveling in Mexico. The protection officer can only advise and assist you in case of need.

The American Benevolent Society at Copenhagen 2-503, in Mexico City (Tel. 14-54-65) is an organization with limited resources set up to aid residents in distress.

TELEGRAPH AND TELEPHONE

International telegrams can be sent through any of the national service telegraph offices in Mexico (see Index), but it is best, in cases of emergency when in Mexico City, to place them directly at the main international office at Dolores 3 (near the corner of Avenida Juárez) in downtown Mexico. Tel. 18-09-60 and 19-59-20. Telegrams may be telephoned in, but not from pay phones. To make an international long distance call, in Mexico City, dial 09. Outside of the Federal District, ask for *larga distancia internacional.*

In this guide doctors and some hospitals are listed under the principal cities.

AMERICAN CONSULATES IN THE STATES OF MEXICO

Mexico City. American Embassy and Consulate. Danubio and Paseo de la Reforma.

Cuidad Juárez, Chih. Edificio Banco Nacional. Avenidas Lerdo y 16 de Septiembre. Tel. Juárez 125 and 766.

Guadalajara, Jal. Av. 16 de Septiembre 489. Tel. 3-29-97, 3-29-98.

Matamoros, Tamps. Av. 3a and 5a, Colonia Jardín. Tel. Matamoros 241.

Mérida, Yuc. Paseo Montejo 453. Tel. 60-30.

Mexicali, B.C. Av. Madero 299. Tel. 63-12.

Monterrey, N.L. Edificio Roble, Av. Juárez Sur 800. Tel. 3-60-50.

Nogales, Son. Av. A. Obregón 61, Altos. Tel. 305-3-05.

Nuevo Laredo, Tamps. Calle Madero y Av. Ocampo. Tel. Nuevo Laredo 5.

Piedras Negras, Coah. Calle Hidalgo 107 Sur. Tel. 34.

Tampico, Tamps. Díaz Mirón 106, Oriente. Tel. 2-2087 and 2-2187.

Tijuana, B.C. Agua Caliente 470, San Ysidro, Calif. Tel. 2286, 2287, 3912.

Veracruz, Ver. Arista y Malecón. Tel. 30-40.

PART TWO

Physiography, History, and Culture

15. The Physiography and Climate

Geographically, Mexico is a unique country straddling the Temperate and Torrid Zones, crisscrossed by towering mountain ranges, by broad plateaus and unexplored jungle lowlands. It is a country between frontiers. It is sandwiched between diametrically different cultures — the mercantile-industrial civilization of the north, and the Spanish-Indian societies of the south. It is also a country with numerous internal frontiers separating diverse peoples and cultures.

In Mexico people frequently do not say north or south when offering directions to the traveler. They'll say up or down. The country is set on edge; straight lines and plane surfaces are absolutely homeless. There are always mountains between any two places of real importance. The topography and climate are the despair of engineers and roadbuilders, and this, principally, has saved Mexico from becoming anything else but itself.

The physical conformity of the country resembles a horn with its broad mouth to the north, the better as some observers have remarked, to catch the flow of tourist gold as well as for northern entrepreneurs to dip into the country's natural riches.

The Mexican Republic extends from latitudes north 32° 42′ and 14° 30′, and from 12° 18′ 46″ of E. longitude to 18° 6′ 15″ of longitude west of the meridian of Mexico City, or between 86° 46′ 8″ and 117° 7′ 8″ west of Greenwich. Its 8300 miles of boundaries are continguous with the United States on the north, the Gulf of Mexico and the Caribbean Sea on the east, Guatemala and Belice (British Honduras) on the southeast and the Pacific Ocean on the south and west. The country has an approximate area of 758,259 square miles and is about one quarter of the size of the United States. It ranks fourth in size among the republics of the Western Hemisphere.

Although Mexico has one mile of coastline for every 250 square miles of territory, it is scarcely a maritime nation. Its coastline along the Pacific Ocean extends 4438 miles; along the Gulf Coast and Caribbean sea, 1774 miles. In October 1945 the president of the Republic, General Avila Camacho, incorporated the submarine coastal platform, to a depth of 140 feet, into the territory of the republic, claiming all riches therein.

Mexico's greatest length, represented mainly by the gigantic dorsal ridge of the Sierra Madre range, is 1970 miles as the crow flies, from the northern extremity of Lower California to the southern border of the state of Chiapas. Its maximum breadth from east to west on a line of N. latitude 26° is about 750 miles; its minimum width at the Isthmus of Tehuantepec is 140 miles.

The Río Grande, called the Río Bravo by Mexicans, forms part of the dividing line between Mexico and the United States. By treaty between Spain and the United States (1819), the northern boundary was placed at the mouth of the Sabine River in Texas. In 1848, by the Treaty of Guadalupe, the dividing line was fixed at the Río Grande. Prior to this treaty the area of Mexico was 1,650,000 square miles. The U.S. gained over half this area as a result of the Mexican-American War and other negotiations. In 1853 the United States gained an additional 45,535 square miles of Mexican territory by the Gadsden Purchase Convention. The present U.S.-

Mexican border follows the Río Grande to Ciudad Juárez (El Paso, Texas), then along treaty lines to the Pacific Ocean. This latter line is indicated by 258 international markers.

The main body of the Mexican territory is a vast tableland comprising the central and northern portions of the republic. It is traversed by extensive mountain chains rising to remarkable heights. The tableland gradually rises from an altitude of about 3000 feet near the U.S. border to the 8000- and 9000-foot-high central region around Mexico City.

This central area, crossed by a broad band of volcanic mountains called the Sierra Volcánica Transversal, which extends from San Blas on the Pacific Coast through Guadalajara, Morelia, the Valley of Mexico to Veracruz, contains the highest peaks in the country and effectively divides the north from the south. Among the major peaks are: Orizaba (also called Citlaltépetl) 18,851 feet, and Popocatépetl, 17,716 feet. They are exceeded in height only by Mount Logan and Mount McKinley in the Northern Hemisphere.

The so-called central plateau is the most densely populated area of Mexico and, with few exceptions, contains the country's principal cities. The plateau is actually a series of seven basins or valleys forming seven population clusters. The basin of Mexico (the Valley of Mexico) has an elevation of some 7500 feet. It is the only one of the basins that is not naturally drained to the sea.

To the west of it, separated by high mountains, is the basin of Toluca, the highest of the seven valleys, about 8700 feet above sea level. To the north and west lies the basin of Guanajuato, also called El Bajío. It is the largest of the valley complexes, encompassing rich farming country and important silver mining areas. To the northwest of this is the Aguascalientes basin. Farther to the west is the basin of Jalisco, centered around Guadalajara, Mexico's second largest city. In the region south and east of the Valley of Mexico lies the Morelos basin, with its capital city of Cuernavaca, and the Puebla basin, the gateway to the Gulf of Mexico.

In these seven valley clusters, an area covering less than an eighth of the country, the bulk of the population has lived since pre-Hispanic times. Rainfall, soil, and climate here have favored the growth of civilization. Yet, even in this fairly densely populated region, the mountainous nature of the country has ever been a hindering factor in its social and economic development, creating tremendous problems in transportation and communications as well as determining the principal agricultural areas.

Concerning the two coastlines, the Pacific Coast area, although longer and generally narrow, is the less fertile and productive. The climate along the west coast is considered healthier than the Gulf Coast. The shoreline possesses some splendid harbors, chief among them: Acapulco, Manzanillo, Mazatlán, Salina Cruz, and Guaymas. In recent years these and small fishing ports have become increasingly attractive as resort areas, especially, Zihuatanejo, San Blas, Puerto Angel, San Benito, Barra de Navidad and La Paz, and Ensenada in Lower California.

The Gulf of Mexico and Caribbean coastal area, although blessed with a wider and fertile plain (average width 65 miles), and excellent ports — Tampico, Veracruz, Coatzacoalcos, Campeche, Carmen, and Progreso — is far less attractive from the point of view of tourist fare. Resort facilities are less well developed and the region is at the mercy of violent tropical storms. The coastal plain and the tropic forests of this area embrace some of Mexico's most important resources: rich farm land, hardwood forests, and enviable petroleum and sulphur deposits.

In addition to the great central plateau, the northern desert country, the coastal lands and the southern, isolated region of Oaxaca and Chiapas, two peninsulas complete Mexico's land terrain. The peninsula of Baja California (Lower California), with the exception of its southern tip, is arid mountain and desert country. The Yucatán Peninsula at the southeast extremity of the republic is a tremendous flatland, slightly above sea level. It is thinly soiled and poorly developed. Until a decade ago the Yucatán region was completely cut off from the main body of the nation by impassable jungles. Now a railroad and highway link it to the center.

The Mexican river system is neither varied nor extensive. The rugged configuration of the country converts most rivers into impetuous torrents which cut through deep canyons *(barrancas)* to the sea. Even the longest rivers are navigable for but a short distance. Shallow draught steamers ply inland on some of the southern rivers — the Usumacinta, the Coatzacoalcos and the Papaloapan. The longest river is the Río Balsas which rises in the state of Tlaxcala and flows into the Pacific Ocean. Many Mexican rivers, though useless for navigation, have become important sources for hydroelectric power and for irrigation.

Mexico contains few important lakes. Most of them are high among mountains or on the great central plateau. Lake Chapala, a short distance from Guadalajara, is the country's largest natural lake. Small, yet noted for their beauty and attractive surroundings, are Lake Pátzcuaro and Lake Cuitzeo in Michoacán; Lake Tamiahua and Lake Catemaco in Veracruz; and, completely unknown to tourists, a series of magnificent small lakes in the state of Chiapas, near the Mexican-Guatemala border — Lagunas de Montebello, (see Index).

There are two spectacular canyon groups within the Mexican territory which are comparable to the Grand Canyon of Arizona. The larger, in the state of Chihuahua, is known as Las Grandes Barrancas de la Tarahumara (see Index); the other in Chiapas is called El Sumidero (see Index).

STATES AND TERRITORIES IN THE MEXICAN REPUBLIC

STATE OR TERRITORY	ABBREVIATION	AREA IN SQ. MILES	APPROX. POPULATION	CAPITAL
Aguascalientes	Ags.			
Baja California	B.C.			
(northern section	"	2,528	243,363	Aguascalientes
or state)		27,979	520,165	Mexicali
(southern section	"	28,307	81,594	La Paz
or territory)				
Campeche	Camp.	19,903	168,219	Campeche
Chiapas	Chis.	29,068	1,210,870	T. Gutiérrez
Chihuahua	Chih.	95,942	1,226,793	Chihuahua
Coahuila	Coah.	58,748	907,734	Saltillo
Colima	Col.	2,009	164,450	Colima
Durango	Dgo.	48,250	760,836	Durango
Guanajuato	Gto.	11,943	1,735,490	Guanajuato
Guerrero	Gro.	25,719	1,186,716	Chilpancingo (Ciudad Bravo)
Hidalgo	Hgo.	8,152	994,598	Pachuca
Jalisco	Jal.	31,517	2,443,261	Guadalajara
Mexico	Mex.	13,381	1,897,891	Toluca
Michoacán	Mich.	23,474	1,851,876	Morelia
Morelos	Mor.	1,939	386,264	Cuernavaca
Nayarit	Nay.	10,671	389,929	Tepic
Nuevo León	N.L.	25,431	1,078,848	Monterrey
Oaxaca	Oax.	36,801	1,727,266	Oaxaca
Puebla	Pue.	13,280	1,793,837	Puebla
Querétaro	Qro.	4,484	355,045	Querétaro
Quintana Roo (territory)	Q.R.	19,861	50,169	Chetumal
San Luis Potosí	S.L.P.	24,704	1,048,297	San Luis Potosí
Sinaloa	Sin.	22,847	838,408	Culiacán
Sonora	Son.	71,310	783,378	Hermosillo
Tabasco	Tab.	9,897	496,340	Villahermosa
Tamaulipas	Tamps.	31,095	1,334,182	Ciudad Victoria
Tlaxcala	Tlax.	2,515	346,699	Tlaxcala
Veracruz	Ver.	28,084	2,727,899	Jalapa
Yucatán	Yuc.	15,042	614,049	Mérida
Zacatecas	Zac.	28,454	817,831	Zacatecas
Federal District	D.F.	579	4,870,876	Mexico City

NOTE: 1960-64 population figures from the Dirección General de Estadística, Secretaría de Economía.

THE CLIMATE OF MEXICO

Although many people imagine Mexico as lying entirely south of the United States and as being a hot, tropical country, actually one half of the Mexican area is north of the southernmost point of the United States. Even a great deal of the Mexican territory, though extending into the tropics, remains cool and temperate. Variations in altitude have as much to do with the country's temperature and rainfall as does its geographic position.

The seacoast regions and the lower altitudes of the interior are often intensely hot, except during the winter season. Their mean temperatures range from 75 to 88 degrees F. In some sections the temperatures reach above 100 F and along the coastal areas this heat is accompanied by high humidity.

The temperate zone is found at altitudes from about 4000 to 6000 feet, where the mean temperature ranges between 60 to 70 degrees F. The cool zone (above 6000 feet) has a mean temperature of 58 to 60 degrees F. On the central plateau the days are generally comfortably warm; the nights chilly to cold. Guidebooks and tourist agencies have always portrayed Mexico as a paradise of eternal sunshine where, if it rains, "it rains for an hour or so in the late afternoon, then instantly clears." Travelers should be forewarned that Mexico, like any other country, has "weather." There are periods, especially in the late summer and fall, during climatological disturbances in the Gulf of Mexico and along the Pacific Coast, when the sky will be overcast for days and the weather can be miserable and dreary. Sometimes for a week or two during the winter the cold can be bitingly intense.

Rainfall in Mexico ranges from a few drops a year in the northern desert of Altar (Sonora), to an annual precipitation of 16.4 feet at Usumacinta in the Grijalva River Valley in the south. Throughout most of the country the rainy season extends from late in May to October. From November to April rains are rare. May is generally Mexico's hottest month.

MEXICAN RAINFALL AND TEMPERATURES

AREA	JANUARY		FEBRUARY		MARCH		APRIL		MAY		JUNE		JULY		AUGUST		SEPTEMBER		OCTOBER		NOVEMBER		DECEMBER	
	Temp.	*Rain*	*Temp.*	*Rain*	*Temp.*	*Rain*	*Temp.*	*Rain*	*Temp.*	*Rain*	*Temp.*	*Rain*	*Temp.*	*Rain*	*Temp.*	*Rain*	*Temp.*	*Rain*	*Temp.*	*Rain*	*Temp.*	*Rain*	*Temp.*	*Rain*
Acapulco, Gro.	78	0.4	78	—	79	—	80	—	83	12.0	83	17.2	83	8.6	83	9.8	82	14.3	82	6.7	81	1.2	79	0.4
Ciudad Victoria, Tamps.	60	1.4	64	1.0	70	0.8	76	1.5	79	5.0	81	4.8	81	4.1	82	2.7	79	7.9	74	4.3	67	1.7	60	0.7
Colima, Col.	72	0.5	72	0.3	74	—	77	—	79	0.3	79	5.7	78	7.7	78	7.2	77	7.7	78	3.1	76	0.9	73	1.3
Cuernavaca, Mor.	65	0.1	67	0.2	70	0.3	72	0.3	74	2.1	70	7.8	68	8.6	68	8.7	68	9.7	66	3.1	67	0.3	66	0.1
Chihuahua, Chih.	49	0.1	52	0.2	59	0.3	65	0.3	74	0.4	79	1.0	77	3.1	75	3.7	72	3.7	65	1.4	56	0.3	49	0.6
Durango, Dgo.	53	0.5	56	0.4	60	—	65	0.1	69	0.5	72	2.4	69	4.9	69	3.6	66	4.0	64	1.2	58	0.6	54	0.7
Fortín, Ver.	61	1.9	64	1.5	67	1.6	70	2.1	72	5.0	71	13.8	71	15.0	70	15.9	70	17.5	69	8.5	64	3.5	62	2.4
Guadalajara, Jal.	58	0.7	61	0.2	65	0.1	70	—	72	0.7	71	7.6	69	10.0	68	7.9	67	7.0	65	2.1	61	0.8	59	0.8
Guanajuato, Gto.	57	0.5	60	0.3	64	0.2	68	0.2	71	1.1	68	5.4	66	6.6	66	5.5	65	6.0	63	2.0	60	0.7	59	0.6
Guaymas, Son.	63	0.3	66	0.2	69	0.2	73	0.1	78	0.1	84	—	87	1.8	87	3.0	86	2.1	81	0.4	72	0.4	61	1.1
Manzanillo, Col.	75	0.9	74	0.5	74	—	76	—	79	0.1	81	4.0	83	5.4	83	7.4	81	15.0	81	5.0	79	0.7	77	2.1
Mexico, D.F.	54	0.2	56	0.3	61	0.4	63	0.5	65	0.2	63	4.2	61	4.9	61	4.1	60	4.6	59	1.3	56	0.6	54	0.3
Mérida, Yuc.	73	1.2	74	0.6	78	0.8	81	1.0	82	3.2	81	5.9	81	5.5	81	5.1	81	6.0	79	4.0	75	1.2	74	1.2
Monterrey, N.L.	58	0.8	62	0.9	68	0.6	74	1.1	78	1.7	81	3.3	81	2.9	82	2.5	78	8.1	72	4.3	63	1.0	57	0.8
Morelia, Mich.	57	0.5	60	0.3	64	0.3	67	0.3	69	1.7	67	5.2	65	6.8	64	6.4	64	6.2	63	2.3	60	0.8	58	0.2
Oaxaca, Oax.	63	0.1	66	0.1	70	0.4	72	1.0	73	2.5	71	4.9	70	3.7	69	4.1	69	6.7	67	1.6	65	0.4	64	0.4
Puebla, Pue.	54	0.2	60	0.2	62	0.5	65	0.5	66	2.9	64	6.2	63	5.4	63	5.8	62	7.4	61	2.2	58	0.8	56	0.3
Saltillo, Coah.	54	0.5	56	0.6	59	0.2	66	0.7	69	0.9	72	1.9	72	2.8	72	1.4	68	2.0	63	1.0	56	0.7	54	0.6
San Cristóbal las Casas, Chis.	54	0.3	55	—	57	0.4	60	1.4	60	5.1	60	10.0	60	5.6	60	6.3	60	9.9	61	6.0	55	0.9	55	0.6
San José Purua, Mich.	57	0.7	60	0.6	63	0.3	67	0.3	70	0.2	71	6.3	70	7.1	69	6.6	68	7.0	65	2.5	64	0.8	60	2.5
Taxco, Gro.	66	—	69	0.2	72	0.4	75	0.9	76	3.0	72	10.7	70	12.0	70	13.6	69	13.1	69	3.5	68	0.2	67	0.1
Veracruz, Ver.	70	0.9	71	0.6	73	0.3	77	0.8	79	2.1	80	10.7	81	13.8	81	12.0	81	13.7	79	5.9	74	3.5	72	1.0

NOTE: Figures represent official averages covering a ten-year period, furnished by Mexican Meterological Bureau at Tacubaya. Temperatures are in Fahrenheit; rainfall, in inches.

16. A Digest of Mexican History

During the three or four thousand years before the *Mayflower* deposited its shipload of prolific ancestors on the New England coast, a multitude of important civilizations had already left their mark upon the vast territory of Mexico.

While the Essenes were hiding their biblical scrolls in caverns near the Dead Sea of Palestine and while most of Europe was a savage backwoods, splendid cities had risen in Mexico; calendars were devised and great arts created. The story of Mexico's ancient cultures and the dramatic events of more recent times makes Mexico's history one of the most vivid and exciting in the world.

Although much of the country's remote past is still shadowy, the painstaking efforts of archaeologists and anthropologists have now put together glimpses of New World civilizations that were undreamed of even fifty years ago. The early horizons of man's history in Mexico have been steadily pushed back. The bone of the Tepexpan Man and a nearby elephant, found not far from Mexico City, date back some ten to twelve thousand years. The 1959 discovery of petrified mummies in a cave near Yécora in the northern state of Sonora will shed further light on early man in Mexico.

Where did the first inhabitants of the Americas come from? Were they homegrown? Did they come from abroad? Scholars still argue this point, for no one is sure. The most widely accepted theory is that the American continents were peopled by successive immigrations of tribes from Asia, crossing over a narrow neck of land that once spanned what is now the Bering Strait. This explanation has been somewhat modified in recent years by the hypothesis of the French anthropologist Rivet, who has suggested possible Malay-Polynesian or even Australian migrations; the latter using Antarctica as a steppingstone to Tierra del Fuego at the tip of South America; the former, a kind of island-hopping operation across the Pacific Ocean. The most important mass movement nevertheless seemed to have been that of the northern Asiatics pushing steadily across the Bering landbridge.

On the Mexican plateau, in the southern jungles and in the high Andes, certain mysterious conditions occurred, turning these nomadic tribes toward the path of civilization. Men learned to cultivate maize, to weave garments of vegetable fibers, to fashion pottery and to erect stone buildings. Complex civilizations flowered and wilted with a sort of tropical exuberance. In Mexico the central tableland and southern jungleland become a Grand Central Station through which a variety of civilizations passed to their appointed destinies.

Almost anywhere in Mexico you can dig up examples of ancient pottery and crude tools representing what is called the Middle-Culture or Archaic Period which included groups of cultures that were well advanced on the road to civilization in the dim era before recorded history. This period covers early cultures which terminated at the time of Christ, and extended back perhaps two or three thousand years. The round, pyramid-like Cuicuilco ruin at the edge of Mexico City is of this period. Cuicuilco is the oldest construction on the American continent. It was abandoned about 500 B.C., when it was partially covered by a lava flow from an erupting volcano — but only after centuries of previous occupation!

In addition to the archaic cultures, Mexico has been the cradle for some twelve or more full-blown civilizations which succeeded or grew out of the Archaic. Many were distinct from one another in language, the areas occupied as well as their cultural outlook. They were amazingly complex and advanced in certain social techniques, especially the arts. The most important among these civilizations were: the Olmec, the Teotihuacán, the Mayan, the Toltec, the Zapotec and Mixtec, the Aztec, the Totonac, the Tlahuican, the Tarascan, the Tlaxcala, and the Texcoco cultures.

The oldest and most mysterious of these is the Olmecan. Olmec is a term meaning "citizens of Olman," from *olli* or rubber. They are called the rubber-country people for they lived in the tropic regions. Their culture flourished before and at the time of Christ and, very likely, was the seed or mother-culture for later civilizations such as the Mayan, Totonac, and Zapotec.

Archaeological remains of this shadowy civilization have been found principally along the Gulf Coast in the states of Veracruz and Tabasco.

What disturbs scholars is that the Olmecs seemed to have popped up, a fully developed civilization, for there seem to be no traces of a primitive development. They were amazing craftsmen and lapidaries. They carved colossal stone heads with jaguar baby faces, that is, a squarish face with fat neck, mongoloid eyes, a large mouth drawn down at the corners and a full upper lip that is both sulky and snarling in a way that resembles the face of both infant and jaguar. Some of the most beautifully and skillfully carved jade figurines found in Mexico are of Olmec origin. Oddly, the jade they worked seems to be of Oriental origin and many of the characteristics of their sculpture are also Oriental. Little jade-carved human figures are frequently seated cross-legged, like Chinese gods.

The Mayan culture, one of the two greatest of Mexico's ancient civilizations, may have connections with the Olmecs. The origins of the Mayan people is still uncertain. One investigator, Salvador Toscano, claims their culture was born in the Petén region on the Guatemala-Yucatán border. They dominated a huge area extending over parts of Honduras, Guatemala and the Mexican states of Tabasco, Campeche, and the peninsula of Yucatán.

Earliest recorded Mayan date is August 6, year 613 — before the birth of Christ. However, their calendar figured time from about 3373 B.C., and it is supposed that the Mayans occupied the tropical rain forests and the peninsula country for more than five thousand years. Their civilization flowered in three distinct zones and times.

The pre-Classic (First Empire) culture (before 3000 B.C., to 317 A.D.) occupied an area now marked by the Mexican state of Chiapas, northern Guatemala, and Honduras. Remains of this early culture are represented by the magnificent archaeological ruins at Copán, Uaxatún, Palenque, Tikal Quiriguá, and Dzibilchaltun.

What is called the Middle or Classic Empire (317 A.D. to 987 A.D.) was situated in the high valleys of the Guatemalan plateau where we find the ceremonial sites and cities of Zaculeo, Yuyú, and Utatlán.

The last great period of Mayan culture, called the New Empire, (987 A.D. to the Spanish Conquest), centered in what are now the Mexican states of Campeche, Tabasco, Yucatán, and the territory of Quintana Roo.

The Mayans were driven from region to region, possibly because of drought and the leeching out of corn-growing land. In Yucatán they found a kindly environment and marvelous cities were constructed there. The late or New Empire also received a healthy cultural infusion from the Toltecs who migrated from the center of Mexico, helped build the great Mayan center of Chichén Itzá and later founded the city of Uxmal around 1261 A.D.

During their long history the Mayans developed one of the greatest civilizations of the Americas. They were extraordinarily advanced in mathematics, astronomy, and related sciences. Given enough time they probably would have invented a Sputnik. They developed a hieroglyphic writing (which we still haven't deciphered) and a system of chronology that was unique. In architecture they were pre-eminent among the New World civilizations, constructing vast cities unlike those found anywhere else.

At about the same time that the Mayans became the greatest civilization in the Western Hemisphere, two other cultures — the Totonac and Zapotec — were also at the height of their development.

The Totonacs inhabited the Gulf region north of what is now Veracruz. Our knowledge of their history is still sketchy. It is believed that they were related to the mysterious Olmecs and also to some of the peoples in the Valley of Mexico. Some experts suggest that the great pyramids of the sun and moon at Teotihuacán (north of Mexico City) were constructed by Totonacs; others disagree. It is known that they inhabited the Valley of Mexico, but were driven out by stronger tribes and they settled in the vanilla jungle country of Veracruz which they called Totonacpan. Their religion was closely related to that of the central plateau people. On Totonac temples along the Gulf Coast there are representations of the ancient gods, Quetzalcóatl and Tlaloc, both revered by the cultures of Central Mexico also.

The most important Totonac archaeological ruins we can visit today are: El Tajín, the Niches Zempoala, Huilochitla, and Tepetzintla. Tajín is a remarkable seven-story pyramid with curious exterior niches like dormer windows. A curious Totonac religious dance and acrobatic ceremony is still celebrated in this region. It is the *palo voladores* or flying pole dance, a fertility and sun worship exercise now incorporated in the Christian fiesta calendar and done usually for the Feast of Corpus Christi.

Less than an hour's drive north of Mexico City at Teotihuacán, meaning "place where all go to worship the gods," one can visit the most massive and impressive man-made monument in the Americas — the Pyramid of the Sun. It is a huge rubble-filled, stone-surfaced structure measuring almost seven hundred feet at the base and rising to a height of two hundred feet. This pyramid and its smaller sister, the Pyramid of the Moon, are surrounded by an extensive sacred city which the Aztecs believed was built by the gods. In later years historians attributed it to the Toltecs who did occupy and embellish the site for a while. But the Toltecs were not the original builders. Hard-headed, toiling archaeologists have come to the conclusion that an earlier civilization which they call the Teotihuacana were the original pyramid builders.

They guess that the Teotihuacana culture bloomed sometime between 1 A.D. and the ninth century of our era. It may have been Olmec influenced. The Teotihuacán agriculture was well developed; they wove cotton cloth as fine as linen and they produced pottery and ceramic figurines of unusual artistic merit. Their houses and palaces were substantial, having been built of stone and mortar, and they were often decorated with mural paintings. This culture apparently had trade routes that extended well beyond the central plateau.

The Teotihuacán culture was undoubtedly the foundation upon which more vigorous tribes from the north built the important Toltec, Texcocoan, and Aztec civilizations.

Almost as enigmatic as the story of the rubber people, is the role of the Toltecs in Mexico's ancient history. The Toltecs were a nation of great builders who centered their culture at the storied city, Tollan, now the Tula in the State of Hidalgo. Their influence was widespread, reaching as far southeast as Yucatán.

Until a few years ago almost everything written about the Toltecs was erroneous. Who were they? Where did they come from? No one really knew. Some believed they were originally Olmecs, or that they were the fierce Chichimeca Indians who had come down from what is now the United States. It is now generally accepted that they were a vigorous branch of the Nahoas, a group of tribes less civilized than the Olmecs and Teotihuacanas. The clouded beginning of their civilization is dated roughly between 245 and 752 A.D.; the end, between 969 and 1168 A.D., when famine forced them to emigrate to other regions. From about the time in which Charlemagne was a power in Europe to the period of the Holy Crusades, the Toltecs flourished in Mexico. They absorbed the Teotihuacán culture, founded their metropolis, Tollan; they embellished the Teotihuacán pyramid center and made it their sacred city.

Their civilization, considering the times, was a peace-loving one. They condemned human sacrifice, preferring offerings of fruit and flowers. They were master mathematicians, knew a great deal about medicine and, above all, were great artisans. Centuries later the Aztecs used the term Toltec to denote a man skilled in the arts or crafts.

According to Toltec mythology a northern chieftain named Mixcoatl married a southern woman called Chimala. The union produced a son who was called Quetzalcóatl, who became the principal god of the Toltecs. Quetzalcóatl is one of the fascinating and mysterious puzzles of ancient Mexico. Known as the Plumed Serpent, he was the patron of arts and culture and his name has shuttled about in the mythology of numerous Mexican cultures like an important bolt rattling around in a complex machine. Other tribes believed he came from across the sea and was unlike any person seen before in Mexico; he was light-skinned, had a beard and blue eyes. Legend also had it that this king-god was driven from Tollan by a rival deity who got him drunk on *pulque*. He was said to have gone back across the seas, but before leaving, had prophesied he would someday return and conquer Mexico. This legend, so potent and so remembered, played a significant part in the Spanish conquest of Mexico.

Pulque, the amusing ferment of maguey juices, is said to have been invented by the ancient Toltecs. It played a role in the downfall of Quetzalcóatl as well as the Toltec civilization. At least, this is what certain temperance-minded historians would have us believe. However, a more likely reason for the decline of Toltec power in the twelfth century was the steady, warlike pressure of a barbaric tribe called the Chichimeca.

Contact with the Toltecs and intermarriage and alliances with other tribes of Central Mexico turned the Chichimecas to more civilized pursuits. They established the city of Texcoco and dominated the Valley of Mexico for some two hundred years. Texcoco prospered and became a kind of Athens of its day. Most famed of Texcocoan rulers was Netzahualcóyotl, a remarkable man by any standards. He was a poet, a builder and a great leader. He was also something of a free-thinker, for in an epoch of idolatry and human sacrifice, he believed in one powerful god and in a heaven without corruption.

During Netzahualcóyotl's rule one of the most influential institutions of the city was the Academy of Music. Despite its name the academy was dedicated to the study of science, astronomy, and history as well as the arts. All intellectual works had to be submitted to the academy's judges for approval.

While the Chichimecas consolidated their power in the Valley of Mexico, no one paid much attention to the half-starved, nomadic tribe called Mexicas who wandered into the valley from the north. Small and weak though they were, this branch of the Aztec peoples eventually built the most powerful of all pre-Hispanic civilizations and also gave their name to the country.

For a long while the Mexicas moved from place to place in the valley because, according to legend, their gods had ordered them to seek and settle in a place where they would see an eagle poised upon a prickly pear cactus and devouring a serpent. They finally beheld the sought-after sign on an island in Lake Texcoco and settled there, founding, in 1325 A.D., their island city of Tenochtitlán (now Mexico City). For a half-century the Aztec-Mexica were ruled by chieftains in the manner of semi-nomadic tribes, but by 1376 A.D. a prince named Acamapichtli founded the royal dynasty that ruled until the city was conquered by Hernándo Cortés.

Until 1428 three of the city states situated around Lake Texcoco, namely Tenochtitlán of the Mexica, Texcoco, and Tacuba, had all been paying tribute to the powerful king of Azcapotzalco. They formed a triple alliance and overthrew the Azcapotzalco rule. From this date on the Aztec-Mexicas grew in power, dominating the other city-states as well as other distant communities, welding them into a confederation that extended from the far north to the region of Guatemala.

The civilization of the Aztecs, as these people came to be called, was based on a highly organized, religion-controlled, efficiently administered "empire." Garrisons dotted the land; military and trading missions were constantly abroad, waging war or gathering tribute from subject nations. The king wielded absolute power over all his subjects and their possessions. Aztec law was severe: theft, adultery, disobedience in war were all punishable by death; drunkenness was punished by loss of property or public ridicule.

As with the Mayans and other Indian nations, religion completely dominated the lives of the Aztecs. It was their philosophy, their science, and their morality. The pantheon of Aztec gods was huge and complex. The most important of the deities were the blood-thirsty Huitzilopochtli, the god of war; Tlaloc, the rain god; and Chalchiuhtlicue, the goddess of lakes and rivers. The universe itself was conceived in a religious rather than a geographic sense and was divided horizontally and vertically into areas of religious significance. The religious cults were characterized by ferocious human sacrifices required to keep the world from being extinguished and to satiate the needs of the gods.

The very core of their religion was the calendar, or three calendars: the *tonalámatl,* a religious calendar consisting of 260 days, the *xituitl* or civil calendar based on solar observation, and consisting of eighteen twenty-day months and five nameless days to make up a 365 day year. The third calendar was based on the Venus count of 585 days. The Aztec century or *xiuhtonalli* extended over fifty-two years and was considered a life cycle for the world. On the final night of such a cycle all fires throughout the country were extinguished, people fasted and feared, awaiting the decision of the gods as to whether the world would end or a new cycle would begin again.

The elaborate Aztec school system was in the hands of the priests. There were three types of schools: the *calmécac,* a sort of monastic organization for the sons of nobles; the *telpochcalli* or military college for training warriors; the *cuicacalco,* a school of dance and music for the bulk of the youth not destined to be warriors or priests. The Aztec system of writing remained quite primitive, consisting of ideograms or picture writing and phonograms which were graphic expressions of sounds. Their literature included historical codices, songs, laws, speeches, poetry, and drama. (See Index.)

The Aztecs had a fairly good knowledge of medicine and of the medicinal uses of plants. After the conquest their medicinal plants more than doubled the pharmacopoeia of Europe. They were highly skilled artisans in metal, pottery, weaving, and stonecutting. Their capital, Tenochtitlán, had become one of the largest and most beautiful cities in the world when Cortés first saw it in 1519.

A less important culture was that of the Tlaxcalans, contemporaries of the Aztecs, and their deadly enemies. The Tlaxcalan nation played a role in ancient Mexican history well out of proportion to its size. They were a branch of the Chichimecas who had been driven over the mountains from Texcoco to the area encompassed by the present state of Tlaxcala. Although completely surrounded by Aztec allies, they never submitted to Tenochtitlán's domination. When Cortés began his attack on the Mexican capital he was joined by thousands of Tlaxcalans, and without their help he might never have overthrown the Aztecs.

Far to the south in isolated country that is now the State of Oaxaca, another of Mexico's great civilizations flourished. It was known as the Zapotec-Mixtec culture. Some two thousand or more years ago, while the tribes of Central Mexico were still in their earliest stages of development, the Zapotecs began to fashion a fabulous civilization in the south. Their first great center was at Teotitlán del Valle where they built a magnificent palace and temple. Today Teotitlán is a small but interesting serape-weaving village, a favorite stop for tourists.

According to Dr. Alfonso Caso, Mexico's leading archaeologist, the heyday of Zapotec culture dates from about 534 A.D., to 1125 A.D. These people built three important religious centers — Mitla, Monte Albán, and Zaachila — the ruins of which are as fascinating as those of the Mayas and Aztecs. Their government was a theocracy; a high priest living in the sacred city of Mitla ruled all the kings and tribal chiefs. People dared not look at him lest they die. He lived in complete retirement, something like the old dalai lamas of Tibet. His successor was a son born to him by a virgin daughter of a chief who was presented to him during a religious ceremony.

The Zapotecs had developed a calendar consisting of 260 days, and divided into four seasons. Each season had five thirteen-day weeks. For each day there was a god who controlled the fortunes of any events occurring during those twenty-four hours. It made for a great number of gods and a religion that was unusually complicated and confusing.

At the end of the fourteenth century the Aztecs pushed into the Oaxaca region in order to seize control of trade routes to the south. Their hold upon the Zapotecs and Mixtecs was never very secure for there were constant wars and revolts.

Much of the fascinating work in jade and gold, which for years was attributed solely to Aztec artistry, seems to have been Zapotec and Mixtec inspired. These people were superb artisans when the Aztecs were still nomads. They built some of the most spectacular cities and religious centers in the country. They were unsurpassed potters. They developed the lost-wax technique in goldwork which Europe had to learn from the Chinese. No one in recent years suspected their remarkable skills until the discovery of the famed Tomb 7 at Monte Albán. On January 9, 1932, Dr. Alfonso Caso opened this Mixtec tomb and uncovered a treasure that made world history. In it he found a fabulous cache of splendid jewelry: masks and breastplates of solid gold, delicate lost-wax gold objects, strings of pearls as big as pigeon eggs, finely carved jade, mosaics of turquoise, ornaments of pure crystal and alabaster most exquisitely carved.

Another pre-Hispanic civilization, as isolated as the Zapotecs, lay to the northwest of the Aztec capital. This civilization was known to the Aztecs as the Michhuaca, and to the Spaniards as the Tarascans. The people of this culture had no name for themselves in their own idiom. Their region covered the present states of Michoacán, Colima, and parts of Jalisco. Their language was entirely unrelated to any other tongue in Mexico, and the origin of these people is still a mystery.

The Tarascan culture was based on family units. Their principal city, Tzintzuntzán, lay on the edge of Lake Pátzcuaro. The Tarascans were skilled workers in lacquer, copper, wood, and pottery. They were also masters of a curious art, feather-painting (see Index), which was one of the few pre-Hispanic arts which completely captured the imagination of their Spanish conquerors.

THE CONQUEST OF MEXICO

In the years between 1492 and 1519 Spanish adventurers had spread among the Caribbean islands and touched points along the South American coast. In 1517 an expedition organized by Governor Diego Velázquez of Cuba and commanded by Francisco Hernández de Córdoba, landed on the coast of Yucatán and fought with the natives, presumably Mayans. A second expedition led by Juan de Grijalva explored the Mexican coastline from Yucatán to San Juan de Ulúa, an island opposite the present port city of Veracruz. The 1518 Grijalva party traded beads for gold and gathered information concerning a fabulous Mexican empire that lay inland. Prompted by these reports, Velázquez outfitted an elaborate expedition which was commanded by a man who was to become the hero of one of the greatest adventure stories of all times — Hernán Cortés.[1]

From the very beginning the expedition was plagued with uncertainties. Velázquez distrusted Cortés and planned to remove him from its command. Cortés, in a surprise move, set off without permission. His tiny force which, with the aid of a legend and the support of Indian allies, was to conquer the powerful Aztec empire, included five hundred and eight Spanish infantry, thirty-two archers, thirteen musketeers, sixteen horses for the officers and two hundred Cuban Indian packbearers.

The expedition first touched at the island of Cozumel near the tip of Yucatán, then sailed northward along the Gulf Coast. Two events of great importance occurred during these early steps. At Cozumel the Spaniards rescued Jerónimo de Aguilar. Aguilar had been captured by Indians during a previous expedition and he had lived with them long enough to learn the Mayan tongue. Farther along the coast in what is now the State of Tabasco the Spaniards defeated an Indian war party, and as part of their booty they were presented with twenty young girls. Among them was a handsome, intelligent young girl who eventually became Cortés' chief aid, mistress, and interpreter. She spoke both Mayan and Náhuatl (the language of the Aztecs). Combining her talents and Aguilar's knowledge the Spaniards had expert interpreters.[2]

Cortés' fleet reached the island of San Juan de Ulúa on Holy Thursday, April 21, 1519. A short distance up the coast the Spanish founded their first settlement on this date, calling it La Villa Rica de la Vera Cruz, the Rich City of the True Cross. This site, later abandoned, is now the village of Antigua. The present-day Veracruz is located at the point opposite the island of San Juan de Ulúa where Cortés first landed. Here Cortés had his ships dismantled and burned so there could be no retreat from the great adventure.

Meanwhile disturbing rumors about this race of white men had already reached the Aztec capital ruled by Moctezuma.[3] The Indian belief that the Spaniards and their horses were demigods, belief that the old prophecy about Quetzalcóatl returning to conquer the country and the hatred that many subjugated Indians felt toward the Aztecs, all combined to aid the Spanish in their conquest.

After two months of bitter fighting, reckless courage, and amazing diplomacy, the small Spanish force found themselves in the 12,000-foot-high pass between the volcanoes Iztaccíhuatl and Popocatépetl. Spread beneath them was Tenochtitlán, a jewel-city set in the glistening waters of Lake Texcoco. Bernal Díaz, chronicler of the expedition, wrote: "Not even Venice is richer or more beautiful."

[1] Cortés at the time of the expedition was a thirty-four-year-old *encomendero*, a landowner-colonist, in Cuba. He was born at Medellín, Estremadura, Spain, in 1485. His father, Martín Cortés de Monroy, was a captain of infantry. His mother was Dona Catalina Pizarro Altamarino. At the age of nineteen Cortés left Spain for Cuba where for many years he was a prominent figure in the new crown colony. He died in the Spanish village of Castilleja de la Cuesta (near Seville), December 2, 1547. His remains were removed to Mexico in 1562 and interred in the Monastery of San Francisco in Texcoco. In 1620 they were removed again to the church San Francisco in Mexico City, remaining there until 1784 when they were transferred to the Hospital Jesús Nazareno in the capital. Thirty-nine years later, at the close of the War of Independence, when a mob threatened to break into the vault and scatter the remains of the Conquistador, his bones were secretly removed. It is generally believed that the remains were hidden in the family vault of the Duke of Terranova at Palermo; however, some authorities insist they are still hidden in Mexico.

[2] Cortés' mistress was baptized and named Marina. The Indians called her Malintzin, meaning "rain," a title of honor. The Spanish in turn mispronounced it, Malinche. She has become one of the most romantic and attractive figures in Mexican history and legend. She became Hernán Cortés' devoted slave. Legend has it that because of her treachery to her race she was condemned to three hundred years of martyrdom, her days to be passed beneath the waters of Lake Texcoco, her nights wandering the countryside in agony and tears. She has been personified in Indian song and poetry as La Llorona, the weeping woman. Her name is still a potent force in Mexican life and politics. The word *malinchista* is a term of contempt applied to people who have a preference for foreigners or ways other than Mexican.

[3] Early English chroniclers, unable to cope with Indian names, called him Montezuma.

On November 8, 1519, without having fought an engagement with Moctezuma's forces, Cortés entered the Aztec capital. He was received reluctantly by the Aztec ruler who came to meet him in a jeweled canopy carried on the shoulders of his nobles. The Spanish guests were lodged in the ancient palace of Atzayacatl on the site where the National Pawnshop now stands.

Aware that his welcome would not endure, and to guarantee the safety of his small force, Cortés persuaded Moctezuma to take up residence among the Spanish, thus becoming a voluntary hostage. Meanwhile news reached Cortés that a force of 1200 Spaniards sent by Governor Velázquez had landed at Veracruz. Their purpose: to arrest Cortés. Leaving a small garrison in Tenochtitlán, Cortés hurried to the coast to meet the new threat. He came upon them at Zempoala, overcame them, and persuaded the soldiers to join forces with him.

In Tenochtitlán the corporal's guard of Spaniards under the command of hot-headed Pedro de Alvarado had provoked the local citizens. The Aztecs besieged Alvarado in the Atzayacatl Palace. Cortés returned to the city just as the garrison was reaching its breaking point. The following day, when the Aztecs renewed their attack on the palace, Cortés persuaded Moctezuma to go on the palace roof and appeal for peace. The chieftain was accused of cowardice and was showered with stones and arrows. He died a few hours later of wounds received.

A full-scale siege was mounted by Moctezuma's cousin and son-in-law, a twenty-year-old noble named Cuauhtémoc. On June 20, 1520, a date that has been memorialized in Mexican history as the Noche Triste, (the Sad Night), the Spaniards and their Tlaxcalan allies decided to retreat from the city. Loading themselves with the treasures of gold and jewels which they had received from the Aztecs, they set out across the causeways connecting the city to the mainland. The alerted Aztecs attacked in force along causeways and by boat. Badly mauled in the nighttime fighting, the Spaniards had to abandon their treasures, their gunpowder and cannons. More than eight hundred Spaniards (including many of Cortés' new reinforcements), eighty horses and uncounted thousands of Indian allies were lost during that long night.

The survivors retreated to Tlaxcala where, among loyal friends, they were able to rest, re-equip themselves and prepare for another attack upon the Aztec stronghold. While preparing a fleet of small ships which were to be carried over the mountains and launched on Lake Texcoco in order to attack the island city, Cortés sent out small forces to disrupt and capture outlying Aztec strong points. At last, strengthened by new arrivals from Cuba, Cortés laid siege to Tenochtitlán itself.

Cuitláhuac, the "emperor" who had succeeded Moctezuma, had died during a smallpox plague that paralyzed the Aztecs while the Spaniards were recuperating in Tlaxcala. His successor, Cuauhtémoc, bitterly rejected all of Cortés' peace offers.

On August 13, 1521, following seventy-three days of bitter siege and fighting, the Spaniards overran a city that was completely leveled, scorched by fire and infested with plague. More than three centuries were to pass before the Western Hemisphere would again see a city so vast.

The destruction of Tenochtitlán signified not only the collapse of the Aztec empire, but also the virtual obliteration of the ethos of the Indians all over Mexico. The conquest destroyed their leaders, their priests, the artisans, the values, arts and sciences of the Indian world. The Indian, deprived of his gods, was to survive as a stranger in a stranger's house.

THE COLONIAL PERIOD

The conquest of Tenochtitlán was followed by a series of expeditions that firmly established the hold of Spain in this hemisphere. In the succeeding years Alvarado marched down the Pacific Coast, capturing strongholds in Guatemala and Salvador. Cortés completed an adventurous march through dense jungles to the Gulf of Honduras. Yucatán was secured. The cruel Nuño de Guzmán undertook the conquest of Michoacán and provinces to the north. Coronado led his men up into the land of the Pueblo Indians.

The establishment of Spanish rule began a long, relatively peaceful period in Mexican history during which the foundations of modern Mexico were laid. The Spanish empire in Mexico lasted three hundred years. During its heyday the great colonial cities, the beautiful churches, and historic buildings were constructed. Also, during this time Spaniards and Indians began the long process of amalgamation which was to produce the present-day Mexican.

The first ruler of New Spain was Cortés. The king awarded him the title of Governor and Captain General. He rebuilt Mexico City and divided the country's land among his lieutenants and other colonists. On occasions he got into trouble, had to return to Spain to clear his name and finally died there at the age of sixty-two.

For a short period of time the government of the colony was invested in a group called the *Audiencia,* made up of three appointed magistrates called *oidores* or "listeners." When Antonio de Mendoza arrived, in 1535, to become the first of 61 viceroys who governed New Spain, he was the first of a 300-year series of successions, a period of little political significance, yet one of important sociological development.

In many ways the viceregal period fixed the forms and customs of today's Mexico. The seeds of many of contemporary Mexico's problems were planted at that time. Many observers feel that Mexico's difficulties in achieving a working democracy, despite its being a republic, stems from the fact that both in pre-Hispanic times and during the "Coloniage" there was no self-rule. The viceroy was a powerful figure, and the whole political tone of the Spanish colonies was different from that of the British colonies. The governor or viceroy was the source of all lay preferment and favors, a tradition which has persisted in Mexico.

Instead of fostering small independent farms and farmers, as occurred in the New England colonies, New Spain divided up the land in *encomiendas* or huge landholdings. The *encomendero,* often an absentee landlord, was entitled to the labor of all the Indians on his land. He ruled like a king.

To counteract the greed and ruthlessness of lay colonists, the Catholic kings of Spain sent groups of friars — Franciscans, Dominicans, Augustinians, and finally Jesuits. Though the Roman Catholic Church was eventually to grow excessively powerful, in later years controlling an estimated fifty per cent of the land and wealth of Mexico, during the early colonial period the friars won the affection and admiration of the Indians whom they defended with vigor. The Church recognized the religious needs of the Indians, offered them a theology acceptable to them, and more important, a role in the communion of men. Without the Church, Mexico's new race, the *mestizo,* might never have come into existence or thrived as it did.

The society of the colonial period was made up into four distinct classes or castes: *gachupines,* creoles, *mestizos,* and Indians. The Indians were looked upon by the Spaniards as an inferior race. It took a strong stand by the Church to grace them with savable souls. In the community they were little more than slaves, working in mines and on farms. The *mestizo,* largely the product of Spanish and Indian blood, was hardly better off than the Indians. They could only hold menial posts in government and private enterprises. All the important political jobs and Church offices were held by the Spanish-born *gachupines.* The creoles, born in Mexico of Spanish parents, were able to hold lesser salaried positions in the government and own property.

Toward the end of the Spanish rule the *mestizo* group had grown to some two million (by 1800). many of them had attained education and some wealth and they became restless. Although an internal explosion was inevitable, it took a violent change outside of Mexico to precipitate a shifting of class forces within. The French Revolution, the rise of Napoleon, and the collapse of the Spanish monarchy when the French invaded Spain, were the levers that tipped Mexico into its War for Independence.

INDEPENDENCE

When Napoleon installed his brother Joseph on the Spanish throne, the Spanish people refused to recognize him. In Mexico the municipal government of Mexico City submitted a plan to the viceroy, Iturrigaray, to the effect that Mexico should govern itself (with the viceroy as king), until another Spanish king should occupy the Spanish throne. *Gachupines,* fearful of losing control of the colonial government, seized Iturrigaray and imprisoned him. The independence movement was crushed momentarily.

In 1810, in the towns of Querétaro, San Miguel el Grande, and Dolores — an area now called the Cradle of Independence — a group of conspirators began meeting under the pretext of literary studies. One of their leaders was a priest, Miguel Hidalgo y Costilla, who was to become one of Mexico's great national heroes. Others in the group were Miguel Domínguez, the Corregidor (mayor) of Querétaro and Ignacio Allende and Ignacio Aldama, officers in the King's Regiment. They planned to start a revolt on October 1, but the plans were betrayed to the authorities in Mexico. Doña Josefa Ortiz de Domínguez, the wife of the Corregidor, sent a warning to the towns of San Miguel el Grande and Dolores. During the early morning hours of September 16, Father Hidalgo called his parishioners together by ringing the church bell and raising the cry of freedom.[4] He got together a small band and marched to San Miguel where Allende's regiment joined him. Celaya surrendered on September 21. The army headed for Guanajuato.

Guanajuato, with a population of 80,000 and some of the richest silver mines in the Americas was, in point of wealth, second to Mexico City. After a desperate siege this prize fell into the hands of the revolutionists. Hidalgo then turned toward Mexico City. In spite of the fact that his forces routed the Spanish army and could have taken the city, he retreated for some unaccountable reason. While moving toward the interior of the country his force encountered an artillery train and 10,000 well-equipped creole troops at Aculco. Again Hidalgo's generalship proved faulty and his army was badly mauled.

By this time the viceroy and the Church authorities began fighting back bitterly. The Bishop of Michoacán hurled edicts of excommunication against the *insurgentes.* The Holy Inquisition, still operating in Mexico, charged Hidalgo with subversion. A reward of 10,000 pesos was offered for his capture, dead or alive.

Hidalgo retreated to Guadalajara where he published a decree abolishing slavery. He suffered another defeat near Guadalajara, then marched to the north, hoping to get supplies from the United States. On March 21, 1811, at Acatita de Baján, Chihuahua, Hidalgo, Allende, and Aldama were betrayed, captured, taken to Chihuahua, then shot.

Another priest, José María Morelos, a former student of Father Hidalgo, kept the revolt alive. Morelos, who historians have begun to look upon as

[4] The *Grito de Dolores* or Cry of Freedom is commemorated each year in every town in Mexico at 11 P.M., September 15, when government officials unfurl a Mexican flag and shout Hidalgo's words, "Mexicans, viva México!"

the outstanding man of the War of Independence, proved himself a brilliant leader and tactician. In 1813 he installed the first National Congress at Chilpancingo and published a decree declaring Mexico to be an independent republic. Later, he was captured by the royalist commander Iturbide and was executed on December 22, 1815. The leadership of his forces passed to Vicente Guerrero, one of his lieutenants. Guerrero continued the fight in the rugged mountains of the south.

Meanwhile events had occurred which made the Spanish conservatives and the clergy in Mexico suddenly desire separation from Spain.[5] General Agustín de Iturbide, the royalist commander in the south, met with Guerrero and proposed that they should unite in proclaiming the independence of Mexico. On February 24, 1821, they jointly issued the Iguala Plan of Independence which declared the country an independent constitutional monarchy; throne to be offered to Ferdinand or a reigning European family. The plan upheld the Catholic religion, granted equal citizenship to all inhabitants in New Spain. Though the viceroy opposed the plan, it proved popular, and by the end of September 1821 when Iturbide and Guerrero entered the capital, Spanish rule in Mexico came to an end.

THE REPUBLIC AND CHAOS

For the next hundred years Mexico was to be either in constant turmoil or under the thumbs of homegrown and imported emperors and dictators.

Unlike the thirteen North American colonies where men had some idea of the workings of democracy and the functions of elected legislatures, Mexicans had no tradition at all of self-government. No one had ever voted; no one had ever debated in parliament; few natives had ever held a responsible government post.

The new nation promptly got off to a bad start. Iturbide had been made regent of the government until a suitable monarch could be found. Within a short time he dissolved congress and proclaimed himself Emperor Agustín I. On July 21, 1822, he had himself and his wife anointed and crowned with great solemnity in the Mexico City Cathedral. For a brief moment his empire was one of the largest in the world, extending from the southern borders of Guatemala to the present northern boundaries of the United States. The Emperor Agustín idea did not please Mexico. Soon Iturbide was in trouble and, under pressure of a rebellion led by Guerrero and General Antonio López de Santa Anna, he was forced into exile.

A new congress convened in 1823 and drew up a constitution that made Mexico a popular, representative, federal republic (See Index). Félix Fernández, who styled himself Guadalupe Victoria (in homage of the Virgin of Guadalupe) became the first president of Mexico. He served a full and fruitful term. It was many years before another Mexican president succeeded in serving out a full term.

For some thirty-five years Mexico was plagued by revolts, invasions, and civil wars. During this time General Santa Anna, a fabulous personality, headed revolts, popped in and out of the presidency, sold part of his country, got it involved in a ruinous war with the United States.

Although there were numerous causes which brought on the war with the United States, the immediate irritant was a frontier dispute. Texas had enjoyed nine years as an independent republic and, in 1845, became the twenty-eighth state to join the Union. Mexico considered the Nueces River as the legal border between Texas and herself, whereas Texas and the United States considered the Río Grande as the border. President James K. Polk in his political campaign had claimed he was going to regain the territory up to the Río Grande and he aroused his country against Mexico. He sent General Zachary Taylor to the Río Grande in March of 1846. General Stephen W. Kearny was sent to occupy the Mexican Province of California; Colonel Alexander W. Doniphan proceeded toward Chihuahua and General Winfield Scott besieged Veracruz and eventually marched to the Mexican capital. Santa Anna, who had been in Cuba in exile, returned to Mexico, became president again, took all commands in his hand. Although poorly equipped, the Mexican soldiers fought with amazing valor, yet were defeated at every turn.

On September 14, 1847, after three weeks of furious battle, American troops secured the city. The following February, the Treaty of Guadalupe was signed, and by virtue of it, Mexico lost not only Texas (up to the Río Grande), but the area that now covers Arizona, New Mexico, Nevada, California, and parts of adjacent states. This war, largely forgotten by Americans, left in the Mexican unhealed wounds that still influence the Mexican personality. The country was cruelly dismembered, the war was fought on Mexican territory, and the behavior of American troops toward Mexican soldiers and civilians was often excessively brutal.

Although Santa Anna was exiled again, and the country was exhausted, the endemic civil wars and revolts continued, culminating in what is called the War of the Reform.

THE REFORM

During the 1850s, a taciturn Zapotec Indian named Benito Juárez emerged as one of Mexico's great

[5] In Spain, the Duke of Wellington had finally driven out Napoleon's armies and King Ferdinand had returned to the throne, but as a limited monarch. He was forced to accept the Constitution of 1812 which abolished the Inquisition, seized Church properties and permitted freedom of the press. The Mexican clergy, feeling their privileges were menaced, made an about-face and demanded freedom from Spain.

statesmen and leaders. His place in the hearts and minds of Mexicans compares to that of Abraham Lincoln in the United States. Juárez early made a name for himself as an effective leader of the Liberal party which opposed the power of the Church and wanted to abolish the special powers and privileges of colonial-minded leaders.

On February 5, 1857, Mexico adopted a constitution which ever since then has been regarded as a landmark in the nation's history. This Liberal document provoked a bitter three-year civil war, one of the country's bloodiest; perhaps, because for the first time it was more a struggle of ideologies than of personalities. Juárez, who had become president, was captured by Conservative rebels and was about to be shot at Guadalajara. He managed to escape, took a ship for Panamá, crossed the isthmus and came back to Veracruz where he set up his government. Juárez promulgated his famous Reform Laws — separating Church and State, abolishing convents and religious orders, expropriating ecclesiastical property, declaring freedom of worship and civil marriage.

Although the Juárez government was able to return to the capital, the Conservatives continued armed resistance and soon enlisted the aid of France, England, and Spain, who prepared to intervene in Mexican affairs. France, under Napoleon III, decided to take advantage of the U.S. involvement with its own Civil War, and planned to set up a monarchy in Mexico under French protection. England and Spain withdrew their threat, but the French invaded Mexico.

Although the French were decisively defeated in a battle at Puebla, they received reinforcements and managed to drive Juárez from the capital. On July 10, 1863, a pseudo-Council of Nobles called together by the Conservatives declared Mexico a monarchy and offered the throne to the Austrian archduke, Maximilian of Hapsburg.[6] Maximilian accepted the offer and came to Mexico with his wife Carlotta, daughter of King Leopold I of Belgium. Backed by some 63,000 French troops, he governed the parts of Mexico under French rule. Events leading to the Franco-Prussian War caused Napoleon III to withdraw his troops from Mexico, and without this support, Maximilian's empire crumbled. He was captured at Querétaro and ordered executed there on June 19, 1867, by the relentless Juárez.[7]

The republic was restored, Juárez was elected for another two terms. Shortly after the beginning of his last term of office he died and the presidency fell to Lerdo de Tejada. When the latter tried for re-election for a full term, a revolt, led by General Porfirio Díaz (who had served under Juárez) in 1867, plunged the country into civil war again. Out of it General Díaz emerged as Mexico's strong man. He remained the head of the government for some thirty years, either as president or, for a short period, guiding a hand-picked yes-man.

The "Porfirian Age," as the dictatorship of the durable Díaz was called, introduced tremendous changes and great misery in Mexico. The dictatorship was tough and repressive on one hand; on the other, it was a period of peace. Foreign capital, especially British, poured into the country; railroads were built, ports improved, trade multiplied. But the laissez-faire policies of the government tended to make the rich richer, the poor far poorer. Despite the peace and the new wealth pouring into the country, it was a regime that could not last because it was as foreign to the nature of Mexico as a French or German dictatorship.

THE REVOLUTION

In November 1910, Porfirio Díaz was a rugged old man of eighty. He had just been elected for another term. His opponent, Francisco I. Madero, a northern cotton planter and intellectual, was officially given 196 votes, arrested, held in jail until after the election. In May of 1911, calling for a revolt and advancing the slogan "Effective Suffrage — No Re-election!" Madero and a handful of cowboys under Pancho Villa struck out of the north. The revolt pushed Díaz out of power within six months.

The revolution that blazed across the country for the next ten years, putting eleven different presidents at the uneasy helm of the country — one held office for 45 minutes — appeared to be purposeless.[8] In 1913 Madero, while serving as president, was arrested and assassinated.

[6] Maximilian was a tall, golden-bearded, handsome idealist who had some well-meaning theories about government. His regime, contrary to the expectations of the Conservatives, was a liberal one. Many of the laws he enacted were similar to the Juárez measures. In refusing to restore Church property, he lost the support of the Conservatives.

[7] Maximilian's Carlotta (Charlotte) had left Mexico on June 13, 1866, to appeal to Napoleon III and Pope Pius IX for aid. According to legend their refusals drove her out of her mind. She retired to the Castle of Bouchotte in Belgium where, on January 12, 1867, she gave birth to a child. Ten years before, when she married Maximilian, the inheritance contract took into account that Maximilian was considered impotent and unable to have children or heirs. The child was baptized and named Maxime, and was given for adoption to a notary named Weygand who lived on the French-Belgian border. Later the child was sent to a French military school, his enrollment and expenses being paid for by the Belgian Royal Court. Half a century after his birth, Maxime Weygand became the brilliant chief of Foch's general staff during World War I.

[8] An interesting and revealing interpretation of the Revolution and Mexican history has been advanced by Octavio Paz, *El Laberinto de la Soledad.* Paz points out that the Revolution was unlike the Socialist and Marxist inspired upheavals in Europe and the Orient. The radicalism of the Mexican revolution rested on its originality: a return to the traditional roots and institutions of the pre-Hispanic and the colonial period, that is, those stable roots still meaningful to the people. It was an attempt to recapture the best out of the past, assimilate it, and make it alive in the present.

In pre-Hispanic cultures the two keystones of Indian society were religion and the *capulli.* The *capulli* was the community system in which land belonged to the community and was apportioned out to individuals to be farmed. Such plots were rotated from time to time so no one was permanently stuck with a bad piece. There was no private property, and after the death of the farmer, the land returned to the community. During the colonial period, though there were huge

Following the death of Madero, Venustiano Carranza, governor of the State of Coahuila, declared himself chief of the Constitutional Army. He was joined by General Alvaro Obregón and Pancho Villa. Carranza became president, but also faced a revolt, led by Villa and Zapata. Obregón defeated them and tranquillity returned until Carranza sought re-election. Fighting broke out again and he was killed. Finally, on November 30, 1920, Obregón became president. He restored peace among the warring rivals and initiated what can be called Mexico's era of modern development.

The Revolution, instead of being a thing of pure chaos, made profound transformations in Mexico. For the first time it has made possible an actual nation, embracing groups and races which neither the Spanish "Coloniage" nor the nineteenth-century liberals were able to incorporate.

Under Obregón, José Vasconcelos, whose ideas and writing have influenced much of Latin America, served as Mexico's first imaginative Secretary of Education. He extended educational facilities into the most remote rural areas and built thousands of new schools. He was also responsible for giving government commissions to muralists Diego Rivera and José Clemente Orozco and others.

In spite of one or two attempted revolts which were quickly put down, and despite various difficult social adjustments, Mexico has steadily progressed in the last forty years. The flare up of church-state religious strife which occurred during the Calles presidency in 1926, the strained relations with the United States when Mexico's oil industry was nationalized, have all smoothed out.

In the past decade, notwithstanding inflation, the wealth and well-being of the country has moved forward on all levels. Farming and industry are booming, great electrification and irrigation projects have been developed, a tremendous network of roads is spreading over the country. For centuries Mexican history has been a kind of oscillation between various universal ideas, deeply rooted institutions and foreign ideals. Now, out of the blood and agony of centuries of turmoil, invasion and occupation and uncertainty, the Mexican people are forming democratic institutions to suit their own needs and temperament.

estates, the king's *Laws of the Indies* protected Indian interests by supporting the *capulli* system which was similar to the *ejidal* system of community lands that existed in parts of Spain.

The Mexican Reform, with its laws inspired by European liberalism—though progressive and good in intent—consumed the benefits of the Independence Movement. It destroyed those institutions that provided a useful continuity in Mexican history. The *capulli* or village held lands were shoved aside to make room for the middle-class idea of private property. The Church was suppressed, thus destroying the religious continuity which it had given the Indians.

During the Porfirian Age, Dictator Díaz surrounded himself with young intellectuals called *científicos*, or apostles of the scientific age. Their positivist philosophy or movement, imported from Europe, undoubtedly was an outgrowth of historical development in Europe, but it had no connection with Mexican history. It was a foreign and meaningless "ism" implanted on Mexico. It succeeded in completing the work of the Reform, destroying the *capulli* and severing the people from their historic traditions.

Apart from the intellectuals who tried to give the Revolution some personal direction, the basic impulse behind the upheaval was an attempt to return or recapture the *capulli* and to break with the imported ideologies of the Reform and the dictatorship. The revolutionary hero, Emiliano Zapata—who has become one of Mexico's great folk heroes—saw this most clearly and embodied it in his famed proclamation, the Plan de Ayala.

17. The People of Mexico—Their Character and Ways

Mexico is a little less than one-fourth the size of the United States and has approximately 35,000,000 inhabitants. Like the U.S., Mexico was a melting pot in which peoples of many different origins and cultures were stirred together. In Mexico it has taken much longer for the broth to blend because of many factors, among them: extremely divergent cultural backgrounds, a violent history, and uneven population growth.

In 1521 when the Spanish conquered Mexico there were some seven to nine million inhabitants in the land. Diseases brought by the newcomers, suppression, and cultural readjustments dropped the population count to four and a half million by 1780. After the Independence the population climbed slowly until the turn of this century when it reached some twenty million. In keeping with the universal birthrate explosion since World War II, Mexico's population has leaped to its present size.

The distribution of the population over the Mexican terrain has always been very uneven, the greatest concentration being on the central plateau, the density declining sharply toward the coasts and borders. In the five central states whose capitals have an average altitude of over 7000 feet, more than 25 per cent of the population is squeezed in less than 4.2 per cent of the area of the country. This imbalance is only now beginning to change as a result of the government's policy of developing the outlying regions with massive irrigation projects, mosquito control, and roads.

Apart from a dozen relatively large cities, Mexico is a country of hamlets. Almost no one lives on an isolated farm as is done in the United States. Mexicans cluster together in towns, hamlets, and *rancherías* (small ranch settlements). Some 75 per cent of Mexico's population reside in villages having less than 200 people; 95 per cent of the people live in towns of less than one thousand population.

The geographic nature of the country, the need for mutual defense, and the difficulty in obtaining water created this system of village organization which has existed in Mexico since pre-Columbian times. Most of the villages, large or small, are self-contained units, capable of existing without much contact or commerce with the rest of the country. They are basically so much alike that one could almost be moved blindfolded from one place to another and always find the village plan the same. Standard village equipment includes: a central plaza, a parochial church near it, a bandstand, a village fountain or well and a space for the weekly street market. Situated around the plaza are the *presidencia* or town hall, a few stores, and the larger, often ornate houses of the wealthier citizens.

In spite of the fact that Mexicans are accustomed to living in towns, villages, or social groups, experts say that less than ten per cent of the population are truly urbanized. Although village loyalty is very strong, there exists a remarkable indifference where community projects such as sanitation, schools, hospitals, public welfare and such are concerned. In a certain sense almost every man, every family, every village is an island. Some of this isolation may be due to the fact that various centuries and various cultures still exist side by side in Mexico.

One is never allowed to forget that Mexico is still part Indian and part European. The European influences have prevailed in the larger cities; the Indian influence, in hamlets and rural areas. The proportions of these two cultures also varies geographically. The northern part of Mexico is *mestizo* and more European; the southern regions are largely Indian in tradition and habit. However, there is no sharp dividing line. In a place as cosmopolitan as Mexico City, especially in the poorer districts, you will find women preparing meals with implements that have not changed since Toltec days; even among the upper class, where Cadillacs are *de rigeur* and the children may be sent to Harvard, when illness strikes, the family may use a folk remedy devised by the Aztecs. At the same time, in some remote Indian village the Singer Sewing Machine and plastic dishes have come into use.

No one knows exactly how many Indians there are in Mexico. Finding the term "Indian" too difficult to define, the Mexican government, for census purposes, merely lists those people who speak Indian tongues. According to Jiménez Moreno, there exist 125 different Indian languages in Mexico. Of these ninety are still spoken (see Index). More than a million people in Mexico speak only one of these languages; another million and a quarter speak both Spanish and an Indian tongue. These people can be considered more or less of pure Indian blood and they definitely reflect the ancient Indian civilizations of Mexico. About 80 per cent of the national population is *mestizo,* people of mixed Indian and European stock for the most part. A large proportion of this group remain Indianist in outlook; their cultural habits, tools, utensils, social organization, and attitudes are more Indian than European.

Although many of the Indian folk are small and live in isolation, others constitute important national groups and they occupy vast regions. According to some estimates there are now in Mexico perhaps ten times more Indians than there were ever at one time within the United States domain.

Some of the principal linguistic families and ethnic groups are the following:

North and northwest: Seri, Tarahumara, Yaqui, Apache, and Mayo Indians. Yuman Indians in Baja California.

Central West Coast: Huichol and Tarascan.

Central Plateau: Náhuatlan, the largest linguistic family in the country. It includes the Aztec or Mexica. Tribes of this stock are found in almost unbroken continuity from Sinaloa in the north to the Guatemalan border, but the principal center of this culture was the Valley of Mexico. Other groups found in Central Mexico are the Otomí, a large ethnic group, the Chichimecas, and others.

Southern Mexico: The Zapotecs and Mixtecs, important groups centered in Oaxaca; Zoques, Chamulas, Huaves; and, along the southwest coast, one tiny group that speaks Sioux.

Eastern Mexico: Totonacs who inhabit part of Veracruz and Puebla. The Huastecan are also of this region.

Peninsula of Yucatán: Mayans, who remain a closely knit, populous group occupying most of the peninsula and areas in Chiapas and Tabasco.

Linguistically and culturally, these and many other groups (some living only a few miles apart) are as often as different from one another as are the Finns from the Brooklynites.

The average tourist, following well-worn travel tracks, rarely has a chance to meet and mix with such indigenous families. If one does meet them, one comes away usually feeling that you have met a marvelous people. Although they often live in isolation, withdrawn from the mainstream of national life, the people of these "little nations" are polite, formal, hard-working, shy — but they are also good hosts.

The Indian is extremely conservative. He jealously guards old customs and traditions. His family structure is a much more tightly knit one than that of the average American, or of the Mexican middle-class. Mexico's Indians seem to live in intense family union. Sexual differences are not as important in their community as in ours. A division of labor based on sex exists, but it is not as sharply or violently drawn as in the *mestizo* society. The family as well as village social organization is simple, direct, and satisfying.

Some people imagine that the Indians are backward or "closed" because they remain apart from the national life. However, it is likely that the trauma they suffered during the Spanish conquest and subsequent events was of such magnitude that their possibility of fighting the new culture was annulled. Aside from the work of the Church, no real effort was made to understand and include Indian society in the national picture until after the Revolution of 1910. Naturally, the Indian's strength and his mechanism of defense has been to accept what there is, and to have no confidence in anything Spanish, foreign or *mestizo.* In his pauperism — having withdrawn to the mountains, canyons, and deserted lands which no one else wanted — he found a margin of interior security. He doesn't rebel too often against poverty because in it he had been able to devise a certain degree of independence. He avoids the cultural conflicts tormenting people above him. His isolation is his defense of his manner of being.

When we speak of the contemporary Mexican, we are speaking of a brand-new race. In the United States the so-called melting pot produced a new nation, but not a new people. The *Norteamericano* is merely another blend of European stocks which had been shuffling and blending for ages in Europe. In Mexico a new race has actually come into being. This new race was at first merely a caste called *mestizo,* that is, someone of mixed European and Indian blood with, at times, a rarer intermingling of Chinese or Negro blood.

Less than a hundred years ago the Mexican Indian outnumbered both the *mestizo* and the European. Since then people of *mestizo* background have become the dominant group; they have actually become *the* nation and will eventually assimilate both the Indian and European. The *mestizo,* or Mexican as he should properly be called, is the only one of the many racial groups in Mexico which has developed a sense of nation — the Indian remains parochial, the European (less than ten per cent of the population) longs for his homeland. This new Mexican is an extremely intriguing, remarkable, and sometimes alarming personality to whom the future of Mexico belongs.

It has been the custom in guidebooks to sketch something of the character of the people visitors will meet in a new country. Often such books refer to the inhabitants of a strange country as "natives," almost implying that they are not quite human beings. Likewise, in order to reassure the traveler, the people of a country are generally described as "gracious, austere, excessively polite, and friendly" — a description that can fit almost anyone and tells us nothing. Part of the enjoyment of travel is to meet and understand new people, to learn something of their ways and how they tick. If you come to Mexico imagining all the people you meet are gallant, gay *caballeros* given to high-flown language, or that they are all Pancho Villas, you will be in for a disappointment.

Mexicans are people — among the most interesting and complex in the world. On the surface their society is often gracious, friendly, and generous to a fault. But also, the individual can be inexplicably violent toward his fellow man or brusque toward a tourist. Many of his attitudes, ways and motivations may be difficult for the North American to fathom. If you spend any time in the country and keep your eyes and ears open you will inevitably come upon such terms as *"machoism"* and *"malinchista"* and many others which are used to describe certain ingrained attitudes and, to outsiders, curious behavior.

You may admire his stoicism, or be fascinated by his indifference toward life. In Mexico there is a curious expectancy of death, death that strikes suddenly and meaninglessly, which makes fatalism and indifference to life a common feature of all groups and all classes. Some of this attitude derives from the very violence of the Mexican scene: the volcanoes sprouting out of cornfields, earthquakes, sudden ruinous tropical downpours, hurricanes, and floods. But it also goes beyond all this to what might be called the "Mexican experience."

The history of the country and the forging of the Mexican race has been peculiarly tragic and remorseless. Time after time an enigmatic evil has abruptly appeared, seeming to make life a gamble that is not always worth living. One such tragedy was the Spanish conquest. It not only killed off the leaders of the pre-Hispanic Indian world; it also destroyed their temples, their cultural records, their ethos and morality. It almost crushed their identity with their own past. It was a traumatic experience on a racial scale.

Other such seemingly destructive and purposeless experiences followed — the long, bloody War of Independence which destroyed many of the values implanted during the years of colonial teaching; the Reform Period, with its imposition of strange and foreign ideas; the French Occupation; the war with the United States and the consequent loss of huge territories which was like dismembering a living body. Events such as these, piled one upon another, can stretch man's faith in the future beyond endurance. To cope with vast disasters men set up defenses which become deeply ingrained, and are retained even after the threats are gone. Such things have conditioned the Mexican character.

Mexicans live in a world where skepticism and cynicism are a means of survival. The Mexican man often assumes that the worst is to be expected from any new experience or contact so he withdraws into himself. He is undoubtedly stung by the memory that not long ago he (the *mestizo*) was practically an outcast in his own homeland. Being neither pure Indian nor European, he was rejected by both groups, and his actual caste status was most uncertain.

The beginnings of this new race — El Mexicano —

were difficult and character-searing. Usually, the father was Spanish; the mother, Indian. The father was tough and lordly; the mother, submissive and almost a chattel. According to the Mexican psychologist Santiago Ramírez, "the culture of the Spanish father, his way of life, dominated both the nation and the household. He looked upon his *mestizo* offspring more as a product of sexual necessity than a perpetuation of his line." Such a father might be envied and admired for his indomitable courage, manliness, and ruthlessness. But he was also hated by the rejected sons. The history of Mexico's sons has been one of being dominated by a succession of fathers — Spanish, French, European, and North American. He has feared and hated them, but at the same time, he would like to emulate their power and their ways.

Such a background, repeated and repeated among millions of people could not help but make for a curious, often somewhat warped personality. Mexicans themselves have said that their history has fostered a kind of national servility, a nation-wide inferiority complex, a series of historical wounds that never quite heal. The Mexican has devised many defenses, some of them forms of overcompensation.

One of the defenses is the habit of negation, a form of cynicism. The Mexican often rejects or denies the very things that are deeply important to him. The frequently heard *"no importa"* ("it's of no importance") has almost become a symbol in the country.

Yet another defense is the cult of elusive language. Spanish is naturally flowery, ceremonious, and complex. The Mexican, however, often carries it to extremes never dreamed of in Spain or other Latin American countries. At times he utilizes speech in such a way that it goes nowhere, says nothing, in order to hide his true intent of feeling. The scatology of the great Mexican comedian, Cantinflas, carries this to its ultimate. His double-talk, like that of the adolescents, veils, defends; it is also a weapon to confuse, confound, and defeat those in power. Cantinflas, incidentally, has become a popular national hero as well as an inviolate symbol representing the underdog, the outcast, the *mestizo,* who will eventually come into his own.

In most countries the qualities of manliness, particularly in male adults, is taken for granted. The man who has to prove constantly that he is tough and forceful is considered to be somewhat childish or adolescent. In Mexico the reverse is true. The cult of *machoism* (maleness) is pursued with passion, terrible compulsion, and dedication. It colors thousands of aspects of Mexican behavior, social relations and attitudes.

It is basically a defense mechanism against insecurity; an overcompensation, an attempt to emulate the ways of the conqueror, the Spaniard, the father or the foreigner. In the daily behavior of the Mexican man it appears in many forms and frequently without the person realizing the basis for his actions or attitudes. It appears in extreme ostentation, in the seignioral show of wealth, in wanting to grab the bill in a restaurant even though one cannot afford it. When a Mexican says "My house is your house," most foreigners take it to be a sign of wonderful hospitality. Mexican psychologists claim it goes beyond hospitality and is another way of proving one's maleness, or one's social predominance. Mexicans are always testing one another's courage or forcefulness in the most minute ways: in forcing another to drink with one, whether it is desired or not. If you refuse a proffered drink it can be a terrible insult to your host's maleness. *Machoism* even appears on the street and highway; the driver who forces another to give way on the road or at a crossing proves his maleness. According to Dr. Ramos, it is the Mexican's most driving compulsion.

Visitors in Mexico may be confused or dismayed or charmed by Mexicans who make grandiloquent statements or promises, then forget about them. Some guidebooks have created a kind of cartoon-strip Mexican who is always gay, effervescent, "who loves companionship and whose aim, at any cost, is to be amiable and to please everyone."

The reason behind such behavior runs deeper and is a bit more human. According to Octavio Paz, "Mexicans live in themselves like taciturn adolescents. They are suspicious, wary and cynical." Mexico is a country of difficult contacts. People maintain relations, but they rarely live in relationship with one another. They are constantly maneuvering and defending themselves and their isolation. They mask their features and mask their smile, or, the smile is a mask, too. Everything serves as a defense: irony and resignation, courtesy and discourtesy, silence and speech. The Mexican often builds a wall between reality and his person. "He," says Paz, "is always distant; distant from the world and all; distant even from himself. We Mexicans are not only enigmatic to outsiders, but to ourselves, too. A Mexican is always a problem for another Mexican as well as for himself."

Various commentators on the Mexican personality have written about a phenomenon they call "the Mexican lie," that is, the exaggerated statement without basis in fact, or the eloquent promise not meant to be kept. It, too, is a defense mechanism. It is not really a lie and cannot be judged by our puritan, ethical, or moral standards. It is basically a fantasy, the creation of a wall to hide behind. The excessive courtesy of Mexico, the excessive sincerity which is carried to extremes, is all part of it — a refined form of the so-called "Mexican lie."

It has been said that the Mexican man never leaves himself open to the world in a natural manner; he opens up only in the release of delirium and the fiesta, or from alcohol, or when touched by death or violence. For him life is a matter, plain and simple, of being ravished, or of ravishing, that is, to humiliate, punish, and offend, or the reverse. This black-and-white concept of society has influenced the structure of Mexican social orders, making for sharp divisions between the strong and the weak. It leads to adhesion to chieftains and personalities rather than to principles. Mexican history has long reflected this. *"Isms"* (republicanism, Catholicism, communism, etc.) are less important to the Mexicans that *"istas,"* (Villistas, Carranzistas, etc.). They will be moved, and follow a Francisco Villa or a Venustiano Carranza, or the image of a saint, more readily than they will be moved to action by some abstract ideal.

During this last generation the Mexican personality has begun to change and open to the world. Much of the old insecurity has gone, being replaced by a sense of confidence, of worth and of nation. In the larger cities and towns men are becoming more cosmopolitan and less worried about proving their *machoism.* This does not mean that the distrust, fatalism, and uncertainly has been entirely wiped out. The word *"malinchista"* is still a potent and feared word.

A decade ago Octavio Paz pointedly summed up the Mexican character and personality by contrasting it with the North American personality. He wrote:

"Whereas Americans are ready to believe, we are believers; they love stories of enchanted nymphs, and detective yarns, we like myths and legends. The Mexican lies are fantasies done out of desperation or to surmount a sordid life; Americans do not lie, they substitute the true truth for the social truth. We get drunk to confess; they to forget. They are optimists; we are nihilists — but our nihilism isn't intellectual, but rather an instinctive reaction, therefore irrefutable. Mexicans are suspicious; Americans are open. We are sad and sarcastic; they are happy and jovial. Americans always wish to understand everything; we prefer to contemplate. They are activists, we are quiet. We gather the dividends of our wounds while they count the dividends from their inventions. They believe in hygiene, health, work and happiness, but they never experience the true delirious happiness which is both a drunkenness and a tornado. In the celebration of a night fiesta our voices are surrounded by lights, and life and death are mixed; they, on the other hand, let their vitality be petrified in a smile, they deny aging and death, and they immobilize life."

18. The Language of Mexico

With the exception of certain outlying areas where the many ancient tongues of Indian Mexico are still spoken (see *People of Mexico,* Index), the language of Mexico is Spanish.

The lack of a knowledge of Spanish should not deter one from visiting Mexico, as English-speaking persons are to be found in almost all large towns and cities, in the resorts and routes favored by tourists. In addition, Mexico is one of the easiest of foreign countries to travel in, as the people gesticulate freely and expressively; a few key words plus gestures can convey a world of meaning. However, a slight knowledge of Spanish, even badly spoken, can add greatly to the pleasures of a trip below the border.

The Spanish of Mexico is not quite the Spanish of Spain nor the Castilian taught in classrooms. It is notably richer, more flexible, and elegant in expression than the tongue of the mother country. It is softer and more euphonious than the lisping, burring speech of north-central Spain, since the Arabic gutturals still heard there become mere aspirates in Mexico. The Mexican pronunciation of Spanish is closer to the Andalusian pronunciation brought to the New World by the men who followed Cortés and helped to settle Mexico. Blended with this are rich elements of the Indian tongues which add a virile, subtle, and elastic quality to the speech of Mexicans.

Countless Indian words are current in the Spanish of Mexico. The speech of each state or district is sprinkled with its particular *dejo* or manner of usage which the practised ear can detect. The Spanish of Sonora is influenced by the *Yaqui* tongue; that of Chihuahua by the *Tarahumara,* of Nayarit by the *Huichol* and that of Michoacán by *Tarascan.* The *Tlaxcalan, Otomí,* and *Náhuatl* derivatives influence the speech of the central states. *Huastecan* words abound along the Gulf Coast while in Southern Mexico *Zapotec* and *Mixtec* words heavily influence the Spanish there. The rich Mayan language distinctly colors the Spanish of Yucatán.

Náhuatl, the language of the *Nahoas* or *Aztecs* or *Mexica* which most affects the Spanish of the country was, by the beginning of the twelfth century, a language noted for its cultured qualities. It was elegant in expression, polished and sonorous. Although it lacked the consonants *b, d, f, r, g* and *s,* it was full and rich. Its copiousness was demonstrated by the fact that some 1200 different species of local plants, 200 or more species of birds, animals, reptiles and insects, each had its proper name in the language. It was also especially rich in a vocabulary capable of expressing abstract ideas. It contained more diminutives and augmentatives than Italian or Spanish which, even today, influence the Mexican's Spanish. Agglutination or aggregation (making a complex word out of many simple words) was most common. One word of sixteen syllables, the name of a plant —

mihiittilmoyoiccuitlatonpicixochitl — was one of the tongue-twisters of the Aztecs.

In addition to the excessive use of diminutives and the reflex, as well as the elaborate floweriness of expression (which does not occur as strongly in Spain), a host of *Náhuatl* terms have been blended into the Mexican's vocabulary. The *Náhuatl* elements are distinguishable by their structural peculiarities and terminations. For example: *Tepec* or *tepetl* means hill, mountain, as *Chapul-tepec* (*chapulin,* grasshopper) or grasshopper hill. *Popocatépetl (popo-ca-teptl),* smoking-mountain. The terminations *can* and *tlan* signify place, as: *Coyoa-can,* place of the coyote (Aztec, *cóyotl,* wolf); *Ocotlán* (*ocote,* pine), place of the pines. *Milco* is a common termination, as: *Xochimilco (xochitl,* flower); *milli,* seed bed; *co,* (in or place), place of the flowers, or where flowers grow. *Milpa,* meaning a farmer's plot, derives from *milli,* seed bed, and *pa,* place. *Atl* (the pseudonym taken by one of Mexico's revolutionary painters), meaning water, is a suffix to many substantives, as *Chocolatl* (*xoco,* sour; *atl,* water), chocolate.

In the Spanish of Mexico the Castilian lisp *(el ceco),* said to have been perpetuated by Charles V, is not employed. While Castilians declare the lisp to be correct, and the only way to pronounce *decimos* (we say) day-*theme*-ohs, *cepillo* (brush) theh-*peel*-yo and *feliz* (happy) fay-*leeth,* the Spanish-American purists reject this form and say day-*see*-mohs, seh-*pee*-yoh and fay-*lease.* Any Mexican affecting the lisp is looked upon much the same as we would regard an American who affects B.B.C. English.

It should be noted, however, that in order to keep alive the custom and usage of the Spanish stage, the Castilian of the traditional drama is pronounced in the Castilian fashion. Also, along the Gulf Coast, the natives often clip syllables and slur their *s's* after the manner of certain Andalusians.

In Mexico the liquid *ll* is pronounced *y,* as cah-*by*-yoh instead of cah-bahl-yo (*caballo,* horse). In Mexico *b* is often substituted for *v,* as in *buelbo* instead of *vuelvo* (I return), and when there is a question as to which is being used, the two same sounding letters are distinguished by being called *bay-chica, v,* and *bay-grande,* the *b.* (i.e., little b and big b). The lower classes of Mexico frequently slur or smother terminations. They will say *pos* for *pues* (so or then), or *comí-o, querí-o, ganá-o* for *comido, querido, ganado,* or *no vale ná* for *no vale nada.* The educated Mexican speaks Spanish with unusual purity, however, and the American in Mexico should make it a point to practice the pronunciation accepted there as correct rather than the vernacular which is often localized or regional.

Spanish is a beautiful and complex language. Although it may take a scholar years to learn all its subtleties, the fundamentals (for purposes of daily communication) are neither involved nor difficult. The pronunciation is simple and direct. When one hears a word spoken, one knows exactly how to spell it. With very few exceptions it is pronounced exactly as written. (Among the exceptions: the letter *h* is always silent; the letter *j* takes its place and is pronounced nearly like it.)

A list of phrases and useful words is added at the end of this guide to help the traveler in particular situations, such as in restaurants, hotels, shopping, ordering car repairs, etc. For those who would wish to add to their knowledge of Spanish we suggest the following simplified courses and books:

Language Records: The records published by the Mexican-Spanish Academy, or the Linguaphone series.

Books: The Basis and Essentials of Spanish by Charles Duff (Thomas Nelson & Sons, Ltd.). A pocket-size approximation of "basic Spanish" that contains all that should be known of grammar and vocabulary to express the most frequently recurring ideas.

A Graded Spanish Review Grammar by Courtney Tarr and Agusto Centeno (Appleton-Century-Croft, Inc.). A very detailed grammar for advanced students.

Spanish Through Pictures by I. A. Richards (Pocket Books, Inc.). A very satisfactory, simplified, visual approach to Spanish.

When one has acquired a knowledge of the language, one should avoid certain expressions which carry double meanings. For instance, in asking a dining-room waitress for milk, never employ the verb *tener* (to have). Instead, use the impersonal verb *haber* (to have), as follows:

(incorrect) *¿Tiene usted leche?* Have you (a flow of) milk?

(correct) *¿Hay leche?* Is there any milk?

The girl may resent being taken for a wet nurse. Likewise, it is sometimes dangerous to ask in a grocery store or restaurant *¿Tiene usted huevos?* Have you any eggs? This is sometimes interpreted as meaning sexual glands, especially in today's slang. It is better to say *¿Hay huevos?* Or, as people do in some areas, they use the word *blanquillos* (whites), or *yemas* (yolks) in place of the word *huevos.* Also, never employ cryptic remarks overheard on the street unless you know their full meaning. The Mexican argot is rich in subtle and explosive insults which, if not used correctly, can result in troublesome situations.

19. The Mexican Government

Mexico is a Federal Republic consisting of 29 states, two territories, and a Federal District, known as the Estados Unidos Méxicanos, or United Mexican States. The states are free and sovereign in all that concerns them internally, and to the states are reserved all those powers not expressedly granted to the federal government. (See Index: states and territories.)

During Mexico's republican history there have been six constitutions: 1812 (provisional), 1824, 1836, 1837, 1857, and 1917. The constitution of 1857 was in effect until 1917 except for the period of the Empire under Maximilian. The present constitution was adopted at Querétaro on January 31, 1917, and was promulgated on February 5 of the same year by President Carranza. It is similar to the 1857 document as regards to government structure, but it contains important changes, chiefly in the form of guarantees and provisions concerning social welfare, labor, land tenure, and the unusual powers given the president.

The federal government is divided into three coordinate branches — legislative, executive, and judiciary.

The legislative power of the nation is vested in a general congress made up of two chambers, a Senate and a Chamber of Deputies. Deputies *(diputados)* are elected by direct popular vote for a term of three years. There is one deputy for each 150,000 inhabitants; each state must have at least two deputies; each territory, one deputy. Senators *(senadores)* are elected by direct popular vote for a term of six years. There are two senators for each state and the Federal District. Neither senators nor deputies can be re-elected for a succeeding term.

Theoretically, the constitution provided that the Congress legislate on all matters pertaining to the National Government, the territories, and the Federal District. Congress imposes taxes, enacts tariff laws, instructs the executive in matters concerning the public debt, legislates in respect to mining, commerce, credit, citizenship, public health, roads, postal service, coinage, public lands, weights and measures. The legislature includes a Permanent Committee (14 senators, 15 deputies) whose job it is to carry on the work of the Congress during periods of adjournment, as well as to prepare reports concerning upcoming legislation. Congress ordinarily convenes on September 1 of each year and adjourns on the following December 31.

The executive power of the government is vested in a president who is elected by direct popular vote. There is no vice-president. The president must be at least 35-years old, a native-born Mexican, of native-born parents. His term is for six years and re-election is prohibited. In the event of his death or permanent disability while in office, Congress elects a temporary substitute and, if the vacancy occurs during the first half of the term, a new presidential election is called for.

The functions of the president are to promulgate and execute the laws of Congress, appoint and remove cabinet ministers, diplomatic agents, and military officers and to act as commander in chief of the army and navy. He can, upon congressional resolution, declare war and decree new laws. The president's official family, the cabinet, includes 16 ministers who head the following Departments *(Secretarías):* Office of the Attorney General *(Procuraduría General de la República),* Department of Interior *(Secretaría de Gobernación),* State *(Secretaría de Relaciones Exteriores),* National Defense *(Secretaría de Defensa Nacional),* The Navy *(Secretaría de Marina),* Treasury *(Secretaría de Hacienda y Crédito Público),* National Patrimony *(Secretaría del Patrimonio Nacional),* Commerce and Industry *(Secretaría de Industria y Comercio),* Agriculture *(Secretaría de Agricultura y Ganadería),* Communications *(Secretaría de Comunicaciones y Transportes),* Public Works *(Secretaría de Obras Públicas),* Hydraulic Resources *(Secretaría de Recursos Hidráulicos),* Education *(Secretaría de Educación Pública),* Public Health *(Secretaría de Salubridad y Asistencia),* Labor *(Secretaría del Trabajo y Previsión Social),* and the Secretariat of the Presidency *(Secretaría de la Presidencia).*

In spite of the very democratic scheme of the constitution, the actual powers of the president are far broader than is indicated by the constitution. Mexico's long history of *caciquism,* that is, the adherence to political chieftains or leaders rather than to platforms or parties, has resulted in a curious governmental situation: *De Facto.* The government of Mexico *is* the president.

"The president is the government, and all discussions of Mexican politics must assume this fact . . . The legislature takes its politics and its laws from the president, and there is and can be no effective opposition in the Congress. The judiciary takes its views from the administration . . . He [the president] is the effective chief of the administration, the members of the cabinet are simply instruments of his will . . . Traditionally speaking, the President of Mexico must be able to do everything he wants or he will be unable to do anything he wants. He has either all power or no power; there is no middle ground."[1]

The president's power rests on control of the army and, in recent years, on control of labor and other elements. The majority of the unions in Mexico are creatures of the administration and they act as vehicles for the policies of the government, that is, the president.

There are various political parties in Mexico, free speech is unrestricted, political activities and organizations go on — yet, a political campaign and an election in present-day Mexico is in the nature of make-believe. Despite the number of parties there is really only one political party of consequence, the PRI (Partido Revolucionari Institucional), which is the government party. A candidate who has the official approval of the government party is certain of election. Tradition demands that there be a campaign, but no one is fooled by the results. The campaign also serves to familiarize the public with their next representative.

"No one can be elected governor of any state who is not acceptable to the president. This applies likewise to senators and deputies. And under the constitution the Senate has the duty of deciding on the legality of a state government, or of breaking off all federal relations with it. The Senate, therefore, decides who has been elected governor. But the Senate, like the governors of states, is a creature of the president, and the Permanent Committee of the Senate, which acts when the body is not in session, is handpicked by the president."[2]

It is not unusual in state elections to find a situation where there are two or three governors, each with his own legislature, each claiming he was elected by a popular majority. Since the state legislature must decide who has been elected governor and then must have the count accepted by the federal government, the situation can appear ridiculous. Since there may be three legislatures all trying to occupy one state house, it falls upon the Permanent Committee of the Senate to decide who is really "in."

Even after a governor has been seated, the federal executive can remove him at will. The Senate's Permanent Committee can sever relations with a state government by simply declaring that the federal powers in the state have vanished. The president then instructs the local military commander to eject the governor. The president appoints a provisional governor (often the army commander of the area) until a new election is held. Within a single year as many as four state governors have lost their jobs in this manner.

The vast powers of the Mexican president have made him the key figure in both the political and economic life of his country. He is expected to make all the important decisions. He has become the principal legislative agency of the nation. Instead of the president having to submit proposed laws to Congress, the constitution permits the Congress to pass a resolution empowering the president to issue a decree law in a specific case. During the last forty years a large part of the controversial economic legislation in Mexico (petroleum expropriation, land expropriation, etc.) was thus issued by the president under these extraordinary powers.

One Mexican observer has likened Mexico to a kingdom with a time limit on the reign. "The regime has many characteristics of an absolute monarchy, since all power resides in the president and is hereditary. The inheritance does not follow blood line or primogeniture, but follows the line of closest political and friendship ties with the incumbent president and with the ex-presidents, who still retain influence. Though Congress is nearly impotent, the ex-presidents act as moderators with almost senatorial functions."[3]

The third branch of the Mexican government, the Judiciary, has its powers vested in a Supreme Court and in Circuit and District Courts. The 21 members of the Supreme Court are approved by the Senate from candidates appointed by the President of the Republic. District and circuit court members are appointed by the Supreme Court.

The federal courts have jurisdiction over civil and criminal cases arising from enforcement or application of federal laws, cases to which the federal government may be a party, cases between states, cases between a state and the federal government, cases between a state and a citizen of another state and cases affecting members of the consular or diplomatic corps.

The governmental structure of the individual states is patterned on that of the federal government. In addition, each state is divided politically, as a rule, into districts governed by a prefect or *jefe politico* (political chief) who is directly responsible to the governor. The minor divisions are called *municipalidades* (municipalities) and the local authority is the *ayuntamiento* which corresponds to the town council in the United States.

THE NATIONAL FLAG

The Mexican national flag has three vertical stripes of equal width: green symbolizing unity, white for religion, red for independence. In the center of the white stripe the national coat of arms is set.

The coat of arms shows an eagle perched upon a *nopal* cactus and clutching a serpent in its talons. It is based on the legendary omen that led the Aztecs to found their capital city Tenochtitlán on the site now occupied by Mexico City. The eagle is encircled by the words *Estados Unidos Mexicanos.*

THE NATIONAL FLOWER is the Dahlia.

[1] *Mexico: The Struggle for Peace and Bread,* by Frank Tannenbaum (Alfred A. Knopf). One of the most preceptive books in English about contemporary Mexican politics and economics.

[2] Ibid.

[3] *The Mexican—His Psycho-Social Dynamic* by Francisco González Pineda.

20. Mexican Economy, Industry, and Mining

Although Mexico has been developing its industries at a rapid rate, it remains primarily an agricultural country. Over 60 per cent of the working population is engaged in farming and agricultural enterprises. Coffee, cotton, sugar, henequen, and truck produce account for 40 per cent of the value of the national export.

Corn *(maiz)* is the major staple food of Mexico as well as the chief agricultural crop; 3.5 to 4 million tons annually. It is cultivated in almost every section of the county; some 12 million acres are devoted to this crop alone. However, neither corn nor wheat are produced in sufficient quantity to satisfy the internal demands of the nation and each year grains are imported to fill the gap.

Cotton, grown principally in the states of Tamaulipas, Durango, Coahuila, and Baja California, is Mexico's major export crop. It is followed by sugar, then coffee. During the last few years Mexico has so increased its coffee production that she ranks after Brazil and Colombia as one of the world's chief coffee growers and exporters. The truck crop — tomatoes, lettuce, melons — has expanded tremendously in recent years and the bulk of it is shipped to the United States during the winter months.

Cattle raising, one of the nation's basic farming enterprises, has suffered severe setbacks in the past two decades due to an *aftosa* plague (hoof-and-mouth disease), requiring extensive destruction of infected cattle. In the last ten years the government has made a considerable effort to improve breeds through the importation of prize cattle from abroad and by modern techniques of artificial insemination.

Since the Revolution of 1910–18, tremendous changes have taken place in the ownership of Mexican agricultural lands. At the turn of the century less than ten per cent of the total population owned land. The general system up to that time was that of the *hacienda* — huge, self-contained, self-governing units or estates that were like small principalities. They often involved absentee-ownership, and a system of labor similar to peonage. The Revolution initiated the transition from these vast privately owned estates to numerous small tracts owned by individual farmers, or farms worked co-operatively.

The present-day land system includes the following: (1) small individual farms, usually marginal land; (2) large agricultural enterprises under private management or ownership, though the government limits the size of such estates; (3) co-operatives and (4) *ejidos* or collective farm lands. The *ejido* is an ancient form of land tenure that dates back to early Spanish as well as pre-Hispanic times. (See Index.) The modern *ejidos* are made up of land distributed from federal holdings or expropriated private property. The *ejidatario* or farmer cultivates such allotted lands and receives the profits from it directly.

The Mexican government is devoting unusual energies to opening new lands and spurring agricultural development, especially by extending farm credits, establishing centers for agricultural research, rural education, and undertaking huge federal irrigation projects. Several important new dams — the Papaloapan in Veracruz, the Mocuzari Dam in Sonora and the Hidalgo Dam in Sinaloa — are greatly increasing the amount of tillable land. In the last twelve years 8.4 million acres have been converted to agricultural exploitation.

MINING

Although people abroad often think of Mexico as a mining country primarily, in actuality Mexican mineral exploitation contributes less than five per cent to the gross national income. The largest portion of this income is derived from silver mining, Mexico being the world's foremost producer.

The mineral wealth of the country, however, is judged to be vast, needing only adequate financing and techniques to be fully exploited. With the exception of Campeche, Tabasco, and Yucatán, every state in the Mexican territory possesses mines. Numerous of the mines, especially silver and gold, were taken over from the Indians by the Spanish who also opened new regions. The first silver taken from a Mexican mine by Europeans in 1521 came from the still celebrated mines in Taxco, Guerrero. During the three-century period of Spanish domination over three billion pesos in gold and silver were extracted — almost one-third of this total came from the mother lode *(veta madre)* at Guanajuato. The largest silver nugget ever found in Mexico was discovered near a Papago Indian village in Sonora. It weighed 2750 pounds.

Due to the increased industrialization within the country and an expanding world market for nonferrous and ferrous metals, the production of lead, zinc, copper, iron, and some coal has achieved more prominence in Mexico. The country is now the world's second greatest producer of lead, third with zinc, fifth with copper. Proven iron ore deposits are estimated at 275,750,000 tons, with an additional probable reserve of 292,140,000 tons. The most important ferrous deposits lie along the Pacific continental slope and over the northeast and center of the highland plateau. The most important coal reserves, still unexploited, are in the northern part of the country, plus a newly discovered coal basin in Oaxaca that is estimated to have a probable 100,000,000 tons.

The recently discovered and exploited gigantic sulphur deposits in the Isthmus of Tehuantepec have given Mexico the world's largest sulphur reserve. In a matter of a few years she has become the second largest sulphur producer in the world.

Mexico was the first Latin American country to become an important oil producer. Because of poor exploitation of coal reserves, petroleum has been one of the principal sources of industrial power in Mexico. The proven oil reserves are estimated at somewhat over 2.8 billion barrels, with new fields being continually found.

Since the expropriation of the foreign-owned petroleum properties in 1938, Mexican petroleum production has been controlled chiefly by a government corporation, Petroleros Mexicanos (Pemex).

INDUSTRY

Mexico can boast of one of the highest long-term rates of industrial growth in the Western Hemisphere. The industrialization which began in the 1880s with the construction of railroads expanded before the Revolution to include a wide variety of industries: chemicals, brewing, cigarette manufacture, pulp and paper, petroleum refining, etc. Since the 1920s, and especially after World War II, there has been a phenomenal increase in manufacturing, including new pharmaceutical plants, automobile assembly plants, rolling mills and appliance plants. Most of these have been concentrated around Mexico City, Monterrey, Guadalajara, Puebla, and Veracruz.

The nation's leading steel plant, Altos Hornos de México, S.A., in Nuevo León, accounts for one-third of Mexico's steel production. It is presently turning out a million tons annually.

In that Mexico seriously lacks sufficient private investment capital, and because there is a deep-seated fear of foreign capital controlling the country if it were allowed to invest freely, the government itself has made up for this shortage by investing heavily in new industry and projects. However, in recent years the government investment has been designed so as not to compete with, but rather, to pave the way for private investment. Due to the vastness of necessary expenditures in certain fields — electrification, irrigation, and transportation — the government has begun financing basic projects in order to provide power and other facilities for private industry.

The government also contributes to the financing of private enterprises through its national credit institutions such as agricultural banks, transportation banks, and specialized long-term lending agencies. The Nacional Financiera, a government-sponsored investment bank, has granted credits for the development and expansion of private industry in excess of 7,838,000,000 pesos.

The bulk of the nation's industry and capital is still concentrated in the Federal District, plus a few progressive cities such as Monterrey, Puebla, and Guadalajara. Unfortunately, smaller towns, states, and outlying districts are hampered in their development by lack of funds which might be spent in improving roads and sites that might attract industry and commerce. Part of this trouble is due to the curious tax situation in Mexico. The federal government, even today, remains somewhat like the ancient Aztec regime, exacting unusual tribute from subject regions. In a recent year, for example, the total tax income from municipal, state, and federal sources came to 12,789,419,754 pesos. Of this total, the federal administration absorbed 79.7 per cent for its uses; 11.1 per cent went to other federal entities such as territorial and island administration; 6.2 per cent was allotted to the Federal District. Meanwhile, of this tax fund, less than 3 per cent went back to all the municipalities in the country.

In addition to larger industries and manufactories, Mexico is also a country of vast home industries or cottage crafts which are of special interest to travelers. The people produce a tremendous volume of hand-loomed textiles, hand-wrought ironwork, colorful ceramics, artistic glass, tiles, jewelry, and other native crafts. The native crafts, along with the tourist industry — often called the industry-without-chimneys — has become an important factor in the national economy. During the past decade the income from tourism has rapidly risen, and since 1958 it has outstripped the petroleum industry, mining, farming, and manufacturing as the nation's principal source of foreign income. Tourists are spending over $590,000,000 annually in Mexico.

21. The Arts of Mexico. Architecture and Sculpture, Painting, Folk Arts, Music, Songs and Folk Dances, Fiestas

ARCHITECTURE AND SCULPTURE

The story of architecture and sculpture in Mexico is essentially one of the creation of monuments, for the most part of a religious nature. It is also a story of departed cultures, of cities and temples built and deserted one after another, of pagan temples turned into stone quarries for Christian churches and palaces.

When you travel in Mexico you are struck by the countless towers and domes of churches and by the seemingly endless archaeological sites. No other country in the world is so jammed with enduring architecture of so monumental a character.

One of the reasons behind the creation of so much fascinating building and sculpture is stone. Mexico is blessed with an abundance of building material that lends itself to expressions in substantial and permanent form. The country is like a huge slag heap of volcanic and other rock, always at hand, tempting to the mason and artist. Notable among these basic materials is a peculiar, porous, volcanic traprock called *tezontle.* The name is derived from the Aztec, *tezontli,* meaning "stone of hairs." Its composition is somewhat like pitted pumice and it does resemble petrified hair. In color it ranges from pink to a deep maroon. It is the seared-looking stone you see on all the old palaces in Mexico City. It was also the primary construction material of the Aztecs. Mortar joins with it so perfectly that a wall constructed of *tezontle* becomes a lightweight, earthquakeproof, homogeneous mass. As a contrasting trim, a hard gray stone called *chiluca* is used for cornices, doorways, and lintels.

Other parts of the country have their special stone, each of which impart an atmospheric tone to entire cities. In Oaxaca it is a soft, pale green stone which makes you feel that the city of Oaxaca has been rained on for centuries. On the central plateau a pinkish limestone called *cantera* and a hard, blueish limestone lend buildings a rich sunny appearance.

Long before the Spanish conquered Mexico, the pre-Columbian inhabitants had mastered stonecutting and many of the principles of great architecture. They developed certain motifs and forms — pyramids, sculptured columns, and bas-reliefs — which were repeated through the various Indian cultures.

The earliest examples of important architecture appeared in the jungles of Guatemala and on the Yucatán Peninsula where the ancient Mayans built elaborate structures for ceremonial purposes. They showed a keen conception of the value and beauty of architectural order. Their typical religious cities, Uxmal, Chichén Itzá, and others, were constructed around a great plaza or square. At one end there were large terraced mounds serving as bases for temples. The remaining sides were occupied by palaces, monasteries, nunneries for the temple maidens and usually an astronomical observatory. During the early Mayan periods the buildings were covered with thick layers of stucco painted in brilliant colors. The central plazas were dotted with sculptured monoliths engraved with figures of priests, warriors, and religious symbols. In the latter Mayan period (New Empire), less attention was paid to the formal arrangement of the buildings. Also, instead of being covered with stucco, the stone façades of buildings bore richly carved geometric patterns so that the entire structure appeared as a massive form of sculpture.

Although the Mayans, despite their engineering skill, never hit upon the principles of the arch and keystone, nor the corbelled arch, they showed amazing advancement in applying other scientific and engineering principles to art. They were not inferior to the Greeks in utilizing optical refinements to balance line and perspective. Like the Athenians, they made their long horizontal lines, such as the steps of temples, slightly convex to overcome the illusion of sag in the middle. Instead of building courtyards to purely rectangular and horizontal forms, they built the side walls closer together at the rear and sloped the floor upward toward the rear to create an effect of greater depth. They even took into account the effects of sun, light, and shadow in placing their sculptured decorations on buildings.

On the central plateau of Mexico the Toltec peoples evolved their own forms of architectural embellishment which were eventually to influence both the late Mayans and the Aztecs. Their ceremonial cities at Tula and at Teotihuacán were distinguished for their massive proportions and sculpture. At Teotihuacán, just north of Mexico City, they extended and refurbished pyramids of an earlier civilization and built a sacred city which left no doubt as to its careful preconceived planning. In raising the grandest of all pyramids in the Americas, the Pyramid of the Sun, they did not use cut stone to the same lavish degree as the Mayans. However, in the handling of mass and the treatment of planes to gain the effect of awe, the Toltecs were master architects. The sloping sides of their huge pyramids were set at different angles so that when seen from below the structures create an effect of infinite height. When priests climbed the pyramid, to the populace waiting below, it appeared as if they were disappearing into the heavens.

In the deep south the Zapotec civilization built a remarkable holy city, Monte Albán, which in planning shows certain resemblances to the Mayan centers and the Tula of the Toltecs. It has the broad central plaza, the temples on their individual mounds, the low pyramids and bas-relief sculpture. In striking contrast to Monte Albán, the nearby Mixtec religious center of Mitla offers a type of temple architecture that evokes memories of Greece in the mind. At Mitla, instead of the great pyramids and platforms, the ancient builders left an arrangement of well-preserved temples set in groups-of-four around paved courtyards. In place of sculptured human figures and symbols, the walls are a mass of geometric designs similar in pattern to the Greek fretwork.

With the exception of ceramic figures and jade carvings, almost all pre-Hispanic sculpture was closely related to architecture. Few statues were created to stand alone; almost all were destined to be architectural embellishment. The pre-Columbian Indian's concept of sculpture was quite different from ours: their ideas of beauty were based more on rhythmic proportions, repetition and symbolism, than on naturalism or realism. Sometimes they did produce sculpture that was realistic, but these remain more the exception than the rule.

The purpose of sculpture was religious — to portray natural forces, the gods, the symbols of belief. The early Mexican artist and sculptor worked from within rather than from without. According to their ideas of esthetics the artist had to become what was called *yoltéotl,* that is, "one-with-a-heart-rooted-in-God." He had to "learn to converse with his heart," all of which meant that his ideas, forms, and symbols sprang from an inner religious impulse.

Although the wellsprings of the pre-Columbian arts were often similar, the art and sculpture of each culture were quite distinctive.

The mysterious rubber-country people, the Olmecs, appeared on history's tapestry not as primitive artists, but as highly skilled sculptors. Their work puzzles archaeologists because they seem to have popped up out of nowhere like full-fledged Michaelangelos. They carved fifteen-ton monumental stone heads, delicately sculptured figures in clay, as well as some of the most beautifully carved jades the world has known.

The Mayan artist, less individualistic than the Olmec, turned sculpture to architectural use. In their early period the Mayans sculpted delicate, realistic human figures. In their use of perspective, especially in the carving of low reliefs involving interlaced figures, they were far in advance of the Assyrians and Egyptians for they could carve the human figure face-on, full-profile or three-quarter view without distortion. Like the Greeks, they painted their sculpture to bring out line.

The sculpture of the Toltecs had neither the grace nor the subtlety of Mayan work. It was powerful and dramatic, relying on massive forms and grotesque effects. The gigantic columns at Tula, carved in low relief so that the finished figure suggests the original stone, is an example of this; likewise the wonderfully executed serpent heads with collars like flower petals, at Teotihuacán.

Magnificent examples of the ancient sculpture of Mexico — Olmec, Mayan, Zapotec, Toltec and the delightful ceramic sculpture from the Colima and Jalisco regions — can be seen at the National Museum of Archaeology in Mexico City.

The Spanish conquest of Mexico completely severed the native architectural and sculptural genius, replacing it with a type of Spanish architecture which came to be known as "colonial." During the next three hundred years, from 1520 to 1820 and later, a mixture of European styles with certain native embellishments flooded the New World.

According to Trent E. Staford, "If one could generalize, we might sum up the architectural styles and centuries in Mexico as — 16th Century: Gothic and Romanesque, with early Plateresque application or decoration; 17th Century: a brief period of severe classic renaissance, the Herreran Classic, overtaken by the Baroque and ultimately replaced by the Ultra-Baroque (which extended into the eighteenth century); 18th Century: the glorious, wealthy, and lavish Ultra-Baroque or Mexican Churrigueresque, (particularly the latter half of the century)."[1]

During the first generation following the Conquest the colonial architecture was Gothic-Franciscan, so called after the friars who built the first Christian churches and monasteries in Mexico. Their churches were used both as a religious center and as a defensive citadel against Indian attacks. The buildings were distinguished by great walls and massive Gothic buttresses reaching the full height of the structure, and by battlements all along the parapets of the roof. The few windows were placed high and widely spaced. The interiors were simple, having rib-vaulted ceilings or simple barrel vaults. In general they were without aisles and terminated in a polygonal aspe.

There was usually a monastery connected with the church. It was built around an enclosed cloister or patio featuring two-story arcades supported by columns and carved stone arches. The ceilings were generally simple barrel vaults or wooden beams. A noteworthy exception is the lovely Augustinian monastery at Yuríria in the State of Guanajuato where

[1] *Architecture in Mexico* by Trent E. Staford, W. W. Norton & Co., Inc.

the lower cloister has an exceptionally fine Gothic rib-vaulted ceiling.

Throughout most of the colonial period, while Mexico was at its height of architectural activity, renaissance tastes in decoration dominated the country. During this time several distinctive forms and decorative motifs were developed, chief among these: the dome and tower and Plateresque decorations.

The dome and tower, a most pleasing combination that strikes the eye of the traveler everywhere in Mexico, is almost like an architectural signature. Outside of the Orient and the Near East no other part of the world can boast of so many beautifully formed domes and towers. Called *cúpulas* or *media-naranja* (half-orange), the Mexican domes are beautifully arched, solid masonry. Some are set on drums; many are covered with glistening green, blue, or orange tiles.

The Plateresque, a peculiar Spanish style of decoration characterized by delicate ornament, heraldic and floral designs, usually placed about portals, was a forerunner of the more exuberant Churrigueresque decorations of the eighteenth century. It gets its name from the Spanish word for silversmith, *platero,* since the decoration somewhat resembles the design work of Spanish silversmiths. Among the best examples of Mexican Plateresque are the portals of San Agustín Acolmán (north of Mexico City) and the portals of the old Montejo Palace in Mérida, Yucatán.

The enormous wealth extracted from silver and gold mines, and reaped from the huge estates of Mexico, financed one of the wildest sprees of magnificent palace and church construction known in any country. During the seventeenth and half of the eighteenth centuries this lavishness was expressed in the Baroque style, typified by its capricious proportions, its accidental profiles, twisted columns, and the constant interruption of straight lines.

Mexico City is graced with a lavish number of such Baroque monuments. One of the finest is the Church of Santo Domingo, noted for its handsome dome, fine tower, and stately carved façade. The Iturbide Palace on Avenida Madero (now an office building) is also an excellent example of the Baroque applied to civil architecture.

A problem that the visitor must keep in mind is that, during Mexico's colonial building spree, the particular styles of one period overtook another. On buildings such as palaces and churches, which took hundreds of years to complete, a multitude of styles will appear; an exterior may be Gothic or early Baroque and the interior may be a mixture of Churrigueresque and anything else, perhaps even as in recent years, Hollywood Mudéjar and Miami Cabin Cruiser styles.

The Baroque forms lasted well into the eighteenth century, finally being overtaken by the Ultra-Baroque or Mexican Churrigueresque as it is sometimes called. The name Churrigueresque, once used as a term of reproach for overextravagant styles, is derived from a Spanish artisan and builder, José de Churriguera. Oddly, his own work in Salamanca, Spain, was much more restrained than the architectural style in Mexico which adopted his name.

As an outgrowth of the Baroque forms, Churrigueresque styles also involve an interruption of the classical straight lines and the use of broken pediments and entablatures. In the Baroque a column may be twisted, storied, or decorated with foliage, but it remains a column. In the Churrigueresque, the column became so infinitely broken up into a variety of geometric forms, inverted pyramids, covered with scrolls, carved fruit and other decorations, and so interrupted with statues and panels, its basic shape is hardly recognizable. Churrigueresque decoration, like the Plateresque, is concentrated mainly around portals (enlarged to accommodate more do-dads) and around the upper part of the church towers. The style also invaded church interiors, filling them with lavish, intricately carved, gold-encrusted altars, retablos and other decorations of such fantastic exuberance that nothing was left to the imagination.

Fine existing examples of this style are the two façades of the Sagrario Metropolitano in Mexico City, the exterior of the Santisíma Trinidad church, the Chapel of the Kings in the Mexico City cathedral, the interior of the Sanctuary at Tepotzotlán, the church interiors of Santa Rosa and Santa Clara in Querétaro.

Unfortunately for Mexican architecture, the extraordinary enthusiasm aroused by Churrigueresque styles was followed by a pseudoclassic interval at the beginning of the nineteenth century. This movement was inspired by Manuel Tolsa, a Spaniard who became the mentor of the Mexican San Carlos Academy. Moved by a fanatical rage for destruction and regimentation and armed with unusual royal powers, Tolsa had the rich interior trappings of numerous buildings stripped in order to make them classically correct. He succeeded at best in making them naked and forlorn; in the end, doing more damage to Mexican architecture than several revolutions.

Mexico hardly recovered from Tolsa's impact which, of course, was followed by the hundred-year era of civil strife, sterile dictatorship and revolution. During this long interregnum only one or two works of architectural brilliance were to appear.

In Celaya and Querétaro, a man who was an engineer, architect, poet, sculptor, engraver, and musician shone briefly. This man, Francisco Eduardo Tresguerras, is now considered the Michaelangelo of Mexico. He built churches and palaces, filled them with his sculpture and painting. His churches, with their perfect domes and graceful decorations, are among the finest in the country. Especially memorable are his El Carmen church in Celaya and Santa Rosa in Querétaro.

Less important, but nevertheless a curious personality in architecture, was the pure-blooded Indian, Ceferino Gutiérrez, who built one of the strangest church façades in Mexico. Completely untrained in formal architecture, Gutiérrez designed and raised the parochial church in San Miguel de Allende — a crude, illogical attempt at French Gothic which somehow combines monumentality with certain Indian graces and, as Sylvester Baxter suggests, "an undisciplined sense of form and an untutored gift for rich expression."

In addition to these principal styles in Mexican architecture, another purely Spanish style, the *Mudéjar* — developed by the Christianized Moors of Spain — has made its influence evident in much of the architecture of Mexico. It is particularly evident in the polychrome tilework of Puebla. The finest secular example of *Mudéjar* influence is the celebrated Casa de los Azulejos, the House of Tiles, now occupied by Sanborn's Restaurant and shops in Mexico City.

With the exception of the work of Tresguerras, the Gothic interlude in San Miguel de Allende and the beautification of Mexican town plazas at the instigation of Maximilian and Carlotta, from the 1850s to the 1920s very little of architectural interest was created in Mexico. This opinion includes that curious, sinking, wedding-cake monument to the age of Porfirio Díaz — the National Opera House or Bellas Artes.

After the turn of the century, thanks to the Revolution and the Tolteca Cement Company, Mexican architects began to toy with modern functionalism, Bauhaus styles and box shapes. A few horrible examples of monumental construction appeared, and the less said about them, the better. One of these is the elephantine Monument to the Revolution (Mexico City); another is the gigantic figure of Morelos, set on an island in Lake Pátzcuaro, which may be an attempt at architecture or at sculpture, but fails to be successful as either.

Following some thirty-five years of experimenting, Mexican architects have begun to develop a modern Mexican style of their own, perhaps influenced somewhat by Le Corbusier and Neimyer. In recent years several new buildings along the Paseo de la Reforma, also the Main Hospital of the National Railways of Mexico and the Central Library building at University City have shown imaginative design and dignified architectural treatment. Some dramatic examples of home-architecture have been built in the Pedregal section of Mexico City.

In contemporary Mexican church architecture the *Purísima* in Monterrey pioneered the concrete shell construction with a good deal of success. Its lines are graceful, its decorations tasteful. In the last few years Félix Candela, a Spanish-born architect-engineer-artist, now working in Mexico, has made the graceful and soaring shells an important new part in Mexican architecture.

Less pretentious, yet solid and unchanged over the centuries, is the typical Mexican village architecture — the simple homes of Mexico. Their form is more or less the same across the country, with certain variations dictated by the available construction material and the climate. In the tropic regions the house is of a pole skeleton covered with thatch, bamboo stalks or palm fronds. The walls may sometimes be daubed with mud. In temperate regions the building material consists of stone or adobe (a sun-dried brick made of mud and straw). The roofs are usually tiled, or a surface of brick and mortar supported by heavy beams.

The houses are usually rectangular in shape; a single room with one door and sometimes a window. Where there is more than one room, each room has its separate entrance. Floors are of packed earth. There is normally a complete lack of furniture, except for a few basic essentials and, of course, flowers. Mexicans will raise flowers in anything from an old straw hat to a discarded gasoline tin.

In the larger villages and towns a house is more extensive: a series of rooms forming an L, or completely surrounding a patio which often has a carved fountain, trees, and a profusion of plants and flowers. A monumental doorway, large enough to accommodate an automobile, faces on the street. This opens into a passageway called the *zaguán* which in turn leads to the patio. In many houses, at some distance behind the street door, where the *zaguán* opens upon the patio, an elaborate wrought iron or finely carved wooden grill gate is placed. It permits the great street doors to be left open during the day, giving passers-by a glimpse of the flower-filled patio, yet serving as a measure of protection for the house. The city of Morelia is noted for its fine colonial houses with the traditional carved doors, the *zaguán, portónes,* and lovely patios.

The sculpture of Mexico during the colonial and post-colonial seldom equaled that of pre-Hispanic sculpture. The creation of great individual works in stone, bronze or ceramics were rare, indeed.

At the time of the conquest the Indian artists were suppressed. The needs for sculpture were met from Spain. A tide of carved wooden statues of saints came from the mother country. Later, as more churches and palaces were constructed and there was a need for skilled artisans, Indians were again employed, but always under Spanish direction.

For the most part, the sculpture of the colonial era was effective and decorative, contributing to the embellishment of buildings. Taken alone, most of the sculpted figures lacked individuality and animation. During the eighteenth and nineteenth centuries sculptured figures, especially in churches, became so debased they had little to do with art. Figures were skeletal and were covered with clothing and wigs made of natural hair. Usually they were grotesque in pose and form.

For a short period a healthy reaction to this degeneracy in sculpture occurred in Puebla and in Querétaro. In Puebla a group of sculptors known as the Three Coras — José Villegas de Cora, Zacarías de Cora and José Villegas (who took the name Cora as an honorary title), took a serious interest in anatomy and the art of sculpture. Their works were the first native sculpture in Mexico since the conquest to deserve the attention of the art world. There are good examples of the work of José Villegas de Cora in the San Cristóbal church in Puebla: a giant figure of Saint Christopher with the child Jesus, one of the Virgin on the high altar and another of a Virgin of Lourdes.

In Querétaro, another group of skill woodcarvers more or less paralleled the work of the Puebla artists. These were called the Three Marianos — Mariano Perusquía, Mariano Arce, and Mariano Montenegro. They carved a wood called *zumpantle,* an almost grainless medium as light as cork. The figures were coated with plaster and polychromed. Of the three, Mariano Perusquía was the most skilled. His work shows fine, painstaking detail, the exact opposite of Arce's bold and virile style. Examples of their work can be seen in the Santa Clara church in Querétaro.

One might note with a touch of irony that the most famous post-conquest statue, also the first important statue to be cast in bronze in the New World and one of the greatest equestrian figures anywhere was done by Manuel Tolsa, the same man who destroyed so much fine Mexican architecture. His huge, bronze equestrian statue of Charles IV of Spain, now popularly called "El Caballito," ("The Little Horse"), stands at the juncture of Avenida Juárez and Paseo de la Reforma in Mexico City.

It is curious that in sculpture Mexico has developed no artist comparable to Rodin or Maillot. Most statuary has been pleasing and public, but not very inspiring. The Revolution thrust up great Mexican painters and muralists, but no sculptors.

Among contemporary Mexican sculptors the work of Ignacio Asúnsola commands interest, especially his work on the Obregón Monument in the capital. A more individual sculptor is Germán Cueto, whose imaginative "La Tehuana" is in the permanent collection at the Palace of Fine Arts. Perhaps the most exciting of the younger sculptors working in Mexico is German-born Lothar Kestenbaum whose powerful human and animal figures contain a vigor and meaning which is often missing in modern-day art.

PAINTING

Early Mexican painting was for the most part fresco or mural painting. Because of their religious and ceremonial nature, and because they were applied to exterior walls, most of them suffered destruction, either at the hands of overzealous Spaniards or due to the ravages of the elements. However, in recent years enough of the ancient murals have been uncovered so as to offer a visitor an ample picture of the skills of pre-Columbian painters.

Some of the earliest examples of Mexican fresco art (200 A.D. to 800 A.D.) can be seen on a ranch property near the great pyramid at Teotihuacán. At Tula there are both polychromed low-relief murals and mosaic murals done by Toltec artists sometime between 800 and 1200 A.D. A few Aztec murals dating from 1200 A.D. to the conquest can be seen at the archaeological site at Tenayuca near Mexico City. Others have been located in the far north, in the Jalisco region and in the south.

For many years these, and some fragmentary Mayan murals at Chichén Itzá in Yucatán, were considered the best examples of pre-Hispanic painting. However, less than a decade ago, following the discovery of a secret burial vault in the temple-pyramid at Bonampak in the State of Chiapas, excellently preserved examples of Mayan painting have been revealed. The Bonampak murals (dated about 1000 A.D.) are magnificent statements of the power, imagination, and skill of the ancient artists. They are rich in color; the designs and execution exhibit a wonderful artistic freedom.

Modern artists have been impressed by the technical command the ancient Mexican muralists had over their medium. Their pigments and fixing agents were apparently superb. The Bonampak frescoes, for example, were true frescoes done with the wet-technique in which the design, pigments, and preserving agents become an integral part of the wall surface rather than simply being painted on a wall.

Another important Indian art form, from which we have gained valuable historical information as well as an insight into Mexican art, is the Codice. The pre-Hispanic Codice is an Indian document, a kind of blending of writing and miniature painting. They were usually done on doeskin or a papyrus type paper made from maguey fibers or the pulpy center of the amatl tree. The skin or paper sheets were about 13 inches wide and from 5 to 12 feet long. The surface was treated with a thin varnish made of vegetable gum and powdered stone.[2]

Both the *tlacuilo* or picture-writer (Codices) and

[2] The Indian codices generally treated epic or historical happenings: wars, perigrinations, tribal history, etc. The great pre-Columbian libraries of Codices were burned by the Spanish. Those that remain in existence are rare and immensely valuable. They are scattered throughout the world, held in private and museum collections in Rome, Paris, etc.

From time to time limited edition reproductions of the Codices are published, along with appended scholarly interpretations of them. Two of the most recent and interesting publications of this sort are the full-color reproductions of the famous *Bourbon* and the *Bodleian Codices.* The commentaries were written by Dr. Alfonso Caso. The *Bourbon Codice* (published by Delpire in Paris) is one of the most important of the amatl paper documents, being a résumé of what the calendar meant to the ancient Mexicans. The *Bodleian Codice* reproduction, published by the Mexican Society of Anthropology, deals with the geneology of the Mixtec kings and princes from 670 A.D. to the conquest.

the muralist developed a unique, often very formalized style of painting which, hundreds of years later, greatly influenced the modern Mexican muralists. The draftsmanship of the pre-Hispanic artist, especially when delineating figures, exhibited all the directness and simplicity of a cartoon. They captured and froze moods as well as motion and color. Perspective was not understood or used, except in sculpture. Instead of showing diminishing forms and spaces to create the illusion of depth and reality, all figures were painted the same size. The artist devised a different kind of "reality" through the arrangement of figures in patterns. His palette was exceptionally brilliant,[3] and he knew how skillfully to juxtapose colors. He made free use of obvious symbols: God, earth, and element symbols; or to indicate time or movement in space, footprints meandered over a painting; or to indicate speech, song or music, little curlicues of clouds representing sounds issued from a mouth. If the cloud curled upward it indicated happy sounds or pleasant speech. If it curled downward, anger was evident.

A quite spectacular kind of decorative art that flourished before the conquest, and died out immediately afterward, was the feather painting or feather mosaic. Pictures were made by fixing countless tiny hummingbird feathers upon amatl paper, on cloth or copper. Of all the ancient Mexican arts this seemed to have been the one that most impressed the Spanish conquerors. A number of feather pictures were sent back to Spain as gifts to the royal court.

Mexican native arts all but died with the coming of the Europeans. Indian artisans were forbidden to express themselves in the old ways, being put on "parole" until they learned to see things in a Christian manner. Some who accepted conversion quickly were set to work painting murals and doing carvings for the new churches, but they always worked under Spanish guidance. European-style painting was first taught in New Spain at the Indian School established in the famous San Francisco monastery in Mexico City. This school, founded in 1521 by the Flemish padre, Fray Pedro de Gante (Peter of Ghent), also employed Rodrigo de Cifuentes, the first Spanish painter to set foot in the new world.

During the sixteenth century a sizable school of painters was active in Mexico, but not much can be said in their favor except that they used a lot of oils and canvas. They daubed indistinguishable copies of the Flemish and Spanish masters with pigments that were so inferior and faded so rapidly scarcely any examples of these junior masterpieces are recognizable today.

In the early part of the seventeenth century, after a brief period when the most highly esteemed painters in Mexico were those who could copy a good Italian like Titian or Tintoretto, tastes again changed and artists began copying Spain's Murillo, Ribera, and Zurburán. At this time several painters in Mexico, mostly Spanish-born, began to create on their own (as well as copy). The most noted were: Baltazar de Echave, called "El Viejo" ("The Elder"), and his son, Baltazar, "El Mozo" ("The Lad"). The older Echave showed a great deal of power in his composition, was an excellent draftsman and good colorist. He was zealously copied by his students and contemporaries. Along with the Echaves, Sebastián Arteaga and Luis Juárez (a native-born artist) shared honors. The works of all four hang in the Academy of San Carlos Gallery in Mexico City.

During the 1640s the eminent Spanish painter and architect, Pedro García Ferrer, paused in Puebla long enough to design the dome of the cathedral there, to carve the high altar (since destroyed) and paint six large pictures for the altar of the Chapel of the Kings. At about the same time two artists of about equal merit, Cristóbal de Villalpando and Juan Correa, collaborated in producing the outsized paintings which decorate the walls and sacristy of the cathedral in Mexico City. Correa, a very prolific painter, was also the teacher of two of Mexico's most important colonial masters — José Ibarra and Miguel Cabrera.

Ibarra (1688–1756), a clever colorist, a prolific worker, was an admirer of the Spanish master, Murillo. He was often called the Murillo of the New World and it is our suspicion that a number of the paintings attributed to Murillo, which awed early travelers in Mexico, were probably Ibarra copies. A quantity of Ibarra's canvases (as well as Murillo-school paintings) hang in the San Carlos Gallery. The four large murals that decorate the walls of the coro in the cathedral at Puebla are by Ibarra.

Miguel Cabrera (1695–1768), a Zapotec Indian, born in Oaxaca, was the more brilliant of these two artists. He had one weakness, however; he was overproductive. His work was so much in demand, he flooded the churches and private collections of Mexico with murals and canvases. As a result, much of his later work betrayed a superficial execution and handling of color, almost to the point of formula.

The establishment of the San Carlos Academy in 1778 — Académia de los Nobles Artes de San Carlos de la Nueva España — served as the deathblow to Mexican painting. The only artist who escaped its deleterious regimentation was that remarkable genius from Celaya, Francisco Eduardo Tresguerras (1745–

[3] The palette of the muralist working in true fresco techniques rather than encaustics, was limited to the earth colors. For other mediums — Codices and textile painting and polychroming of bas-reliefs — the pre-Hispanic artist developed an amazing collection of colors and dyes. At and before the time of the conquest, Aztecs, Mayans, and Zapotecs surpassed the Europeans in this field. Chief among some of their color mediums were: cochineal *(nochitzli)*, vivid permanent reds and purples compounded from an insect that feeds on the nopal cactus; blue was made from the *matlalxihuitl* flower; while indigo was pressed from the sediment obtained after soaking branches of the impossibly named *xiuhquiliptzahuac* plant in water. Other shades of red, yellows, oranges, and so on were produced by combining the juices of plants, adding alum or nitrates. As a mixing agent they used the oil from *chia* seeds, a Mexican sage.

1833). His murals in the Santa Rosa Church, Querétaro, are among the finest ecclesiastical paintings in Mexico.

During the violent years that followed the War of Independence, churches and monasteries were looted to provide funds for revolutionary groups. To carry on his disastrous war with the United States, General Santa Anna plundered churches and chapels to fill his war chest. A bit later the French marauders of the lesser Napoleon swept Mexico clean of every picture they could lay their hands on. When unable to take their booty out of the country, they destroyed the art work, as in the case of the Santo Domingo Convent in Oaxaca City where, for the sake of the canvas only, they soaked them in water and beat the paint off against stones. It is said that in the century of turmoil scores of priceless pictures were sold abroad or destroyed. A notable few escaped; for example the "Assumption of the Virgin" by Murillo which was hidden in the walls of the cathedral at Guadalajara to protect it from the repeated attempts made to gain possession of it; also preserved were the two thousand or more pictures of varied merit which now repose in the vaults and gallery of the San Carlos Academy.

While the struggle for independence raged over Mexico, followed by the epidemic of civil wars, occupation, and the Díaz dictatorship, no real painting raised its head in the country. The Academy dictated what the official art should be, namely, an aping of European styles, but unfortunately, the most middle-class, sterile and saccharine modes of Europe. During this era hardly an artist thought that Mexico was a worthy subject to paint, and only one artist reflected anything of the country.

The one exception was José María Velasco (1840–1912), an accomplished landscapist who chose the Valley of Mexico as his favorite subject. On canvas he was an excellent organizer, skilled at holding the observer's eye on the picture plane with a decorative use of rich flora, then cutting his planes to distant mountain vistas with a Poussin-like clarity.

While Mexican "official" art grew stilted, in many provincial towns and villages unrecognized portraitists and primitive painters managed to produce a kind of folk art that was vital and esthetically of high value. In a sense they proved to be a more vital link than the urban painters in joining what was good in the past to what would prove important in the future. Some of the best of this grass-roots art are the ex-voto paintings to be found in village chapels, the carved and polychromed *santos* or religious figures and the *pulquería* painting which have all but vanished in the past several decades.

The ex-voto or miracle pictures popularly called *retablos*[4] are primitive, almost perspectiveless paintings done on oblongs of tin, wood, or cardboard. Such works are commissioned by the poor, usually as a thanksgiving and commemorative offering, celebrating a miraculous escape from injury, recovery from an illness and so on. They are executed by a *retablero,* a village artist who may lack formal training, yet who often paints with a deep sincerity and innocent expressive power. Chapels often have entire walls covered with these pictures; vivid primitive illustrations of robberies, train wrecks, people falling from buildings, and always with the saint who saved the victim hovering in one corner. There is a large display of such *retablos* in the Sanctuary of Guadalupe in Morelia; a small but fine collection in the village museum in Pátzcuaro. One of the largest and best collections is exhibited in the Freida Kahlo Museum, Mexico City.

Similar in expressive feeling are the crudely carved and painted *santos* or religious images done in villages by an artisan called a *santero,* a saint-maker. These popular works rarely go into churches. They are made for altars and shrines in private homes and for the tiny Indian chapels that dot the Mexican countryside. In recent years the older saint-figures have become collectors' items.

The last of the village art forms, *pulquería* painting, was once one of the most popular of Mexican provincial arts. These were vivid, native murals, executed upon the exterior walls of village *pulque* or grog shops. Though often crude, yet colorful, they served as an important bridge between the fresco painters of ancient Mexico and the modern muralists.

During the last quarter of the nineteenth century and the early years of this one, a major figure suddenly burst upon Mexico's dormant art world. He was José Guadalupe Posada (1851–1913), a notable engraver and political caricaturist. Posada was as Mexican as a jumping bean. Full of vitality, he thoroughly shook the country with his acid caricatures and lusty portrayals of popular life. His work helped pave the way for what is frequently called the Mexican Renaissance — the flowering of the vigorous mural painting movement which has brought world fame to Mexico.

The spark that set off this renaissance was the Revolution of 1910, which pushed Porfirio Díaz out of office, turned the country upside down for a number of years and captured the imagination of practically every worthwhile Mexican artist. Prodded by the colorful Doctor Atl — Gerardo Murillo, a strange man of many talents including his passionate fixation for Mexican volcanoes — Mexico's younger artists turned their backs on the Academy and took their inspiration and cues from José Guadalupe Posada. They began to re-examine Mexico's deep-rooted traditions; they took their colors and some forms and themes from pre-Hispanic and colonial murals. Then they began to create the controversial "shouting walls," the vivid murals of contemporary Mexico.

[4] Not to be confused with the fancifully carved and gilted Churrigueresque altar backings which are also called *retablos.*

Their murals were intensely dramatic expressions of popular history, a glorification of the revolutionary spirit, of its heroes and its martyrs. They abandoned European subtleties and sophistication for easily understood symbolism as well as persuasive narrative forms and themes. They tried to be as direct as an Aztec Codice or a Bonampak mural. They did all this, as well as reviving world interest in the ancient art of true fresco.

Many of the values, as well as much of the bombast and froth that accompanied Mexico's vigorous art renaissance, can be attributed to three famous exponents of the mural arts — Orozco, Rivera, and Siqueiros.

Of the three, José Clemente Orozco (1883–1949), was the lone wolf or revolutionist-in-isolation of Mexican painting. Born in Zapotlán, Jalisco, he studied agriculture before finding his career in art. He was an ardent patriot, a passionate humanitarian and something of a caustic recluse. His paintings, always filled with intensity and violence, often lacked the mural quality of Rivera's frescoes, yet they contained a universality and a kind of abstract protest that is more in the tradition of Michaelangelo. In addition to several important mural commissions executed in the United States, his best at-home murals are in the Chapel of the Orphanage and in the assembly hall of the University, both in Guadalajara. Other Orozco murals can be seen in the National Preparatory School, in the Palace of Fine Arts and at Sanborn's House of Tiles, all in Mexico City. His home and studio in Guadalajara have been turned into a museum.

Diego Rivera (1886–1958), the second of the big three, was born in Guanajuato. Of the triumvirate, Rivera was probably the greatest interpreter of modern fresco painting. Unlike Orozco, he was an outgoing man of strong individuality and equally strong self-expression. Between 1907 and 1921, except for a brief return to Mexico, he studied and worked in Europe. In 1921 he returned to his homeland and became involved in the revolutionary movement. For almost four decades he dominated the Mexican art world with works that are both social and political propaganda.

Although some of Rivera's early murals were encaustics, most of his paintings were true frescoes (painted on wet plaster), which limited his palette to the earth colors, plus blues, greens, and blacks. His complete command of these materials and his ability to organize his subject matter into a decorative mural unit (one which can be viewed satisfactorily from any angle), is apparent in all his work. The finest of his frescoes are in the chapel at the government agricultural school at Chapingo, near Texcoco. It has been called the Sistine Chapel of the Revolution. Its massive figures of Earth and the Elements are touched with a pervading warmth resulting from the powdered red *tezontle* stone which he used as his pigment.

Other Rivera murals can be seen in the Palace of Fine Arts, in the Ministry of Education Building, at the Insurgentes Theatre, the Lerma Waterworks, all in Mexico City. Rivera was also a prolific portrait and easel painter. Especially charming are his warm scenes of Indian rural life.

Rivera's influence upon the revival of fresco paint in the United States has been due in no small degree to those frescoes he executed in San Francisco, in Detroit, and for Rockefeller Center in New York City. The latter have been destroyed, but smaller copies of them, done by the artist, are preserved in the Palace of Fine Arts in Mexico City.

David Alfaro Siqueiros (1898–), is, according to some art critics, the potentially most powerful of the big three. However, his potential has always been seriously hampered by the amount of time he has spent in jail or has devoted to revolutionary activity. The only durable Communist of the three — Rivera flitted in and out of the Communist Party as his whims dictated — Siqueiros has consciously reflected his intense proletarian leanings in his sculpturesque mural paintings. His works which are frequently left unfinished, due to appointments in prison, also reflect a preoccupation with techniques and an interest in developing new mediums as well as perspectives.

Siqueiros' murals can be seen in the Electrician Union building, in the Social Security Hospital, in the Rectory Building at University City, and in the Palace of Fine Arts, all in Mexico City.

More or less contemporary with the big three, but overshadowed by them, are a number of other painters of considerable stature in Mexico's art world, among them: Roberto Montenegro, Adolfo Best-Maugard, French-born Jean Charlot, and Miguel Covarrubias. These and other painters joined forces in 1922, forming a Syndicate of Painters and Sculptors, with the aims of having no more to do with "outmoded" European art and to create a vital Mexican art rooted in Mexican tradition. The post-Revolution governments commissioned them to cover the walls of schools and public buildings with paintings, leaving it up to the artists to choose their themes.

In the 1930s and 1940s the names of younger artists began to push forward. By this time the vigor of the Revolution began to wane. Although many of the artists were to continue doing murals, their works were often more decorative than propagandic. The themes, however, were still rooted in Mexican tradition. Among these artists the most noteworthy are: Juan O'Gorman, an architect and painter responsible for the striking acre-large stone mosaic mural on the central library building at University City and also the recently completed historical mural in the Hall of Independence in Chapultepec Palace; Chavez Morado, the author of important murals on the Ministry of Communications Building and at University City in Mexico, D.F., as well as a mural in the museum in Guanajuato.

As so often happens in art movements, a vigorous trend may become "official" and fixed in its ways. This seems to have occurred in Mexico. The art inspired by the Revolution and the social ferment of the 1920s has become academic in its own way, and with all that the word implies — disapproval of new tendencies, artistic hardening of the arteries, and so on.

There are, however, a number of Mexican artists who have gone their own way, but not without a bitter struggle with the newer academies. Often recognition within their own country has come only after recognition was gained abroad. This, to some extent, has been the case of one of Mexico's greatest modern artists, Rufino Tamayo (1899–), a man of Zapotec blood and a contemporary of Rivera and Siqueiros. Tamayo has worked a semi-abstract vein, using Mexican colors, Mexican lighting and native themes as a source of his inspiration. Although he has done murals in Mexico City (Palace of Fine Arts, Sanborn's Restaurant, etc.) he is primarily an easel painter. Another "unnoticed" yet magnificent painter is the late Francisco Goitia. Although he was of Rivera's generation, his work seems more closely related to Rouault. He remained throughout his life more or less the mystery man of Mexican contemporary art. No one noticed him much until he won the first Mexican Biennial shortly before his death.

In Mexico City there are a number of art galleries exhibiting and selling the works of contemporary painters and sculptors. See List, Index. Among the Mexican artists worthy of attention are: José Luis Cuevas, Guillermo Meza, Rufino Tamayo, Fernando Castro Pacheco, Antonio Rodriguez Luna, Hector Alaya, Juan O'Gorman, and Leopoldo Méndez. The latter is one of the most skilled and powerful printmakers of this generation.

FOLK ARTS AND HANDICRAFTS

Mexico is a land of gay and meaningful handicrafts. From pre-Hispanic times to the present each region has nurtured its traditional cottage or village crafts. Unfortunately, a great amount of the so-called crafts that tourists usually see and buy is not representative of the country's fine traditional popular arts. Souvenir shops are generally cluttered with a kind of debased folk art especially created for tourists. The worthy pieces, produced in tiny villages for village consumption and pleasure often contain a great deal of vivid artistry.

A visitor will find that much of the truly native work offers more than the immediate delights of surprising colors, pleasing forms and unusual textures. Often there is incredible and imaginative workmanship expressing a unique vision of Mexico, for the folk arts are rooted deeply in the nation's traditions.

Shopping for native craftgoods is one of the great tourist pastimes in Mexico. The city shops, the village outdoor markets, and the workshops of artisans constitute a vast treasure house of vivid hand-loomed textiles, piquantly decorated ceramics, inexpensive silver jewelry, handsome lacquerwork, leather, masks, basketry and unique toys. Each area of Mexico has its specialties. You will find tucked-away villages where everyone is weaving a certain type or color serape; others where the whole town is busily making guitars, or still another where for hundreds of years the men produce eye-dazzling, hand-hammered copperware.

The products of Mexico's indigenous artisans will be discussed in detail under the regional sections of this book. As a preview, however, here is a brief chart indicating where you may get your best buys in Mexico's colorful popular arts and crafts.

BASKETRY: Toluca, Oaxaca, Yucatán.
TINWARE: San Miguel de Allende, Mexico City.
SERAPES AND RUGS: Tlaxcala, Oaxaca, Toluca, San Miguel de Allende, Saltillo, Guadalajara, Pátzcuaro.
TEXTILES AND WEARING APPAREL: (Hand-drawn and embroidered blouses) Morelia, Pátzcuaro, Guadalajara, San Miguel de Allende, Aguascalientes, Puebla. (Resort wear and hand-loomed cottons) Mexico City, Cuernavaca, Oaxaca, Chiapas, Acapulco, San Miguel de Allende, Pátzcuaro, Guadalajara. (*Rebozos,* stoles) Morelia, San Miguel de Allende, Oaxaca, Puebla, Guadalajara, Mexico City.
STEEL CUTLERY: Morelia, Oaxaca.
CERAMICS: Oaxaca, Pátzcuaro, Puebla, Tonalá (near Guadalajara), Metepec (near Toluca), Texcoco, Dolores Hidalgo, Mexico City.
HAND-BLOWN GLASS: Guadalajara and Mexico City.
LACQUERWARE: Pátzcuaro, Uruapan and Olinalá.
COPPERWARE: Mexico City, Guadalajara and, for native hand-hammered copper, Santa Clara del Cobre, Mich.
WOODCARVING: Paracho, Mich.
SILVER: Mexico City, Taxco, Guadalajara, Oaxaca, San Miguel de Allende, Pátzcuaro.
GOLD FILAGREE: Tehuantepec, Oaxaca City, Mérida.

Before purchasing Mexican handicrafts you should visit the Museum of Popular Arts (Museo Nacional de Artes e Industrias Populares), Av. Juárez 44, Mexico City. The museum has exhibits of the best of Mexican handicrafts, and there you can familiarize yourself with regional work. The museum also has a sales section. Prices are somewhat high. In Uruapan, Tlaquepaque, and Los Alamos, there are smaller regional branches of the museum.

The most complete and up-to-date book in English on Mexican arts and crafts, including a history of their development and where to buy them, is *In Mexico,* by James Norman, (William Morrow & Company, New York).

MUSIC

From the colonial period until recently Mexico's musical development, excepting folk music, was closely tied with musical trends in Europe. Continental composers, operas, and artists were brought to

Mexico and were the principal influences on native-born composers. It was not until the turn of this century that a nationalist musical movement developed in Mexico.

This movement, utilizing popular folk airs and themes in composed music, was introduced by Manuel Ponce (1886–1948). Ponce, a sensitive and talented artist, is best remembered for his orchestral compositions "Chapultepec" and "Ferial," for his chamber music and songs. Most people abroad are familiar with his lovely lieder-type song, "Estrellita."

Perhaps the most brilliant, although sometimes uneven, Mexican composer was Silvestre Revueltas (1899–1940). He embraced native themes and, as one musicologist has said, "he was a pessimistic lover of the picturesque." His best known works for orchestra and for ballet are the striking "Cuauhnahuac," "Colorines," "Janítzio," "Ventanas, Caminos y Esquinas" and the sensitive string quartet composition, "Magueyes."

Since 1928 Carlos Chávez (1899–) has led Mexico through a stormy intensification of musical activity. Noted both as a composer and conductor, Chávez has variously headed the government's department of Fine Arts, the National Conservatory of Music, the fine arts section of the Department of Public Education, the Symphony Orchestra of Mexico, as well as conducting abroad. His "Concerto for Piano and Orchestra," composed in 1942, did for Mexican music internationally what De Falla's "Concierto para Clave" did for Spain. His ballet-symphony "H.P." was first played by the Philadelphia Grand Opera Company in 1932. Chávez has done a great deal toward arousing interest in pre-Columbian themes, utilizing old Indian legends and music, especially in his ballets "Four Suns," "New Fire," and through his imaginative re-creation of the pre-Hispanic orchestra (utilizing ancient instruments) in his composition "Xochipili-Macuilchitl."

Other important contemporary composers in Mexico are: Luis Sandi, conductor of the excellent Coro Madrigalista, and composer of choral and orchestral works; Miguel Bernal Jiménez, a student of colonial church music, and composer of the opera, *Tato Vasco;* also, José Moncayo, Eduardo Hernández Moncada, and Blás Galindo.

Although a truly Mexican vein in formal music is relative new, the folk, popular, and dance music of the country has had a considerably longer and indigenous history. The mysterious property that music has of absorbing the sights, sounds, and moods of a country is outstandingly apparent in the case of Mexico.

The traditional songs and tunes of the different regions are primarily a blend of Spanish and Indian elements or, as the perceptive Zapotec writer, Andrés Henestrosa, puts it, "Mexican songs are Indian inside, European outside — Spanish tears in native eyes. All are *mestizo;* Spanish melody and Indian melancholy." Of course, there is much more to Mexican popular music than this simple duality. The people of Mexico are musical blotters; they soak up anything and everything that contains rhythm or melody. A wide variety of exotic influences have been fused in the popular music: pre-Hispanic rhythms, tinges of flamenco and Moorish embellishments, the beat from Africa and the tunes from northern Spain and even Italy.

Mexicans undoubtedly inherited much of their feeling for percussion rhythms and for the dance from their Mayan, Zapotec, and Aztec ancestors. Of that ancient music, not too much is known yet. No musical notations were left for historians to pour over. However, we do know that music played an usually important role in the lives and ceremonies of the pre-Columbian people. Their music was not written to be played simply as music, like our quartets and symphonies. Music was always linked with song and dance. The Aztecs, for example, maintained the *cuicacuilli,* houses-of-song, where singing and dancing were taught. All children at the age of twelve were required to attend or suffer severe punishment. The Náhatl name for poet, *cuicani,* also meant a singer. Poetry was always sung, or during recitation, accompanied by musical instruments.

The ancient instruments were primarily percussions: clay and wooden drums, rasps contrived of notched bones and sticks, various rattles, turtle-shell drums, as well as conch-shell horns and simple flutes. Many of these instruments still play an important part in the ceremonial music of the present-day Seri, Yaqui, Huichol, and Tzotzil Indians. This is especially true of the drums.

Like Haiti and Africa, Mexico is a country of drums. All important fiestas are heralded in advance by drum sounds. You hear the repetitious, utterly mesmerizing beat echoing through narrow village streets, day and night, before a fiesta. Then, during the fiesta dances, again there are drums. For ceremonial dances two unusual drums are played, the same drums the Indians used a thousand years ago. One is the *huehuetl,* a vertical war drum with a skinhead and a tone so resonant it can be heard miles away. The other, the *teponaztle,* is a rather long, horizontal instrument hollowed from a log. It is usually beautifully carved and has a slotted playing surface with two wooden tongues that are partially free. Four different tones can be gotten from the drum, depending on where the tongues are struck.

The flutes you will undoubtedly hear during fiestas are made of clay, of bone or reed. These have hardly changed since pre-Hispanic times. The most common type, called the *chirimía,* looks like a short wooden flageolet, though it is actually a primitive oboe with a double palm-leaf reed.

The present-day folk orchestra has absorbed some of these ancient instruments and has added several imports: the brass horn and trumpet, guitars, violins, harps, and, in the Chiapas region, the African marimba. Of all of these, the guitar and its numerous variations have become the most popular instruments in Mexico. Among the fanciful variations are: the *guitarrón,* a huge hunched-back guitar resembling a bass viol; the *vihuela,* a half-sized guitar; the *jarana,* a small ukulele-guitar that is popular along the Gulf Coast; and the *concha,* an Indian ceremonial guitar which has an armadillo shell for a soundbox. In the far south, the Chamula and Tzotzil Indians fashion a twelve-string guitar, which, when played, sounds like the rushing of water in a deep canyon.

Of Mexico's popular music *(música popular* or *música folklórica),* the songs of the more isolated ethnic groups or Indian tribes are least influenced by European melodies. The songs of the Tarascan Indians in Michoacán and the Seri Indians in Sonora are unusually melodic and have haunting qualities to them. Seri songs are often sung without accompaniment.

In Mexico singing is almost a disease. Bus drivers, mule-skinners, your cook and your maid sing all day; songs burst out of taverns; pilgrims afoot on the road sing. Mexicans seemed to be blessed with perfect pitch. The Mexican male, especially, often has a rich, bel-canto voice. Even the singing cowboys and matinee idols of the silver screen can *actually* sing. They put our Sinatras and Crosbys to shame.

The song bag below the Río Grande is quite rich. In addition to the primitive Indian songs, there are chants and religious songs heard in village *coloquias* (an indigenous medieval miracle or mystery play); there are the *corridos;* the *cancíon popular* and *ranchera* songs; popular dance songs, the *sones* (tunes), the *jarabes* and *huapangos* from the hot country, from Jalisco and the south.

The *corridos* are of unusual interest because they reflect so much of the life of rural Mexico as well as the outlook and moods of the people. These songs are folk ballads, the name coming from the word *ocurrida,* meaning "happening." Until the advent of the radio, they served as a kind of news service; the ballad singer wandering from village to village, exchanging his songs which included bits of sly local gossip and news for food and tortillas. Although they are descended from the Spanish romances, they lack the literary style of the latter. Their themes run the gamut of historical events; the Revolution, the agrarian movement, politicians, love, executions, bandits, brave men and so on. Some of the most famous *corridos* are: "Benito Canales" (with more than forty-five verses), "The Suicide of Julian Ramírez," "Delgadina" and "Siete Leguas." This last, now a jukebox favorite, is an excellent *corrido* and the commercial version is well sung by Miguel Aceves Mejía.

The *canción ranchera* (ranch song) grew out of the *corrido* and is rapidly replacing it. It reflects much of the anguish, bittersweet melancholy and violence of Mexico, being full of references to *tequila,* doves, adultery and unrequited love.

The *sones* or tunes are mostly derived from nineteenth-century Spanish waltzes, so spiced to Mexican tastes they are now recognizable only as Mexican. They come in all varieties: *sones de Jalisco, sones abajenos, sones* from the tropic or Gulf region. Those from around Veracruz are tempered with African rhythms; those from Oaxaca and the Isthmus take on a gracious quality. One *son* from Tehuantepec, the "Zandunga," has almost become a national air. One should dance barefooted to this haunting melody, as the women do there.

In the State of Jalisco and throughout much of the central plateau, groups of wandering minstrels, the *mariachis,* dominate the field of the *ranchera* and love song. Dressed in the traditional *charro* costume (See Index) and equipped with fine voices, guitars, fiddles and a trunkful of songs, they hire out for serenades and parties. The most popular of their numbers is "Las Mañanitas" ("The Little Mornings"), a dulcet, sentimental thing, sung for birthdays or to welcome someone to the community. Usually the musicians gather in the street before dawn, and wake the entire neighborhood with their tribute.

Another traditional serenade, the *gallo* or rooster, is the young man's way of courting in Mexico. Sometimes alone, or accompanied by a small army of *mariachis,* an ardent lover appears beneath his girl's window shortly after midnight — the hour when the cock crows. The opening song that is sung is "Si Estás Dormida" ("If You Are Asleep"). The serenaded girl may peek cautiously from behind curtains and should be overjoyed to be so rudely awakened. Following the rendition of a sizable number of other songs, the young man is supposed to leave his calling card on the window sill, if he can reach it. In Guadalajara, where such things are done with élan, the suitor may fire his pistol a few times to make sure the young lady is awake or, as in one instance, he may show up with the entire Don Cossack chorus.

Here is a brief list of recorded Mexican folk music. The records can be purchased in music shops in Mexico or ordered directly from the recording companies.

Folkways Records and Service Corp., 117 W. 46th Street, New York 36, N.Y., has issued the following records:

Songs of Mexico, 3 vols. LP FW6815 and FW6853
Ten Mexican Corridos, LP FW6913
Yaqui Dances, LP FW6957
Indian Music of Mexico (ethnic series), LP FW4413
Folk Songs of Mexico, LP FW8727
Music of the Indians in Mexico, LP FW8815
Tarascan and other Music of the Mexican Plateau, LP FW8867

The Cook Laboratories, 101 Second Street, Stamford, Connecticut, has issued the following:

Blind Troubador of Oaxcaca, (Mexican Love Songs by Alonzo Cruz and guitar) LP 5019
The Voice of Mexico, (the classical guitar of Gustavo Zepoll) LP 10248

Capitol Records has the following:

Mariachis de México, (Dora María and Pepe Villa's Mariachis) LP T10035
Marimbas Méxicanas, (marimba from Chiapas) LP T10043
Mexican Rancheras, (Los Centaros and Dora María) LP T10102
Sones Méxicanos, (with Antonio Maciel, Los Aguillas and the Mariachi México, conducted by Rafael Carrión) LP T10135
Los Tres Caballeros, (popular songs) LP T10152

RCA Records:

Mexican Folk Songs, (Miguel Aceves Mejía singing) LPM-1077
Memories of Jorge Negrete, LPM-1363
The Man from Mexico, (Miguel Aceves Mejía) LPM-1460

Vanguard Records:

México, Alta Fidelidad! (Conjunto Medellion and Lino Chavez, and other folk ensembles) LP VRS-9006
Mexican Panorama, (200 years of folk songs) LP VRS-9014

FOLK DANCES

There are few countries in the world where native dances are as varied, brilliant, and long-historied as the dances of Mexico. Such dances, among the most vivid attractions for visitors in Mexico, include a great number that are pre-Columbian Indian in origin, and many that were brought from Europe and modified in the Mexican climate.

Although the Spanish conquerors tried to suppress the pagan rituals, the early Franciscan and Dominican fathers allowed the Indians to continue their chants and dances, often incorporating them into Catholic ceremony and celebrations. Although the ancient dances remained more or less the same, there occurred subtle changes. For example, the Aztec conflict dance which symbolized the eternal struggle between good and evil, night and day, became a Christian dance; the old gods were put aside, being replaced by the Church and the devil, or Moors and Christians. The dances honoring the Aztec Earth Mother, Tonantzin, were celebrated around a hill called Tepeyac. Today the same dances, the same vivid costumes, and the same music joins at Tepeyac to honor another mother, the Virgin of Guadalupe, whose shrine was built there.

For the tourist anxious to see some of the more colorful indigenous dances, your best bet is to find a town or village where an important fiesta is in progress. See Index — Fiesta Calendar — for principal fiesta dates. Some hotels in Mexico frequently have regional dancers in to entertain their guests. These are not floor shows. The dancers are the same men and women you'll see in a tiny village fiesta.

Here, briefly, are descriptions of the more colorful Mexican folk and indigenous dances:

Los Voladores — part dance, part ritual and part acrobatic entertainment. According to George C. Vaillant,[5] in pre-Hispanic times it was an important Aztec and Huasteca ceremony "involving the erection of a high pole at the top of which a movable platform was socketed. Men dressed as gods or the birds into which the gods transformed themselves, and, fastened by ropes wound around the platform, leaped off into space. As they did so, the ropes, unwinding, rotated the platform and gave the effect of flight to the circling performers."

Nowadays the performance is done by Otomí, Huastecan, Totonac, and Mexican Indians. The pole they swing from is some thirty feet high. Four to six fliers, young men costumed as hawks (at Pahuatlán, Hgo., one of them is dressed as a woman — Cortés' mistress, Malinche), climb to the revolving platform where a musician sits. Following a short ceremony, a kind of dance on the cramped platform, the fliers swing out into space making thirteen revolutions around the pole, the number symbolizing the thirteen months of the Aztec calendar.

The Deer Dances (pascolas) — performed at most Yaqui and Tarahumara Indian festivals in northern Mexico, was originally a ceremony to induce good luck on the hunt. In the more progressive settlements the dance takes place beneath an open-sided thatched arbor which also shelters the patron saint of the community. A barefooted dancer, naked from the waist up, and wearing a kind of kilt and a stuffed deerhead, is accompanied in the dance by two or more *pascolas* or clowns. The dance is a formalized pantomime of a deer hunt. In the High Sierras the Indians do without the thatched arbor and clowns. Instead, their ceremony occurs at night around a huge bonfire over which the dancers leap. In this more primitive dance the *pascolas* are replaced by coyotes and the dance is a vivid mimicry of an exciting hunt, at times done so eerily and magnificently one gets the impression that the dancer has actually turned into a deer.

The Matachín Dances — are masquerade and coyote dances performed by the Coros, Mayos, Yaquis, and Tarahumaras in northern and northwest Mexico. Less complicated and impressive than the deer dances, they are nevertheless important ritual dances. The *Matachines* or masqueraders are formed in a semireligious brotherhood called Soldiers of the Virgin. They wear a variety of elaborate costumes: white shirts with colored ribbons woven across the front, red bandannas upon the head and crowns of flowers. They perform at funerals, at all important church fiestas. In some villages they do a ribbon dance around a kind of maypole.

[5] *The Aztecs of Mexico,* George C. Vaillant, Doubleday.

The Conchero Dances — the *conchero* dancers who take their name from the *concha* or armadillo shell guitar which accompanies the dance, are by far the largest ceremonial dance organization in the country. It is estimated that there are some 30 or 40 thousand *conchero* dancers in the central states of Mexico, Guanajuato, Querétaro, Hidalgo, and Tlaxcala. They are much more sophisticated than most Mexican indigenous dancers for many of the dancers are *mestizo* and the organization has included some North Americans. This army of dancers is formed in groups called *mesas* (from the table or altar that each group gathers around in its chapel or captain's home).

The *concheros* have elaborate initiations, observe stiff regulations and meet regularly to practice their dances. Their costumes are vivid adaptations of pre-Columbian dress: capes, brilliant feathered headgear, sandals, shields, curious skirts — and when the spirit moves them, BVD's. Their musical instruments include the concha guitar, the vertical *huehuetl* drum, the horizontal *teponaxtli* drum, and a variety of rattles. Their dance steps, disarmingly complicated, are full of religious symbolism — crosses, the four winds and so on.

The Sonajero Dances — Dance of the Bows and Rattles, popular in the northwest and some of the central states. Although there are many regional variations of these dances, they are generally marked by an almost machinelike drive and vigor. In the Aguascalientes region the dancers are young men selected for their endurance and hardness. They wear bright red skirts and pants decorated with rows of reeds tipped with colored wool, red woolen socks, and sandals. They all wear crowns adorned with mirrors, beads, and feathers. Each dancer carries a painted rattle or a toy-size bow and arrow. They dance to *sones* played on a violin and a crude drum called a *tepenaje*. The dance steps and figures are as usual symbolical of the cross and the elements.

Dance of the Moors and Christians — *Los moros y los cristianos,* — a popular fiesta dance which was introduced immediately after the conquest and replaced the ancient pagan "conflict dances." In the various versions of the dance the actors, some dressed as Moors, others as Christian soldiers, enact battles, fighting with machetes and other weapons. The costumes are often full of anachronisms and one will see French Zouaves with kepis and other rare outfits.

A similar "conflict dance," *Los Santiagos,* re-enacts the story of Saint James fighting the heathens. The principal dancer has parts of a small white wooden horse tied around his waist so that it appears as if he were riding it.

The Quetzales — which takes its name from the brilliantly plumed tropical quetzal bird, is a simple dance made remarkable by the dazzling costumes of the celebrants. The costumes consist of vividly colored three-quarter-length short trousers, white or colored shirts trimmed with ribbons, silk capes that fall over the shoulders, colored stockings and sandals. But most extraordinary is the quetzal headdress, a huge wheel-like affair measuring some five feet across made with interlaced colored papers, slender reeds and vivid feathers. It is attached to a conical cap which rests on the head of the dancer and is tied under the chin by ribbons.

Los Viejitos — the dance of the little old men, celebrated in the Michoacán country, is said to date back before the conquest. The dancers are boys or young men who wear elaborately carved and lacquered masks representing old men. They wear long flaring trousers handsomely embroidered at the bottoms, a tunic with a red sash, a *chaleco,* a broad-brimmed straw hat, and each dancer carries a staff with an animal's head carved at the handle.

The dancers begin by acting like rheumatic old men, but in the course of the dance their pace quickens, the steps become lively and they end up doing a series of gay *zapateados.*

Each district, each region in Mexico has its special ritual dances and their number is legion. In almost all, the costumes are among the glories of Mexican popular arts. There is no end to their variety and brilliance. And in the dances themselves one finds traces of both irony and humor, a delicate softness as well as a driving violence.

Besides the many hundreds of ritual dances, Mexico has numerous traditional popular dances which come closer to the Western idea of folk dancing. These Mexican counterparts of our reels and polkas are based on tunes and steps of Spanish provenance. The more noteworthy among them are:

The Jarabe Tapatío — which originated in Guadalajara, Jalisco, has become the national folk dance. It is the dance form that most Americans visualize when they think of a Mexican fiesta.

The costumes worn are: for women, the *china poblana* dress; for men, the *charro* or horseman's outfit consisting of silver-embellished tight suède trousers, a leather jacket with silver embroidery, a huge sombrero, gun belt, pistol, and spurs. The dance itself consists of nine lively melodies and dance figures, the participants moving around one another, but always a reserved distance apart. The final figure, The Dove, is a gay, flirtatious finale in which the man follows his partner as she dances around the broad brim of his sombrero which has been placed on the floor. As the girl stoops to pick up the hat the man passes his right leg over her. They end the dance by stealing a kiss behind the shelter of the hat.

The Zandunga — meaning elegant or graceful, is the favorite folk dance of the Isthmus of Tehuantepec region. The music, a *son* derived from the Spanish waltz, is sentimental and romantic, with a touch of melancholy. For the dance the girls wear the traditional Tehuantepec fiesta costume, including the lacy headdress (see Index). They move about with stately grace, the girls never looking at their partners and the latter, as though exasperated, dance about the barefooted girls in a variety of quick heel-and-toe clicking steps.

The Huapangos — a rhythmic dance performed on a platform or wooden floor which serves as a kind of drumhead or sound box. It is one of the most popular of folk dances, especially in the Veracruz region. The name is derived from the Aztec *cuah-panco-cuaitl,* meaning wood-over-place. The tunes however are of European origin with Afro-Cuban elements added.

During fiestas in the idyllic town of Tlacotalpan, up the River of Butterflies, in Veracruz, there are four dance platforms, one at each corner of the plaza. On a fiesta evening musicians gather and begin playing their small *jaranas,* guitars, and a tiny harp called a *requinto.* They turn out an energetic, flowery music, often accompanied by song. When a man invites a woman to dance the *huapango,* he doesn't bow or take her hand or beg permission — he simply takes off his hat. The woman takes her place opposite him on the platform. Without conversation, and with facial expressions as fixed as stone sculpture, they begin to dance. The steps are sharp and deliberate, the couples wind in and out, their heels stamping a rhythm that has the proud force of an Aragonese *jota.*

If the woman gets tired — you can never tell if she is enjoying the dance or is bored for her expression never changes — she merely walks off of the platform without so much as glancing at her partner. If someone wants to cut in he simply sets his straw hat on the woman's head. The woman will remove it if she doesn't want a new partner. Or, her partner can remove the hat from her head and hold it until the dance is over. As the night lengthens the singing and dancing become more intense — a dance of stone-faced sonambulists. Even the verses of the songs, growing more improper through the night, seem to have no effect.

Here and there in the crowds around the wooden stands you'll see a pretty girl wearing a peculiar ornament that goes with these dances. The ornament is one that makes a woman's hair sparkle wondrously, as though her tresses were sprinkled with living jewels. These hair ornaments are *cocoyos,* small black beetles with greenish phosphorescent spots that glow. Secured with a bit of thread, the beetles are worn as lapel and hair decorations.

22. *A Thumbnail Sketch of Mexican Literature*

Father Landa, historian of the invasion of Yucatán, says in his *Las Cosas de Yucatán:* "The Maya priests wrote books about their various sciences and imparted their knowledge to those whom they considered worthy of enlightenment. . . . We found a great number of their books, but because there was nothing in them that had not some superstition or falsehood of the Devil, we burned them all, at which the natives were marvelously sorry and distressed."

Since no one as yet has quite deciphered Mayan writing, Father Landa and other Spaniards who destroyed so much of Mexico's pre-Hispanic literature must have been prompted by superstition and bigotry rather than a knowledge of what Mayan and Aztec writings contained. Landa's book-burning was duplicated in Central Mexico where Don Juan de Zumárraga, the first bishop of Mexico, had collected countless Aztec and Texcocoan documents, piled them in the marketplace at Tlatelolco and set the torch to them.

Despite the destruction enough of the ancient texts were saved, or buried and later recovered, to give us some idea of Mexico's earliest literature. According to George C. Valliant much of the pictographic writing of the Aztecs was too simple to record as literature, yet a great body of poetic and dramatic literature was created in the pre-Hispanic world, most of it kept alive through recitations and word of mouth.

Many of the works of the famed Texcocoan poet-king, Netzahualcóyotl, were translated by a native historian, Fernando de Alba Ixtlilxóchitl who was a native of Texcoco and a descendant of the sovereigns of that kingdom.[1] Today, of course, there is some question as to how much of Netzalhualcóyotl's poems were his own, or how much Ixtlilxóchitl added to them.

In recent years there has been intensive research done in the field of pre-Hispanic literature and numerous translations (from Náhuatl to Spanish) have been published. Among them: Brinton's *Ancient Náhuatl Poems,* Angel María Garibay's monumental *Historia de la Literatura Náhuatl* and numerous publications issued by the press of the National University.

For a period immediately after the conquest the development of any worthy literature was hindered by the establishment of the Inquisition and a rigorous censorship which tolerated little else than theological writings and church histories. Among the latter, however, there appeared some excellent accounts of the conquest: Fray Toribio de Benevente's *Historia de los Indios* and his *Historia Eclesiástica,* also Bernal Díaz del Castillo's *Historia Verdadera de la Conquista.* Other historians of merit from whom we get

[1] Fernando de Alba Ixtlilxóchitl is said to have been the son of one of the principal wives (or the queen) of Netzahualpilli. Shortly after the coming of the Spaniards he mastered Castilian, was baptized and acted as interpreter for the Viceroy. He devoted himself to recording and translating Texcocoan songs and histories. He wrote the first history of the Toltecs (see Index).

an ample picture of the religious, political and Indian affairs of the time were: Torquemada, Fray Bartolomé de Las Casas, Fray Baltazar de Medina, and Gerónimo de Mendieta.

In colonial Mexico the import of foreign books was forbidden, while the reading of poetry, novels, and other entertainments was also discouraged. Nevertheless printing in the New World got its start in Mexico. The first printed book was Fray Juan de Estrada's *Escala Espiritual para Llegar al Cielo (Spiritual Ladder for Reaching Heaven),* translated from the Latin and published in Mexico City in 1535. Although the book no longer exists, it was a printing landmark, for it appeared one hundred years before the first press was established at Cambridge, and a quarter of a century before Shakespeare's birth.

The first wood engraving printed in the New World was the title page of Juan Gerson's *Tripartido* issued in 1544. The first sheet music came from the same press in 1566. By 1761 there were six printing presses in Mexico.

During the seventeenth century censorship was relaxed and writers turned to poetry, essays, drama, and criticism as well as history. The three most prominent literary figures of that era were Juan Ruiz de Alarcón, Carlos de Siguenza y Góngora and Sor Juana Inés de la Cruz.

Juan Ruiz de Alarcón (1580–1639) was born in Mexico, studied both in Mexico and Spain and at the age of thirty-three finally settled in Madrid where he distinguished himself as a playwright.

Carlos de Siguenza y Góngora (1645–1700) was a poet, philosopher, mathematician, and essayist in whose work one finds the beginnings of intellectual curiosity and a certain opposition to religious concepts.

Sor Juana Inés de la Cruz (1648–95) was colonial Mexico's most unusual woman. She was born in Nepantla, Mexico, where, as a child, she attracted notice because of her amazing intellectual capacities. Since there was no place in colonial society for a woman of her abilities, she entered a convent where she was able to devote herself to studies in the sciences of the day: music, painting, and literature. Several of her paintings are among the best of that period. However, she is most noted as Mexico's greatest colonial poet.

The first truly Mexican classic was the picaresque novel *El Periquillo Sarniento,* created by José Joaquin Fernández de Lizardi (1771–1827), who wrote under the pseudonym of El Pensador Mexicano. This book, full of quaint humor, biting wit, and gently ironic portrayals of the national character, was first published in Cuba, for the author had already earned the enmity of the Spanish viceroy in Mexico and had been jailed and persecuted as a result of his satiric attacks on the clergy.

Throughout much of the nineteenth century Mexican literature reflected the disorganization of the times. Most published works dealt with Mexican history and social movements, the propagation of European humanism, as well as some poetry of a romantic nature. Between 1849 and 1852 Lucas Alamán wrote his excellent *Historia de México* and his *Disertaciones Sobre la Historia de la República,* the latter still one of the best works on the Mexican independence movement.

In 1840, almost twenty years after Mexico became independent of Spain, the Spanish crown sent a Señor Calderon de la Barca as its envoy to the Mexican Republic. He was accompanied by his wife, a Scottish-English woman who, in 1843, published a book called *Life in Mexico,* one of the most delightful and entertaining books ever written about the country.

During the latter part of the century there was a so-called literary revival, largely romantic, inspired by the lyricism of Spain and France. Its hero was the poet Manuel Acuña who committed suicide over a love affair. Among the noteworthy poets of this period were: Guillermo Prieto (1818–97), *Romancero Nacional* (National Romance) and *Musa Callejera,* (Curbstone Idyls). To some extent the modernist influences of the brilliant Nicaraguan writer, Rubén Darío, and the Cuban, José Martí, were felt in Mexico. Authors such as Justo Sierra (1848–1912) and Manuel Gutiérrez Najera (1859–95) charged Mexican literature with a much-needed new psychological and philosophical depth. However, it was not until the Revolution (1910) and the years after that a widespread vitality infected writers.

Until the 1920s most Mexican novelists, essayists, and dramatists inhabited a rose bower. Little of their work reflected the nature and realities of the moment. They toyed with excessive romanticism and were nourished on moonlight and roses. The Revolution succeeded in shaking up the literary scene much as it did the art world.

In 1925 Mariano Azuela published his *Los de Abajo (The Underdogs)* and it has stood out as the first major Mexican novel since Fernández de Lizardi's earlier classic. Azuela's book, picaresque in form, dealt with ordinary people caught up in civil war. It created what is called "the Mexican Revolutionary novel." It was soon followed in 1928 by Martín Luis Guzmán's powerful novelized autobiography *El Aguila y la Serpiente (The Eagle and the Serpent)* which also dealt with the Revolution. These books broke through the romantic "moonlight curtain" and touched the lives of ordinary people, thus paving the way for other writers who were to deal with various aspects of Mexican life — rural mores, urban realism, and Indian life.

During the past several decades Mexican literature has continued to show remarkable vitality. Numerous works of interest both to the student and tourist have appeared, notably the historical, social, and philosophical writings of Alfonso Reyes, José Vasconcelas, Elí de Gortari, and Octavio Paz. Of especial interest to foreigners who wish to gain a basic understanding of Mexican life and outlook is Octavio Paz' *El Laberinto de la Soledad* (1925).

Among the contemporary novelists and short-story writers the most outstanding are: Augustín Yañez, the former governor of the State of Jalisco, whose *Al Filo del Agua* is a powerful fictional study of village life; Juan Rulfo, whose *Pedro Páramo* and *El Llano en Llamas* sketch out excellent pictures of Mexican mores; Carlos Fuentes, author of *La Region más Transparente;* and Luis Spota, an occasionally powerful but uneven journalist and novelist whose many works *(Casi el Paraíso* and *La Sangre Enemiga,* etc.) are the current best sellers. The most important short-story writer in Mexico at present is Juan José Arreola *(Varia Invención* and *Confabulario),* whose works have a remarkable subtlety and depth. Among the dramatists one of the most important is Rudolfo Usigli.

Although the first book published in the New World came from a Mexican press, Mexico's publishing industry is chaotic and limited. Several publishing houses, including the National University, publish a vast number of important titles in the fields of philosophy, history and critical essays. The average edition of such works, as well as works of fiction, is extremely small — often 500 to 1000 copies. Between 1948 and 1958 only 475 original works of fiction (novels and short stories) were published. Of these, 218 titles were written, edited, and financed by the authors themselves. One of Mexico's best contemporary books, Rulfo's *El Llano en Llamas* (issued by the largest private publishing firm, La Fonda de la Cultura Economica), sold 2000 copies in twenty-five months. Top best-selling author Luis Spota rarely expects a larger sale than 5000 copies.

23. *Archaeology, Ancient Ruins, and Artifacts*

Centuries ago Mexico enjoyed the unique fortune of playing host to some of the greatest of Amerindian civilizations — the Olmec, Maya, Zapotec, Toltec, and Aztec. Such ancient civilizations contributed importantly toward the formation of Mexico's present-day cultural and racial heritage. (See Index: *A Digest of Mexican History.*) The archaeological remains of these cultures have also added a culminating touch to Mexico as a tourist attraction.

Much the same as Egyptian archaeology intrigued the world around the turn of the century, today Mexican ruins have become a subject of world interest. Dozens of universities and institutes are busily digging through Mexico's archaeological treasures which less than a half-century ago were hidden by jungle growth or buried under fields. At present there are some 2000 known and recorded sites — rich constructions, ancient cities, temples, tombs, and ceremonial structures. It is estimated that there are countless others still to be found. When asked what is his favorite archaeological ruin, archaeologist Franz Blom usually replies "The ones we haven't found yet, but may stumble on next week."

Of the known ruins there are many that can be reached easily and are of unusual interest to the tourist, student, artist, or photographer. Travel agents offer well-conducted tours to a handful of interesting archaeological zones: Teotihuacán, Tula, Monte Albán and Mitla, Chichén Itzá, El Tajín, and others. A traveler in Mexico will find it worth his time to spend at least several days browsing, guided or unguided, at such colorful locales.

The more serious traveler, amateur archaeologist, historian, or artist seeking a more rounded picture of Mexico's ancient past should make contact with the Escuela Nacional de Antropología e Historia (the training school for archaeologists in Mexico), as well as the Department of Archaeology of the University of the Americas (see Index: *Study in Mexico*), and also the government department charged with the care of pre-Hispanic monuments, Dirección de Monumentos Prehispánicos.

At the end of this section is a partial list of the more important archaeological sites in Mexico. Many of them can be easily reached by car, plane or train.

ARTIFACTS

For more than two centuries after the Spanish conquest, Mexico's ancient treasures — sculpture, ceramics, Indian jewelry, and idols remained buried and unwanted. But in the late 1860s when Maximilian's troops returned from Mexico to France, carrying with them countless unique figurines, European collectors began to take an interest in Mexican archaeological artifacts. One of the most famous of these art objects was the stone statue of the goddess Tlazolteotl in the act of giving birth to a child. A French soldier sold it to a Parisian collector for a few francs. Since then it has passed through many hands and is now in the private collection of the American connoisseur Robert Woods Bliss. The figure is presently insured for $80,000.

Such treasures are now considered better investments than diamonds. During the past decade world

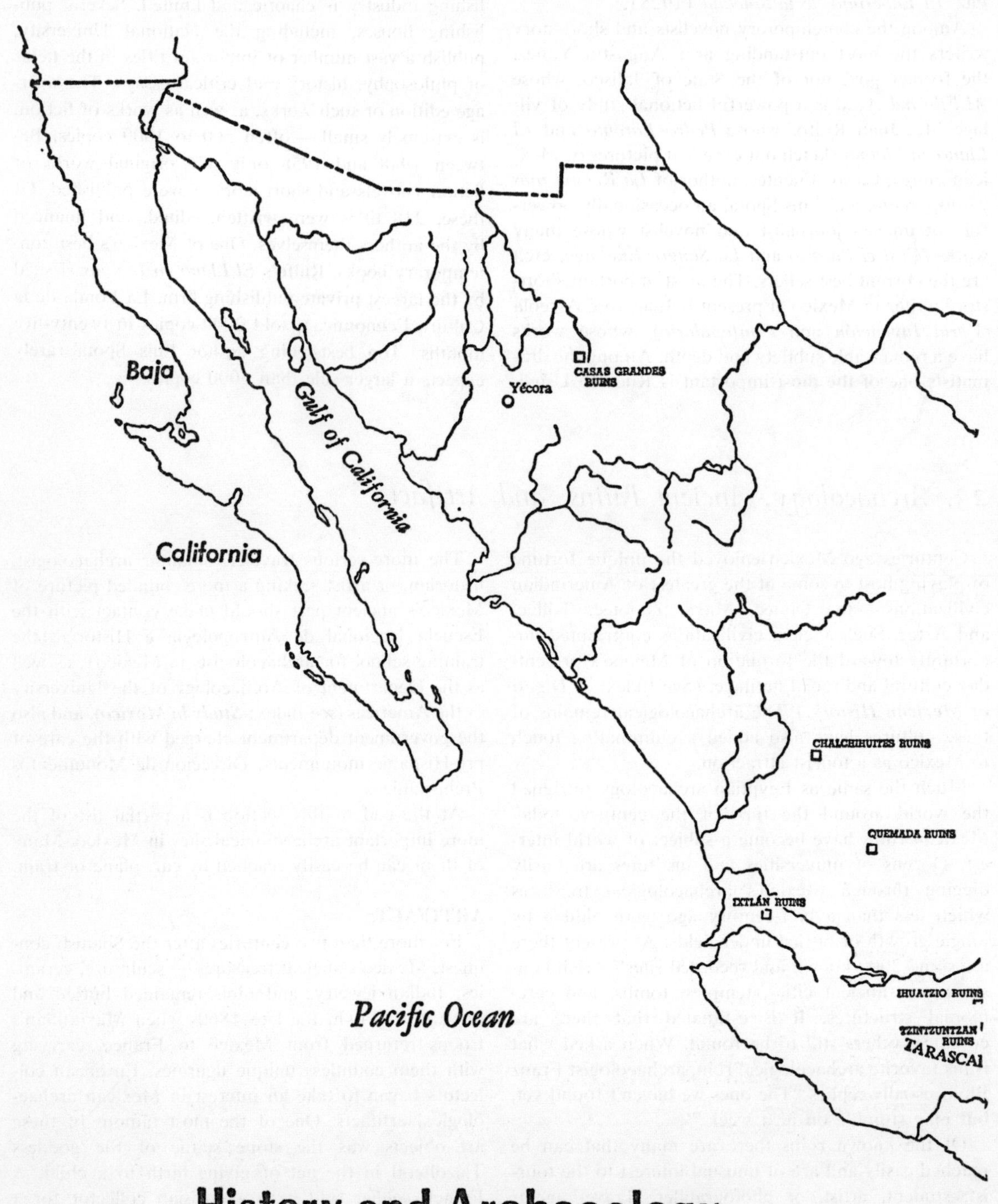

History and Archaeology

UNITED STATES
Nueces R.
Gulf of Mexico
TAMUÍN RUINS
Dolores Hidalgo
Querétaro
Guanajuato
TOLTEC
Zempoala
TOLLAN RUINS
TEOTIHUACÁN
TEXCOCO RUINS
TEOTIHUACÁN
TACUBA
TLALOC
COPILCO
YIZATLÁN
TLAXCALA
Tlaxcala
TENOCHTITLÁN
CHOLULA RUINS
TEPOZTLÁN
CALIXTLAHUACA
MALINALCO
XOCHICALCO
TEOPANZOLCO RUINS
LOS MONOS RUINS
CUICUILCO
TEXCOCO
AZTEC
EL TAJÍN RUINS
CASTILLO DE TEAYO RUINS
HUATUXCO RUINS
ZEMPOALA RUINS
SAN JUAN ULÚA (ISLAND)
TOTONACPAN RUINS
TOTONAC
OLMEC
HUEYAPAN RUINS
LA VENTA RUINS
Chilpancingo
MIXTEC
MONTE ALBÁN RUINS
YAGUL RUINS
ZAPOTEC
MITLA RUINS
GUIEN-GOLA RUINS
ZAACHILA RUINS
Gulf of Tehuantepec
Bay of Campeche
DZBILCHALTUN RUINS
MAYAPAN RUINS
CHICHÉN-ITZÁ RUINS
Cozumel Island
ISLA DE JAINA RUINS
UXMAL RUINS
LABNÁ RUINS
ZAYIL RUINS
TULUM RUINS
MAYAN
XPUHIL RUINS
UAXAYÚN RUINS
PALENQUE RUINS
TONINÁ RUINS
TIKAL
QUIRIQUÁ RUINS
YAXCHILÁN RUINS
BONAMPAK RUINS
BR. HONDURAS
GUATEMALA
COPÁN RUINS
HONDURAS

interest in pre-Columbian treasures has fostered a lively hunt for them and a huge trade in them. Thousands of artifacts are smuggled across the border each year.

When you travel in Mexico you may be offered such art objects. Be cautious about purchasing them. According to Mexican law (designed to protect national treasures), no item of pre-Hispanic culture may be unearthed without official authorization and no pre-Columbian artifacts of value may be taken out of the country. Often you can buy such treasures in shops. Unscrupulous dealers may fail to inform you that, though you may own an idol, to take it home you must have proper clearance papers from the National Institute of Anthropology and History. These are very difficult to secure.

You should also bear in mind that an estimated 70 per cent of all the so-called pre-Columbian figures now being sold in shops, at archaeological sites, and through dealers in Mexico and abroad are but skillfully rendered fakes. Some of them are so incredibly well made that even qualified archaeologists are fooled by them.

A similar law is in effect regarding the export of colonial art objects, paintings, and sculpture. Likewise, there is a lively trade in skillfully executed copies of colonial treasures — which are sometimes offered to the unwary as authentic colonial pieces.

PRINCIPAL ARCHAEOLOGICAL ZONES

The following list includes only the most important ruins, most of which can be reached by automobile, plane, or train. For additional details regarding these, and other sites not listed here, see the regional sections of the guide.

Bonampak, Chis. Mayan. Famed for its magnificent murals, pyramid and tomb. Difficult to reach.

Calixtlahuaca, Méx. Pre-Aztec and Aztec. Noted for its unusual circular temple.

Castillo de Teayo, Ver. Toltec. Pyramid.

Copilco, D.F. Archaic. Remains of extremely old culture found under lava beds.

Cuicuilco, D.F. Archaic. Oldest structure in Americas.

Chalchihuites, Zac. Teotihuacán. Pre-Aztec fortress structures.

Chichén Itzá, Yuc. Mayan with later Toltec influences. Most famed of Mexico's ruins.

Cholula, Pue. Various cultures. Gigantic pyramid and religious center.

Guien-Gola, Oax. Zapotec. Large and important archaeological zone.

Huatuxco, Ver. Aztec. Pyramid and temple, well preserved.

Hueyapan, Ver. Olmec. Constructions pre-dating the birth of Christ. Huge Olmec heads.

Ihuatzio, Mich. Tarascan. Pyramidal bases.

Ixtlán, Nay. Toltec. Unusual circular structures.

Island of Jaina, Camp. Mayan. Important for its quantity of artifacts and huge clay figures.

Labná, Yuc. Mayan. Notable tenth-century architecture.

Malinalco, Méx. Important zone near Tenancingo. Unusual sculpture.

Mayapán, Yuc. Mayan. Architecture not as lavish as at Uxmal or Chichén Itzá.

México, D.F. Aztec. Scattered remains of Tenochtitlán, base of main Aztec temple near the cathedral.

Mitla, Oax. Mixtec. One of the famed sites. Architecture unique in Mexico.

Monos (Los--,) Arcelia, Gro. Extensive and interesting zone, difficult to reach, not yet fully explored.

Monte Albán, Oax. Zapotec. One of the most impressive and beautiful archaeological ruins. The famed Tomb 7 jewels were found here.

Palenque, Chis. Mayan. Extraordinary ruins in the jungle. Hard to reach.

Quemada (Chocomoztoc) Zac. Teotihuacán. Well-preserved fortress settlement.

Tajín, Veracruz. Totonac. Pyramid of the Niches.

Tamuín, S.L.P. Huastecan. Pyramids, altars.

Tenayuca, Méx. Chichimecan. Northwest of Mexico City. Pyramid and interesting sculpture. A wall of stone serpents.

Teopanzolco, Mor. Aztec. Pyramid on outskirts of Cuernavaca.

Teotihuacán, Méx. Teotihuacán and later, Toltec. The great pyramids of the sun and the moon. etc.

Tepoztlán, Mor. Aztec. Temple or pyramid of Tepozteco.

Tizatlán, Tlax. Tlaxcalan. Noted for its altars and early paintings.

Toniná, Chis. Mayan. Difficult to reach.

Tres Zapotes, Ver. Olmec. Monumental Olmec sculpture.

Tula, Hgo. Toltec. Ancient capital of Toltec. Ruins, colossal sculpture, frescoes.

Tulum, Q.R. Mayan. One of most beautiful archaeological zones in the Mayan country.

Tuxtlas (Los--) Ver. Olmec. Near Lake Catemaco.

Tzintzuntzán, Mich. Tarascan. Ruins and remains of this capital of the Tarascan empire.

Uxmal, Yuc. Mayan. One of the most important of the Mayan centers. Extraordinary architecture.

La Venta, Tab. Olmec. Area in which the most notable of Olmec artifacts have been found. The museum at Villahermosa has most of the statuary now.

Xochicalco, Mor. Toltec (?) ruins of a magnificent city that flourished about 1000 A.D.

Xpuhil, Camp. Mayan. Pyramids and city. Difficult to reach as yet.

Yaxchilán, Chis. Mayan. Remote and notable Mayan ruins on Guatamalan border.

Zayil, Yuc. Mayan. Ninth- and tenth-century ruins.

Yagul, Oax. Mixtec. Similar to Mitla. Site just off the highway between Oaxaca and Mitla.

Dzibilchaltun, Yuc. Mayan. A "new" important site representing some of the earliest of Mayan construction. Off road between Mérida and Progreso.

24. Fiestas

One of Mexico's most fascinating social activities is the fiesta — a way of commemorating men and events that involves gay fun as well as a blending of ritual, ceremony, and pagentry. Mexico is one of the few countries in the world where the art of the fiesta has not been debased. It is one of the few places where a visitor can take part in almost any of the countless great civil or religious celebrations with their vivid and violent primary colors, their spectacular fireworks, their curious ceremonies and spontaneous gaiety.

Year around, the Mexican calendar is crowded with fiestas. In addition to the official national holidays when the entire country from the most remote village to the largest city bursts forth with shouts, dancing, and bizarre costumes, each city and village has its own fiesta dates. Some towns have as many as thirty celebrations spread through the year, and some of them are week-long events.

The fiesta with its inexhaustible surprises: the delirium of activities, the things sold in the open-air market, piquant toys, candies, fruits, and other objects is an event no tourist in Mexico should miss. It is one of those rare times when the Mexican opens out to the world, shouting, laughing, dancing, and discharging his pistol in the air. As described by Octavio Paz, "It is the time when friends who have not exchanged more than the most formal courtesies throughout the year get drunk together, trade confidences, weep together, laugh together, discover they are brothers and, sometimes to prove it, kill each other. Guitars are brought out, the day and night rings with music. There is a steady mounting delirium, an explosion of the community soul. The Mexican fiesta, shot through with vivid colors, lights and sounds, is a brilliant reversal of the reticence and silence of ordinary living."

Fiestas are governed by their own rules. They are not precisely organized with timetable regularity as are the celebrations we are accustomed to in the United States. The Mexican fiesta has its own traditional, mysterious logic and ethic. It encompasses an enchanted world in which almost everything takes place as if it were not so, or as a dream. In some fiestas even the notion of order vanishes and chaos rules supreme. A barrage of fireworks will shatter your sleep at unaccountable hours, Indian dancers in gaudy pre-Columbian costumes burst out of nooks and side streets when you least expect them. In the Mexican fiesta you will find that pomp, circumstance, laws, even death, are toyed with and ridiculed.

The most important and widely celebrated fiestas are the following: Independence Day (Sept. 15–16); The Day of the Dead (Nov. 2); The Christmas *Posadas* (Dec. 16 to 24); Carnival Week (just before Lent); Holy Week; Corpus Cristi.

Independence Day, in most towns, means a speech, the traditional *grito* or Cry of Independence, parades, fireworks, and dancing. In Mexico City there is always a gigantic turnout for this celebration. On the night of September 15, the Zócalo or plaza fronting the National Palace and Cathedral is brilliantly lighted. At 11 P.M., the President of the Republic appears on the balcony of the National Palace, repeats the combustible words first shouted in 1810 by Father Hidalgo, then he rings the liberty bell. The plaza, jammed with countless thousands of people, bursts in a delirium of shouts. On the following day there is a ceremony at the Monument of the Independence on the Paseo de la Reforma.

In Dolores de Hidalgo, Querétaro, and San Miguel de Allende, the cradle cities of the Mexican independence movement, the celebration is even more elaborate. In San Miguel, for example, the evening of September 15 opens with a band concert or *serenata* (serenade) in the plaza. At 11 P.M., heralded by brilliant showers of fireworks, runners bearing torches and a scroll arrive from nearby Querétaro, re-enacting one of the memorable scenes in Mexico's story of the Independence (the message sent by Doña Josefa to Captain Allende that the plot for the revolution had been prematurely discovered). The following day is given over to parades, tableaux, and elaborate floats depicting great moments in Mexico's history. There are also Indian dancers, sporting events and one of the season's major bullfights.

In this same town, two weeks later, the festival honoring the town's patron saint is celebrated. Visitors who have been to the Mardi Gras at Cannes and New Orleans will find them pale compared to this three-day spree. And this is true of fiestas honoring the patron saints of towns from one end of the country to the other.

During the week preceding such a fiesta basket weavers, toymakers, peddlers, and ranchers jam the roads and donkey trails leading into town. A rash of smaller celebrations break out here and there: anticipatory rockets sail into the night sky while Indian dancers try a step or two. Then, one day comes a thunderous *alborada,* the dawn-fireworks that literally shake the entire town. This sets off what is almost a continuous round of parades, street dancing, and parties. No one sleeps for twenty, thirty, forty hours — there is too much to see and do. The colorful pre-Conquest *conchero* dancers, the Indian dancers from Oaxaca and Mitla, the *voladores* from Papantla and many other places appear in strength. Sometimes as many as three hundred regional dancers will fill the various plazas of a town, gyrating tirelessly, hour after hour, in swirls of color. On the final day of such a fiesta, usually a Sunday — and if the town can afford it — there is a bullfight. Always, the final evening is capped with a display of pyrotechnics, the setting off of huge *castillos* (a tower supporting the fireworks).

Each fiesta, depending on the region, the season, the indigenous groups involved and the event being commemorated, displays subtle variations. No two Mexican fiestas, no matter how traditional or ritualistic they are, have ever, or will ever be exactly like another. The reader will find further details regarding specific regional and village fiestas in the regional sections of this guide.

The calendar of the Catholic Church is one's best guide to Mexico's religious fiestas. When you are in Mexico and want to see a fiesta, simply pick the day you want to go fiesta-ing, look up which saint's day it is, then locate the nearest town or church bearing that name. One should keep in mind, however, that the fete may not be celebrated exactly on the saint's calendar day. If it falls on a weekday the principal festivities may be celebrated the following weekend so as to give the men who work in the country a chance to get into town to enjoy it.

Listed below are some of the more colorful fiestas. They represent but a tiny fraction of all the fiestas that take place daily in one part of Mexico or another.

MEXICAN FIESTA CALENDAR

DATE	LOCATION	EVENT
January		
1	All Mexico	New Year.
1	Mitla, Oax.	Zapotec Indians celebrate New Year's Eve and Day, called, "Wishing Night" with an all night vigil and fires. Wishes are displayed in miniature models set at foot of a cross at entrance to the village.
1	Dolores Hidalgo, Gto.	New Year fair. Dancers.
1	Tehuantepec, Oxa.	Commercial fair. *Serenata* in the Hidalgo Park.
3	Totolac, Tlax.	Important religious fiesta and native dances. (Sunday following date.)
5–7	Irapuato, Gto.	Fiesta commemorating founding of city.
6–7	Chalma (Sanctuary)	Religious fiesta honoring Our Lord of Chalma. Native dances.
6	All Mexico	Day of the Three Kings *(Santos Reyes)* when Mexican children get their Christmas toys.
6–15	Temascaltepec, Mex.	Fiesta with regional dances.
8	Ahila, Pue.	Fiesta. Pre-Hispanic *voladores*.
10	Temax, Yuc.	Fiesta for the Virgin of Buctozotz. Folk dances.
15	Jocotepec, Jal.	Village fiesta on shores of Lake Chapala. Regional dances.
15	Teotitlán del Valle, Oax.	Fiesta for Señor de Esquipula. Feather Dancers.
16	Tepoztlán, Mor.	Santa Catarina fiesta. Native dances.
17–25	León, Gto.	Fiesta honoring San Sebastian and founding of city.
17	All Mexico	St. Anthony's Day. Children take animals to church to be blessed.
18	Taxco, Gro.	Fiesta with fair and dancing.
20–25	Tehuantepec, Oax.	Local fiestas.
20–28	Mitla and San Pablo, Oax.	Fiesta with feather dancers.
February		
2	San Juan de los Lagos, Jal.	Nation-wide peregrinations end here, honoring patroness of the town. Religious ceremonies, fiesta.
2–8	All Mexico (especially at:) Tlacotalpan, Ver. Teotihuacán, Mex. Tzintzuntzán, Mich.	Fiesta, Virgin of La Candelaria. Processions, bullfights, dancing, blessing of seeds and candles.
5	National Holiday	Constitution Day. Parades.
22–25	Matías Romero, Oax.	Colorful annual tropic fair.
24	National Holiday	Flag Day. Parades.

Note: The Mexican *carnavales* (Mardi Gras) take place in late February or early March, the days just preceding Ash Wednesday, a movable feast. The best carnivals are held in Veracruz, Ver., Mazatlán, Sin., Tampico, Tamps., Campeche, Camp.

DATE	LOCATION	EVENT
March		
1	Durango, Dg.	Very old fiesta honoring the Soldier's Christ, plus annual commercial fair.
3	Amecameca, Mex.	Native fiesta and market conducted on Hill of Sacromante. Dances.
4	Chalma, Mex.	Pilgrimages to shrine of Señor de Chalma. Indian dances.
4	Taxco, Gro.	Religious festival. Pastorals and dances performed by children dressed as roosters.
9–13	Etla, Oax.	Local fiesta honoring an image called Lord of Sorrows.
9–13	Talpa, Jal.	Local fiesta. Dancing.
15	Coyutlán, Col.	Spring festival begins.
18	Tepaltzingo, Mor.	Famed market day noted for sale of primitive ceramic animal figures.
18–31	Antiguo Morelos, Tamps.	A prolonged traditional fiesta.
19	All Mexico	Feast of San José. Celebrations by everyone named José, as well as fetes at churches and villages of that name.
21	National Holiday	Birthday of Benito Juárez.

Note: Late in March, or early in April, Passion Week and Easter Sunday fall due (movable feasts). In Mexico they are observed with solemn religious ceremonies, colorful processions, Passion Plays, and fiestas. The most interesting events take place in Taxco, Gro., Ixtapalapa, Mex., Tzintzuntzán, Mich., San Miguel de Allende, Gto.

DATE	LOCATION	EVENT
April		
1–7	San Cristóbal Las Casas, Chis.	Popular fair commemorating founding of this picturesque city.
1	Etla, Oax.	Indian market day. Folk costumes and dances.
15–17	Fortín de Las Flores, Ver.	Traditional flower festival.
15–30	Progreso, Yuc.	Spring festival.
16	Ticomán, Mor.	Fiesta with colorful Dance of the *Chinelos.*
21–26	Tuxtla Gutiérrez, Chis.	Colorful fair, regional dances.
25 on	Aguascalientes, Ags.	San Marcos Fair, one of Mexico's most lively and large fiestas. Fair ends May 5.
May		
1	National Holiday	Labor Day. Parades.
3	All Mexico	Feast of the Holy Cross. Fiestas in honor of masons and builders. Endless fireworks and drinking.
3	Ozumba, Mex.	Half-pagan, half-Christian ritual held on crest of Zempoatltepetl hill to evoke rainfall and good crops.
1–5	Nogales, Son.	Annual flower festival.
5	National Holiday	Commemorating Battle of Puebla.
6	Tepoztlán, Mor.	Fiesta of the *Chinelos.* Dancers.
10	Cuautla, Mor.	Horseman's festival and fete honoring Emiliano Zapata.
15	All Mexico	Day of San Isidro, patron of rain and agriculture. Village priests bless livestock previously decorated with garlands of flowers. Dances.
15–25	Juchitán, Oax.	Spring festival, dancing, regional costumes.
June		
1	Port towns	Navy Day. Port cities honor Mexican naval heroes.
Corpus Christi	All Mexico	A movable feast. Children in native costumes bring 1st fruits to be blessed by parish priests. Plazas filled with toy stands.
Corpus Christi	Papantla, Ver.	Flying dancers *(voladores)* perform famed aerial dance.

DATE	LOCATION	EVENT
13 on	Río Verde, S.L.P.	Old style annual fair commemorating the construction of village church.
13	Casas Grandes, Chih.	Fiesta, dances of the pastores, etc.
13	Various villages	Fiestas in honor of Saint Anthony.
24	All Mexico (esp.) Huixquilucan, Mex. San Luis Potosí, Guanajuato, Gto. San Juan del Río, Qro. Navojoa, Son. Puebla, Pue.	Feast of St. John the Baptist. Called "Bath Day." Villagers take celebratory baths, women cut tips of hair in memory of Salome's dance. Regional dances, etc.
July		
4	Lagos de Moreno, Jal.	Fiesta honoring Our Lord and Lady of Refuge. Matachine dancers.
6	Tlacotepec, Pue.	Indians from several states gather in traditional costume to make offerings of hair and personal belongings on top of a nearby hill.
8	Teotitlán del Valle, Oax.	Fiesta and Feather Dance.
15	Teotihuacán, Mex.	Feast of Divine Redemptor, Indian dances, fireworks.
16	All Mexico, but especially in Oaxaco City, Ciudad del Carmen, Camp., Coyoacan, D.F.	Fiesta, Virgen del Carmen. Folk dances.
18	National Holiday	Anniversary of death of Juárez.
22	Tlaxcala, Tlax.	Impressive torchlight pilgrimage to Chapel of Christ the King.
25	Silao, Gto.	Fiesta for St. James. Dances, flower battles, etc.
25	Cuilapan, Oax.	Feather Dances.
29	San Pedro Actopán, D.F.	Fair honoring St. Peter. Dances.
25–31	Querétaro, Qro.	Fiestas honoring St. Anne. Bullfights, dancing, etc.
August		
5	Ixtantepec Nieves, Oax.	Festival honoring Virgin of the Snows.
6	Lagos de Moreno, Jal.	Religious fiesta.
1–6	Saltillo, Coah.	Annual fair. Matachine dancers.
2–9	Tulancingo, Hgo.	Annual fair and fiesta.
8	Paracho, Mich.	A curious fiesta in which a feted bullock becomes the main fiesta food.
8–12	Ciudad Juárez, Chih.	Fiesta honoring St. Lawrence.
15	Various towns	Feast of the Assumption. In the Tlaxcala region villagers weave huge carpets of flowers to cover church floors.
13–16	Juchitán, Oax.	*Vela de Agosto* fiesta. Dances, costumes.
21	Zacatecas, Zac.	Week-long fair.
25	San Luis Potosí, S.L.P.	Brilliant fiesta honoring St. Louis.
28	Chalma, Mex.	Religious festival, dancing, etc.
31	All Oaxaca	Day for blessing animals. Feast of San Ramón.
September		
1–8	Los Remedios, Mex.	Fiesta, ceremonies and dancers, honoring tiny statue of Virgin said to have been brought by Cortés.
1–30	Mexico City	Gala festivals, music, regional dancers staged by Mexican Tourist Department in Chapultepec Park. Daily.
1	Acatlán, Pue.	Traditional fiesta, Tocatines and Santiago dancers.
1–8	Cuzamá, Yuc.	Week-long religious and civic festival.
3–4	Juchitán, Oax.	*Vela Pineda* fiesta. Tehuantepec dances, costumes, and flowers.
4	Mulegé, B.C.	Fiesta honoring Santa Rosalia, dancing, sports events.
8	Tepoztlán, Mor.	Local fair and Aztec war dances and recitations in Náhuatl.
6–14	Chicxulub, Yuc.	Local fiesta in pleasant port town.
8	Tlaltenango, Mor.	Fete honoring Our Lady of Miracles. Processions, native dancers.
9–11	Chalma, Mex.	Pilgrimages and festivities.
10	Ramos Arizpe, Coah.	Fair, Matachine dancers.
14	Querétaro, Qro.	Fiesta at Convent of the Cross. *Chinchín* dancers.
14–30	Campeche, Camp.	Annual fiesta honoring Cristo de San Roman.
15–16	National Holiday	Independence day. Fireworks and gaiety everywhere. Best places to be: Zócalo in Mexico City, Querétaro and San Miguel de Allende.

DATE	LOCATION	EVENT
29	San Miguel de Allende, Gto.	Weekend carnival honoring Saint Michael. Dancers, bullfight, etc.
30	Morelia, Mich.	Fair honoring birth of José María Morelos.
October		
1–7	Ciudad Delicias, Chih.	Annual cotton fair, dancing, floats, bullfights.
4	Various towns	Feast of San Francisco.
4–12	Zapopan, Jal.	The tiny Vírgen de Zapopán returns to her church after wandering.
3–7	Constancia del Rosario, Oax.	Religious festival and folk dances.
10–12	Tlacolula and Sta. María del Tule, Oax.	Two-day fiesta moving from one village to the other.
12	National Holiday	*Día de la Raza* (Day of the Race) commemorating discovery of America.
22–25	Ciudad Guzmán, Jal.	Fiesta, dancers.
17–24	Alvarado, Ver.	Gay fiesta beside the sea.
November		
1–2	All Mexico	The Day of the Dead (All Souls and All Saints), the most important religious and Indian festival in Mexico.
1–2	Janitzio, Mich.	A magnificent spectacle of glowing candles in the cemetery.
1–2	Yecapixtla, Mor.	Important market day and Day of the food and toys.
11	San Martín Texmelucan, Pue.	Regional dancers and fair.
8–13	Yekax, Yuc.	Religious fiesta and dancing.
13	San Diego de la Unión, Gto.	Local fiesta.
20	National Holiday	Anniversary of Revolution 1910.
22–26	Santa Catarina, Gto.	Religious fiesta, processions, fair.
23–30	Comonfort, Gto.	Traditional fiesta, dancers, etc.
25 on	Pátzcuaro, Mich	Festival honoring Vírgen de la Soledad. End Dec. 16.
30	Texcoco, Mex.	Annual fiesta and native dances.
December		
8	All Mexico (esp.) Pátzcuaro, Mich. San Juan de los Lagos, Jal. Tenancingo, Mex.	Feast of the Immaculate Conception.
12	All Mexico (esp.) Shrine of Guadalupe in Mexico City	Feast of Mexico's patroness, the Virgin of Guadalupe.
12–15	Autlán, Jal.	Semi-pagan fiesta, dancing, etc.
12–24	Celaya, Gto.	Annual fair.
13	Joanacatepec, Mor.	Fiesta of *La Vaquerita,* fair, and native dances.
16–18	Oaxaca	Fiesta honoring the Vírgen de la Soledad, patroness of the State. Processions at the Soledad church, Oaxaca City.
23	Oaxaca City, Oax.	Radish Night.
24	Quiroga, Mich.	Fiesta.
16–24	All Mexico	The nine days of traditional *posadas,* or religious celebrations. Most impressive in Oaxaca, Querétaro, and San Miguel de Allende.
25	National Holiday	Christmas.
31	All Mexico	Traditional midnight suppers and religious services.

25. *Traditional Food and Drink*

No visit in Mexico would be complete without sampling some of the regional cookery and traditional beverages. Although Mexicans are partial to highly seasoned food and very hot *(picante)* peppers, nevertheless, a great number of regional dishes are mild, subtle or dramatic and do not require a hard-cased stomach of the traveler. It must also be remembered that authentic Mexican cookery has almost no cousinship with the so-called Mexican food of the border states where cauterizing chili powder takes the place of imagination and art.

True Mexican cookery is a blending of dishes that

are pre-Hispanic in origin, along with recipes that were brought from Spain. Often the recipes are marvelous creations involving artful proportions and seemingly incompatible ingredients. Doctor Atl, the Mexican painter and folklorist, once aptly said "Mexican cooking merits in itself an entire volume — not just simply a dictionary of recipes, but a philosophic treatise."

Although the people of Mexico have been subjected to conquests by Spaniards, Frenchmen, Americans and, lately, by Coca-Colas, they have sturdily resisted most imported kitchen innovations. A large portion of the people still eat exactly as did their forefathers centuries before the arrival of Columbus in the New World. The staples then, and now: corn products, herbs, a minimum of meat, beans, carloads of tomatoes, subtle as well as explosive chili peppers, beverages made of the cocoa bean and the juices of the *maguey* plant.

Even the dining hours have scarcely changed. The typical Mexican rises and puts away several hours of work before breakfasting at about 10 A.M. This mid-morning repast, the *merienda,* consists of beans, fresh *tortillas,* coffee or a thickish cornmeal brew called *atole.* The afternoon main meal is usually a stew swimming in tomato sauce, beans, and *tortillas.* Supper is as light as breakfast: hot chocolate or coffee, beans, *tortillas* or sweet rolls.

Today the wealthier Mexicans eat more à la European, with a cuisine that is closer to the Spanish or French. In pre-Columbian times the upper-class also dined amply. Each day, for example, some 300 plates of various delicacies were prepared for the Aztec chieftain, Moctezuma. In describing the variety of dishes an Aztec cook had in his repertoire, Jacques Soustelle[1] reports that a chef could make seven types of *tortillas,* six of *tamales.* He or she had twenty ways of preparing fowl, countless recipes for vegetables, fruits, and meats. Such a cook could turn out a multitude of unpronounceable stews and sauces — the *molli, chilimolli* and *ahuacamolli* — from which today's national dish, *mole poblano,* was evolved. For ceremonial feasts there was even an exotic stew, *tloco pozole,* made of hominy, spices, chili peppers and the tender thigh of a freshly captured young warrior. For centuries before 1521 Mexican cooks either boiled, roasted, or stewed their food. Oils and fats were little used. The fry cook who has done such great damage to the Mexican cuisine was a foreign import.

Both Europe and the United States are indebted to the industry and gastronomic fearlessness of the pre-Columbian Indians for much of our most flavorful tablefare. Countless spices, corn, beans, the avocado, vanilla, yams, tomatoes, and some very delicious maggots are all Indian gifts to the modern kitchen. Without the ancient Mexican's *uexólotl* — which the Spanish renamed *guajolote* (turkey) — we would have no traditional Thanksgiving dinner bird. The tomato, too, was an Aztec export. It is thought to have come from the west coast village of Tomatlán (near Manzanillo). When tomatoes were introduced into Europe during the sixteenth century they were called "love apples." The French promptly suspected them of having aphrodisiac properties and they took to them with enthusiasm. The puritanical British and North Americans frowned on the tomatoes for years until it was discovered that they contained vitamins — which made them acceptable.

In many parts of Mexico the Indians still observe their curious and ancient way of classifying whether food is hot or cold, which has nothing to do with temperature. Foods that are considered easy to digest, and which stimulate body heat, are tabbed as hot. Honey, *pinole,* beef, and coffee are among these. Although served piping hot, wild turkey, venison, rice, boiled eggs, and certain bananas are considered cold.

For countless centuries the Mexican bread has been the *tortilla,* which should not be confused with the Spanish omelet bearing the same name. The Mexican *tortilla* is a flat, usually thin pancake made of corn that has been soaked in lime and water, then ground on a stone grinder *(metate)* until it forms a moist paste called *masa.* This dough is patted by hand to the proper shape and thinness, and is then baked on a clay or iron platter *(comal).* In larger towns the dough may be machine-ground and the *tortillas* shaped mechanically. These tend to be rubbery, losing the fine texture and delicate flavor of the hand-patted kind.[2]

In addition to being the country's indispensable daily bread, as well as serving as a spoon for scooping up stews, the *tortilla* is the frame or foundation for the following inviting snacks:

Tacos — a between-meal snack made of shredded meat, eggs, cheese, chili, or vegetables folded into a *tortilla* and fried crisp in deep oil.

Huevos Rancheros — ranch-style eggs, fried and served upon a *tortilla* raft and covered with a cauterizing sauce made of green tomatoes *(tomate)* or red tomatoes *(jitomate),* and chili peppers.

Enchiladas — *tortillas* rolled around a filling of shredded meat or cheese, and cooked in a sauce made of ground tomatoes, chopped onions, and chili. To add an alpine touch, *Enchiladas Suizas* are served in individual casseroles and are topped with sour cream.

Quesadillas — the traditional way to make these is to blend cheese into the *nixtamal* dough before making the *tortillas.* The *tortilla* is then filled with meat, beans or fried, tender yellow squash flowers. The

[1] *La Vie Quotidienne des Aztéques a la Vielle de la Conquete Espagnole.*

[2] *Tortillas* play an important role in the Mexican psychology and have been known to influence the course of revolutions. At the turn of the century, when the men of Juchitán, Oax., revolted against the government of Porfirio Díaz, the uprising was effectively shattered without a shot being fired. The simple strategy was to arrest and jail all the women of Juchitán, thus cutting off the supply of *tortillas.*

edges of the *tortilla* are then crimped together like a tart and it is baked over charcoal.

Chalupas — the ancient Mexican version of canapes. It is an open-faced snack, the base is a crisply fried *tortilla* upon which beans, tomatoes, shredded lettuce, and chili are sprinkled. It is topped with grated cheese.

Mexican gourmets are most moved to poetic utterances by their *moles,* complicated sauces related to the pre-Columbian *molli.* They are concocted of a variety of puréed red tomatoes and green tomatoes, chilis, and other ingredients. Among the most touching are:

Mole Verde — a hot *(picante)* green sauce made of green tomatoes, green chili, onions, garlic, cummin seed, coriander, and chicken broth.

Mole Romerito — a vivid red sauce prepared from red ingredients: ripe tomatoes, red chilis.

Mole Pipián — composed of puréed green tomatoes, green chilis, plus toasted pumpkin seeds.

Mole Poblano — a celebrated and subtle dark brown sauce which, when combined with turkey, becomes the Mexican national dish *guajolote con mole poblano.* It is brought out with fanfare for fiestas of importance. The recipe for this famed dish calls for a young turkey that has been slightly inebriated on brandy before slaughter, plus a sauce that takes about three days to compound and includes some twenty-six incompatible ingredients. The makings include four types of chili peppers, cinnamon, garlic, bananas, onions, peanuts, almonds, sesame seeds, raisins, cloves, whole pepper, cummin seeds, coriander seeds, and chocolate.

The Mexican *tamale,* made of cornmeal molded around tidbits of meat, chili or other fare, then wrapped in corn husks and steamed, vary in style from region to region. The *tamale veracruzano* served along the Gulf Coast comes out as a soft pudding of cornmeal served on a banana leaf. A depression in the center is filled with a lagoon of rich meat sauce. The *tamales* of Oaxaca have chili, tomato, and spices mixed in a thin cornmeal gruel that is steamed in a banana leaf. In Yucatán one may encounter a jumbo-style *tamale* called *muc-bil.* It houses a half of a boned chicken.

Mexican women have an incredible gift for being able to blend spices and ingredients into delicate and flavorful sauces and stews that the best French chefs might envy. Delectable stews are among the crowning glories of the Mexican cuisine. They travel under the names of *guisados* (a meat stew, usually simmered with tomatoes); *pozoles* (a traditional stew made with pork, hominy, and herbs); and *menudos.* The latter are made of tripe or giblets, and are considered excellent hangover preventatives. Late at night, near important *cantinas* and saloons, you will come upon little cook-stands offering tripe stews. For many years, near the Indianilla streetcar barns in Mexico City, there were dozens of these stands, and it was not unusual to see the poor and the rich, women in rags and in minks, sitting side by side on crude benches during the wee hours of the morning. *Menudos* recognize no class lines.

The gourmet has no trouble finding endless exotic fare in Mexico. Among some of the "spooky foods" the most amendable to American taste are the *chiles rellenos,* flavorful chili peppers *(chili poblano)* stuffed with either cheese, or a meat mixture consisting of ground beef, cactus candy, ground almonds, and spices. These are dipped in an egg batter, deep fried, and served with a covering sauce made of ground green walnuts blended with cream cheese.

The mildly curious tourist should make some effort to taste *papat zules,* a dish from the Yucatecan region. It is made of *tortillas* rolled around hard boiled eggs and is served with a subtle-flavored turquoise sauce made of sunflower seeds and *epazote,* a long-leaved herb like our coriander. It is one of the most delightful of Mexico's regional dishes.

For the really adventurous trencherman there are numerous Aztec and Zapotec hand-me-downs which almost all Mexicans delight in, but tourists prefer to reserve as conversation pieces. Among these are:

Gusanos de maguey — plump little white maggots that feed on the *maguey* plant. When crisply fried they turn golden in color and are as tasty as cracklings. You will find them in the better bars.

Iguana — an ugly, monstrous lizard native to the tropic regions. They grow up to five feet in length. In the south of Mexico both their eggs and flesh are prized. The meat tastes somewhat like Louisiana frog legs.

Cactus — the numerous species of cacti make their way to the Mexican table in various forms: as fruit, candies, vegetables for stews, and salads. The *nopal* cactus is especially favored in the Lenten cuisine. Among the most popular dishes prepared from the tender pads of the *nopal* are: *nopales navegantes,* in which the sliced pads navigate about in a sea of tomato broth and chili; *revoltijos,* a main dinner course of chopped *nopal* pads, rosemary, potatoes, dried ground shrimp, and beaten egg that is served with a *mole romeritos; ensalada de nopalitos,* a delicious chilled salad made of boiled cactus pads, onions, coriander, *chili serrano,* olive oil, and vinegar.

The red, green, and maroon fruit that sprouts from the rim of the *nopal* pad is used both as a fruit and also the makings of a kind of cactus cheese. The fruit, called *tuna,* is often candied, but may be eaten fresh. The maroon-colored ones taste the best. When boiled with sugar, the *tuna* forms a cheeselike substance which is pressed into flat cakes called *queso de tuna* (tuna cheese).

MEXICAN BEVERAGES

The principal beverages consumed by Mexicans are: chocolate, coffee, fruit drinks, *pulque,* beer, *tequila*, and *mezcal*. The last four are alcoholic. Mexican beer, less carbonated and "green tasting" than American beer, is quite inexpensive. The better grades, (Superior, Carta Blanca, Dos Equis, Corona, etc.) compare with the best of German brews.

Before the conquest the national beverage was *xoco-atl* or chocolate. Today Mexicans still whip it up in more delicious frothy ways than anywhere else in the world. *Chocolate méxicana* is the favored type, made with water, chocolate, vanilla, cinnamon and sugar. It is beaten with wooden whirlers to a wonderful foam. When prepared with milk it is called *chocolate francés*. Cocoa is considered a travesty on chocolate and is not widely popular.

Atole, a thickish beverage made of water and cornmeal, flavored with cinnamon, chocolate or other spices, is a favorite of the rural people.

Refrescos, native soft drinks made of natural fruit juices diluted with water and sweetened with honey or sugar. The colorful *refresco* stands with their vivid juice jars which graced most Mexican parks and plazas are rapidly disappearing, being replaced by commercially bottled soft drinks.

Pulque. Of the three alcoholic drinks secured from the *maguey* plant, *pulque* (a whitish ferment of low alcoholic content) is the only one boasting of pre-Hispanic lineage.[3] It seems doubtful that any drink elsewhere has ever elicited so many violent reactions. Writer Anita Brenner once described it as tasting like "wallpaper paste laced with mucilage." Charles Flandrau called it "a thin fluid resembling water that has been poured into a receptacle in which a little milk has been carelessly left, and, tasting like a kind of degenerate buttermilk." The descriptions are apt, but erroneous.

If you visit in a village where good, fresh, unadulterated *pulque* is made, you'll find a flavorable beverage. It is pleasantly refreshing. The alcoholic content is about six per cent. A good *pulque* reaches its peak of perfection shortly after it has come from the fermenting vats. It begins to sour or degenerate very shortly afterward. It is advisable to skip the "cured" or "prepared" *pulques* sold in the larger cities. They are doctored with fruit juices to disguise the fact that they are going bad.

The production of *pulque* is a tedious, long-drawn-out and tradition-bound labor. The *maguey* or "century plant" is cultivated during a 7–10 year unproductive period. (For description of the species see *Wildflowers, Orchids & Cacti*, Index.) When the plant is about to flower it sends up a giant central stalk or lance, 20 to 30 feet high, upon which cluster countless greenish yellow flowers. After this crowning effort the exhausted plant dies. It is when in the throes of borning the flower that the central shoot is cut off and then, for two or three months, the sap (*aguamiel* or honey-water), which was destined to give brief life and beauty to the plant's brilliant offspring, flows into the basin prepared for it. The stem is cut off short and the heart of the plant is scooped out, leaving only the thick outer rind, which forms a small hollow in which the juice gathers. In a *maguey* field these mutilated plants are readily distinguishable by the fresh heart which is stuck on one of the sharp spines of the plant — as a signal to the workers that the plant is ready for attention. The *tlachiqueros*, (field workers) who harvest the *aguamiel*, know by unmistakable signs, almost to the hour, when the central stem, destined to produce the flower, is about to appear. If the extraction of the heart of the plant is performed too soon or too late, the plant dies.

A productive plant will yield from ten to fifteen pints of unfermented juice every day until it dies. The liquid is drawn from it two or three times a day by means of a long tubelike gourd called *acocote* or *guaje* which has a reed tube at each end. The tube at the bottom is placed into the liquid. The man sucks on the other tube, drawing the liquid up into the gourd. From this, the *aguamiel* is transferred to pigskins and sent to the *tinacal*, or fermenting room of the hacienda. Fermentation is hastened by the introduction of a mother culture, or *madre pulque*, which has been kept for a fortnight and is rank and sour. Within 24 hours the mass becomes the *pulque* of commerce. Twenty-two of the 33 species of *maguey* produce *aguamiel*, and six produce fine *pulque*.

Much ceremonial activity accompanies the making of *pulque*. In some regions women are not permitted in the *tinacales* while the *pulque* is fermenting; the taboo is doubly rigid if the woman is pregnant. Men

---

[3] *Pulque* is said to have been invented by the Toltecs in the tenth century. According to legend, a kinsman of Tepancaltzin (8th ruler of the Toltecs) observed a field mouse gnawing a hole in the central bulb of the *maguey* plant. He secured some of the curdy juice oozing from the hole and he sent his daughter, Xochitl, with a bowl of the juice to the palace. King Tepancaltzin seemed more impressed by the girl than by the juice. He held the girl captive and from their union was born a child called Meconetzin (Child of the *Maguey*). It has been said that Xochitl's liquid gift eventually brought down the kingdom of the Toltecs. They became addicted to *pulque*.

The Aztecs, who called the ferment *cocti*, considered it a semi-divine brew. In their mythology there was a *pulquería* or saloon, where the gods were accustomed to gathering, in one corner of the night sky. This heavenly tavern, which had four hundred udders, was operated by Mayauel, the goddess of *pulque*. In Aztec society, the drinking of *pulque* was vigorously proscribed. Only old men and women whose useful life lay behind them were allowed to get drunk on it. The unfortunate average citizen could only drink to excess on the feast of Mayauel. If he or she were caught drunk at any other time the punishment included stoning and sometimes death.

The Aztec ban on *pulque* ended with the coming of the Spanish and, as a result, drunkenness became a serious national problem. At first the Spanish made some attempt to abolish *pulque* imbibing as being pagan. At one time a law was passed limiting the number of *pulquerías* in Mexico City to one hundred, each to be operated by a widow of good repute. Even as late as the turn of this century various attempts were made to limit or prohibit the sale of the brew. Ironically, the popularization of bottled soft drinks and beer had done more to reduce the number of *pulquerías* than government edicts.

bare their heads on entering a fermenting room as if it were a church. A figure of the patron saint of the *tinacal* occupies a prominent place above the vats.

Mezcal is a potent, clear liquor fermented from the hearts of the agave or *maguey* plants after they are baked. It is most popular in the State of Oaxaca. It is marketed in small, squat, black clay jugs and is called *mezcal de olla.*

Tequila, a fiery distillate, is the national aperient of Mexico, as is bourbon to the U.S. or vodka to the Russians. It is made from the *maguey* plant in and around the village of Tequila, Jal. It is customary to take *tequila* with salt and lemon, licking the salt held between the thumb and forefinger and sucking on the lemon. It is also delicious taken with slices of green mangoes.

Wines: Mexicans are not wine-drinking people. Vineyards are limited and their output is not of especially fine quality. There are several adequate table wines produced mainly in the northern states. Compañía Vinícola de Saltillo makes red and white table wines, the best being their *Alamo Rosado* and their white wines marketed under the label *Generosos.* Compañía Vinícola de Aguascalientes produces white and red and purple wines, the best being their Spanish claret-type wines *Noblejo* and *Rancho Viejo.* The Bodegas Santo Tomás S.A. make an excellent white and red Chianti.

26. Wild Flowers, Orchids, and Cacti

The traveler with an eye for color and an irrepressible yen to photograph or collect unusual flowers and plants will find Mexico a tailor-made paradise. The countryside seems to be in endless, exuberant bloom, a spectacular open-air greenhouse harboring hundreds of varieties of parasitic orchids, weird cacti, the delicate tendriled spider lily, vivid coral-tree flowers, vast fields of marigolds, lantana, passion flowers and a curious flower called "Hair of an Angel."

A casual knowledge of some of the flowers native to Mexico greatly increases the pleasures of travel below the border, as well as throwing light on some of the picturesque traditions of the people. Mexicans are an avid flower-picking and flower-growing nation; it is one of their great national pastimes. The *maguey,* cactus, and wild flowers play an incredibly important role in their daily life.

In the land of Cortés and Cantinflas, blossoms are more than garden and table embellishments. Men wear flowers as costume decorations. They garland their beasts of burden with wreaths and bouquets. They'll cover an entire church floor with a huge carpet, a mosaic painting made entirely of wild flowers. In village markets you can purchase plant and flower remedies for almost every known illness.

The Mexican's passion for flowers dates back to the ancient Mayan and Aztec cultures which attributed a civic importance to flowers rarely found elsewhere in the world. In the Aztec capital, Tenochtitlán, the patios of temples, the plazas surrounding the great pyramids, the upper and lower stories of palaces and homes were planted with exquisite gardens so that the city resembled a vivid cascade of colors.

The pre-conquest Mexicans devised curious practices and taboos involving flowers. Certain plants — the vivid Frangipani, the Aztec Lily and the Mexican Magnolia — were reserved for the gardens of the nobility. When an important Aztec man-about-town went out for a stroll he was followed by servants who carried assorted bouquets of fragrant flowers. Throughout the course of his busy day the Aztec gentleman took time out to sniff blossoms, just as we pause to smoke or take a coffee break. Flower-smelling was an important element in the cultivated man's education.

Certain native flowers were also reserved for the exclusive use of the priesthood and religious rituals. The deeply hued yellow, red, or orange Mexican Marigold, used throughout Mexico today for the Feast of the Day of the Dead, was cultivated by priests who also compounded a powder from it which had anaesthetic properties. In the Aztec's human sacrifice, this powder, *yauntli,* was thrown in the face of the victims to stun them.

The Aztec hierarchy of gods included two important Flower Gods — Xochipilli (literally, Five Flowers) and his female counterpart, Xochiquetzal, or Flower-Quetzal-Feather, who reigned over the pastimes of flower-picking, singing, and dancing.

One of the strangest of the ancient rites was the Aztec ceremony "the buying of the rains." In this ritual held at the end of the dry season, large groups of children were carried on flower-decked litters to mountaintop temples where they were sacrificed. Oddly, for weeks previous to this ceremony, it was illegal for anyone to smell a flower.

The present-day Mexican has lost none of his ancestors' passion and reverence for flowers. Elaborate floral displays are one of the important features of all fiestas. In many regions there are fiestas dedicated to flowers. The most colorful of these flower fetes are those held at Huauchinango near Pachuca (February), in Comitán, near the Guatemalan border (February) and at San Angel, a picturesque suburb of Mexico City (April).

For the impressive Feast of the Day of the Dead (November 2), the most important Indian religious holiday in the country, literally millions of native marigolds, the *Cempoalxochitl,* are gathered and woven into flower arches, displays and beds to decorate household shrines and church altars as well as cemetery graves. Other important flower-using fiestas are: Día de la Cruz (Holy Cross), the fete of Mexico's construction workers who decorate buildings they are working on with crosses and brilliant flowers; the spring festival of San Isidro Labrador, patron of agriculture, when Indian farmers lead their flower-decked oxen into village churchyards to be blessed. On December 12, at the Shrine of the Virgin of Guadalupe, pilgrims from Ixtlapa lay a huge carpet of flowers upon the shrine floor.

Since pre-Columbian times plants and flowers have been the Mexican's most important source of medicine. Handed-down Mayan and Aztec folk remedies are still widely used. The Aztecs were noted for their voluminous herbal pharmacopoeia. In the Badianus Manuscript (an important illustrated medical treatise of the Aztecs), there is a unique prescription utilizing various flowers to treat an ailment called "fatigue of statesmen and those holding public office." Fatigue and melancholy were considered serious ailments and they were often treated with fragrant flowers which are still considered a mild stimulant.

Among the most prized of Mexican wild flowers are the native orchids. Mexico and Central America vie with Southeast Asia as the world's most bountiful orchid area. Some 800 species of orchids have been classified in Mexico. Their distribution, especially the epiphytic orchids, occurs in the south and east regions of Mexico, mostly along the 3000-foot contour where the mountains have reasonable humidity. The richest orchid state is Chiapas, a veritable treasure house of orchids. It is followed by Veracruz, Oaxaca, Guerrero, Michoacán, Puebla, San Luis Potosí, and the State of Mexico. In most of these states you can drive along roads and count thousands of orchids growing wild.

The collector may encounter some difficulties when making excursions in the field because there is a great deal of confusion regarding orchid names in Mexico. Many of the plants have Mayan or Náhuatl names. The old Indian names were descriptive and exact. The Spanish names, added later, contributed nothing, generally being confusing and nondescriptive. And, of course, the natives of a particular region are completely unaware of the Latin names used to classify all Mexican orchids.

Along with orchids, the most Mexican of native plants are the cacti *(Cactacea,* an order of *Calycifloral dicotyledons)* which grow in great profusion in many parts of the Republic (see Index: *Orchid and Cactus Hunting*). The hundreds of Mexican species of cacti form the dominant vegetation of certain vast plains which stretch along the Great Central Plateau. Some thrive best on the sandy lowlands of Yucatán, others on the yellow plains of Sonora. Most prominent among the latter are the species *Cerei,* which rise to a height of 60 feet or more; their straight, rigid, and spiny trunks supporting great branches like candelabra — whence comes the name *Candelabra cacti.* Others creep along the ground and some species, while showing but a small bunch of leaves or pads above ground, will possess, beneath the surface, a taproot as large as a barrel.

If unmolested, nearly all the cacti develop brilliant flowers; almost all are covered with spines and some are strangely grotesque in shape.

Many cultivated, as well as uncultivated varieties, produce considerable private and national wealth. Others serve the people in a variety of ways, providing food, drink, material for weaving, thread and fuel. Certain of them produce delicious fruits — notably the *Nopal* and *Pitahaya* — and from the roots of others a variety of sweetmeats are prepared. Most prominent among the cacti is the *Maguey* (Aztec, *metl*), the generic name for 33 species which thrive on the Mexican plateau.[1] Of these species the *Aloe* or *Agave* or *Pulque*-plant is best known and the greatest wealth producer. In some regions it matures so slowly and flowers so rarely, it has been called "century plant." No vegetable product of the Mexican plains is so imposing as the *maguey* and the Greek — *agave* (noble) — is fittingly applied to it. From the equitant leaves and roots, juices and a variety of useful products are obtained: paper, vinegar, molasses, twine, fine thread, candy. The fine fiber called *pita* — a name also applied to the plant — makes very serviceable rope, though less pliable and water resistant than hemp. Some of the most valuable Aztec manuscripts were written or painted on paper made from *maguey* and this parchment was long considered the equal of Egyptian papyrus. Fermentation of the heart juice produces *pulque* and distillates of the lower leaves and root become *mezcal* and *tequila* (see Index: *Mexican Food and Drink*).

Almost equal in importance, especially as a food source, is the *Nopal Manso* or *Cactus Opuntia* which figures on the Mexican National Coat of Arms. It thrives best on the elevated tableland and reaches its greatest perfection in the State of Hidalgo. An odd feature of the plant is that each oval pad is a unit from which the entire tree is composed. With age the lower internodes produce a false kind of bark before merging into the semblance of a tree trunk. It usually presents a variety of shadings from deep greenish-brown at the base to bright green at the

[1] Although the *Maguey* or *Agave* is popularly classified with cacti, it is really a genus of plants of the natural order *Amaryllidaceae.*

terminal pads. When a branch is broken off a bundle of delicate, lacelike fibers is exposed instead of splinters and decayed wood. Around the edges of the prickly pads grows a delicious fruit — the *tuna* (prickly pear, to Americans; Indian fig, to the English; Barbary fig, to the French). It is about the size of a duck or turkey egg, covered with fine prickles, and as full of seeds as an ordinary fig and of a color ranging from whitish-gray to a rich crimson. A peculiarity of the fruit is that it is always cool when plucked, although it may have been taken from a plant exposed to desert heat and in the direct rays of the sun.

The organ cactus *(Cereus excelsus)* is common on the windswept highlands of the Central Plateau. It attains considerable height, is often found in bizarre shapes and its deep-ribbed spiny branches usually grow in clusters on a single parent stem — pointing straight upward like naked fingers, with thorns and flowers, in lieu of leaves and foliage.

The *Biznaga* or barrel cactus is somewhat rare and is noted for its thin, short taproot with an enormous upper reservoir in which it stores water. It possesses a most formidable armor of fishhook-shaped spines that no beast or bird dare penetrate. These vegetable porcupines, bristling with hooks and spines, produce a mass of lovely yellow flowers that later turn to orange and then to dark red. The meat of the plant, candied and flavored, is a popular sweet.

The *Echino* cactus *(Echinocactus horizonthalonius)*, popularly called *Peyote,* or mescal button *(Lophophora Williamsii)*, is one of the most curious among the species. It is one of the strongest stimulants known. It produces Technicolor dreams, allays hunger and thirst, is said to produce a direct effect on the genital organs and it is a powerful aid to abstinence. The Tarahumara and Huichol Indians make a cult of the plant and use it in their pharmacopoeia and religious rituals. They undertake long arduous pilgrimages to secure it, make offerings to it and worship it as a demigod.

The *Pitahaya* cactus *(Cereus pitahaya)* is an ever-present feature of the plains of Sonora and Lower California. It often grows from one to three feet in diameter and may attain a height of 60 feet. It is a first cousin to the organ cactus, and produces a fruit (soft, sweet, and nourishing) somewhat similar to the *tuna.* It ripens at the height of the dry season (June) and the harvest lasts about a month. Oddly, the lovely white flowers of the plant are never found growing on the north side of the stem. Also, the fruit, when picked early in the morning, tastes quite different than if it is picked at midday. The fruit is used by the Tarahumara Indians in their religious rites. They gather the fruit with long reed sticks armed with four prongs, then pack it in crates of split bamboo.

Amole, a species of *agave,* also called soapweed because a native soap is made of it, grows in many parts of Mexico. Although scarcely larger than a big pineapple it sends up a gigantic flower stalk, 12 to 15 feet high and from 20 to 30 inches in circumference. One of these huge spikes will bear as many as 20,000 beautiful yellow blossoms, each as large as a tulip. A multitude of hummingbirds usually feed on them. Certain Indian groups used to pound the freshly cut leaves and use the extracted juice as a poison. Indian fishermen crush the leaves, expose them to sunlight for a few hours, then throw them into a shallow stream in order to stupefy fish.

The *Cochineal* cactus *(Opuntia coccinellifera)* (see Index), was at one time of great value to the Mexicans who exported a vivid red dye taken from a louse that fed upon the cactus.

The *Agave fourcroydes (Henequén* plant) (see Index).

From several cacti, especially the *Biznaga,* the Indian methods of extracting water is interesting. They will select a *Biznaga* plant about five feet high, cut the top off, then use a blunt stake to pound the white pulp into the standing trunk. This flesh is then removed and the juice squeezed from it into a receptacle. Two or three quarts of clear, bitter, and slightly salty water can be thus secured. To extract water from tall, log-shaped cacti, the Indians will cut one down, place it on two stones, one at each end. The heavy plant sags in the middle and there a small hole is made. Fires are built at each end and the heat drives the water to the center, where it drips into a receptacle placed to catch it.

The wildflower, orchid, and cacti fancier can gather further information regarding the Mexican species from the following books:

Wildflowers of Mexico by Helen O'Gorman.

Orchidicea of Mexico and Guatemala by James Bateman (London, 1843). An exhaustive study, unfortunately out of print, but may be found in public libraries.

Las Cactaceas de Mexico by Helia Bravo H. (University of Mexico Press, 1937). The most complete book on Mexican cacti. In Spanish.

Further information can be gained from the Botany Department of the Biological Institute in Chapultepec Park, Mexico, D.F.

27. *Semiprecious Gem Stones*

Baron Alexander von Humboldt in the early 1800s called Mexico the "Treasure House of the World" because it is one of the most highly mineralized regions known. With the exception of Campeche, Tabasco, and Yucatán, every state in the republic possesses mines. Over 22,000 have been recorded. In addition to its nonferrous and ferrous deposits, obviously Mexico should be a bountiful source for semiprecious stones so avidly sought by amateur rock hounds. Igneous rocks of almost every geologic epoch form, to a large extent, the superstructure of the Great Central Plateau where many of the most celebrated mines are located. This great tableland seems to consist mainly of matamorphic formations, which have been partly upheaved, partly interpenetrated and overlaid by igneous masses of all epochs, and which are chiefly represented by shales, graywacke, greenstones, siliceous schists and unfossiliferous limestones. The highest ranges are formed mainly by volcanic rocks, such as granites, syenites, diorites, mineral-bearing trachytes, basalts, porphyries, obsidian, pearlstone, sulphur, pumice, lavas, tufas, and other recent volcanic discharges.

Unfortunately, despite the suspected gem-stone wealth of Mexico, since Humboldt's day no really thorough survey has ever been made of the country's mineral potential. Commercial geologists have generally restricted their investigations to the commercially valuable ore-bearing formations, and they have either ignored or failed to report the less important deposits that might contain gem-stone material. At the same time, geologists connected with Mexican educational centers have lacked the forces, time, and finances to do extensive field work. Mexico cries aloud for an army of dedicated rock hounds capable of snooping through the vast ranges of mountains and collecting this needed information.

At the present moment Mexico's semiprecious stone inventory includes: opals, amethysts, quartz crystals, apatite, agates, some garnets, nephrite, some forms of topaz, suspected deposits of jadeite. Although there are no proven deposits of sapphires, emeralds, rubies, nor of beryl and of diamonds, experts are confident they will eventually come upon some.

Visitors shopping for semiprecious stones often encounter street peddlers hawking a whole rainbow of colorful stones. This applies also to shops which try to palm off either synthetic or imported emeralds, rubies, smoky topazes and sapphires as native Mexican stones. One should shop with caution. The smoky topaz or golden topaz offered at bargain prices is actually either a smoky quartz or citrine. Almost all the jade and much of the nephrite is imported. Even the green-colored onyx is dyed.

The principal native stones mined in any quantity are opals from around Querétaro, amethysts from the State of Guerrero, turquoise and turquoise-matrix from Zacatecas, agates from the U.S.-Mexico border area, and quartz crystal. Other non-gem stones used for decorative carvings and in jewelry are obsidian and onyx.

Opals: The opal or *ópalo,* a birthstone (October) emblematic of Faith and Hope, is one of the most prized of Mexican gem stones. The largest known deposits are in the State of Querétaro where the first opal discovery was made in 1835 near San Juan del Río. The first opal mine, La Esperanza, which is still being worked, is in this region. There is still no large-scale opal mining done in Mexico. Most of the mines are one- or two-man operations. The Indian miners bring their finds down to the market in the village of Tequisquiapan, Querétaro, where they sell them to visiting dealers, or they take them directly to gem-stone workshops in Querétaro and Mexico City.

The quality and value of Mexican opals range from a few cents to some that are worth thousands of dollars. The finest opal of commerce is the fire opal *(girasol del fuego),* an exquisitely beautiful stone displaying emerald tints upon a basic color of fiery red and often flashing a fine flame from a rich crimson center. Other native opals include the brilliant harlequin opal *(arlequines);* the cloudy opal *(lechoso,* or milky); the so-called cat's-eye opal.

Agates (ágates): fossilized wood and bone which are opalized. They are often called agate opals and wood opals. The Mexican agates are generally of a better quality than those found in the United States. The best come from the northern border states.

Amethysts (amatista): This purple or violet gem stone rates after opals as Mexico's next most profuse and commercially important semiprecious stone. The principal mines and largest deposits are located in the State of Guerrero.

Turquoise (turquesa): a celebrated, beautiful sky-blue birthday stone (December) which has been mined in Mexico since before the conquest. The finer grades of Mexican turquoise are equal to the products of the famed Nishapur and Khorassan mines. One should be cautious, however, when purchasing this stone. The finer grades are of a sky-blue color inclined slightly to green. The inferior stones are of a pale, muddy, yellowish green. The blue tints so much prized may alter to green, (both naturally by exposure to weather or artificially by heat). Ordinary turquoise should be kept for some time before mounting for jewelry, to see if the color is permanent. It should be worn with care, especially as to contact with soaps, perfumes, and body oils which are apt to alter the color. Perhaps the best turquoise in Mexico comes from the Santa Rosa area around Zacatecas.

Jade, (Jadeite) and Nephrite: Although jade and nephrite are both popularly known as jade by the less discerning, there is a qualitative, and in Mexico, a quantitative difference. Jade or jadeite *(piedra de ijada)* is a monoclinic mineral, a member of the piroxine group of minerals, ranging in colors from white to various shades of green and blueish green. Nephrite is a less valuable stone belonging to the amphibole group. The colorings are often similar to jadeite.

One of the great archaeological and minerological puzzles in Mexico is that the pre-Hispanic Indian artisans created magnificent artifacts and jewelry of jadeite, and yet no worthy deposits of this mineral have been located within the borders of the republic. In addition to this many of the carvings, and some of their ceremonial uses, are disturbingly similar in concept and ceremonial use to those of the Orient. Some authorities rely on this as one of the proofs that there existed some sort of cultural or missionary trans-Pacific interchange between Mexico and the Orient, long before the conquest, yet many years after the Alaskan landbridge migrations from Asia had ceased. On the other hand, although no important jadeite deposits have been found by minerologists in the four and a half centuries since the conquest and although the jades found in Mixtec and Aztec tombs are similar to the fine Oriental jadeite in quality, feel, appearance, and even structure, nevertheless, spectographic analysis has indicated that these Mexican jades differ from jades having their origin in China and Burma. Where they came from remains a mystery.[1]

Travelers in the Mexico of today are offered quantities of so-called jade carvings, jewelry, and beads, often purported to be of ancient workmanship. Although good examples of ancient jadeite handiwork may sometimes be found, the bulk of what is offered is neither ancient, nor is it jadeite. Most such pseudo-antiques are made of nephrite, a less valuable stone which is native to Mexico. Also, many of these carvings are made of nephrite imported from the United States and Alaska.

[1] There is no mention of jade in European literature before the discovery of America by Columbus. The early Spanish navigators brought back specimens of a green stone which was highly valued by the natives of America and which was worn by them as a badge of rank, or as an ornament, and as a safeguard against certain diseases. The Indians attributed curative properties to the stones, especially for renal diseases. From this the Spaniards named the stone (the name first appeared in the works of *Monardes,* a physician of Seville, in 1565) *Piedra de hijada* or colic stone.

The Aztecs, Mayans, and Zapotec considered jade as the most precious of all stones. In their tongue it was called *chalchihuitl,* or also *quetzalitzli,* from the *quetzal,* or bird of paradise *(Trogon resplendens)* and *itzli,* stone — because of the similarity of the stone to the brilliant metallic green plumes (worn by the rulers of Mexico as a regal insignia) of this splendid bird. In some parts of Mexico the stone was also called *quetzal-chalchihuitl.* The Chinese, by a curious coincidence, no doubt accidental, derived the name *fei-ts'ui* from a kingfisher, the peacock-green plummage of which they often inlaid in jewelry.

Bernal Díaz says that among the presents which Moctezuma gave to Cortéz for the King of Spain there were some jadeite pieces. Moctezuma said, when handing them over, "To this I will add a few *chalchihuis* of such enormous value I would not consent to give them to anyone save to such a powerful emperor as yours. Each of these stones is worth two loads of gold."

Juan de Torquemada *(Monarchia Indiana,* 1613) says that "when a great dignitary died in Mexico his corpse was richly decorated for burial with gold and plumed feathers, and that they put in his mouth a fine *chalchihuitl,* as a heart. A great law-giver and high priest of the ancient Mexicans was miraculously begotten by a *chalchihuitl* placed in the bosom of the goddess Chimalma, and if a similiar stone is laid upon the tongue of a deceased person it will help the soul pass the seven ordeals before reaching Quetzalcoatl in heaven."

Incidentally, the jade stone placed on the tongue of the deceased in ancient Mexico was painted a bright red cinnibar. A similiar cinnibar-painted jade is used in China to weigh the tongue and eyelids of the dead.

28. The Bullfight

The *corrida de toros* (meaning "a running of the bulls") should not be regarded as a sport, nor as a cruel baiting of a helpless animal. The bullfight or *fiesta brava* is a traditional festival as well as a tragic ceremony celebrating bravery and death. It is staged and played out with symbolic artistry and vivid pageantry.

The fighting bulls, *toros bravos,* who appear in the ring are of a very special sort. They are bred for only one purpose, and that is to fight and die in the bullring. The bravery of these animals is the primal root of the entire spectacle. They battle not because they are cornered, ill-tempered, or panicky, but because they welcome a fight. In character they are about as far removed from the domestic bull as the timber wolf is from a collie. They possess incredible speed, muscle, fighting strength, consistent anger, and a cunning unknown in the domestic animal.

Both in Mexico and in Spain there are ranches devoted exclusively to the raising of fighting bulls. The greatest care is taken in keeping the bloodline of such fighting animals pure. Until the moment of their appearance in the ring, the bulls have led a life of animal luxury; they eat well, have the freedom of an excellent range and they have no contact with man, except once, when at the age of two they are tested for their qualities of bravery.

During the testing or *tienta,* held at the ranch, the young bull is driven into a corral where a *picador* or horseman offers him the lance tipped with a very small goad — it is considerably shorter than the *garrocha* offered in the ring proper. In the testing, the horseman doesn't move. No one makes a sound and nothing is done to excite the young bull. The point is to determine the bull's willingness to charge without being annoyed. If the bull charges at the horseman with frankness, if he ignores the pain of the lance and returns for another charge, he is marked as *aprobado* in the rancher's record book, that is, he is an approved candidate for the bullring. He is immediately released to the range again. Young bulls that fail to show bravery are cut out of the herd as *desecho de tienta* (rejected in the proof). Some of these rejected animals are sold to the *novilladas,* that is, for the fights where novices or aspiring bullfighters take part. Occasionally such bulls put on a surprisingly good showing in the ring.

The mature bulls that you see in a formal *corrida de toros* are between four and five years old. They weigh between 400 to 600 kilos — a half a ton or over. The best of the Mexican fighting bulls are descendants of the Spanish bulls. Sometimes the bull-breeding ranches welcome visitors. If you can wrangle an invitation to visit one, especially during a *tienta,* it is well worth the time. Some of the better Mexican breeding ranches are: Pastejé, Xajay, Santa María, Peñuelas, etc.

In Mexico City and the larger cities throughout the country the bullfights begin promptly at four o'clock. The best fights *(corridas formales)* are held in the winter season, between November and March. Noted *toreros* or bullfighters perform throughout the country. Between April and October, the *novilleros* (novices) have their season. However, during these off-months, for special fiestas, many of the noted *toreros* make guest appearances.

The elaborate ceremony of the bullfight has not changed much over the years. First, there is the *desfile* or opening parade. A judge or supervising official (the *presidente*) takes his seat in a central box. Then a rider on horseback, the *alguacil,* emerges from a gate, rides across the ring to a point just below the judge's box. He salutes and petitions the authorities for permission to begin the spectacle. He rides back to the portal through which the principal actors appear: the three matadors, their assistants, and peons. The colorful parade of the bullfighters, known as the *paseo de las cuadrillas,* follows the strictest tradition. Foremost comes the *alguacil* upon his capering stallion; close behind come the *matadores* (also called *espadas,* or swords) striding three abreast. Their costumes, *trajes de luces* or suits-of-lights, are tight-fitting, beautifully embroidered with silver and gold thread. By usage, the eldest of the fighters to have taken the *alternativa* (a so-called doctorate degree in bullfighting) always marches on the left, the next oldest on the right and the newest fighter in the middle. The men wear their heavily embroidered, glittering *capotes de paseo* or parade capes flung over their left shoulders. The *matadores* are followed by the *banderilleros* who wear less costly but similar uniforms. They are followed by the *picadores,* the mounted lancers whose garb is infinitely plainer, consisting of a broad brimmed, round crowned hat with a pompom, a short jacket of colored velvet, light yellow breeches, a scarf about the waist, a frilled shirt and protective leather boots. These are trailed by the lesser ring attendants and the *arrastres,* the team of mules who eventually drag away the dead bull.

During the parade across the ring the band plays the stirring two-step "La Virgen de la Macarena," a tune that has the same emotional effect on bullfight fans as "Mother Machree" has on Irish-Americans. Arriving before the *presidente's* box, salutes are exchanged, then the procession breaks up. Picadores, mules, attendants abandon the ring to the principal fighters and their assistants.

The *presidente* waves a handkerchief and a trumpet signals the coming of the first bull into the ring. As the bull rushes from the *toril,* an attendant plants a hooked dagger festooned with gay ribbons into the hide of the animal. These are the colors of the ranch that bred the bull.

The first rush of the bull is an exciting thing to see. The *matadores* and their assistants have retired behind a wooden barrier encircling the arena better to observe the characteristics of the animal. The bull is magnificent both while in motion, or in repose. His hide is strong, thick, and glossy; his head is small, his forehead wide, his horns curve forward. His neck is short and powerful and there is a great hump of muscle upon his shoulders which erects when he is angry.

The stages of the fight are divided into three *tercios,* or acts, which are carried out with each bull.[1]

---

[1] Originally bullfights were far less formal. The earliest bullfights were celebrated on the island of Crete in the Mediterranean, before the time of Christ. They were introduced into Spain by the Moors around the twelfth century.

The Moors fought the bull on foot, but in a quite different manner than is used today. The Moorish bullfighter carried a cloak over the left arm and he threw a harpoon-like weapon at the bull. This javelin, the *rehilete,* has since then evolved into the present-day *banderilla.*

Until the early eighteenth century bullfighting was the prerogative of the aristocracy. Noblemen, armed with short lances (the *rejón*), fought the bull from horseback. This early style, requiring brilliant equestrianship and highly trained horses, is still practiced. Mexico's famed *matador,* Carlos Arruza, has done much to popularize this technique.

In the early history of the festival accidents were frequent. In 1512, no less than ten knights lost their lives in a single *fiesta de toros* in Spain. It was not unusual for kings and princes to descend into the arena and display their skills.

Each *tercio* is necessary for preparing the bull for his death, but so that it is accomplished with art and bravery. When the animal first comes into the ring he is lofty in bearing, or *levantado,* as it is called. His head is held high, he is confident; he charges quickly, but without careful aim. At this time he is least dangerous, but his horns are held too high to permit the fighter to go in over them with the sword.

During the first act the assistants to the *matador* run the bull to test his behavior. They observe which horn he favors, how straight he charges and any other quirks he may exhibit in the ring. The *matador* stands behind a *burladero,* (a wooden shield or barrier) and watches carefully. Finally he steps out and works the bull himself. If the animal responds well, he may indulge in a series of passes with the heavy cerise-and-gold fighting cape. Generally these passes will be *verónicas,* the mother of all two-handed passes with the cape. Following these preliminaries, the mounted *picadores* are introduced and the bull's attention is diverted toward them. The *picador's* role is to ward off the fierce charges of the bull by placing the tip of his lance *(vara)* in the powerful *morilla* or shoulder muscle of the animal. Several such pics serve to weaken the tossing muscle and bring the bull to a condition called *parado,* in which he is at bay and his head is carried somewhat lower. When the bull has reached this stage a fighter can perform brilliantly with him.

A trumpet signal ends the first *tercio* and announces the second act — the placing of the *banderillas* (short lances, gaily decorated with colored paper and having barbed points that hook underneath the bull's heavy hide).

Usually the assistants to the *matador* place the barbs, but sometimes a *matador* will do it himself. If he does it he is expected to add something extra to the spectacle. If performed with grace, skill, and daring, the *suerte de banderillas* can be one of the brilliant moments of the bullfight. The actor must stand alone, facing the bull and exciting him. He raises the pair of barbs at arm's length and at the same time rises slightly on his toes. When he does this he is said to be *alegrando,* or cheering the bull. Suddenly the bull charges and the fleet-footed man moves toward the animal at a slight tangent. Just as they meet the *banderillero* raises his arms above his head, his hands are almost together and the short javelins are held poised above the bull. For an instant the man appears to hang perilously over the bull's horns; he drives the barbed javelins into the shoulder muscle of the animal, then deftly escapes the horns. Three pairs of javelins are placed in this manner.

The third and final act of the fight consists of passing the bull with a small red cloth called the *muleta* and the climactic kill. This *tercio* begins with another traditional ceremony. The *matador,* holding the sword and *muleta* in hand, presents himself below the authority's box and asks permission to kill the bull. He then dedicates the death of the animal and the risking of his own life to someone in the stands.

Tradition dictates that he should be left completely alone in the ring to face the bull. By now his adversary has been somewhat slowed and his head lowered, but at the same time, the animal is most dangerous. With the *muleta* draped over a short stick (the *ayudado*), the bullfighter begins a series of passes designed to establish his complete dominance over the animal. Although there are numerous passes, the finest is called the *pase natural,* a left-handed movement in which the *matador,* his feet fixed, draws the bull past his undefended body. To be really effective, any pass should be done in series. To do a series of three or four *naturales* requires exceptional skill and artistry, to say nothing of courage. As Ernest Hemingway once expressed it, "All spectators hope to see a complete *faena* (a perfect sum of passes); the *faena* that takes a man out of himself and makes him feel immortal while seeing it, that gives him ecstasy . . . To see a great *faena* followed by a great *estocada* (the kill) happens once in a lifetime."

The *muleta* passes should make the bull *aplomado,* that is, heavy, short-winded, slower, yet without loss of strength. This is the moment for the kill. The *matador* stands directly before the bull and sights along the blade of his sword while, at the same time, holding the bull's attention with the *muleta.* The fighter then goes in over the horns, delivering the sword thrust into a small target area between the bull's shoulders. At the same time, he escapes to the left. All these critical movements must be done with smoothness and artistry, almost as a continuous flow. At times the sword may hit bone and fly out. The next attempt to kill then becomes far more dangerous. Even with a cleanly planted sword thrust, the bull very seldom dies instantly. Often the thrust of a dagger or a sword into the base of the skull is required to finish him.

In the larger cities of Mexico the bullrings are

Risks were apparently so great that in 1567 Pope Pius V issued a Papal Bull threatening excommunication to all princes who permitted bullfighting.

During the early eighteenth century bullfighting was taken over by professionals. The modern style of fighting is accredited to the little city of La Ronda in Spain, where Francisco Romero introduced the *suerte de la muleta,* the use of a small brilliant red cloth to play and place the bull in position so he could be killed with a single sword thrust.

Seville, Spain, soon became the rival of La Ronda. Each city had its school and its particular style of fighting. The Sevillians were considered *arrojo* (daring), while the La Ronda fighters developed a style noted for its *serenidad* (coolness). The Sevillians fought *a pié movido,* that is shifting their feet as they made the kill. The La Ronda men made the kill *a pié quieto,* without moving a foot.

From these two basic styles, the refinements of today's bullfight evolved. To suit the more showy modern techniques, the gigantic bulls of the past had to be changed. Today's bulls have been bred down in size and in length of horn. In many ways their suavity of charge and fierceness has been so improved it has made for a more spectacular and graceful fight.

stone or concrete amphitheaters consisting of a circular arena carpeted with sand. The tiers of seats are separated from the arena by a wooden barrier *(barrera)* about five feet high. Behind this is a narrow passage, then a higher cement or stone *contrabarrera.* The first rows of seats (ringside) are called *asientos de barrera.* They are the most prized and expensive. The next nine or so rows above them are called *tendidos,* and rank next in cost. The following twenty or so rows — *segundos tendidos* — are reserved, but less expensive. All seats above this area are general admission. In most rings there is also a section of covered box seats called *palcos.* Since the bullfights take place in the late afternoon when the sun is declining, one half of the plaza is in shade, the other exposed to the glare of the sun. The best reserved seats *(localidades de preferencia)* are on the shady side.

29. Jai Alai or Frontòn

The famous Basque ball game of *pelota,*[1] masquerading in the New World under the Cuban name of *jai alai,* or also *frontón,* is a unique and favorite spectator sport in Mexico. It is played by professionals who use curious wicker baskets as a kind of extended bat and glove to catch and hurl a hard, leather-covered rubber ball at incredible speeds on a seemingly block-long concrete court.

The game is one of the fastest, toughest, and most skill-demanding games ever devised. It is played on a long three-walled court called a *frontón.* The fourth side of the court is usually screened in with wire. The long 100-yard side wall, at right angles to the *frontís* or front wall against which the ball is hurled, is marked out in spaces or *cuadros.* The back or rebound wall is called the *rebote.* The parallelogram-shaped playing floor is known as the *cancha* or cockpit.

The game is played between teams of two men each. Each player uses a *cesta,* a long boat-shaped basket made of tough woven reeds. It is attached to a leather gauntlet that is laced over the player's hand. The *cesta* is used to catch the ball and to whip it back against the wall at terrific speeds. At the beginning of the game the players toss for position; those winning the place nearest the front wall are called *delanteros,* the couple stationed behind, *zagueros.* The serve is termed *el sáque;* a good one being called *limpio* or clean, a poor one, *sucio* or dirty. Volleys are known as *boteas* and the rebounds *rebotes.* The ball may hit the two end walls or side wall within the marked white lines. Each team takes turns serving and receiving. The first to miss gives the other side a point. Usually, games are played to 29 points, *partida a 29 tantos.*

In each professional *frontón* program there is usually a *quiniela* in which six men play winner-stay-up until one man wins six points.

Betting at Mexican *jai alai* matches is as lively as the play itself. Wagering is done on the basis of 100 pesos for the favored team, against lesser amounts for the underdog. As the game progresses the odds change rapidly and are flashed on an electric scoreboard. In the *quiniela,* if you happen to pick the winner and runner-up, you are in for a happy daily-double reward. (For additional information regarding location of *frontón* centers, hours, prices, see Entertainment and Recreation listings under individual cities, i.e., Mexico City, Tijuana, etc.)

Frontenis or *frontón* tennis is a version of *jai alai* that is played on a smaller court, and with rackets. Many private residences and sports clubs throughout the country have their own *frontenis* courts.

[1] Since the Aztecs played a similar game called *tlaihiyotentli,* some historians have claimed that Cortés introduced the game into Spain from Mexico. However, since Philip I of Castile died in 1501 as the result of an accident incurred while playing *pelota,* (thirteen years before Cortés reached Mexico), it would appear that the game is of Old World provenance. The original game somewhat resembled our lawn tennis. It was not until the nineteenth century that the present form of *jai alai,* utilizing the *cesta* or basket, was developed in the Basque regions of Spain.

30. Cockfights, Football, Baseball, and Golf

COCKFIGHTS

The *pelea de gallos* is not an especially popular entertainment in Mexico, except in rural communities. There is one pit where cockfights and the accompanying betting take place in Mexico City. (See Entertainment, Mexico City.) The staging is drab and depressing. If you really want to see a cockfight, it is suggested that you take one in at a country fair, a village festival or during a fiesta at someone's ranch.

FOOTBALL

Mexican football *(futbol)* is actually the international game of soccer. It is one of Mexico's most popular sports. Wherever you travel below the border, whether it be through a remote village or the distant desert, you'll inevitably spot the oblong playing field and pair of goal posts. The game, far more exciting and speed-packed than our American football, now draws bigger crowds than most bullfights.

Mexican professional soccer teams are on a par with the best of the European teams and international matches are frequently played in the larger Mexican cities. In Mexico there are two leagues, a major *(primera división)* and a minor *(segunda división)*. For the convenience of sports fans here is the list of teams often in the first division and their home cities:

TEAM	CITY	STATE
Guadalajara	Guadalajara	Jal.
América	Mexico City	D.F.
León	León	Gto.
Toluca	Toluca	Mex.
Atlas	Guadalajara	Jal.
Irapuato	Irapuato	Gto.
Oro	Guadalajara	Jal.
Necaxa	Mexico City	D.F.
Tampico	Tampico	Tamps.
Zamora	Zamora	Mich.
Zacatepec	Zacatepec	Morelos
Atlante	Mexico City	D.F.
Morelia	Morelia	Mich.

Each year the team that ends up in the first division cellar is transferred to the second division for the following season. The top team in the second division then plays in the first division league.

The teams have eleven players each. The game, consisting of two 45-minute halves, is scarcely interrupted for time out; the players are almost in constant motion. A team scores one point each time the ball is sent through the opposition's goal. To touch on some of the mysteries of the game for visitors unfamiliar with the rules: (1) the players move the ball toward the goals by kicking it, using their head, shoulders, or other parts of the body. However, if they touch it with their hands they are penalized. The ball is turned over to the opposing team. (2) *Off-side:* a penalty which results in the loss of the ball to the opposition. It occurs when a player is in the opposition's zone and he is running ahead of all the opposition team players. If he receives the ball from one of his teammates in this area, without it having been touched by an opposing player, the penalty occurs. (3) *Corner:* when the ball touches a player and it then goes out of bounds near his own goal. A player from the opposite team takes possession and may kick it from the corner. (4) *Foul:* when a player pushes, kicks, or strikes an opposing player deliberately. The opposing player takes possession of the ball and puts it into play again.

The main season for professional football in Mexico is the summer and fall.

BASEBALL

An extremely popular game in Mexico, played much as it is above the border, but often with a dash of hot sauce. There is a Mexican league made up of eight teams and they play in various cities of the republic. There are two seasons: summer and winter. Frequently, during the winter season, top U.S. ball players contract to play with the Mexican teams.

Of interest to North American fans are the linguistic changes and adaptations that go with the game below the border. Games are called *juegos de beisbol*. Home run becomes *jomrón*. A hit is spelled *jit*. A strike out is a *ponche*. Innings are *entradas*.

GOLF

There are no public links in Mexico. There are, however, a number of excellent courses sprinkled throughout the country. These belong to hotels or private clubs. Visitors are welcome to play them in most cases. According to the rules you should be introduced by a member. However, it has been our experience that a visitor can walk in, make contact with the club "pro" who will make arrangements for you to pay the green fees and rent clubs if needed.

Clubs affiliated with the Mexican Golf Association

NAME AND ADDRESS	HOLES
Campestre de Chihuahua, S.C. Aptdo. 257, Chihuahua, Chih.	9
Campestre Juárez, S.A. Aptdo. 146, C. Juárez, Chih.	9
Centro Campestre Lagunero, S.C. de R.L. Aptdo. 35, Gómez Palacio, Dgo.	9
Club Campestre de Aguascalientes, A.C. Portal Juárez 6, Aguascalientes, Ags.	9
Club Campestre de Avándaro, Avándaro, Valle del Bravo, Mex.	9
Club Campestre de Durango, A.C. Aptdo. 24, Durango, Dgo.	9
Club Campestre de la Ciudad de Mexico, S.A. Aptdo. 100 bis, Mexico, D.F.	18
Club Campestre de Mazatlán, Aptdo. 105, Mazatlán, Sin.	9
Club Campestre de Nuevo León, S.A. de C.V. Prolongación Ote. Fraccionamiento Club Campestre, Nuevo Laredo, Tamps.	9
Club Campestre de Puebla, S.A. de C.V. Aptdo. 172, Puebla, Pue.	9
Club Campestre de Querétaro, A.C. Aptdo. 86, Querétaro, Qro.	9
Club Campestre de Saltillo, A.C. Aptdo. 271, Saltillo, Coah.	9
Club Campestre de Zacapu, A.C. Aptdo. 6, Zacapu, Mich.	9
Club Campestre de Monterrey, A.C. Aptdo. 1448, Monterrey, N.L.	18
Club Campestre Tampico, S.A. Aptdo. 605, Tampico, Tamps.	18
Club Deportivo Campestre de Tijuana, A.C. Aptdo. 439, Tijuana, B.C.	18
Club de Golf de Acapulco, Escudero 3, # 4, Acapulco, Gro.	9
Club de Golf de Cuernavaca, S.A. Av. Morelos 73, Mexico, D.F.	9
Club de Golf de Hermosillo, A.C. Aptdo. 54, Hermosillo, Son.	9
Club de Golf Esmeralda, Aptdo. 130, Parral, Chih.	9
Club de Golf de Irapuato, S.C. Aptdo. 23, Irapuato, Gto.	9
Club de Golf Ruiz Galindo, Fortín de las Flores, Ver.	9

Club de Golf Santa Gertrudis, Aptdo. 170, Santa Gertrudis, Ver. 9
Club Potosino de Golf, S.C. Aptdo. 359, San Luis Potosí, S.L.P. 9
Country Club Los Mochis, Aptdo. 14, Los Mochis, Sin. 9
Chapultepec Golf Club, S.A. Aptdo. 23515, Mexico, D.F. 18
Frisco Club, San Francisco del Oro, Chih. 9
Guadalajara Country Club, A.C. Aptdo. 700, Guadalajara, Jal. 18
Valle Alto, A.C. Club de Golf, Aptdo. 1924, Monterrey, N.L. 18
Club de Golf Peñafiel, Hoteles Unidos S.A. Tehuacán, Pue. 9

31. Bibliography

The following is a small selection of books on subjects of interest to the traveler in Mexico. Other works of local value are mentioned throughout the Guidebook.

A Basic Ten Books, to outfit the traveler with a broad peek at Mexican history, customs, arts, and economics.

Ancient Mexico by Frederick Thompson, a new and very good picture of Mexico's pre-Hispanic past. *History of Mexico* by Henry B. Parkes (Houghton Mifflin), an exciting, perceptive general history of the country. *The True History of the Conquest of New Spain* by Bernal Díaz del Castillo. It is the piquant, classic "I was there" account of the conquest. *El Laberinto de la Soledad* by Octavio Paz (in Spanish). The best study of the Mexican character. *A Treasury of Mexican Folkways* by Frances Toor (Crown). A rich accounting of the peoples, customs, dances, arts, and outlook. *The Story of Architecture in Mexico* by Trent E. Sanford (Norton). *In Mexico* by James Norman (Morrow), Mexican popular arts and crafts and where to find the best of them. *Mexico — Struggle for Peace and Bread* by Frank Tannenbaum (Knopf), covers the labyrinth of contemporary Mexican politics and economics. *Arte Mexicano, de sus orígenes a nuestros días* (in Spanish) by Justino Fernández. The most comprehensive history of Mexico's art from ancient times to the present. *In Indian Mexico* by Fredrick Starr. An old and still excellent account of off-trail exploration.

Regional Books: *Zapotec* by Helen Augur (Doubleday). A sensitive and poetic appreciation of the Oaxaca region. *Mexico South — the Isthmus of Tehuantepec* by Miguel Covarrubias (Knopf). Lively travel, folklore, and history that has become a classic. *Yalalag — a Zapotec Village,* by Julio de la Fuente (in Spanish). *Tepoztlán — A Mexican Village* by Robert Redfield (University of Chicago Press). *Lower California Guidebook* by Gerhard and Gulick. A meticulous exploration of Baja California. *Central America, Chiapas and Yucatán* and *Incidents of Travel in Yucatán* by J. N. Stephens.

History, Archaeology and Anthropology: *The Conquest of Mexico* by W. H. Prescott. A vivid classic, though now somewhat inaccurate. *Aztecs of Mexico* by George C. Vaillant (Doubleday). *El Pueblo del Sol* by Alfonso Caso (English version published by University of Oklahoma Press). *History of the Mayas* by Thomas Gann and J. Eric Thompson. *La Vida Cotidiana de los Aztecas* by Jacques Soustelle (in Spanish and English). One of the best accounts of Aztec life. *Relación de las Cosas de Yucatán* by Fray Diego de Landa (Spanish). *Historia General de Las Cosas de Nueva España* by Fray Bernadino de Sahagún (in Spanish or English). *A Comparative Study of the Mayas and Lacandones* by Alfred M. Tozzer (University of Chicago Press). *The Tarahumara* by W. C. Bennett and R. M. Zingg (University of Chicago). *Religious Aspects of the Conquest of Mexico* by C. S. Braden (Duke University Press). *Idols Behind Altars* by Anita Brenner (Payson & Clarke).

Personal Accounts: *Life in Mexico* by Madame Calderon de la Barca. A delightfully refreshing account of Mexican mores shortly after the Independence. *Viva Mexico* by Charles Flandrau.

Political and Social Works: *El Perfil del Hombre y la Cultura en México* by Samuel Ramos (Spanish). One of the most important studies of the Mexican character. *The Eagle and the Serpent* by Martín Luis Guzmán. *Children of Sánchez,* by Oscar Lewis (Random House), an exceptional study of the Mexican family.

The Arts and Literature: *The Art of the Ancient Mayas* by Alfred Kidder II and C. S. Chinchilla (Crowell). *Mexican Manuscript Paintings of the Early Colonial Period* by Robertson Donald (Yale), the best study of the old codices yet done in English. *Mexican Pre-Hispanic Paintings* by J. Soustelle and Ignacio Bernal (New York Graphic). *Mexican Music* by Carlos Chaves and Herbert Weinstock (Doubleday). *Colonial Architecture in Mexico* by Sylvester Baxter. *Made in Mexico* by Patricia F. Ross (Knopf). The story of Mexican folk arts and crafts for young readers. *20 Centuries of Mexican Art* published by Museum of Modern Art, N.Y. *Historia de la Literatura Náhuatl* by K. Garibay (Spanish). The most complete study of Aztec literature.

Flora and Fauna: (See Index for books about Mexican Cacti and Orchids.) *Wildlife in Mexico* by Dr. Starker Leopold (University of California Press). A magnificently illustrated and documented book on game birds and animals. *Mexican Birds* by George Sutton (University of Oklahoma Press). *Fishing in Mexico* by Hart Stillwell (Knopf).

PART THREE

Routes

Although accommodations and the general condition of roads are indicated at the beginning of each log, it is advisable to make local inquiries while traveling, concerning temporary detours due to weather damage, road-widening projects, and repairs. The American Automobile Association booklet *Mexico and Central America* (available to members of affiliated motor clubs *only*) carries detailed road reports. The information regarding detours, however, is not always up to the minute due to the time lag between the period when the highways are checked and the publication date of the booklet. For timely road-condition reports, Sanborn's Travel Service, McAllen, Texas, issues up-to-the-minute mimeographed highway bulletins.

Mileages between points may vary from those logged herein due to detours, new road construction and recent short-cuts.

Symbols: In the following condensed logs the boldfaced letters: **G, H,** and **R,** separately, or joined, **GHR,** indicate gasoline, hotel, and restaurant stops. These are included, not as firm recommendations, but for emergency purposes. Best stops for overnight and eating stops are listed at the beginning of each log. Further information regarding hotels and restaurants are included in Part Four, the regional sections of the guide. Where you see the asterisks, these refer to Part Four of the guide where detailed descriptions of points of interest, hotels, etc., mentioned in the logs, may be found.

Of the highways entering Mexico, those with port of entry at Laredo, McAllen, Brownsville, and Eagle Pass are recommended for motorists coming from the East, Midwest, and Rocky Mountain states. The El Paso and Nogales ports are best for motorists coming from Western states, and who are anxious to see as much of Mexico as possible. However, if you are in a hurry to get into Central Mexico and have no interest in dawdling along the road, you will find that the Eagle Pass entry and highway is much the fastest route to Mexico City, whether you come from Chicago or San Francisco.

ROUTE

Laredo to Mexico City (Pan American), CN–85
— from McAllen, CN–40 & 85
— from Brownsville, CN–101 & 85
— from Roma-Falcoln Dam to Monterrey, CN–12

Eagle Pass to Mexico City (Direct) CN–57
— via Toluca, CN–57 & 71 & 15
— via Ixmiquilpan, CN–57 & 45 & 85

El Paso to Mexico City, CN–45 & 57

Nogales to Mexico City (Pacific Coast), CN–15
— via Morelia and Querétaro, CN–15, CE–20 & 45, CN–57
— Tijuana-El Centro to West Coast Highway Route

Monterrey to Mazatlán (Coast to Coast), CN–40

Tampico to Yucatán and Quintana Roo (Gulf Circuit) CN–180

Mexico City to Acapulco, CN–95

Mexico City to Oaxaca and Chiapas (Cristóbal Colón) CN–190 (via Puebla)
— via Cuautla, CN–95, 138, 115, 190

Mexico City to Veracruz (via Texcoco, Jalapa)
CN–136 & 140
— via Puebla, Jalapa, CN–140
— via Puebla, Tehuacán and Cordoba,
CN–190 & 150

Pachuca to Tuxpan or Tecolutla (Vanilla Route)
CN–130

Salina Cruz to Coatzalcoalcos (Trans-Isthmus)
CN–185

Ciudad Mante to Guadalajara, CN–80

Tijuana to La Paz, CN–1

Special Maps: For normal vacation travel in Mexico the general maps issued by the American Automobile Association and by the Humble Oil Company are satisfactory. In the republic, gasoline stations do not give away maps — nor even have them on hand. The Mexican petroleum monopoly, Pemex, publishes road maps, but frequently these are quite inaccurate. For off-trunk-highway travel the Goodrich-Euzkadi tire company issues an excellent book of gate-fold maps entitled *Caminos de Mexico.* It is sold in bookshops. Price $20 MN.

The best of the really detailed maps of Mexico, for off-trail exploring, are the Mexican and Central American sheets, scaled at 1:5,000,000, published by the U. S. Government.

32. Laredo to Mexico City

This is the original and oldest leg of the Pan American highway, a scenic and spectacular road, an engineering marvel cut through difficult mountain terrain. *Length:* 765 m. *Road:* narrowish two-car width. Entirely paved. Occasional short detours where road is being widened. Due to several stiff gradients, not recommended for trailer travel. Highway CN-85. Driving time about 2½ days. *Best stopovers:* Monterrey, Ciudad Victoria, Ciudad del Mante, Ciudad Valles, Tamazunchale, Zimapan, Ixmiquilpan.

MILES FROM LAREDO — TRIP LOG

0 *NUEVO LAREDO.** **GHR.** Port of entry. Customs and immigration offices. To avoid customs inspections at the two substations farther along the road, do not break open the customs seals placed on your baggage. Near S. end of town Calle González leads to a road going to the Don Martín Dam and lake 80 m. away.* Driving time, Nuevo Laredo to Monterrey about 3½ hrs. First 47 m. of highway is flat and straight.

17 *Customs Inspection Station.* Only the car papers are usually checked.

42 *La Gloria.* A crossroad here leads to Don Martín Dam, 75 m., and to Sabinas on the Eagle Pass-Mexico City highway, 116 m.

67 *Vallecillo.* Beyond here road begins ascent into Sierra Madre foothills.

82 *Sabinas Hidalgo.* **GR.** Town a former mining center. Road crosses Río Salinas and soon begins climb to Mamulique Pass, alt. 2300 ft. About 2½ m., winding road.

107 *Federal Inspection Station.* No stop for northbound cars. After passing station seals can be broken on baggage.

124 *Ciénaga de Flores.* **G.** Pretty village with a nice parkway. Road crosses Río Salinas. 5½ miles beyond is a Dept. of Agriculture Inspection Station. You may have to stop and open your car trunk.

146 *MONTERREY, N.L.** **GHR.** Junction with CN-40 to Saltillo and McAllen. See Index: Highway Routes — McAllen to Monterrey. The fastest route to Mexico City is via Saltillo and down CN-57; see Index: Highway Routes — Eagle Pass to Mexico City. However, following the scenic Pan American, we leave Monterrey for Ciudad Victoria, CN-85. Driving time 4 hrs.

150 *Huajuco Canyon.* Saddle Mountain to the E., the Sierra Anáhuac range on the W. About 20 m. of canyon road.

166 *Villa Santiago.* Two miles beyond, at El Cercado, there is a turn-off to W., to Cascada Cola de Caballo or Horsetail Falls.*

195 *Montemorelos.* **GR.** A citrus center. The highway is joined by state highway, CE-89, a shortcut between McAllen and this point, bypassing Monterrey. The highway passes through rich farm country to:

288 *Linares.* **GHR.** From here side trip can be made to the picturesque villages of Iturbide and Galeana.* The two villages are reached over a new road connecting Linares to the high-speed Eagle Pass-Mexico City CN-57.

324 *CIUDAD VICTORIA.** Capital of State of Tamulipas. **GHR.** Junction with CN-101, a good short cut between Brownsville and this point. Driving time from C. Victoria to Tamazunchale, 5 hrs. 5 m. from Victoria the highway crosses the Tropic of Cancer. 10 m. beyond it enters *Galeana Canyon* and gradually drops into tropic country dotted with sugar-cane *haciendas.*

400 *El Limón.* Lowest town on the highway. Alt. 187 ft.

407 *CIUDAD DEL MANTE.* **GHR.** Junction with CN-100 (1½ m. south), the best paved road to Tampico. Its 97 m. are smoother than the shorter alternate road between C. Valles and Tampico.

425 *Antiguo Morelos,* **GHR.** Junction with the westbound leg of the Tampico-Guadajalara highway CN-80. Side-trip to El Salto Falls.*

469 *CIUDAD VALLES.** **GHR.** A popular overnight stop. Junction with CN-110 going to Tampico, 87 m. The road is paved but in poor condition. South of C. Valles the highway traverses vivid Huastecan Indian country and there are several off-the-highway Indian villages worth a brief visit. At 497 m. is a junction with an all-weather road going E. to the village of Tancanhuitz. At 510 m. there is a graveled junction with CE-55 which goes 15 m. west, climbing to the colorful isolated villages of Xilitla and Xilitia.

474 *Villa Fierro.* Two miles beyond village are thermal springs, golf, hotels, and restaurants. Hotel Covodongo, best. El Bañito next.

533 *TAMAZUNCHALE.* **GHR.** Generally pronounced Thomas-and-Charley, the village is pleasantly tropical and the best overnight stop before beginning the real climb to the Mexican plateau.*

The highway leg between Tamazunchale and Ixmiquilpan, driving time about 6 hrs., is the most spectacular of the route. There is a big climb into the Sierra Madres, from an altitude of 675 ft. to over 5000 ft. in a matter of 60 m. This first part of the drive should be covered between the hours of 8 A.M. and 5 P.M. to avoid the heavy fogs that sometimes blanket the area. The road is good and there are steel guardrails. For some 10 m. out of Tamazunchale the road hugs the turquoise Río Moctezuma.

550 *Chapulhuacán.* **GR.** Now begins the scenic climb.

592 *Jacala.* **GHR.** An old mining town perched on the edge of a lovely valley. Restaurants and accommodations are only fair.*

633 *ZIMAPÁN.** **GHR.** A charming colonial town about 3 m. west of highway. Good motel.

648 *Tasquillo.* **G.** ½ m. east of highway. Ancient capital of the Otomí Indians. Interesting colonial bridge over the Tula River gorge.

654 Junction with CN-45 going to Querétaro. Five miles farther there is a Federal Customs Inspection Station. Car papers.

649 *IXMIQUILPAN.** **GHR.** Colonial town and Otomí center. From here to Mexico City, driving time about 2½ hrs., the climb is by easy stages through picturesque country.

687 *Actopan.* **G.** Site of famed colonial convent. Junction with CE-126, going west 35 m. to the archaeological ruins at Tula. Paved. From Tula you can continue via the new toll road to Mexico City in one hr.*

702 Turn-off to *Pachuca,* 5 m.* In Pachuca one can join CN-130 leading to Tuxpan, the Flower Route.*

704 *Hacienda de la Concepción.* Highest point on route. Alt. 8206. Nearby, on r. Monument to Mexican-American Friendship.

709 *Colonia.* Paved road to the l. goes to Pachuca.

744 *Venta de Carpio.* **G.** on l. junction with CN-132 going to pyramids at Teotihuacán, 12 m., and to Convent of Acolmán.*

The highway traverses the great stone dike built by the Spaniards to separate Lake San Cristóbal from Lake Texcoco (both dry now). At 746 m., *San Cristóbal Ecatepec,* on r. is a colonial building called "House of the Viceroys." The revolutionary hero, Morelos, was imprisoned here. House is now a museum.

752 *Santa Clara.* Road forks here. Left to Villa Madero and the Shrine of Guadalupe.* Surface not in good condition. Right-fork goes directly into Mexico City.

Via McAllen to Mexico City. This is simply a variation of the old Pan American. The motorist enters Mexico at McAllen, Texas (Reynosa, on the Mexican side), and joins the Laredo to Mexico City highway at Monterrey or at Montemorelos.

MILES FROM REYNOSA — TRIP LOG

0 *REYNOSA.** **GR.** Customs and immigration offices on Mexican side of the International Bridge spanning the Río Grande. Follow CN-40 to Monterrey. Driving time 3½ hrs. Paved and good.

15 *Federal Inspection Station.* Car papers checked.

61.5 *General Bravo.* **G.**

70 *China,* **G.** In plaza, junction with CE-89. If you wish to skip Monterrey, turn left here and follow 89 to Montemorelos. For Monterrey you continue

straight ahead on CN-40. 1½ m. beyond China the road crosses the Río San Juan.

119 *Customs Inspection Station.* The last one.

121 *Cadereyta.* **G.** A dusty town that always seems to have detours. It is Mexico's broom-making capital.

140 *Guadalupe,* a suburb of Monterrey. Just beyond, the highway crosses the usually dry Santa Catarina River.

145 *MONTERREY.* **GHR.** Junction with CN-85. Turn S. toward Mexico City. For description of route see Index: Highway Routes — Laredo to Mexico City.

Brownsville, via C. Victoria to Mexico City. Another variation of the old Pan American route. The motorist enters Mexico at Brownsville, Texas, (Matamoros on the Mexican side), following CN-101 to Ciudad Victoria where the road joins CN-85 or the Laredo-Mexico City Highway. The road is paved and good. Driving time to C. Victoria about 4½ hrs. for the 198 m. There is little of scenic interest, and very few suitable rest-stops. It is advisable to fill your gas tank before leaving Matamoros.

MILES FROM MATAMOROS — TRIP LOG

0 *MATAMOROS.** **GHR.** Mexican customs and immigration offices.

14 *Federal Inspection Station.* Car papers.

71 Junction with gravel road, CE-97, connecting with Reynosa.

88 *San Fernando.* **G.** South of the town the road crosses Río Conchos.

139 *Jiménez.* **G.** Some 22 m. beyond Jiménez the road crosses the Río Purificación and enters Padilla.

198 *Ciudad Victoria.** **GHR.** Here you join the Laredo-Mexico City highway and proceed south.

33. Eagle Pass to Mexico City

Mexico's newest and best north-south highway, passing mostly through flat to rolling country, with a minimum of mountains. Sections of the road are superhighway width, while other parts are still the typical narrower two-car Mexican style. *Length:* 816 m. *Road condition:* fair to excellent. Entirely paved. Occasional short detours where bridges and old sections are being widened. The best trailer highway to Mexico City. *Best stopovers:* Saltillo, Matehuala, San Luis Potosí, and Querétaro. A new hotel at Monclova has also just been opened. The road is posted as CN-57.

MILES FROM PIEDRAS NEGRAS — TRIP LOG

0 *PIEDRAS NEGRAS.* The Mexican port of entry opposite Eagle Pass. Custom and immigration offices. Best hotel and restaurant accommodations are on the U.S. side of the border. Driving time for the 278 m. section between Piedras Negras to Saltillo is about 6 hrs.

14 *Federal Inspection Station.* Car papers. The road traverses flat farm and range country that is not too interesting. The rangeland is unfenced so motorists should be cautious of straying animals.

34 *Morelos.* **G.** Four miles beyond, the highway passes through Allende where there is a junction with a paved branch road to Múzquiz.

76 *Federal Inspection Station.* The last permanent one on this leg.

77 *Nueva Rosita.* **G.**

85 *Sabinas.** **GHR.** Junction with branch road leading to Don Martín Dam on the Salado River. Road not recommended.

157 *MONCLOVA.** **GHR.** The home of Mexico's largest steel plant. Load up on gasoline here. After Monclova the road begins the gradual climb to the plateau country.

278 *SALTILLO.** **GHR.** Capital of the State of Coahuila and popular resort and university center. Junction with CN-40, eastward to Monterrey, or westward to Torreón and Durango.

The second section of the highway, Saltillo to Querétaro, 400 m., driving time about 8 hrs. Except for a 65-mile stretch between Huizache and San Luis Potosí (being widened), the road is roomy and fast. Leaving Saltillo the road passes through a lovely canyon, then on into rolling country.

360 Junction with CE-60 going east to Galeana.

437 *MATEHUALA.** **GHR.** Old mining center. A popular lunch and overnight stopping place. From here the road stretches across flat desert country flanked by dry mountains.

488 *Huizache.* Junction with CN-80 which runs E. to Ciudad El Mante on the Laredo-Mexico City road, or W. thru San Luis Potosí to Guadalajara. CN-80 and 57 share the next 65 m. to San Luis Potosí.

560 *SAN LUIS POTOSÍ.** **GHR.** One of Mexico's richest mining centers and capital of the state of the same name. At San Luis Potosí there are a series of bypasses. You have a choice of going through the city, or skipping by it and continuing on CN-57 toward Querétaro. The stretch to Querétaro is fast and good.

590 *Santa María del Río.* A charming craft village 1 m. off-the-road, r. Noted for its *rebozo.** A mile farther on the l., a dirt road leads to Lourdes, a hot springs resort. Modest hotel and restaurant.

635 Road Junction. Turning l. the paved byroad goes to San Luis de la Paz, 5 m. Fifteen minutes beyond over a gravel road lies Los Pozos, a picturesque ghost town. The paved byroad to the r., goes to Dolores Hidalgo, 25 m., Mexico's cradle of liberty.* Four miles before Dolores a paved road to the l., goes 20 miles to the colonial town and art center, San Miguel de Allende. Excellent accommodations in San Miguel.* Continuing on CN-57.

671 On r. paved side road, CE-36, also leading to San Miguel de Allende, 22 m.

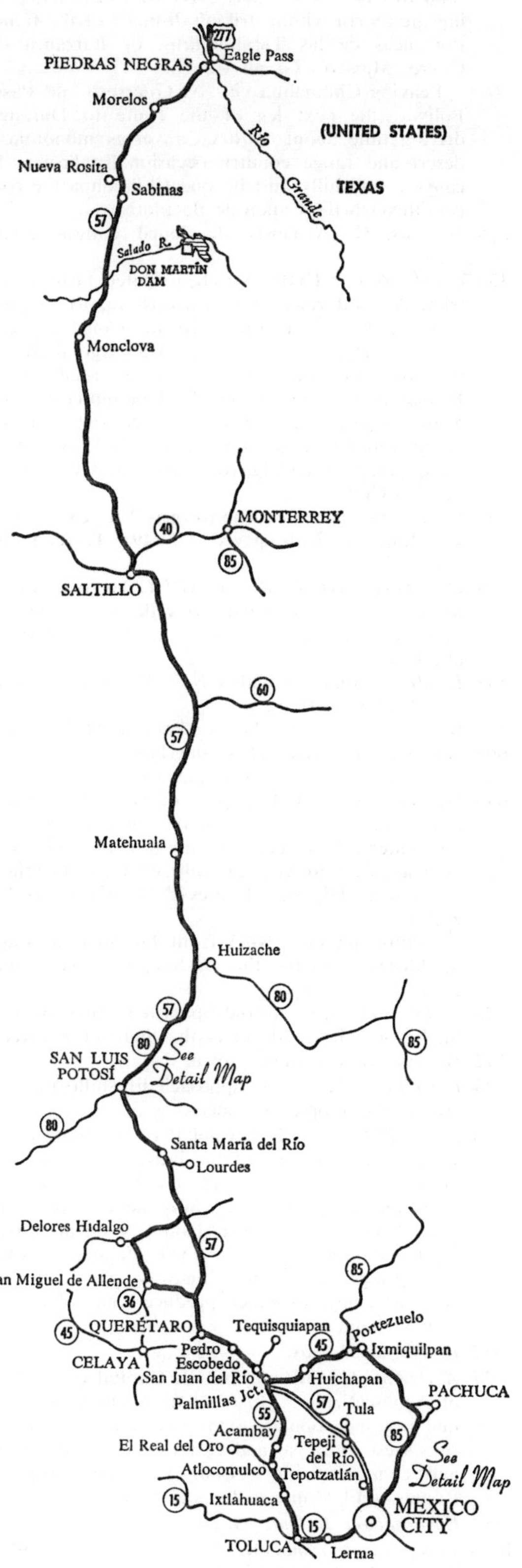

687 *QUERÉTARO.** **GHR.** Capital of the state of the same name. A charming colonial city noted for its architecture. A mile west of the city CN-57 and CN-45 junction. Both by-pass the town. For description of CN-45, see Index: Highway Routes—El Paso to Mexico City. From Querétaro to a point 5 m. east of San Juan del Río the two routes share a handsome, new and wide road.

704 *Pedro Escobedo.* A shrine on the left where truck drivers pay homage to the Blessed Virgin.

716 *SAN JUAN DEL RIO.** **GHR.** Opal and reed-weaving center. Junction with CE-122, northeast, 12 m. to Tequisquiapan, a picturesque village and hot springs spa.*

722 Junction. CN-45 continues eastward to Ixmiquilpan and the old Pan American Highway. The shortest route to Mexico City is to bear to the right. Two miles south of the junction there is a Federal Inspection Station. Car papers. Just beyond the station a paved road branches off to the right. This is CN-55, going to Toluca (for route description, see below). CN-57 continues straight ahead. One hundred yards farther it becomes a toll road. Passenger cars $15. MN; with trailer, $20. MN. The toll road is fast and wide. Driving time to Mexico City, less than 2 hrs. There are no tourist facilities on the toll section, except for a gas station at the north entrance. Keep your receipt for you must surrender it at the exit gate.

798 *Tepeji del Río.* **G.** The toll road bypasses the town. At the north edge of the town there is a turn-off, 9 m., paved, to the famed Toltec archaeological ruins, *Tula.**

814 *Toll Booth.* Surrender your receipt. Just beyond the toll station there is an over-pass and a paved branch road, 3 m., to Tepotzotlán, one of Mexico's most magnificent colonial convents.*

820 *MEXICO CITY.** The highway passing through the new suburban development, Ciudad Satélite, is divided. It passes the El Toro bullring, Hipódromo Las Americas Race Track, the imposing Military Hospital and joins the Paseo de la Reforma at the Petroleros Fountain. Turn left at the fountain.

Via Toluca to Mexico City

This road, CN-55, connecting San Juan del Río, Toluca and Mexico City, although paved, fair, and passing through some lovely country, is little traveled since the opening of the toll road described above. It is mountainous and time consuming. Beginning at the cut-off, r., just before the toll booth.

0 Turn right on to CN-55.

16 *Acambay.* **G.** A pretty valley village.

29 *Atlocomulco.* **G.** Junction with good sideroad, 19 m. to El Real del Oro, a fascinating semi-ghost mining town. A half hour beyond El Oro there are good trout lakes.

47 *Ixtlahuaca.* **G.**

69 *TOLUCA.** **GHR.** Capital of the State of Mexico. Noted for its Friday Market and nearby craft-art villages. Junction with CN-15, the Pacific Coast Highway. Taking the southern exit along CN-15, the road to Mexico City passes through Lerma, 10 m. from Toluca, then begins an abrupt ascent into wooded mountains, and near the monument to Hidalgo on the site of the Battle of Las Cruces, the highway climbs to nearly 10,000 ft. Shortly beyond El Zarco, a federal trout hatchery and picnic area, the road drops toward Mexico City,

entering the capital via the handsome Paseo de la Reforma.

110 *MEXICO CITY.**

Via Ixmiquilpan

A longer variation of the Eagle Pass-Mexico City route may be made by following the highway as described above, to San Juan del Río. Six miles east of San Juan, at the Palmillas Junction bear left on CN-45 to Ixmiquilpan. The road is paved and in fair condition.

0 *Palmillas Junction.*

24 *Huichapan.* **GR.** The road winds through hilly country offering charming vistas.

75 *Portezuelo.* The road bypasses the village on l., and just beyond junctions with the Pan American Highway CN-85. Turn right. Ixmiquilpan is 5 m. south of the junction. For continuation of the route see Laredo to Mexico City Highway.

34. *El Paso to Mexico City*

This highway, often called the Columbus or Central Route, was the second major highway built from the U.S.-Mexican border to the Central Plateau. It is just over a decade old. Although long, it is a popular highway for it passes through important historical areas and there is a minimum of mountain driving. Highway is numbered CN-45.

Length: 1270 m. via Tepeji del Río. *Road condition:* Paved, two-car width; some sections being widened and repaved. Recommended for trailer travel. Driving time about 3 to 3½ days. *Best stopovers:* Chihuahua, Ciudad Camargo, Hidalgo de Parral, Durango, Zacatecas, Aguascalientes, León, San Miguel de Allende, Querétaro.

MILES FROM CIUDAD JUÁREZ — TRIP LOG

0 *CIUDAD JUÁREZ.** **GHR.** The Mexican port of entry opposite El Paso. Customs and immigration offices. The Mexican customs open from 7 A.M. to 11 P.M. M.S.T. U.S. customs open around the clock. Driving time for the first lap — El Paso to Chihuahua, about 5 hrs. There are few tourist accommodations along this section and it is advisable to fill up on gas before leaving Ciudad Juárez. Leaving C. Juárez the highway turns south near the airport.

18.5 First *Federal Inspection Station.* Car papers. The road continues thru semi-desert range country.

32 *Samalayuca.* To r. and just south of the village colorful desert sand dunes edge near the road.

80 *Villa Ahumada.* **G.**

113 *Moctezuma.* **G.** Refreshments.

134 Side road to r. CE-10 leading to Casas Grandes archaeological site. Not of great tourist interest.*

175 Last *Federal Inspection Station.* A little beyond it the road crosses the Río del Sauz and approaches Chihuahua.

233 *CHIHUAHUA.* **GHR.** You enter town via Medina Boulevard and Avenida Carranza. Chihuahua is the capital of the state of the same name, and a center of the Yaqui and Tarahumara Indian country.* From Chihuahua there is a partially improved road to Cuauhtémoc and Creel (dry season), placing the tourist within striking distance of the famed Barrancas de las Tarahumaras, or Barranca del Cobre, Mexico's Grand Canyon.*

Leaving Chihuahua via Av. Guerrero and Paseo Bolívar, the next leg of the route to Durango, driving time about 10 hrs., traverses monotonous desert and range country occasionally broken by canyons and hills. Just beyond Chihuahua the road cuts through the Cañon de Bachimba.

286 *Delicias.* **G.** A newly developed cotton-growing area.

330 *CAMARGO.** **GHR.** A rich, irrigated farming district. A good road to r., goes 18 m. to Boquilla and the large San Francisco de Conchas Lake. Good fishing. Leaving Ciudad Camargo there are two roads to Ciudad Jiménez: a new road runs to E. and parallel to CN-45. Though unmarked and 5 m. longer, it is the best choice for motorists going from Camargo to Torreón. CN-45 is best for those going to Hidalgo de Parral and directly to Mexico City.

372 *Ciudad Jiménez.* **GR.** The town is 2 m. east of CN-45. Junction with paved CN-49, Torreón and Saltillo.*

428 *HIDALGO DE PARRAL.* **GHR.** Historic mining town and spot where Pancho Villa was killed.

457 *Federal Inspection Station.* Car papers may be checked.

543 *La Zarca.* Junction with CN-53 E. to Torreón, all paved, about 101 m.

548 Branch road, all-weather, to Palmito Dam on r.

609 *San Juan del Río.* (Not the basket-weaving San Juan of the State of Querétaro.)

690 *DURANGO.** **GHR.** Capital of State of Durango, a sixteenth-century city and one of Mexico's mining centers. At E. edge of city, Junction with CN-40 (northeast to Torreón, and west to Mazatlán). See Index: Highway Routes — Monterrey to Mazatlán.

Continuing on CN-45 from Durango to Lagos de Moreno, driving time 6 hrs., the road climbs easily but steadily.

723 *Nombre de Dios.* An old Spanish mining town. 19 m. beyond the road enters the State of Zacatecas.

772 *Sombrerete.* **G.** Mining town.

843 *Fresnillo.* **GR.** As you approach Fresnillo the road crosses the Tropic of Cancer.

880 *ZACATECAS.** **GHR.** Capital of the State of the same name, and one of the most interesting cities on the route. A side-road, CE-11 runs SW., to Jalpa and Moyahua, deep into the interior of the state. Continuing southward on CN-45, after passing Guadalupe, 884 m., and Ojocaliente, 901 m., a hot springs center, the highway passes through acres of vineyards which produce some of the fine Aguascalientes wines.

932 *Rincón de Romos.*

957 *AGUASCALIENTES.** **GHR.** Capital of the State of Aguascalientes. Alt. 6260 ft. An attractive colonial city and popular stopover. Branch road, CE-50 runs west to Jalpa, and east to Ojuelos de Jalisco and connects with CN-80, see Index: Highway Routes — El Mante to Guadalajara.

982 *Encarnación de Díaz.* **G.**

1008 *Lagos de Moreno.* **G.** Junction with CN-80, r. through Lagos to Guadalajara, l. to San Luis Po-

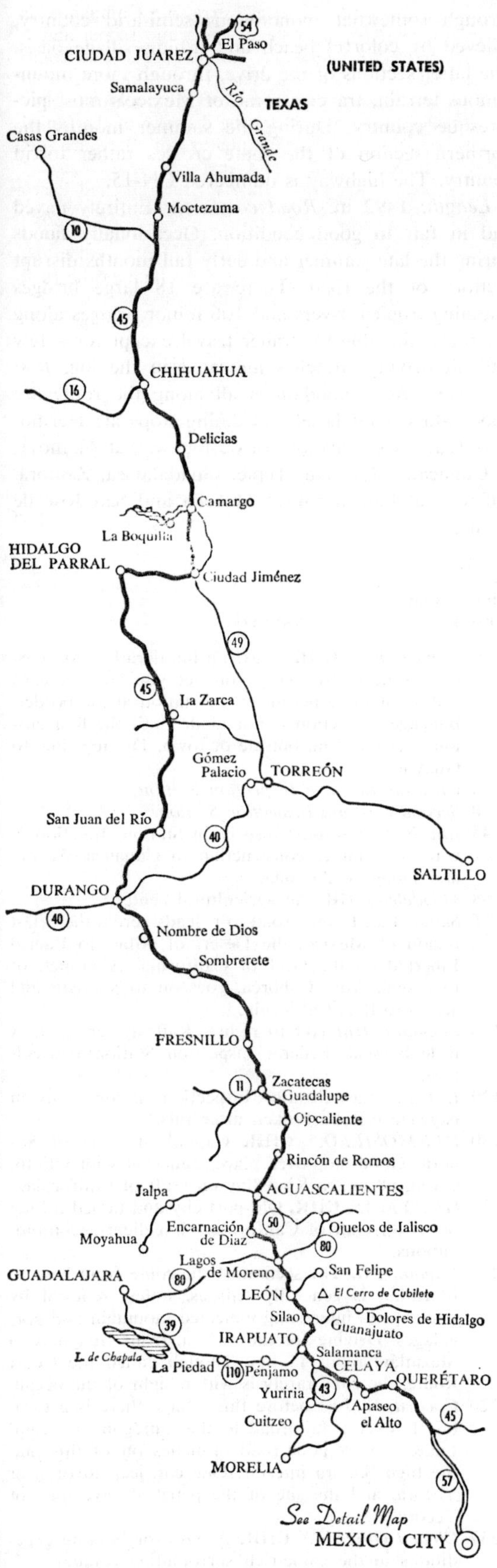

tosí. For route description, see Index. CN-45 continues southeast to Querétaro, driving time about 3½ hrs. This section of the route runs through some of Mexico's most attractive and historically interesting areas.

1037 *LEÓN*. **GHR.** Largest city in Guanajuato State. A branch road (jeep recommended) goes northeast 122 m., to San Felipe, then by new highway (in construction) to Dolores de Hidalgo.

1044 Branch road, l. 5 m., to thermal spa, Comanjilla. Good small hotel.

1054 *Silao*. **G.** A noted serape-weaving town. The highway has now entered the verdant, storied El Bajío region, an extensive basin in the Central Plateau.

1055 A mile beyond Silao, Junction, 1, with CE-110, leading 16 m. to Guanajuato, Mexico's most picturesque colonial city. A good overnight stop.

1061 If you missed the Silao turn-off to Guanajuato, here you have another chance to turn left and still get there. This branch turn-off is numbered CE-29, after 6 m. it joins up with CE-110. Bear right at the junction.

The mountaintop statue you see to the west is El Cristo Rey (Christ the King) upon El Cerro de Cubilete, said to be the geographic center of Mexico.

1077 *Irapuato*.* **GHR.** 1 m. right off highway. In this old city, Mexico's strawberry center, there is a junction with CE-110, leading westward to Pénjamo, La Piedad and Guadalajara. Though parts of this road are new, much is in very poor condition and not recommended.

1090 *Salamanca*. **G.** The industrial works on N. edge of the town are Pemex refineries. In Salamanca a branch road leads westward, connecting with the Pénjamo, La Piedad route to Guadalajara. Condition: poor. Another branch road, CE-43 short-cuts across very beautiful country via Yuriria and Cuitzeo* to Morelia and the West Coast Highway, see Index: Highway Routes — Salamanca to Morelia.

1115 *Celaya*.* **GHR.** A busy, unattractive town possessing several distinguished examples of architecture by Tresguerras, Mexico's greatest architect. Junction with an unnumbered, excellent paved road to south leading through picturesque Salvatierra, Yuriria to Morelia.* Junction also with paved CE-49, 28 m., to *SAN MIGUEL DE ALLENDE*.* Here the motorist can leave CN-45, stopover at San Miguel and rejoin Highway 45 at Querétaro.

1130 *Apaseo el Alta*. **G.**

1150 *QUERÉTARO*. **GHR.** One of Mexico's noteworthy colonial cities. Here the El Paso Highway joins with the direct Eagle Pass-to-Mexico City Highway, CN-57. See Index: Highway Routes — Eagle Pass to Mexico City.

35. *Nogales to Mexico City*

(Pacific Coast Route)

For U.S. motorists coming from the states north and west of Arizona and who have time to dawdle along the way, this is an attractive route into Mexico. It is called variously the Pacific Highway, West Coast Highway and the International Highway as well as the Nogales Route. The early laps of the route pass

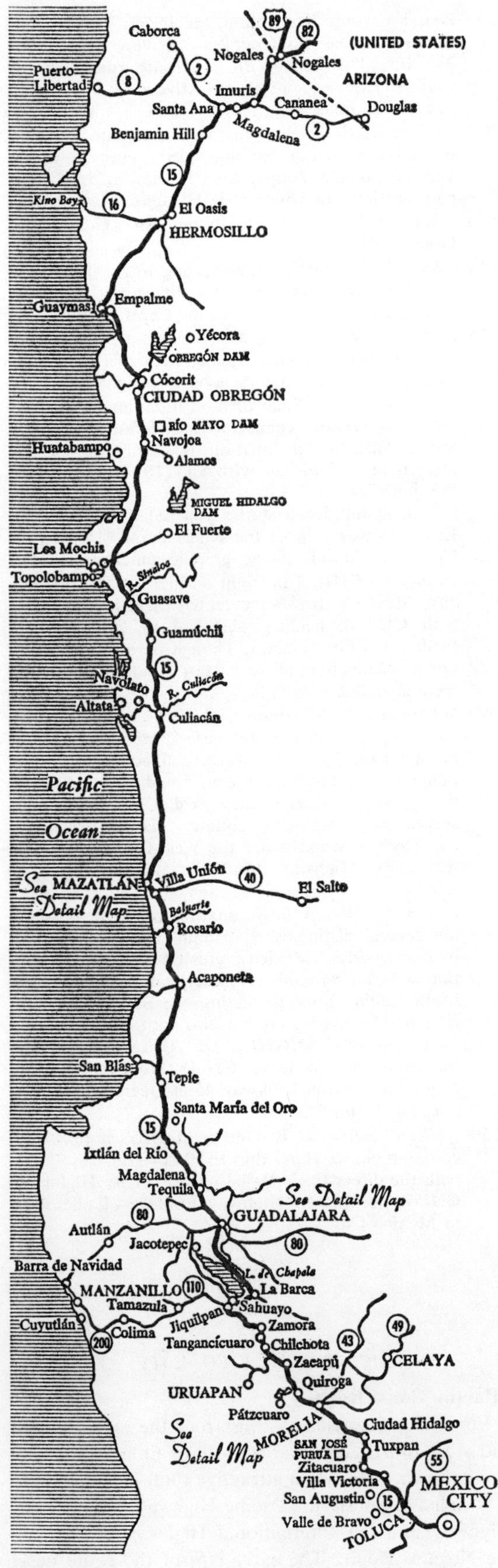

through somewhat monotonous semi-arid country, relieved by colorful beach and fishing-village oasis. The latter sections of the drive, through more mountainous terrain, traverse some of Mexico's most picturesque country. During the summer months the northern section of the route crosses rather torrid country. The highway is numbered CN-15.

Length: 1492 m. *Road condition:* Entirely paved and in fair to good condition. Occasionally floods during the late summer and early fall months disrupt sections of the road. There are 18 large bridges spanning tropical rivers and 106 minor bridges along the route. Suitable for trailer travel except for a few difficult driving stretches indicated in the log. *Best stopovers:* Accommodations all along the route are good. Make your hotel and dining stops at: Hermosillo, Guaymas, Navojoa (or off-highway at Alamos), at Culiacan, Mazatlán, Tepic, Guadalajara, Zamora, (off-road at Pátzcuaro), at Morelia and San José de Purua.

MILES FROM NOGALES — TRIP LOG

0 *NOGALES.** **GHR.** Mexican immigration and customs offices. Normally you get your tourist card and automobile permit at the station at the border. Baggage inspection is not made until the first customs station 4 m. outside of town. Driving time to Guaymas, 6 hrs.

4 *Customs Baggage Inspection Station.*

8 *Second Customs Inspection Station.*

45 *Imuris.* **G.** Customs Inspection Station. Junction 1. with road under construction to Cananea, 51 m., and Douglas, Arizona.

58 *Magdelena.* **GR.** An agricultural center.*

75 *Santa Ana.* Branch road to r. leads across the driest region of Mexico, the Desert of Altar, to Puerto Libertad on the Gulf of California. A branch of this road, from Caborca, goes on to Sonoyta and across to Baja California.

100 *Benjamin Hill* (off to right). Railway terminal. A little beyond, Federal Inspection Station: agriculture.

129 *El Oasis.* Last Customs Inspection Station. Seals on baggage can be broken after this.

180 *HERMOSILLO.** **GHR.** Capital of State of Sonora. Good stop-over place. Junction with CE-16, paved, 68 m., to Kino Bay on Gulf of California.*

258 *GUAYMAS.* **GHR.** Old port city and famed fishing resort on Gulf of California.* Excellent accommodations.

265 *Enpalme.* **G.** The section of the route from here to Mazatlán is generally tedious, unless relieved by side trips to interesting indicated mountain and port villages. Driving for the 485 m. from Guaymas to Mazatlán about 11 hrs. Though called the Coast Route, the road rarely is within sight of the ocean.

326 *Cocorit.* **G.** Just before this village there is a turnoff, 1, over a fair road to the Obregón Dam and Lake. A very poor road branches off of this into the high Sonora interior. One can jeep to or near Yecora, and the site of the petrified cave men of Yecora.*

337 *Ciudad Obregón.** **GHR.** A base for hunting expeditions in the game-rich surrounding country.

380 *NAVOJOA*. **GR.** A Mayo Indian center.* Junction with branch road east, 34 m., part paved, part gravel, to popular and picturesque mountain town of *Alamos*. Well worth visiting; good accommodations in season. A dry-weather branch of this road, 18 m. from highway, leads to Mocuzari and Río Mayo Dam. Another branch-road, W. from Navojoa, 20 m., goes to the interesting Gulf of California port village of Huatabampo. From Navajoa the highway continues southward through agricultural country, entering the State of Sinaloa.

476 Junction. 3½ m. to left is Los Mochis.* **GHR.** From Los Mochis via paved road, 15 m., is Topolobampo, a tiny picturesque fishing port and shrimp center. Another improved road goes from the Junction, west, 50 m., into the hills to El Fuerte, a picturesque, colonial, semi-deserted mining town. No accommodations. Beyond El Fuerte is the huge Miguel Hidalgo Lake and Dam.

514 *Guasave*. **G.** Near here road crosses Río Sinaloa. Temporary wooden toll bridge. New bridge should be finished in 1962.

540 *Guamuchil*. **G.**

605 *CULIACÁN*. **GHR.** Capital of State of Sinaloa.* On entering city, route crosses Río Culiacán via a concrete causeway. During high-water, cars cross via the railway bridge. A branch road via Navolato westward leads to the fishing village of Altata, about 38 m. Leaving Culiacán, the highway crosses small rolling hills, and at 725 m., crosses the Tropic of Cancer.

746 *MAZATLÁN*. **GHR.** Mexico's largest Pacific port. Fishing and beach resort.* A popular stopover.

The next section of the route, Mazatlán to Guadalajara, 330 m., driving time about 8 hrs., traverses both tropic and mountain terrain. Off-highway visits to interesting small ports and beach resorts can be made.

760 *Villa Union*. Junction with CN-40, the Coast-to-Coast Route from Matamoros on the Gulf of Mexico, via Torreón and Durango to Mazatlán. For description of this route see Index. The route will offer motorists some of the most spectacular mountain scenery in Mexico.

786 *Rosario*. **G.** Silver mining center on the Buluarte River.

841 *Acaponeta*. The road climbs into pretty mountain country.

906 Junction with CE-54. You can turn right, E., 23 m., via paved road to pleasant old port and resort village of *San Blas*.*

928 *TEPIC*. **GHR.** Capital of the State of Nayarit. A charming colonial town. Good stopover. Leaving Tepic, a time zone is crossed. Adjust watches from M.S.T. to C.S.T.

948 *Santa María de Oro*. **G.** Old silver mining village. From here on the highway steadily climbs.

977 *IXTLÁN DEL RÍO*. **G.** The region around is rich in archaeological ruins. Beyond the town begins dramatic barranca and lava country, and deep gorges lush with tropical vegetation.

1022 *Magdalena*. **G.** Occasionally an inspection station operates near the town. Car papers.

1035 *Tequila*. **GR.** Picturesque valley town noted for its fiery distillate of the same name.* The countryside is dotted with maguey haciendas.

1071 *GUADALAJARA*. **GHR.** Capital of State of Jalisco and Mexico's second largest city.* Junction with CN-80 leading to San Luis Potosí and El Mante and connecting with the El Paso, the Eagle Pass and the Laredo to Mexico City Highways. (See Index: Highway Routes.) Junction with CE-35 to Lake Chapala.

Leaving Guadalajara via CN-15, the lap to Morelia crosses some of Mexico's most picturesque country, noted its forests, lakes and unique Tarascan villages. Driving time, 226 m., about 6 hrs. Plans should be made for off-highway stop at Pátzcuaro.

1091 Junction with CE-33 on r., leading west to Autlán, to the off-trail beach resort Barra de Navidad and to Manzanillo. This road is not recommended now; when completed it will be the best short-cut from Guadalajara to Manzanillo and the coast.

1106 Branch-road to left, CE-94 — one mile to Jocotepec, 13 m., to Ajijic, and 5 m., more to Chapala, there connecting with CE-35, making the circuit to Guadalajara.

The highway continues along the south shore of Lake Chapala, passing Cojumatlán, a picturesque fishing village beside the lake. The road has entered the State of Michoacán, home of the Tarascan people.

1163 *Sahuayo*. **G.** An interesting sixteenth-century church here. Junction with poor road northeast to La Barca.

1167 *Jiquilpan*.* **GH.** Interesting town and market. Junction with CN-110, paved and good, to Manzanillo.

Manzanillo Route: There are no recommendable stopovers on the road to this popular seaport and resort.

From Jiquilpan the distance is 199 m., about 5 hrs. driving time, winding terrain and tropics. *Log:* 0—Jiquilpan. 25 m. — road crosses state line, Michoacán to Jalisco. 61 m. — Tamazula. **G.** 68 m. — junction on r. with road to Ciudad Guzmán, and to Guadalajara. A good short-cut. 68 m. — road crosses Tuxpan River. 119 m. — route crosses Naranjo River and enters State of Colima. The majestic snow capped Colima Volcano can be seen. 136 m. — *COLIMA*. **GHR.** Capital of the State of Colima.* 161 m. — branch road, l., to Tecomán resort area. 171 m. — branch road, l. to Cuyutlán, about 5 m. A modest beach resort.* 199 m. — MANZANILLO. **GHR.** Colorful old port and seaside resort area.*

There are now two shorter routes connecting Guadalajara to Barra de Navidad and Manzanillo. Both leave Guadalajara S on CN-15. 25 m. from the city turn W on paved road to Acatlán (4½ m.). From Acatlán an excellent paved road runs S, 75 m., via Sayula and Ciudad Guzmán, joining the Jiquilpan-Manzanillo road described above. This short-cut eliminates some tedious mountain driving.

The newest, direct route to Barra de Navidad branches westward from Acatlán, via Autlán to Barra de Navidad. Parts of this short route are still under construction (1964). Motorists should check on road condition.

Leaving Jiquilpan, the Nogales-Mexico City Highway traverses well cultivated highland country to:

1203 *ZAMORA*.* **GHR.** An attractive agricultural center town.

1213 *Tangancícuaro*. Nearby is Lake Camécuaro, tree-surrounded and scenic. The road begins to wind through picturesque country, often called "the Switzerland of Mexico."

1221 *Chilchota*. The road runs through the broad La Cañada de los Once Pueblos, the famed Eleven Villages (noted for their pottery and home-crafts).

1226 Carápan. Junction on r. with CN-39, a paved and beautiful drive, 57 m. to URUAPAN, a lush garden-city noted for its lacquer crafts, and for the nearby, now inactive, Parícutin Volcano. (See Index for description of route and Uruapan Region.) Fair accommodations in Uruapan.

1245 *Zacapú.** **G.** A rich agricultural town. Nearby archaeological sites.

1283 *Quiroga.** **GR.** Junction with CN-41, right, to Pátzcuaro, about 15 m. Before reaching Quiroga, jewel-like Lake Pátzcuaro is visible from the highway. Branch road CN-41 skirts around the lake, passing through several charming and important villages. (For description of the road and region see Index.)

From Quiroga to Morelia the road continues through hilly wooded country. Enroute, to r. is a vista of the Cerro Quincero. Alt. 10,878 ft.

1298 *MORELIA.** **GHR.** Excellent overnight stop. Capital of State of Michoacán and one of Mexico's most beautiful colonial cities. Junction with CE-43, leading north to Salamanca or Celaya and the El Paso-Mexican City Highway.*

The last section of CN-15, Morelia to Mexico City offers more breathtakingly beautiful scenery than any other route entering the national capital. Driving time, about 6 hrs. As the highway leaves the city it flanks the magnificent many-arched colonial aqueduct, then crosses the beautiful Guayangareo Valley and climbs into the Sierra de Ozumatlán.

1332 *Puerto Garnica.* Highest point on the road. Alt. 9469 ft. The road winds on, entering Atzimba National Park.

1341 *Mil Cumbres.* High point in the park. Alt. 9179 ft., is called Mirador de las Mil Cumbres (View of a Thousand Peaks).

1361 *Ciudad Hidalgo.* **G.** An old Tarascan town with a pretty sixteenth-century church.

1372 *Tuxpan.* **G.** The road follows the deep gorge of the Tuxpan River for a short distance.

1379 Sideroad on r., to SAN JOSÉ DE PURUA, 4 m. Thermal spa, excellent hotel and restaurant.*

1389 *Zitácuaro.** **G.** Historic old city.

1421 *San Agustín.* 4 m., off road to left is Villa Victoria, noted for its embroidery work. Nearby Aztec ruins.

1445 Turn-off to r. CE-56, about 44 m. to Valle de Bravo* — magnificent mountain setting and lake.

1446 Turn-off on r. Paved road to village of Zinacantepec. From there a narrow road leads to the summit of the imposing Nevado de Toluca, alt. 13,621 ft.*

1451 *TOLUCA.** **GHR.** Capital of the State of Mexico. Junctions with CN-71 to San Juan del Río* (see Index); CN-55 (southward) to Neuva Ixtapan.* The latter, though in somewhat poor condition continues on to join the Cuernavaca-Taxco-Acapulco Highway, bypassing Mexico City.

If you wish to bypass Toluca, as you enter the city on CN-15, at the Niños Heroes Monument, take the posted truck-route, a good, fast four-lane artery. It rejoins CN-15 at the Flag Monument, opposite end of town. Description of remainder of route to Mexico City (see Index: Highway Routes — Toluca to Mexico City).

36. Monterrey to Mazatlán

(Coast to Coast Route)

Via this route one can travel from the Gulf Coast (Brownsville or McAllen) directly across the northern states of Mexico to the Pacific. At various points it makes connections with all four of the major north-south highways, and serves as a short-cut to these for motorists from the Lower Río Grande Valley. *Length:* 792 m. from Brownsville. *Road condition:* Paved. *Best stopovers:* Monterrey, Saltillo, Torreón, Durango, Mazatlán.

The highway is numbered, CN-40. Approximate driving time, two days.

MILES FROM BROWNSVILLE — TRIP LOG

0 *Brownsville-Matamoros.* For description of the route between Brownsville or McAllen to Monterrey, see Index: Highway Routes — McAllen-Monterrey-Mexico City.

200 *MONTERREY.** **GHR.** The drive from Monterrey to Torreón takes about 5 hrs. The road crosses semi-desert country. Near Monterrey and Saltillo the pavement is badly worn and traffic is heavy. Leaving Monterrey for Saltillo:

203 Branch road to l., leading 13 m. up to Chipinque Mesa, a 4000 ft., cabin resort area. Road paved but narrow. There is a toll of $2.30 MN per person on the road.

209 *Santa Catarina.* Branch road l., to Huasteca Canyon,* 2 mi. From Santa Catarina the route begins its ascent to the tableland.

213 Junction with paved sideroad N. to Villa de García and the García Caves.

244 *Ramos Arizpe.* **G.**

254 *SALTILLO.** **GHR.** Capital of the State of Coahuila. A popular resort and summer school town. Junction with Eagle Pass to Mexico City Highway, CN-57. Leaving Saltillo for Torreón, the road is fairly fast, crossing semi-arid mountain and desert terrain.

336 *Paila.* **G.** Paved sideroad to l. goes 16 m. to the colonial town of Parras de la Fuente, birthplace of Francisco I. Madero.

385 *La Cuchilla.* Road fork. The road to the left, via the village of Matamoros, is the more direct and better route into Torreón. The other goes via the village of San Pedro, and its surface is in poor condition.

434 *TORREÓN.** **GHR.** Largest of the "Triplet Cities" of the Laguna cotton district, (Torreón, Gómez Palacio and Lerdo). As the route enters the city it connects with Boulevard Miguel Aleman, a new four-lane road that bypasses the center of the city and connects with CN-40 on the west.

Leaving Torreón for Durango, driving time about 3½ hrs., the highway bypasses Gómez Palacio, w. of road.

For a fast short cut to Ciudad Jiménez and Chihuahua one can enter Gómez Palacio and make connections with the Jiménez road, CN-49. At Bermejillo, CE-30 branches l. to La Zarca on the

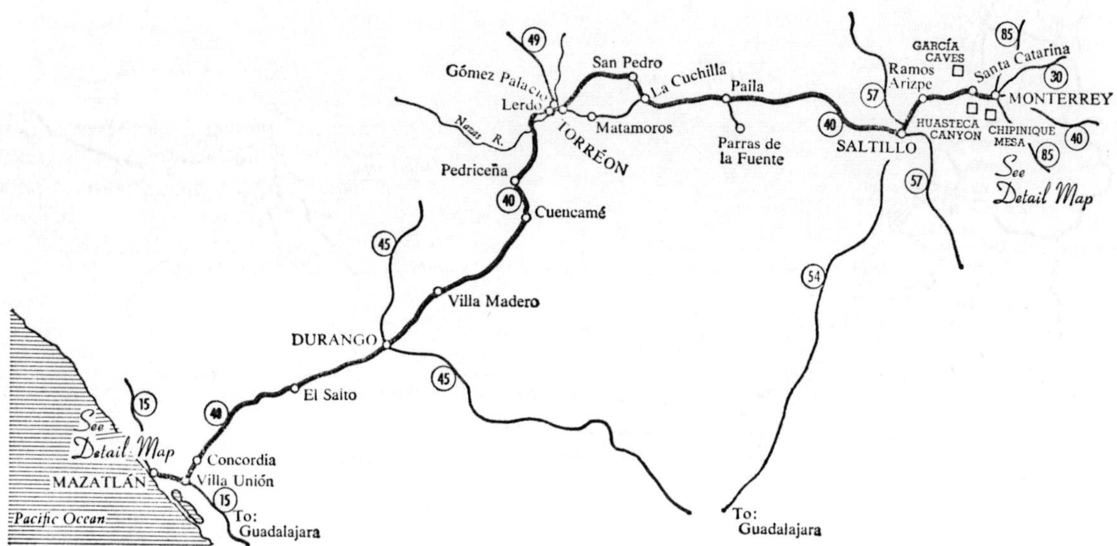

El Paso Highway. However, it is better to continue on CN-49.

Continuing southwest on the main highway to Durango, the road traverses the Nazas River Valley.

436 *Lerdo.* **G.**

484 *Pedriceña.* Good speeds can be maintained through most of this area.

500 *Cuéncame.* **G.**

556 *Villa Madero.* **G.**

593 *DURANGO.** **GHR.** Junction with El Paso to Mexico City Highway, CN-45 (route description see Index).

CN-40 continues on to Mazatlán. This lap is one of the most spectacular scenic drives in Mexico. Paved. Under fair conditions the driving time is approximately 6 hrs. for the 199 mile leg. It is advisable to load up on gasoline before leaving Durango.

622 Provisional bridge over Los Mimbres River.

656 *El Salto.* **G.**

764 *Concordia.* **G.**

778 *Villa Union.* **G.** Junction with Nogales to Mexico City Highway, CN-15. Turn right for Mazatlán; left for Guadalajara.

792 *MAZATLÁN.** **GHR.**

37. *Tampico to Yucatán and Quintana Roo*

This route, called variously the Gulf Coast Route, the Gulf Circuit and the Caribbean Circuit, is the Mexican section of an envisioned Circle Tour which will permit a motorist to enter Mexico through one of the Texas ports of entry, drive the entire distance to the southeast tip of the peninsula of Yucatán, then put his car aboard a ferry, cross the Yucatán Channel to the southwest tip of Cuba, drive again to Havana, ferry to Florida's Key West, and motor back around the U.S. shore of the Gulf.

Utilizing some established roads and some brand-new highways cut with great difficulty through vivid jungles, the Mexican Gulf Route is now almost complete. One can drive from Laredo or Brownsville to the proposed ferry embarkation point (to Cuba) at Puerto Juárez in Quintana Roo. The road is passable now during most seasons. By late 1962 it should be entirely paved.

Length at present: 1686 m. *Road condition:* Mostly paved from Laredo to Puerto Juárez, Q.R. Champotón to Mérida, Yuc., and beyond Valladolid, Q.R., all paved. *Best stopovers:* Monterrey, Ciudad Victoria, Tampico, Tuxpan, Papantla, Teziutlán, Jalapa, Veracruz, Catemaco, Villahermosa, Ciudad del Carmen, Campeche, Mérida, Isla Mujeres, Chichén Itzá.

The route offers a variety of magnificent scenery, tropical beaches, dense mangrove jungle, and an opportunity to motor to the rich archaeological ruins of the Huasteca, Totonac, Olmec, and Mayan civilizations.

Driving time, about 6 days. Best season is from December to February. Remaining months are excessively hot. The route has no official posted number yet. Highway numbers are indicated in the log.

MILES FROM BROWNSVILLE **TRIP LOG**

0 *Brownsville-Matamoros.* For description of first sections of route, see Index: Highway Routes — Laredo to Mexico City; Brownsville to Victoria.

139 *Jiménez.* Junction on 1. with planned road to Soto La Marina, Aldama and joining the Ciudad Mante-Tampico road at Manuel, thus bypassing Victoria. As yet, not passable.

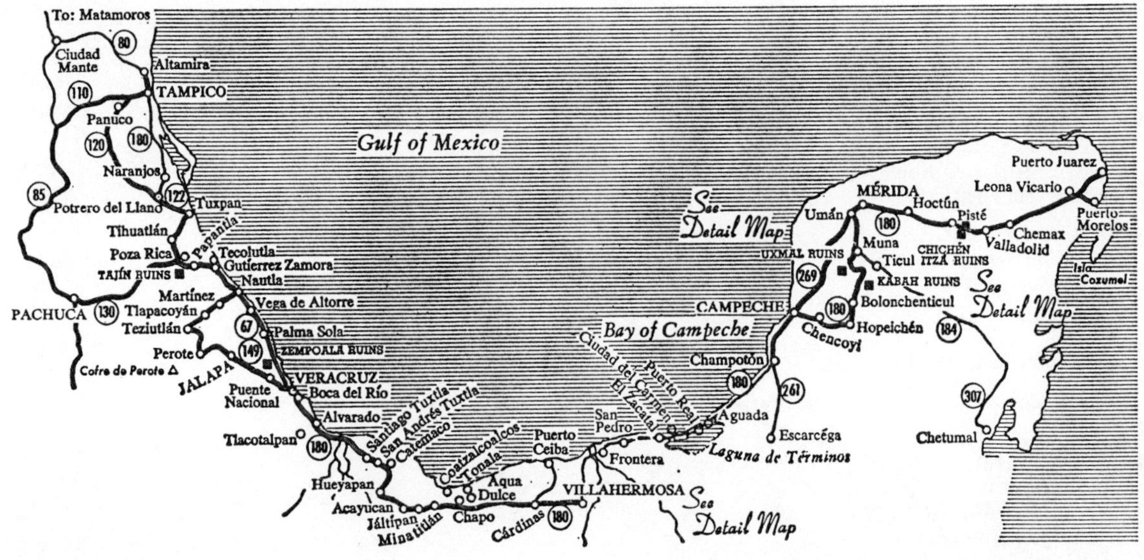

198 *VICTORIA*. **GHR.** The Gulf Route joins CN-85, the Laredo Highway.

281 *Ciudad Del Mante*. **GHR.** Here 1½ m. south of Mante, junction with CN-100 to Tampico, 197 miles. Good paved road. Following CN-100:

316 *González*. **G.**

326 *Manuel*. **G.**

364 *Altamira*. **GR.** Interesting colonial church and monastery.

378 *TAMPICO*.* **GHR.** Center for rich oil region and a popular fishing resort. Leaving Tampico the Gulf Route follows CN-180 to Veracruz.

The new road skirts along the Gulf shore and the Laguna de Tamiahua, traversing flatlands to:

446 *Naranjos*. **G.**

469 *Potrero del Llano*. The new section joins the "inside road," Tampico-Panuco-Tuxpan. Turn left.

497 *TUXPAN*.* **GHR.** Interesting port town on the Tuxpan River. Leaving Tuxpan you cross the Río Tuxpan, ferry rate $2. MN. A new bridge was completed in 1961. Follow CN-130 southward; paved and excellent. The country becomes less monotonous. There are rolling hills covered with tropic verdure.

518 *Tihuatlan*. **G.** Here the highway enters the oil rich Poza Rica region, dotted with oil rigs, and at night the eerie glow of natural gas jets.

530 Junction. CN-130 continues east toward Pachuca (for route description see Index: Highway Routes — Pachuca-Tuxpan-Tecolutla). CN-180, the Gulf Route turns left (to the south) two miles to Poza Rica.

532 *POZA RICA*. **GHR.** A spanking new, lively city built by Mexico's oil monopoly, Pemex.* A paved side road goes from the city, 11 miles to the important archaeological ruins of Tajín.* This road to Tajín is far superior to the Tajín road from Papantla. Leaving Poza Rica the highway traverses lush, hilly tropical terrain, the Vanilla Forests of the Totonac Indians.

544 *PAPANTLA*. **GHR.** Home of the Totonac Indians, a charming tropical town and vanilla center of the world. Noted for its famed Corpus Christi (*voladores*) flying-pole dancers.

563 *Gutiérrez Zamora*. **G.** At this picturesque river town the highway parallels the Río Tecolutla.

570 *Tecolutla*.* **GHR.** A rundown but interesting beach village at the mouth of the Tecolutla River. Ferry across the river, $2. MN.

Leaving Tecolutla the highway parallels the shore and many beaches excellent for camping. On this stretch villages are tiny, tourist facilities slim. There is a good beach at Reachuela, a hotel halfway to Nautla (Hotel el Palmar de Susana), and ten minutes drive farther, at Paraíso, Hotel Playa Paraíso.

599 *Barra de Nautla*.

601 Road junction (no signs). To left road approaches the ferry crossing the Nautla River.

602 *Nautla*. **G.** The 111 m. stretch along the coast from here to Veracruz.

668 *Zempoala*.* Nearby are the Zempoala archaeological ruins.

713 *Puente Nacional*. **HR.** Here the road joins CN-140, Mexico City to Veracruz. Turn left.

750 *VERACRUZ*.* **GHR.** Mexico's most important seaport. A popular resort and stopover.

THE LOG FOR THIS INSIDE ROUTE IS:

0 *Road fork*.

25 *Martínez de la Torre*.

38 *Tapacoyán*.

58 *TEZIUTLÁN*.* **GHR.** An interesting colonial city,

noted for its market. At Teziutlán, take the paved road to Perote and Jalapa. It winds through vivid mountain country. In the distance ahead the imposing volcanic *Cofre de Perote* is visible.

69 *Perote.* **G.** Junction with the Mexico City-Veracruz Highway. CN-140 (description of this route, see Index: Highway Routes — Mexico City to Veracruz). Turn left.

101 *JALAPA.** **GHR.** Capital of State of Veracruz. A charming semitropical city.

144 *VERACRUZ.** Leaving Veracruz via CN-180, for Alvarado.

753 *Mocambo.* **HR.** A pleasant beach and fair hotel.

764 *Boca del Río.** **GR.** Beaches, seafood, etc.

793 *Alvarado.** **GR.** A fishing port at the mouth of the Papaloapan River. Boats can be taken up-river to picturesque Tlacotalpan.* Ferry across to Ciudad Zerde. Fee: $6 MN. per car. A bridge is in construction. From Alvarado to Minatitilán the excellent paved highway passes partly through coastal brush country and some vivid tropical hill country. This 136 m. lap can be done in 3 hrs.

Ten minutes beyond Alvarado, on r., there is a ferry crossing the river to Tlacotalpan. The road from the ferry landing to the village is poor.

836 *Santiago Tuxtla.* **G.**

844 *San Andrés Tuxtla.** **G.**

852 *CATEMACO.** **GHR.** Tiny lake village and one of Mexico's most beautiful natural lakes. A good stopover.

877 *Hueyapan.* **G.**

902 *Acayucan.* **G.** Junction with the Trans-Isthmus Highway connecting the Gulf and the Pacific Ocean. For description see Index: Highway Routes — Salina Cruz to Coatzacoalcos. Bear left and continue on CN-180.

916 *Jáltipan.** One of Mexico's new, important sulphur centers.

927 *Minatitlán.* **G.** Road bypasses the town.

933 *COATZACOALCOS.** **GHR.** A gulf port and terminus of the Trans-Isthmus Highway and railway. Coatzacoalcos is a staging point from which motorists can ship their cars via Sureste Rry. to Campeche or Mérida (see Index: Sureste Railway).

941 *Chapa.* There is a turn-off here on a secondary road to Agua Dulce and the pleasant seaside village of Tonalá. Not far from Agua Dulce is the archaeological site of La Venta,* principal Olmec ruins. *Note:* most of the La Venta figures have been moved to the outdoor museum at Villahermosa.

The 119 m. stretch from Coatzacoalcos to Villahermosa is flat and fast, passing through heavy tropical verdure. Fine pavement, driving time 2 hrs.

1015 *Cárdenas.* Unimproved sideroad on 1. goes north, 40 m. to South Sea Island style Gulf villages of Paraíso and Puerto Ceiba.* Recommended only in dry weather.

1052 *VILLAHERMOSA.** **GHR.** Capital of the State of Tabasco. Best stopover. Take-off point for the fabulous Palenque Ruins.

Until the opening of this highway and, a few years earlier, the Sureste Railway, this entire region was jungle-bound and cut off from the rest of Mexico. Tourist facilities in Tabasco, Campeche, and Yucatán are generally still limited, the region remains quite unspoiled and fascinating.

Leaving Villahermosa, the route cuts back to the Gulf Coast, there running east and north along unspoiled beaches, occasionally island-hopping, and lancing through dense mangrove jungles. The first lap of this section, to the port of Frontera is 43 m. The motorist passes several interesting tropical thatch-hut villages.

1095 *Ferry Landing* at mouth of joined Grijalva and Usumacinta Rivers. Ferry service day and night. Rate: $15 MN.

1096 *FRONTERA.* **GHR.** A rundown port. The beach is about a 20-minute drive from the town. In a pinch, the only half-passable hotel and restaurant is the San Agustín on the plaza. Rates: $30 to $40 MN. per double, EP.

From Frontera to El Zacatal, 59 m., the road skirts the ocean while on the right are dense mangrove jungle and swamps. The tropical vegetation and exuberant birds are brilliant.

1125 *San Pedro Ferry Landing.* Ferry crossing this lovely river costs $15 MN. Crossing service from 6 A.M. to 10 P.M. A mile north of the ferry landing (dirt road) is the village, San Pedro, and the Barra de San Pedro, a magnificent expanse of beach.

1155 *El Zacatal.* Ferry crossing to Isla Carmen.

During heavy weather and northerners the service is halted, and motorists are sometimes stranded at the landings (without hotel or restaurant facilities. The ferry rate at present is $50 MN. Daytime service. The crossing takes approximately an hour. By 1962 modern auto-ferries were expected to replace the primitive *pangas.*

1158 *CIUDAD DEL CARMEN.** **GHR.** A picturesque fishing port and the only city on the island of Carmen. Best available stopover.

Leaving C. Carmen, the road runs the length of the island, 23 m., passing through lush coconut palm haciendas.

1181 *Puerto Real.* Ferry Landing at E. end of Isla Carmen. No tourist facilities.

1183 *Aguada.* Ferry Landing. A picturesque palm-shaded fishing village. The waters around Aguada, Isla Carmen, and the Laguna de Terminos are considered a fisherman's paradise. Though there is no gas station here, gasoline can be procured from Sr. Polo Rejon, in the village.

The paved road from Aguada continues along the ocean, the length of what is called Aguada Island (actually a long fingerlike peninsula parallel to the mainland).

1251 *Champotón.* **GHR.** A charming old fishing village. Junction with a new graveled road going south deep into the jungle country of Campeche, to Escárcega and Laguna de Silvituc. Dry weather only. The hotel in Champotón, El Popular, is primitive but clean. The seafood is good.

Leaving Champotón and crossing the Champotón River, toll fee, 1 peso, the highway follows the coast north.

1295 *CIUDAD CAMPECHE.** **GHR.** Good stopover. Capital of State of Campeche. An old, fascinating port town.

Leaving Campeche the highway turns inland (E.) passing through low tropical verdured hills.

1314 *Chencoyi.* Junction to left with secondary road leading through the Mayan bush country to Becal, Umán, and to Mérida. Take it only if you want a rough ride.

1348 *Hopelchén.* **G.** The highway turns north in the village.

1359 *Bolonchenticul.** **G.** Famed for its 9 Cave Cenotes.

1362 State Line — leaving Campeche, entering Yucatán. There is a triumphal arch over the road. The highway winds through a low-hilled region covered with sparse growth.

1367 *Kabah.* One of Yucatán's principal Mayan ruins. The temples are on each side of the road.*

1370 *Uxmal.* **HR.** Fabulous Mayan ruins, left of road. To right, excellent hotel and restaurant.

1380 *Muna.* **G.** Junction on right, road to Ticul, and to Chetumal, Q.R. (for description of this route, see Index: Chetumal, Q.R.). The main highway continues northward, passing huge *henequén* plantations.

1408 *Umán.* **G.**

1419 *MÉRIDA.** **GHR.** Capital of State of Yucatán. Famed for its colonial architecture, pretty women, pleasant mode of life. A comfortable base from which to make motor trips to Uxmal, Chichén Itzá, Progreso.

Leaving Mérida, CN-180 continues across the vast pancake-flat Yucatecan peninsula, past Chichén Itzá, across jungle-dense Quintana Roo to its terminus on the Caribbean shore at Puerto Juárez.

1450 *Hoctún.* **G.**

1493 *Pisté.** **R.**

1494 *CHICHÉN ITZÁ.* **HR.** The archaeological area extends over a vast area on both sides of the road. A few hundred yards beyond the entrance, and up the road, is an excellent hotel and restaurant.

1519 *VALLADOLID.* **GHR.** An interesting Yucatecan town with some good colonial architecture.

1528 *Chemax.*

1658 *Leona Vicario.* (*Note:* At press time, up to this point the highway was fast, paved, and excellent. The remaining 45 m. to *Puerto Juárez* has now been paved.) From Leona Vicario there is a road through jungle to Puerto Morelos to Caribbean village opposite Cozumel Island. This is a jeep road at present.

In the stretch between Vicario and Puerto Juárez, around what is known as kilometer 102, near the tiny village of Cristóbal Colón, there is a dirt road leading into the jungle, south, to Agua Azul, a great rundown hacienda with a huge old church and nearby Mayan ruins.

1686 *PUERTO JUÁREZ.* The Caribbean terminus of the highway. A collection of palm-shaded shacks and a custom's office. Across the narrow channel is the cocoanut isle, *Isla Mujeres.** **HR.**

38. Mexico City, Cuernavaca, Taxco to Acapulco

Since early colonial days the tour to Cuernavaca, Taxco, and Acapulco, has always been the most popular with new visitors in Mexico. Via the express toll road the run to Acapulco can be done easily in one day; however, visitors should plan to spend more time along this route to enjoy its unique side excursions. If the trip is taken during the height of the "tourist seasons" it is advisable to have confirmed reservations in advance.

Length: (direct to Acapulco) 267 m., or (via Taxco) 284 m. *Condition of road:* Paved. *Best stopovers:* Tepoztlán, Cuernavaca, Taxco, Acapulco.

MILES FROM MEXICO CITY — TRIP LOG

0 *MEXICO CITY.** The best route from the city's center to Cuernavaca is via Av. Insurgentes Sur, going past the gigantic bullring, the Obregón Monument, the Pedregal, and University City. The road is marked, CN-95, and CN-95CP. The *CP* in CN-95CP stands for *camino de paga* (toll road).

Three miles beyond the University, a turn-off to l., leads to Cuicuilco, the oldest construction in the Americas.*

11 Junction. CN-95 bears to r. This is the old road to Cuernavaca. It is paved, narrow, full of turns. Continue straight ahead ½ m. for the toll road. Toll fee is $8 MN. to Cuernavaca. The highway is divided and excellent.

There is a spectacular but easy 15 m. climb into pine covered mountains. The summit of the pass is Estación Parres (El Guarda), 9920 ft. The State of Morelos.

36 *Tres Cumbres.* On the old road, CN-95, there is a cut-off to the r., to Las Lagunas de Zempoala. Beyond this point the road drops swiftly, 5,000 ft. to the semitropical Valley of Morelos.

48 *Toll Booth.* There is a new by-pass around Cuernavaca, connecting with the next leg of the toll road. Surrender your receipt.

49 *Junction.* A paved road to the left leads to picturesque *TEPOZTLÁN,** 10 m.

53 *CUERNAVACA.** **GHR.** Capital of State of Morelos and sundrenched weekend haven for Mexico City's well-to-do.

Visitors going only as far as Cuernavaca can return to Mexico City via an alternate route — *Cuautla, Amecameca* and *Chalco.*

Leaving Cuernavaca for Acapulco, 2½ m. south of town the motorist has a choice of two routes. CN-95CP, a wide, fast road, bypasses Taxco. Driving time to Acapulco less than 5 hrs. The other road, CN-95, leads through Taxco and Iguala, there rejoining the toll road. From this junction to Acapulco the road is posted CN-95 and there are no further toll fees.

Via Taxco (old road):

55 *Junction* and Toll Gate. Bear right.

65 *Alpuyeca.* **Junction:** paved road to left leads to *Lake Tequesquitengo.** **Paved road to right goes to-**

ward Xochicalco pyramid,* and 20 m beyond to Cacahuamilpa Caves.* Just beyond the caves turn-off is the junction with the Nueva Ixtapan to Toluca highway (see Index: Ixtapan de la Sal).

88 *Puente de Ixtla.* **G.** A charming Indian village. Junction on right with road connecting with Nueva Ixtapan-Toluca highway.

101 *TAXCO.** **GHR.** One of the most popular and picturesque towns in Mexico, noted for its silver crafts, its Sunday market, etc.

118 *El Naranjo.*

122 *IGUALA.** **GHR.** Just off highway to r. Junction with unpaved road W. to Ciudad Altimirano and the wild Balsas River Basin.

124 Iguala Interchange. Here the toll road and CN-95 join.

Via CN-95CP from Cuernavaca to Iguala Interchange.

55 *Cuernavaca toll gate.* Fee: $8 MN. to Taxco turn-off.

67 Turn-off from toll road to CN-95 toward Taxco. Just beyond is a second toll booth. Toll fee: $10 MN. from here to Iguala.

112 Iguala Interchange. Toll road ends. Highway posted CN-95.

121 *CHILPANCINGO.* **G.** Capital of State of Guerrero. Junction with unimproved road E. to Chilapa.

The highway winds through tropical country and just beyond Tierra Colorada begins the drop to the Pacific Coast lowlands.

225 *ACAPULCO.** **GHR.** Mexico's most beautiful and popular seaside resort.

39. Mexico City to Oaxaca and Chiapas

(Pan American)

The southern extension of the Pan American Highway leading to Guatemala and the republics to the south. This section is officially called the Carretera Cristóbal Colón (Christopher Columbus Highway). It extends through much of Mexico's least visited, yet most interesting and beautiful country. The road is posted as CN-190.

Though the posted highway goes through Puebla, a comfortable alternate route, goes via Cuernavaca, Cuautla, and joins the Columbus Highway at Izúcar de Matamoros.

Length via Puebla: 938 m. to Guatemalan border; *Condition of roads:* Paved and excellent to San Cristóbal de las Casas, Chiapas. *Best stopovers:* Puebla, Cuernavaca, Oaxaca, Mitla, Tehuantepec, Tuxtla Gutiérrez, San Cristóbal las Casas.

Via Puebla

MILES FROM MEXICO CITY — TRIP LOG

0 *MEXICO CITY.** The best route out of the city toward Puebla is via Av. Fray Servando Teresa de Mier, (posted, CN-190) a wide, double-laned boulevard.

A new, Mexico City to Puebla toll-road was opened May 1962.

14 *Los Reyes.* Junction, left, CE-136 to Texcoco and Veracruz.

The road traverses the area which was once the basin of Lake Texcoco. To N. are the swampy remains of this once important lake.

21 *Santa Barbara.* **G.** Just before the town there is a turn-off to r. toward Cuautla via CN-115.

20 *Zoquiapan.* The climb over the Sierras begins. Nearing the summit to the W. are beautiful views of the Valley of Mexico. On the eastern slopes, views of the snowcapped volcanoes, Popocatépetl and Iztaccíhuatl.

42 *Puerto del Aire.* Summit of the pass and Continental Divide. Alt. 10,486 ft.

41 Río Frío. Famed, old-time bandit hangout.

45 *La Venta.* **G.** Beautiful early nineteenth-century bridge here.

59 *San Martín Texmelucan.** **G.** Colonial monuments, interesting market on Tuesdays. Shops. Junction: CN-188, paved, branches off NE. to *Tlaxcala.** From Tlaxcala one can go directly to Puebla via another paved road.

68 *Huejotzingo.** Colonial church and museum.

78 *CHOLULA.** City of churches and once center of the Toltec kingdom. Town is off the highway to r. There are two turn-offs, one a mile before town, one opposite the town.

86 *PUEBLA.** **GHR.** Capital of State of Puebla, and fourth largest city in Mexico. Noted for its distinctive architecture and its tile and ceramic works.

Before entering Puebla, at mile 82, there is a new bypass to the right which avoids all city traffic. Two miles beyond this CN-190 turns r. (SE.)

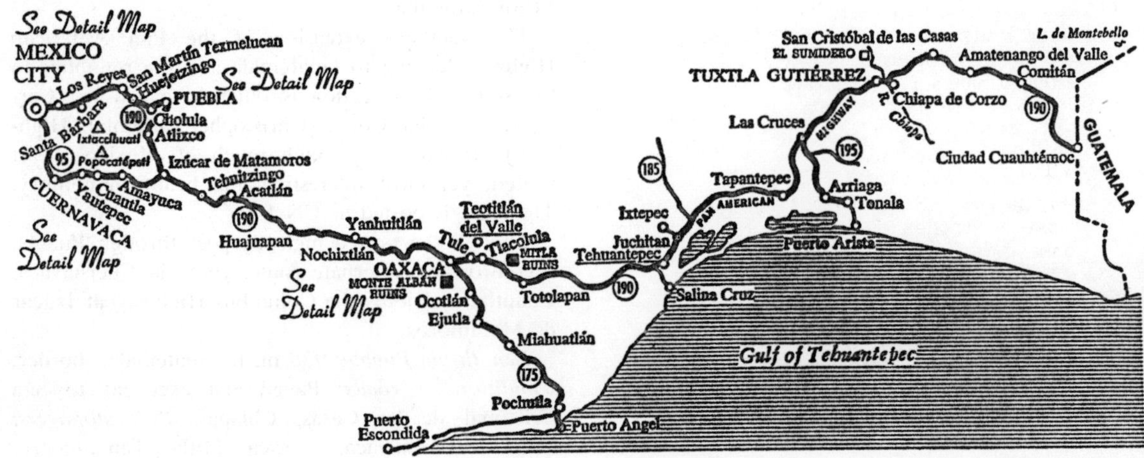

toward Oaxaca. The bypass connects with it. Motorists bound for Veracruz continue on through the city. Driving time to Oaxaca City, approximately 7 hrs. This section of the road is generally winding, and in good condition.

92 *Acatepec.* **G.** Indian village with an interesting Indian church. Junction with paved road to NW. to *Tonanzintla,** 1 m. Site of the Church of Sta. María de Tonanzintla — an architectural jewel.

104 *Atlixco.* **G.** A textile center in a fertile valley.

125 *Izúcar de Matamoros.* **G.** Potters here are noted especially for their "Tree of Death" candelabras. Here, just before entering town, on r. road junction with alternate route via Cuautla to Mexico City. See below.

Alternate to Oaxaca, via Cuernavaca and Cuautla

Motorists can skip the round-about and mountainous Puebla leg of the journey, taking the following route.

0 *MEXICO CITY.* Leaving Mexico City via Insurgentes Sur, follow CN-95CP, the toll road to Cuernavaca.*

53 *CUERNAVACA.* Here take paved CN-138 toward Cuautla.

69 *Yautepec.* **G.** A picturesque village.

79 Junction with CN-115. Turn right.

81 *CUAUTLA.** **GHR.** A popular bathing spa.

94 *Amayuca*

111 Bridge over Arroyo del Muerte. Morelos-Puebla state line.

116 From here to Atencingo the road is unpaved. Slippery in wet weather.

124 *Atencingo.* **G.** Resume pavement.

139 *IZÚCAR DE MATAMOROS.* **G.** Junction with Oaxaca-Chiapas Highway, CN-190. Turn right.

Continuing toward Oaxaca. (Mileage count via Puebla.)

125 *Izúcar de Matamoros.* The highway winds southward passing through the towns of *Tehuitzingo, Acatlán* (**G.** and noted for its pottery).

219 *Huajuapan.* **GHR.** Fair, new *viajero-type* hotel and restaurant. *Hotel Laredo,* Antonio de Leon 13.

266 *Yanhuitlán.* **G.** There is an imposing sixteenth-century Dominican convent here. Worth visiting.

276 *Nochixtlán.* **G.** Town is off the road to 1. Beyond here the road climbs to 8000 ft., then begins a panoramic descent into the Valley of Oaxaca.

342 *OAXACA CITY.* **GHR.** Capital of State of Oaxaca, center of the Mixteca-Zapoteca culture. One of Mexico's most charming and interesting colonial cities. Nearby are the important archaeological ruins of Monte Albán and Mitla. (See Index: Oaxaca Region.)

From Oaxaca City several new roads are being projected into the interior reaches of the state. A road south via Ocotlán, Ejutla and Miahuatlán, winds down toward Pochutla and the picturesque Pacific Coast village of Puerto Angel. Another (incomplete, but jeep-passable) goes to the idyllic Pacific hideaway, Puerto Escondido. (See Index for descriptions.) Another road crosses the high sierras to the Papaloapan Basin and the Gulf Coast.

Leaving Oaxaca City for Chiapas, the next lap to San Cristóbal las Casas is a 12-hour driving stretch, and should be broken at Tehuantepec. Most of the route winds through mountainous country. Continuing on CN-190:

348 *Tule* or *Santa María del Tule.** Noted for its gigantic *ahuehuete* tree. A few miles beyond El Tule is a turn-off, on l., dirt road, to the picturesque serape weaving village of Teotitlán del Valle, and in the High Sierras beyond it, fascinating *Yalalag.*

359 *Tlacolula.** Off road to r. The Sunday market is one of the most interesting in Mexico.

365 *MITLA* road fork. Turn left, 5 m., paved to *MITLA,** important pre-Columbian temples and ruins. Good restaurant and small inn.

386 *Totolapan.* **G.** Beyond here, almost to Tehuantepec the road is an endless series of "S" curves.

499 Road junction and Customs Inspection Station. Car papers. The fork to the right, CN-185, goes

to Salina Cruz, the Pacific port on the Gulf of Tehuantepec.

500 *TEHUANTEPEC.** **GHR.** An interesting tropical city on the Río Tehuantepec, noted for its regional fiestas and the unique costumes of the women.

516 Junction. To left, road goes to Ixtepec,* one of points for rail shipment of cars to Guatemala. To right, the cross road leads to nearby *Juchitán,** an interesting Isthmus of Tehuantepec City.

525 Junction. The Trans-Isthmus Highway which began at Salina Cruz and shared the road with CN-190, turns off to left (N.) at this point. For description of this route, CN-185, see Index: Highway Routes — Salina Cruz to Coatzacoalcos. Beyond the junction good speeds can be maintained until Tapanatepec.

582 *Tapanatepec.* Road begins to climb again.

596 *Los Amates.*

615 *Las Cruces.** Junction. CE-200, paved, goes south (r.) toward Arriaga, Tonalá, and Puerto Arista. Cars can be shipped via rail from Arriaga to Guatemala. The new road from Tonalá to Guatemala, following the railroad is in fair condition and easier than the route via Comitán.

687 *TUXTLA GUTIÉRREZ.** **GHR.** Capital of State of Chiapas. Leaving Tuxtla the road crosses the Grijalva River. Up the river a short distance is the magnificent El Sumidero Canyon.*

696 *Chiapa de Corzo.* **G.** An interesting colonial town with two architectural gems — a fountain and a church.

707 Road junction on left. A new road, gravel, is being built from here to Villahermosa, Tabasco. It is passable as far as Pueblo Nuevo, on this side; Pichucalco to Villahermosa on the other side. In between is magnificent and scenic jeep country.

738 *San Cristóbal de las Casas.** Former capital and oldest Spanish city in Chiapas. A charming town, rich in regional color. Interesting villages nearby.

766 *Amatenango del Valle. Note:* the highway from Las Casas to the Guatemalan border is all-weather, but remains to be paved in part.

800 *Comitán.* **GHR.** Tropical town noted for its orchids, and the famed, nearby *Montebello Lakes.** The road from Comitán to the border is paved but in wretched condition.

847 *Ciudad Cuauhtémoc,* formerly El Ocotal. Mexican village at the Guatemalan border.

40. Mexico City to Veracruz

The motorist has three choices of routes to Veracruz, each possessing certain touristic attractions. For centuries the principal route was via Puebla and Jalapa, (CN-140). Within the last decade a shorter route via Texcoco, bypassing Puebla, has been opened. It is less mountainous and faster. It joins CN-140 east of Puebla. A third very long and interesting route takes off from Puebla, skirting to the south through Tehuacán, Orizaba and Cordoba. Motorists will increase their enjoyment of a trip to Veracruz by making a circuit tour, going by way of the Tehuacán-Cordoba road and returning via the Texcoco route.

Length: via Puebla-Jalapa, 294 m.; via Texcoco, 274 m.; via Tehuacán-Cordoba, 330 m. *Road condition:* paved throughout. Being old roads, the surfaces are ripply and extensively patched. *Best stopovers:* Puebla, Jalapa, Tehuacán, Fortín.

All three routes leave Mexico City via CN-190 (Av. Fray Servando Teresa de Mier). 16 miles from the city, 1 m. beyond the village of Los Reyes there is a road fork. Bear left on CE-136 to Texcoco. The Puebla route keeps to the right on CN-190. The following is the Texcoco road:

MILES FROM MEXICO CITY — ROUTE LOG

0 MEXICO CITY. Leave city via CN-190.

16 Road Fork. Turn left on Texcoco Highway, CE-136.

26 Branch Road to r., leads one mile to Coatlinchán, from which point there is a 3-mile trail to the Idol of Tlaloc, a gigantic, carved monolith so large, all attempts to move it have failed.

27 *Chapingo.** The National Agricultural School housing Diego Rivera's finest murals.

29 *TEXCOCO.** **G.** Historic capital of the Texcocoan Indian kingdom. The city is now a pottery and weaving center. Nearby is Molino de Flores, a famed hacienda and now a national park.

53 *Calpulalpan.*

87 *Ocotoxco.* Junction: paved road to r. leads 10 m. to Tlaxcala.*

91 *Apizaco.*

108 *Huamantla.* **G.**

137 *Zacatepec.* **G.** The route makes a junction here with CN-140 (Puebla to Veracruz highway).

Mexico City to Veracruz (via Puebla and Jalapa)

0 Leave Mexico City via CN-190.

16 Road Fork. To left, via Texcoco. Straight ahead for *Puebla,* following CN-190. (See Trip Log of Mexico City to Puebla section.)

86 *PUEBLA.** **GHR.** Leave Puebla, east on CN-150. The country is fairly flat, but pretty.

95 *Amozoc.* Village noted for its pottery and craftsmen who silver and gold-chase on steel.

110 *Junction:* Here CN-140 begins. Turn to l. on 140 toward Zacatepec. (CN-150 which continues ahead goes to Tehuacán and Cordoba, see route description below.)

144 *Zacatepec.* **G.** Junction with CE-136, the Mexico City-Texcoco-Veracruz route. Continue on CN-140. The road traverses a vast, high plain to Alchichica.

157 *Alchichica.* Nearby is an extinct volcano which has in its crater Alchichica Lake. From here there are excellent views of snowcapped Mount Orizaba (Citlaltépetl), towering about 18,851 ft. above sea level.
172 *Perote.** **G.** An interesting town at the foot of Cofre de Perote, an extinct volcano. Junction: a paved road to the left goes to Teziutlán.*
185 *Las Vigas.* **G.** Road begins descent into the Valley of Jalapa.
201 *Banderilla.* Home of the extensive botanical gardens, the Jardín Lecuona. Noted for its orchids.
205 *JALAPA.** **GHR.** Capital of State of Veracruz. A picturesque, interesting city and good stopover. Leaving Jalapa the road drops steadily and rapidly to the tropic coastal plain, passing rich coffee plantations, etc.
247 *Puente Nacional.* **HR.** Side road to l. to the archaeological ruins at Zempoala, and beyond to the excellent beach at Chachalacas.
294 *VERACRUZ.** **GHR.**

Mexico City to Veracruz (via Puebla, Tehuacan, Cordoba)

0 *MEXICO CITY.* Follow route from the capital to Puebla described above. Road surface is excellent.
86 *PUEBLA.* Leave Puebla via CN-150.
110 Junction with CN-140, going to Jalapa and Veracruz. Bear right, continuing on 150 toward Tehuacán.
117 *Tecamachalco.* **G.** An interesting village with a nice Franciscan church.
154 Turn-off to r. 2 miles to *TEHUACÁN.** Thermal and mineral springs area. Good stopover. Beyond the turn-off the road climbs to the Cumbres de Acultzingo, then a spectacular descent to Acultzingo begins, the highway dropping some 2000 feet in less then five miles. Fogs are encountered on the road in the early mornings.
180 *Acultzingo.* Gorgeous view of the valley and Mount Orizaba.
197 *ORIZABA.* **GHR.**
208 *FORTÍN DE LAS FLORES.** **GHR.** Tropical climate, garden country, and endless flowers, plus gardenia-filled swimming pools.
212 *CORDOBA.** **GHR.** A charming city in beautiful surroundings. From here the highway drops to almost sea level.
248 *Las Tinajas.** A new paved road branches to the right, leading 50 m., to the Papaloapan River basin.
280 Junction with CN-180, the Gulf Coast Highway. Turn left for Veracruz.
287 *Boca del Rio.*
293 Junction with CN-140 to Jalapa. Continue straight ahead to Veracruz.
300 *VERACRUZ.**

41. Pachuca to Tuxpan and Tecolutla

(The Vanilla Route)

This, one of the most worth-while motor trips in Mexico is scarcely known to the average tourist. It is a comfortable, scenic drive that takes in beautiful mountain country, vivid tropics, and unique towns.

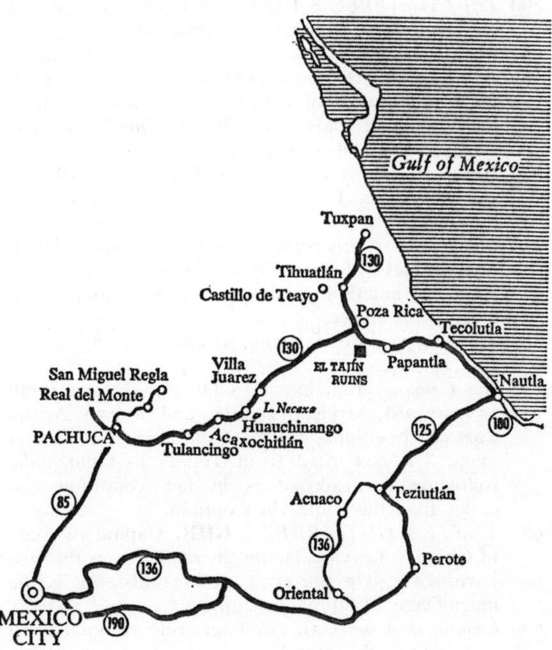

The traveler interested in getting somewhat off-trail, yet in comfort, can follow this route to Tecolutla, then return by another road (Nautla, Teziutlán) to Mexico City.

Length: (from Colonia, the turn-off on the Pan American Highway), 165 m. to Tuxpan; 175 m. to Tecolutla. *Condition of road:* Paved and good. *Best stopovers:* Villa Juárez, Tuxpan, Poza Rica, Papantla, Tecolutla, Teziutlán, (and on return) Puebla. Although the drive to the Gulf of Mexico can be made in a day, it is suggested that several days be taken for the entire circuit drive.

The turn-off for this route is at Colonia on the old Pan American Highway, CN-85, about 53 m. north of Mexico City.

MILES FROM COLONIA — TRIP LOG

0 *Colonia.* Junction; CN-85 and CN-130. Turn east toward Pachuca.
6 *PACHUCA.** **GHR.** Capital of the State of Hidalgo and noted mining center. From here an interesting short side-trip can be taken to Real del Monte, a picturesque silver mining town, and to San Miguel Regla,* a lovely hideaway resort.

Leave Pachuca via Av. Madero, CN-130, for Tulancingo, Tuxpan, etc. The road traverses rolling hill country and lovely valleys.
35 *Tulancingo.* **G.** A woolen mill center.
50 *Acaxochitlán.* **G.** Famed for the cider from its apple orchards. Here the road begins the climb into the cool pine forests of the Sierra de Zacapoaxtla.
69 *Huauchinango.** **GHR.** A colorful town, noted for its wealth of gardens and surrounding orchards.

Beyond the town the road skirts the beautiful Lake Necaxa.

82 *VILLA JUÁREZ.** **GHR.** Best stopover. Town is famous for its flowers, fruit wine and Friday market. The road winds down into exciting tropical country.

132 *Road Junction:* CN-180 (the Gulf Coast Highway, see Index), and CN-130. For Tuxpan, turn left. Routes 180 and 130 share the road to Tuxpan. Gas.

144 *Tihuatlán.* From here a good side-road leads left (NW) 7 m. to the archaeological ruins of Castillo de Teayo.*

165 *TUXPAN** (also written Tuxpam). **GHR.** An interesting Gulf port on the Tuxpan River. Excellent fishing and swimming.

From Tuxpan you return via the same route to the road junction (33 miles). Here turn left (E) toward Poza Rica and Tecolutla. Follow CN-180.

132 Road Junction.

134 *POZA RICA.** **GHR.** Mexico's lively petroleum metropolis. Side trip from here to *El Tajín,* one of Mexico's most important archaeological zones.

146 *PAPANTLA.** **GHR.** Charming tropical town, center of the Totonac Indian country, and important vanilla center. Noted for its Corpus Christi fiesta and its flying-pole dancers.

172 *TECOLUTLA.** **GHR.** A rundown fishing and beach resort that retains a certain charm.

The motorist interested in returning to Mexico City via a different route may continue along the coast on CN-180 (see Index: Highway Routes — Tampico to Yucatán), or at Nautla, turn right, continuing up through *TEZIUTLÁN.* At Teziutlán there is a choice of roads, one going to Perote and there joining the Mexico City-Veracruz Highway; or, one may continue over a good but winding secondary road going through Acuaco, Oriental, and not far from there, joining the Texcoco-Zacatapec Highway.

42. Salina Cruz to Coatzacoalcos

(Trans-Isthmus Highway)

The new Isthmus of Tehuantepec highway, the shortest link between the Pacific and Atlantic, with the exception of the Panama Canal. You can drive from coast to coast in about 4½ hrs. *Length:* 189 m. *Road condition:* Paved and generally good.

MILES FROM SALINA CRUZ — TRIP LOG

0 *SALINA CRUZ.** **GHR.** Pacific Coast port. Leave Salina Cruz via CN-185 for Tehuantepec.

11 *Junction* with CN-190, the Mexico City to Chiapas Highway. Turn right. CN-185 and 190 share the road for some 26 m.

12 *TEHUANTEPEC.** **GHR.**

28 *Junction.* Road to left goes to Ixtepec; branch to right goes to Juchitán.

37 *Junction.* CN-185, the Trans-Isthmus Road branches off left here. The road is flat, wide and high-speed.

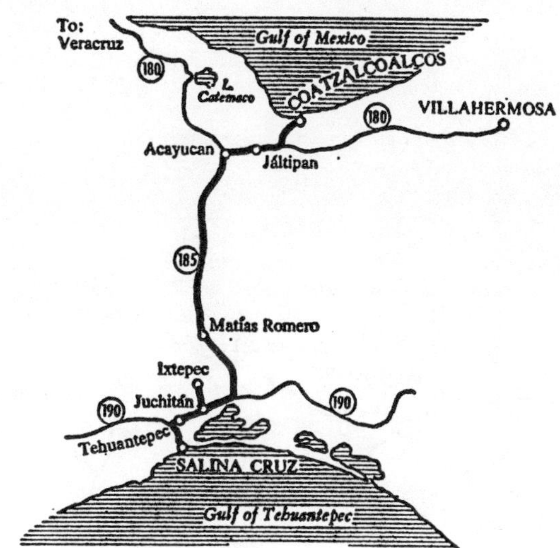

65 Branch road to *Matías Romero** (1 m. to left). An interesting old railway town noted for its annual fair.

147 *ACAYUCAN.* **G.** Junction of CN-180 and CN-185. Turn left to go to Lake Catemaco and Veracruz. Turn right to continue toward Coatzalcoalcos.

160 *Jáltipan.*

185 Junction. Road to right leads to Villahermosa.

189 *COATZACOALCOS.** **GHR.** The Atlantic or Gulf of Mexico port and terminal of the highway.

43. Ciudad Mante to Guadalajara

This is another of the trunk roads linking Mexico's north-south highways. Running southwest from C. Mante, it provides a good paved connection to San Luis Potosí and Guadalajara for tourists coming from the eastern United States. *Length:* 434 m. *Road conditions:* Entirely paved. In sections the road is old and narrow, the surface battered. Between Huisache and San Luis Potosí, the road is being widened and there are occasional delays due to the construction work. Driving time about 12 hrs. *Best stopovers:* San Luis Potosí, Guadalajara.

MILES FROM C. MANTE — TRIP LOG

0 *Ciudad Mante.* **GHR.** On CN-85, the old Pan American Highway, about 407 m. from Laredo. Leave C. Mante on 85, going toward Antiguo Morelos and Mexico City.

20 *Antiguo Morelos*. **GHR.** Here the route, posted CN-80, branches off right (W).

39 Branch road to right, CE-45, unpaved, goes 7 m. to El Salto Falls.* Admission $5 MN. per car to Falls.

40 *El Naranjo*. **HR.** There is a pleasant motel and restaurant here on the river's edge. The highway continues through spectacular tropical valleys and hills.

74 *General Cedillo*. **G.** Here the road has reached the Central Plateau. Elevation, 4500 ft.

102 *Tepeyac*. **GR.** A desert stop. The lunchroom is fair.

146 *Huizache*. Junction with CN-57, the Eagle Pass to Mexico City Highway, (see Index). Both routes 80 and 57 share the road to San Luis Potosí. Continue straight ahead. The road remains monotonous, relieved only by a few small villages.

214 *SAN LUIS POTOSÍ*.* **GHR.** Capital of State of San Luis Potosí. Leaving S.L.P., for Guadalajara, via CN-80, the highway traverses somewhat more mountainous terrain.

248 *Villa de Arriaga*. **G.** Just beyond the town the boundaries of four states meet — San Luis Potosí, Zacatecas, Jalisco, and Guanajuato.

265 *Ojuelos de Jalisco*. **G.** Branch road to r. CN-70, leads to Aguascalientes and the El Paso-Mexico City Highway. Paved.

307 Junction with the El Paso-Mexico City Highway, CN-45 (see Index). Road to left leads to León, Querétaro, and Mexico City.

309 *Lagos de Moreno*. **G.** CN-80 continues through the town. At the northern edge of the town there is a new and recommended bypass, avoiding the town center.

336 *San Juan de los Lagos*.* **G.** Noted for its famed perigrination fiesta and for its needlework. A new bypass circles the town to the south.

383 *Tetpatitlán*. **G.**

409 *Zapotlanejo*. **G.** Junction on left with paved CE-86 to Soledad and Irapuato.

428 *Tlaquepaque*.* **G.** A suburb of Guadalajara. Once noted for its usual pottery (which has deteriorated), its furniture crafts and glassware.

434 *GUADALAJARA*.* **GHR.** Capital of State of Jalisco. Mexico's second city.

44. *Tijuana to La Paz*

(Lower California)

The peninsula of Lower California (Baja California) is largely desert country with a few oases thrown in. Travel by car to the southern tip of the peninsula is possible, but only under the most ideal conditions — that is, in dry weather, in a high-chassis, and best, four-wheel-drive vehicle. About 152 miles of road is paved; the remainder is dirt, sand and nothing. There are few stopover facilities and gasoline is not available for long stretches. It is camping country where extra gas, water and supplies must be carried.

Length: approximately 964 m. *Road condition:* Tijuana to Santo Tomás, paved; Santo Tomás to Arroyo Seco and to San Telmo, paved; from San Telmo to somewhat north of Santo Domingo, trail; from Querétaro to La Paz, paved.

APPROXIMATE MILES FROM TIJUANA — TRIP LOG

0 *Tijuana*.* **GHR.** Mexican border town opposite San Isidoro and San Diego, Calif. Customs and Immigration offices. For motorists going as far as Ensenada, tourist cards are not required, and generally there is no baggage inspection. The exits from the city are poorly marked and the motorist must take care not to get on the paved road running along the border to Tecate.

16 *Rosarito Beach*. **GHR.** The beach hotel is attractive, when opened.

30 *Descanso*. **G.**

65 *ENSENADA*.* **GHR.** A popular port and beach

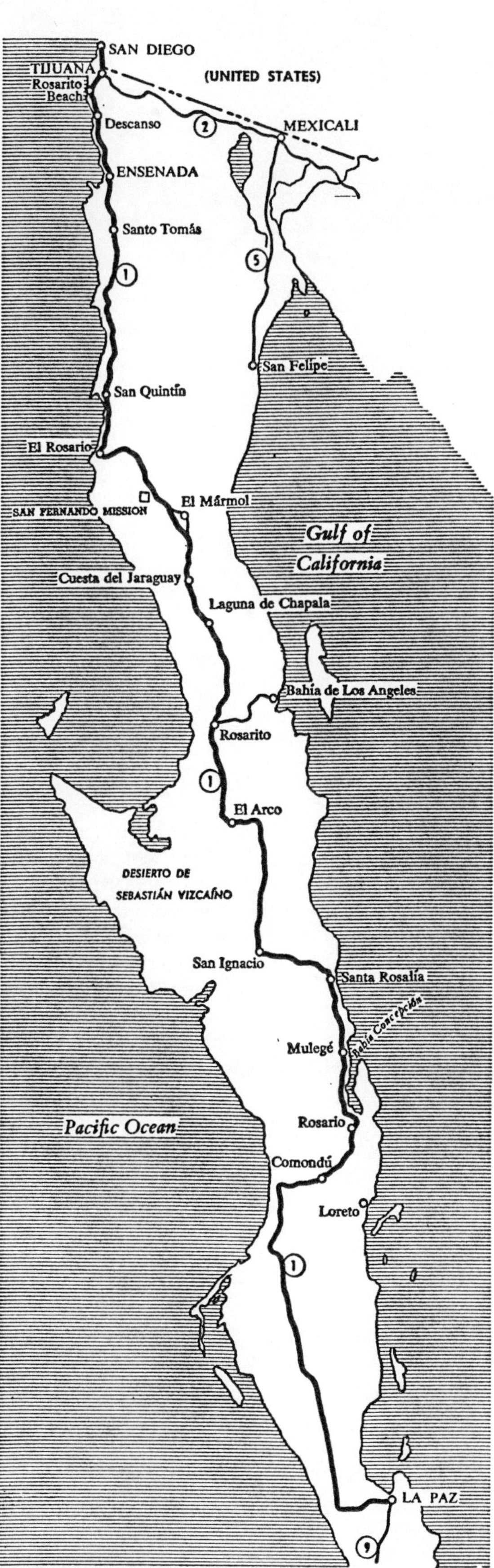

resort. Beyond here the paved road continues over several low ranges.

94 *Santo Tomás.* **G.**

172 *Hamilton Ranch.* A guest ranch patronized by Americans.

186 *San Quintín.** A semi-abandoned port. The road continues through farming country.

195 Entrance to Santa María Sky Ranch. A guest ranch.

227 *El Rosario.* **G.** Small settlement near Rosario Bay. At Rosario Arriba there are primitive tourist cabins and a restaurant. Here road turns inland. It is one of the worst stretches.

270 *San Fernando Mission.* Food available at nearby San Agustín Ranch.

292 *El Mármol.* An onyx mining camp. It has what is perhaps the only school in the world made entirely of onyx.

323 *Cuesta del Jaraguay.* Stiff grade to the peninsula's central plateau.

348 *Laguna de Chapala.* (Side road to San Felipe, left, very rough.) Route continues across the lake bed in dry weather; skirts it when it has rained.

371 Branch road left to *Bahía de Los Angeles.**

440 *Rosarito.* Small settlement.

498 *El Arco,* lying just S. of the boundary between the State and the Territory of Baja California. Last place where U.S. gasoline is available. Beyond here road continues in long straight sections skirting the Desierto de Sebastián Vizcaíno, a desert covered with weird cacti and yucca.

578 *San Ignacio.* **GHR.** A fair size settlement. From here side trips can be made to Turtle Bay.

626 *Santa Rosalía.** **GHR.** The most important town in Central Baja California. Leaving Santa Rosalía the route crosses unusually rugged but pretty terrain.

667 *Mulegé.** **G.** An attractive settlement situated 2 m. from the Gulf of California. Leaving here the road skirts Bahía Concepción (Conception Bay).

730 *Rosario** (or *Rosarito*). Branch road goes to interesting Loreto.

765 *Comondú.* Oasis village. Road is difficult along here.

990 *LA PAZ.** **GHR.** Capital of Territory of Baja California, pleasant fishing resort.

PART FOUR

The Regions of Mexico

45. Geographical Areas and Accommodations

This section of the guide is your detailed exploration of Mexico, an intimate prowl through the cities, the villages, the resorts, and the vivid, ever-changing countryside. For convenience's sake we divide the country into arbitrary regions, taking one at a time, rather than skipping around, and casing it thoroughly. Our regions may include several states, and even segments of others, as long as they seem either geographically or touristically related. Here are the regions and the states, territories or districts they encompass:

REGIONAL DESIGNATION	STATES
1. NORTHWESTERN MEXICO	Baja California, Territory of Baja California, Sonora, Sinaloa, Nayarit.
2. NORTH-CENTRAL MEXICO	Chihuahua, Coahuila, Durango, Zacatecas, the northern half of San Luis Potosí.
3. NORTHEASTERN MEXICO	Nueva León, Tamaulipas, a small section of eastern San Luis Potosí.
4. CENTRAL MEXICO	Aguascalientes, the NE corner of Jalisco, San Luis Potosí, Guanajuato, Querétaro, Hidalgo, Mexico, Tlaxcala, Morelos, Puebla.
5. MEXICO, D.F.	Mexico City, the Federal District and immediate environs.
6. CENTRAL WESTERN MEXICO	Western half of Jalisco, including the Guadalajara-Lake Chapala country. Michoacán, Guerrero, Colima.
7. EASTERN MEXICO	Veracruz, Tabasco.
8. SOUTHERN MEXICO	Oaxaca, Chiapas.
9. PENINSULA OF YUCATÁN	Campeche, Yucatán, Territory of Quintana Roo.

With new roads laid each year, exciting new areas being opened to travelers, a guidebook to Mexico can no longer trot along trunk highways or railways and be satisfied that it has offered a reader the best there is. As a convenience for travelers *Terry's Guide to Mexico* utilizes a more convenient and effective way of covering the regions of Mexico.

For each region you will find a brief description, an easy-to-digest thumbnail history, and a preview of the most important attractions there. Each region has certain centers of interest which can serve as a comfortable base from which a traveler can explore the surrounding area. For example, CENTRAL WESTERN MEXICO has four well-defined areas of tourist importance: the Guadalajara country, the Colima-Manzanillo country, the Michoacán country, and, the vivid area around and leading to Acapulco. Rather than listing all the points of interest alphabetically and letting the frustrated reader try to pin them to a map, or, instead of leading you on a tedious spin through endless highway towns, we simply plunk you down upon a comfortable base and help you explore it and the region around it. At the beginning of each of the regional sections which follow there is a list of the most interesting areas or districts and a base from which you can begin your explorations.

ACCOMMODATIONS

(See Index, *Hotels and Restaurants.*) The system of rating hotels and restaurants with stars or other arbitrary symbols strikes us as both unrealistic and unsatisfactory. The tastes, demands, and habits of travelers vary too much. Instead of grading establishments in such a manner we try to typify them with a brief comment, offering some idea of the general atmosphere, how they are run, and the service proffered.

In the following sections certain words are repeatedly used as a kind of shorthand to tip you off regarding hotels and restaurants. The most used terms are:

Chilly — meaning that the general atmosphere, the service, the attitude of the management, is distant. Few attempts are made to see that you are enjoying yourself or made to feel at home. In some instances a *chilly* hotel may be otherwise well operated.

Friendly — management is present and goes out of its way to help you, to give information, etc.

Chrome-plated style — establishment where a good deal of money has gone into the plant, décor, and fixtures, yet the whole doesn't fuse happily and there is something lacking. This is a peculiar Mexican phenomenon. Usually the thing lacking is managerial presence, warmth, and service know-how.

De luxe — a place that combines first-class equipment, facilities and good standard hotel or restaurant procedure. It is usually expensive.

Homey — a small place, something like the three-star European pension, where the equipment may be modest, even old, but the establishment is clean, the cuisine simple and good, the atmosphere friendly.

Viajero-type — this is a particular, inexpensive type, thoroughly Mexican hotel patronized by *viajeros* (traveling salesmen). Some of these are clean; others not so well kept. In most of them the comforts are minimum — no floor coverings, Spartan furniture, poor lighting fixtures, no ashtrays, no wastebaskets, haphazard service, uncertain plumbing and hot water. Generally, their only saving grace is their low prices.

All hotel and restaurant rates are given in pesos (MN) unless otherwise indicated.

In most cases this guide only lists rates for double occupancy in hotels, abbreviated *dble.* Hotels have very few single rooms with one bed. The charge for single occupancy is about ¼ to ⅓ less than the double rate, European plan. In *viajero-type* hotels you pay by the bed. You can occupy a room containing five beds but you pay only the rate for one. Most hotels charge extra for garage.

The rates indicated hereafter in the guide were those officially posted during our inspection tour of hotels in 1961.

46. Northwestern Mexico

This region of Mexico which includes the Peninsula of Lower California (Baja California) with its two political entities, the State of Baja California Norte and the Federal Territory called Baja California Sur, and furthermore includes the States of Sonora, Sinaloa and Nayarit, all together might be typified as a sprawling tourist-resort noted for its rooms with views. Each of its districts has seaside frontage — the Pacific Ocean and/or the Gulf of California. If one were to cruise along its shores from Tijuana to Cabo San Lucas (Cape San Lucas, S. tip of Baja California), then up the Gulf to the mouth of the Colorado River and finally, down the beaches of Sonora, Sinaloa, and Nayarit, the ship's log would read well over 3000 miles.

Since a good part of this region has always been a frontier, both in pre-Hispanic times as well as until very recently, there are no impressive ruined cities, temples, nor even many colonial monuments to mark the occupation of great civilizations. The northwestern region has little to offer the seeker of quaint historical mementos, great art, or architecture, or for that matter, even impressive scenery. It is principally a region for vacationers — deep-sea fishermen, avid hunters, and people who like to laze on sunny shores.

There are various avenues of communication into the distinct parts of the region. Several airlines link the region with Mexico City and U.S. cities. The Ferrocarril del Pacifico (formerly the Southern Pacific Railway) runs from Nogales, at the Arizona border, to Guadalajara, Jal., where it connects with the Mexican National Railways (to Mexico City). The fairly new West Coast Highway also runs down from Nogales to Guadalajara and on. Boat transportation, though it exists, is less comfortable and regular. Tourist accommodations are quite good. The only exception is Lower California, from Ensenada to a bit north of La Paz, there are still no roads and no accommodations. The new Chihuahua-Pacific Railway adds a spectacular east-west link between Presidio, Texcel and the west coast port of Topolobampo.

Outstanding Attractions: The beach and fishing resorts at La Paz, B.C.S., Guaymas, Son., Mazatlán,

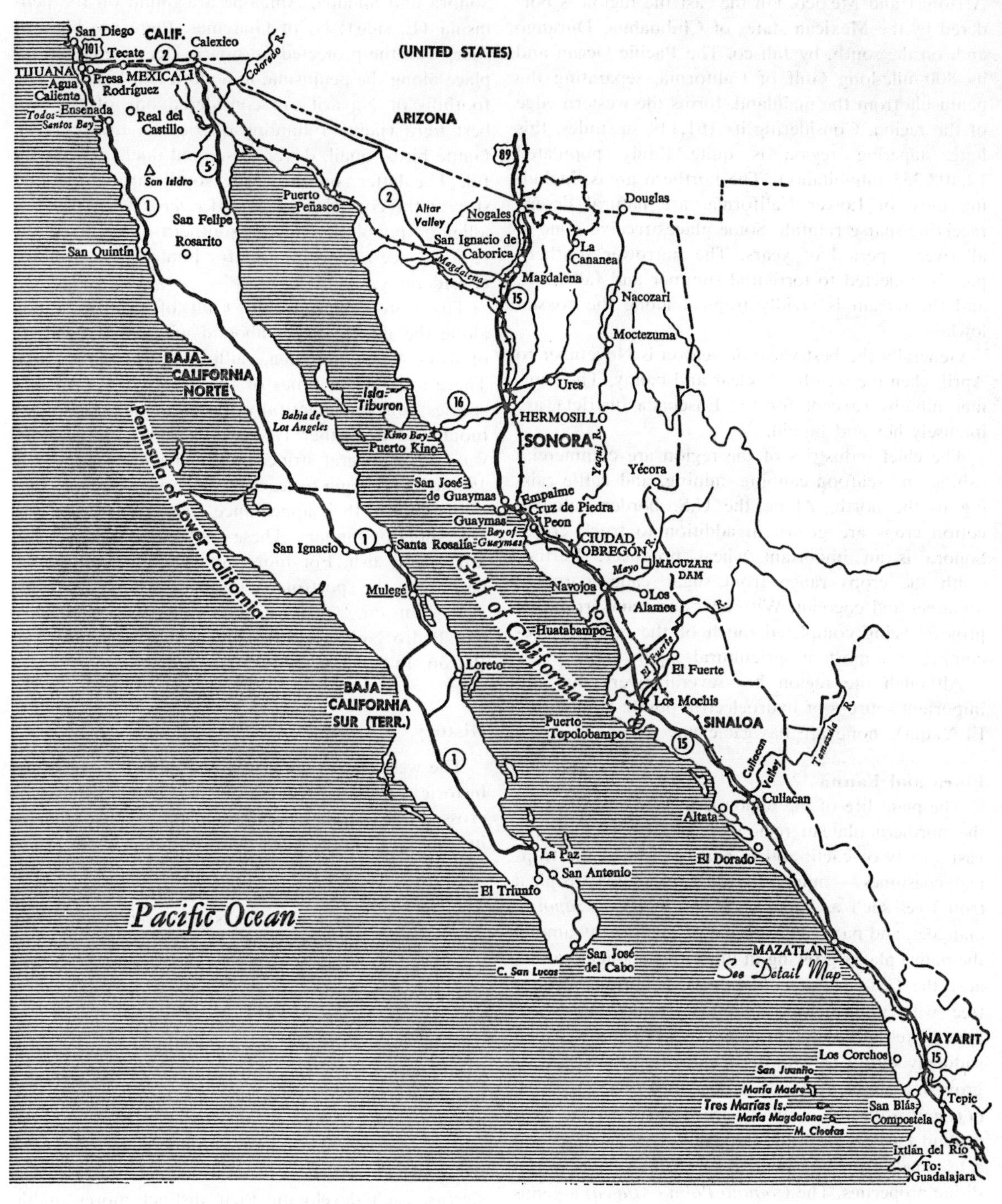

Sin., and numerous smaller fishing villages. The picturesque semi-ghost colonial mining towns of Los Alamos, Son., and El Fuerte, Sin. Bear, deer, antelope, and jaguar hunting, especially in Lower California, and the Sierras of the coastal states.

AREAS OF MAXIMUM INTEREST	BASE
Lower California	Ensenada
Sonora Country	Guaymas
Sinaloa-Nayarit Country	Mazatlán

The Region

The northern boundary of the entire region is the International Border between the U.S. (California, Arizona) and Mexico. On the east the region is bordered by the Mexican states of Chihuahua, Durango and, on the south, by Jalisco. The Pacific Ocean and its 800-mile-long Gulf of California, separating the peninsula from the mainland, forms the western edge of the region. Considering its 161,114 sq. miles, this long, tapering region is quite thinly populated (2,408,353 inhabitants). The northern areas, including most of Lower California, are natural desert, receiving sparse rainfall. Some places receive none at all over a period of years. The narrower southern part is subjected to torrential summer and fall rains, and the terrain is vividly tropical along the coastal lowlands.

Generally the best vacation season is November to April when the weather is clear and balmy. The summer months (except for the Ensenada district) are intensely hot and humid.

The chief industries of the region are commercial fishing and seafood canning, mining, and cattle raising in the north. Along the U.S. border valuable cotton crops are grown in addition to truck crops. Sonora is an important wheat producer. Farther south the crops range from sugar cane, corn, to tomatoes and coconut. With new dams and irrigation projects being completed much of the region is becoming an important agricultural export area.

Although the region has several rivers that are important sources of hydroelectric power (El Fuerte, El Yaqui), none are navigable any distance.

Flora and Fauna

The plant life of the region is in part typical of all the northern plateau region of Mexico, including a vast variety of cacti; and in part, typical of the tropical coastlines — numerous types of palms, tropical fruit trees such as bananas, dates, mameys, *zapotes,* mangoes, and papayas. Unusual or noteworthy among the native plants growing in this vast botanical garden are: the *Cirio (Idria columnaris),* a curious slender tree with unbranched columnar trunks and short pencil-like horizontal branches near the top which suddenly sprout leaves after a rain. Its yellow flowers grow in a plume at the tip of the trunk. The *Damiana (Turnera diffusa),* a small shrub native to the area around La Paz. Both the liqueur flavored with it and a tea made from the twigs is reputed to have aphrodisiac properties. The *Coquito Palm (Attalea)* a genus of palm allied to the coconut and distinguished by the fact that each of the *coquitos* (little nuts), about 3 to 4 inches long, contain three cells each enclosing a single seed. The nuts hang below the fronds of the palm in great datelike clusters. Their oily, edible kernels, gathered between October and June, are expressed for the valuable soap oils obtained from them.

Wild game in the area has long been a magnet attracting both Mexican and U.S. sportsmen. Black bear (*oso negro*) are met with in the higher sierras, Sonora and Sinaloa. Antelope are found on the peninsula (E. side); N. of Guaymas, there are bighorn sheep (on the protected list now). Deer are commonplace along the peninsula, in Sonora and Sinaloa. The foothills of Nayarit are considered one of the two best *tigre* (jaguar) hunting districts in the republic. Game birds, quail, dove, geese, and ducks are plentiful. The latter, on their way south during the fall, stop at the coastal lagoons and *esteros* (ponds). The alligator population in the southern segment of the region, once a favorite prey for hunters, has declined considerably.

The waters both in the Gulf of California and along the Pacific coasts abound with a great variety of fish — albacore, tuna, sailfish, shark, marlin, etc. There are certain times of the year when a specific species will run plentifully in certain areas, while a month later another type will abound in the same waters. In general striped marlin begin to appear in January and begin to leave about April. During April sailfish put in their appearance and are plentiful until December or January. These are the two most sought-after game fish. For more detailed fish-running and best areas, the sportsman can secure fish charts from: Tom Jamison, % Cia. de Botes de Pesca Deportiva San Pedro Nolasco, S.R.L., Guaymas, Son.; or Luis Patrón, Indian Fleet, Mazatlán, Sin.

History

The west coast region was undoubtedly one of the historic avenues down which the Asiatic tribes who crossed the Alaskan landbridge must have traveled in the dim, unrecorded past. Among them, most likely, were the Toltecs who may have reached the Culiacan Valley, Sinaloa, some 500 years before Christ. It is said they established a settlement there called Tlapallan, before moving on to Central Mexico. Likewise, the Nahoas (mother-family of the Aztecs or Mexica) may have passed along the coast, pushing toward Central Mexico. Later, when they became powerful and dreaded, ruling a vast Indian Confederacy from Tenochtitlán, their power extended north up into the west coast, and the region was one of their principal sources of wealth. When the Aztecs moved southward splinter groups from the main tribal stream settled in the coastal region and nearby sierras, each developing their distinct mores, habits and ways. (See below, *People.*)

Following the conquest of Tenochtitlán the Spaniards soon set out to add new territories to the crown and the west coast was one of the first regions to attract them. In 1524 a kinsman of Hernando Cortés, Francisco Cortés, captured the Indian settlement of Tepic, Nayarit, and waged war against the strongly entrenched Nayarito tribe who continued to resist the European encroachment until 1722. Francisco Cortés was soon followed by Captain Nuño de Guzmán, and later by Pedro Almindez Chirinos, who sailed along the coast. Reports of vast gold treasures in Sonora sent Vásquez de Coronado into the region to conquer it. By 1563 fortresses were being built along the coast and at river mouths, and Jesuit and Franciscan friars were setting up their strings of missions. Often these missions never amounted to much, the native tribes frequently rejecting the teachings of the indefatigable friars and preferring their freedom and traditions to the Inquisition and Iberianism. In Nayarit the Indian groups jealously maintained their independence, and it was not until July 1876 that they finally submitted to the Mexican Government.

In Baja California the situation varied somewhat due to the forbidding terrain and poverty and backwardness of the Indians on the peninsula. The first Spanish expedition touched peninsular soil near La Paz in 1534. The following year Cortés himself landed in La Paz Bay, which he named Santa Cruz. Though pearls were found there, and numerous attempts were made to colonize the peninsula, almost all the settlements failed until 1697 when the Jesuits, led by Father Juan María Salvatierra, founded the first permanent settlement at Loreto in 1697. For some seventy years the Jesuit order tightly controlled the peninsula and the twenty missions they had set up. No one, including crown representatives, was allowed in the region except with their special permission. Even the crown soldiers who kept order in the area were hand-picked by the order. In 1768, when the Jesuits were expelled from all Spanish dominions, they were replaced in Baja California by Franciscan friars led by Junípero Serra. The Franciscans founded one mission, then moved on to upper California (present state of California) and were succeeded in Baja California by the Dominican Fathers.

At various times, during the French invasion of Mexico, and later, foreign troops and even freebooters attempted to seize control of Lower California and parts of Sonora. American forces occupied key ports during the war of 1846–47. In 1853 an American adventurer, William Walker, invaded Lower California and proclaimed himself president of a new "republic." He was ejected the following year. In 1911 an army of "socialist" adventurers invaded the northern part of the region in a vain attempt to set up a socialist regime.

The People: Today the inhabitants of Lower California are almost entirely Mexican (mestizo stock), whereas the inhabitants of the mainland coastal states are Mexican, plus a strong sprinkling of Indian tribes who have maintained their customs and traditions.

When the Spaniards discovered Lower California there were some 80,000 Indians, distinguished by the fact that they were undoubtedly the most primitive peoples in America. Most of the tribes had no agriculture, few shelters, they wore no garments. Their weapons were so crude that they were forced to subsist for long periods on insects, reptiles, grubs, and the seeds of wild plants. When they luckily killed an animal they tied a string to a piece of meat, chewed, swallowed, then pulled the morsel back and let another man have his turn at it. With certain seedy fruits, it was the custom after having eaten them, for the Indians to gather up their own stools to recover the seeds, which were ground into a meal and eaten again. Most of these original inhabitants of Sonora and Baja California were wiped out by epidemics during the eighteenth century. The peninsula, for example, remained almost deserted until the arrival of Mexican immigrants from the mainland during the nineteenth century.

Along the mainland coast (States of Sinaloa and Nayarit) there remain several important ethnic groups whose customs, folkways, and handicrafts are of interest to the traveler, These tribes, living in the highlands mostly, and diminishing in population, are the Mayos, Coras, and Huicholes.

The Mayos, living in the foothills and sierras of Sonora and Sinaloa, are related to the potent Yaqui tribes of North Central Mexico. Their customs and traditions are very similar (see Index). They carve interesting wooden ritual masks and weave heavy wool serapes.

The Coras, farther south, are related to the Huichol Indians. They consider themselves somewhat superior to neighboring tribes and entertain a strong dislike to being confounded with them. They are a handsome people, skilled weavers, noted for their woollen serapes and intricately woven and embroidered bags. Although much of their folklore is similar to that of the Huicholes their dances are altogether different. One of their most interesting ritual dances is Los Maromeros, an acrobatic dance of pre-Hispanic origin performed to the eerie music of a small drum and flute played by a single musician.

The Huicholes, living mostly in the Sierra de Nayarit, remain one of the most interesting of Mexican indigenous groups. They, like their Cora neighbors, entertain a folk tradition of a great deluge, along with a Noah-like personage, and ark, and birds involved in the aftermath of the flood — much of the story disturbingly like our biblical tale, yet it existed among these people long before the coming of the Spanish. Their customs and rituals, hardly affected by the overpowering advance of modern civilization in their country, are of exceptional interest. They still police their own tribal groups and Mexican law has little meaning to them. In cases of serious crimes the Huichol governors or headmen act as judges.

Decades ago they punished offenders cruelly on whipping posts introduced by the missionaries centuries ago. Now-a-days drunks are put in old-fashioned stocks until they sober up. Both whipping posts and stocks are kept in the local Christian temples because the Huicholes still connect them with Christianity and the Santo Cristo.

Though very strict in the ritual, the Huicholes are lax in their social relations. Young girls are often seduced during fiestas and no one seems upset by it. The custom of asking for a bride is observed, but only in the case of virgins. A Huichol man often takes two or three wives. However, when a man adds a wife to the household, he must secure the consent of the other wives.

The Huicholes are noted for their imaginative and unique ritual art — the objects which they use in order to speak to their gods. They devise beautifully decorated prayer arrows; poetic god's-eyes woven of vividly colored wool yarn and used to protect children; votive bowls made of gourds decorated with colored beads set in a beeswax base; and intriguing yarn paintings. Equally interesting are their native costumes, fabulously decorated hats, and the pouches woven of cotton or wool and elaborately decorated.

The Huicholes, like the Tarahumaras who live hundreds of miles to the north and with whom they have no contact, are peyote worshipers. Both people use the peyote plants, (a small cactus, *Lophophora Williansi,* which lives for months after being uprooted), in their religious ritual. The peyote when eaten allays hunger and fatigue, produces Technicolor visions and often, an exalted state. Both tribes worship the plant as a demigod and, though they speak different tongues, they both refer to the plant as *hikuli.* The peyote button does not grow in the Huichol region and they are forced to make long (43-day) pilgrimages to the Real de Catorce area in the Central Plateau state of San Luis Potosí to obtain the singular little cactus. (For further information regarding the Huichol peyote rituals and other tribal ceremonies, consult *A Treasury of Mexican Folkways* by Frances Toor, and *Unknown Mexico* by Carl Lumholtz.)

PENINSULA OF LOWER CALIFORNIA

This area, the western-most part of the northwestern region, extends from the U.S. border on the north some 800 miles southward to the tip of the peninsula. It is separated from the body of Mexico by the Gulf of California, except for a narrow desert belt along the U.S. (Arizona) border where it joins the State of Sonora. The region for the most part is mountain-rugged, a moonlike desert country with little rainfall and a sparsity of vegetation. The population is concentrated in a few favored areas — the fertile Mexicali Valley and the Pacific Coast in the north, and the La Paz region in the south. The entire central area, over 600 miles in length, from slightly south of Ensenada to La Paz is virtually without inhabitants except in a few tiny mining and oasis settlements.

HIGHLIGHTS: Except for a few resorts, Ensenada and La Paz, Lower California has little to offer as far as sightseeing and casual vacationing goes. The only suitable roads are in the north and the only comfortable means of reaching the southern tip is by air. The peninsula, however, is fascinating region for sportsmen, experienced campers, and off-trail explorers who enjoy rugged vacationing.

The tourist should be reminded that a visit in the northern section offers nothing of the real Mexico — neither customs, traditions, picturesque villages, fiestas, etc. Being so close to the U.S. it is the most "Americanized" of Mexican regions. You go there not to see Mexico, but merely to swim, fish, hunt or explore.

Tijuana, B.C. Pop. 65,000. Alt. 125 ft. The principal port of entry on the U.S. (California)-Mexico border.

HOW TO GET THERE: Via highway — U.S. 101 from San Diego, Calif. *Via bus* — Greyhound from San Diego to San Isidro (U. S. Customs side), thence by foot or taxi into Tijuana. *Via air* — regular daily flights by CMA to Los Angeles, Mexico City, Mexicali, Hermosillo, Mazatlán and Guadalajara. Aeronaves de Mexico S.A., has flights to Acapulco, La Paz, Mazatlán, Mexicali, Guaymas, Nogales, and Guadalajara.

HOTELS: *Agua Caliente Travelodge,* across from the Agua Caliente race track, 60 rooms, air-conditioned dining room, cocktail lounge, heated pool. A first-class motel. Rates: EP, $100 to $187.50 MN, dble. Tel. 4951. *Rancho la Gloria,* 7 m. S. on Ensenada highway. Pleasant 31 unit resort hotel with heated pool, dining room, and cocktail lounge. Rates: $62.50 to $162.50 dble, EP. *La Sierra Motel,* 2 blocks farther south on Ensenada highway, 60 rooms, pool, cocktail lounge, dining room (closed Mondays). Nice atmosphere and first-class accommodations. Rates: EP, $100 MN to $125 MN, dble. *Tropicana Motel,* Ensenada Highway, 31 units, pool. Well-run and pleasant atmosphere. Rates: EP, $100 MN to $125 MN. *Hotel Cesar's,* Calle 5 and Revolución (in town). A popular, fair hotel, 70 rooms, good dining room. Rates: EP, $100 MN and up, dble. *Other Hotels — Hotel Nelson,* 100 rooms, restaurant, bar . . . *Motel León,* Calle 7, 144.

RESTAURANTS: *Cesar's,* in Hotel Cesar. *Capri,* Av. Revolución 366.

DIRECTORY: *Banco Nacional de Mexico,* Calle 2, 139. (U.S. currency is generally used in Tijuana and also Ensenada.) *Auto Service* — Central del Norte, (Ford), Av. Madero and Calle 4. *Motores de Tijuana,* (GM), Blvd. Agua Caliente 1. *American Consulate* — Av. Revolución and Calle 3. *Car Rentals* — Hertz Drive Yourself, Calle 2 and Av. Madero. *Travel Agencies* — Multi-Tours, Av. Revolución 100. *Bus Lines* — Transportes Amarillos de Pasajeros, S.A., Calle 1. Tel. 60-20 (Ensenada-Mexicali routes, Mexicali to San Luis, Son.). Transportes to Baja California S.C.L., Calle 1, 111. (Routes to Ensenada, Mexicali, Tecate, Santa Rosalia.) *Airlines* — CMA, Av. Revolución 426. Tel. 16-25. Aeronaves de Mexico, Av. Revolución and Calle 2. Tel. 46-21.

THE CITY AND ENVIRONS: Tijuana, pronounced tee-who-AH-nah, and derived from the Indian name *Tee Huana* (city near the sea), sprouted from a ranch settlement into a tawdry collection of bars and brothels, and is now gradually changing into a busy commercial center with modern buildings, good hotels, restaurants, and residential areas. Because much of its prosperity is still dependent on American visitors, tourists attractions, savory and unsavory, play an important part in the city's activities.

Avenida Revolución is the Great White Way, busy with curio shops, bars, night clubs, and the palatial jai alai *(frontón)* stadium. (The *frontón* games are held from Thursday through Sunday. The players are top men in the field. There is pari-mutuel betting.) In the shops most of the curios are frankly geared to North American purses, and the so-called native crafts-arts are debased. In that Baja California is a free-zone, savings can sometimes be made on the purchase of European goods (cameras, binoculars, watches) which come into the area duty-free.

About 1½ m. E of the center of town at Agua Caliente *(Hipódromo de Tijuana),* the Saturday and Sunday horse races are a prime attraction. Tipsters along the road offer handicap sheets at an exorbitant 50 cents apiece. Nearby is the Club Campestre (Golf Club), with a fair course, and a quite good dining room. Other entertainment offered by the city are: dog races (Wednesday through Sunday night), bullfights at the Plaza de Toros, east side of town. Best performances on holidays.

About 9 m. E of town on CN-2 (continuation of Av. Revolución) is the Presa Rodríguez, a dam and artificial lake, a favorite weekend spot. The lake is well stocked. Boats, fishing tackle, etc., available. Fourteen miles from Tijuana, on same road, is the entrance to El Florido, one of the palatial ranches belonging to former President Miguel Alemán.

East of Tijuana there are several points of minor touristic interest — the progressive border town of Tecate, Mexicali (state capital), and the fishing port of San Felipe at the head of the Gulf of California.

Tecate, B.C. Pop. 4000. Alt. 1600 ft. On CN-2, 31 m. E of Tijuana. A somnolent border town if compared with Tijuana or Laredo. Customs and Immigration offices open at 8 A.M., close at 6 P.M. The town is noted for its brewery, Cervecería Tecate, one of the largest in Mexico. *Hotels* — Motel Las Cabañas and San Carlos. Rates from $75 MN dble, EP.

Mexicali, B.C. Pop. 85,000. Alt. sea level. Seat of the state government of Baja California del Norte.

Once a sprawling, vice-ridden town with bar and other grim accommodations catering to ranchers from the Imperial Valley across the border, Mexicali has since changed into a busy and progressive commercial center.[2] The Mexican and U. S. Immigration and Customs are open 24 hours.

HOTELS: Most U.S. visitors stay in Calexico (across the frontier). There are several good establishments in Mexicali, among them: *Del Norte,* Av. Madero and Calle Melgar, new and has good coffee shop. *Palacios,* Av. Madero 366. *Rancho Motel,* at km. 11, road to San Luis. Rates average $60 MN to $100 MN, dble, EP. *Hotel Cucapah,* Av. Madero 222. New, a/c, 40 rooms, bar, dining. Rates: $60 MN, dble, EP.

RESTAURANTS: For Mexican food, *The Restaurant 19,* Av. Juárez 28.

DIRECTORY: *U. S. Consulate,* Edificio Banco de Comercio. *Banks* — Banco Nacional de México, corner, Altamirano and Lerdo; Banco de Mexicali, Calle Morelos and Av. Reforma. *Car Repairs* — Cia. Automotriz de Mexicali (Ford), Calle México 237. Motores de Mexicali (GM), Av. Juárez 158. *Airlines* — CMA, Calles México and Reforma.

San Felipe, B.C. Pop. 990. Alt. sea level. 125 m. S. of Mexicali, good paved road. A hot, sandy fishing village attracting more and more U.S. campers and fishermen. San Felipe is one of the few places in the world where the prized *totuava* can be caught (a fish about 5 feet long and having delicious meat). Accommodations are primitive except at Augie's Riviera, a modern hotel with bar and restaurant. (Closed June to October.)

Rental boats are available for local fishing. Larger boats may be chartered for trips to Bahía de Los Angeles.

Ensenada, B.C. Pop. 23,000. Alt. 10 ft. Baja California's most popular holiday resort town.

HOW TO GET THERE: *Via highway* — the Peninsular Highway, CN-1, from Tijuana to Ensenada, 67½ m., all paved and a delightful drive. *By bus* — Camionetas Amarillas, first class, from Tijuana. Also, Camionetas Verdes plying between Tijuana, Ensenada, and Santa Rosalia. *Via sea* — freighters with limited passenger space occasionally call at Ensenada. The *Spruce,* a Mexican Mail Line motor vessel makes one trip a month between Los Angeles and Mazatlán, calling at Ensenada and La Paz. Space for six cabin passengers. Agents in California are the Southern Terminals Company, Pier D, Berth 34, Long Beach,

---

[1] Only a small part of Baja California is spanned by railway lines. None are comfortable, nor are schedules predictable. Two short lines of the Southern Pacific system dip below the border (Tijuana to Tecate, and Mexicali to Algodones). A new railway, *Ferrocarril Sonora-Baja California* (completed in 1948), makes it possible to travel by land from Central Mexico to Baja California without having to cross into the U.S. The line runs from Mexicali to Algo-Colorado Delta, skirts the Gulf of California at Puerto Peñasco, Son., then traverses desert country to Benjamin Hill, Son., where it joins the main line of the Ferrocarril del Pacifico (Nogales to Guadalajara). Mexicans call the Mexicali-Benjamin Hill run the *antesala del Infierno* (the anteroom of Hell) because of the intense desert heat, badly aired cars, poor service. Although some of the coaches are of new German vintage, they are mixed with coaches that could date back to the days of the American Civil War. The lights, water, and air-conditioning are frequently inoperative.

[2] During the Prohibition years in the U.S. Mexicali was so "wide open" the local government licensed gambling, prostitution and opium refining in order to finance public works and the first automobile road across the mountains to Tijuana. Gambling is now outlawed, and prostitution and drug-peddling have been curtailed.

Calif. In Ensenada, Servicos Marítimos del Pacifico, Call 2a 363.

HOTELS: *(Note — the larger Ensenada hotels require two to three day cancellation notice for deposit refunds. No refunds are made on cancellation of holiday reservations.)* By far the most spacious, luxurious, and interesting hotel is the *Hotel Riviera del Pacífico* on the beach at the S edge of town. This rambling block-long colonial establishment occupies what was once Ensenada's lavish short-lived gambling casino. The building is jammed with colonial treasures — grills, old doors, woodwork, and tennis-court-size Oriental rugs robbed from Old Spain and Cuba. Hotel service is good, atmosphere friendly. Rates here and at the annex, *Hotel Playa Riviera:* EP $100 MN to $135 MN for dbles. and suites. AP $275 MN to $425 MN. Tel. 80. *Bahía Resort Hotel,* de luxe and modern, near 1st and Alvarado St. 73 rooms, pool, dining room, and bar. Nightly floor shows. Rates: EP $100 to $181.25 MN dble. Tel. 711. *Casita del Mar,* a tiny (6 room) very tidy and reasonable hotel, a favorite of California newspaper men and fishermen. Located near the breakwater. Excellent restaurant. Rates: EP $90 MN dble. *Villa Marina,* Calle 1 and Blancarte. Modern, de luxe. 90 rooms, dining room, bar, heated pool. Rates: EP $87 to $156.50 MN, dble. Tel. 167. *Cortéz Motel Apts.* A cheerful, attractively furnished motel, 26 rooms, 10 kitchenettes, coffee shop, pool, nice gardens. Rates: EP $100 MN. Tel. 765. *Hotel del Paseo,* downtown at 1st and Ruiz Streets. 30 rooms, incl. 4 kitchenettes, pool, cocktail lounge. ½ m. from beach. Rates: EP $87 MN to $125 MN dble. Tel. 625. *Quintas Papagayo,* 2 m. N of town on beach. A delightful cottage colony, overlooking the sea, secluded, beautifully landscaped grounds, pool, private beach. Kitchenettes. EP $150 MN dble. Tel. 1231. *Villa Carioca.* A very good 2-story motel, 2½ m. NE of town. Rates: EP $100 to $150 MN, dbles. and kitchenettes. Tel. 1230. *Estero Beach Resort,* 6 m. S on CN-1. 34 units and suites on the beach. De luxe accommodations, but made somewhat juke-boxish by the layout of the grounds and the trailer park impinging on the hotel. Rates: EP $125 MN to $162 MN, dble.

Other motel-hotels, comfortable, sometimes less well kept, and with rates ranging from $75 MN to $125 MN dble. *Hussong's El Morro,* N of town; *La Playita Cabins,* 3 mi. N of town; *Granada Cove Beach Resort,* 2½ m. N.

RESTAURANTS: *Enrique's Restaurant,* 2 m. N. and just SW of CN-1. Good seafood, Mexican regional dishes, and U.S. style steaks. Open 8 A.M. to midnight, except Tuesdays, *Carlos' Café,* on Beach Boulevard near Breakwater. Carlos is an exceptional cook and does wonders with seafood and steaks. *Restaurant Calmarisco,* on Calle 3, ½ block S of Calle Ruiz. A seafood house right in the center of town. Never closes. Inexpensive and no fancy frills. Seafood excellent, especially lobster and tacos made of breast of turtle. *El Rey Sol,* on Beach Boulevard, connected with Casa del Sol Motel. Good French cuisine and pastries. *Cafe Colonial,* 352 2nd Street. Good Mexican food.

DIRECTORY: *Bank* — Banco Nacional de México, Calle Ruiz 202. *Telegraph and Telephone,* Central office on Calle 5 between Av. Gastelum and Mirimar. Tel. 0-92. There are those Mexican rarities, public phone booths, at Av. Obregón and Calle 3a. *Red Cross* — First Street and Av. Azteca. Tel. 9-56. *Municipal Hospital* — Av. Ruiz and Calle 14. Is well staffed and equipped. Offers ambulance service to the U.S., except cases of infectuous diseases. *Airlines* — Trans-Mar de Cortés, Av. Ruiz and Calle Frente. Tel. 529. *Bus terminal* — Camionetas Amarillas, Av. Ruiz and First St. *Auto repairs* — Super Servicio Ensenada, Juárez and Placante; Automotriz Ezroj, Av. Ruiz 555 (Ford); Ensenada Motors, Av. Ruiz 7 Seventh St. (GM). *Post office* — Calle 5, between Gastelum and Mirimar. *Churches* — Catholic services on Sunday: La Purisima, Av. Obregón and Calle 3a, at 6, 8 and 11 A.M. and at 7 P.M. Our Lady of Guadalupe, Calle 6a and Av. Guadalupe, Mass at 7 A.M., noon, and 5 P.M. Protestant services: Church of the Nazarene, Av. Ruiz and Calle 11a, Sunday 10 to noon and 8 to 9:30 P.M. Baptist Church, Calle 6a and Av. Hidalgo. Sunday, 10 to noon, and 8:30 to 9:30 P.M.

THE CITY AND ENVIRONS: *Ensenada* (en-seh-NAH-dah), the third largest city in Lower California is a colorful Pacific port noted for its fine commercial and sport-fishing and its pleasant climate, especially from April through October. The winter months are apt to be raw. The town is located on the NE side of Todos Santos Bay protected by low barren hills, and the rugged Todos Santos Islands. To the S of the town there is a ten-mile-long, perfect half-moon beach of hard sand.

The bay was discovered by Rodríguez Cabrillo in 1542. There was an Indian settlement on the shore. During the colonial era the port was occasionally visited by whalers and traders, but the area remained undeveloped until 1804 when the surrounding country was given to José Manuel Ruiz, a seaman, who developed it into a prosperous cattle ranch. In 1852 when the peninsula was divided into two federal territories Ensenada became the northern capital. In the 1880s it became a boom town, and headquarters of an American (and later) an English land company which attempted to colonize the region. Some of the weathered, wooden Midwest-style buildings in the town date from this period. Following the Revolution of 1915 the land grants were canceled and the capital was moved to Mexicali, and Ensenada became a sleepy fishing port.

During the past decade the increased agriculture and commercial activity in Baja California, plus sizable influxes of vacationers from Southern California, has sharply awakened the town. It has become a popular resort area boasting of spanking new hotels and trim California-style residences. The principal street, Avenida Ruiz, is lined with glittering shops, numerous motels, a few night clubs and boat-and-tackle stands catering to sports fishermen.

THINGS TO DO: Ensenada and the area around have none of the charms, the picturesque architecture, folklore, nor interesting customs that are among Mexico's chief attractions. Scenically it is about as exciting as a blank picture postcard, and tourist-wise the town is just a rather high-class honky-tonk that manages to offer fair bathing, good hunting in the back country and excellent deep-sea fishing.

FISHING INFORMATION: Almost all the charter-boat offices and bait houses are on Calle 1a, S of Av. Ruiz. Tickets for fishing trips (a few hours or more) cost $6.50 per person. Children half price. Tourists need no license nor need pay a fishing tax. There are a dozen or so charter-boat operators running fully equipped launches (diesels, ship-to-shore radio, refrigerators, tackle). Rate for the larger launches run between $80 to $175 per day. The more important operators are: Santa Monica Boat House and Caribe Sports; Thomas Moreno (Aztec Boat House), Tel. 560 and 967.

Ensenada is known as "the yellow tail capital of the world," and this seems not to be an understatement for those who have fished the local waters. Tuna, mackerel, bonito, and sailfish are also in plentiful supply during certain seasons. For up-to-date information regarding best seasons and areas, the airline Trans-Mar del Cortés issues weekly fishing reports which they'll send to you free. The Automobile Club of Southern California has also published an excellent detailed sportsman's map of the peninsula and the shoreline areas of the NW region of Mexico indicating the best fishing and hunting areas. Address inquiries to 2601 S. Figueroa, Los Angeles, Calif.

Some of the best fishing waters around Ensenada are: the San Isidro waters south of the town, El Farito, the bay itself and the waters around Todos Santos islands.

VISITS TO THE PIERS: Tourists may visit the fishermen's pier and docks at any time. To visit the government docks special permission is required. Apply at the office of the Captain of the Port.

PORT FACILITIES: The port is in the process of being enlarged so as to provide all the necessary facilities for visiting yachtsmen, including a new floating pier. Port procedure for yachts can be procured from the Captain of the Port, corner of Av. Gastelum and Av. Frente. Incoming yachts may receive visits from officers representing the Port Health Inspector, Port Captain, and Customs. Proper documentation to visit other Mexican ports can be procured from the Port Captain.

EXCURSIONS FROM ENSENADA: Trips east and south of the resort are strictly for the sportsman and off-trail traveler equipped with a rugged vehicle or boat, and possessing a gift for roughing it. A few off-trail highlights are:

Real del Castillo, B.C. 26 m. E of Ensenada via dirt road. Alt. 2000. An interested, semi-deserted ghost town in a valley hemmed in by barren, lunarlike mountains. The town was once a thriving settlement as the result of a gold strike in 1870, and was for some eleven years the seat of government of the frontier area.

Hamilton Ranch. About 106 miles from Ensenada on the Trans-Peninsular Road. A popular guest ranch patronized by American sportsmen. 17 m. farther S is *San Quintín,* an interesting ghost town on the edge of a large shallow bay. Small landing strip nearby. In the 1800s the port was often visited by American ships involved in contraband trade. About 1885 an American colonization project was started here. The forlorn cemetery with graves of American and English colonists is all that remains of the project. Good fishing here. Accommodations in a badly rundown motel.

Bahía de Los Angeles, B.C. Pop. 60. On the Gulf of California side of the peninsula. 302 m. from Ensenada a branch road leaves the Peninsular route, going SE 46 m. to Los Angeles Bay. A beautiful harbor, swimming and fishing spot. Excellent for oysters, crabs, lobsters, turtle. For rough cabins, see Sr. Antero Díaz. Sr. Díaz also serves good meals and rents boats. Best season: winter and spring.

The Lost Mission. An intriguing passion pursued by many Baja California visitors is to hunt for the so-called "lost mission of Santa Isabel," believed to be in the barren hills north of Bahía de Los Angeles and east of Laguna Chapala. According to legend, the Jesuits who worked in and ruled the peninsula (1697–1767) almost as a closed corporation, accumulated vast stores of gold and pearls. Yarn-spinners tell the story that shortly before their expulsion from Mexico the priests received advance word of the king's order. The order came from Rome that they should submit, but at the same time, not give up their reputed treasure. Accordingly, the wealth from the various missions was collected and transported to a secret mission called Santa Isabel, located in an almost inaccessible gorge. Just before their expulsion they sealed off the valley by means of a landslide and gracefully submitted to exile in Europe. As yet no one had found the "lost mission headquarters," and it is most likely that no one will. According to carefully documented investigations the Jesuits had little chance to accumulate wealth during their stay in Baja California. Their missions were always on the verge of economic collapse and they had to rely on alms to keep them going. However, the quest still continues.

San Ignacio, B.C. Pop. 950. Alt. 500 ft. About midway between Ensenada and La Paz, on the Trans-Peninsular Road. A happy oasis town set in bleak country. The village, clusters of thatch-roof adobe houses around a central plaza dominated by a massive stone Dominican church-mission, is shaded by huge groves of date palms and other fruit trees. Overnight accommodations available at the house of Señora Leree, and at other private homes.

San Ignacio is the favored base for trips to Turtle Cove (Bahía Tortugas), about 45 m. W. Pacific Coast. There is a good harbor, a small fishing village, an abalone cannery, and an air strip. The great sea turtles for which the area was famous are no longer in large supply. Fishing and hunting excellent.

Santa Rosalia, B.C. Pop. 6000. Alt. sea level. On Trans-Peninsular route, 540 m. from Ensenada. Located on Gulf of California, the town is the most important commercial center between Ensenada and La Paz. Climate is pleasant in winter, and like the anteroom of Hades in summer. Sports fishing excellent in the gulf waters. *Hotels:* Hotel Francés, small, with fair restaurant. Hotel Central, across from the church. Neither are attractive. *Air transportation:* Trans-Mar de Cortés makes regular scheduled stops here.

THE SOUTHERN BAJA CALIFORNIA AREA

The southern half of the peninsula, from the 28th Parallel down, politically designated as a federal territory, is more closely related to and influenced by the Mexican mainland than it is by the U.S. Of all of the peninsula, it reflects the customs and mores of the republic more exactly than the northern area. Its climate differs from the north in that its summers are hot and more humid, its winters delightfully tepid.

La Paz, B.C. Pop. 30,000. Alt. sea level. Capital of the Territory of Baja California. It is by far the most attractive seaport and resort on the entire Baja California Peninsula.

HOW TO GET THERE: Via road — CN-1, the Trans-Peninsular Road from Ensenada. Recommended only for the well-equipped adventurer. See Index: Highway Routes. Aeronaves de Mexico, S.A., offers daily service between Mexico City, Acapulco, and La Paz, and Mexico City, Guadalajara, and La Paz. The line does not accept local passengers between La Paz and Tijuana or viceversa. *Via*

Sea — see Index for Mexican Mail Line information, trips between Ensenada and La Paz. There are local motor vessels carrying passengers and ferrying cars between La Paz and the eastern shore of the Gulf of California, Guaymas, and Mazatlán. The two largest are owned by the Ruffo Brothers *(Perla de La Paz)* and run weekly schedules. Passenger fare (cabin) about $75 MN; cars $350 MN and up. The independent *Estrella Costera* makes two to three round trips to Mazatlán a month. Rates: $125 MN and up, cabin, or $50 MN, deck passage. The trip takes 30 to 35 hours.

HOTELS: With the exception of the Hotel Guayacura, all the principal hotels in La Paz face on the Bay of La Paz. Most have some air-conditioned rooms. Hotels operate on either European or American plan. *Hotel Los Cocos,* 2 m. S at Playa Sur. First-class modern accommodations, 18 rooms, good dining room, beach, bar. Rates AP $310 MN, dble. *Hotel Los Arcos,* on Av. Alvaro Obregón. 32 attractive rooms and cottages. Dining room, bar. Rates: AP $125 MN to $200 MN. *Hotel Misión de la Paz,* Alvaro Obregón 220. 10 rooms, a pleasant colonial style inn. Dining room, bar. EP $60 to $85 MN dble. Air-conditioned rooms $25 MN extra. *Motel Guaycura,* N edge of town on main highway. 10 units, dining room, pool. Rates: AP $100 to $175 MN dble. (Closed from July 1 to September 15.) *Hotel Perla,* Av. Obregón 150. A *viajero-type* hotel, 85 rooms, some comfortably modern, others old. AP $200 to $225 MN dble.

Other hotels, less expensive and with uncertain service but often comfortable during the cool seasons — *Viosca,* on waterfront. Rates: EP from $50 MN. Also, *La Yéneka* and *La Central.*

RESTAURANTS: The best food (and stick to seafood) is served in the hotels. Other fair restaurants are the *Aero-Cafe* at the airport; and *El Flo,* in town. *Restaurante El Bucanero,* at Palmar de Abaro, a palm grove along the bay just south of town, serves seafood, mariachi music, offers dancing.

TAXIS: Taxi fares in the city are reasonable — $3 to $5 MN; to Coromuel Beach about $10 MN round trip. For longer trips, around $250 to $275 MN per day. Bargain and agree on price beforehand.

DIRECTORY: *Banks* — Banco Nacional de México, Calles Puerto and Ezquerro. La Perla de La Paz (Ruffo Brothers store — a bank, garage, general store, etc., operated by the principal merchants in town). *Auto repairs* — Baja California Motors (Ford), Av. Obregón and Calle Bravo. *Airlines*—Aeronaves de México, Belisario Dominguez. Tel. 8. *Doctors* — Hospital Salvatierra, the municipal hospital, is well equipped and has good doctors on duty.

LA PAZ AND ENVIRONS: The largest town in Baja California Sur, La Paz is attractively situated on a series of low bluffs facing the shallow Ensenada de los Aripes (a kind of appendix to the Bay of La Paz). A low sandspit protects the Ensenada from the open gulf and bay. The town is more charmingly Mexican than any other in Lower California; the older section along Av. 16 de Septiembre is a maze of twisting tree-shaded lanes, while the *malecón,* the coconut-palm-lined walk along the waterfront makes a pleasant promenade.

Although the bay was visited by the Spanish as early as 1533, and Cortés camped on the shore in 1535, and for a period of years the Jesuit mission, Nuestra Señora del Pilar de la Paz, existed here, it was not until 1800 that permanent inhabitants began to settle in. In 1830 the territorial government was moved from Loreto to La Paz. The town, always small, was deemed important enough to be occupied by American troops during the war of 1847–48. Five years later the notorious adventurer William Walker and his followers again seized the port town.

The principal attractions of La Paz, in addition to its tropical charm and weather, are water sports and deep-sea fishing. The best beach for swimming is Coromuel Beach, 2 m. N of town.[3] Fishermen in the know consider the waters around La Paz and the Gulf of California the most exciting big-game fishing grounds along the Mexican west coast. Numerous world's record catches have been landed here. Marlins crowd the waters between mid-March and November; sailfish from May through November.

BOAT RATES: Rental rates for motor skiffs and charter launches are set by the Port Captaincy. At present the prices are: $2.50 per hour for 16-foot outboard skiffs which accommodate two persons and the skipper. Large deep-sea cruisers charter for $50 and up, per day, and take four passengers. Tackle and bait are provided.

Skin-diving is especially good due to the warmth of the waters and absence of seaweed and kelp. Diving equipment can be rented; there is a compressed air service, and instructors are available. One of the favorite diving pastimes is pearling.[4]

EXCURSIONS OUT OF LA PAZ: A worthwhile auto trip is the "four-day loop" south of La Paz, that goes down the Gulf side of the peninsula to Cabo San Lucas (the southern tip of Lower California), and returns on the Pacific side by way of Todos Santos. The route crosses through mountainous mining country and lush tropics. Among its most interesting points and stop overs:

El Triunfo and *San Antonio,* almost deserted, picturesque mining towns which were once thriving silver centers. El Triunfo once had over 10,000 population, and now has about 500 inhabitants. The towns are at a cool 18 and 13 hundred foot elevation. *Buenavista,* a fishing resort with good beaches and hotel accommodations. Rates at *Hotel Buena Vista,* AP $150 MN single. Nearby is *Hotel Bahía de Palmas,* rates somewhat lower, has launches and tackle for rent. *San José del Cabo, B.C.* Pop. 1900. Alt. 70 ft. Almost at the tip of the peninsula and one of the loveliest towns in Lower California. Excellent sport fishing, fair accommodations. *Hotels:* in town, Guest House of Señora de Fisher. Rates $60 MN, single, AP. 6 m. W on Palmilla Bay, *Hotel Las Cruces Palmilla,* a good fishing resort with air strip and deep-sea cruisers. Rates: AP $225 MN and up, per single.

North of La Paz the country is rugged and there are few towns of interest. Travelers on the Trans-Peninsular trail will delight in the oasislike *Mulegé, B.C.* Pop. 1000.

---

[3] The word *coromuel* is also used by local citizens to refer to an almost clocklike evening breeze that springs up during the hot months. Heavier winds, the tropical hurricanes, are called *cordonazos.* These usually occur in September.

[4] *Pearls:* La Paz was until the turn of the century noted for its fabulous pearl fisheries. Some of the world's most valued translucent-gray (black) pearls were brought up here. Since the 1914 Revolution commerical pearling has died out, but individual divers still bring up valuable pearls. Tourists should be cautioned regarding the purchase of La Paz pearls, however. A story is told in La Paz about an American who forked out lavishly for a handsome "black pearl" only to discover he had bought a ball bearing.

Alt. 25 ft. The village is 2 m. from the Gulf. It is a charming garden spot resembling some South Sea paradise. There is a tranquil plaza, a nearby lake, a mission and even a federal prison. The prisoners can work for wages anywhere in town. They seem so captivated by Mulegé that none ever want to escape. *Hotel* — Club Mulegé, 1 m. E on Gulf. A nice sportsmen haven. Write for rates.

Loreto, B.C. Pop. 1500. Alt. sea level. About 130 air miles north of La Paz, and on the gulf. An attractive settlement now becoming popular with American fishermen and hunters. Loreto was the first permanent Spanish settlement in Lower California and was established by Jesuit Father Juan María Salvatierra in 1697. For 132 years it was the capital of California.

HOTELS: Guest House of Doña Blanca de Garayzar, across from the church. Modest and clean. Rates: AP $30 MN and up, per single. *Flying Sportsman Lodge,* 1 m. S of town. An American-style resort having private baths, pool, bar, an airstrip, and charter boats. Rates: from $175 MN per single, AP.

THE SONORA COUNTRY

This section of Mexico's northwest region, the State of Sonora, covers an area of 71,310 sq. miles and has a population well over 783,387 inhabitants. It is bounded on the north by the U.S. frontier (Arizona), on the east by the Mexican State of Chihuahua, to the west by Baja California del Norte and the Gulf of California, and to the south by the west coast State of Sinaloa.

Once noted primarily for its mineral wealth and important gold, silver, and copper mines, and its deserts, it has — since the opening of the Nogales-Guadalajara Highway and the building of the Obiachi and Abelardo Rodríguez dams — developed rapidly as one of Mexico's most important wheat, cotton, rice, and corn-producing areas.

The area is served by networks of new roads and by the West Coast Highway, CN-15, which enters the State at Nogales (frontier) and touches most of the important towns and places of tourist interest. The Ferrocarril del Pacifico (connecting with the Southern Pacific Railway at Nogales) more or less parallels the highway. Several airlines connect Guaymas, Hermosillo, Cd. Obregón with Mexico City, Tijuana, and El Paso, Texas.

VACATION HIGHLIGHTS: The Sonora country offers little to the tourist in the way of cultural or scenic attractions (at least in areas the tourist can reach). Its beach and fishing resorts along the Gulf littoral are, on the other hand, incomparable. For the traveler making a brief sortie below the border, or traveling on south, Sonora's two most interesting points are: the Guaymas resort and surrounding district, and the picturesque mountain village of Alamos, one of Mexico's most fascinating colonial mementos.

The most suitable base for an extended stay in Sonora is the port of Guaymas.

Guaymas, Son. Pop. 19,000. Alt. 10 ft. Most important seaport and resort on the Sonora Coast.

HOW TO GET THERE: *Via highway* — From the U.S. (Nogales), the West Coast Highway, CN-15 (258 m. from Nogales). *Via air* — de México offers daily flights from Mexico City and Tijuana. *Railway* — Ferrocarril del Pacifico line between Nogales and Guadalajara runs daily trains which leave Nogales at 5:30 P.M., arriving at Empalme at 1:55 A.M. From Empalme it is a short taxi drive to Guaymas. *Via bus* — Transportes Norte de Sonora operates first-class service between Nogales, Guaymas, and Guadalajara. Autotransportes Tres Estrellas de Oro runs first-class buses between Tijuana, Nogales, Guaymas, and Guadalajara.

HOTELS: Guaymas is really two communities — the town with its port and commercial facilities, and divided from it by a hilly peninsula, the resort area on Bocochibampo Bay. The better hotels are situated around the shore of the bay, with a few good motels on the highway before the resort area turn-off.

Hotel Playa de Cortés, on Bocochibampo Bay 2 m. W off of CN-15. Although old, founded by the Southern Pacific Railway in 1936, the hotel is by far the most pleasing and comfortable in Guaymas. It remains one of the finest establishments in the country. Colonial in style, with a lavish use of colorful tiles, antiques, lovely gardens, its 64 rooms (6 cottages) are homey and well kept. Some rooms air conditioned. The hotel has its own docks, swimming pool, air-conditioned cocktail lounge, travel service, shops, lawn games. The dining room serves excellent meals. Rates: AP $248 MN to $403 MN, dble. Reservations advised for December-April season. Tel. 121.

Posada San Carlos, a few miles N of Guaymas, on beach, pleasant accommodations, reasonable.

Guaymas Inn, on highway 3 m. N of town. A new, de luxe motel without ocean view or facilities. Swimming pool, good dining room, cocktail lounge, air conditioned. Friendly atmosphere. 24 units. Rates: EP $75 MN dble. *Motel Marlin,* on highway. 24 units, air conditioning, dining room, pool. Newly opened. No information on rates or service. *Motel Flamingos,* on highway. New 40-unit motel, some kitchenettes. Very glossy. Some rooms air conditioned. Rates: EP, from $60 MN dble. Tel. 6-26. Less expensive but quite comfortable and clean is *Motel Armida,* on highway, 25 units, pool, and good restaurant. Rates: EP $65 MN and up, dble. *Hotel Mirimar Beach,* 100 rooms, some old and badly rundown. Though nicely situated on the beach the hotel is poorly managed and badly maintained and is mentioned only as a last resort. Expensive for what you get. *Escalante Trailer Park,* on the bay. Trailer connections, showers, etc. Rate: $15.50 per day, $108 MN per month.

RESTAURANTS: The best food is served at the hotels, particularly *Hotel Playa de Cortés, Guaymas Inn,* and *Motel Armida.* Seafood and snacks are also served at a pavilion at the N end of the bay, across from Hank's Boat Stand.

DIRECTORY: *Banks* — Banco Nacional de México, Av. Serdán and Calle 46. *Auto repairs* — Guaymas Automotriz (Ford), Av. Serdán 452; Guaymas Motor (GM), on highway at entrance of town. *Airlines* — Trans-Mar de Cortés, Av. Serdán and Calle 24. Tel. 348. Aeronaves de México, Av. Serdán 52. Tel. 1-23.

GUAYMAS AND ENVIRONS: Though visited by Spanish explorers as early as 1535, and although it became a mission base under the direction of Fathers Salvatierra and Kino, the present town site of Guaymas de Zaragoza was not settled until 1769. As a Spanish-Mexican free port and outlet for the mineral riches of Sonora, the town prospered and was prized by various governments and adventurers. The most dramatic of such events involved a French freebooter, Count Gaston Raousset de

Boulbon,[5] with a force of some 400 adventurers made two expeditions in order to seize Guaymas and Sonora. During the second siege of Guaymas, and in the grim house-to-house battle that ensued, Boulbon was captured. The local defender of the port, General Yañez, ordered the adventurer to be executed. Eleven years later the French, under Maximilian, again occupied the port for a year. During the American Civil War supplies for troops fighting in Arizona were brought down from San Francisco and shipped up through Guaymas. Following the 1914 Revolution the town seemed overcome by lethargy, and it was not until the opening of new roads in the past few decades that it has come to life as the center of a productive agricultural region, a fishing port and resort.

Situated on two bays — *Bahía de Guaymas* and *Bahía Bocochibampo* (Serpent Bay) — with a low peninsula dividing the commercial and recreational halves of the community, Guaymas is a handsome place. The view from the terrace of the Hotel Playa de Cortés is one of the loveliest along the coast. Although the town itself is dusty and nondescript, the shrimp docks are of interest, as well as the eighteenth-century Church of San Fernando and the Municipal Palace.

About 3 m. NE of the airport is *Aranjuez,* a fascinating pre-revolution hacienda. Some nine miles beyond is *San José de Guaymas,* the original mission settlement. Nearby is the great *Saguaro Forest,* a unique, brooding forest of cacti which is the favorite breeding place of colorful parakeets.

RECREATIONS: Guaymas' chief attraction is sport fishing. As at La Paz, across the Gulf, the waters team with a bewildering variety of fish — marlin, sailfish, totuava, mackerel, etc. Between April 15 and May the marlin run and a colorful Fiesta de la Pesca (fishing festival) is held in May. During September there is an international fishing tournament.

Charter boats range in price from $50 to $90 per day. There are several fleets. The largest and most efficient is Tom Jamison's Cia. de Botes de Pesca Deportiva "San Pedro Nolasco." Offices in the Hotel Playa de Cortés and Hotel Miramar. Tel. 121 and 684. Jamison's charter rates are from $6.50 to $7.50 per hour, (minimum 6 to 8 hours). Capacity, 6 persons. The charter boats are equipped with ship-to-shore radio, refrigerators, galley, experienced English-speaking crews. Tackle and bait furnished. The fleet also operates two party boats which go out on six-hour fishing cruises (twice a day). Rate: $6.50 per person for the trip.

A glass-bottom boat makes a trip around the bay each morning. Rate: $12.50 MN (one dollar). Speedboats for water-skiing, and skin-diving equipment also available.

During the height of the fishing season a $20 per boat deposit is required to hold reservations. If you send in reservations personally, deduct 10 per cent agent's commission.

SHELL COLLECTING: Guaymas is noted the world over for its abundance and variety of shellfish. Each year numerous conchologists visit the area during the low tide period, November to March. Another favorite recreation is clamming. The best clam areas are the lagoons of *Puerto San Carlos* and the *Estero del Soldado,* both west and north of Bocochibampo Bay. Both can be reached by boat in an hour, or via fair road, in 20 minutes. To get there take the highway toward Hermosillo, 6 m., then turn left. On the way you pass *San Francisco Beach,* a fine, camping, picnicking and surf-fishing beach. For the famed Guaymas oysters (in season) you must go to the lagoons south of *Empalme*. Drive past *Cruz de Piedra,* and just before *Peon,* turn right to *Las Guasimas*. At low tide the oyster pickings are fabulous.

[5] Some chroniclers refer to the Count as Count Rascourt de Bourbon.

AREAS NORTH OF GUAYMAS: The vast sun-baked areas extending north of Guaymas to the U.S. border contain very little of important tourist interest, except possibly Hermosillo, the state capital, and Nogales, the U.S.-Mexico port of entry. There are also some fishing villages and spots for motor adventurers, indicated below.

Nogales and Hermosillo as well as other towns of secondary interest can be visited by motorists and bus travelers on their way to Guaymas. Somewhat apart is *Puerto Peñasco, Son.,* a somewhat bleak fishing resort at the head of the Gulf. It is most easily reached via paved highway from the Arizona border. (U.S. 80, through Gila Bend, Ajo, and Organ Pipe Cactus National Monument, connects with the Puerto Peñasco road.) There are several motels, a good beach, and camping areas 6 m. N at *Cholla Bay*. Hotel Playa Hermosa. Attractive, 34 rooms, bar, good restaurant, a/c. Rates: AP $70 MN, up, dble.

Nogales, Son. Pop. 25,000. Alt. 3870 ft. Typical Mexican border town, across from Nogales, Arizona. The Mexican customs offices open from 8 A.M. to midnight. U. S. Customs open 24 hours daily. Though tourist and car import permits are issued at the border office, the Mexican customs inspection occurs at the first checkpoint several miles after leaving the city for Hermosillo.

HOTELS AND RESTAURANTS: There are motels on the American side of the International Boundary. The Mexican side hotels are: *Hotel Fray Marcos de Niza,* Campillo 34. Tel. 651. 100 rooms, some air conditioned, 2 dining rooms, bar, parking. Rates: from $55 MN up, EP. *Hotel Olivia,* Obregón 81. Rates, EP, $50 MN dble.

Restaurante La Caverna, at Calle Elías 43, in the underground cellars of a former prison. Specialty: wild duck, quail, and turtle soup.

DIRECTORY: *U. S. Consulate,* Calle Obregón 31, altos. Tel. 305. *Bank* — Banco Nacional de México, Calles Internacional and Plaza. *Auto repairs* — Distribuidora Automotriz de Nogales (Dodge), Obregón 381; Nogales Automotriz (Ford), Obregón 344. *Airline* — Aeronaves de México, Edificio Josefina. Tel. 2-55. *Bus lines* — Transportes Norte de Sonora (to Guaymas, Mazatlán, and Guadalajara), Calle Pesqueria 6. *Railway* — tickets at the depot, Ferrocarril del Pacifico.

THE CITY: Nogales (No-GAH-lehs), meaning walnut trees in Spanish, is the northern trading center for the State of Sonora, the terminal of the West Coast Highway and of the Pacific Railway of Mexico (formerly the Southern Pacific, or more popularly called "Southern Patience" due to its snail-like pace). Points of interest in the town are its market, the shops, the La Caverna restaurant where (when it was a jail) Geronimo was held, the Old Custom's House and the Sacred Heart Church. Most of the shops are on Av. Alvaro Obregón.

Between May 3 and 5, both the U.S. and the Mexican Nogales have an annual flower fiesta featuring floats, flower battles, parade, bullfights.

Magdalena, Son. Pop. 7000. Alt. 2460 ft. On CN-15, 58 m. from Nogales. A pleasant, semi-colonial town, noted for its fine mission building, the Church of San Francisco Xavier. An important fiesta is held here early each October. *Restaurant:* Los Tres Tambores has fair food.

A fair road leads from here to *San Ignacio de Caborca,* another Kino mission town.[6]

Hermosillo, Son. Pop. 55,000. Alt. 780 ft. Capital of the State of Sonora. On CN-15, about 180 m. from Nogales, 78 m. from Guaymas.

Hermosillo (air-mo-SEE-yo), named after José María Gonzales Hermosillo, a patriot in the War of Independence. The colonial aspects of the city have almost vanished as a result of a recent building boom. Save for its semitropical weather (best in winter) the city has few attractions. Somewhat interesting is the Plaza Principal with its old-fashioned bandstand, its worse than mediocre cathedral and the quaint Palacio del Gobierno with its two-story Moorish-arched, tree-filled patio. A pleasant promenade is along the Boulevard Centenario which passes the plaza.

Though there are parking meters on the streets in the center of town, tourists are excepted from putting in coins. The principal shopping district is along Calle Serdán. The Market is at Calle Vildosola and Matamoros. The University of Sonora is in the northwest section of the city. The State Museum (part of the university) is housed in a modern building of unusual proportions and decorated with a lacelike concrete screening.

The most important exhibit in the Museum is El Hombre de Yécora (Man of Yécora), a prehistoric, petrified mummy roughly estimated to be 10 to 12 thousand years old. A group of such figures, remarkably well preserved and lifelike, were found in a decorated cave near Yécora (SE Sonora), early in 1959. The figures of these primitive men, surrounded by cave paintings and tools or weapons, have aroused intense interest among anthropologists for the Yécora men long antedate the Seri, Pima, and Opata cultures of the northwest region.

Across the street from the museum in a pleasant park there is a statue (bronze) entitled "La Madre," done by Ignacio Asunsola, one of Mexico's leading contemporary artists.

HOTELS: *Motel el Encanto,* on CN-15 NE edge of town. An excellent, attractively furnished, colonial style establishment with 25 air-conditioned units, pool, and good dining room. Rates: EP $72.50 MN dble. Tel. 3-6535. *Motel Bugambilia,* in the same area, 30 units, air-conditioned, nice gardens, pool, fair restaurant. Rates: EP $55 MN to $75 MN, dble. *Porter's La Siesta Motel,* same area, well-operated motel with 21 air-conditioned units, restaurant, some kitchenettes, pool. Rates: EP $60 MN to $72.50 MN, dble. *Hotel San Alberto,* center of town. 135 rooms, some air conditioned, dining room, pool. The hotel is old and not too well-kept. The outdoor terrace, shaded by old trees, is a pleasant place to take refreshments. Rates: EP $60 MN and up, dble.

Other hotels: *Hotel Motel Gandara,* on highway NE of town. 60 rooms, air conditioned (not always working), dining room, bar, pool, night club. New chrome-plated style, but the service and atmosphere does not recommend it except as a last resort. *Hotel de Anza,* in town, 60 rooms, fair dining room. *Viajero* style. In the lower brackets: *Hotels Moderno, Kino,* and *Posada México.*

DIRECTORY: *Banks* — Banco Nacional de México, Serdán 39 (across from Hotel San Alberto). Banco de Comercio de Sonora. Serdán and Yañez. *Airlines* — CMA, Av. Serdán 171 Pte; Aeronaves de México, Juárez y Monterrey. *Bus lines* — Transportes del Norte de Sonora. Tel. 7-48. *Auto repairs* — Sonora Motors, Juárez and Yucatán; Super Autos, Blvd. Rodríguez and Av. Constitución. *Church services*—the Cathedral (Catholic).

EXCURSIONS FROM HERMOSILLO: A few miles from the capital, the well-stocked *Rodríguez Lake* (artificial) has become a favorite bass fishing area.

Kino Bay, 61 m. W of Hermosillo via a good all-weather road. This lovely bay and primitive little fishing village, *Puerto Kino* will someday be one of the coming resorts along the gulf coast line north of Guaymas. There are rough accommodations, skiffs to rent. 6 m. to N at *Cerro Prieto* there is another fine beach and a cantina where boats can be rented. Across a narrow channel lies *Isla Tiburón,* (Shark Island) inhabited by the dwindling Seri Indian tribe.

EAST OF HERMOSILLO: An extensive area east of the Nogales-Hermosillo highway has been opened during the last few years by a network of unpaved roads. The region is inviting to motor-explorers, but requires cars with good road clearance. Fair roads link the highway via *La Cananea, Son.* to Douglas, Arizona. La Cananea is a busy mining town dominating what has been called the largest contact-copper deposits ever discovered. The road from Cananea runs 40 m. N to the U.S. border, crossing through Naco, Arizona. A fair hotel in La Cananea is the New Hotel Alameda, 35 rooms, good dining room. Rates: from $35 MN, dble, EP.

Just E of Hermosillo reasonably fair roads reach into the interior, opening desert-foothill country similar to the Tucson area. About 10 m. N of the capital on CN-10 there is a turn-off, E to *Ures.* Two miles beyond there are three unmarked roads. The one to the right goes to Ures and Moctezuma. *Moctezuma, Son.,* once an important city, is now a somnolent agricultural center. It has a lovely plaza, a cathedral-like old church, and is noted for its leather industry, especially the tooling of saddles.

North of Moctezuma a road continues up through *Nacozari, Son.,* once a booming copper center, and on toward Douglas, Arizona. Instead of turning N toward Douglas, after leaving Moctezuma the off-trail traveler can continue E over regularly traveled jeep roads to Gallego, Chih., on the Central Highway.

AREAS SOUTH OF GUAYMAS: This area — a flat alluvial plain along the coast and rugged mineral-rich mountains to the E — is made prosperous by the Yaqui and Mayo Rivers and the new irrigation and hydroelectric works established here by the federal government.

Ciudad Obregón, Son. Pop. 31,000. Alt. 230 ft. A dusty boom town on CN-15, about 80 m. S of Guaymas. The town is a base for hunters seeking deer, wild turkey, and bear in the foothills 50 m. E of the city. Between October and February ducks swarm in the rice fields near the town making it one of the best duck-hunting areas in Mexico.

HOTELS AND RESTAURANTS: *Motel Costa de Oro,* N edge of town, on highway. 36 units, completely new and just opened. Dining room and cocktail lounge. Rates:

[6] *The Kino missions:* The remains and reconstructions of early missions founded by Jesuit Father Eusebio Kino are scattered across the Altar Valley and Magdalena River Valley. Kino, a remarkable explorer, horseman, builder, and successful rancher, in addition to being a priest, has left an indelible 250-year-old mark on Sonora where before his death (1711) he founded 25 missions.

Many of the missions fell into ruin and were later reconstructed by Padre Francisco Garces, a Franciscan priest who worked in the region during the latter half of the eighteenth century. The principal missions, most of them off the highway, are: Misión San Ignacio de Caborca, Misión San Diego del Pitiquito, Misión La Concepcion de Nuestra Señora de Caborca, Misión San Antonio de Oquitoa, and Misión San Pedro y San Pablo Tubutama.

EP $75 MN dble. *Hotel San Jorge,* N edge of town, highway. Fair motel-hotel, 60 rooms, some air conditioned, pool, cocktail lounge. Rates: EP from $75 MN dble. *Hotel Colonial,* Guerrero 102 (center of town). Older hotel, 100 rooms, *viajero* atmosphere and reasonable prices.

Navojoa, Son. Pop. 17,350. Alt. 118 ft. An old Mayo Indian center and new agricultural focal point. The *Nacozari Dam,* nearby, is part of a tri-river federal irrigation project (Yaqui, Mayo, and El Fuerte Rivers) that will eventually entice an estimated two million population to the area.

HOTELS AND RESTAURANTS: *Motel del Rio,* 1 m. N on CN-15. A nice 35-room motel in pretty gardens. Pool, dining room. Rates: EP $80 MN dble. *Motel El Mayo.* 40 rooms. Fair. *Hotel Aguilera,* 36 rooms, some air conditioned. *Viajero-type.* Reasonable rates.

FIESTAS: About June 24 each year, the Mayo Indians (related to the Yaquis) celebrate Saint John's Day with a lively fiesta, displays of their basketry and serape weaving and the famed Deer Dance.

Alamos, Son. Pop. 2872. Alt. 1276 ft. One of Mexico's most charming colonial towns. 34 m. E of Navojoa. Turn-off in Navojoa. Road is paved. One of Sonora's two most important attractions.

HOTELS: *Casa de los Tesoros,* Av. Obregón 10. (P. O. Box 12.) An unusually delightful and well-run colonial inn; restful, friendly atmosphere. 18 rooms, small pool, excellent dining room. Rates: AP $250 MN dble. (Closed May 1 to October 1.) *Motel Alamos,* N edge of town. Dining room, cocktail lounge, pool. A typical, somewhat chrome-style motel, rather out of place in Alamos. No report on services. Rates: moderately high. *Hotel Los Portales,* on main plaza. 14 rooms in a famous old colonial mansion. Bar, fair food, furnishing not in especially good taste. Rates: AP from $150 MN dble.

THE TOWN AND ENVIRONS: Declared a national colonial monument, Alamos (AH-la-mos) retains the patina of past grandeur. Of all the colonial cities along the west coast it is almost the only one to have escaped modernization over the centuries. Though there is electricity, a few telephones, good hotels, and an airstrip outside of town, the fact remains its newest building is over one hundred years old.

Alamos (meaning, cottonwood trees) is one of the oldest white settlements in the New World. It served as a campsite for Coronado's explorers in 1531; later was settled by miners. The development of the rich gold and silver deposits in the area brought wealth and fame to the town. By 1791 it was one of the "silver capitals" of the world with a population of some 30,000. Embellished by men of wealth and lavish tastes, it became one of Mexico's colonial jewels, replete with fabulous mansions, fine churches, parks, and plazas.[7] However, following floods, Indian raids, civil war, and the decline in silver prices Alamos became almost a ghost city. Ruins of magnificent old buildings line the deserted streets. The town's present occupants are so thinly scattered one is hardly aware of their existence. During the past few years the vivid sunshine and graceful old houses have caught the eyes of American visitors. More and more people from the north are settling in Alamos, restoring its old buildings and enjoying the unpretentious and unsophisticated life in a colonial monument.

THINGS TO DO AND SEE: The most intriguing sight in Alamos is its charming Plaza de Armas, surrounded on three sides by arched *portales* and fine buildings, and at one end by the "Cathedral," the Church of La Señora de la Concepción. The imposing church with its lovely simple façade and bell tower dates back to 1784. It was constructed on the site of the original mission burned by Indians.

An interesting visit is to the colonial cemetery with its quaint above-ground vaults and beautiful wrought iron crosses.

Other nearby favored spots are: *La Uvulama,* a cluster of thatch huts called the "pottery village." Clay bowls are made here by women potters. *La Aduana,* a ghost town around the great smelter works where Alamos silver was cast into ingots. Note the large cactus growing out of the wall of the church here. According to legend, the cactus was on the site before the church was built, and at one time an apparition of the Virgin appeared on it to point out a rich silver lode. Each November 20 an important Mayo Indian festival takes place at Aduana. *Río Cuchujaqui* (7½ m. via rough but passable road from Alamos). A favorite bathing spot. This woodland paradise is surrounded by great sabino trees.

The hills around Alamos are a hunter's paradise, and also a rockhound's heaven. Information regarding local gem stones and rock specimens can be gotten from Albert Maas, a resident in the town. Fanciers of Mexican jumping beans will also find their prey here. Alamos is the jumping-bean center of the world, the curious worm-filled bean being a local product.

On the Navojoa-Alamos road, 18 m. E of Navojoa, is a dirt road turn-off to nearby *Mocuzari* and the Río Mayo dam and lake which offers good fishing.

To the west of the West Coast Highway, a branch road goes from Navojoa, across flat farm country to an undeveloped but interesting little fishing port, *Huatabampo.* Hotel accommodations: *Casa de Huespedes la Region,* Calle Hidalgo. *Casa Rosita,* Calles Iturbide and Morelos.

---

[7] A story is told concerning silver baron Don José María Almada, whose mansion overlooked the *Plaza de Armas,* that as many as 500 silver bars were sometimes stored in the house. There is a legendary tale that for a wedding which took place after a heavy rain, when the cobbles of the plaza were submerged in rushing water, Don José had a path of silver bars laid from the steps of his house to the church in order to secure a dry passage for the dainty shoes of his ladies.

The history of the old mines is full of interest. The *Doña María Mine* (Huacal District) was once exploited by a Spanish widow, Doña María de Rodríguez, who accumulated a vast store of ingots. Planning to pass her latter days in Spain, she loaded the treasure on the backs of 40 mules, and surrounded by a small army of retainers, she traveled to Mexico City. It was estimated each mule carried about 200 lbs. of gold and silver bars. According to the old chronicles the industrious woman did not breathe freely until she had deposited her fortune in the hands of the Spanish Viceroy; soon thereafter she ceased to breathe entirely, for she suddenly and mysteriously disappeared.

Another mine belonging to the Estrella del Norte Mining Company (near Arispe) was "lost" for many years. The only record touching its location was a notation on an old Jesuit map to the effect that "the opening of the tunnel can be seen from the door of the mission church." For years the hillside opposite the church door was searched with no results. In 1905 a side wall of the old church crumbled and disclosed a hidden door. From this door a prospector searched the opposite hillside with field glasses, located the lost mine, and made a fortune.

SINALOA-NAYARIT COUNTRY

This section of the Mexican northwest region includes the narrow, ocean-front states of Sinaloa (22,847 sq. m.) and Nayarit (10,671 sq. mi.). The area is bordered in the north by Sonora, to the east by the states of Chihuahua, Durango, and Zacatecas, and on the south and SE by the State of Jalisco. The coastal area is largely farm country, and in Nayarit, quite tropical. The eastern flank of the area rises to the great dorsal ridge of the Sierra Madre Occidental. Except for a new highway from Mazatlán to Durango there are no normal motor roads linking this region with the states to the east.

The continuation of the West Coast Route, CN-15 links the principal towns and ports. There is good air service to the larger cities, and likewise rail service via the Ferrocarril del Pacifico.

VACATION HIGHLIGHTS: As in the Sonora country, the best vacation fare in this area has to do with sports—fishing and bathing in the coastal towns, and spectacular big-game hunting in the back country. If you were to visit only one or two places, these should be the colorful port town and resort, Mazatlán, and the idyllic South Pacific style fishing village, San Blas. Of secondary interest are the colonial highway cities of Culiacan and Tepic.

The heart of the area and our base town is Mazatlán.

Mazatlán, Sin. Pop. 60,000. Alt. 9 ft.

HOW TO GET THERE: *Via road*—on CN-15, West Coast Route, 745 m. from Nogales, 326 m. from Guadalajara. *Via air*—CMA, daily flights from Tijuana, Hermosillo, Guadalajara, and Mexico City. Aeronaves de México, flights from El Paso, Monterrey, and Tijuana. *Via bus*—Nogales to Mexico City run, Autotransportes Tres Estrellas de Oro; Transportes del Norte. *Via boat*—weekly passages to La Paz, B.C.

HOTELS: In Mazatlán there are two hotel areas, the first along *Olas Altas,* facing the ocean, and near the center of town activities, and second, *Playa Norte* (North Beach), about 1½ m. from town. Most newer hotels are here. Reservations should be made during winter months. Off-season rates available during June to October. Rates quoted below are in-season rates.

Hotel La Siesta, Olas Altas 11. Tel. 26-40. An older hotel, 79 rooms, balconies facing ocean, some air-conditioning. Nice patio. A very friendly, well-operated establishment. It has one of the best dining rooms in the city. Rates: EP $70 MN to $100 MN dble. *Hotel de Cima,* 1½ m. NW on Av. del Mar. 108 rooms. New and nicely furnished, some air conditioned. Cocktail lounge, fair dining room, pool. EP from $100 MN dble. Tel. 33-88. *Hotel Belmar,* Olas Altas 66. Tel. 20-66. 86 rooms, bar, dining room only fair. One of the oldest and very Mexican style hotel. Has the most comfortable rocking chairs in the republic. Rates: from $50 MN up dble, EP. *Hotel Eldorado,* on Av. del Mar. 36 rooms, some air conditioned, dining room, cocktail lounge, pool, balconies facing sea. Rates: EP $115 MN dble. *The Sands,* Av. del Mar, a glossy new motel, 18 rooms, fair dining room, pool, bar. Rates: EP from $90 MN to $110 MN. *Hotel Freeman,* Olas Altas 79. A pleasant, older hotel, 90 rooms, fair dining room. Skyroom cocktail lounge. Dancing. Rates: EP from $45 MN to $80 MN. *Hotel Posada Colonial,* a little off the hotel belt, on Av. Miguel Alemán 11. Pleasant, very nicely kept motel. 31 units. Very good dining room. Rates: EP $40 to $60 MN dble. Tel. 36-33. (Closed during September.) *Hotel Playa Mazatlán,* 4 m. from town on Las Gaviotas Beach. 93 units, some air conditioned. So-so service. Rates: EP $85 MN dble. *Motel Agua Marina,* Av. del Mar. 44 rooms, some air conditioned. Dining room, bar. Rates: EP $90 MN. *Motel Los Flamingos,* on CN-15, N of town. 30 units, dining room, pool, cocktail lounge. New and modernistic. Rates: EP $90 dble. *Motel del Sol,* new, very comfortable, on ocean drive.

Very inexpensive, *viajero-style: Hotel Milán,* Canizales 10; *Hotel Central,* Angel Flores and Dominguez; *Hotel Avenida,* Av. Miguel Alemán 39.

There are a number of modern apartments where units can be rented per day, week, or month. Most are in the Paseo Clausen area and Paseo Centenario district. Among them: *Lido Apartments, Lincoln Furnished Apartments, Capri Apartments, Tropical, Hotel Freeman Apartments.* Rates range from $100 MN per day, up.

RESTAURANTS: Seafood is of course *de rigeur,* and the visitor's best bet. Excellent food at the *Hotel La Siesta Restaurant* and at *Hotel Posada Colonial.* On Olas Atlas, *La Copa de Leche,* air conditioned, somewhat glossy restaurant, fair cuisine. *El Puerto Azul,* on Paseo Clausen, overlooking ocean. Specialty, seafood. *Los Comales,* Calle de Carnaval corner Angel Flores (downtown). Inexpensive, tidy, clean spot serving Mexican fare, *Jonkol's,* Angel Flores 254. Good coffee shop. *O'Brien's,* Centenario 16, saloon and restaurant. An informal American hangout. Good lobster.

DIRECTORY: *Banks*—Banco Nacional de México, on Olas Atlas and Constitución; Banco Commercial del Pacifico, B. Domínguez 260. *Auto repairs*—C. J. Felton y Cia, (Ford) Constitucíon and Azueta; Federico Partida, Norte Km. 132 Ote. *Airlines*—CMA, B. Domínguez & Escobedo. Tel. 15-11. Aeronaves de México, B. Domínguez 11 Sur. Tel. 25-46. *Bus lines*—Autotransportes Tres Estrellas de Oro; Transportes del Norte; Transportes Monterrey, Saltillo. The new bus depot is at Calles Serdán and México. *Doctors*—Dr. Roberto Romero Dousset, Angel Flores 29 Pte. Tel. 32-25. (He did postgraduate work at Memorial Hospital, New Jersey); Dr. José Arteaga Zamorano. *Drugstore*—Rex Farmacia, on Leandro Valle facing city market. English spoken. Has all American medicines. *Church services*—Daily and Sunday Catholic services at the Sanctuary of St. Joseph, Calzada Gabriel Leyva, and at the Basilica on the Plaza Principal. The Basilica has a special Sunday Mass for fishermen at 5 P.M. *Christian Science* center, corner of 5 de Mayo at Melchor Ocampo. Evangelist Church, on Zaragoza Street. Baptist Church, Hidalgo and Francisco Serrano. *Golf club*—Club Campestre de Mazatlán. 9 holes, par 36. Tom Garcia the club professional. Green fees. $25 MN per day. *Hunting and Fishing Guides*—Gil and Bob Aviles. Licensed. Contact them through hotels. They furnish equipment. Speak English.

TAXIS AND ARAÑAS: Taxi fares within city, $5 MN per trip; to Flamingo Motel, $6 MN; Airport, $7 MN; Hotel Playa Mazatlán and Los Gaviotas Beach, $12 MN; by the hour, $13 MN. The two-wheel, horse-drawn, surrey-like *arañas* (spider wagons) are a most enjoyable way to tour the port. Fares: $1.60 MN for trip within city. If

the horse has to go up hill there is a $2 MN extra charge; if it rains, 50 centavos is tacked on to your bill. By the hour, $6 MN. Bus fares: within the city, 60 centavos; to the Gaviotas Beach, 75 centavos. You can rent bicycles by the hour, half day, or day. Rates: 1 hr. $3 MN; ½ day, $20 MN; by the day (24 hrs.), $30 MN. These rates set by the municipal authorities — *pay no more!*

FISHING AND BOATS: Mazatlán is one of Mexico's most important sport-fishing centers. International competitions held here annually. Best seasons: January to March for striped marlin; April for sailfish and marlin; May to July for some blue (black) marlin.

The best boat fleets (some equipped with ship-to-shore radio, refrigerators, tackle and bait furnished) are: *The Star Fleet,* operated by Bill Heimpel, contact La Siesta Hotel; *The Marlin Fleet,* run by Gil and Bob Aviles; *La Flota Indio* (Indian Fleet) operated by Luis Patrón; and *Bibi Boats,* run by Ernesto Coppel. Average cost per day of a charter boat is $50. Boats usually set out about 7 A.M. and return between 3 or 4 P.M. Fishing licenses ($10 MN) can be purchased at the docks.

THE TOWN AND ENVIRONS: Mazatlán (Mah-zat-LAHN, from the Náhuatl, place of the deer), lying on the Pacific littoral, just S of the Tropic of Cancer, and about parallel with the southmost tip of Baja California, is one of the three most interesting of Mexico's larger west coast ports and resorts. The history of the city is relatively brief. Though the Jesuit missionaries and Spanish explorers stopped off in the area, originally inhabited by an Indian tribe called the Chibchas, and the settlement was occupied successively by pirates, filibusters, and U. S. Forces, the town really got its start in the middle of the last century when enterprising Germans selling agricultural equipment settled in the port to do business with the neighboring regions. The colony grew and prospered, along with its brewery — Cervecería del Pacifico. For many years there was brisk trade with the Orient, and as a result, the port reflects overtones of this.

The city is situated on a peninsula jutting into the sea. The bay *(La Bahía)* on the SE side of the port is shallow and includes the area between *Crestón Island* at S and *Chivo* (Goat) *Island* at SE. Creston Island, now linked to the peninsula by a fill-in passage, is also called *El Faro,* from the lighthouse crowning its summit. It is said to be one of the tallest lighthouses in the world; is 515 feet above high water, and the light is visible 30 miles at sea. The W side of the peninsula with its ocean front boulevards — Paseo Centenario, Olas Altas, Paseo Clausen, and Av. del Mar — has become the tourist and vacation belt. Lined along it are shops, hotels and restaurants. (*Note:* In some guides these various linked boulevards are all referred to as Centenario.)

An isolated peak called *Cerro de Nevería* (Icebox Mt.) separates the Olas Altas beachfront from the Paseo Clausen and North Beach.

The center of town reflects the busy restlessness of a port city. There is no architecture of consequence. The so-called cathedral, Basilica of the Immaculate Conception (on the Plaza), begun in 1875, recommended by some guides as one of the beautiful churches in NW Mexico, is actually a mediocre structure.

THINGS TO DO AND SEE: The pleasures of Mazatlán are primarily recreational: fishing (see above), riding in the *arañas,* boat trips to the outlying islands, swimming. The best beaches are: *Las Gaviotas* (the sea gulls), N of town; *Olas Altas,* directly in front of the downtown hotels. At low tide it is rocky. *Playa Sur,* below the lighthouse, is popular with the townspeople but has not been taken up by visitors. An interesting excursion (boat) is to the bird paradise on *Palmito de la Virgen Island.*

AREA NORTH OF MAZATLÁN: The area from Mazatlán northward to the Sonora state line has several interesting points, most of them lying athwart the highway, or down toward the coast.

Culiacán, Sin. Pop. 49,000. Alt. 216. Capital of the State of Sinaloa. On CN-15, about 140 m. N of Mazatlán. Culiacán (Coo-lyah-CAHN, from the Aztec, *Colhua-can* — place where the god Coltzin is revered) was built on an ancient Indian settlement, that of the *Colhuas,* one of the Náhuatl tribes that helped settle the Valley of Mexico. At present it is a burgeoning mining and agricultural center. Huge quantities of tomatoes are exported from here to the U.S. The architecture and town layout retain flavors of the colonial era: the quaint portales, some of the public buildings and the massive and pretty cathedral overlooking the Plaza de la Constitución are all worth pausing to view.

HOTELS AND RESTAURANTS: Best, *Los Tres Rios Motel,* N edge of town. Lovely gardens, nice atmosphere, good dining room. 40 rooms, air conditioned, pool. Rates: EP from $80 MN dble. *Hotel El Mayo,* Blvd. Madero 623. Tel. 10-14. 48 rooms, some air conditioned, bar, restaurant. Rates: EP from $70 MN dble. *Motel San Luis,* S edge of town. Ultramodern, 26 air-conditioned units. Swimming pool, bar, dining room. Rates: EP from $70 MN dble. *Hotel San Luis,* 2 blocks S off CN-15, on Alvaro Obregón. 16 units, modest, tidy, and pleasant without the garish chrome. Good dining room, pool, rooms air conditioned. Rates: EP from $55 MN.

DIRECTORY: *Auto repairs:* J. M. Hiser y Cia, Riva Palacio 43 Nte; Sinaloa Motors, Blvd. 5 de Febrero 113. *Bank* — Banco Nacional de México, Rosales & Gen. Juan Carrasco. *Airline* — Aeronaves de México, Obregón 567 Nte. Tel. 4-60.

RECREATIONAL AREAS AROUND CULIACÁN: On the outskirts of the city are two thermal resorts: the *Carrizalejo Hot Springs,* and, 12 m. beyond, the *Ymala Hot Springs,* on the right bank of the Tamazula River. In a canyon a few miles below Ymala (foot trail) are walls with Aztec picture writing on them. There are several ocean bathing resorts. The best is *Altata,* 42 m. E (road is paved 30 miles, improved the remainder). Another popular ocean resort is *El Dorado* (43 miles SE paved road). Accommodations at both are unfortunately not too good.

Los Mochis, Sin. Pop. 22,300. Alt. 50. Center of a rich agricultural region supplied by waters from the El Fuerte River Basin project. Mexico's largest west coast sugar cane refinery is located here, NW edge of town. Visitors welcome. Present western terminal of the new Chihuahua-Pacific Railway.

HOTELS: *Santa Anita,* on Av. Leyva in center of town. 120 rooms, air conditioned, dining room, cocktail lounge. First-class accommodations. Rates: EP from $70 MN dble. *Motel Chapman,* 2 m. W. Has 22 rooms, some air conditioned. No dining room yet. Rates: EP from $65 MN.

To the E of Los Mochis, 14 m. via paved road is the interesting fishing village of *Puerto Topolobampo,* completely unspoiled by tourist traffic. There is a shrimp-packing plant. Excellent fishing in nearby waters.

Yacht Motel, on bay, away from village, 20 units, a/c, guest beach, fishing pier, dining room. Rates: $55 MN and up, EP. Write Box 209, Los Mochis, Sin.

To the W of Los Mochis a road goes (50 m.) to *El Fuerte, Nay.*, an old mining town in the foothills. Though smaller, it is remindful of Alamos, Son. Explorers with rugged cars can continue N via the rough remains of the old colonial *El Camino Real,* to Alamos. There are plans to eventually surface these fascinating back roads so tourists can leave the flat Coast Highway at Navojoa, drive up to Alamos, continue to El Fuerte, then rejoin the highway at Los Mochis.

THE AREAS SOUTH OF MAZATLÁN: The country south of Mazatlán, lying mostly in the State of Nayarit takes on a tropic exuberance — palm trees semaphore against the sky, Ebony, rosewood, mahogany, and other tropical trees are gaudy with vivid flowers. In this area there is one city of interest (Tepic), an archaeological zone, (Ixtlán), a South Pacific style fishing village and, as yet, unspoiled resort (San Blas).

San Blas, Nay. Pop. 1800. Alt. sea level. A sleepy, delightful, tropical fishing port on the Pacific, still more or less "undiscovered" by most visitors in Mexico.

HOW TO GET THERE: *Via road* — Turn off CN-15 (West Coast Highway) at junction 22 m. N of Tepic. The branch road, CE-46 goes west 23 m. to the town. *Via air* — Aeronaves de México flights from Mexico City or Tijuana to Tepic. From there taxi or bus to San Blas. *Via rail* — Ferrocarril del Pacifico to Tepic. Taxi to San Blas (*Note:* there is a San Blas, Sinaloa, on the rail line. Don't get off there by mistake. It is bleak.)

HOTELS AND RESTAURANTS: *Hotel Bucanero,* Av. Juárez, block W of Plaza. 28 rooms around a pleasant patio. Nothing to shout about, but atmosphere is friendly. Pool, cocktail lounge, dining room. Food not exceptional. Rates: EP $35 MN to $60 MN dble. Lower rates June to November. Tel. 1. *Hotel Playa Hermosa,* out from town on Borrego Beach. 100 rooms in modern shell of a building. The best that can be said is it is near the water. Rates: EP $50 MN dble. *Hotel Casino Colon,* out from town on Matanchén Beach. 20 rooms, bar, restaurant, air conditioning (sometimes), pool. Rates: from $70 MN dble, EP.

Seafood is the thing to eat here — turtle, planked shrimp, pompano, oysters. Best restaurant is *Torino's* a block down from the Hotel Bucanero. Also a fair seafood place across from the hotel, *The Beachcomber.*

THE TOWN AND ENVIRONS: The approach from the highway to San Blas is one of the delights of a visit to this tiny port. The paved branch road drops rapidly from 1000 feet, passing vivid vegetation and the stately coquito palms which flank the road for several miles and form a living green canyon. As you approach the sea there are estuaries and dark mangrove swamps, the exposed roots crusted with oysters. The town itself sprawls informally, adobe and thatch houses, sandy streets, lazy palms lending it a Tahiti-like air.

Above the town, on a small hill, are the ruins of "Old San Blas," built by the Spaniards. The crumbling remains of the old fort, church, and other small buildings are overgrown with vegetation. During the coloniage the Spanish made San Blas one of their principal shipbuilding centers. Many of the ships that sailed in the Philippine trade were constructed here.

The beach is about one m. from town. There are bathhouses and stands where food is sold. For more isolated swimming and good camping spots — Matanchén Beach and Bay, S of town. A number of interesting excursions can be taken through jungle waterways via dugout or outboard boat: (1) through dense mangrove swamps to a large banana plantation, (2) up the Conchal estuary to *La Aguada,* a small boat landing. Time, about 40 minutes. The boat landing is close to one of the beautiful Matanchén Bay beaches.

Small fishing boats are available for estuary and deep-sea fishing. One of the best boats is *La Perla* operated by Sr. Eduardo Victoria Peña, Apartado (Postal Box) 10, San Blas, Nay.

The best season is from October to April. Summers are humid to torrid. From around sunset to early morning it is advisable to avoid the beaches or to use insect repellents. Tiny gnats *(jejenes)* swarm during those hours.

Tepic, Nay. Pop. 25,000. Alt. 3000 ft. Capital of State of Nayarit.

On West Coast Highway, CN-15 (183 m. from Mazatlán, 143 m. from Guadalajara). Air connections with Tijuana and Mexico City via Aeronaves de México.

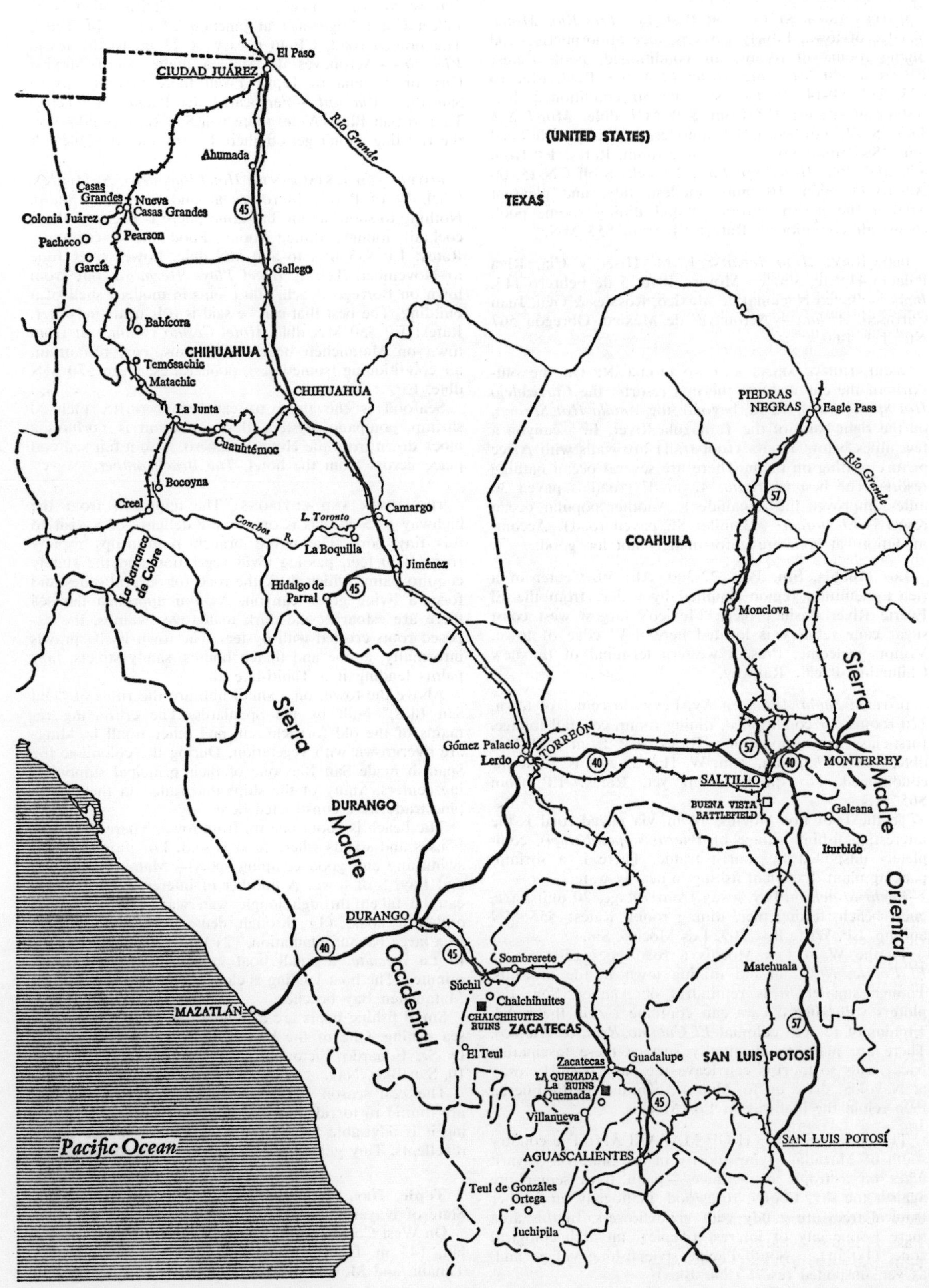
El Paso
CIUDAD JUÁREZ
Rio Grande
(UNITED STATES)
TEXAS
Ahumada
Casas Grandes
Nueva Casas Grandes
Colonia Juárez
Pacheco
Pearson
García
Gallego
45
Babícora
CHIHUAHUA
Temósachic
Matachic
CHIHUAHUA
La Junta
Cuauhtémoc
Bocoyna
Creel
Conchos R.
L. Toronto
Camargo
La Boquilla
Jiménez
La Barranca de Cobre
Hidalgo de Parral
PIEDRAS NEGRAS
Eagle Pass
Rio Grande
57
COAHUILA
Monclova
Sierra
Madre
Oriental
Sierra
Madre
Occidental
Gómez Palacio
Lerdo
TORREÓN
40
57
40
MONTERREY
SALTILLO
BUENA VISTA BATTLEFIELD
Galeana
Iturbide
DURANGO
DURANGO
40
45
MAZATLÁN
Sombrerete
Súchil
Chalchihuites
CHALCHIHUITES RUINS
ZACATECAS
El Teul
Zacatecas
Guadalupe
LA QUEMADA RUINS
La Quemada
45
Villanueva
Matehuala
57
SAN LUIS POTOSÍ
SAN LUIS POTOSÍ
AGUASCALIENTES
Teul de Gonzáles Ortega
Juchipila
Pacific Ocean

HOTELS: Tepic rarely counts on tourists staying long so its hotels are modest and make no flashy play for the dollar. Offering most comfort is, *Motel Cora,* opposite Loma Park. 14 rooms, good dining room. Rates: EP from $50 MN dble. *Motel Loma,* same area, 14 unit old motel somewhat refurbished. Has dining room and cocktail lounge. *Hotel Imperial* and *Hotel Sierra De Alica,* both old, limited services. Rates: moderate.

DIRECTORY: *Bank* — Banco Nacional de México, Av. Veracruz 263. *Auto repairs* — Nayarit Motors, (Ford), Lerdo 149 Pte; Ricardo L. Garate y Cia. (GM), Puebla and Hidalgo; Valdes Motors, (Plymouth) Hidalgo 118 Pte. *Airlines* — Aeronaves de México, Av. México 174. Tel. 3-09. *Bus lines* — Tres Estrellas de Oro, Allende 60. Autotransportes de Nayarit. Av. México 18; Autotransportes del Pacifico, México 212 Nte.

THE TOWN AND ENVIRONS: Tepic (Teh-PEEK, from the Náhuatl, *tetl,* stone, and *pic,* hard) is a curious mixture of the old and the new. It remains one of the quaint and surprising cities of the west coast. Standing at the foot of the quiescent volcano of Sangangüey, it is the center of an attractive region destined to grow in touristic importance.

The town came into history in 1542 when Francisco Cortés occupied the Indian *pueblo* which stood on the site of the present city. Though the Spanish king gave it the title of *Noble y Leal Ciudad* (Noble and Loyal City) in 1711, it nevertheless took the whistle of the first locomotive that reached it in 1912 to impart more life to it than it had ever felt before. The seventeenth and the twentieth centuries have blended here rather well. Many of the houses, streets, public buildings, even customs of the people are those of viceregal times. Added to this, there is always the feel of surprise on seeing Huichol and Coro Indians who come down from the back country in their unique costumes to trade in the town.

Points of interest in the city are the Plaza Principal with its colonial atmosphere. The *Cathedral,* on the Plaza, built in 1750 and dedicated to La Purísima. It is noted for its two very fine Gothic towers. Interesting also is the *Church of the Holy Cross* which was once a part of the imposing Franciscan Convento de la Cruz founded in 1741.

On July 25 the townspeople celebrate the traditional Fair of Santiago.

Places of interest in the nearby area include San Blas and its beaches (see Index), the little-known coastal villages — *Los Cocos, Los Corchos* and *Miramar* — the formerly rich mining town of *Compostela* (via good road, 25 m. directly south) with its old red *tezontle* church built in 1539. Just N of Tepic there are lovely waterfalls on the Tepic River.

Ixtlan del Rio, Nay. Pop. 5960. Alt. 3395 ft. On CN-15, about 49 m. S of Tepic; 74 m. NE of Guadalajara. Ixtlán (Ix-TLAHN) lies on the edge of the spectacular *barranca* country to S. It is surrounded by a rich archaeological zone (1 m. from town).

THE RUINS: The architecture of the zone is considered post-Classic (900 A.D. and later), that is, contemporary with the Toltec culture. The structures that remain are of a circular type rarely encountered elsewhere.

THE TRES MARÍAS ISLANDS *(Islas Marías),* about 60 m. off the coast of Nayarit, due W of Tepic. A lofty, rugged group of islands of which the largest (*María Madre,* 10 m. long, 3½ wide) is used by the federal government as a maximum security penal colony. The other islands of the group are *Magdalena, Cleofas,* and *San Juanito.* The islands can be reached by boat from San Blas, and by mail plane from Tepic. There are several beaches on María Madre that charm the few tourists who manage to reach the island.

47. North Central Mexico

North Central Mexico, in which we include the states of Chihuahua, Coahuila, Durango, Zacatecas, and a bit of San Luis Potosí (lying N of the Tropic of Cancer), is a vast area where points of unusual tourist interest are separated by great distances or, in instances, are still almost inaccessible. It is a region that most travelers hurry through over high-speed highways or via air routes to the more picturesque, crowded country to the south.

The region has almost no tropical lowlands. There are vast plateaus, rugged mountains, huge cattle grazing and farming areas, as well as fabulous mining sections. Its cities are far apart and on the whole the region is one of the most sparsely populated in the country. Three major highways serve the region: the new Constitution Highway, CN-57, linking Eagle Pass (Piedras Negras) to Mexico City, the Central Highway, CN-45 and 57, from El Paso (Ciudad Juárez) to Mexico City; and the East-West Highway linking NE Mexico to the NW coast (Mazatlán) via Monterrey, Saltillo, Durango. (See Index: Highway Routes.) Trains of the National Railways of Mexico connect the principal cities of the region with Mexico City as well as the U.S. border cities of El Paso and Eagle Pass. A small branch line goes from C. Juárez, through Pearson and connects with the Ferrocarril Chihuahua-Pacifico. The latter (the old Kansas City, Mexico and Oriente Line), until 1960, extended only as far as Creel, Chih. The final links from Creel, through the Sierra Tarahumaras to the Pacific port of Topolobampo, Son., were completed in the fall of 1961. It passes near the famed Barrancas de la Tarahumaras. Airlines — Aeronaves de México ties most of the cities of this region with the capital and the U.S. border.

The climate of the region is temperate to cold in

winter, hot along the Mexican-U.S. frontier areas in summer, to moderately hot the farther south and higher you go.

Hotel accommodations along the various routes are ample, ranging in quality from fair to very good.

TOURIST ATTRACTIONS: Although spread over vast distances, the more important points of interest in the region tend to be spectacular, and these come under the heading of natural beauties: the *Caída de Basaseáchic,* third highest waterfall on the North American continent; and a complex of canyons rivaling the Grand Canyon of Arizona, the *Grandes Barrancas de la Tarahumara.* Both of these unusual attractions are in the State of Chihuahua. Next in interest are the cities of Chihuahua, Saltillo, and Zacatecas — each noted for some fine examples of colonial architecture, and also for their historical associations. Although the archaeological ruins in this region lack the haunting fascination of the great ruined cities farther south, several are of interest — *La Quemada* and *Chalchihuites* in Zacatecas, *Casas Grandes* in Chihuahua. The vacation prospector searching for unusual or quaint mining towns can stake out claims to a number of picturesque hideaways in the mineralized mountains. For the sportsman, the region boasts of the best trout fishing and black bass fishing in the country. Likewise, the high back country is game rich — black bear, grizzlies, deer, and wild fowl. This is also the country of the Tarahumara Indians, the largest and perhaps the least known tribe north of Mexico City, and one of the most amazing indigenous people below-the-border.

AREAS OF MAXIMUM INTEREST	BASE CITY
Chihuahua Country	Chihuahua
Durango-Zacatecas Area	Zacatecas
Coahuila	Saltillo

GEOGRAPHY OF THE REGION: This region, one of the most homogenous in Mexico, is actually a continuation to the south of the basin and range province of Arizona and New Mexico. It is a gently sloping tableland, rising from about 3000 feet at the northern border to an average of some 6000 feet at its southern sections. Physically it is bounded on the north by the U.S.-Mexico border which generally follows the course of the Río Grande River. Along this border there are two principal ports of entry — at El Paso, Texas (Ciudad Juárez), and at Eagle Pass, Texas (Piedras Negras). On the west the region is bounded, and cut off from the Pacific Coast by the forbidding Sierra Madre Occidental range; on the east it is flanked by the Sierra Madre Oriental, through which there are several passes to the northeastern Mexican states.

FLORA AND FAUNA: Sand and alkali are a salient feature of the plains, and where the soil has not been reclaimed and irrigation provided, much of the vegetation is of a desert-range variety — buffalo and crab grass, endless types of cacti, the spiny bushes and trees such as the *mesquite* (Aztec, *mesquitl*), the *tornilla,* the *fouqueria,* the *agaves,* and the *yuccas.* Interesting among the plants is a small agave with ash-covered leaves covered with livid spots. It is known to the Indians around Chihuahua as *Cebadilla* (sneeze wort) and the juice of its leaves, which contain a strong alkaloid, is said to serve as an excellent antidote for the bite of any poisonous animal or reptile. Snakes flee the plant, and when irritated by the Indians into biting it, they are said to die of convulsions.

In the mountain areas fine stands of timber are found, ranging from oaks to pines. In the timber area, mostly along the still unopened west and northern flank of the region, lies one of Mexico's great wildlife reserves. It is the only part of the country where the grizzly bear, and a dwindling number of big horn sheep may be spotted. Other game in the region are deer, mountain lion, wolf, antelope, quail, dove, and ducks.

HISTORY: The story of North Central Mexico was for countless centuries one of violence, conquest, and rapine. The region existed as a kind of no man's land across which tribal expeditions, Spanish conquerors, latter-day armies and even bandits passed back and forth on their way to somewhere else. Before the conquest, Indian tribes passed through the region on their way to the paradise-like Vale of Anáhuac. The few stragglers and latecomers who remained in the region found the land too hard to gain more than a bare existence from it. They had no incentive or leisure to create great cultures or erect lasting cities. The early Spanish expeditions found little to interest them except gold and silver. They were men with built-in divining rods. Their only settlements were established where there was gold. Both tragic and glorious pages of Mexico's latter history were written in this region.

Here, in 1811, Miguel Hidalgo y Costilla, the father of Mexican independence, met his tragic end. When the sorely beset priest and his patriotic adherents met with reverses in Central Mexico (1810), they retreated northward to unite their torn and scattered forces at the Hacienda de Pabellon. Here Hidalgo, a notoriously bad military tactician, turned over the military command to Ignacio de Allende, and it was decided to try to reach the United States and endeavor to obtain help from the northern neighbor. The ragged army marched through Zacatecas, and on reaching Saltillo, it was met by Lieutenant Colonel Ignacio Elizondo, who had but recently joined the insurgent ranks and who now requested a colonelcy under Allende. For some reason this was refused; embittered, Elizondo again transferred his allegiance. He made an alliance with the Bishop of Monterrey (Primo Feliciano María), planned an ambush, and captured Hidalgo and his adherents at Acatita de Baján, March 21, 1811. Father Hidalgo and his companions were taken to the city of Chihuahua, were there executed and decapitated.

Some 25 years later the north region was again ravaged by battle, and part of the region was lost to Mexico when Texas gained its independence. Again, in 1847, the region suffered invasion by American forces and one of the major battles of the Mexican War was fought at Buena Vista near Saltillo.

In 1866, when Maximilian and the French intervened in Mexico, the northern region became the national base when President Juárez brought his government to Chihuahua, and from there began the drive that forced Maximilian to defeat. Even during moments of national peace, those who had settled in the north central area had little rest. The region was repeatedly subjected to raids of Apache Indians. Early in the nineteenth century hordes of Apaches and Comanches poured across the Mexican border from the U.S., to winter like troublesome tourists in the balmy climate of Chihuahua and Coahuila. They raided even as far south as San Luis Potosí and Zacatecas.

A final chapter of civil strife took place in this century when Francisco I. Madero of Coahuila sparked the revolution of 1910, and aided by hard-riding Pancho Villa (Doroteo Arango), succeeded in overthrowing the Porfirio Díaz dictatorship.

THE PEOPLE OF NORTH CENTRAL MEXICO: With the exception of a few extremely isolated Indian tribes, notably the Tarahumaras and some Yaqui Indians on the Chihuahua-Sonora line, the Mexicans of this region are far less Indianist and traditional in outlook, customs, and manners than their kinsmen farther south. To a great extent their cultural ties are much closer to the United States and the mores of the Río Grande border country. In agriculture, industry, and economics their methods tend to be more like those of their northern neighbors than of the south. A new agricultural economy is developing the potentially fertile soil. Mexicans here do large-scale farming, and there is little comparison between the modern mechanized methods they use, and the old-fashioned operations one observes in the central and southern portions of Mexico.

Although the future of Mexico rests with the progressive elements of its people, nevertheless, some of the most interesting are those who have retreated from the stream of progress. By far the most fascinating are the Tarahumara Indians who live in the southwest part of the State of Chihuahua and range as far north as Temosachic.[1]

The 40,000 or so Tarahumaras are the lees of a populous nation which the Spanish Conquistadores found in possession of the region of Chihuahua. They are, today, a timid lot, and have little or no community life, preferring to live alone with their immediate family. One usually gets one's first sight of the Tarahumaras in Chihuahua City where they go to barter. Both men and women wear long, flowing, jet-black hair, usually tied with a narrow headband. The clothing of the men consists of little more than the colored headband, a rough white shirt and a *tapote,* or glorified loincloth.

Bashfulness seems to be one of their tribal traits and there is a great deal of reserve between the sexes. Unless there is a close relationship, men and women usually only talk to each other at a respectful distance, and with faces averted. The Tarahumara woman is extremely shy about giving birth; often she goes to some isolated spot in the woods, prepares a nest of grass to receive the child and, holding to the branch of a tree, she crouches and delivers her offspring. She generally resumes her household duties within 24 hours. Her husband, on the other hand, does not work for three days after the event, lest some accident might occur to his work implements or animals. The umbilical cord, believed to have some magical connection with the child's future, is never thrown away. If the child is a girl the cord is buried near the hearth so she will become a good housewife. A boy's cord is hung on a tree so the lad will become a good hunter. Or, sometimes, the cord is buried near where the child was born so he will not grow up stupid.

Like the Huichol Indians of the West Coast, the Tarahumaras consider the peyote cactus (*Echinocactus* or *Lophophora Williamsi,* also called "mescal button") as sacred. Though the two people live hundreds of miles apart and speak different tongues, they both refer to the peyote as *hikuli.* Even where the Tarahumara are Christianized, in their chapels they will have the peyote demigod placed on the altar beside the cross or statue of a saint. They believe the tiny plant possesses human attributes, as well as the powers to cure, to purify and bring luck. They often call the peyote "uncle." And they also believe the peyote is modest, and to avoid shocking the little plant it is kept in a jar or separate storehouse so it won't be shocked by the things it might see going on in a home. At times the plant is offered food and drink, is dressed in bits of blanket, and is offered cigarettes to smoke. When the Tarahumaras go on pilgrimage to seek the peyote, they put the picked plants in separate bags lest the peyote fight with each other. The peyote evidently likes to be picked, for it is said that they sing charmingly to attract the attention of the peyote-seekers.

The Tarahumaras are exceptional runners.[2] They have been known to run hundreds of miles, nonstop,

[1] The numerous towns and villages in the state with names terminating in *chic* pertain to, or were formerly inhabited by these Indians.

[2] The name of the tribe alludes to their running ability. *Tarahumara* is a Spanish corruption of *ralámari,* meaning foot runner.

taking nothing more than pinole and water to keep going. They catch deer by running after them for days until they exhaust them, and at the end of the chase, the men seem comparatively fresh. They often hold running competitions, and do not measure their running time in long races by the clock, but by the evolutions of the heavenly bodies. A fairly short race lasts about 12 hours, and it is nothing for a race to extend over three days and nights, covering several hundred miles of rugged mountain country. Popular among them is a ball-game foot race in which they kick a small ball ahead of them for miles over the mountains, from sunrise to sunset. When four Tarahumara runners were induced to represent Mexico in the 1928 Olympics at Amsterdam, they failed to take the first places in the 25-mile marathon because they didn't realize the race was over after so short a distance. The bewildered comment of one of them was, "Too short! Too short!"[3]

Other tribal groups of the North Central region include the Pima Indians, who are allied in customs and language to the Tarahumaras, and dwell to the south of the Tarahumara region in the Sierra Madre Mountains. Still further south, near the border of Chihuahua and Durango, around the village of Nabogame, are the fast dwindling remnants of the Tepehuane tribe. These Indians somewhat resemble the Tarahumaras, and many of their beliefs and customs are unusual. Finger- and toe-nails are permitted to grow long — Chinese mandarin fashion — for fear that cutting them will produce blindness. A sleeper is never wakened, as his soul may be absent and may be wandering around, etc.

To the west, along the Chihuahua state line, and branching over into Sonora, are the Yaqui Indians, a division of the Piman stock of North American Indians. They speak a Cahita dialect. They were once a powerful people and were prone, like the Apaches to whom they are related, to indulge in endless warfare. From earliest colonial times they fought the Spanish relentlessly and continued to fight the federal troops until almost the turn of this century. It has been said that they are the only North American tribe which, surrounded by enemies for centuries, has never been subdued. The death of their chief, Luis Matuz in June 1927, seemed to have been a great blow to the tribe, and now they are settled and have become agriculturists.

THE CHIHUAHUA COUNTRY

Chihuahua is one of the two states of this region having a border with the U.S. It is the largest and one of the richest states in Mexico, covering an area of 95,942 sq. m., and with a population of over 1,226,793. Its climate is as hot and dry as that of Texas while its altitude varies from 3000 feet in the eastern tablelands to 10,000 feet in the western Sierra Madres. It is an important mining state — silver, zinc, lead, and other minerals. It is also a leading cattle and agricultural state.

Its thriving border city, Ciudad Juárez, opposite El Paso, Texas, is one of the chief tourist ports of entry into Mexico.

VACATION HIGHLIGHTS: Most noteworthy of Chihuahua's tourist attractions are: (1) Chihuahua City's historical and colonial monuments, (2) hunting and trout fishing in the western sierras, bass fishing at *La Boquilla* (Lake Toronto) near *Camargo,* (3) for off-trail explorers — *La Cascada de Basaseáchic* (Basaseachic Waterfalls) and the great *Barrancas de la Tarahumara* (Tarahumara Canyons) SW of Chihuahua City.

AREA NORTH OF CHIHUAHUA CITY: The area between Chihuahua City and the U.S. border to the north is monotonous desert country. The only points of interest are Ciudad Juárez, and branching westward from the Central Highway at Ahumada, side trips to the archaeological zone, Las Casas Grandes, and beyond that in the sierras, grizzly bear and trout country.

Ciudad Juárez, Chih. Pop. 122,600. Alt. 3700 ft. Mexican port of entry on the Río Grande, opposite El Paso, Texas. Juárez (WHA-rez) is reached by two international bridges. Toll: auto and driver 10 cents, passengers 2 cents each. The Mexican Customs and Immigration offices are opened from 8 A.M. to midnight, C.S.T.; the U.S. offices are open 24 hours daily.

Long known as Paso del Norte, and one of the historic stops on the old Santa Fe Trail that linked Independence, Missouri, via Santa Fe, to Chihuahua, Ciudad Juárez has grown into a lively border city possessing an interesting Mexican-American atmosphere, some worthy monuments and the usual assortment of border-town bars, night clubs and other places of dubious pleasure.

The town recalls one of Mexico's greatest presidents — Benito Juárez, a Zapotec Indian. In the principal park there is a monument to Juárez, a tall shaft surmounted by a heroic bronze figure of the patriot and reformer. The tablets let into the base of the shaft typify scenes in his life. Other points of interest in and near the city are: Plaza de Toros Monumental, the large and handsome bullring 3½ m. from the center of the city on the Central Highway. Bullfights are held on Sundays, during the season. There is good parking. Misión de Nuestra Señora de Guadalupe, the historic mission built by Father García in 1659. The building is well preserved and has handsomely carved beams and altar.

In Ciudad Juárez, in addition to the normal national and religious fiestas there are two other important celebrations: the fiesta of Santa Barbara on December 4, and the fiesta of San Lorenzo on August 10. In the nearby village of San Lorenzo the latter fiesta extends from August 8 to 12, and is well worth attending to see the Indian matachina dancers.[4]

HOTELS: Most visitors prefer to overnight on the El Paso side of the border. Ciudad Juárez has a number of

[3] Report of Enrique Aguirre, coach to the Mexican Olympic team, 1928.

[4] According to tradition, during the colonial epoch a statue of San Lorenzo (Saint Lawrence) was always carried from Chihuahua City to San Antonio, Texas, to celebrate the anniversary of the saint. The village of San Lorenzo was an important rest-stop for the pilgrims. Once, while making the stop the Río Grande flooded, preventing the march from continuing. The people took it as a sign that the Saint preferred to stay in the village. A chapel, and later, a church were built to house the image.

fair hotels, none de luxe, but you will find the rates somewhat lower than across the river. Rates in the following hotels range from $45 MN, dble, EP, to about $100 MN. *Campo Turista Jardín Fronterizo,* on road to Chihuahua, 5 m. from International Bridge. Fair bungalows. *Hotel Koper,* Av. Juárez 124. 60 rooms, some air conditioned. Near bullring. *Hotel De Luxe,* Lerdo and Galeana. 72 rooms, some air conditioned. Elevators. Central. *Hotel Moran,* Av. Juárez 238 Nte; 3 blocks from the bridge. 44 rooms, some air conditioned.

DIRECTORY: *U. S. Consulate,* Lerdo and 16th Septiembre. Tel. 125. *Auto repairs* — Automotores de Juárez, (Olds, Pontiac, Vauxhall), Calzada del Valle and Av. Hipodromo; Juárez Automotriz, (GM) 16 de Septiembre 642; Juárez Comercial (Ford), 5 de Mayo 105. *Bank* — Banco Nacional de México, 16 de Septiembre and Lerdo. *Insurance* — At the AAA border offices across the river, or, La Azteca, Cia. Mexicana de Seguros, 16 de Septiembre, 1111 Ote. *Bus lines* — Transportes Chihuahuenses, Av. 16 de Septiembre 204 Ote. (this is one of the top Mexican lines, connected with Greyhound, running de luxe coaches to Mexico City); Autobuses Flecha Roja, 16 de Septiembre and Anáhuac, (first class buses to Mexico City and to Guadalajara). *Airlines* — Aeronaves de México, Edificio Banco Nacional. Tel. 6-14 (connecting flights to Monterrey, Tijuana, Mexico City, Chihuahua, etc.). Trans-Mar de Cortés, Calle Lerdo Nte. 205b. Tel. 2-50-99 (flights on Tuesday and Friday to Guaymas and La Paz). *Railways* — National Railways of Mexico (central route to Mexico City), tickets at Depot. Tel. 5-67; Ferrocarril Noroeste de México, R. Corona & 20 de Noviembre, Tel. 1-88. (Route to Pearson, Nueva Casas Grandes, and S toward the Barrancas de la Tarahumara.)

Casas Grandes, Chih. (Archaeological site) 4 m. from the town of *Nuevo Casas Grandes.* To get there turn right (W) off Central Highway, CN-45 at *Gallego* (137 m. S of C. Juárez). This road, marked CE-10, traverses level country, 123 m. to Nuevo Casas Grandes. The town may also be reached via the Ferrocarril Noroeste de Mexico Railway, or by air via Aeronaves de México planes.

THE RUINS: Until recently Casas Grandes (Big Houses) was regarded as a somewhat mysterious ruined village once peopled by an equally mysterious race. The ruins, on the crest of a ridge commanding a wide sweep of territory, resemble much more the constructions of the Indian pueblos of Arizona and New Mexico, than the grandiose and sophisticate buildings of Mayas in Yucatán. The building material is mud mixed with gravel molded into large adobe bricks. The rooms are superimposed on each other like those of the Zuñi Indians. Recent archaeological excavations have uncovered unsuspected pyramids, a large ball court, an irrigation system and artifacts of apparent Toltec and pre-Aztec origin.

HOTEL: In the nearby town of Nuevo Casas Grandes there are fair accommodations and restaurant. Best is the quite comfortable *Motel Casa Grande,* 38 rooms, air conditioning, good dining room. Rates: EP, from $60 MN dble.

The Sierra Madre Hunting and Fishing Area. *Nuevo Casas Grandes* is a good take-off point for a little known but fabulous hunting area (bear and deer) and trout fishing waters to the west along the Sonora-Chihuahua state line. This highland region, beautifully forested and crisscrossed with excellent streams, centers around the remote villages of *Colonia Juárez, Pacheco* and *García,* SW of Casas Grandes, and the area E of *Babícora.* A vestige of road leads in from Casas Grandes to Colonia Juárez. The road was the brain child of English entrepreneurs who set out to lumber the area before the Revolution. They laid out a rail bed which, today, is maintained as a jeep road extending to Pacheco and some 70 m. farther south toward *Estrella.* A guide is needed since you must leave the road and pack into the best trout stream areas. Best season is from May to mid-October. The elevation for much of this region (headwaters of the Yaqui and Mayo Rivers) is from 7000 to 9000 ft. You find brook trout in the four tributaries of the *Bavispe River* (north fork of the Yaqui, just W of García). Best rainbow streams are the San Juan de Dios, Tres Ríos, Gavilán, Paraíso, Largo, and the Canada del Oro. At a box canyon where the Gavilán, Negro, and Chichupa Rivers join to form the Tres Ríos there are magnificent trout ranging up to 20 inches. At García, 35 miles south of Pacheco (wagon road) there are several good streams.

To reach this area by train take the Ferrocarril Noroeste de México from C. Juárez and get off either at Pearson (also called Juan Mata Ortíz) or at Babícora. You can rent a car that will take you up to the Mormon settlements on the flank of the fishing country. There you can arrange for pack outfits and guides.

Chihuahua, Chih. Pop. 86,970. Alt. 4600 ft. Capital of the State of the same name and the metropolis of North Central Mexico. 230 m. S of the U.S. border on the Central Highway, and first large stopover point on the route.

HOW TO GET THERE: *Via Highway* — see route description, Central Highway or Independence Highway, CN-45, see Index. *Via air* — Aeronaves de México offers direct daily flights to Mexico City and to C. Juárez. *By bus* — daily first-class service to C. Juárez and Mexico City on the Transportes Chihuahuenses buses, and Autobuses Flecha Roja. There is also bus transportation to Monterrey and Saltillo. *Railway* — Mexican National Railways, route from C. Juárez to Mexico City. Chihuahua-Pacific Railway from Presidio, Texas and Los Mochis, Sin.

HOTELS: *Hotel Palacio Hilton,* center of town, facing the plaza. Old hotel, but still our favorite. 125 comfortable, air-conditioned rooms; good service, cocktail lounge, air-conditioned restaurant, garage. Rates: EP $70 MN to $90 MN dble. *Motel Mirador,* N edge of town on CN-45, new, excellent accommodations, a/c, dining room. Moderate rates. *Motel el Capitán,* 2 m. N on CN-45. 22 air-conditioned units. Bar and restaurant. Tel. 2-35-60. Rates: EP $50 MN to $65 MN dble. *Santa Rita Motel,* 3 m. N on highway. 30 air-conditioned units, nicely furnished, pleasant grounds, pool, cocktail lounge, dining room, and patio. Tel. 20-58. Rates: EP $40 MN to $70 MN dble. *Motel La Cima,* highway, N of town. 40 units, not always too well kept. Rates: EP from $35 MN dble. *Hotel Victoria,* Av. Juárez y Colon. Once one of the show places of Chihuahua. We have had several reports from travelers that the service was poor and the attitude of the staff chilly to rude.

RESTAURANTS: *Caballo Bayo,* Av. Independencia 617. Fair. *El Parador,* Juárez 3901, cattleman's restaurant serving some of the best steaks in Mexico. *Hotel Fremont,* center of town, new and very good, a/c. Rates: moderate.

DIRECTORY: *Banks* — Banco Nacional de México, Libertad 100; Banco de Chihuahua, Independencia and Victoria. *Auto repairs* — Chihuahua Motors, (Ford), Victoria 114; Distribuidores Generales, (Chevrolet), Carranza y Corregidora 1703; Automotriz de Chihuahua (Buick, Olds, Pontiac), Av. Carranza 1101. *Travel agency*

— Agencia de Turismo Rivas, Hotel Victoria. *Airlines* — Aeronaves de México, in Hotel Palacio Hilton. Tel. 33-19. *Railway* — Mexican National Railway, ticket office, Calle 3a 206. Tel. 33-19. *Bus lines* — Autobuses Flecha Roja, Carranza and Allende. Tel. 6-65; Transportes Chihuahuenses, Bolivar 714. Tel. 10-54; Transportes Monterrey-Saltillo, Coronado 507, Tel. 3-21 (routes to Torreón, C. Juárez, Saltillo and Monterrey). *Doctors* — Dr. Ricardo Guardia R. (bilingual) Clínica del Parque, Calle 12 and Llave. Tel. 2-07-39. *Church Services* — daily and Sunday services in the Catholic Cathedral.

THE CITY: Chihuahua (Che-WAH-wah), founded in 1709, is the center of a rich silver mining and ranching district. Silver was first found in the area in 1679. The curious name of the city is derived from two Tarahumara words signifying "Place of the Workshop." According to legend, and possibly fact, some of the older buildings in Chihuahua contain enough silver in their walls to render demolition and reduction a profitable undertaking. The early Spanish method of extracting the ore was so crude that much rich mineral was discarded with the dross after reduction of the ores, and in the absence of a better material, this slag, mixed with silver scoriae, was used to construct many of the houses.

One of the city's curious claims to distinction results from the breeding of the tiny, vivacious dogs, *Perros Chihuahueños.* These little canines somewhat resemble the *Chin Koro* of Japan and the *Sleeve Dog* of China. They are of a delicate fawn, or fawn-and-white color, with large erect ears, standing out like the wings of a butterfly. Their eyes are large and soulful. The expensive, pure-bred specimens, weighing from 14 oz. to 2 lbs., are distinguished by a depression *(mollera)* about the size of a pea in the forehead, and by the possession of 20 nails, five on each foot. Travelers should beware about purchasing "Chihuahua Dogs" offered to them by street peddlers. These young pups sometimes grow into large and lusty, St. Bernard-size mongrels.

The most imposing building in the city, an excellent reliquary of colonial times, is the cathedral, facing the Plaza de la Constitucion. The church is dedicated to San Francisco de Asis, patron saint of the city. The structure, (begun in 1717 and completed by 1789) represents the Baroque style. It has a profusely ornamented façade adorned with 13 statues (St. Francis and the Twelve Apostles) placed in niches between twisted columns. The tall, twin, 146 ft. high, bell towers rise above their plain base in three gracefully diminishing stories of columns and arches. Tradition avers that an inclined plane of earth was laid, and as fast as the building stones were dragged into position the plane was increased, so that when the last stones of the towers were placed the entire structure was buried and the runway extended beyond the edge of the plaza.

The interior of the cathedral is Doric in style, and though most of the fabulous silver and gold furnishing have been lost, the place is attractive. The main altar *(altar mayor)* is supported by 16 Corinthian columns in groups of four, with a statue of Saint Francis. Permission can be gotten to ascend one of the cathedral towers where a breath-taking view of the city and surrounding country is obtained. The great colonial aqueduct (built in 1790) which stretches 3½ m. across the valley to the hills, can be seen from here.

The Palacio de Gobierno (State Capitol Building), N side of the Plaza de Hidalgo. This handsome building was originally constructed in 1891 on the site of the Jesuit Colegio de Loreto, which dated back to 1713. When the Jesuits were expelled from Mexico the Loreto became a military hospital. Here Father Hidalgo and other leaders of the Independence movement were imprisoned after being captured at Acatita de Baján, March 1811. There is a tablet in the lower corridors commemorating the spot where Hidalgo was executed. Of additional interest in this building are the handsome carved panel walls and ceilings in the Sala de Cedro (Cedar Room). Due to a destructive fire the Palacio was completely reconstructed between 1941–47.

Palacio Federal (Federal Palace), on Calle de la Libertad. An interesting colonial building, reconstructed, containing the cell where Hidalgo was held during his trial, and from which he was taken to be shot. . . . The handsome monument in the center of Plaza Hidalgo is dedicated to the heroes of the War of Independence. This Corinthian monument, 45 ft. high, is made of marble from Orizaba. The life-size bronze figure of Hidalgo and the smaller figures of his adherents were cast in Brussels.

Other points of passing interest in the city include: *San Francisco Church* on Calle Libertad, begun by Franciscan missionaries in 1721. Here, in the Chapel of San Antonio, there is a tablet with the inscription, *"Don Miguel Hidalgo y Costilla, Father of Mexican Independence, was shot in Chihuahua July 31, 1811, and his decapitated body was laid here. The remains were exhumed for transportation to Mexico City in 1827."*[5]

La Quinta Luz, the house of General Francisco Villa (Pancho Villa), now the property of his widow, Señora Luz Corral de Villa. The residence has been converted into a private museum exhibiting the auto Villa was riding in when assassinated, his arsenal of weapons, clothing, and documents.

FIESTAS: Among Chihuahua's more colorful fiestas: Fiesta de Santa Rita, May 22; Cotton Fair, September 7–16; and Fiesta de San Francisco, around October 4.

AREA WEST OF CHIHUAHUA CITY: **Basaseáchic Falls.** An excursion to the falls (La Cascada de Basaseáchic), although one of the fabulous sights in Mexico, is recommended primarily for active young tourists for it is definitely off-trail. It is camping country. There are no accommodations of any sort near the falls.

TO GET THERE: Take the Ferrocarril Noroeste de México to *Matachic,* or, second-class buses from Chihuahua, via Cuauhtémoc (center of famed Mennonite Settlements), to Matachic. If you follow this route by automobile the road is fine to Cuauhtémoc, fair to Matachic. Light standard cars (Fords, Chevrolets, Vauxhalls) can navigate it. At Matachic you leave your car, or the train, and go by truck or jeep SW to *Concheño.* Here you can hire pack horses or walk the last leg to the falls (a five-hour walk).

THE FALLS: The river, a branch of the Río Mayo, follows a deep narrow channel, and for a hundred yards before the brink of the falls it runs straight as an arrow. At the cliff's edge the erosion has formed an arch from which the top has long since fallen. The Río Basaseáchic pours through this and shoots out in a spectacular 1010-ft. drop. At the bottom there are a series of jade green pools, and a precipitous path leads from the canyon rim down to the pools. The surrounding valley and pine forest is an area of magnificent solitude.

Barrancas de La Tarahumara. Mexico's breathtaking version of the Grand Canyon. The canyon is also known

[5] Two errors exist in the inscription. According to historians, Hidalgo was shot July 30, and his body was disinterred for removal to the capital in 1823.

as *La Barranca del Cobre* (Copper Canyon), after one of the three gorges that make up this spectacular canyon.

TO GET THERE: From Chihuahua take the Ferrocarril Chihuahua-Pacifico Railway to *Creel* (food and accommodations here). There is also a light-plane airstrip on the rim of the Barranca del Cobre. From Creel there are several routes to various of the 20 vast canyons in the Sierra de Tarahumara. Easiest to reach and the best lookout point is *El Divisadero,* about 28 miles from Creel. It can be done in a not-too-low-slung car, though a jeep is preferable.

THE CANYONS: Of the 20 or so great canyons in the sierras the most breathtaking are the complex of three, seen from *Divisadero* where there is a natural *mirador.* There at your feet lies a giant cut in the earth, some 4000 to 5000 feet deep and about 1 m. across. To the E in the opposite wall of the canyon are the entrances of three narrower, but equally deep canyons. These are: *La Barranca del Cobre* (the northernmost), the *Tarrveca Canyon* and, to the south, *El Cañon de Balojaque* (Urique Canyon). Of these, the first two have been thoroughly explored, the last, because of its sheer vertical walls and formidable torrent, is yet to be conquered. The complex of canyons, with side *barrancas* cover an area (extension) of slightly over 100 m. The rim or surface country ranges in altitude from 7000 to 9000 ft. It is broken into myriads of bluffs and cliffs liberally dotted with giant rocks, some balanced in delicate, weird ways. The ground is covered with crystallized volcanic ash, and the surface flora includes many varieties of cacti, forests of pine, cedar, oak, and juniper. The bases of the canyons are almost tropical. Stands of bamboo, oranges and exotic orchids are found there. Many of the Tarahumara Indians use the canyons as their winter dwelling place.

Of the many "grand" canyons in this region, only two can be navigated from top to bottom by car (jeep) — the remainder require pack equipment. Directly south of the Gran Barranca are two equally spectacular canyons and mining regions: *La Bufa* (75 m. S of Creel, via good but twisting mountain road), and *La Barranca de Batopilas,* reachable via a mining camp trail. *Batopilas,* a most picturesque settlement is famed for its *La Nevada* mine, a producer of so pure a virgin silver it almost needed no processing. The mine, now inoperative because of gases in the tunnels, brought a fortune to a colonial miner, Don Angel de Bustamante, who was made Marqués de Batopilas. At the turn of this century the same mine was exploited by an American engineer named Shepherd who cleared some $22,000,000 out of it.

These breath-takingly marvelous canyons are soon to become a Mexican National Park. There are plans to pave a highway to the canyon area and, eventually, establish hotel and cabin accommodations.

AREA SOUTH AND EAST OF CHIHUAHUA CITY: South and SE of Chihuahua City there are several towns of minor interest strung along the Central Highway. The most important vacation attraction is Lake Toronto (La Boquilla) near Ciudad Camargo.

Camargo, Chih. (officially called, Ciudad Camargo). Pop. 12,000. Alt. 3950 ft. On Central Highway, CN-5, 100 m. S of Chihuahua City.

Camargo (ka-MAR-go) was founded during the Mission period (around 1740) and was originally called Santa Rosalia in honor of the town's patron saint. It is an interesting old settlement which has become the busy center of a vast ranching and agricultural area. There are an important meat-packing plant, textile mills, and other industries in the town. Beginning September 4, and for 8 days, the lively Fiesta of Santa Rosalia is celebrated.

HOTELS AND RESTAURANTS: *Santa Rosalia Courts,* center of town on CN-45, Calle Irigoyen. First class, two-story motel with 33 rooms, air conditioning, good dining room, cocktail lounge. Rates: $50 MN dble, EP. *Hotel Baca,* Guerrero and Abasolo. A fairly well-kept hotel, 35 rooms, so-so restaurant, bleak bar. Some air conditioning. Rates: EP, from $45 MN dble. *Motel Baca,* on highway outside of town. 60 units, some air conditioned. Not too appealing. Rates: EP from $40 MN dble.

DIRECTORY: *Bank* — Banco de Chihuahua, Guerrero and Comonfort. *Bus lines* — Autotransportes Chihuahuenses, Irigoyen and Libertad. Tel. 19. Transportes Monterrey, on Irigoyen, no number. Tel. 1-53. Autobuses Flecha Roja, Irigoyen and Comonfort. *Auto repairs* — Casa Baca (Ford), Guerrero 708; Comercial del Río Conchos (GM), Av. Obergón and 7th.

ENVIRONS OF CAMARGO: About 3 m. from town there are two well-known hot springs — *Ojo Caliente* and *Ojo de Jablali.* Long before the conquest these springs were considered important curative centers by the Indians. Apache tourists from the SW U.S., made regular peregrinations to bathe in these sulphur spas.

La Boquilla (Lake Toronto), 18 m. SW of Camargo via fine paved highway. The lake, one of the largest in Mexico, is formed by waters of the Conchos River, backed up behind La Boquilla Dam. Though officially called Toronto, when the lake was stocked with fish from Toronto, Canada, its popular name remains *La Boquilla.* From the 40 m. long lake, and nearby *Colima Lake,* fishermen take black bass, bluefish, perch, and catfish. The spring months are considered best for fishing. Small boats and launches can be rented by the day. Best fishing is several miles above the dam. The lake is closed to fishing during July and August. At Lake Colima's Club de Esquies boats and equipment can be rented for water skiing.

Hidalgo de Parral, Chih. Pop. 40,000. Alt. 5450. An old mining town on CN-45, 198 m. S of Chihuahua City.

HOTELS AND RESTAURANTS: *El Camino Real Motel.* 1 m. SE on highway. 23 units. A comfortable, clean establishment. Fair restaurant. Rates: EP $35 MN to $55 MN, dble. *Hotel Burciaga,* Coronado and 20th. Commercial type hotel. Moderate rates.

DIRECTORY: *Bank* — Banco Nacional de México, Ojinaga 10. Banco de Londres y México, Plaza Hidalgo 9. *Bus lines* — Transportes Chihuahuenses, Maclovio Herrera 87. Tel. 2-75; Auto Transportes Santa María del Oro-Parral, Plaza Morelos 10. Tel. 7-41 (to the nearby mining towns). *Railway* — National Railways of Mexico. Tickets at depot. *Auto repairs* — Automotriz Parralense, (GM), Ramírez 10; Casa Ramos (Ford), Francisco Moreno 1.

THE TOWN AND ENVIRONS: Parral (pah-RAL) is a somewhat picturesque and relatively primitive town, founded in 1631, and once the capital of the state. Early in the 1600s the town had over 7000 men, mostly Indians, working the rich mines — *Cerro de la Cruz* and *La Negrita* — and wealth poured from the region into the coffers of the Spanish kings. Napoleon's troops occupied the town during the French intervention. On the *Cerro de la Cruz* there are the remains of an old fort of that period.

The famed cowboy-bandit and revolutionary general, Pancho Villa, retired in this district and was assassinated in Parral. His rather ornate city house, now occupied by shops and a grocery store (La Villa de Grados), is a landmark in the town.

There are several buildings of interest in the town: the *Palacio Municipal,* on the central plaza, with a curious clock tower surmounting the N corner of the building. The interior patio and garden are nice. *La Parroquia* (Parochial Church), flanking one side of the pretty plaza, and dating from 1710, is noted for its beautifully carved Churrigueresque altars. The remainder of the interior is rather garish. A curious display in glass cases on one side of the nave is quite startling — one is of Christ, crowned with thorns; the other is of Christ, clad in a woman's white undergarment edged with cheap lace. The latter peers out from a dingy prison with compassionate wistfulness. *La Iglesia de la Virgen del Rayo,* (Church of the Virgin of Thunderbolts), on a deserted square across the river from the town center, is the most noteworthy in town. It is the favorite of the Indians who refer with pride to its history and the stoicism of its founder. Begun in 1690 and completed in 1710, it was largely paid for by an Indian miner who every Saturday brought a gold ingot with which to pay the workmen. No one knew the source of his supply. When the church was finished the taciturn Indian was hailed before the Spanish *commandante* of the district and told he must divulge the secret of the hidden mine; he refused and was tortured to death. From that date the mine was "lost" and it still remains undiscovered. The church itself is quaint. It is minus a dome, has a three-storied tower, curious old buttresses and a crumbling façade adorned with graceful Tuscan columns. One entire end of the single nave interior is filled with a curious old altar, elaborately Churrigueresque in style. A number of figurines stand in railed niches and produce the effect of a gigantic cuckoo clock with figures ready to come forward and announce the time.

Iglesia de Nuestra Señora de Fatima (Our Lady of Fatima Church), a recently built church in which pieces of ore — gold, silver, manganese, zinc, copper, antimony — taken from all the regional mines, are imbedded in the structure. Even the individual seats are made of ore. . . . The house at Calle de Mercaderes 30 is noted as the stopping place of Benito Juárez, when en route to Paso del Norte. . . . More interesting is the *Palacio de Pedro Alvarado,* an incredibly ornate residence (overlooking the river), with a good façade, ornate carvings and Corinthian columns, a sumptuous chapel and a fine onyx stairway. The fabulous building was put up by a poor miner who became a multimillionaire (La Palmilla Silver Mine), and who gained notoriety many years ago by offering to pay the national debt.

To the W of Parral, about 24 m. via paved roads, are the mining towns of *San Francisco del Oro* and *Santa Barbara.* For a half a century before the Pilgrims reached Plymouth Rock these towns were great mining centers, and at present they are still very active. Santa Barbara, lying in a broad hill-girt valley, was founded in 1547 by the Spanish miners Juan de Velasquez, Miguel Iturralde, and Venancio de Castro who discovered gold there. In 1580 it became the seat of the government for the territory of Nueva Vizcaya (New Biscay) which then comprised the present states of Chihuahua, Coahuila, Sonora, as well as Texas, New Mexico, Arizona, Colorado, and California. A number of Americans are connected with the mining companies in the district.

THE DURANGO-ZACATECAS AREA

This section of the North Central region of Mexico is comprised of the states of Durango and Zacatecas. It lies directly S and SE of neighboring Chihuahua — is bordered on the W by the states of Sinaloa and Nayarit, to the S by Aguascalientes and Jalisco, and to the E by San Luis Potosí and Coahuila. The area covered is 76,705 sq. m. (Durango — 48,250 sq. m.; Zacatecas — 28,454 sq. m.). The total population, about equally divided between the two states is 1,564,687. The principal industry of the region is mining, followed by cattle raising, cotton, and in Zacatecas, corn and grapes.

VACATION HIGHLIGHTS: This area has never been very important, touristically speaking. The only unique and attractive city is Zacatecas. In the vicinity of Zacatecas there are several important archaeological zones — *Chalchihuites, La Quemada, Las Ventanas* and *El Teul.* A stop at least one of them is worthwhile.

The Central Highway, CN-45, crosses the region from N to S linking the principal cities, as does the central route of the Mexican National Railways. Aeronaves de México offers air service between C. Juárez, Chihuahua, Durango, and Mexico City. A new East-West highway, linking Monterrey to the Pacific Coast port of Mazatlán, CN-40, has one of the most spectacular scenic drives in the country. (See Index: Highway Routes.)

NORTHERN SECTION — STATE OF DURANGO:

Durango, Dgo. Pop. 60,000. Alt. 5315 ft. Capital of state of the same name. A fair overnight stop for travelers. The city has almost no other attractions.

HOTELS AND RESTAURANTS: *Posada Durán,* Av. 20 de Noviembre 506, Pte. near the plaza. 17 rooms, cocktail lounge and good dining room. Colonial in style, this is the most comfortable and well-run hostel in town. Friendly atmosphere. Rates: EP $50 MN to $80 MN dble. *Hotel San Luis,* Bruno Martínez 109 Nte. 64 rooms, fairly well-kept, 30 units air conditioned. Bar, passable dining room. Rates: EP $35 MN to $70 MN dble. *Campo Mexico Courts.* Modern court with 48 units, well furnished. Atmosphere somewhat chilly. Also, skip the restaurant. Rates: EP $60 MN to $80 MN. Other hotel, *viajero* in style, rates ranging from $40 MN up, dble. *Hotel Elizondo,* Av. Constitución 203 Nte. *Hotel Roma,* 20 de Noviembre 750 Pte. *Hotel Casa Blanca,* Av. 20 de Noviembre 811, Pte.

DIRECTORY: *Banks* — Banco Nacional de México, Constitución 312 Nte. *Bus lines* — Transportes Chihuahuenses, Pasteur 205 Sur. Tel. 23-07; Transportes Estrella Blanca, Pasteur 205 Sur; Flecha Roja, Madero 415 Sur, Tel. 20-16; Autobuses Blancos, Pasteur 205 Sur (route to Torreón and Saltillo.) *Airline* — Aeronaves de México, Constitución 175, Nte. Tel. 23-13. *Railway* — Mexican National Railways, tickets and information at depot.

THE CITY AND ENVIRONS: The city, on the margin of Río Tunal, stands on a level plain formed by the foothills of the Sierra Madre Occidental Mountains. Its name is derived from the old Basque city in Spain, the home of Don Francisco de Ibarra, who founded this Durango in 1563.

Previous to Ibarra's expeditions into this region, Spanish explorers combed the area for mineral wealth. One

Gines Vasquez de Mercado, searching for silver in the Durango district, came upon a disappointing (to him) iron mountain.[6] On the return journey Vasquez de Mercado's party was ambushed by Indians at *Sombrerete* and he died before reaching his base. It remained for Francisco de Ibarra to locate the silver wealth of the area and establish the present city.

The climate of Durango is generally pleasant to cool in winter, with only a short spell of hot weather in early summer. It is noted for its clear skies and sunshine, which has made it a favorite "location" for Hollywood and Mexican movie companies. During very hot weather the city is sometimes plagued by deadly white scorpions. It is one of the few areas in the country where scorpion stings, though painful in most instances, may prove fatal unless treated.

Sightseeing attractions in the city are limited. There is the Plaza Principal, with its attractive gardens and unattractive bandstand. Facing the plaza is the *Cathedral,* a massive Tuscan-style structure, considered by some to be one of the finest in the country. It was begun in 1695 and completed in 1750, therefore reflects a number of different decorative motifs and periods.

The country W and NW of Durango City is noted for its excellent hunting — bear, deer, and big cats, including jaguar. Arrangements can be made for hunting trips through your hotel manager. NW of the city, the country as far as *Tepehuanes* is reachable via a branch line of the Mexican National Railways. Daily trains from Durango, leave 8:20 A.M., arrive at Tepehuanes roughly around 3:30 P.M. From there trails lead on into the Tepehuane Indian country (see Index: Tepehuane Indians).

AREA NE OF THE CITY OF DURANGO: At the NE border of the State of Durango is a section called LA LAGUNA REGION, the site of a large-scale reclamation, resettlement, and co-operative farming project. It is one of Mexico's principal cotton-raising districts. In the Durango part of this section the city of *Gómez Palacio,* Pop. 45,872, is a picturesque old town on the Monterrey-Mazatlán Highway, CN-40.

SOUTHERN SECTION—STATE OF ZACATECAS: Best base from which to explore this district is from the city of Zacatecas, itself worth a touristic pause.

Zacatecas, Zac. Pop. 24,300. Alt. 7377 ft. Capital of state of the same name, and picturesque colonial mining city.

HOW TO GET THERE: *Road* — On Central Highway, CN-45, 880 m. S of El Paso, Texas; 399 m. NW of Mexico City. *Via railway* — Central Line of the Mexican National Railways. *Via bus* — (from El Paso or from Mexico City) Autotransportes Chihuahuenses.

HOTELS AND RESTAURANTS: *Zacatecas Courts,* S edge of town on highway. 16 units, new and modern. Dining room and good room service. Rates: EP $50 MN to $90 MN dble. Tel. 1-15. *Hotel Ruiz,* Av. Juárez 55. 43 rooms, good dining room, bar, pool, tennis courts. An old-fashioned hotel, but pleasant. Rates: EP from $35 MN dble. Tel. 1-22. Other hotels: *Hotel Condesa,* Av. Juárez 5; *Hotel Reyna Cristina,* Av. Hidalgo 7. *Restaurant Los Petates,* Juárez 22. Good Mexican fare.

DIRECTORY: *Bank* — Banco Nacional de México, Av. González Ortega 7. *Bus lines* — Autotransportes Chihuahuenses (bus terminal being moved, no present listing). Omnibus de Mexico, Flecha Roja, Independencia 76. Tel. 2-74. *Railway* — Mexican National Railway, information and tickets at depot. *Auto repairs* — Automotriz de Zacatecas, (Ford), Av. Torreon 56; Casa Lopez (GM), Plaza Independencía 90.

THE CITY AND ENVIRONS: Zacatecas (sah-kah-TEH-kas: from the Aztec *zacatl,* grass or hay, and *tlan,* place; the Indian tribe inhabiting the area were called *Zacatecos*) lies in a narrow ravine at the foot of the *Grillo* (Cricket) and *Bufa Mountains.* The city is a refreshing sight after traveling over dusty plateaus, especially for travelers coming from the N for the approach is from above, by a winding mountain road. The entry into town is eye-filling, as the highway runs through high arches of an aqueduct built in the early 1700s, and passes through the pleasant, small Parque Enrique Estrada.

The houses of the city are packed in a gulch or perched on the slopes, and the steep streets and lanes — many of them pieced out with stone stairs — are medieval in aspect and highly picturesque. Surface water is scarce and, though modern water distribution is replacing the old, a great deal of the water is still brought up from deep, flooded mines in huge, dripping horsehide sacks. Up and down the quaint streets go leather-clad *aguadores,* or water-carriers who obtain the precious liquid from public fountains and sell it from house to house.

Although Zacatecas is surrounded by cattle and agricultural country, it remains primarily a mining city, and has been all its history. Discovering the potential wealth of the region, the Spanish, following a few decisive skirmishes with the natives, quickly added it to the crown. The capital city was founded in 1548 by Juan de Tolsa, Cristóbal de Oñate, Baltazár Temiño de Bañuelos, and Diego de Ibarra. By 1588 the town was given the resounding title of "Very Noble and Loyal City of Our Lady of Zacatecas." It proved loyal by funneling a stream of silver to Spain that could scarcely have been exceeded by a modern pipeline. Between 1548 and 1832 the district yielded 667,348,299 pesos in silver bullion — at a time when the peso was on par with our dollar. Many of the mines are still being worked. Visitors can procure permits to tour them.

Zacatecas has numerous important architectural treasures of the seventeenth and eighteenth centuries. Noteworthy is the *Cathedral,* S side of the Plaza or Jardín Hidalgo. The Cathedral, begun in 1612, occupies the site of an earlier (1559) parochial church. The present edifice was finally completed in 1752 and dedicated to Our Lady of the Assumption. Its construction was paid for by a tax levied on various of the city mines. In Spanish Colonial days the Cathedral was a blaze of gold and silver candelabra, costly vestments, and beautiful pictures brought from Europe — much of which vanished during the reform period and in later revolutions. Time and bad taste in its interior decorations have ruined it for the student of art, but the portico — one of the most elaborate and richly carved in the country — remains a fine showpiece. The side entrance is less exhuberant than the front, belonging to another period.

A block W of the plaza is the handsome *Church of Santo Domingo,* originally the Jesuit church known as *La Compañía.* It is an admirable example of the Spanish Baroque, peculiarly the style of the Jesuits. Its interior is quite well preserved (except for the destruction

[6] *El Cerro del Mercado* (Iron Mountain) is a helmet-shaped hill of colossal proportions rising some 700 ft. above the surrounding plain, just N of the city. It is composed almost totally of iron in different stages of oxidization. The ore is hematite, specific gravity 4.658. Each cubic foot weighs approximately 291⅓ lbs. It is said to be from 55 to 67 per cent pure, and the estimated weight of the mass is 600,000,000 tons.

of the original magnificent high altar with its Churrigueresque *reredos*). The fine old murals and the excellent lateral altars remain intact.

Within walking distance of the center of the city there are several other attractive colonial buildings — the *Theatre of Calderón*, the *Municipal Palace*. In the plaza there is an exceptionally good equestrian statue in bronze of General Ortega, a military hero. On the summit of *El Cerro de La Bufa*, NE edge of town, one obtains a fine view of the city and its mountain setting. This hill is crowned by *La Capilla de los Remedios*, also called *El Patrocinio*, an interesting chapel containing an image of the Virgin to whom the Indians attribute miraculous healing powers.

EXCURSIONS OUT OF ZACATECAS: **Guadalupe, Zac.** Pop. 6083. On the Central Highway, just south of Zacatecas. A tile- and mosaic-manufacturing village. The chief attraction of the place is the Franciscan monastery, the *Convent of Nuestra Señora de Guadalupe*, considered one of Mexico's important colonial monuments. The cruciform structure, with two fine *cimborios*, a pair of quaint belfries and some handsomely decorated chapels merit a visit. The *Colegio* was founded in 1707 by Fray Antonio Margil de Jesus. The present church dates from 1721. The *Capilla de Purísima* has some ornate gold-leaf decorations. There is also a library with a collection of rare hand-printed books, as well as some valuable paintings of the colonial period — notably a fine *Last Supper* by Antonio de Torres (1720). The convent is now a national museum. Hours, daily, 9 A.M. to 1 P.M., 3 to 5 P.M. Admission 2 pesos.

La Quemada or **Chicomoztoc Ruins** (Archaeological Zone). About 28 m. S and W of Zacatecas. Just N of the city an all-weather road branches off of CN-45, to Villanueva, Zac.

THE RUINS: A fortified city, abandoned long before the coming of the Spaniards in 1535. It stands on a terraced hill and somewhat resembles Monte Albán or Xochicalco. Unlike many of the ancient cities in the tropics which have been overgrown and broken by vegetation, the terraces and buildings of La Quemada have been remarkably preserved by the dry air of the region. Architecturally the ruins do not compare with those of *Palenque* (Chiapas) or *Chichén Itzá* (Yucatán), yet the traveler stands amazed at their solidity.

The remains of streets, dwellings, temples, towers, and storehouses extend over a vast area. The majority of the houses are constructed of a hard stone held together by cement made of a peculiar red clay and corn husks. Water still flows from some of the ancient fountains and forms the only active principal in this silent city. In a letter written by one of the Spanish explorers in 1535, we read: "They discovered a large depopulated city of sumptuous edifices built of stone and lime. The streets and plazas were wide, well laid out and of imposing appearance. A quarter of a league from the city stood a *cué* [tower] with a fine *calzada* [roadway] leading therefrom to another tower standing at some distance. There were four towers in all, with their connecting *calzadas*, and they guarded the four corners of the city. In the center was a *cué* of great height, and fronting it was a fountain pouring forth a stream of limpid water pretty to behold."

The ruined city is divided into three parts: *La Ciudadela* (the Citadel), *El Palacio* (Palace), and *El Templo* (Temple). One of the structures includes a wide hall containing round columns, built of small stone slabs in many courses. These columns, which may once have supported a roof, were most likely covered with stucco. Pottery found among the ruins is beautifully finished and resembles cloisonné.

In the region hereabout, it is believed that La Quemada is the legendary Chicomoztoc or "Seven Caves," the place from which (according to mythological legends) the Náhoa tribes, including the Aztecs or Mexicas originally came. According to some versions they were supposed to have emigrated from their original home (Aztlán), thought to be somewhere near the Gulf of California, in 1160. Legend has it that after crossing the Colorado River into Arizona, they founded there a city called Casas Grandes (Big Houses), the ruins of which still remain. Continuing their peregrination southward, they were supposed to have established another Casas Grandes in present-day Chihuahua (see Index). In time this stronghold was abandoned and the restless tribe moved westward toward Culiacan (then Hueicolhuacan), capital of the State of Sinaloa. There they remained three years, reportedly leaving behind them, when they again took up their march, a huge statue of Huitzilopochtli (Aztec god of war, similar to the one in the National Museum). Traveling toward the southeast, they came to the Durango area, where they met a tribe who they attacked and defeated. They remained but a short time on the plains of Chimalco, from which point they moved on to Chicomoztoc (La Quemada). Legend has it that in time six tribes branched out from this stronghold like bees swarming from a hive. These were said to be the Chichimecas, the Tepenecas, Colhuas, Chalcas, Tlahuicas and Tlaxcaltecas. The Aztecs, or Mexica, remained. Here the latter dwelt for nine years, then abandoning the fortress city, they zigzagged across the country, always trending southward, until, in 1196, they reached the famous Toltec city of Tollan (Tula). They conquered the Toltecs, drove them from the country, then spread over the Valley of Mexico.

Imaginative, but hard-headed archaeologists disagree with the legend, of course. They point out that the fortress-like characteristics of La Quemada indicate a long occupancy by a people who were perfectly integrated politically, socially, culturally, and economically, and were not just bumming around the country *à la* Aztecs. From the incomplete data available it is believed that La Quemada had its origins in the Teotihuacán culture (see Index), fourth to sixth centuries A.D.

OTHER ARCHAEOLOGICAL SITES: To the NW near the Zacatecas-Durango state line and directly S of the railway town, *Súchil*, reachable only by mining trail, lies the ruins of another fortress-like city, *Chalchihuites*, Zac. Its characteristics and period are the same as of La Quemada. A visit there is strictly off-trail, calling for the services of a guide. To the SW of the city of Zacatecas, on the same road that leads to La Quemada, but some 100 m. beyond (and the road deteriorates badly) are: *El Teul*, ruins near the village of *Teul de Gonzáles Ortega*, and *Las Ventanas*, ruins near the village of *Juchipila*. Neither of the sites are quite as extensive as La Quemada, nor has there been much investigation and restoring done at them.

THE COAHUILA COUNTRY

In this, the easternmost part of Mexico's North Central region, we include all of the State of Coahuila and a wedge of northern San Luis Potosí served by the Piedras Negras-Mexico City Highway. Excluding the San Luis Potosí bit, the area covers some 914,059 sq. miles, with a population of somewhat over 58,800. The climate as well as history, flora, and fauna are similar to that of neighboring Chihuahua. The State of Coahuila is separated from the United States on the north by the Río Grande. It is the third largest state in the Mexican

Republic. Cattle raising and agriculture (wheat, cotton, corn, and sugar cane) are predominant. There is also a large mining center at Real de Catorce. The country's largest iron and steel mill, Altos Hornos de México, is located at Monclova.

VACATION HIGHLIGHTS: Unless you are a motor or pack-mule explorer in search of picturesque mining towns or rock specimens, there is little in this section to attract a vacationist. Texans often make the capital city, Saltillo, a vacation objective because of its mile-high crisp climate, and to admire some of the colonial buildings that dot the city.

Piedras Negras, Coah. Pop. 27,590. Alt. 792 ft. One of the four principal tourist points of entry from the U.S. into Mexico. It stands across the Río Grande from Eagle Pass, Texas. Piedras Negras (pee-AY-dras NAY-gras — black stones) is fast becoming one of the most popular gateways into the republic. Motorists are attracted both by the courtesy and consideration of the Mexican border officials (often absent at other border stations), and by the excellent Eagle Pass to Mexico City Highway, CN-57. (See Index: Highway Routes.)

From the U.S. side, the river is crossed via the International Bridge. Toll fees: car and driver, 20 cents; passengers, 5 cents each.

Mexican immigration and customs offices are at the Mexican side of the bridge. Visitors not planning to go beyond Piedras Negras need no tourist card. At present the customs sheds and offices are somewhat primitive for this port is only newly opened. Both Mexican and U.S. offices are open daily, 24 hours.

Piedras Negras is typical of border towns — the souvenir shops offering pseudo-native arts and crafts, the bars, a few night clubs, etc. At the moment there is an atmosphere of a boom town for oil has recently been struck in the area.

RESTAURANTS: *Modern Café,* Allende 34 Ote. An excellent restaurant specializing in Mexican food. Good bar, dancing. Open noon to after midnight.

DIRECTORY: *U. S. Consulate* — Hidalgo Sur 56. Tel. PN 34. *Auto repairs* — Adalberto Santos (Chrysler), Av. Hidalgo 48; Auto Camiones (Ford), Av. E. Carranza 8; Mercantil Piedras Negras (GM), Zaragoza Sur 108. *Banks* — Banco de Londres y Mexico, Allende 55 Ote. Banco Nacional de México, Morelos and Allende. *Insurance* (car) — La Azteca, Terán 10, Pte., or at Sanborn's Travel Agency in the Eagle Hotel, Eagle Pass. *Bus lines* — Autobuses Anáhuac, Allende 44 Ote. Tel. 82 (route: Piedras Negras to Mexico City via CN-57).

Monclova, Coah. Pop. 19,048. Alt. 1935 ft. On CN-57, 157 m. S of Piedras Negras. Monclova (mon-CLO-va) was capital of Coahuila when Texas was part of that state, early 1800s. The town is in the center of a vast stock raising region and is also Mexico's principal steel mill town. The great Altos Hornos de Mexico mills are to the E of highway. There is only one good hotel here — *Hotel Buena Vista,* on hill one block W of highway, N end of town. Newly opened chrome-style hotel, all air conditioned. 80 rooms, nicely appointed. Bar. Dining room comfortable, food best available. Rates: EP $100 MN dble.

Saltillo, Coah. Pop. 69,874. Alt. 5145 ft. Capital and leading industrial city of the State of Coahuila. Also, the most interesting tourist stop in this area.

HOW TO GET THERE: *Via highway* — (From Eagle Pass-Piedras Negras) CN-57. (From Laredo or McAllen, Texas, drive to Monterrey, N.L., take CN-40 west from Monterrey to Saltillo. *By air* — Aeronaves de México. *By bus* — there is almost hourly bus service connecting Saltillo with Monterrey, McAllen, Laredo, Eagle Pass, and Mexico City. (See DIRECTORY for lines listed.) *Railway* — trains of the Mexican National Railways connect Saltillo with Piedras Negras, Monterrey and Laredo, and Mexico City. The de luxe once-a-day *Aguila Azteca* train from Laredo to Mexico City passes through Saltillo (S bound) at 1:25 A.M.

HOTELS: *Motel Estrella,* 2½ m. E on CN-40. Nice new motel with 24 units, pleasant grounds, pool, cocktail lounge, fair dining room. Rates: EP $70 MN, dble. Tel. 3-67-42. *Hotel Arizpe Saenz,* on Victoria 216, center of town. A charming, old, colonial-style hotel and still the most satisfying in the city. 56 rooms, cocktail bar, pretty flower-filled patios. The dining room, sometimes disappointing in the past, has improved greatly and can be well recommended. Rates: EP $70 MN to $100 dble. Tel. 3-80-00. *El Paso Courts,* E on CN-40. Fair motel, 15 rooms. No dining room. Rates EP from $50 MN dble. *Motel Huizache,* E edge of city on CN-40. 20 rooms, some new. The older ones should be skipped. Pool. Restaurant. Rates: EP from $50 MN dble. *Hotel de Avila,* a new, small, but nicely kept *viajero-type* hotel overlooking the market plaza. Rates: EP from $30 MN dble. *San Luis,* Abbot and Pablo Flores. 43 rooms, *viajero* clientele. Rates: EP from $40 MN dble.

RESTAURANTS: For a popular resort city Saltillo is sadly lacking in good restaurants. Best bets are the *Hotel Arizpe-Saenz* and the *Estrella Courts.*

DIRECTORY: *Banks* — Banco Nacional de México, Allende and Ocampo; Banco Mercantil de Monterrey, Allende and Ocampo. *Car repairs* — Automotriz Americo (Dodge), Obregón 110 Nte; Autos Santa María (Ford), Oaxaca and Carretera Matamoros. *Bus lines* — Autobuses Blancos (Saltillo-Torreón), Lerdo de Tejada and Allende. Autobuses El Aguila (Saltillo-Piedras Negras), L. de Tejada and Allende; Transportes del Norte (Mexico City to Laredo via Saltillo), Cardenas 504 Pte. Tel. 23-23. Transportes Monterrey-Saltillo (Routes to Monterray, Torreón and Durango), Padre Flores 121. Tel. 9-16. Autobuses Anáhuac (Routes to Mexico City, Piedras Negras, Monterrey), Allende 17 Nte. Tel. 14-00. *Railway* — Ferrocarriles Nacionales de México, tickets and reservations at the station.

THE CITY AND ENVIRONS: Saltillo (sahl-TEE-yo, meaning, Little Falls) was founded in 1575 by an expedition led by Captain Francisco Urdiñola. The Spanish were forced to drive off Indians occupying the area. To reinforce the settlement Tlaxcalan Indians from Central Mexico were sent to the new town. During the early seventeenth century it was a headquarters for further explorations to the north, and from 1824 to 1836 it was the capital of a huge territory which included Texas and the region up to the Colorado line. In 1827 it was named Leona Vicario, after a famed heroine of the War of Independence, born in the town. In its official title, the city still bears her name. During the Mexican-American War in 1847 the city was occupied by American troops, and one of the decisive battles of the war was fought at nearby Buena Vista.

The city is noted for its weaving industries, some of its handicrafts and for its clear, refreshing, dry climate which has made it a favorite health resort for people living in the lower, hot regions. The market in the center of town is of interest for the many kinds of local products and handicrafts sold there. Saltillo is famed throughout the country for the fine wool serapes woven here, though it must be said that the current output of these vivid rainbow-like blankets is often inferior in texture, quality, and subtle color-blending for which the turn-of-the-century serapes were celebrated.

THINGS TO SEE AND DO: A tour of the city can be done in about two hours, including a visit to the market and shops. If you are going farther south, then skip the silver factories and souvenir shops — their products are in unusually poor taste compared to what you will find deeper in Mexico. If you need a guide to show you the sights, get in touch with Señor Victor Carranza, a reliable, bilingual, licensed guide. His rates are $60 MN for 3 hours (in your car). His headquarters are at the Arizpe Saenz Hotel, or across the street at the Urdiñola Hotel.

The only building of architectural consequence in the city is the *Cathedral,* on the main plaza. Constructed between 1746 and 1801, it is one of the best examples of ecclesiastical architecture in northern Mexico, and the farthest north example of good Churrigueresque style. The elaborate façade with its twisted and decorated columns on the first story, its richly carved Churrigueresque "columns" above, and a wealth of carving over-all, is of interest to northerners accustomed to plain, almost puritan architecture.

Other civic points of interest are: *The Alameda,* a pleasing park containing an excellent equestrian statue of General Ignacio Zaragoza, a *Saltillense* who was the hero of the Battle of Puebla . . . *Palacio del Gobierno,* across the plaza from the Cathedral, a nondescript building guides take you into to view unexciting murals by artist Zarazona.

Flanking the highway to Monterrey are the buildings of the *State College of Coahuila* (often called the University). A popular Inter-American Summer School is conducted here (see Index).

FIESTAS: Saltillo's most famed fiesta occurs between August 1 and 6, in honor of the Santo Cristo de la Capilla. There are fireworks, regional Indian dances (the Matachines), bullfights, etc. According to tradition, on August 6, 1608, an unaccompanied donkey appeared in the streets of the town bearing a strange-appearing box. At one point the donkey broke under the weight of the box and collapsed. When people removed the box and opened it they found an image of Christ. Suddenly the donkey vanished. It was taken as a sign that a chapel should be built on the spot, which was done, and which started the annual fiesta.

EXCURSIONS FROM SALTILLO: *Buena Vista Battlefield,* a half-hour drive from the city. The now bucolic scene of one of the most sanguinary and decisive battles between U.S. soldiers under General Zachary Taylor, and the Mexicans under General Antonio Lopez de Santa Anna, in 1847. The American troops engaged numbered 4691; the Mexicans a reported 23,000. The former lost 264 killed and 450 wounded; the Mexicans lost 2500 killed and wounded. This appalling sacrifice of brave and willing men was entirely due to Santa Anna's inefficiency and poor generalship. The victory virtually ended the American operations in the north of Mexico and exercised great influence on the final issue of the American invasion of the republic.

Diamante Pass, 11 m. S of the city, gravel road. A beautiful but rough drive over an 8000 ft. high pass.

Monterrey, N.L. Mexico's NE Region key city, 1½ hours drive from Saltillo.

The area to the W of Saltillo offers no tourist attractions. The highway to Durango and Mazatlán, CN-40, cuts across this country, passing through the rich Laguna agricultural basin, of which the principal city is Torreón.

Torreón, Coah. Pop. 155,234. Alt. 3789 ft. An important mining and agricultural (cotton) center at the western border of Coahuila, on CN-40, about 180 m. W of Saltillo.

Torreón (to-reh-OAN) was founded in 1887 on a ranch known as El Coyote. It is the largest of the so-called "triplet cities" of the Federal Government's vast *La Laguna* cotton and wheat reclamation district. The other cities are *Gómez Palacio* and *Lerdo,* in the nearby State of Durango. Torreón is unattractive and dusty, but the region around when irrigated is marvelously productive.[7]

HOTELS AND RESTAURANTS: *Hotel Río Nazas,* Av. Morelos at Treviño, about 5 blocks from plaza. 160 rooms, hotel completely modern and air conditioned. Cocktail lounge, bar, coffee shop and nice dining room. First class in almost every way. Rates: EP $80 MN to $100 MN dble. Tel. 2-05-40. *Hotel Elvira,* at Morelos and Valdes Carillo, on plaza. A modern and comfortable all air-conditioned hotel, 120 rooms that are well appointed. Coffee shop, bar. A delightful collection of antique clocks grace the lobby. Rates: EP from $50 MN. Tel. 2-04-22. A very modest *viajero* hotel for the budget traveler is the *Naves,* 40 rooms. EP $35 MN and up, dble.

Restaurant Apolo Palacio, V. Carillo 258, facing plaza. Up-to-date restaurant, air conditioned, opened from 6 A.M. to 2 A.M. Cocktails, soda fountain, fairly good American and Mexican fare. *Restaurante de Doña Julia,* on Matamoros, quite good Spanish food. *Restaurant La Rambla,* Morelos and Cepeda, a popular short-order place.

DIRECTORY: *Bank* — Banco Nacional de México, Av. Hidalgo 1300 Pte. *Auto repairs* — Mercantil Automotriz de Torreón, Juárez and Carillo, Up-to-date general repair shop; Distribuidora de Automóviles, (Ford), Blvd. Torreón and Privada Rayon. *Airlines* — Aeronaves de México, Av. Juárez 1109 Pte. *Travel Agency* — Arro, S.A., Cepeda 450 Sur. *Bus lines* — Omnibus Mexico-Aguascalientes, V. Carrillo 459 Sur. Transportes del Norte, Zaragoza 229 Sur. Tel. 26-02.

South of Saltillo, with the exception of scenery, the only points of passing tourist interest are a few off-the-road mining settlements, especially *Real el Catorce* and *Matehuala,* a popular overnight stop. 83 m. S of Saltillo on CN-57, at *San Roberto* (gas station and poor restaurant on left) a very good paved road leads to the E high into the sierras to the fascinating colonial mining towns of *Galeana* and *Iturbide* in the State of Nuevo León (see Index). To Galeana it is about 31 m.

Matehuala, S.L.P. Pop. 34,500. Alt. 5000. A mining center and important tourist service stop on the Piedras Negras-Mexico City route, CN-57. The town itself is

[7] In the *Laguna* district cotton is perennial, and does not require to be planted oftener than once in ten years.

Although cotton (Spanish, *algodón)* is an indigenous plant it is one of Mexico's newest important export crops. When the Spaniards conquered Mexico they found the use of cotton textiles widespread among the Indians. According to Toltec legend, Quetzalcoatl, god of the air, grew a marvelous cotton for which modern textile manufacturers would give a fortune — it grew in all different colors, no dyeing was needed. Among the pre-Hispanic people cotton weaving was a highly developed craft. They made armor of quilted cotton which was proof against arrows which the Spanish finally adopted in lieu of the heavy armor. Many articles of apparel were made of a cotton woven of a fineness and almost the lustre of silk. Even today, some of the most exciting fabrics are handloomed in villages on primative looms.

¾ m. to the W of the highway. The newer motels and better restaurants and some garages are along the highway. The bus stops are in the town.

HOTELS AND RESTAURANTS: (all on highway, NE edge of town) *Motel Las Palmas,* 94 units, spacious grounds, pool, excellent dining room, cocktail lounge and bar, some units air conditioned. Good accommodations. Rates: EP $75 MN dble. Tel. 2. *Motel La Hacienda,* 16 units, a/c, pool, bar, excellent food, friendly atmosphere. Rates: $80 MN, dble. EP. *Motel Pedregal,* next to *Restaurant Pedregal,* just opened. First-class accommodations. Rates: from $60 MN up, dble. EP. The best restaurant in the area is in the *Motel Las Palmas.* Others, new and fair, are *Savoy, Restaurant Pedregal,* and the *La Hacienda* motel restaurant.

FIESTA: Each year on January 6 there is a popular fair and celebration honoring the Three Kings. Beginning December 28 there is an important fiesta honoring El Señor de Matehuala. This fiesta dates back to the 1550s when two Chichimeca chiefs were granted the right to settle in the area and found a town, then called San Francisco de Goathemala. Fiesta activities center around the Purísima Church, called by the citizens *"La Nave."* There are processions, Indian dancers, fireworks, cockfights, and all the trimmings.

To the West of Matehuala, via a rather difficult mountain road (about 3 hours' drive) lies *Real de Catorce, S.L.P.,* a picturesque mountain mining town, narrow twisting streets, etc. The population of the town, depending on the state of mining, has fluctuated from 40,000 to 6000 inhabitants. Real de Catorce can also be reached via the main line of the National Railways of Mexico, Laredo to Mexico City route. There is a flag stop at the village of Catorce, about 14 km. from Real de Catorce.

48. Northeastern Mexico

The northeastern region covers two states — Nuevo León and Tamaulipas — and, for touristic convenience, we include several Pan-American Highway towns in the eastern corner of the State of San Luis Potosí.

This region is one of the least interesting parts of Mexico, containing little of the superb scenery encountered farther south, and few of the dramatic contrasts that make the republic so exciting to visit. Except for the industrial center of Monterrey (the importance of which came only with the advent of the railway and modern highways), there is hardly an important or colorful city in the region. There are almost no great colonial landmarks, no reminders of the vivid pre-Hispanic cultures, and there is a paucity of colorful native arts and crafts which delight the eye elsewhere in the country.

The region, however, is intensely traveled. Its roads and tourist facilities are among the best in the republic. It is important as a kind of anteroom to Old Mexico, for several of the busiest and oldest gateways between the U.S. and Mexico dot its northern border. More than half of all the visitors who head deep into Mexico use it as a convenient corridor to pass through.

TRAVEL HIGHLIGHTS: The following are the principal points of vacation interest. The traveler going deeper into the country should be reminded that none are worth dallying over long when compared to the delights that lie farther south or west. *Monterrey,* a busy industrial city with some overtones of Old Mexico. *Tampico,* a somewhat drab, but popular (with Texans) deep-sea fishing port and resort. The lovely drive through tropical country on the Pan-American, south of Ciudad Valles. *El Salto Waterfalls.* The picturesque mining towns of *Galeana* and *Iturbide.*

The two best base-towns for excursions in this region are: northern part, *Monterrey;* southern part, *C. Mante* or *Tampico.* However, since accommodations are good in almost all the larger towns along the Pan-American Highway, almost any place will do.

PHYSIOGRAPHY OF THE REGION: The northern section of the region, lying along the Río Grande which separates it from the U.S. is hot, arid country covered with cactus and mesquite growths. The western and southern parts of the region, along the slope of the Sierra Madre Oriental are somewhat cooler in climate and receive more rainfall. The southernmost section includes lush tropical canyons and forests. This rather compact region is bounded on the E by the Gulf of Mexico; to the S by the states of Veracruz, and Hidalgo; to the W by San Luis Potosí and Coahuila; and to the N by the rich Texas Río Grande country.

In ratio to area, the population of the two principal states are relatively equal. Nuevo León, with 25,431 sq. m. has a population of 976,348 inhabitants; Tamaulipas, with 31,095 sq. m. has a population of 1,067,191.

The natural resources of the region include some of

the most important petroleum reserves in the country (Tamaulipas), some mining, rich citrus and sugarcane regions, cotton and henequén. Although the State of Nuevo León is less rich in natural resources than many of its neighbors, it nevertheless ranks as the nation's wealthiest region, outside of Mexico City and the Federal District.

FLORA AND FAUNA are extensive, the former ranging from desert plants in the northern districts to tropical forests and orchids in the south. The fauna includes mountain lions, wild boar, jungle cats, and a great variety of game and tropical birds.

HISTORY: Except for the Huasteca Indians (see below) the region seemed to have had no important pre-Hispanic history. The northern districts (Nuevo León) were penetrated by the Spanish, led by Captain Francisco de Urdiñola, during the 1560s. The southern and eastern areas proved a bit more difficult for the Spanish. Several early expeditions were repulsed by the Huastecans until (1523) a group under Gonzalo de Sandoval entrenched themselves in the region. The Provincia de Pánuco was founded, with Tampico as its capital, and the notoriously cruel Nuño de Guzmán was its first governor. In the 1840s the country was subjected to violent Apache and Comanche raids that created havoc as far east as Tampico. In 1846 the northern frontier became the initial battlegrounds of the Mexican-American war.

THE PEOPLE: The southern portion of the region was the homeland of the Huastecas, cousins of the Mayas. Although they spoke the Maya tongue, the Huastecas left almost no architectural or other traces of their culture comparable to those of their southern neighbors, the Totonacs. It is known that about 1400 A.D. the Tezcucans (from around present-day Texcoco) sent an expedition against Hauaxtecapán, with *Chila* (the capital, on the shore of *Lake Chairel*, where Tampico now stands) as the objective point. The Aztec Confederacy under Moctezuma conquered the region and forced the natives to pay an annual tribute.

Present-day Huasteca Indians (wahs-TEH-cah) have a number of settlements in southern Tamaulipas, the northern lowlands of Veracruz and especially in eastern San Luis Potosí. In many villages, notably in the San Luis Potosí area, the indigenous dances are most colorful. One of the principal dances is the flying pole *(volador)* dance which they refer to as *la danza del gavilán* because the performers dress as sparrow hawks, (for further description of this spectacle see Index). Another unique Huasteca dance is that of *La Malinche,* in which a youth dressed as a woman represents Cortés' mistress, and dances to a regional folk tune while enacting remorse and shame for having allied herself with the conqueror.

With the exception of the small and isolated Huastecan pockets the people of the northeastern region are much more progressive, and more influenced by U.S. ways than the Mexicans to the south of them. They have a reputation throughout the country as being the busiest, most industrious and shrewdest entrepreneurs in the republic.

AREAS NORTH OF MONTERREY — THE BORDER TOWNS

The three principal frontier ports of entry for this region are Nuevo Laredo, Reynosa, and Matamoros. Highways from the first two lead directly to Monterrey. The road from Matamoros avoids Monterrey and joins the Pan-American Highway further south at Ciudad Victoria.

Nuevo Laredo, Tamps. Pop. 58,000. Alt. 420 ft. A typical border town, the main eastern gateway into Mexico from the U.S. It is linked to Laredo, Texas, by International Bridge across the Río Grande. Toll Rates: car and driver, 20 cents; passengers, 5 cents each. Mexican and U. S. Customs and Immigration offices at the bridge are open 24 hours daily. Baggage must be inspected at the customs office.[1] Hand baggage of visitors coming in by train is inspected on the train.

Nuevo Laredo, founded by Spaniards in 1767, contains but little to interest the traveler and it should not be viewed as representative of the fascinating country to the south. There are the usual shops filled with debased craft arts, bars, night clubs of dubious repute, and a bullring where first-class *corridas* are occasionally held.

HOTELS AND RESTAURANTS: The most satisfactory are on the U.S. side of the river. In Nuevo Laredo the new *El Río Motel,* S edge of town, is de luxe, 60 suites, a/c, pool, good dining room, cocktail lounge. Rates: $100 MN dble EP. Tel. 16-17. *Hotel Plaza,* Calles Guerrero and Gonzáles, 64 rooms, is fair. Rates: EP from $40 MN dble. *Restaurante La Rocha* at Victoria and Matamoros. Fair. Cadillac Restaurant, center, excellent seafood and game.

DIRECTORY: *U. S. Consulate,* Ocampo and Madero. Tel. 5. *Bank* — Banco Nacional de México, Guerrero 222, and also near the customs. *Travel information and car insurance* — Sanborn's (in Laredo, Texas, at 1920 San Benardo). *Bus lines* — Transportes del Norte, Guerrero 118. Tel. 541. (Routes: first-class service to Mexico City via Pan American Highway, and via Monterrey, San Luis Potosí, Querétaro); Autobuses Flecha Roja, Ocampo 129, Tel. 152 (second class to Monterrey and Mexico City); Transportes Frontera, Ocampo 119. Tel. 242. (Route to Tampico.) *Airlines* — Mexicana de Aviacion (CMA), Hotel Plaza, Guerrero and González. Tel. 20-52. (Flights to Monterrey, Mexico City and Tampico.) *Railway* — Ferrocarriles Nacionales de Méx-

[1] For many years some Mexican Customs and Immigration officials stationed here have made a practice of creating phony difficulties or "irregularities" so as to put the bite *(mordida)* on incoming tourists, thus padding their pockets at the expense of both the visitor and the Mexican Government. Federal authorities are anxious to end such venial annoyances. Tourists encountering unusual rudeness, or unreasonable difficulties, during border crossings should report the incident in writing (include all details — hour, day, officials involved, etc.) to Department of Complaints, Departamento Federal de Turismo, Av. Reforma 35, Mexico, D.F. Or send it to *Terry's Guide.* We'll pass it on to the proper authorities.

ico, tickets and reservation at the passenger depot.[2] *Auto repairs* — Automotriz Laredo (Ford) Av. Guerrero and Dr. Mier; De León Autos (Chrysler), Dr. Mier and Heroes; Laredo Autos (GM), Victoria and Ocampo. *Customhouse broker* — Brennan & Co., Aldama & Arteaga. Tel. 9-59. Brennans will see that baggage and purchases that you send home separately are cleared through customs and expressed to your residence.

Reynosa, Tamps. Pop. 34,076. Alt 125 ft. A popular gateway into Mexico, on the Río Grande, opposite Hidalgo, Texas, and near McAllen. International Bridge toll: car and driver, 25 cents; each extra passenger, 10 cents. Both Mexican and U. S. Immigration and Customs offices opened daily, 24 hours.

The highway linking Reynosa to Monterrey is CN-40 (which also goes on to Durango and the Pacific Coast port of Mazatlán). CMA offers daily flights between Reynosa, Monterrey, and Mexico City.

DIRECTORY: *Hotel San Carlos,* Plaza Hidalgo 134. 44 rooms, poor compared to accommodations in McAllen. Rates: EP from $50 MN dble. *Auto repairs* — Automotriz Reynosa, Oaxaca and Matamoros Road. *Banks* — Banco Nacional de México, Hidalgo and Matamoros. *Bus lines* — Transportes Monterrey Cadereyta Reynosa, Quintana Roo 277. Tel. 55. (Route to Monterrey.) *Auto insurance and travel information* — Sanborn's, Jct. U.S. 83 and Tex-336, in McAllen, Texas.

Matamoros, Tamps. Pop. 46,000. Alt. 25 ft. Important port of entry from the Lower Río Grande Valley. Linked to Brownsville, Texas, by International Bridges. Toll: 20 cents per car and driver; passenger, 5 cents each. Customs and Immigration offices open 24 hours daily.

Matamoros (mah-ta-MOH-ros), settled in 1765, has had a vivid history, having been violently involved in the Texans' struggle for independence, as a battleground in the Mexican-American War and as an active supplier of contraband cotton to the Confederate forces during the American Civil war. The city was burned twice and pillaged several times. Mementos of Matamoros' flamboyant day can be seen in the old fort, the theater built during Maximilian's time, and the cathedral.

Situated in what is considered Mexico's richest cotton-producing region, the town is both progressive and wealthy, evidenced by the modern and lavish homes in the Colonia Jardín suburb. About 22 miles E via good road, is Washington Beach, a good wide white beach for swimming, though not as pleasant as Padre Island to the N on the U.S. side.

DIRECTORY: *U. S. Consulate* — Av. 3a and 5a, Colonia Jardín. Tel. 241. *Auto repairs* — Talleres Mendoza, Calle 6a and Vizcaya. *Bank* — Banco Nacional de México, Calle 6a and Gonzáles. *Bus lines* — Transportes del Norte, Obregón and Puente Nuevo. Tel. 7-77. (Routes to Ciudad Victoria, Monterrey, Mexico City.) Transportes Matamoros, Abasola and González, Tel. 4-17. (Route to Ciudad Victoria.) *Airlines* — CMA, Abasola 89, Tel. 30. Aerolineas Mexicanas, (daily direct flights to Mexico City.) *Hotel* — Hotel Ritz, 100 rooms, air conditioning, cocktail lounge, coffee shop. Fair. Two blocks from main Plaza. *Car insurance and tourist information* — Sanborn's, in El Jardín Hotel, Brownsville, Texas.

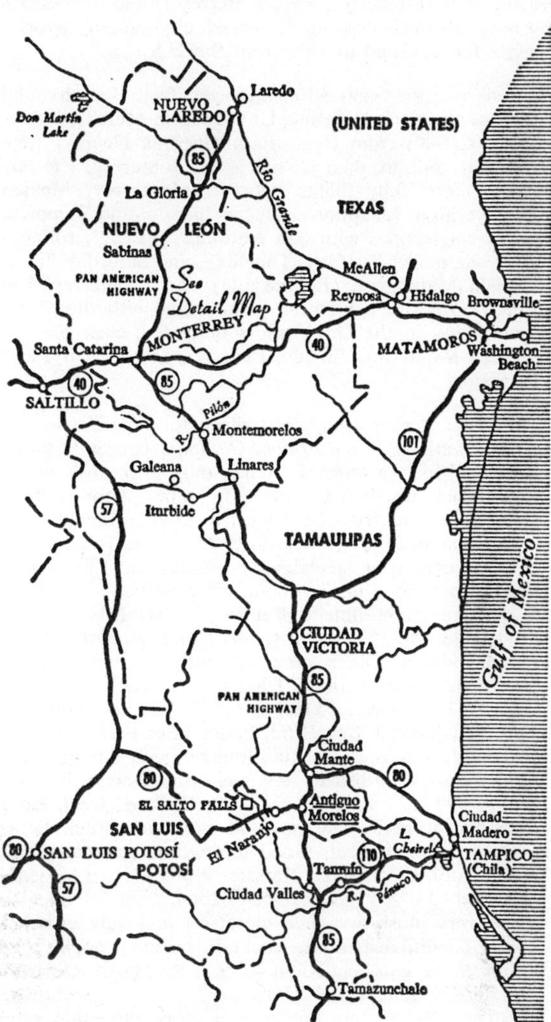

Don Martin Lake *(Presa Don Martín)* This large man-made lake, a favorite fishing spot for people from Laredo and Monterrey, actually lies in the State of Coahuila, close to the Nuevo León line. There is a road (not recommended) from *Sabinas, Coah.* to the lake, and another fair road that leaves the Pan-American, CN-85, at *La Gloria* (42 m. S of Nuevo Laredo). From La Gloria it is 72 m. E to the lake. For a few years the water level has been low and fishing was poor. It is reported, however, that the level is close to normal again and fish are biting. There are bait and boat facilities available. A small-plane landing strip is situated near the dam. For last-minute information regarding fishing and road conditions to the lake, write to Lic. Jesús Santos de la Garza, Republica Dominicanna 444, Monterrey, N.L.

[2] Trains of the Missouri Pacific Line make connections with the de luxe *Aguila Azteca* of the Ferrocarriles Nacionales. Pullmans from the U.S. are connected with the Mexican train so passengers need not transfer. Baggage inspection (hand pieces) occurs aboard the train.

The *Aguila Azteca* is almost the only comfortable train going to Mexico City. It is air-conditioned, has excellent dining service, bar and lounge. The Mexican equipment is Swiss-made. Fares from Nuevo Laredo to Mexico City — $104.40 MN. Pullman lower $59.50 MN, extra. Drawing room, $226.10 MN, extra. Trip to Mexico City takes 26 hours. Route and principal stops: Leaves *Nuevo Laredo* daily at 6:15 P.M. *Monterrey* Ar. 10:23 P.M., Lv. 10:55 P.M. *Saltillo,* Ar. 1:25 A.M., Lv. 1:50 A.M. *San Luis Potosí,* Ar. 9:07 A.M., Lv. 9:30 A.M. *San Miguel de Allende,* 1:11P.M. *Querétaro,* 2:57 P.M. Mexico City, 8:10 P.M.

Monterrey, N.L. Pop. 333,422. Alt. 1762 ft. Capital of the State of Nuevo León, Monterrey (mohn-tay-RAY) is both Mexico's leading industrial city and a favorite mecca for weekend tourists from the U.S.

HOW TO GET THERE: *Via highway:* from Laredo take the Pan-American Highway, CN-85; from McAllen (Reynosa), CN-40; from Eagle Pass (Piedras Negras) take CN-57 to Saltillo, then CN-40 E to Monterrey. *Via air:* CMA offers daily flights between Monterrey, Mexico City, Reynosa, Matamoros, Nuevo Laredo, and Tampico. Direct connections with San Antonio, Texas. Aerolineas Mexicana makes Tuesday, Thursday, and Saturday flights between Matamoros (Brownsville) and Monterrey. *Via bus:* Transportes del Norte (connecting with the Greyhound Line in the U.S.) offers daily first-class passage between Monterrey, Laredo, Reynosa, Mexico City, and Tampico.

HOTELS: Perhaps the nicest place to stay, if you can get reservations, is the *Posada Carápan,* corner Ocampo and Escobeda, downtown. It has only 5 rooms, all air conditioned, no dining room. The atmosphere is most picturesque and friendly. Rates: including breakfast, 2 bedroom suite $300 MN and $125 MN dble. Tel. 2-43-60. *Hotel Ambassador,* Hidalgo and Galeana. 120 rooms, cocktail bar, good dining room, air conditioned. Garage. A de luxe establishment. Rates: EP $60 MN to $115 MN, dble. Tel. 2-20-40. *Gran Hotel Ancira,* off of Plaza Hidalgo. Older hotel, recently refurbished, air conditioned (new section). Dining room, cocktail terrace. Garage. 250 rooms. Rates: EP $50 MN to $180 MN dble. Tel. 3-20-60. *Hotel Rio,* Padre Mier Pte. 89 rooms, air conditioned, pool, cocktail lounge, good dining room. Modern, well furnished, and well run. Rates: EP $75 MN to $90 MN dble. Tel. 2-21-90. *El Paso Autel,* Zaragoza and Ruperto Martínez. 60 unit auto-hotel. Some rooms air conditioned. Good dining room, bar service, heated pool. Free garage. Rates: EP $65 MN to $85 MN dble. Tel. 3-02-04. *Anfa Super Motel,* 6 m. N on CN-85. A very plush first-class motel set in lovely grounds. 89 air-conditioned units, cocktail terrace, pool, good dining room, excellent room service. Rates: EP $75 MN to $90 MN dble. Tel. 3-85-40.

Other good to fair hotels with more moderate rates are: *Motel Alamo,* two-story air-conditioned motel on CN-85. Has 38 rooms, snack bar. Rates: EP from $60 MN dble. Tel. 3-80-81. *Campo California,* on CN-85 N. Old courts, 84 units, a few air conditioned. Pool. Only fair. Rates: EP from $50 MN dble. *Apartamientos La Silla Courts,* on CN-85 south of town. 16 units, some air conditioned. Fair. Rates: EP from $40 MN dble. Tel. 2-54-30. *Monterrey Motel,* south on CN-85, modest 16 unit court. Rates: EP from $25 MN dble. Other budget-priced establishments are: *Hotel Amega,* north end of town (good); *Avenida,* uptown in the Madero district; *Continental,* on the plaza; *Favorita,* on Madero; *Yamallel,* in the Madero district.

RESTAURANTS AND NIGHT SPOTS: Monterrey, with its cosmopolitan atmosphere, has a number of well-established restaurants that strive to meet standards of "international cuisine," though not always with cheering success. Among the best: dining rooms at the *Hotel Ambassador,* the *Ancira,* and *Hotel Río.* Also, *La Luisiana,* on Plaza Hidalgo. Continental style, and sometimes quite good. Noon to midnight. *Santa Rosa Restaurant and Patio,* on Plaza Hidalgo, an atmospheric, old Mexico-style restaurant, air conditioned, lovely patio, *mariachi* music. Very good Mexican food, 6 P.M. to midnight. *Restaurant Mérida,* Zaragoza 522 Nte. Popular and fair Mexican and Yucatecan food. *Chipps,* at Escobeda and Morelos. A de luxe restaurant-supper club and bar. Fairly expensive. *Los Arcos Café,* across from Regina Courts on CN-85. Air conditioned, popular fairly good restaurant. 7 A.M. to midnight. *Holanda,* good coffee shop and ice cream parlor, on Zaragoza and Corregidora. The following cocktail bars and night spots recommended for mixed company. The *Barrio Bar and Lounge* in the Hotel Río. Pleasant atmosphere and music. *Posada Carápan,* Ocampo and Escobeda, charming patio, guitar serenades in the evening. *Calabria,* Av. Morelos 555 Pte. The best supper club. Good food, dancing from 8 P.M. Floor shows on (weekdays) 9:30, and midnight, (Saturdays) 9:30, and 11:30 P.M., and 1:30 A.M. *El Toro,* a new and pleasant night spot, just opened, back of Hotel Ancira.

DIRECTORY: *U. S. Consulate* — Juárez Sur 800. Tel. 3-06-50. *Banks* — Banco Nacional de México, Morelos 235 Sur; Banco Mercantil de Monterrey, Morelos and Zaragoza. *Car insurance and travel information* — Turismo Sanborn's, Hotel Ambassador. *Travel agents* — Sanborn's, Hotel Ambassador; Turismo Regiomontaño, Morelos 564 Ote. Tel. 2-79-13. *Auto repairs* — Automotores (GM), Av. Piño Suárez 351 Nte; Automotriz Monterrey (Ford), Piño Suárez and R. Martinez. Motores Generales, Av. Tecnólogico 982; Vehículos Nacionales, (Nash), Aramberri 615 Pte. *Airlines* — Aeronaves de México, Hidalgo and Escobedo, Tel. 2-30-43; CMA, Morelos and Parras, Tel. 2-07-18. *Bus lines* — Autobuses Anáhuac, Cuauhtémoc 1155 Pte. Tel. 2-33-36; Transportes del Norte, Juan Méndez Nte. 1355. Tel. 3-42-80; Transportes Frontera, Colegio Civil 1153 Nte. Tel. 2-03-58; Transportes Tamaulipas, Cuauhtémoc 1128 Nte. Tel. 3-44-80. *Railway* — Ferrocarriles Nacionales de México — tickets and reservations at depot, or through travel agents.

Churches — English-speaking Catholic Church, Padre Mier 1411 Pte. (Sunday Mass, 11 A.M.) Fr. Harold Coughlin . . . First Baptist Church, Aramberri 114 Ote. Tel. 2-57-67 . . . Trinity Methodist Church of Mexico, Washington 513 Ote. Tel. 2-26-12 . . . Union Church of Monterrey, Larralde and P. González Garza. *Doctors and Hospitals* — Dr. Pedro Rodríguez (G.P.), Zaragoza Nte. 326. Tel. 2-06-30. Dr. Eugenio Mireles Treviño (surgeon), Benavides Bldg., Piño Suárez and Matamoros. Tel. 3-24-40 ext. 117. Dr. Ramón Pera (pediatrics), Carranza Sur 723. Tel. 2-27-91. Dr. José Barragán (dentist), Matamoros Ote. 831. Tel. 3-40-79. Dr. Luis G. Cantu Morales (Int. Med.), Piño Suárez 446 Sur. Tel. 6-06-62. St. Vincent de Paul Hospital, S. Peña 106 Nte. Mexican Red Cross, Washington Pte. 505. Tel. 2-66-62. *Schools, Clubs, etc.* — American Society of Monterrey. Tel. 6-83-66. Benjamin Franklin Library, Juárez Sur. 800. Monterrey Foreign Club, Ocampo 754 and 756 Ote. American School Foundation of Monterrey, Missouri 555 Ote. Tel. 6-87-71. Instituto Tecnólogico de Monterrey, on Pan-American Highway. Tel. 3-21-60. Mexican-North American Institute of Cultural Relations, Hidalgo 317 Pte. Tel. 3-10-49. Pan-American School, Hidalgo 656 Pte. (grammar and high school).

TAXIS AND CARRIAGES: The fare for horse-drawn "calandrias" is $20 MN per hour. Monterrey's fame "Model A" taxis charge $8 MN per hour, $3 MN per trip in the downtown area. Regular taxis charge $15 MN per hour; for single trip, downtown area, $4 to $5 MN; to the brewery, $7 MN. Taxi with English-speaking guide, $25 MN per hour.

THE CITY: The city of Monterrey was a Spanish colonial outpost, named successively Santa Lucia and Ciudad

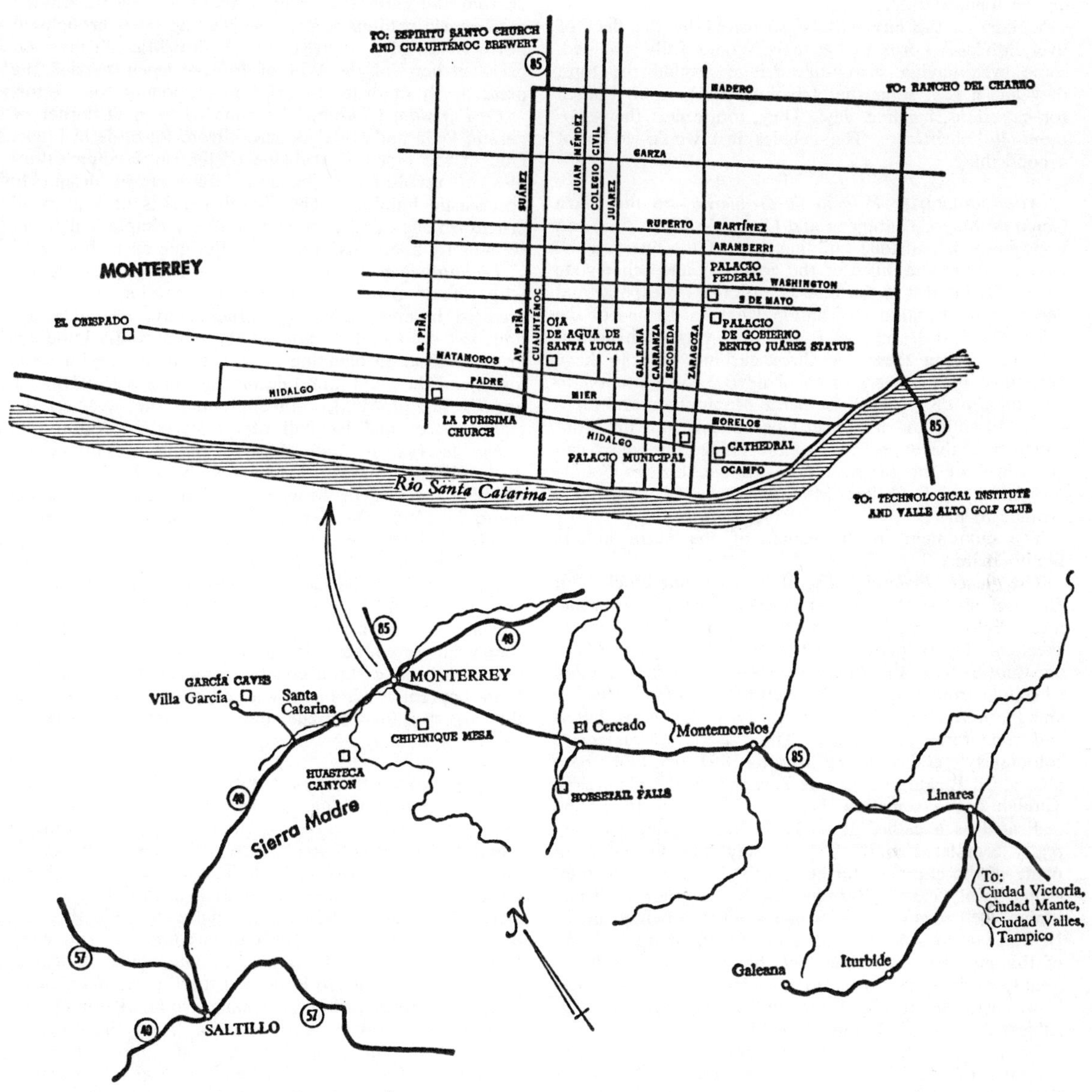

de Léon. In 1596 the Spanish Viceroy of New Spain, Don Gaspar de Zuñiga y Acevado, Count of Monterey, renamed the settlement, La Ciudad Metropolitano de Nuestra Señora de Monterey. The city remained an outpost and trading center until the coming of the railway, and later, highways — then it burgeoned. It has become the richest and busiest industrial city in the country. Although its population makes up a little more than one per cent of the national population, Monterrey pays ten per cent of the federal tax. It has Mexico's biggest brewery, turning out a million and a half bottles of beer a day. It has the country's largest glassworks, is one of the important steel centers, has hundreds of thriving industries, an up-to-date sewer and water system and some of the most modern housing in Latin America.

Despite this energetic development the echoes of Spanish colonial days still sound over Monterrey. It remains a city of narrow streets (almost all, one-way, to handle traffic)[3], there are age-old buildings, countless homes with flower-filled patios, and an interesting observance of many old customs.

The city lies in the mountain-girt valley of the Santa Catarina River. Due to its somewhat peculiar geographic position the climate is variable, temperatures ranging from above 90° F in the summer to 30° F during the short winter. Snows often fall in January and February. The most imposing landmarks are the nearby 5703 ft. *Cerro de la Silla* (Saddle Mountain), and *Cerro de la Mitra* (Miter Mountain), 7806 ft. The former is identified by its saddle-shaped crest. According to many Mexicans the mountain acquired its curious shape because of the thrifty nature of the *regiomontaños,* who are regarded as the Scots of their country. It is said that the saddle-

[3] Blue and white arrows fixed to the walls of buildings on every corner indicate traffic direction. On one-way streets the parking of cars is allowed only on the left side.

indent on the mountain got that way because of the feverish digging of a good citizen who had lost a nickel on the topmost ridge.

Visitors in the city will be surprised by the fleet of lively Model-A Fords used as taxis. Wonderfully groomed, some even having surrey-like fringe around the tops, they add a gay, somewhat frivolous air to a city noted for its serious, bustling ways. They, too, reflect the *regiomontaños'* thriftiness. The cabbies just won't let go of a good thing.

CITY HIGHLIGHTS: *Palacio de Gobierno,* on the Plaza Cinco de Mayo, (Zaragoza and Cinco de Mayo Sts.), an imposing red sandstone building, one of the finest in the city. It houses the office of the governor and other state offices. Of interest is the interior colonial-style patio and decorated halls, statues of national heroes. In one of the *salas,* the Red Reception Room, are various historical exhibits, among these are three carbines said to have been used by members of the Nuevo León battalion to give the *tiro de gracia* to Emperor Maximilian, and Generals Miramon and Mejia, at Querétaro. From the front windows of the upper story of the Palace fine views can be gained of the Sierra Madre Range, bizarre Saddle Mountain on E, Miter Mountain on SW and Topo Grande to the S.

The monument in the center of the plaza honors Benito Juárez.

The *Palacio Federal* (Federal Palace), one block N at Zaragoza and Washington, is an overheavy modern structure. Visitors are admitted to the tower which offers an excellent view of the city and surrounding region. About five blocks S of the *Palacio de Gobierno* is a section wheeling around the small, picturesque *Plaza Hidalgo* and *Plaza de Zaragoza,* where many of the shops, hotels and restaurants are located. The *Palacio Municipal,* a colonial-style edifice dating back to 1853, overlooks both plazas. On E side of Plaza de Zaragoza is the *Cathedral.* Though begun sometime between 1600 and 1603, and dedicated as a cathedral in 1791, the building was not really completed until 1851. It may lack the color of many of the churches farther south, but it has an interesting, richly carved Baroque façade, a graceful "Catalonian" bell tower on the S and a pierced belfry on the N. The interior and decorations are without merit. Some of this may be due to the fact that the church suffered greatly during the American invasion of 1846–47 when it was used by troops as a powder magazine and was subjected to severe bombardments.

In this same district, visitors interested in really fine examples of Mexican native arts and crafts will find the *Carápan* (it is both museum and sales gallery) most interesting. The owner, Sr. Humberto Arellano, a discerning arts-and-craft hunter, is to be commended for avoiding the sort of debased arts that jam most of the souvenir shops in the district. Similar standards are maintained by *Helena's,* at Hidalgo 2727 (some distance out of this district). Some five blocks to the S and W of the Cathedral a new ultramodern market building has replaced the famed old *Colón Market* (River Boulevard and Garabaldi). It still contains pottery, native wares and foodstuffs.

El Obispado (Bishop's Palace) on the crest of Chepe Verea Hill, W side of the city. Take Calle Padre Mier, going west. Built in 1786, to provide employment for Indian victims of a severe drought, it has been in turn the bishop's palace during the coloniage, a fortress, a hospital, and now a museum. During the Mexican-American War valiant Mexican defenders holed up in the building continued to resist the invading U. S. Army two days after the city was lost. It was again used as a fort in 1864 during the war with the French. In 1913 it was again stormed by Pancho Villa who likewise used it as a strong point. Its museum has exhibits depicting the industrial and cultural developments of the region. Among the historic exhibits is the first printing press brought to northern Mexico in 1813 by Padre Mier. The good priest, a hero of the War of Independence, carried the press north in order to print revolutionary manifestos.

La Purísima Church, W section of town at corner of Serafin Peña and Hidalgo, across from Plaza de la Llave. One of the first and still one of the outstanding examples of revolutionary modern architectural design in ecclesiastic buildings. The church consists of a graceful cruciform shell and a slender and very simple bell tower set slightly apart. Its designer is Enrique de la Mora.

Technological Institute, 2 m. S on highway to Mexico City. "Tec," a privately endowed institution, highly accredited in engineering and architecture, is the largest and best school of its type in the country. Its buildings are a fascinating blending of the ultramodern with some forms and the vivid mural decorations of the pre-Hispanic architecture of Mexico. Its stadium is the scene of the major soccer and football games staged in Monterrey.

Ojo de Agua de Santa Lucia, a simple and impressive obelisk-like monument at Cuauhtémoc and Allende Sts., marking the site of Monterrey's first permanent settlement, in 1596. The first white inhabitants were twelve families led by Diego Montemayor.

Espiritu Santo Church, turn left about 2 m. N of Madero Blvd. on the Laredo Highway. An architecturally unique church designed by Armando Rauize. Asymmetrical in concept, its simplicity is such that the church somewhat resembles an aircraft hangar, and the bell tower looks like those concrete practice towers used to train apprentice firemen. The interior contains one of the largest Italian mosaic murals in America, depicting the 14 Stations of the Cross.

THINGS TO DO IN MONTERREY: In addition to sightseeing and night-clubbing, Monterrey offers the visitor a variety of vacation activities. The Chamber of Commerce issues cards for golf and tennis privileges at the lovely 18 hole *Valle Alto Golf Club.* The club pro is Al Escalante. The club is on the road to Mexico City . . . The city has two large bullrings and fights are held throughout much of the year. The *corridas formales* occur between November and March . . . On Sunday mornings you can see the Charro Rodeos at the *Rancho del Charro.* Excellent horsemanship and roping. No admission charge. The *rancho* is reached by driving E on the Reynosa road and at *Villa Guadalupe* turn off, following arrows pointing to *Huajuco* . . . On Sundays local artists exhibit their work in the corridors of the Palacio Municipal . . . To practice your Spanish, you can meet with the Conversation Club of the Mexican-North American Institute of Cultural Relations, Monday, Wednesday, and Friday, 6:30 to 7:30 P.M., at Hidalgo 317 Pte. . . . If you're interested in climbing the inviting peaks around Monterrey contact Sr. Agustin Zorrilla of the Hotel Río. The local alpine club has Sunday excursions.

The Cuauhtémoc Brewery, makers of Carta Blanca and Bohemia beer, invites visitors to see the plant. Regular tours are made at 9, 10, and 11 A.M., and at 2 and 3 P.M., Monday through Friday. Free beer is served in the garden.

EXCURSIONS OUT OF MONTERREY: *Horse-Tail Falls* (Cascada Cola de Caballo): A beautiful natural waterfall, widening toward the bottom like the tail of a horse. Located on a private hacienda named Vista Hermosa, 25 m. from the city. Take CN-85 S toward Mexico City. At the village of El Cercado (22 m.) turn W. There are 3½ m. of winding paved road to a mesa where you leave your car. A path leads to the falls. Burros and horses may be hired ($5 MN round trip on burro, $10 MN on horse). There is a $2.40 MN admission charge to the area. There are very nice cottages for rent, a fair restaurant, and swimming pool. Sunday is the best time to see the falls for on weekdays the local textile mills often use up all the water. *Hotel Cola de Caballo,* 19 units a/c, dining room, bar, pool. Rates: $65 MN and up, dble, EP. Tel. 2-34-90.

Garcia Caves (Grutas de García): about 27 m. from the city; take the road to Saltillo, 13 m. then turn N 15 m. to Villa García, N.L. From the village an all-weather road leads to the parking area. A funicular (accommodates 14 persons) leaves hourly for the caves, between 10 A.M. and 5 P.M. Admission to the well-lighted and ventilated caves: adults, $8 MN; children, $4 MN.

The caves are among the largest and most fantastically beautiful in Mexico. Discovered in 1834 by Father Juan Antonio de Sobrevilla, the caves have only recently been opened to the public.

Huasteca Canyon (hoo-ahs-TEH-ka): A spectacular rock gorge with towering walls 750 to 1000 ft. high, SW of the city. To get there take the Saltillo road to Santa Catarina, turn left, then travel 2 m. over new pavement.

Chipinque Mesa (chee-PEEN-kay): A lovely, wooded, 4200-ft.-high mesa about 13 m. from the city. There is a breathtakingly beautiful view of Monterrey. *Chipinque Inn,* old, clean, offers overnight accommodations and food. To reach Chipinque take the Saltillo road 3 m. W of Monterrey, turn off on the marked toll road (paved, but winding and steep). Toll rate: $2.50 MN per person.

AREAS SOUTH OF MONTERREY

Montemorelos, N.L. Pop. 7580. Alt. 1608 ft. On CN-85, about 49 m. SE of Monterrey in the Río de Pilon Valley and center of Mexico's richest citrus growing belt (orange and lemons). From March 1 to 30 an important annual fair is held here. *Hotel Kasino,* on highway. 60 rooms, rather old and not well kept. An emergency stop. Rates: EP from $35 up, dble. There are good snack bars and fruit-juice stands on the other side of the highway.

Linares, N.L. Pop. 13,496. Alt. 1265. A farming and ranching center, once the seat of the old bishopric of San Felipe de Linares, founded in 1712. The town has some pleasant plazas, and a few interesting buildings, namely the *Casino,* and the *Iglesia del Señor de la Misericordia. Hotels: Escondido Court,* 1 m. N on highway. 18 units, some air conditioned. Dining room and pool. A comfortable, fairly good stop. Rates: EP $50 MN dble. Tel. 555. The following are emergency accommodations only: *Hotel Guidi,* Morelos 201 Ote. 33 rooms, *viajero*-style. *Rodelin Courts,* on highway. 9 units, somewhat run-down. Low rates. *Auto repairs* — Automotriz Monterrey, Hidalgo 803 Nte.

Between February 23 and 25 Linares celebrates a traditional fiesta which no one seems able to recall the origin of. There are bullfights, cockfights, regional dancing, and theatrical functions and a lively market.

Branching W from Linares, via new road through beautiful country (CE-31) is an interesting sidetrip to the picturesque Indian villages of *Iturbide* and *Galeana.* The latter, lying on the slopes of the snow-capped *Cerro del Potosí,* is more easily reached from the Eagle Pass-Mexico City Highway, CN-57.

Ciudad Victoria, Tamps. Pop. 31,807. Alt. 1470. Capital of the State of Tamaulipas, and important tourist overnight stop. The town straddles the Pan-American route, CN-85, 178 m. S of Monterrey. CN-101, the road from Matamoros (Brownsville) joins the Pan-American here.

There are no highly recommendable points of interest warranting an extended stopover. Of only passing interest are the *Palacio del Gobierno* (State Capitol), the *Cathedral,* the *Plaza de Armas,* and nearby: *Salto de Juan Capitán,* a waterfall, and *La Peñita,* a rustic picnic spot. The city is the center of the largest henequén (sisal) producing area in Northern Mexico.

HOTELS AND RESTAURANTS: *Hotel Sierra Gorda,* center of town, 83 rooms, some air conditioned. Fair dining room, cocktail lounge. The best in town, though only fair. Rates: EP from $50 MN up, dble. Tel. 240. *San Antonio Motel,* on highway, 30 units some air conditioned. Fair accommodations and good café. Rates: EP $45 MN and up, dble. Tel. 311. *El Jardín Motel,* passable, no food. *Turner's Restaurant,* at jct. CN-85 and 101. Old, established, and popular with tourists. The food is safe but not very inspiring.

DIRECTORY: *Bank* — Banco Nacional de México, Hidalgo and Puebla. *Auto repairs* — Automotriz Sierra Gorda, Aldama and Tijerina (Chrysler); Automotriz Victoria, Torres and Tijerina (Ford); Victoria Motors, Highway and Allende (GM). *Airline* — CMA, Hidalgo and Tijerina. Tel. 4-80. *Bus lines* — Transportes del Norte, Guerrero and Calle 8a. Tel. 3-49. Transportes Frontera, Hidalgo and Morelos. Tel. 4-73. Transportes de Matamoros, Hidalgo and Morelos 9. Tel. 3-75.

Ciudad Mante, Tamps. Pop. 21,300. Alt. 295 ft. in the heart of a vast sugar-cane region, tropical Mante (MAHN-teh) lies 260 m. S of Monterrey on CN-85. Here there is a junction with a highway going E to Tampico. Only points of interest in the town are Mexico's largest, modern sugar refinery. (It operates from November to April. Visitors welcome.) To S of the town, a large government nursery *(Viveros)* where a great variety of tropical trees are cultivated.

HOTELS AND RESTAURANTS: *Los Arcos Courts* one m. S on highway. A friendly, very well-kept motel, 12 units, pool, good dining room. Rates: EP $60 MN dble. *Hotel Naola,* center of town, old but fair. *Hotel Mante,* Guerrero 500 Pte. 40 rooms, old, some rooms air conditioned. Pool, poor dining room. Rates: from $35 MN, dble, EP. Best food available is in *Los Arcos.*

Car Repairs — Mexicana Automotriz, Juárez 200 Ote.

About 18 m. S of C. Mante, on CN-85, is *Antiguo Morelos, Tamps.* Pop. 925. A turn-off here, to the E (CN-80) leads to *El Salto Falls* (27 m.). The falls are among the most charming in Mexico, being surrounded by beautiful tropical verdure and mountains. The cascades have a drop of about 200 ft. The side road to the falls is 1½ m. E of *El Naranjo, S.L.P.,* over a 6 m. rough but passable road. Admission: $5 MN per car.

Ciudad Valles, S.L.P. Pop. 14,383. Alt. 295. Founded in 1533 and originally called Villa Santiago de los Valles de Oxitipa, is a popular Pan-American Highway overnight stop. It is a railroad center on the Río Valles and a distribution point and market for the produce from the sierras. A road leads E to Tampico.

HOTELS AND RESTAURANTS: (In town) *Hotel Casa Grande,* center, 42 rooms, some air conditioned. Excellent swimming pool, good dining room, cocktail lounge. A modest but good hotel. Rates: EP $35 MN to $80 MN dble. Tel. 66. *Hotel Valles,* on highway, N edge of town. 50 rooms, 15 air conditioned. Beautiful grounds, tropical dining room, pool, cocktail lounge. Rates: EP from $45 MN dble. *Palma Motel,* highway. 30 units, inexpensive, no frills or service. (Out of town) *Hotel Taninul,* 9 m. E via CN-110, and 1 m. off highway. An excellent spa-hotel with fabulous grounds. 250 rooms, endless archways. Cocktail lounge, good dining room. Warm sulphur water pool. Tennis, riding, 9-hole golf. Hunting and fishing guide available. During winter season a night club in a natural cave is featured. Rates: AP $225 MN dble. P. O. Box 87. Comment: a fascinating and comfortable hide-away. *Hotel Covadonga,* 7 m. S of Valles on CN-85. A pleasant resort hotel on extensive grounds. 33 rooms (cottages), some air conditioned. Cocktail lounge, sulphur water pool, 9-hole golf, riding, rifle range, bowling. Air strip. Rates: AP $145 MN dble.

DIRECTORY: *Bank* — Banco Nacional de México, Hidalgo and Galeana. *Car repairs* — Auto Ideal Valles, Av. Mexico-Laredo 30; Automóviles de Valles, Av. Mexico-Laredo 24 Nte. *Airline* — CMA, Casa Vitela. *Railway* — Ferrocarriles de Mexico (Monterrey to Tampico Line), tickets at depot.

In the C. Valles area, E of the village of *Tamuín,* and near the edge of the Río Tamuín, there are the ruins of the most important Huasteca archaeological site yet discovered. The ruins, somewhat inaccessible, are such that their appeal is limited to archaeological fans. There are a few fragments of early paintings, rubble-covered platforms and altars. The site is post-Classic, dating somewhat after the tenth century.

For some 70 to 80 miles S of Valles lies a region of endless canyons, mountain barriers and vivid tropical valleys seemingly eternally cut off from the world, except for the narrow ribbon of Pan-American highway lancing through it. This is Huasteca country. The Indians live in tiny, pocket valleys, in almost complete isolation. The only road stop of importance in this section is *Tamazunchale,* reasonably pronounced "Thomas and Charlie" by knowing travelers.

Tamazunchale, S.L.P. Pop. 5817. Alt. 390 ft. Tamazunchale (ta-ma-soon-CHAH-leh, meaning, "Place of the Governor" in the Huasteca tongue), is a colorful and quaint tropical town that seems to exhude an air of antiquity. Its sixteenth-century church, the Sunday market, and vivid walks through jungle paths are its principal attractions. The area around is a paradise for ornithologists and butterfly collectors.

HOTELS: *Hotel San Antonio,* S edge of town, a well-run, neat hotel. Friendly atmosphere. 20 rooms, swimming pool, quite good dining room. Rates: $60 MN, dble, EP. *Quinta Chilla,* S edge. 10 units, cottages overlooking the river. Budget rates, EP from $35 MN up, dble. *Hotel Mirador,* 30 units, very plain. Reasonable. The same can be said for the *Texas Hotel,* on highway near the bridge crossing the Moctezuma River.

On June 24, "bath day," the town celebrates in honor of San Juan Bautista (St. John the Baptist).

About 90 m. to the E of the Pan-American highway, in the State of Tamaulipas, lies the Gulf of Mexico port of Tampico, a once popular fishing resort.

Tampico, Tamps. Pop. 94,500. Alt. 31 ft. Largest city in Tamaulipas and one of Mexico's important Gulf ports.

HOW TO GET THERE: *Via highway* — from the Texas border, CN-85 to Ciudad Mante, then E on CN-100 to Tampico, or CN-85 to Ciudad Valles, then E on CN-110. The Mante road, though a bit longer, is in better condition. From Mexico Ciy, take the Pachuca to Tuxpán road, CN-130, from Tuxpán continue N on CN-180. *Via bus* — there is first-class bus service from Nuevo Laredo and Monterrey and Mexico City. Lines — Transportes del Norte. *Via air* — CMA offers daily flights between Mexico City, Tampico, Monterrey, and Matamoros (Brownsville, Texas). *Via sea* — Ward Line and other ships call at the port, schedules uncertain.

HOTELS: Hotel *El Camino Real,* edge of town on El Mante highway. A de luxe new hotel, fine dining room, bar, a/c. Rates medium expensive. *Colorado Courts,* Calle Miraflores 204 and 206. Small, 11 unit, modern and pleasant cottage-motel. Nice atmosphere. Pool. Good dining room. Rates: EP from $45 MN to $75 MN dble. Older but fair — *Hotel Imperial,* Aurora and Capitán Carranza. 100 rooms, bar, restaurant. Rates: EP from $50 MN dble. Tel. 2-29-10. *Hotel Inglaterra,* corner Díaz Mirón and Olmos. 140 rooms, some air conditioned. Bar, dining room. Garage extra. "Normandie" night club. Rates: EP from $50 MN dble. *Hotel Tampico,* Carranza 513 Ote. Just fair. Reasonable.

RESTAURANTS: Tampico, the crab port, as it is fondly called, offers some of the best sea-food dining in the country, whether it be luscious stuffed crab *(jaiba rellena)* in countless nondescript lunch counters, or lobster thermidor in the modestly appointed better restaurants. *La Gruta Azul,* Carranza 513 Ote. *Hotel Imperial Restaurant,* Aurora and Carranza.

DIRECTORY: *U. S. Consulate* — Díaz Mirón 106 Ote. Tel. 2-2087 and 2-2187. *Banks* — Banco Nacional de México, Madero 403 Ote. Banco de Comercio de Tampico, D. Mirón and Aduana. *Airlines* — CMA, Mirón and Colón. Transportes Aeros de Tampico, Altamira 202 Ote. *Buses* — Transportes del Norte, Carranza 216 Pte. Tel. 2-33-39. Transportes Frontera, Madero 110 Ote. Auto Transportes Lineas Guadalajara-San Luis Potosí-Tampico, Madero 112 Ote. *Railway* — Ferrocarriles Nacionales de México, ticket and reservations at new passenger depot. *Shipping* — Ward Line, Edificio Luz, 2nd floor; Representationes Maritimas, Edificio Luz, Room 510. *Travel agents* — Inglaterra Tourist Service, Hotel Inglaterra; Agencia de Viajes Tampico, D. Mirón 114 Ote. *Auto repairs* — Auto Ideal (GM), Corner of Muelle and Altamira; Nacional de Automóviles (Chrysler), A. Obregón and Avila; Superservicio (Ford), Av. Hidalgo 310. *Tourist and Fishing Information* — Sr. Joaquin Cicero, Tourist Bureau, Palacio Municipal. (He is an avid sportsman.)

THE CITY AND ENVIRONS: Tampico (Tahm-PEE-co) on the N bank of the *Río Pánuco* (named for a one-time Indian Chief), was for many years Mexico's largest and busiest port, a turbulent shipping, fish and petroleum center, with a climate that is apt to be hot and muggy through the spring and summer months.

The history of the city has been that of a people subjected to unusual man-made and natural violence. The original Huasteca Indian settlement on the site of the present city was laid waste by Cortés' forces in 1523. In 1530 Fray Andrés de Lomos united the remnants of the Indians and founded Tampico Colonial. Twenty years later Spanish settlers arrived from San Esteban del Puerto (now Pánuco, Ver.). The tranquillity which prevailed for a long period was shattered by the famed pirate, Lorencillo, who destroyed the village and scattered the inhabitants. The town was not reestablished until 1823. In 1829 the place was captured by the Spanish general Isidro Barrandas, in an attempt to recapture the country for Spain. He was defeated the same year by Mier, Santa Anna, and Terán, thus ending the Spanish domination of Mexico. In later years the town was occupied by American forces. Early in the century, with the discovery of oil in the region, Tampico grew in wealth and importance, becoming a boom town with international atmosphere. Less than a decade ago the town suffered severely from a hurricane and a disastrous flooding of the Río Pánuco.

In 1909 and subsequent years *Terry's Guide* viewed Tampico as a charming Mexican-American flavored city and Mexico's "premier fishing resort on the Atlantic Coast." It no longer is that, and most tourists can afford to bypass it. The boom days are over, and the party has quieted down. There are still touches of Old World atmosphere, turn-of-the-century dignity, somewhat mixed with the new, smart shops, oil refineries, Coca-Cola plants and dry cleaners. The local society is exclusive and worldly. Its Business Men's Club is coldly welcoming, with a somewhat north-of-the-border accent.

THINGS TO DO: Tampico offers excellent swimming facilities, especially at Miramar Beach, linked to town by a fine paved road that goes through the petroleum town of *Ciudad Madero*. Bathing is good the year around. The beach extends over 2 m. There are bathing establishments and restaurants where you can get regional dishes and seafood. At the Casino de Miramar, during the summer, there are dances.

Hunting in the region behind Tampico is quite good — jungle cats, some deer, but the best is for *javelina* or wild boar. In season the lagoons in the region are jammed with northern ducks.

For years Tampico was noted as a top deep-sea and river fishing center. The sea fishing is still good — red snapper *(huachinango)*, snook, yellowtail, sea bass, shark. The Pánuco River, noted for its tarpon (the world's record tarpon was caught here), has in recent years been fished out, largely by commercial seiners. It is reported that the big fish are coming back again. General Gonzales Santos, former governor of San Luis Potosí and owner of the Taninul resort near Valles, has been appointed as chief of the Fish & Maritime Department, and he has clamped down on the seiners.

The *Corona Yacht Club,* located on pretty *Chairel Lagoon* behind the city, sponsors the annual International Tarpon Rodeo. Outside the club entrance there is a public boathouse which rents launches and skiffs by the day or hour. One of the best charter boatmen is Albert Rock, an old-timer in the area. Best tarpon fishing occurs during the months of February and March on any of the four rivers in the area.

FIESTAS: The Fiesta de la Covadonga is celebrated with great élan each September 9 and 10. The carnival, just before Lent, is also very lively. In the village of Altamira, a short distance N of Tampico, (the place where people took refuge when Lorencillo sacked the port), is a very colorful fiesta honoring Santiago, July 25.

94. Central Mexico

This region, the hub of the country, wheels around the national capital, Mexico,[1] and includes a complex of high valleys or basins in which is concentrated the bulk of Mexico's most important cities, the largest percentage of population, the finest colonial and modern architecture, the best tourist accommodations, and an unusually heavy concentration of sightseeing attractions.

For convenience sake Mexico City is not included in this section, but is treated separately. (See Index: *Mexico City and Environs.*)

We include in the Central Region the following states or parts of states: Aguascalientes, the bulk of San Luis Potosí, Guanajuato, the eastern third of Jalisco (the Guadalajara-Chapala area is treated under CENTRAL WESTERN MEXICO), Querétaro, Hidalgo, the states of Mexico, Tlaxcala, Morelos, and Puebla.

[1] For the sake of clarity, in this book we usually refer to the capital as Mexico City. The proper name for it is simply, *México*. For legal purposes and addressing correspondence, one should write, México, D.F. *(Distrito Federal,* i.e., the Federal District), as we say, Washington, D.C.

Communications in this region are the best in Mexico. The north-south trunk highways, with the exception of the new Gulf Coast route, cut through or converge upon the Central Plateau. An ample network of good roads pokes into every corner of the region. First-class buses link most of the principal points of interest with almost hourly schedules. And, of course, a dozen international and Mexican airlines make their target the center of the republic.

VACATION HIGHLIGHTS: In that there are so many things to see and do in this region, the high points will be covered in detail in each separate section. See also, WHERE TO GO vacation suggestions at the beginning of the *Guide*. Mexico City is the natural base for trips out into the various areas. Very few places are more than three to five hours away by car, bus, or train. For a more minute or extended exploration of the region, here are the main areas of interest and their base cities or town.

AREAS OF MAXIMUM INTEREST	BASE CITY
The Bajío Country (incl. Aguascalientes, San Luis Potosí, Querétaro, a bit of Jalisco and Guanajuato)	Guanajuato, Querétaro or San Miguel de Allende
The Hidalgo Country (State of Hidalgo)	San Miguel Regla
The Puebla-Tlaxcala Country (states of Puebla and Tlaxcala)	Puebla or Tehuacán
The Mexico-Morelos Ring (states of Mexico and Morelos — excluding Mexico City and immediate environs)	Mexico City or Cuernavaca

PHYSIOGRAPHY OF THE REGION: The only factors geographically unifying the various portions of this region are: the states surround the *Vale of Anáhuac*[2] and Mexico City, they are on the Central Plateau, and for the most part (Morelos excepted) their altitudes are roughly similar, ranging between 5000 and 8000 feet. The entire region is chopped up by volcanic peaks, mountain chains and gorges. See Index for description of the principal valley basins.

The region contains a number of lakes and artificial lakes. The most famed, but now dried up, were Lake Texcoco and Lake Chalco. Today the largest lake is man-made, the lake at Valle del Bravo near Toluca. There are no navigable rivers in the region, though several rivers of importance have their sources in the mountain folds overshadowing the various basins. The Lerma River has its headwaters in the Sierra de Toluca, winds through the state and on into the Bajío Country, making the latter the granary of Central Mexico, then empties into Lake Chapala, and from there continues on to the Pacific Ocean. Similarly, the Río Balsas, rising in the State of Puebla, winds westward through the State of Guerrero to the Pacific. Likewise, the Río Moctezuma starts on the plateau, then plunges through vivid canyons to join the Río Pánuco which flushes into the Gulf of Mexico near Tampico.

CLIMATE: The climate of the Central Plateau is temperate (except in Morelos and parts of Puebla which are subtropical). The hottest months are May and June, with the summer months becoming pleasantly comfortable as the season of rains set in. From October to late May there are very few rains, the countryside become more parched as the dry season extends. During the winter months the days are pleasantly warm, the nights chilly to cold. Often, in December or January there may be a few weeks of intense cold, with snow falling above the 8000-foot level.

FLORA AND FAUNA: The flora of the region ranges from desert plants (cacti, mesquite) to the trees and plants found in temperate climates (oaks, pines, etc.). Wheat, corn, fruit of all types, and even coffee are grown. The wildlife in the various areas (deer, geese and duck, quail, dove, rabbit) is limited mainly to the more inaccessible spots, having been pushed back by centuries of cultivation and hunting.

HISTORY OF THE REGION: is essentially that of Mexico itself for here the great Toltec, Texcocan, and Aztec cultures flourished, here the Spanish fought their decisive battles for the conquest of Mexico, and here they laid the foundations of Mexico's colonial world. Here also, the Independence movement was born, and its major battles were fought. Mexico's vivid and violent history (see A DIGEST OF MEXICAN HISTORY, Index) is reflected in the ruined pre-Hispanic cities, the colonial monuments and towns of the central region.

THE PEOPLE OF THE REGION: Broadly speaking the people of the Central Plateau reflect most accurately the characteristics of the new nationality and race we call "The Mexican." (See THE PEOPLE OF MEXICO — THEIR CHARACTER AND WAYS, Index). In the larger towns and cities there is exhibited a continual effort to be modern and progressive, to throw off the imprint of colonial ways and traditions which still exist, and to submerge the influences of the Indian world which once prevailed. At times, through some gesture, act or way of doing things, it is obvious that the Indian influence is still there, even in the most modern Mexicanized home. In the rural areas of the region the process of transformation is still going on. The "Indianist" outlook remains strong, even among those who can no longer be considered Indian.

With the exception of a few pockets where indigenous groups have holed up, as it were, the so-called pure Indian is no longer a predominant force in Central Mexico, as he is, for example, in Yucatán or in Oaxaca. Generally, the descendants of the Toltecs and Aztecs have been quite thoroughly absorbed into the new nationality. In certain small communities, for example, Tepotzlán, Mor., and in the highlands of the State of Puebla the Aztec tongue, Náhuatl, is still widely spoken. To the north of Mexico City, in Hidalgo, a large indigenous group, the Otomí Indians — one of the most backward and poverty-stricken of Mexico's tribes — continue to remain outside of the national stream of life. Descendants of the Huasteca still control the mountain and tropical districts in eastern San Luis Potosí, and similarly, but less influential, the sons of the warlike Chichimecas dot the Bajío Country.

[2] *Vale of Anáhuac,* the basin or Valley of Mexico. Originally the area which the Toltecs and Aztecs called Anáhuac included only the oval basin surrounding what is now Mexico City. It extended some 30 m. E and W, by 50 m. N and S. As Aztec power spread, it eventually came to include all the regions under their domain.

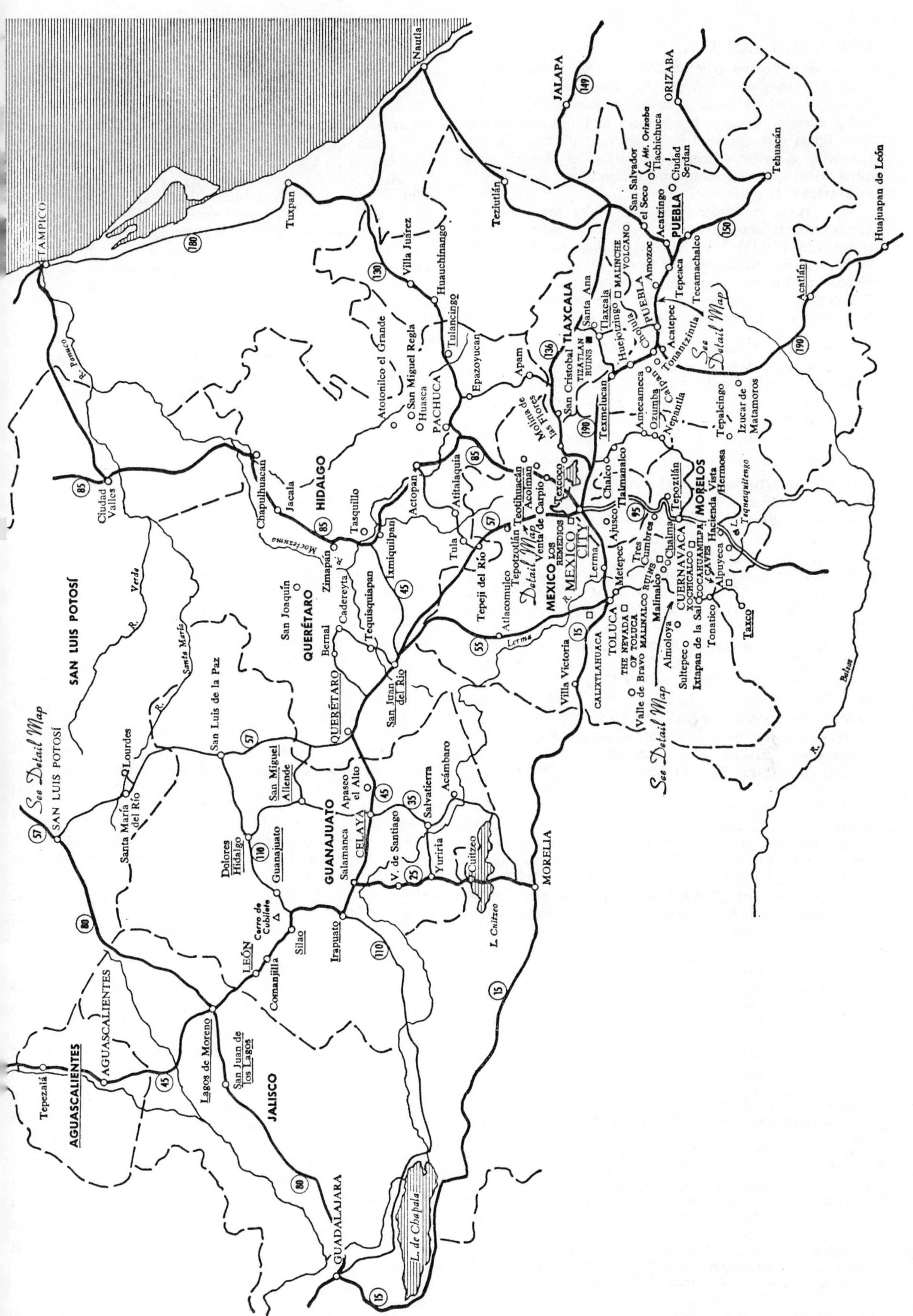
TAMPICO
Tuxpan
Nautla
Villa Juárez
Huauchinango
Tulancingo
Atotonilco el Grande
San Miguel Regla
Huasca
PACHUCA
Epazoyucan
Apam
Teziutlán
JALAPA
ORIZABA
Mt. Orizaba
San Salvador el Seco
Tlachichuca
Ciudad Serdan
Acatzingo
Amozoc
PUEBLA
Tehuacán
Tecamachalco
Tepeaca
Acatepec
Tonantzintla
Cholula
Huejotzingo
MALINCHE VOLCANO
Tlaxcala
Santa Ana
TLAXCALA
San Cristobal
TIZATLAN RUINS
Texmelucan
Amecameca
Ozumba
Nepantla
Tepalcingo
Izucar de Matamoros
Acatlán
Huajuapan de León
Molina de las Flores
Texcoco
Chalco
Tlalmanalco
Teotihuacán
Acolman
Venta de Carpio
LOS REMEDIOS
MEXICO CITY
MEXICO
Tepotzotlán
Lerma
Ajusco
Tepoztlán
MORELOS
Tres Cumbres
Chalma
CUERNAVACA
XOCHICALCO
COCAHUAMILPA CAVES
Hacienda Vista Hermosa
Tequesquitengo
Alpuyeca
Metepec
MALINALCO RUINS
Malinalco
TOLUCA
THE NEVADA OF TOLUCA
Almoloya
Tonatico
Taxco
Ixtapan de la Sal
Sultepec
Valle de Bravo
CALIXTLAHUACA
Villa Victoria
See Detail Map
Atlacomulco
Tepeji del Río
Tula
Atitalaquia
Actopan
Ixmiquilpan
Tasquillo
Zimapán
HIDALGO
Jacala
Chapulhuacan
Ciudad Valles
SAN LUIS POTOSÍ
San Joaquín
QUERÉTARO
Cadereyta
Bernal
Tequisquiapan
San Juan del Río
San Luis de la Paz
San Miguel Allende
Apaseo el Alto
CELAYA
GUANAJUATO
Salamanca
V. de Santiago
Salvatierra
Acámbaro
Yuriria
Cuitzeo
L. Cuitzeo
MORELIA
Irapuato
Silao
Guanajuato
Dolores Hidalgo
Cerro de Cubilete
LEÓN
Comanjilla
Santa María del Río
Lourdes
SAN LUIS POTOSÍ
Lagos de Moreno
San Juan de los Lagos
JALISCO
AGUASCALIENTES
Tepezalá
GUADALAJARA
L. de Chapala
R. Verde
R. Santa María
R. Moctezuma
R. Lerma
R. Balsas
R. Panuco

THE BAJÍO COUNTRY

This area, N and NW of Mexico City, is one of the most charming and historically fascinating parts of Mexico. Called La Cuna de la Independencia (Cradle of Independence), because the movement for independence from Spain was nurtured in its colonial cities, it is fast becoming a favorite region appealing to visitors who have tired of the over-commercialization one finds closer to Mexico City.

This region is bordered on the W by the states of Michoacán, Jalisco; to the W and N by Zacatecas and Nuevo León; to the E by Hidalgo, and on the S and SW by Mexico and Michoacán. It covers an area of roughly 33,655 m. and has a population upward of 3,500,000. The center of the Bajío[3] Country is Guanajuato, one of Mexico's most picturesque and unique cities.

Guanajuato, Gto. Pop. 27,500. Alt. 6855 ft. Capital of the state of the same name.[4] Formerly a wealthy mining city, noted for its opulence, its monumental buildings and high living. Its narrow, tortuous streets climbing up mountain sides lends an atmosphere that is a blend of Provençal France, the hill towns of Italy and a touch of Montmartre.

HOW TO GET THERE: Guanajuato (gwah-na-HWAH-toh) lies some 300 m. NW of Mexico City by road. From the national capital, *via highway* — take CN-57 (Eagle Pass-Mexico City Route through *San Juan del Río* to the W edge of Querétaro. Here you have a choice of two routes. One follows through *Celaya, Salamanca,* and *Irapuato* on CN-45. About 6 m. S of *Silao,* a branch road, CE-29 (paved) leads 16 m. to Guanajuato. An arm of this branch road also leads into Silao and can be taken by motorists coming from the north. The alternate route from Querétaro is to follow CN-57 northward, about 46 m. to junction with CE-111, branch road (paved) to *Dolores Hidalgo.* From Dolores a new road, paved and time-saving, winds through spectacularly scenic country to Guanajuato. Motorists coming down from the States via the El Paso route, turn off at Silao. Motorists coming from Eagle Pass, or Laredo via Saltillo, turn off on the Dolores road.

Via bus — at present none of the de luxe bus services between the U.S. and Mexico City stop in Guanajuato. Connections can be made at Silao or Querétaro. From Mexico City the Estrella Blanco line offers fair direct service to Guanajuato. *Via train* — Ferrocarriles Nacionales de México runs through trains from Mexico City to Guanajuato on holidays and for special events, otherwise you are in for tedious train-changing.

[3] *El Bajío* (depression) is the largest of the seven valley basins making up the Mexican Central Plateau. Strictly speaking it is made up of the lowlands surrounding Celaya, Irapuato, and León as well as the mining center of Guanajuato, Querétaro, and Morelia. For touristic convenience we leave out Morelia, but extend the Bajío perimeter to include San Luis Potosí and Aguascaliente which is in its own basin.

[4] *State of Guanajuato* often called the "Colonial State" because of its picturesque and historic cities, is one of the most favored of Central Mexican States. It has a population of 1,640,976, and an area of 11,943 sq. miles. Its boundaries are: San Luis Potosí on the N, Querétaro on the E, Michoacán on the S, and Jalisco on the W. The topography is varied, giving rise to equally varied climate. Guanajuato is one of the important Mexican mining states, as well as an exceedingly rich agricultural area. Curiously, the state is renowned throughout the republic as the place where life has no value *(la vida no vale nada),* the refrain taken from a popular song about Guanajuato, which has managed to make the Guanajuatenses as feared throughout the country as though they were all armed to the teeth.

Note: There are a number of tours (bus or limousine) out of Mexico City to Guanajuato. If you don't have your own transportation these are by far the most convenient way to make the trip. Check with any of the listed Mexico City travel agents. (See Index.)

HOTELS AND RESTAURANTS: *Posada de la Presa,* Paseo de la Presa 138 (1½ m. from plaza and across from Hotel Orozco). An informal, very modest, but popular inn. Most friendly atmosphere. 11 rooms, family-style dining (some of the best food in town). Free parking. Reservations advised during summer and winter seasons. Tel. 4-41. Rates: AP $125 MN dble. *Motel las Ambajadoras,* Paseo de la Presa, 1 m. from center. 12 units, modest, informal and friendly. Recommended for its cleanliness and for the well prepared food served. Steaks are tops in the city. Rates: EP $60 MN dble. Add $30 MN per person for American Plan. *Hotel San Diego,* Jardín de la Union 1, new colonial-style hotel, fair dining room, bar. Moderate rates. *Castillo Santa Cecilia,* 2 m. from center on road to La Valenciana. 34 rooms in a gloomy pseudo-castle. Cocktail lounge, pretty pool, dining room. Rates: from $160 MN, AP, dble. *Hotel Orozco,* Paseo de la Presa, 1½ m. from plaza. 100 rooms, bar, pool, nice gardens, elevators, dining room (latter is only fair). The hotel is *viajero* type, but okay. Rates: AP from $160 MN dble. No EP. *Posada San Diego,* Jardín de la Union, new, modest but good. Rates: reasonable.

DIRECTORY: *Banks*—Banco Nacional de México, Plaza de la Paz 69. *Car repairs* — Rangel de Alba (Ford), Jardín del Cantador 152; J. Jesús Arroyo, 5 de Mayo 144. *Bus lines* — Autobuses Estrella Blanca, Hotel Reforma, Juárez 113. Tel. 4-69. Autobuses Flecha Roja (first class, to Guadalajara and C. Juárez), Hotel Palacio, Plaza de la Paz 10. Turismo Corsario del Bajío, Angeles 14 (first class, Mexico City to Guanajuato. Tel. 1-04). Autobuses del Bajío, Angeles 80 (first class, Guanajuato to Morelia. Tel. 1-56). *Railway* — Ferrocarriles Nacionales de México, ticket office at station, a fair distance from center of town. Have hotels make reservations. Tel. 1-55. *Red Cross* — first aid station, Juárez 73. Tel. 4-67.

THE CITY AND ENVIRONS: Guanajuato is a sightseer's heaven. It makes no attempt to attract the sportsman, athlete, or gay-time tourist. Its Old World charm, exciting views, and tucked-away sights amply make up for its lack of other vacation facilities. It is one of those wonderful towns, small enough to wander about on foot, day or night, offering enthralling surprises at every turn. One should allow at least two to three days for a visit here.

The town is situated in a narrow mountain gorge traversed by the Guanajuato River. The approaches to the city are picturesque, the roads winding through gorges and precipitous hills dotted with homes and churches and mining works. The streets of the town are so narrow and tortuous and sloping, sometimes two people cannot pass abreast, and often the streets are merely endless series of winding steps. The roofs of certain houses are on a level with the ground floor of those contiguous. Such sights, coupled with intimate small plazas and an opulence of colonial architecture and embellishments give the place a curiously medieval aspect, leaving one with the feeling that every corner of the town is a brilliant setting for a theatrical work by Cervantes.

The area was originally occupied by Otomí Indians who were driven out successively by Tarascan Indians from the west, and later by Aztecs. The Tarascans called the place *Cuanaxhuata (cuanex,* frog; *hutta,* hill — Hill of the Frogs) for one of their deities, the rain god, was represented by a frog. Apparently, in ancient times there was a great carved figure of a frog in the vicinity. The Spanish converted the Tarascan name to *Quanashuato* (mentioned in the manuscripts of Fray Balthasar de Mendoza), and finally simplified it to *Guanajuato*. The town, one of the oldest in Mexico, was founded soon after the conquest. Nuño Beltrán de Guzmán poked through the area in 1529, claiming it for the Spanish crown. In 1548 silver and gold were discovered, the San Bernabé mother lode, and later the celebrated *Veta de Rayas* vein. Soon mine after mine was opened and Guanajuato became one of the great silver- and gold-producing centers of New Spain, bringing in such wealth that the mine owners could squander it on fine homes, great churches, and lavish living. The Conde de Rul, owner of *La Valenciana* mine, was said to have spent a million gold pesos a month for incidentals, and he had enough left over to build lasting monuments. During its heyday the VIP's of Mexico and Europe paid court to this fabulous little city. Great opera stars bypassed Mexico City as too provincial and came directly to Guanajuato; viceroys, presidents, the ill-fated Maximilian, that indefatigable genius, Baron von Humboldt,[5] all came to visit this regal city which, for a brief spell (1858), was also the capital of the nation.

WHAT TO SEE: It is recommended for your first day in town that you use the services of a guide recommended by your hotel or the university. Fees are: $25 MN for a tour of the city's highlights (in your car); $25 MN for a guided tour in a cab (2 people minimum). After the guided tour, then wander on your own, exploring the *plazas* and *plazuelas,* the steep, zigzagging tributary streets that drop to the winding main street threading through the valley floor of the city. And by all means, do some wandering after dark. It is the nearest thing on the American continent to being in Montmartre, Dijon, or Toledo.

Jardín de la Union is the heart of the town, one of the smallest and loveliest *zócalos* in Mexico. The pavements are tiled, the Indian laurels are carefully trimmed and the iron benches lend a frivolous air. It is a favorite promenade. There are band concerts on Tuesday, Thursday, and Sunday evenings. Facing the plaza, S side, is the *Teatro Juárez* or opera house, one of the most romantic and thoroughly delightful buildings to be found anywhere in the country. Constructed on the site of the old Convent of San Pedro de Alcántara, the theater was begun in 1873 and completed in 1903. For its dedication the most lavish production of *Aida* ever seen in Mexico was put on for an audience that included the President of the Republic, the cabinet and most of the diplomatic corps. The exterior is Roman-Doric, with an added French flavor. Its columns and façade are made of a handsome green stone of local origin. The eight allegorical figures in bronze which crown the edifice are the work of W. H. Mullen of Salem, Ohio. The unique foyer and breath-taking interior are vivid and lavish beyond imagination, reminding one of a vast Persian tapestry. *El Templo de San Diego* (San Diego Church), next to the opera house, originally begun by the Franciscans in 1663, badly damaged by flood waters in 1780, was finally completed in its present form. Its façade is a jewel—one of the most exquisite examples of Churrigueresque art to be found in Mexico. You can skip the interior. From one side of the plaza one can view the monumental (not very attractive) 30 foot high *Statue of Pípila* which dominates the city.[6] A road leads to the statue, and an excellent view of the city is obtainable.

Plaza de la Paz, 1 block NW of Jardín Union, is noteworthy for the fine buildings surrounding it, some now occupied by banks. Facing the plaza is the *Basílica de Nuestra Señora de Guanajuato,* also called *La Parroquia.* It was begun in 1671 as the Church of San Francisco, and completed in 1696 as the Church of San Juan de Dios. In 1828 it was taken over by the Franciscans and suffered devastating reconstructions. The sacristy and adjacent baptistry are at present the best portions of the interior and are comparatively unspoiled. In the sacristy there is a large painting of the *Last Supper* by Vallejo, dated 1777. The venerated image of the Virgin of Guanajuato[7] is housed in an adjacent chapel. On one side of the plaza is the former palace-like home of the Conde de Rul. The building is the work of Mexico's Michaelangelo, Eduardo Tresguerras. Baron von Humboldt slept here in 1803. At No. 48 is the house where Mexico's most distinguished historian, Don Lucas Alamán, was born. Aside from the church, the most commanding building on the plaza is the former *Palacio del Gobierno* (now used by the State Legislature and other

[5] Fredrich Heinrich Alexander von Humbolt (1769–1859), German statesman, naturalist, geographer, geologist, and explorer, traveled through much of South America and Mexico, collecting plant and mineral specimens, as well as touristic data. The information he compiled was of unusual value, and his writings remain an important and delightful source of information concerning Latin America. He was, in a sense, the first "Kilroy-was-there" man. The author of this revision of *Terry's Guide* traveled over 30,000 m. in Mexico, gathering data—almost everywhere he went, he found that Baron von Humboldt had been there first.

[6] Pípila (José Barajas) a local miner became a hero of the War of Independence. When the insurgent forces under Father Hidalgo took Guanajuato by storm, the last defense point of the Castilians was the fortress-like *Alhóndiga* (see below). With its massive walls and heavy doors it was almost impregnable. Hidalgo called for volunteers to brave the hail of missiles that fell from the walls, and to set fire to the huge doors.

The sturdy young workman called Pípila volunteered. He had a broad slab of flagstone tied to his back, and with this as a shield, braved the fierce gunfire and attained his objective. The revolutionaries were able to rush into the building where a fierce hand-to-hand struggle ensued. The royalists contested every foot of the great stairway, were forced to the roof, where they were all killed. Thus, the city was secured (momentarily) September 28, 1810.

A few days after the capture of the *Alhóndiga* an infuriated populace broke into the fortress and murdered 247 defenseless Spanish soldiers imprisoned there. This barbarism inflamed the Spaniards. They reunited their scattered forces, besieged the city and recaptured it. Their leader, Calleja, ordered that every person captured, regardless of age or of sex, should be slain. So many innocents were slaughtered by the royalists that Fray José María de Jesús Belaunzaran, a local priest, placed himself between the executioners and victims, stopping the blood bath with no other weapon than his courage, faith, and a cross he held aloft.

[7] *Nuestra Señora de Guanajuato* is one of the oldest and most venerated religious figurines in Mexico. Its history, if true, is curious. It existed in Spain in the seventh century, at which epoch it was held in great veneration at Santa Fe, near Granada. When Spain was invaded by Moors in 714, the image was hidden in a cave to save it from desecration by the infidels. It remained hidden for eight and a half centuries; its miraculous origin and qualities being proven by the fact that the subterranean hiding place was damp, ill ventilated, and of a nature to destroy wood or iron. But the figure was preserved from the slightest disfiguration. In 1557, Felipe II, pleased by the vast royalties received from Guanajuato, presented the figure of the Virgin to the settlement. After years of being venerated by the Guanajuatenses, in 1907 it was officially declared the city's Patroness by Papal sanction. The wooden figure, crudely made, is scarcely handsome. Nevertheless, it is beautifully vested, wears a gem-studded gold crown (weight about 5 lbs.), and is esconsed on a silver pedestal.

government offices). Its rooms contain numerous paintings of national heroes. The building is the work of architect Luis Long.

Via a shoulder-width street, one block NE of the plaza is the *University of Guanajuato,* a brand-new, striking plant constructed of a white stone flecked with green, much in keeping with the architectural tone of the city. A most impressive and endless bank of stairway leads up to the principal building. The university has an excellent summer school for foreign students, and is also the springtime Mexican home for special sessions conducted by Ohio's Antioch College (see Index).

Nearby is the great Jesuit *Church of La Compañia,* begun in 1747. A building of magnificent proportions, designed by Fray José de la Cruz and completed by architect Don Felipe Acuña. The front of the church, placed on a narrow platform, is a beautiful blending of the Baroque and Churrigueresque forms, and the theatrical design of the stumpy belfry is not so detrimental as it might be. The original dome, said to have been strikingly majestic, crashed into the church interior when its supports were weakened during some reconstruction work. The present dome, though equally imposing, with a two-story drum and colonnades, is hardly in keeping with the general design of the building. It is the most visible landmark when viewed from the surrounding hills. The spacious interior of the church is interesting for its simple, classical lines, rather than its decorations. The proportions are deceptively perfect: the church is 207 ft. long by 94 ft. in width, and 66 ft. high.

Following Calle Sopena from Jardín de la Union, SE the street leads up into *Paseo de la Presa,* a pretty residential district. The present-day *Government Palace,* situated in the former residence of the Marqués de San Clemente, is located here. The Paseo ends at some romantic parks built around the two dams *(Presa de la Esperanza* and *Presa de la Olla)* which protect the city from and contain the waters of the Guanajuato River.[8] On the way back from the *presas* the one-way road turns into the *Calle Belaunzaran,* picturesque sunken-street (formerly the river channel) with stone walls, arches and bridges. It is remindful of corners of Jerusalem.

On the western side of the city, one block from the interesting *Municipal Market,* stands one of Guanajuato's memorable monuments — the *Alhóndiga de Granaditas.* This massive pile, begun in 1798 and intended as a grain exchange and warehouse, has served variously as a fortress, a prison, and today as a historical museum. It stands at the foot of the *Cerro del Cuarto* (quarter mountain), so named because prisoners were formerly drawn and quartered here and the leg, or quarter, was nailed to a post for the contemplation of evildoers. The building forms a parallelogram, 210 ft. on its longest side. The upper stories are lined with quaint Moorish windows. The ground floor is Tuscan, the upper Doric, with a stone balustrade between the columns.

During the War of Independence it was the last royalist stronghold in the city and was successfully breached after Pípila's heroic burning of the gates. A few months after this event, when the patriots Father Hidalgo, Allende, Aldama, and Jiménez were executed in Chihuahua, their heads were brought here and hung from hooks high up at the four corners of the building. The hooks are still in place. At the end of the long war for independence, March 28, 1821, the heads were removed at the instance of Colonel Anastasio Bustamente, and solemnly buried in the cemetery. They remained there until April 31, 1923, when they were removed to Mexico City.

Recently converted into the *State Historical Museum,* the *Alhóndiga* has been somewhat refurbished. On the walls of the main interior stairway artist Chavez Morado has executed a vivid mural painting with representational themes of the Independence movement and later revolutions. The upstairs rooms are devoted to displays of historical mementos and include some rather fascinating (especially for children) scale-model reconstructions of colonial villages, etc. *Museum hours:* 9 A.M. to 6 P.M. Admission free.

The *Panteón* (cemetery) on the *Cerro del Trozado* (W of city) has become, oddly enough, one of the most pushed tourist "sights." The walled cemetery itself resembles the Campo Santo of Genoa and the Roman catacombs, in the manner of disposing of the dead. Bodies of those who can afford it are placed in the cemetery wall for a period of five years, or in perpetuity. Unless the crypts are rented for all time the bodies are removed at the end of five years, the bones being thrown in a common ossuary. Certain of the bodies which have mummified due to the dryness of the region are placed in standing rows along the walls of an underground chamber. The *momias* (mummies) are the "sight" guides first offer to take visitors to, and of course, they tell some wild and ghoulish stories. There is no charge to view the mummies, but a caretaker of the crypt waits for a small remuneration, unless, as during this writer's last visit there, the man was a bit tipsy and refused to either take money or go down into the crypt simply because, as he explained in a sobbing voice, "All my friends are down there." The trip is recommended only for travelers with a fairly strong stomach, for it is indeed macabre.

About 3 m. NW of the city on CE-30 (the new road to Dolores Hidalgo) is a church that outshines all in the city and is considered one of the most perfect ecclesiastical buildings in all Mexico. It is *La Iglesia de San Cayetano,* also called *La Valenciana,* after the fabulous mine that made it possible. The church stands on a wind-swept eminence far above the twisting, climbing streets of the city, and being a distance away it has fortunately escaped the hands of overanxious restorers.

La Valenciana was built by the Conde de Rul, owner of the Valenciana mine, just across the road from the church. The architect of the church remains unknown. According to records the expensive edifice was paid for both by the *conde* and his workmen; each of the thousand workmen employed in the mines contributed each week the value of a *piedra de mano* — a piece of ore the size of his fist. And the church construction was expensive! It is even locally said that silver powder and choice Spanish wines were mixed in the mortar (as one writer has commented — an obvious attempt at buying off the Supreme Deity, and getting him drunk at the same time). The church was dedicated August 7, 1788, after some difficulties. The original plan was so imposing that the jealousy of the parish *cura* in Guanajuato was aroused. He claimed that license had been given for a chapel, not a basilica. A compromise was finally reached, and the rank of the church was lowered by having only one tower complete. It was thought at one time that San Cayetano stood upon a rich mineral deposit and the *conde* was offered enormous sums for the property on which the church stood. Moreover it was proposed to take down the church, stone by stone, and reconstruct it on another site — free of charge. The *conde* disdainfully refused the offer.

The decorative treatment around and above the entrance of the church is what attracts expert attention.

[8] The Guanajuato River formerly plunged down through the center of town, frequently causing serious floods. In 1760, 1885, and 1905 floods caused tremendous damage and loss of life. Since then an immense tunnel has been cut to divert the overflow from the dams and provide against a recurrence of disasters. Throughout the center of town there are markers placed on buildings indicating the height of the flood waters *(inundacion)* in the disaster years.

The relief work is Churrigueresque, but so orderly and refined, one authority has called it "Ultra-Plateresque." It is the finest late-period Churrigueresque façade in Mexico. Within the building there are three splendid Churrigueresque altars with their magnificently carved and gilded *retablos* filling the full height of the chancel and transepts. The coloring of the interior, cream-white stonework is elaborately carved and charming. The pulpit is one of the best examples of fine, wood inlay-work to be seen in the country.

La Valenciana Mine is just across the road from the church. The old stone buildings, workshops, and administration offices, surrounding an immense patio where the ore was processed, are now in ruin. Here can be seen the pit-mouth, a hole about 12 yards across and dropping straight down over 1000 feet. At its bottom numerous tunnels branched out a mile or more in various directions. The tunnels and shaft are now flooded. Other mines in and about Guanajuato are still being operated and visitors can secure permission to see them.

Marfil. About 3 or 4 m. from the city (CE-110, road to Silao) lie the ruins of Marfil, once the Beverly Hills-like suburb of Guanajuato. Less than 50 years ago it was a place of luxurious estates, lovely parks, and promenades. The wealthy of Guanajuato had their summer homes or *quintas* there, and some lived on such a large scale it was nothing to stage a bullfight in the patio of a home or to have a European opera company put on an entire production of *Carmen* as after-supper entertainment. The 20,000 people who once lived in Marfil have dwindled to a few hundred as a result of disastrous floods and the decline in the silver market. Weed-grown and half-wild, with a pleasant stream winding through the ruins, it has become an idyllic place to picnic, or in which to dawdle and reflect upon the fleeting glories of mankind. In recent years a remarkable Italian-American artist, Sr. George Belloli, has moved into the ruins, and has exerted unusually good taste in restoring many of them. When he is not too busy, he is charmingly ready to show interested visitors the best of Marfil.

FIESTAS AND SPECIAL EVENTS: No matter where you might be in Mexico during the months of April and May, an absolute *must* is to get to Guanajuato to see the *Entremeses Cervantinos* which are staged weekly during those months. The *Entremeses* are witty, brilliant little plays and sixteenth-century sketches (some written by Cervantes, the creator of *Don Quixote*), presented out-of-doors, at night, utilizing Guanajuato's picturesque colonial little plazas as the setting. Mostly in pantomime, and wonderful comedy, they are easily followed by people without any knowledge of Spanish. To create the illusion of the sixteenth-century world, even the people whose homes face on the stagelike *plazuelas,* are required to don medieval costumes, monks habits, etc., when they wish to go in or out. The spectacles are brilliantly executed by the drama department of the University of Guanajuato. For the *Entremeses* the National Railways of Mexico frequently run special through trains from Mexico City to Guanajuato.

Good Friday — Fiesta of Flowers in the Jardín Union.

May 31 — Fiesta of the Virgin of Guanajuato. Begins nine days before this date, ending on May 31. Regional dances, fireworks.

June 24 — Fair at the Presa de la Olla.

July 31 — Día de la Cueva, an important and colorful fair held on Bufa Hill.

EXCURSIONS OUT OF GUANAJUATO: About ten miles W of Guanajuato there rises the *Cerro del Cubilete,* considered the geographic center of Mexico. Atop the 2600-meter-high peak stands an enormous sculptured figure of Christ the King *(El Cristo Rey)* which can be seen for miles around. The figure, cast in bronze, and having a hollow concrete core stands approximately 75 ft. from toe to head. It weighs 200 tons. The sculpture was executed by Fidias Elizondo. The figure stands on a gigantic ball-shaped base or structure. There is an interior stairway and one can climb to approximately the figure's heart where there is a small chapel. Another chapel on the first floor of the pedestal is dedicated to the Virgin of Guadalupe.

The *Cristo Rey* monument was begun in 1922 and completed some seven years later. It is told in the region that when engineer Carlos Olvera, in charge of the construction, encountered difficulties because there was no nearby available water, Monsignor Valverde y Téllez (initiator of the project) repeatedly replied, "Just keep on working. God will supply us with water." Some weeks later an ample flow of water was found near the top of the mountain in a place now called *El Pocito* (little well). Since its dedication *El Cubilete* and its monument have become an important target for numerous religious peregrinations.

Other excursion points in the Guanajuato area are nearby *Silao* (pop. 18,463), on CN-45, noted for the colorful serapes woven there; and the Cradle of Independence towns treated below.

AREAS SOUTH AND EAST OF GUANAJUATO CITY: For any extended vacationing and exploring in the historic Cradle of Independence region, the most comfortable base-town for a motorist is San Miguel de Allende. If you must rely on public transportation (trains or buses) your best accommodations are in nearby Querétaro.

San Miguel de Allende, Gto. Pop. 12,000. Alt. 6400 ft. A picturesque, regal town, one of the few to have been named a national monument in order to preserve its distinctive colonial atmosphere.

HOW TO GET THERE: San Miguel de Allende (sahn MEGEHL deh ahl-YEHN-deh) is about 200 m. NW of Mexico City, and stands midway between the El Paso-Mexico City and the Eagle Pass-Mexico City highways. From the El Paso route, CN-45, turn off at Celaya, on paved CE-49, 28 m. to San Miguel. From the Eagle Pass route there are two turn-offs: one about 71 m. S of San Luis Potosí, leading to Dolores Hidalgo and to San Miguel, paved, about 41 m. The other turn-off is 17 m. N of Querétaro, on CE-36, paved, 22 m. *Via railway* — the de luxe *Aguila Azteca* of the Mexican National Railways (Laredo-Mexico City line) stops at San Miguel. *Via bus* — Corsarios del Bajío, from Mexico City, twice daily.

HOTELS AND RESTAURANTS: *Posada de San Francisco,* on main plaza. A pleasant colonial-style inn. Good service, friendly atmosphere. Lovely patio, nice cocktail lounge and good dining room. The Spartan-furnished rooms are apt to be cold in winter unless you have one with fireplace. (This applies to all hotels in the region.) Rates: AP $150 MN to $160 MN dble. Tel. 72. *Instituto Allende,* S edge of town. 60 rooms, some suites, modestly furnished. Dining room, cocktail area. Hotel set on lovely, spacious grounds. Since the hotel is connected with the Instituto Allende Art School, reservations suggested during winter and summer season. Tel. 149. Rates: AP $160 MN dble. *Hotel Rancho Atascadero,* in the hills, E edge of town. A modest, charming ranch-type inn with lovely patios and grounds. 27 rooms, good dining room, cocktail lounge, swimming pool, horseback riding. Very friendly atmosphere. Rates: AP $125 MN dble; $75 MN single. *Motel Siesta,* 1½ m. S on

Celaya road. A new, neat motel with 24 comfortable units, fireplaces, pool, dining room. Rates: EP $80 MN dble. *Posada de Sierra Nevada,* Hospicio 7, Tel. 55. A delightful colonial-style inn, excellent cuisine and service, 8 suites, cocktail service. Rates: $125 MN, AP single.

Other hotels offering minimum service and comforts, *viajero*-style, or appealing to student pocketbooks. Rates range from $25 MN up, per single, EP. *Hotel Vistahermosa. Hotel Colonial, Casa Sautto.*

Aside from the three first hotels, the pleasantest place to dine (steaks, chops, etc.) and to wine is *El Patio,* an inviting, colonial-style bar-restaurant ½ block from the plaza on Calle Correo. Hours: noon to midnight. *Restaurant La Flama,* San Francisco 50, new de luxe restaurant, charcoal broiled steaks. Hours: 4 P.M. to 11 P.M. *La Terraza,* SE corner main plaza. Good snacks and fountain specialties.

DIRECTORY: *Bank* — Banco del Centro, on the plaza. *Telegraph office* — Mesones near Reloj. *Doctors* — Dr. Francisco Olsina, Hernandez Macias 48, Tel. 80.

THE TOWN AND ENVIRONS: San Miguel de Allende, the first Spanish settlement in the State of Guanajuato, was founded in 1540 by the Franciscan friar Juan de San Miguel. It was originally designated as a military outpost in hostile Chichimeca Indian country, but as the place prospered it came to be known as San Miguel el Grande (to distinguish it from a half-hundred other San Miguels in New Spain). The Allende was added to its name in honor of Ignacio Allende, one of the patriot-conspirators who joined with Padre Hidalgo in leading the revolutionaries during the War of Independence, 1810 (Index). The town had long before this become the home of many noble families who drew wealth from Guanajuato silver mines, and embellished the city with palatial homes and a wealth of churches.

Clinging to the slopes of the *Cerro de Moctezuma,* and overlooking the Laja River valley, the town is blessed with both a pleasant climate and sufficient water to make its plazas and flower-filled Mudéjar patios especially attractive. The town being a national colonial monument, the local citizens make an effort to maintain its colonial façade. Here there are no twentieth-century Aztec temples neighboring some hybrid-Bauhaus movie palace, no echoes of medieval Spain squeezed between garages and bottling plants.

Today, San Miguel has become a popular Mexican-American art center, attracting painters and art students from the U.S. and Canada. (See school listings, Index.)

The principal points of interest in the town are within a few blocks' walk of the central plaza, called the Jardín. The most conspicuous edifice, among the many extraordinary examples of monumental architecture in San Miguel, is the *Parroquia* (parochial Church of San Miguel), S side of the plaza. Originally the church was a plain Franciscan building, but during an architectural building spree in the last century the building had its face lifted by an unlettered Indian mason named Ceferino Gutiérrez who was undoubtedly an architectural genius. Gutiérrez based his unique pink stone monument on post-card impressions of French cathedrals, creating an imaginative façade that is Gothic in feeling, yet full of the charming plastic freedom native to the Indian artist.

The interior of this imaginative, "gothesque" false front (begun, October 1880) has little to recommend it. It is rather gloomy, and has been tastelessly refurbished over the years. The church is the home of a much venerated relic, a crucifix called Señor de la Conquista (Lord of the Conquest) which, like its counterpart in the Mérida Cathedral, is supposed to have come over with the Conquistadores.

To the W of the church, on the corner, is the colonial home where Ignacio Allende was born (1779). It has a monumental stone entrance with a curved pediment. Above the door is an inscription: HIC NATUS UBIQUE NOTUS (Here was born He who is widely known). The block-long street starting from the door and going S is called Calleja de la Cuna de Allende (Little Street of the Cradle of Allende). Facing the NW corner of the plaza stands a huge building that was once the opulent residence of the so-called Counts of Canal. The Canal family were granted the title of *Conde,* but it was never confirmed for one of them was accused of aiding the 1810 revolutionaries. The massive entrance-way on Calle Canal has sumptuous portals, beautifully carved wooden doors. The *zaguán* and interior patio are also examples of fine colonial architecture.

One block to S (on Canal) stands the *Church and Convent of the Conception,* popularly called *Las Monjas* (The Nuns). Though the church was erected between 1755–65, its magnificent dome was not completed until 1891. The dome, perhaps the masterwork of mason-architect Ceferino Gutiérrez, is an imposing composition. It is dodecagonal and has a drum of two stories — a rarity in Mexico, and the finest of them all. The adjacent monastery with its impressive tree-filled patio and two-story arched corridors, abandoned for many years, has now been converted into a fascinating museum and cultural center — Centro Cultural Ignacio Ramirez.

Other exemplary buildings include the *Church of San Francisco* (one block S of market), the *Church of la Salud* and the *Oratorio of San Felipe Neri,* both N of and facing the market. The San Francisco, begun in 1779, has an exceedingly richly carved Churrigueresque portal and a neoclassic tower often attributed to Tresguerras. This church was built with donations of wealthy families and assessments on bullfight tickets. Near the Oratorio of San Felipe is the *Chapel of the Santa Casa de Loreto* having a towerlike construction of superposed domes with lanterns, and a notable *camarín* with a vaulted ceiling in a style similar to that of the camarín of Tepotzotlán.

Almost every street has its liberal sprinklings of historic houses memorialized with plaques indicating that "secret revolutionary meetings were held here under the guise of fancy balls" (NE corner of the plaza), or, noting that national figures — El Nigromante, the great liberal writer, General Bustamante, General Escobeda, etc. — had been born or had resided in the town. There are numerous picturesque parks and plazas and nooks to delight the eye of a painter or photographer. The town is a natural movie set and it has attracted both Hollywood and Mexico movie makers who have used it as a backdrop for *The Brave Bulls, Serenade, Wonderful Country,* and other pictures.

FIESTAS: Since colonial times the town has been famed for its fiestas. Some people insist these are San Miguel's major industry. The official town calendar of events lists over thirty celebrations throughout the year, some of them almost week-long affairs. Among the most brilliant or unique are: Independence Day celebrations (September 15–16); Vivid two-day Fiesta of San Miguel, (September 29-week-end); Day of the Dead (November 1–2); the Christmas Posadas, considered among the most colorful and traditional in the country, (December 16–24); Dia del Conquistador, with a brilliant array of Indian dancers (first Friday in March). This celebration honors Our Lord of the Conquest, not Cortés. Two weeks before Easter there is a moving procession from the Sanctuary of Atotonilco to the Church of San Juan de Dios, bringing the image of the Señor de la Columna; Easter Week; Corpus Christi with its charming dance of the gardeners (June — a movable feast).

EXCURSIONS FROM SAN MIGUEL DE ALLENDE: Many of the places of interest listed below are also within one to two and a half hours' drive of the city of Guanajuato.

Sanctuary of Atotonilco. 7½ m. from San Miguel on road to Dolores Hidalgo. Atotonilco (ah-toh-toh-NIHL-coh, meaning, place of hot water) is considered by art historians to be of unusual interest, partially for its architecture, and in part because of the amazing decorations and mural painting of a primitive religious nature covering its walls and ceilings. These works, little jewels of popular art, were painted by Miguel Antonio de Pocosangre. The sanctuary was constructed between 1740 and 1748. It figured in Mexican history as the site where Ignacio de Allende was married (1802), and as the first stopping point of Hidalgo's raggle-taggle army on its way to glory.[9] For centuries the sanctuary has been a focal point for nation-wide peregrinations. Even today bands of pilgrims trudge hundreds of miles over mountain and desert to attend religious exercises at the sanctuary, which, frequently, houses as many as four to five thousand *perigrinos* in a week.

Dolores Hidalgo, Gto. Pop. 10,000. Alt. 6300 ft. On CE-110 — about 25 m. W off of the Eagle Pass-Mexico City Highway; 32 m. from Guanajuato (E), or 25 m. N of San Miguel de Allende (all roads paved).

There being no recommendable restaurants or hotels in Dolores, visitors should arrange to stop either in Guanajuato, Querétaro, or San Miguel.

The town is situated in the valley of the Río Laja. Although not a pretty town, it is a national mecca for here the Independence of Mexico was proclaimed on September 16, 1810, when the parish priest, Don Miguel Hidalgo y Costilla sounded the *Grito* and led his small band of citizens against the Spanish. By tradition, at least once during his term of office, every Mexican president is expected to appear in Dolores on the fiesta date and re-enact the *Grito*.

Points of interest in Dolores are: *Casa de Don Miguel Hidalgo,* Morelos 1, at corner with Hidalgo. The home of the patriot, now a national museum containing many historic items pertaining to Hidalgo's life. *Hours:* 9 A.M. to 1 P.M.; 4 to 6 P.M. Sundays and holidays, 9 A.M. to 1 P.M. Admission: one peso.

Parroquia de Dolores Hidalgo, the parochial church, with a fine eighteenth-century Churrigueresque façade, faces on the pleasant Plaza de Independencia. It was on the steps of the church (marked by a plaque) that Hidalgo proclaimed Mexico's Independence. Within the church there are two handsomely carved *retablos,* one of them left in its natural state rather than being gilded. Across from the church, in the plaza, there is a fine statue of Hidalgo. The heroic statue is said to stand on the site where once there was a small bullring in which the priest himself fought.

The newly dedicated monument at the S edge of town, by the late architect-sculptor Santacilla, could better have been left undone.

THE MARKET: The town market is at its best on Sundays when there is an unusual display of the pottery for which Dolores is noted throughout the country. Both on Sunday and weekdays visitors can also go through the pottery "factories."

FIESTAS: On January 1 a popular fair is held in the town. Indian dancers perform *Los Comanches, El Torito,* and *Los Compadres.* On September 15 and 16 occur the important Independence Day celebrations.

Pozos, Gto. A fascinating, little-known ghost town NE of Guanajuato and San Miguel de Allende. Pozos (the Wells) had an estimated population of some 40,000 until not too many years ago. At present the number of inhabitants may come to about 300, so thinly scattered they are hardly noticeable. The town, once a prosperous silver-mining center, boasted of regal homes, lovely plazas, and a number of interesting churches — now all slowly falling into ruins, but with the peculiar grace and appeal that seems to occur in Mexico when things deteriorate.

To reach Pozos, turn E off of the Eagle Pass-Mexico City Highway, CN-57 (also the Dolores turn-off), 53 m. N of Querétaro. Go 5 m. to *San Luis de la Paz.* From here an improved road leads 6½ m. S to Pozos.

Twenty-eight miles S of San Miguel Allende is the prosperous agricultural, highway town of *Celaya,* noted throughout the republic for a sticky candy, and as the birthplace of Mexico's famed architect-genius, Francisco Eduardo Tresguerras (see Index). Several of his most outstanding works are to be found here.

Celaya, Gto. Pop. 34,426. Alt. 5930 ft. On CN-45 (El Paso to Mexico City route).

HOTELS AND RESTAURANTS: *Royal Courts,* E edge of town, on highway. 32 units, fairly well kept. Dining room, bar, pool. Rates: EP from $50 MN dble. Tel. 79. *Hotel Isabel,* Hidalgo 15. 80 rooms. Restaurant, bar, garage. A rather old and run-down establishment. Rates: EP from $45 MN dble. *Motel Campestre,* E edge of town. 20 units, new. Rates: from $40 MN, dble, EP. *Restaurant El Gaucho,* same area. Good Argentine-style broiled meats.

DIRECTORY: *Bank* — Banco Nacional de México, corner of Obregón and Góngora. *Auto repairs* — Automotriz Celaya, Morelos 257. *Bus lines* — Autobuses Flecha Roja, Hidalgo 15. Tel. 96 (first class: Mexico City, Torreón, Guadalajara, C. Juárez); Autobuses Estrella Blanca, Madero 27 and 29. *Railway* — Ferrocarriles Nacionales de México. (Direct service to Mexico City.)

THE TOWN AND ENVIRONS: Celaya (sa-LAH-yah — Basque for flat land), one of the busiest small cities in the center of the fertile Bajío basin, was founded in 1570 by sixteen Spanish Basque families. Although the town is quite flat and lacking a pretty natural situation it nevertheless has several pleasant parks and plazas and a few memorable examples of Baroque architecture.

The present-day *Plaza Principal* or *Jardín,* with its stone bandstand and carefully trimmed Indian Laurels is flanked on four sides by arched *portales.* At the SE corner is the new city hall, noteworthy only because in the building previously located on the site, Father Hidalgo was officially proclaimed commander-in-chief of the revolutionary army of 1810. A block to the E is another somewhat chopped-up plaza (formerly the principal plaza) containing the remnants of a lovely formal garden and the striking *Monument to Independence* designed by Tresguerras. This impressive shaft is demeaned by shoddy civic improvements surrounding it, particularly a gigantic steel water tower. A remark of architect Tresguerras concerning his work shows that city authori-

[9] After sounding the famous *Grito de Dolores,* Father Hidalgo aroused a small, poorly armed band of peons and marched from Dolores to San Miguel. On the way they stopped at Atotonilco and took a banner having the image of the Virgin of Guadalupe on it, from one of the chapels. It became the standard for the Revolutionary army. The Spaniards (royalists), on the other hand, chose the *Virgen de los Remedios* as their representative and made her a captain general in their army, even giving her a marshal's baton.

ties were considered a fair target even in his day. The eagle on the monument has his head turned backward, and a friend asked the reason for this peculiarity. "So he may not see the barbarities committed by our municipal authorities," replied Tresguerras. Flanking this plaza are the *Church of El Tercer Orden,* as well as that of *La Cruz.* The attached colonial convent has been restored and is at present a theological seminary.

The Church of Nuestra Señora del Carmen, chief point of interest in the city, is also one of the most famous edifices in Mexico. It is the masterwork of Francisco Eduardo Tresguerras. The present structure, built to replace an older church which had been destroyed by fire, was begun in 1803 and completed in 1807. It is a large and impressive building, with a nave 220 feet long, 55 feet wide, and 69 feet high. In spite of its size, it achieves an effect of great simplicity, grace, and unity. The main dome is the church's crowning achievement. As Trent Stafford has written, "There are literally thousands of domes in Mexico, the land of domes, but this is the queen of them all." In it Tresguerras showed his greatest artistry, achieving a soaring unity and perfection of line rare in this world. In addition to doing the over-all structure of the building Tresguerras sculpted all the figures and *retablos* as well as executing all the murals in the church.

In the *Capilla del Juicio* (Last Judgement) in the Carmen there are three important Tresguerras frescoes. The largest of these, *The Last Judgement,* appears to have been done sketchily and off-handedly, yet the concept is forceful and there is an unusual element of humor underlying the dramatic realism. In it the artist ironically represents himself as a central figure in the last awakening — emerging from a yawning tomb in the middle foreground between hosts of the elect on one side and of the condemned on the other, and peering out with an expression of anxiety and uncertainty on his countenance, as if doubtful as to which party he might be assigned. The other two frescoes represent the *Entombment of Tobias* and the *Resurrection of Lazarus.* This chapel also contains a memorial to Tresguerras in the form of two medallion portraits in fresco that flank the main entrance, one representing him at the age of thirty-five and the other at sixty-three — the latter when he had just finished the church.

Other Tresguerras embellishments in the city include the lovely colonial bridge over the Laja River, 2 m. E of town on highway. It was constructed in 1800 and is still in use. *San Francisco Church and Convent* — a cathedral-like parochial church in which Tresguerras designed a chapel, various altars, and painted some murals. He should not be blamed for the somewhat sad façade and dome, despite what local guides tell you.

Celaya's other chief claim to national fame is a sweetmeat called *cajeta* or *dulce de Celaya. Cajeta* (kah-HAY-tah) is a pale carmel-like sauce made of burnt sugar and milk and flavored variously with vanilla, wine, etc. It is sold (bottled) in syrup form, or in candified form, in pretty wooden boxes called *cajetas.*

FIESTAS: Several colorful fiestas and fairs are celebrated in the town — May 15, Fiesta de San Isidro Labrador; December 12, religious fiesta in the Barrio de Piedras Negras; December 16–25, Christmas celebration and fair, including regional dances, etc.

To the E of Celaya, just off the highway (CN-45), is an interesting village named *Apaseo el Alto* (midway between Celaya and Querétaro), noted for its skilled *santeros,* (carvers of saints). The admirable polychromed figures of saints produced here are sold in a number of shops throughout the region.

An interesting drive can be taken S of Celaya, which includes pretty country, several interesting towns and a famed monastery. Motorists can take CE-35 (paved), southward from Celaya to *Salvatierra,* 26 m. At Salvatierra there is a picturesque colonial bridge spanning the Lerma River. Just W of the river there is a road junction — CE-35 continues to *Acambaro,* a noted pottery-making town. From here a rough gravel road continues on to *Morelia, Mich.* Not recommended. From Salvatierra another state road, CE-66, leads westward, 19 m. to *Yuriria.*

Yuriria, Gto. Pop. 8120. This picturesque, rarely visited village, pronounced you-rhee-RHEE-ah, is situated on the charming small Lago de Yuriria. The town was originally an important Tarascan Indian city called Yuririapúndaro, governed by a Tarascan chieftain who was quick-witted enough to realize that his life depended upon his rapid conversion to the Catholic faith when the Conquistadores came through the area. He promptly became so devout that even his name was changed and in history he is known as Alonzo de Sosa (Alphonso Soda).

Yuriria is noted for its lovely and massive Augustinian Convent begun in 1570. This ancient religious center is remarkable for its imaginative, Indian-style Plateresque façade, its interesting Italian-like *loggias* and the Gothic rib-vaulted ceilings of the lower cloister. The architect was Pedro de Toro. The convent is now a national colonial museum. VISITING HOURS, 9 A.M. to 1 P.M., 4 to 6 P.M. ADMISSION, one peso.

From Yuriria motorists can swing back via CE-25 to Salamanca, on the El Paso-Mexico City Highway, or drive S on the same road (SE-25) to Morelia and the Lake Patzcuaro area (see Index). A description of the Salamanca to Morelia route linking the El Paso-Mexico City, and the Nogales-Guadalajara-Mexico City Highways, follows.

Salamanca to Morelia Route
CE-25 (Gto.) and CE-45 (Mich.)

MILES FROM SALAMANCA	LOG
0	*Salamanca.* On CN-45.
13	*Valle de Santiago.* Colorful fiesta honoring Santiago on July 25th.
29.2	*Road Junction.* Left 2 m. to Yuriria. Continue ahead toward Morelia.
34	*Uriangato.*
39	Guanajuato-Michoacán state line.
47	*Cuitzeo.* Just beyond the village the road crosses the beautiful Lake Cuitzeo via an interesting colonial causeway.
61	Sideroad turn-off to r. ½ m. to Tarímbaro. This village, originally Tarascan Indian, is startling. The motorist visiting it discovers that all the signs on stores and shops are in English, and they make you think you have entered a Western town of the 1870s. Some years ago a Hollywood studio made a movie here and redecorated the town. No one has bothered to change anything.
68	*Morelia* (see Index).

Salamanca, Gto. Pop. 20,586. Alt. 5806. On El Paso-Mexico City Route, CN-45. About 42 m. from Guanajuato. Salamanca (sah-lah-MAHN-cah) is an important highway town on the N bank of the Lerma River. It is the site of one of Mexico's largest oil refineries. The petroleum is piped in from the Poza Rica fields in the State of Veracruz. The town possesses several examples of interesting colonial architecture: the *Iglesia y*

Convento de San Agustín, with its enormous Churriguresque *retablos;* and the *San Bartólo Church* which has a lavishly carved façade (the niches have been stripped of the sculptured figures they once must have held). The town is otherwise rather characterless and squalid.

In nearby **Irapuato, Gto.** (Pop. 49,400), just off CN-45, there are some worthy examples of colonial architecture, notably the Baroque façade of *El Hospital,* the neoclassic *Palacio Municipal* and the *Church of San Francisco* which contains a painting of the Virgin of Guadalupe by Miguel Cabrera, and a painting of the Virgin of the Apocalypse by Tresguerras.

On CN-45, 1 m. S of junction leading into Irapuato is the attractive colonial-style motel, *Posada de Belém.* It has 40 nicely furnished units, heated pool, quite good dining room, cocktail lounge. Rates: EP $75 MN dble. *Restaurant El Rancho,* at N junction leading into town, charcoal broiled specialties.

Just to the E of the rich *El Bajío* basin lies the State of Querétaro, with its capital city (Querétaro) which is usually included in the historic *cuna de la Independencia* triangle, and which also possesses several points of historic and touristic interest. The State of Querétaro though small — population 328,775 in an area covering 4,484 sq. mi. — is both a rich agricultural region and an area noted for its opal and mercury mines.

Querétaro, Qro. Pop. 64,000. Alt. 6160 ft. Capital of the state of the same name. One of Mexico's prettiest colonial cities, as well as being an important industrial center, highway junction and railway stop.

HOW TO GET THERE: *Via road* — both the Eagle Pass and the El Paso trunk highways to Mexico City pass through Querétaro. From Mexico City the shortest route is via CN-57 to Querétaro, about 135 m. *Via bus* — The following bus lines serve the area: Transportes Chihuahuenses (Mexico City to El Paso), The Flecha Roja line, Transportes del Norte, Autobuses Estrella Blanca. *Via railway* — The de luxe *Aguila Azteca* train on the Nacional Railways' Laredo-Mexico City route stops at Querétaro, as do the direct trains between Guadalajara and El Paso to Mexico City.

HOTELS AND RESTAURANTS: *Casa Blanca Motel,* on CN-45 and 57, ½ m. W of town entrance. A new and attractive motel with 30 units, fair dining room, cocktail lounge, heated pool. Rooms on highway side apt to be noisy due to night-trucking. Rates: EP from $60 MN to $80 MN dble. Tel. 11-34. *Motel El Baron,* on CN-57, ¾ m. W of town. Recently opened, quite nice motel with good dining room. Rates: EP from $50 MN. *Flamingo Motel,* on CN-45 and 57, ½ m. W of town. New, comfortable, with fair service and dining room. On noisy highway. Rates: EP $50 MN up, dble. *El Jacal,* on CN-45 one m. W of town. Old motel with good dining room, pool, bar. Rates: EP $60 MN up, dble. In town the *Gran Hotel* on the plaza is old, cater to *viajero* trade. Rates reasonable.

The motel restaurants are fairly good. Add to these *Flor de Querétaro,* on plaza, a fair café.

DIRECTORY: *Bank* — Banco Nacional de México, 16 de Septiembre and Juárez. *Auto repairs* — Automotriz de Querétaro (Ford), Juárez 12 Nte. Luis Escobar (GM), Av. Colón and Highway. *Railway* — Ferrocarriles Nacionales de México, ticket office at station. *Bus lines* — Transportes Chihuahuenses, at Genova Restaurant. Autobuses Estrella Blanca, Zaragoza and Colón. Tel. 5-03. Servicios Unidos Flecha Roja, 2a Zaragoza 3, Ote. Tel. 9-00. Transportes del Norte, near the Alameda Gas Station. Tel. 4-00.

THE TOWN AND ENVIRONS: Querétaro (que-REH-tahro) was an important Indian town long before the Spanish discovery of the New World. The town was founded by Otomí Indians, became part of the Aztec Empire in the fifteenth century and was captured by the Spanish in 1531.[10] The name is thought to be derived either from the Tarascan Indian word, *querenda* (place of the stony peak), or from *queretaro,* meaning, a ball game. By royal order of Felipe IV, Querétaro was designated as a city in 1655. In 1808 it sprang into prominence as one of the cradle cities of Independence for several of the revolutionary plotters lived and met there. In 1867 Archduke Maximilian was captured in the city and shot there.

The city lies in a fertile valley at the foot of a long hill called *Sangremal.* When approaching it from the W or N the city can be seen from afar, white and gleaming, somewhat remindful of Madrid. When approached from the E the most conspicuous feature is the great and graceful colonial aqueduct which brings water from the neighboring hills. The aqueduct was begun in 1726 and completed October 17, 1738. There are over 74 soaring arches, some being 94 feet high. Connected to its terminal within the city is *The Fountain of Neptune* created by Tresguerras.

In addition to its fascinating Old World streets, tree-

[10] The story of Querétaro's capture is embroidered with a curious embellishment. When the Spanish and certain Christianized chieftains from the province of Xilotepec (Baltazar del Campo, Juan de Luna, and Miguel de la Paz) approached the Otomís with peace proposals, the latter were loath to give up their city, but they knew their arrows would be ineffective against Spanish armor. Someone proposed the fate of the city be settled by a fist-fight. Accordingly, a representative from each side faced each other for this incredible battle. However, during the fray, a great cross of red and gold appeared in the sky. In some versions of the tale an angel was seen near the cross, in others, Santiago (Saint James) carried the cross. This miracle converted the population to the new faith. Santiago became the patron saint of the town, and a chapel to the Cross was constructed on the site. The present structure, the *Templo de la Cruz,* was built in 1682.

filled plazas, seignorial houses, and unusual vistas, Querétaro is an exciting reliquary of Mexican history and exceptional colonial architecture.

The *Plaza Obregón* (Plaza Principal), formerly called the *Jardín Zenea,* is the heart of the city. Facing the plaza, on the E is the *Cathedral.* Built in 1698 as the Church of San Francisco, it was later enlarged and made a cathedral in 1862. With the exception of its fine old tower and dome, both tiled, the church has been so injured by alterations it has become somewhat nondescript. Perhaps the most noteworthy feature of the interior is a polychrome statue of San Diego de Alcalá (carved in wood by Arce, the celebrated Querétaro sculptor) which perhaps dates from about 1606. The elaborate iron *reja* enclosing the organ loft, and the metal adornments on the organ itself are interesting. In the adjoining monastery, now the *Museum Pío Mariano,* there is an important collection of colonial religious art and artifacts—huge parchment choirbooks, a painting by Miguel Cabrera, and an 8000-book library dating from the seventeenth and eighteenth centuries.

One of the city's most attractive spots is the tiny, tree and flower-filled *Plaza de la Independencia* (2 blocks E of Plaza Obregón). On one side of the plaza stands the former residence of the Marqués de la Villa del Villar del Águila, the public benefactor who caused the great aqueduct to be built. His house is an unusually fine example of the Baroque seignorial mansion. A statue to the Marqués stands in the plaza. Also facing on the plaza is the *Palacio Municipal,* once the *Casa Real* of the Spanish governors and home of Doña Josefa Ortiz de Dominguez, wife of the Spanish *Corrigedor* and heroine of the Independence Conspiracy.[11] The building is at present both City Hall and museum.

Perhaps the most unusual and architecturally important building in Querétaro is the *Collegiate Convent of Santa Rosa de Viterbo,* on Calle de Santa Rosa, SW edge of town. The present building is a reconstruction of an older building, done by Tresguerras. The dome, the tower, cloisters as well as exterior decorations are his. The extraordinary flying buttresses which help support the dome are among the most curious in the country, being almost theatrical. The fine dome, with its polychrome tiles, is altogether quaint. In the church interior Tresguerras put aside his experimentations with the Baroque and Oriental, and devoted himself to Churrigueresque designs that are indeed a triumph. The rich embellishments are remindful of the Santo Domingo in Oaxaca. In the sacristy the artist's carvings are carried out with a splendid luxuriousness, but most notable is the artist's great mural that entirely occupies the head of the room. The subject shows nuns and their pupils working in a garden, and lambs receiving white roses from the Virgin and carrying them to the feet of the crucified Savior to be turned red by the blood from his wounds. The work, entitled *Hortus Conclusus (The Closed Garden),* is considered by many authorities to be one of the finest examples of mural art in the New World.

The *Church and Convent of Santa Clara* (on the Plaza de Santa Clara, W of Plaza Obregón). Founded in 1633 and reconstructed in part by Tresguerras in the eighteenth century. It was once one of the largest conventual buildings in Mexico, sheltering, it is said, over 8000 nuns. Tresguerras' work was probably confined to the glazed tile dome and tower, and perhaps the small, barrel-vaulted interior. The latter is richly decorated in elaborate Baroque style rather than Churrigueresque. The delicate ironwork, the carved altars, and richly carved and polychromed pulpit are notable works of colonial art. The church contains a wealth of sculpture by Perusquía and Arce, the two most famous of the Mariano trio (see Index). Particularly fine is the group of *La Piedad* by Arce, notable for the masterly handling of the draperies as well as the monumental quality of the composition and the contrast between the Virgin Mother's intensity of grief and the repose expressed in the relaxed form of the dead Savior.

Other points of architectural as well as historical interest are: the *Templo de la Cruz,* highest point in the city and place where the curious, decisive fist-fight for control of the city is said to have occurred. The better architectural features of the building have been destroyed by inept restorers. The attached convent was used by Maximilian and his beseiged troops as a barracks, and later became Maximilian's prison. The nearby *Church and Monastery of San Agustín* is an interesting Baroque structure. The monastery part is now the *Palacio Federal.* It has a handsome patio and rooms serving as a museum of Maximilian relics.

Cerro de las Campanas on the W edge of the city (Hill of the Bells) is the spot where the romantic and tragic Maximilian Interlude came to an abrupt end. A brown-stone chapel, *La Capilla de Maximiliano,* placed there by the Austrian Government marks the spot where Maximilian and his generals were executed.

QUERÉTARO OPALS: Numerous guidebooks further the fiction that the amethysts, opals, topazes, and aquamarines sold by sidewalk vendors and shops in town are mined in the area. The only semiprecious stone mining that occurs in the area is for opals, and most of these come from the eastern part of the state. Querétaro is, however, an important gem cutting center. Stones imported from the U.S., Brazil and other parts of Mexico are cut and polished here. It is advisable to avoid the street vendors and make your purchases at a reputable shop. Recommended: *Abbott's,* on the highway next to the Genova Restaurant; *El Rubio,* Av. Madero 3, Pte. (For description of Mexican gem stones see Index.)

FIESTAS: Querétaro is noted for its colorful fiestas which draw visitors regularly from as far as Mexico City. Chief among the celebrations are: May 15, fiesta celebrating the capture of the city by Juárez' troops. July 18–26, important religious fiesta honoring Nuestra Señora Santa Ana, includes important bullfights, regional and Indian dances, fireworks. September 14, Fiesta at the Convent of the Santa Cruz. September 15–16, Independence Day celebrations. December 24, Christmas Fair, processions, floats, regional dances, bullfights. The festivities begin the first Sunday of December and last until January 6.

To the SE of Querétaro, on the route to or from Mexico City, are two points of travel interest: *San Juan del Río,* a fascinating reed-weaving town, and *Tequisquiapan,* a colorful hot springs resort-village.

San Juan del Río, Qro. Pop. 8000. Alt. 6500 ft. On the Central Highway, 102 m. from Mexico City, 31 m. from Querétaro. San Juan del Río (sahn-JUAN-del-RHEE-o) lies in a rich valley through which runs the San Juan River. The town, along with nearby Tequisquia-

[11] Doña Josefa and her husband, the mayor or *Corrigedor,* were charter members of a group called "The Society for the Study of Fine Arts" whose members (including Hidalgo and Allende) were more involved in conspiracy against the Spanish than with art. It was Doña Josefa who, on learning that the club's conspiracy for independence had been discovered, sent word on September 15, 1810, to Allende and Hidalgo, which in effect touched off the spark of rebellion. The Mexican copper 5 centavo coins bear her profile and are popularly called *"Josefinas."*

pan, is one of the few willow-reed *(mimbre)* weaving centers in the country. Numerous stands with a vivid variety of baskets and other articles can be found in the *portales* flanking the highway. On market day (Sunday) a variety of regional goods are available in the market plaza, 2 blocks N of the highway.

There are various interesting colonial buildings and homes in the town. Of colonial architecture the most notable are the colonial bridge built by the architect Arrieta in 1720 (W entrance of town), and *La Parroquia* (the Parochial Church). Also, in this region is the Trinidad Opal Mine, and La Esperanza, Mexico's first important opal mine, discovered in 1835.

HOTELS AND RESTAURANTS: *Hotel San Juan* is fair and inexpensive. *Auto repairs* — Auto Servicio Camacho, Av. Juárez 14.

Tequisquiapan, Qro. Pop. 2043. Alt. 6200 ft. This tiny, picturesque Otomí village, noted for its thermal springs, lies 12 m. N of San Juan del Río, via paved road, CE-17. A small American colony has settled in the town and there are several small, satisfactory hotels or inns. Craftsmen in the village produce finely woven willow basketry, excellent serapes, and beautiful handmade lace. On Sunday mornings (market day) the pleasant tree-filled plaza becomes a kind of Wall Street of the Mexican opal trade. Indian miners come down from the opal mines in the nearby hills with their bags and bottles of uncut opals, and dealers from Mexico City and Querétaro meet them here. The trading follows a curious ritual, almost like the mating dance of certain exotic birds.

A dealer will sit in his car or on a bench in the plaza. The Indian with his bag of matrix-bound opals will stroll around several times, staying a good distance away from the dealer. Eyes may meet, occasionally they will nod. The dealer does nothing. He may have bought from the Indian miner the week before, but still the curious dance is repeated. Finally the Indian comes close and exhibits his treasure. There is no logic at all in the bargaining that follows. If the Indian had had a good week he might ask 10,000 pesos for a 100 peso opal. If he has had a bad week he might literally give away a really valuable opal for a dollar.

HOTELS AND RESTAURANTS: During national holidays and weekends it is advisable to make hotel reservations as well as transportation reservations to and from Tequisquiapan, pronounced teh-keys-KEYA-pahn. *Posada Tequisquiapan,* Moctezuma 6. Tel 10. A small, neat, friendly atmosphere inn. 11 rooms and suites. Lovely garden and rustic swimming pool. Fair dining room, untrained bar service. About the best place in town. Rates: AP $125 MN dble. Other inns roughly similar in size, accommodations and rates are: *Hotel Posada del Virrey,* Guillermo Prieto 9, *Casa Elizabeth,* two doors away. Has excellent hot baths. *El Relox,* Morelos 8, service here about nil. *Hotel Río,* edge of town, new, 58 rooms, dining room, bar, swimming pool. Reasonable rates. *Posada Maridelfi,* nine rooms, pleasant. Reasonable.

DIRECTORY: *Bank* — Banco Mercantil del Bajío, on Guillermo Prieto. *Bus lines* — *Note:* to reach Tequisquiapan from Mexico City it is best to take a first-class bus going through San Juan del Río (Transportes del Norte, Transportes Chihuahuenses of Flecha Roja), and from San Juan taxi out to Tequisquiapan, or transfer to a local or second-class bus. *Shops and regional information* — Artes Tequis, Centenario 44.

EXCURSIONS FROM TEQUISQUIAPAN, from Tequis local guides can take you to the opal mines, including *La Esperanza,* reachable by car. A short distance north via paved byroad is the picturesque village of *Bernal* which sits at the foot of a curious sombrero-shaped hill. Local weavers produce excellent heavyweight loosely woven serapes. Beyond Bernal a road leads to *Cadereyta,* a mining town. It is a base for off-trail jaunts to important Toltec archaeological ruins *Las Ranas* (near the village of *San Joaquín, Qro.*) and *El Pueblito* (near the village of *Villa Corregidora*). The ruins have hardly been investigated. No restoration has been attempted. From Cadereyta they are reached by rough mining roads.

AREAS NORTH AND NORTHWEST OF GUANAJUATO CITY: The country to the north and northwest of Guanajuato one must necessarily travel through enroute from El Paso or Eagle Pass to Mexico City, however, except for casual stops it had little to offer in the way of sightseeing or vacation spots. To the NW the most important points are *León, Gto.* and *Aguascalientes, Ags.* To the N the city of *San Luis Potosí,* S.L.P.

León, Gto. Pop. 122,700. Alt. 6183. The largest and most important commercial city in the state of Guanajuato. León (leh-ON) lies about 30 m. NW of Guanajuato City, on the Central Highway, CN-45. The city was founded in 1756. In spite of its growth and industrialization it contains a number of pretty parks, charming old buildings and churches. The city was the birthplace of Ignacio Aldama, a co-patriot of Father Hidalgo in the Independence movement.

León is celebrated through Mexico because of a great flood which threatened its existence on the night of June 18, 1888. A cloudburst caused the Río Gomez to overflow its banks, and in a twinkling of an eye a huge wall of water and debris rushed over the city, sweeping away 2230 houses, drowning more than 200 persons and rendering 20,000 homeless. The fine bridge known as *El Puente del Coecillo* and the huge dyke of heavy masonry (nearly a mile long and 10 ft. thick) were erected to prevent a repetition of the disaster.

The city is one of the chief leather-manufacturing centers in the republic. Although the handicrafting of leather goods (inlaid saddles, pocketbooks, etc.) is still done, the town's output is largely industrialized.

The principal points of interest in the city are the market, the old *portales* around the central plaza, the *Palacio Municipal* (City Hall), on the plaza, noted for its richly carved façade. The *Cathedral,* facing the plaza, was begun by the Jesuits in 1746, and was dedicated to Nuestra Señora de la Luz (Our Lady of Light). The edifice has a fine dome and two tall towers. The proportions of the nave are somewhat awkward. Of interest to students of art is the *Nuestra Señora de los Angeles Church* embellished by interesting carvings of a native craftsman.

HOTELS AND RESTAURANTS: *Hotel León,* in center of town at Madero 113. 92 rooms. Air-conditioned dining room. Garage. A well-run friendly hotel. The food served is simple but quite good. Rates: EP $80 MN dble. Tel. 32-10. *Hotel Capri,* Belisario Domínguez 107. 42 rooms, just fair. Rates from $55 MN dble, EP. Tel. 37-56. *Yolanda Courts,* on highway, S edge of town. 30 units, fairly new but not too well kept. Skip the restaurant. Rates: EP from $60 MN dble.

DIRECTORY: *Bank* — Banco Nacional de México, Madero 19 and 21. *Car repairs* — Automotriz del Centro (Ford), Calz. J. de Obregón 413 Pte. Automóviles y Camiones de León (GM), Calz. Guadalupe and J. de Obregón. Ernesto Martinez (Nash), Morelos 101. *Bus lines* — Transportes Chihuahuenses (check with hotel); Flecha Roja, Hotel Mexico, Portal Delicias, Tel. 33-41; Transportes Nacionales del Centro Estrella Blanca, Gante 107 and 109; Transportes Estrella de Occidente, Morelos 306. *Railway* — Ferrocarriles Nacionales de México, tickets and information, Hotel Condesa, Portal Bravo 14. Tel. 20-14 and 40-14.

Comanjilla, Gto. A very pleasant, inexpensive hot springs resort a few miles off CN-45 22 m. SE of León, or 31 m. NW of Guanajuato. The Hotel Balneario de Comanjilla is operated by the German-Mexican family of Sr. Winfried Gabriel. 62 rooms, very good restaurant, bar, pool, and baths, nice grounds, horseback riding. Rates: AP $130 MN dble. Tel. 47-08.

Lagos de Moreno, Jal. Pop. 13,220. Alt. 6370 ft. About 26 m. N of León at the junction of the Central Highway, CN-45 and CN-80 (San Luis Potosí-Guadalajara). The town is somnolent and picturesque, having retained much of the colonial atmosphere from the days when it was an important stagecoach stop. *Emergency hotel* — *Hotel Paris,* on the plaza, 35 rooms, poor restaurant, bar. Rates: $45 MN dble., EP.

San Juan de los Lagos, Jal. Pop. 7795. Alt. 6115 ft. On the Guadalajara-San Luis Potosí Highway, CN-80, about 29 m. E of the Central Highway.

San Juan de los Lagos (sahn-HWAN deh loss LAH-gos) is a quiet colonial town with narrow, medieval streets, but a town that suddenly bursts with visitors several times a year during its famed religious fiestas. In the *Parroquia* (Parochial Church) on the plaza is an image of the Virgin of San Juan de los Lagos. The image is said to be miraculous, and it attracts thousands of pilgrims each year. For the religious celebration which usually begins about January 20 and builds up to an almost delirious climax, February 5, pilgrims in groups of 25 to several hundred persons walk for hundreds of miles, day and night, chanting, camping in the open, until they reach San Juan. The atmosphere of such pilgrimages is quite medieval, or remindful of the great Moslem pilgrimages to Mecca.

Other San Juan fiestas are: August 1–16, religious celebration; around November 20, a month-long fair honoring Nuestra Señora de San Juan de los Lagos. During this event there are Indian dancers, bullfights, gambling, *serenatas,* etc. From November 28 to December 8, a similar religious festival occurs.

There are no comfortable accommodations in the town. Tourists attending the San Juan fiestas should seek accommodations at León, Comanjilla, or Guanajuato.

Aguascalientes, Ags. Pop. 93,500. Alt. 6229 ft. Capital of the state of the same name. An attractive colonial city, famed for its annual Spring Festival, the Fería de San Marcos. On the Central Highway, CN-45 (957 m. from El Paso, Texas. 322 m. from Mexico City). The city is also a principal stop on the Ciudad Juárez-Mexico City line of the Mexican National Railways.

HOTELS AND RESTAURANTS: *San Marcos Motor Hotel,* ½ m. S on CN-45. A quite good motel with 27 units and suites, fair dining room, cocktail lounge, good room service. Rates: EP from $40 MN to $65 MN dble. *Hotel Paris,* on the plaza. 36 rooms, nicely maintained, pleasant atmosphere. Good dining room, cocktails served. Affiliated with the Country Club. Garage. Rates: EP from $50 MN to $70 MN dble. Tel. 11-21. *Campo Medrano Courts,* on highway, S edge of town. 19 units, some air conditioning, pool, bar, dining room poor. Motel seems not too well run. Rates: EP from $45 MN dble. Other hotels that will do during the fiesta period: *Hotel Francia,* Plaza Principal. 60 units, fairly old. *Hotel Imperial,* 5 de Mayo 10, *viajero* style. *Restaurant Fausto,* Madero 1. Will do.

DIRECTORY: *Banks* — Banco Nacional de México, 5 de Mayo 37. *Auto repairs* — Automotriz de Aguascalientes (Ford), J. M. Chavez 325; Automotriz Victoria (Chrysler), Chavez 101. *Bus lines* — Transportes Chihuahuenses, tickets at Hotel Imperial. Estrella Blanca, 5 de Mayo 146, Tel. 54. Flecha Roja, corner República and Plaza Principal, Tel. 5-47. *Railway* — tickets and reservations at the station.

THE TOWN AND ENVIRONS: Aguascalientes (AH-gwahs-kahl-YEN-tes) takes its name from the hot waters, thermal springs that abound in the area. The city itself is celebrated for its almost perfect climate, the fine nearby orchards, lovely plazas and colonial buildings. It is sometimes referred to as La Ciudad Perforado (the Perforated City) because of the extensive system of tunnels beneath it. This labyrinth of catacombs, excavated by some pre-historic, unknown tribe, has never been thoroughly explored, although it is known that some tunnels are subdivided into many ramifications. They are closed to the public. It is said that neither Toltec, Aztec nor Tarascan annals refer to them or to their builders. The people who dug them evidently followed some well-defined plan, for at intervals throughout the city the tunnels connect at the surface by shafts which formerly admitted light and air.

The first records of Aguascalientes date from about 1522, soon after the fall of the Aztec Confederation. Cortés sent Pedro de Alvarado to conquer the western territories. Near the site of present-day Aguascalientes the Spanish were badly mauled by well-armed Indians and had to retreat. The city was founded in 1575 by royal decree. For many years it remained little more than an outpost in the Chichimeca Indian country. The real importance of the place dated from early 1800 when rich silver mines were discovered at *Tepezalá.* Coincidentally the Jesuits took a keen interest in the spiritual welfare of the people at this time. The city was made the capital of its state in 1835.[12]

The most important landmarks in the city are the *Palacio del Gobierno* (Governor's Palace), the old feudal castle of the Marqués de Guadalupe; the *Palacio Municipal* (City Hall); the curious, almost Byzantine *Church of San Antonio;* and the *Church of San Marcos* which contains an important painting, *The Adoration of the Kings* by José Alzíbar. The pretty *Jardín de San Marcos* is the focal point each April 25 to May 5 for the famed San Marcos Fair. Aguascalientes is also noted for its Grape Festival, July 27 to August 5. Arrangements to visit the wineries can be made through local hotels.

Of interest, also, is a visit to *Las Peñuelas,* one of Mexico's most famous bull-breeding *haciendas.* If you are fortunate you might see a *tienta* (testing), a kind of

[12] *State of Aguascalientes,* with a population of 214,961, and an area of 2,528 sq. miles, is one of the smallest of the Mexican states. The adjoining state of Zacatecas almost surrounds Aguascalientes on the NW and NE while Jalisco delimits it on the SE. The state is an important agricultural producer — corn, wheat, sweet potatoes, fruit, and grapes. It is noted for its many hot springs such as San Nicholas de la Cantera, Ojo Caliente, and Colombo. The chief constituents of the mineral waters are sulphate of soda, sulphate of lime, carbonate of lime, chloride of sodium, magnesia, and some sulphuric acid.

fiesta during which the young fighting bulls are tested and selected for future glory in the ring. Arrangements can be made through the Motel San Marcos to visit the *hacienda.*

Aguascalientes is known through the country for the fine hand-drawn work done in the region. The embroidery, drawn-work, and crochet of the women is said to rival that of Belgium and Switzerland.

Directly west of Aguascalientes, via paved road CN-70, lies the capital of the State of San Luis Potosí (also on CN-57, Eagle Pass-Mexico City Route). Although it is not attractive enough to be a travel-objective in itself, motorists, train, and bus travelers coming through it will find it an interesting overnight or half-day stop.

San Luis Potosí, S.L.P. Pop. 125,900. Alt. 6290 ft. Capital of the state of the same name, important railway, highway junction, and mining center. It is also noted for its well-preserved colonial architecture.

HOTELS AND RESTAURANTS: *Santa Fé Motel,* ½ m. SE of Juárez Glorieta on CN-57. A de luxe establishment, perhaps the best along the entire route 57. Has 21 units, good dining room, cocktail lounge. Rates: EP from $80 to $100 MN dble. *Motel Cactus,* same area, new and ultramodern, 40 units, good coffee shop, dining room, cocktail lounge, room service. Tel. 45-06. Rates: EP from $80 MN to $100 MN dble. *Hotel Concordia,* at Othon and Morelos, 1 block E of main plaza. 42 rooms, fair dining room, cocktail bar. Parking. Rental TV. A well-run, new, friendly hotel. Rates: EP from $45 to $80 MN dble. Tel. 60-65. *Hotel Gante,* 5 de Mayo 10, just off plaza. 45 rooms, older, but nice hotel. Rates: EP from $60 MN to $80 MN dble. Tel. 64-91. *Motel Tuna,* 3 m. W on CN-80. An older, but very comfortable motel with lovely grounds and 55 nicely furnished units. Good dining room, cocktail lounge, room service, pool. Rates: EP from $60 MN to $80 MN dble. Tel. 29-65.

Other hotels, less pretentious but satisfactory: *Hotel Colonial,* Madero and Aldama; *Hotel Napoles,* Juan Sarabia 6; *Hotel San Luis Rey,* Zaragoza and P. A. Santos (difficult to find, but low priced); *Jardín Motel,* E edge of town, skip unless you're really desperate.

Café La Lonja, Madero and Aldama. An old restaurant, noted for its cuisine. Has recently changed hands. No recent report. *Restaurante Colonial,* Madero 14. Sometimes good. *McCall's Restaurant Dormac,* in Soledad suburb of S.L.P. 2½ m. NE. American operated. *Restaurant Virreina,* on V. Carranza 830 (CN-80) an excellent colonial-style restaurant.

DIRECTORY: *Banks* — Banco Nacional de México, Obregón 39; Banco Mercantil de San Luis Potosí, J. de los Reyes 17. *Auto repairs* — Automotriz Potosina (Ford), Av. Carranza and Urasti (shop at A. Obregón 67); Herrera Motors (GM), D. Carmona and Arista; Servicio S.A. (general repairs), Arista 85. *Travel agent* — Almanza Travel Service, Lobby of Hotel de Gante. *Bus lines* — Transportes del Norte, Bravo and Constitución, Tel. 40-61. (Mexico City to Laredo); Autobuses Anáhuac, Los Bravos 66, Tel. 41-42. (Mexico City to Eagle Pass.) *Airlines* — Aeronaves de México, Jardín Hidalgo 15. Tel. 60-57. *Railways* — Ferrocarriles Nacional de México, tickets and reservation at the station. (Best transportation between S.L.P. and Mexico City is via the once-daily *Autovía* train. The crack *Aguila Azteca* — Laredo to Mexico City — stops in S.L.P. also.)

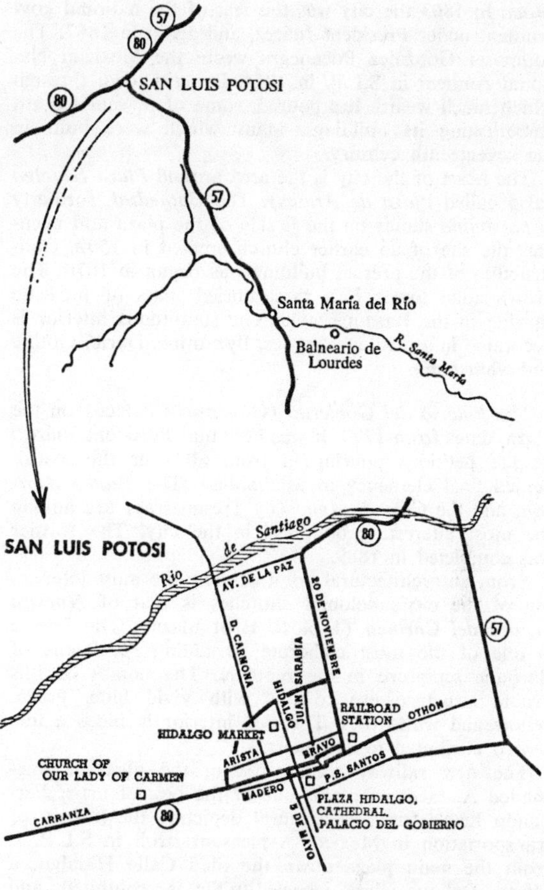

THE CITY AND ENVIRONS: San Luis Potosí (sahn-luis-po-toe-SEE), both city and state,[13] though little visited by tourists are of historical and sightseeing interest. In spite of its growth and commercial importance, San Luis Potosí has retained much of its colonial charm.

At the time of the conquest of Mexico by Spain the San Luis region was unknown to — or at least unconquered by — the Aztecs. In about 1589 Franciscan missionaries entered the area, and a number of missions were founded, chief among them that of *San Luis.* In 1590 gold mines of astounding richness were discovered in the *San Pedro Hills,* and because the enormous production of gold recalled the fabulously productive mines of Potosí, in Bolivia, the new town was named San Luis Potosí. Its original site was in the San Pedro Hills, 12 m. from its present location, whence it was moved because of lack of potable water.

[13] State of San Luis Potosí is one of Mexico's medium-sized states, having an area of 24,707 sq. miles and a population of 1,051,064. The state is quite mountainous, particularly in the east where rise the vast ranges of the Sierra Madre Oriental. The central and western areas are part of the dry, vast tableland, while in the north the country is arid with salt marshes. In the eastern Huasteca Indian area, centering around Ciudad Valles, is Mexico City's primary source of beef. (This area and tropic Tamazunchale are treated under Northeastern Region of Mexico section of the *Guide.*) The central and western parts of the state is one of Mexico's key mining regions, yielding gold, silver, lead, copper, and mercury. The state is bounded on the N by Coahuila, on the E by Nuevo León, Tamaulipas, and Veracruz, on the SE by Jalisco, on the S by Hidalgo, Querétaro, and Guanajuato, on the W by Zacatecas.

The new town flourished as hordes of gold-seeking Spaniards invaded the area. The first building occupied the site of the present Jesuit *Church of La Compañía de Jesus.* In 1863 the city was the seat of the national government under President Juárez, and again in 1867. The composer Gonzalez Bocanegra wrote the Mexican National Anthem in S.L.P. in 1854. Being a town through which much wealth has poured, some of it went toward embellishing its buildings, many which were built in the seventeenth century.

The heart of the city is the area around *Plaza Hidalgo* (also called *Plaza de Armas*). The *Cathedral,* formerly *la parroquia* stands on the E side of the plaza and occupies the site of an earlier church erected in 1592. Construction of the present building was begun in 1670. The brown-stone tower is a three-storied mass of intricate carving in the Baroque style. The sumptuous interior is decorated in a medley of styles, Byzantine, Doric, Gothic and what not.

The *Palacio del Gobierno* (Governor's Palace) on the plaza, dates from 1770. It was here that President Juárez, despite petitions pouring in from all over the world, denied final clemency to Maximilian. The *Teatro Alarcón,* and the *Caja de Agua* (by Tresguerras) are among the most interesting buildings in the city. The former was completed in 1889.

From an architectural point of view the most interesting of the city's colonial churches is that of *Nuestra Señora del Carmen* (1 block E of plaza). The façade is one of the most elaborate remaining specimens of Baroque sculpture in the republic. The domes of this ornate structure are covered with vivid blue, green, yellow and white tiles. The rich interior includes a fine *reredo* attributed to Tresguerras.

The new railway station, facing the pleasant tree-shaded Alameda, contains one of the best of artist Fernando Leal's frescoes, a mural depicting the history of transportation in Mexico. A pleasant stroll in S.L.P. is from the main plaza down the tiled Calle Hidalgo, a street of shops where wheeled-traffic is prohibited, and which is somewhat remindful of the Serpentina in Sevilla. Hidalgo street leads to the *Hidalgo Market,* usually of interest to tourists.

FIESTAS: From August 18 through 26 the traditional Fería Potosina is held. On July 25, the Barrio Santiago fiesta honoring Saint James. During September, the fiesta of the Seven Barrios.

EXCURSIONS FROM SAN LUIS POTOSÍ: Approximately 31 m. SE of the city, via CN-57 (Eagle Pass-Mexico City Road), and ½ m. off highway to W lies *Santa María del Río,* a tiny, charming village in a small valley filled with masses of trees. The village has one of the most relaxing plazas in Mexico. The local women are noted for their production of fine *rebozos.*

A few miles S of Santa María del Río there is a turn-off to the E dirt road leading seven miles to *Balneario de Lourdes,* S.L.P. (formerly Hacienda de La Labor del Río), a rustic thermal spa. The road from the highway is poor, passing through lovely scenic country along the Río Santa María (the river empties farther on into the Río Verde, and sheds toward the Gulf of Mexico near Tampico).

The hotel, built in 1931, is on the bank of the river, has gardens and two unheated pools (one filled with rusty-looking mineral water, the other with crystal-clear river water). Hotel accommodations simple; 36 rooms, large and clean, dining room only fair. Bar service. Rates: AP $55 MN per person. The Lourdes waters, famed through Mexico, are said to be good for ulcers, kidney stones, etc. The *Balneario* is a pleasant, low-priced retreat far off the tourist-beat. The only jarring note here is the bottling works.

THE HIDALGO COUNTRY

This area, lying N and NE of Mexico City covers the small State of Hidalgo (Pop. 994,598; area, 8152 sq. miles), and the northern corner of the State of Puebla. The area is unusually mountainous, especially in the eastern part, and is one of Mexico's wealthiest mineral sections. Hidalgo itself is bordered on the N by the state of San Luis Potosí, on the E by Veracruz and Puebla, on the S by Tlaxcala and Mexico, and to the W by Querétaro. Part of the area, along the easternmost slopes, is beautiful tropical country.

The chief highways serving this area are the Pan-American (CN-85); the Vanilla Route (CN-130), going from the Pan-American, through Pachuca to the Gulf of Mexico. The Central Highway (CN-45) cuts across the northern part of Hidalgo, connecting with CN-85. The Constitution Route (CN-57, Eagle Pass-Mexico City) cuts through a corner of the area near the Toltec ruins at Tula. The best public transportation to points of interest is by first-class bus or private car. Though the railways connect some of the points, service is slow and uncomfortable.

TRAVEL HIGHLIGHTS: In this area are to be found several of the outstanding attractions of Mexico; (1) *Tula,* the ancient Toltec capital, (2) the fascinating silver mining villages around *Pachuca* and, *San Miguel Regla,* a unique hideaway resort, (3) the little-traveled, breath-takingly beautiful mountain and tropic country around *Villa Juárez, Pue.*

The Tula and Pachuca sections can be comfortably visited in a day from Mexico City. With the exception of San Miguel Regla, overnight accommodations are poor so Mexico City is the traveler's best base. An ideal circuit tour from Mexico City is the following:

Leave Mexico City via CN-57. Stop at *Tepotzotlán, Mex.,* to see one of the country's most famous sanctuaries (see Index). Continue on to *Tula* (see Index). From Tula a paved byroad (CE-126) leads to the *Pachuca-San Miguel Regla* area. From here you can either branch off to *Villa Juárez* and the Gulf of Mexico, or continue back to Mexico City via CN-85. Excluding the Villa Juárez junket, the round trip can be made in one rather long day, or very comfortably in two days.

Tula, Hgo. Pop. 6000. The archaeological zone is on a hill across the river from the town, about 2 miles.

HOW TO GET THERE: *Via highway* — take CN-57, to *Tepeji del Río,*[14] about 42 m. N of Mexico City. ½ m. N of Tepeji is paved turn-off NE (CE-126) going 9 m. to Tula. From the Pan-American Highway (CN-85) turn-off to W at *Actopan.* Tula lies 35 m. W. *Via railway* — trains on the Laredo and El Paso lines of the National Railways pause at Tula. It is a flag stop. *Via bus* — take Autobuses Anáhuac to Tepeji del Río, thence by

[14] Tepeji del Río, a rather nondescript town nicely situated on a hillside has an interesting sixteenth-century church noted for its lovely Plateresque façade featuring primitive adornments, sculptures of biblical personages, among them Adam and Eve. During Holy Week, Tepeji stages a fabulous Passion Play, actors wearing hooded costumes as in Sevilla, Spain.

taxi to Tula, or, directly from Mexico City via a conducted tour. See your travel agent.

The ruins of Tula have been so recently discovered, accommodations have still to catch up with the tourist trade. The only hotel in town, the *Posada de la Luz*, Calle Ocampo 26, is primitive and recommended only in an emergency. Of the restaurants, *El Cisne*, Calzada Melchor Ocampo and Juárez, is the best (but far from good).

In the center of Tula (the Spanish town) stands a great walled church and monastery said to have been begun by Fray Antonio de San Juan in 1550. It is an impressive, thick-walled, fortress structure in Renaissance style with some Gothic details. The luxurious Mexican-Spanish Baroque had not yet appeared then. The interior of the church has a beautifully vaulted ceiling. There is little decoration, only purity of line. This massive conventual establishment, so out of proportion to the smallness of the town, was one of the clues that led to the so-called discovery of the Toltec capital across the river.

THE ARCHAEOLOGICAL ZONE: The history of Tollan (Tula), the legendary lost city of the Toltecs is one of the most fascinating in the annals of Mexican archaeology. Investigation has indicated that Tula was the chief Toltec center approximately between 896 and 1168 A.D. (See *Toltex Culture*, Index). Internal strife and famine were undoubtedly the causes bringing to an end this great metropolis. According to legend a powerful king, Huemac (Great Hand), ascended the throne in 1100. Though he was a tyrant, his reign prospered for many years until his avariciousness caused a famine. According to the story, while playing ball one day with the Tlaloques (Rain Gods), Huemac won and was awarded corn kernels. He refused the prize and insisted on feathers and jade beads. The gods gave him his choice, which filled Tula's coffers with treasures but left the people hungry. Civil war broke out and the Toltec metropolis came to an end — the Toltecs wandered off to teach the Chichimecas, help the Mayas and build other temples all over Mexico.

For centuries the city was lost, though the name Tollan kept appearing in ancient codices, chronicles and tradition. Some imagined Tollan was Teotihuacán, others thought it was the Tula near Toluca. In the sixteenth century a Christianized Indian scholar and noble, Fernando de Alba Ixtli-Xóchitl, wrote a work concerning Tollan: portraying the life of the people in the lost city, their government, descriptions of the streets and their industries. It ended Fernando de Alba's career as a man of science. He was bounced from the pantheon of the erudite to the ghetto of poets. He was accused of taking the legend of Tula at face value, just as ancient Troy was considered the fruit of the imagination of a talented liar named Homer. As with Troy, Tollan waited centuries for its Schliemann.

In the latter part of the nineteenth century a colorful traveler, Desiré Charnay, came upon Tollan. Unfortunately, Charnay was of rather dubious character. He had been a spy for Napoleon III, and was now treasure-hunting, financed by a Franco-American millionaire named Lorillard. At Tula he used methods of archaeology better designed to mutilate than to preserve — but he did uncover important Toltec figures. He hadn't consulted Mexican authorities so they doubted his findings. Tollan still remained lost until around 1938 when one of Mexico's leading archaeologists, Jiménez Moreno, defied the doubters, sifted much data and predicted Tollan was at Tula. In 1940 funds were made available to investigate. Even after the site was established some scholars claimed that the pyramids and colossal figures at Tula were falsified. In 1950 further excavations conducted by archaeologists Jorge Acosta and Hugo Moedano proved Tula to be one of Mexico's major archaeological sites. They have uncovered definite links between Tula and the Toltec structures at Chichén Itzá in Yucatán, and that the artistic quality of the bas-reliefs and sculpture at Tula are in many ways superior to those at Chichén Itzá.

The center of the archaeological zone, crowning the hill overlooking the town, is topped by a five-terrace pyramid. There is a plaza and smaller pyramids that are still to be uncovered. Nearby is a court of square columns and several *Chac-Mool* figures (the Toltec Rain God, also found in Yucatán and for a long time believed to be of Maya origin). Near the court of columns, protected by tin roofs are the foundation walls of buildings with the remains of magnificent frescoes and bas-reliefs. Several of the Tula trademarks, the majestic stone figures which originally served as supports at the entrances of temples, have been placed atop the principal pyramid.

To the N beyond the pyramid is the large ball court, thought to be the earliest ball court constructed in the Americas. Recently a partly cylindrical temple-pyramid has been discovered, as well as other constructions several miles to the NE of the metropolis.

The archaeological zone is open daily from 8 A.M. to 6 P.M. Admission, 2 pesos.

Atitalaquia, Hgo. A tiny picturesque village about 15 m. SE of Tula via paved, unnumbered road. The town, completely off tourist routes has one of the loveliest, undamaged, Baroque Franciscan churches in the region. The church is called San Miguel de Atitalaquia.

Pachuca, Hgo. Pop. 58,653. Alt. 8225 ft. Capital of the State of Hidalgo and center of one of Mexico's most picturesque silver-mining areas.

HOW TO GET THERE: *Via road* — Pan-American Highway, CN-85 to *Colonia* turn-off (53 m. N of Mexico City), then E 6 m. *Via railway* — daily slow trains from Mexico City, leaving at 9:45 A.M., arriving at 1:05 P.M. A daily train goes from Tula to Pachuca, taking about 3½ hrs. *Via bus* — the Líneas Unidas de Primera Clase buses run directly to Pachuca and Villa Juárez.

HOTELS AND RESTAURANTS: Considering Pachuca's size, age, and that it produces about 15 per cent of the world's silver supply, hotel accommodations are definitely not elegant. No hotel in the city is recommended except for emergency. Best is *Hotel Noriega*, Matamoros 23, 29 rooms, *viajero* style. Nearest to fair food is served at the *Casino Español*, Matamoros 11. Travelers intending to spend several days in this region should take accommodations at the Hacienda de San Miguel Regla (see below).

DIRECTORY: *Bank* — Banco Nacional de México, Hidalgo and Leandro Valle. *Car repairs* — Auto Servicio, Matamoros 26. Pachuca Motors, Xicotencatl 2. *Bus lines* — Líneas Unidas, Matamoros 13. Tel. 5-55. Turismo Pachuca, Real del Monte, Hidalgo 20. Tel. 2-23-00.

THE CITY AND ENVIRONS: Founded in 1534 by Spanish silver and gold seekers, Pachuca (pa-CHEW-ka) rapidly became one of the country's most productive silver centers. The old Trinidad mine alone produced silver to the value of 40 millions of pesos in ten years, at a time when the peso was equal to the dollar. Hundreds of mines, many of them now inoperative, honeycomb the hills which encircle three sides of the town. The place has all the aspects of a mining camp. It lies at the head of a wide gulch, and the hills which rise sharply upward from the ends of narrow streets form a sort of a pipe through which there almost continuously draws a thin, disagreeable wind. The mines have been operated successively since the sixteenth century by Spanish, English, Mexican, and American operators. The *patio* process (now replaced by a more efficient cyaniding process) for the reduction of ore was invented here in 1557 by Bartolomé de Medina.

Although Pachuca is more picturesque when seen from a distance, there are a few buildings of minor interest, among them: *Casas Colorados* (red houses), built toward the end of the eighteenth century by the Conde de Regla, and now used for government offices. *La Caja,* a bizarre, fortress-like structure erected in 1670 as a treasury for the Royal tribute.

The environs of Pachuca are more interesting than the town itself. Beyond the hills rimming the city is the celebrated *Xixi Mountain,* at the foot of which are curiously shaped rocks of immense size, the *Peñas Cargadas* (Loaded Rocks). The area is a favored picnic spot.

Real del Monte, Hgo., 6 m. from Pachuca, via paved mountain road, is an exciting, colonial mining town in a most picturesque setting — a delight for photographers and artists. The town grew around the Real del Monte mine, one of the most extensive mining properties in the world. The original owner Romero de Terreros, a nobleman, bought the main mine in 1739 for about $60,000. Soon afterward it came into bonanza, and by 1781 had yielded nearly 15 millions of pesos.

Terreros gained international fame by his extravagances. He loaned the King of Spain a million pesos and presented him with a fully equipped warship, for which he received a patent of nobility as the Conde de Santa María de Regla. The Conde's son was unable to maintain the prosperity of the mines and they were closed during the disturbances arising from the War of Independence. An English firm under John Taylor, perhaps inspired by Baron Von Humboldt's reports concerning the mines, reopened them from 1824 to 1848. Still to be seen in the area are vestiges of the 250 Cornish miners and their families who came from Europe, particularly in the high-peaked roofs of many of the houses and buildings in Real del Monte. After losing 10 millions of pesos the English company liquidated. A local company purchased the property and shortly afterward made the rich Rosario strike. At present the property is owned by the U. S. Smelting and Refining Company. Visits to the mine properties can be arranged by applying to the office of the director, Cía. Real del Monte y Pachuca, at V. Carranza 10, in Pachuca. Tel. 2-18-51.

San Miguel Regla, Hgo. A tiny village in the lovely Huasca Valley, 25 m. NE of Pachuca, and lately noted for its secluded, picturesque resort hotel, the Hacienda San Miguel Regla, belonging to the Club Panamericano de Doctores. The hacienda was formerly one of the properties of the Conde de Regla. The grounds are spacious and restful. There are good recreational facilities: swimming pools, trout ponds, golf, lawn games, boating, horseback riding. The hotel has 41 rooms, some first class, some quite modest. Dining room. Members of the Doctors' Club have preference reservations. Rates for nonmembers: AP from $210 to $240 MN dble. Singles, AP from $110 to $130 MN. Children 2 to 6 years, $60 MN; from age 6 to 12, $80 MN. Tel. Huasca 2.

HOW TO GET THERE: The *Hacienda* has its own small airstrip for light planes. Via car or taxi from Pachuca — take the road to *Atotonilco el Grande* (CE-105), passing through *Real del Monte.* 17 m. from Pachuca, at road-marker Km. 110, gravel road forks off to right. The road is rough but passable. Follow it through the delightful, photogenic town of *Huasca* to San Miguel Regla.

Atotonilco el Grande. Hgo.[15] Pop. 3160. An interesting, seldom-visited village N of Pachuca, reachable by paved road, CE-105 (21 m. from Pachuca). The village has an excellent sixteenth-century convent representing the Renaissance style, and an interesting open-chapel. There are early colonial murals on the stairway of the cloister. The City Hall is noted for its gallery or *mirador* (like the Italian *loggia*). Comparatively few examples of this sixteenth-century architectural form remain in Mexico. The Atotonilco *loggia* has richly carved capitals supporting molded arches.

N of Atotonilco lies one of the least explored and interesting areas of Mexico, noted for its small *barrancas* and vivid valleys and tiny villages where the natives fashion interesting gold jewelry, do excellent primitive weaving. Accessible only by jeep.

AREA EAST OF PACHUCA: Directly E of Pachuca, along CN-130, lies one of the most scenic and easily accessible areas of Mexico, a marvelous drive that has yet to become popular with tourists, even though accommodations along the way are good to excellent. For route log, see Index: Highway Routes — Pachuca to Tecolutla. The villages are noted for their markets and handicrafts, and those along the Puebla slope of the Gulf are the flower-treasury of Mexico.

Epazoyucan, Hgo. Nine m. E of Pachuca a paved branch road leads south toward *Apam* and the pyramids at *Teotihuacan.* A few miles from the turn-off from CN-130 is Epazoyucan (aye-pah-zoh-YUH-kahn), noted for its sixteenth-century monastery, open-chapel, and the excellent frescoes in its cloister. On November 30 the town celebrates a lively fiesta.

Tulancingo, Hgo. Pop. 22,000. Alt. 3600. A busy industrial and agricultural community on CN-130, 29 m. from Pachuca. Tulancingo (two-lahn-SEEN-go) was once a flourishing Toltec city. The town is noted for its serape weaving, fruit wines, and cider. *Emergency hotel* — Hotel Colonial, Juárez and Zaragoza. *Auto repairs* — Delgadillo, 1 de Mayo 52.

Market day in the town is on Thursday. Around August 2 the town celebrates its annual fair.

Huauchinango, Pue. Pop. 18,000. On CN-130, 63 m. E of Pachuca. The approaches to the town through the pine forests of the Sierra de Zacapoaxtla are magnificent. The town lies in a valley dotted with fruit orchards and vivid flower gardens.

Huauchinango (woah-chee-NAHN-go) is charmingly semitropical, its picturesque tiled-roof houses seeming to blend into the riot of flowers which have made the town the flower-center of the republic. There is a lively market on Saturdays. During the week beginning with the third Friday of Lent the town has its famed Fería de las Flores (Flower Festival) which attracts visitors from all over Mexico. Wonderful Indian dances.

Worth visiting is El Cantil Florido at Calle Vicario 30, one of the town's most famous flower gardens. Also, at nearby *Necaxa Lake,* the gardens and orchards of Dr. Vargas. This entire area is an orchid collector's paradise.

Emergency hotels — Hotel Morales, Portal Hidalgo 5, or *Hotel Vargas,* Guerrero 6. *Eugenia Restaurant* at Guerrero 8 has fair Mexican food. Visitors coming for

[15] THE ATOTONILCOS. There are numerous villages in Mexico called Atotonilco, and several are noted for their shrines or churches. In the State of Hidalgo there is another Atotonilco, called *San Jerónimo Atotonilco* (near Tula), noted for its walled monastery which has a severe and rather massive Plateresque entrance, and above it a rare and unusually beautiful rose window of Gothic tracery.

the flower festival will do better stopping at Villa Juárez (see below). *Car repairs* — Automotriz Huasteca, Hidalgo 11. *Bus lines* — Autotransportes de Primera, Guerrero 6. Tel. 61. (First class, direct route from Mexico City.)

A few miles beyond (E) Huauchinango one finds unusually scenic pine-clad country. The highway parallels the lovely Necaxa Lake for several miles. At Ramal Necaxa, just S of the highway, is located the Necaxa Dam. Boating and swimming facilities.

Villa Juárez, Pue. Pop. 7000. Alt. 3908 ft. A picturesque semitropical town. The region around is ideal for hiking, orchid hunting, and camping. Market days are Thursday and Sunday. Extraordinary handloomed cottons and beautiful embroidery can be found here. Local fiestas of importance are: Holy Week, and a popular fair held June 24.

In 1960 Villa Juárez was officially renamed Xocotepec de Juárez (cho-KO-tay-pek day WAH-rays) in an attempt to confuse tourists. It will take some time before the new name sinks in or appears on road maps.

HOTEL: *El Hotel "Mi Ranchito,"* SW edge of town on CN-130. This is one of the nicest, small, bungalow-type hotels in the country, comparable in many ways to the kind of first-class pensions one finds in Europe. 16 bungalow units surrounded by 30 acres of gardens, lovely vistas, dining room, cocktails, pool. The best cuisine in this region, plus local boysenberry wine. EP or AP rates. AP $140 MN dble. Tel. 12. Reservations recommended for the hotel is always filled.

DIRECTORY: *Bank* — Banco Nacional de México, on plaza, Portal Norte 6. *Auto repairs* — Ramirez, 5 de Mayo 31. *Bus lines* — Buses from Mexico City and Pachuca stop in the plaza.

AREA NORTH OF PACHUCA: Most of the accessible points of interest north of Pachuca lie along the Pan-American Highway. None are sufficiently interesting to warrant special trips out of Mexico City or from Pachuca, but can be touched by motorists driving down from Laredo. Beginning with the northern part of the State of Hidalgo and moving southward toward Pachuca the principal points of interest are:

Chapulhuacan, Hgo. Pop. 1450. Just E of CN-85, the Pan-American Road, 550 m. from Laredo. A very quaint, photogenic village, worth pausing at if you have a camera.

Jacala, Hgo. Pop. 1700. Alt. 4590 ft. A picturesque ranching town on CN-85, 592 m. from Laredo. Jacala (hah-CAH-la) is set in the scenic mountain-girt valley of the Río Quetzalapa. The name is derived from the word *jacal* (shack) and dates from the period when Spanish miners, seeking a reputed gold vein in the nearby canyons, built themselves a huge shack or shelter to serve as their base.

Simpson's Court and Restaurant, ½ m. N of town. Modest accommodations in attractive setting, 9 units. Fair dining room. Rates: EP $30 MN dble.

Zimapán, Hgo. Pop. 2400. Alt. 6415. Just off Pan-American Highway, 633 m. from Laredo. Zimapán (seem-ah-PAHN), founded in 1522, is a most picturesque mining town, almost hidden in a region of scenic valleys and mountains of the Zimapán Range. The village's old buildings, tree-shaded streets and plaza exude an atmosphere of age. Noteworthy is the *Parroquia* (Parish Church) built in the sixteenth century. It is almost East Indian in style. The façade and tower of red stone contrast strikingly with the white background. The first-story columns of the portals are interestingly broken up into groups of horizontal moldings which could have been imported from India. These, coupled with the Moorish arch at the entrance, and the rather chaste Churrigueresque decorations on the upper story, create a bewildering composition difficult to find anywhere else in Mexico. Also of interest in the town is the old *Palacio Municipal* (City Hall) and a gigantic cypress tree measuring 40 feet in circumference at the base.

HOTELS: *Hotel Posada del Rey.* 47 rooms, colonial-style, nice patio, heated pool, excellent dining room, Spanish-style tavern-bar. A very fine, first-class, semi-resort hotel. Friendly atmosphere and well operated. Tel 61. Rates: from $45 MN to $80 MN, dble, EP. *Hotel Fundicion,* in town, reported to be nice, but we have made no check on it.

Tasquillo, Hgo. 15 m. S of Zimapán, just off of CN-85. Tasquillo (tahs-KEEL-yo) is a picturesque tree-shaded village, once the old capital of the Otomí Indians. Just N of the town a fine old colonial bridge spans the impressive gorge of the Río Tula.

Ixmiquilpan, Hgo. Pop. 2000. Alt. 5579 ft. On the Pan-American Highway, 111 m. N of Mexico City. Ixmiquilpan (is-mee-KEEL-pan), once one of the capitals of the Otomí kingdom, and still an important Otomí Indian center, is a somewhat primitive town containing some interesting colonial structures. There are two colonial bridges spanning the Tula River, the most picturesque being the one at the E edge of town where huge cypress trees overhang the river. Noteworthy also is the sixteenth-century Augustinian monastery and church, founded in 1550. On Monday, market day, the town is quite colorful. Both interesting handbag weaving and some coolers made of *Lapis Mexicanus* can be found in the market.[16]

HOTEL AND RESTAURANT: *H. R. Dobbs Restaurant,* on highway. An old, well-known tourist stop. Clean, good rest rooms, fair food, curio shop. Also 4 motel units. Reasonable. Café hours: 7 A.M. to 10 P.M. *Car repairs* — Cano Brothers, a few doors north of Dobbs.

Actopan, Hgo. Pop. 5000. Alt. 6529 ft. On the Pan-American Highway; 63 m. N of Mexico City, 26 m. N of Pachuca. Actopan (ahk-TOE-pahn) is a small Otomí town with an interesting Wednesday market. Road junction here with highway running W to Tula.

The town is noted for its sixteenth-century Augustinian monastery and church (usually included on conducted tours from Mexico City). The monastery was built in 1546 as a fortress and mission in the Otomí lands. The architect was Fray Andrés de Mate. The edifice or group is interesting for its diversity of styles. The tower is remindful of North African or Saracenic works; the massive walls and battlements are like those of a medieval fortress; the cloisters and interior arches are Gothic; the entrance of the church itself has a monumental Plateresque façade — all which somehow blend harmoniously. There are frescoes depicting the life of San Agustín. A small museum contains some excellent religious art.

[16] *Lapis Mexicanus:* for years the "lapis mexicanus" a kind of stone considered to have magical properties for the distillation and refrigeration of liquids achieved an international fame. Europe went wild about it, buying vast quantities. The Jesuit, Martel de Blois, wrote learned treaties on this filter, as did a Dr. Schatz of Strasbourg, both suggesting the stone possessed elixir-of-life properties. In Ixmiquilpan jars or water-coolers made of lapis mexicanus can be bought for from 5 to 10 pesos.

THE PUEBLA-TLAXCALA COUNTRY

This section of the Central Region of Mexico covers the states of Puebla and Tlaxcala, to the E and SE of Mexico City. It is one of the areas of the republic richest in colonial settlements and colonial architecture, and it has long been the most traveled-over region, having been the first area the Conquistadores and early Spanish settlers crossed on their way to Mexico City. The parts directly E of Mexico City are well covered by roads, often dotted with souvenir stands. The northern and southern sections of Puebla are much more isolated.

The principal highways traversing this country, with the exception of CN-190 (going S toward Oaxaca), all run eastward from Mexico City to the Gulf of Mexico.

TRAVEL HIGHLIGHTS: The city of Puebla, one of Mexico's regal cities is the natural base for extended touring and exploring in this region. From Puebla most of the highlight points are within one to three hours travel. First among the points of interest is *Puebla* itself. Then the famed Indian chapel at nearby *Tonanzintla,* the *great pyramid* and shrine city of *Cholula, Tlaxcala* and its *Ocotlán sanctuary,* and finally the *Tehuacán* spa.

Puebla, Pue. Pop. 211,985. Alt. 7050 ft. Capital and principal commercial center of the State of Puebla. Often called "the city of tiles" for its fancifully talavera-tiled colonial buildings.

HOW TO GET THERE: *Via highway*—From Mexico City CN-190, about 86 m. *Via railway*—the Mexican National Railways runs two first-class trains daily, one leaving Mexico City at 7:15 A.M., arriving in Puebla at 1:30 P.M.; the other, leaving at 4 P.M., arriving at 9:43 P.M. Fare one way: $4.85 MN. *Via bus*—"A.D.O." buses; Transportes Sureste Cristóbal Colón; the Mexico-Puebla-Veracruz "Flecha Roja"; Autobuses del Sureste; run frequently daily service from the capital to Puebla. Riding time, 3 hours. Fare: around $7 to $10 MN, depending on the line.

HOTELS: Although hotels in Puebla are comfortable, the city, after four centuries of innkeeping, has yet to produce a de luxe or really first-class hostel. Best available is the *Hotel Lastra,* Calzada de los Fuentes, (1¼ m. NE of Zócalo). 51 rooms, cocktail bar and lounge, heated pool, roof garden, dining room, shops. We have found the food and service fair to indifferent, with similar reports from other travelers. Rates: EP from $70 MN dble. Tel. 1-72-75. *Hotel Royalty,* center of town facing Zócalo of plaza. 56 rooms, rather old. Garage. Dining room not recommended. Rates: EP from $55 to $70 MN dble. Tel. 1-44-45. *Hotel Palace,* 2 Oriente 13, old, but recently modernized. Comfortable. Bar and restaurant. Rates: EP from $50 MN dble. *Pan-American Courts,* Reforma 2114. Modest and inexpensive. *Reforma Agua Azul,* Prolongación Av. 11 Sur. Fairly new resort-type hotel with its own sulphur springs. Poorly managed.

RESTAURANTS: *El Merendero,* in Hotel Lastra. Hours: 7 A.M. to 10 P.M. *Ritz,* plaza, Portal Morelos. Fair. Mexican food. *Café Madrid,* plaza, Portal Hidalgo. Good Mexican food. Open until 10 P.M.

DIRECTORY: *Banks*—Banco Nacional de México, Reforma 135; Banco Mercantil de Puebla, Reforma 113. *Car repairs*—Auto-Pue (Nash), 2 Poniente 906; C. Montoto (Chevrolet), Av. 7 Poniente 1703; Hermanos Sanchez (Ford), 3 Poniente 527; L. Hace (Chrysler), Av. 7 Poniente and 19 Sur. *Travel agents*—Centro Méxicano de Turismo, Lobby Hotel Royalty. *Bus lines*—Autotransportes del Sureste Cristóbal Colon, Hotel Imperial, 2 Oriente 202; Autos Pullman "A.D.O.", Av. Avila Camacho and Av. 6 Norte. Tel. 23-44; Auto-Camiones Puebla-Cholula, 5 Norte 406, Tel. 43-09. *Airlines*—Aerolineas Vega, 24 Sur 2103, Tel. 39-76 M. (Route: flights to Oaxaca, Acapulco.) *Railways*—Ferrocarriles Nacionales de Mexico, tickets and reservations at the station. Tel. 1-43-11 Ext. 22; Ferrocarril Méxicano, 11 Norte 1009 (this line makes a spectacularly scenic run via Tehuacán to Veracruz, but train comforts are almost nil).

THE CITY AND ENVIRONS: Puebla (poo-EH-blah), in addition to being an important commercial center, is also the Rome of Mexico because of its striking ecclesiastical architecture. There are about 60 churches and conventual buildings, some of them exceptionally attractive. A liberal use of Moorish and Persian tiles (*azulejos*—ah-zoo-LEH-hohs) imparts an Andalusian aspect to the city—where not alone the churches but the private residences, fountains, and many other structures are adorned with these polychromatic embellishments. Puebla was the first city in Mexico to manufacture the Talavera tiles and ware, and is still one of the principal producers of it.

The city is nicely situated on the gradual slope of the Sierra Madre foothills. Striking views are obtainable on all sides. Mexico's most imposing volcanoes (Orizaba, Popo, and Izta) overlook the city. The usually spick-and-span streets of the city are straight and run at right angles to each other. Most E and W streets are designated as avenues *(avenidas)*; those running N and S are streets *(calles)*. Calle del 16 de Septiembre, which becomes Calle del 5 de Mayo N of Reforma, divides the east and west sections of the city. Even-numbered streets are found E of this dividing line, odd-numbered streets in the W part.

Puebla was founded about ten years after the fall of Tenochtitlán when the Spaniards decided to build a fortress-town midway between the Aztec capital and the coast. A Franciscan friar, Toribio de Buenavente—better known to history as Father Motolina—was delegated to select a suitable site. He chose the plain near the Indian holy city of Cholula. According to church chronicles he was greatly aided in his task by a dream which came to Fray Julián Garcés, Bishop of Tlaxcala and first bishop in Mexico, who saw two angels with rod and line pacing off a beautiful plain surrounded by tall volcanoes. Accordingly, Motolina staked out the new city as dictated in the good bishop's dream, and thus the place got its official name, Puebla de los Angeles (Place of the Angels). Some 8000 Tlaxcalan Indian allies came from nearby missions to erect huts for the workmen. At the same time (1531), about 40 Spanish families came to settle there. The place prospered, the bishopric was moved there, and for many years Puebla became Mexico's second city.

During the War of 1847 the American General, Winfield Scott, captured the city. While Scott's main force continued on toward Mexico City a contingent of wounded troops (from the Battle of Cerro Gordo) under Colonel Thomas Childs, remained in Puebla, encamped in the plaza or Zócalo surrounded by a hostile city of 80,000 inhabitants. Anticipating trouble, Childs secured some 30 cattle, 400 sheep plus army supplies and barricaded his small group in the square. Shortly afterward the Mexican General, Santa Anna, with a force of about

2500, attacked the holed-up Americans who refused to surrender. Santa Anna opened a fierce artillery fire on the plaza encampment while a persistent and galling musketry fire was poured upon the sick and besieged troops from the surrounding housetops. The church bells sang joyously, and the unequal battle was watched eagerly by the entire population. The heartrending struggle lasted for thirty days until the approach of Colonel James Lane with reinforcements from Veracruz forced Santa Anna to withdraw.

During the French Intervention the city again became a battleground. On May 5, 1862, Napoleon's troops were soundly beaten off by the Mexican General, Ignacio Zaragoza. That date, *Cinco de Mayo,* marks a national holiday, and in almost every Mexican town a street bears that name-date. The following year the French again besieged the city and after a two-month struggle captured it (May 17, 1863). On April 2, 1867 it was once more the scene of a furious battle when Mexicans led by General Porfirio Díaz took the Puebla fortress.

THINGS TO SEE: The *Zócalo* (Plaza de la Constitución), in which U.S. soldiers under Colonel Childs made their heroic stand, is the focal center of the city as well as one of the most imposing large plazas in the country. It is flanked on one side by the Cathedral, on the others by the handsome *portales* of rich colonial buildings. It is shaded by unusually tall and noble trees, has a number of fountains, a bandstand and some parterres of semitropical flowers. A number of shops and souvenir stalls are to be found in the *portales.*

The *Cathedral,* flanking the Zócalo, undoubtedly one of the largest and richest Catholic temples in America, though less elegant than the cathedral in Mexico City, has far greater unity of design. Its exterior exhibits a well-ordered stateliness, marred only by the fact that the twin towers stand too far apart and are too tall, and by a gloomy feeling imparted by the rather lifeless blue-gray stone used in the building. This dreary effect is added to by the barren, stone terrace upon which the cathedral is built, and the surrounding iron fence surmounted by winged angels. The carvings on the front portal are of white marble, done with simplicity and taste. Even better is the portal of the N transept. The *Campanario* or bell-tower (erected in 1678) contains nearly a score of bells, with various dates up to 1828. The largest weighs 9 tons and was cast in 1729.

The interior of the church makes up for the gloomy outside. It is resplendent and magnificently kept. The proportions are impressive, covering 295 ft. E to W and 153 ft. N and S. The central nave is 83 ft. high, and is separated from the lateral naves (63 ft. high) by unusually massive, but graceful columns. There are 14 chapels, all as richly embellished and well-cared for as the great nave. The floors are of Puebla marble. Of outstanding beauty is the splendid choir *(coro)* with a magnificent wrought-iron screen done by Mateo de la Cruz in 1679. The choir stalls, bishop's seat, lectern, and doors of the side entrances are masterpieces of fine marquetry and woodcarving done by Pedro Muñoz between 1719 and 1722. The original High Altar by Ferrer has been replaced by a not very successful structure of gilded columns and of onyx and marble designed by Tolsa.

The cathedral was begun in 1562 and completed in 1649. Historians quibble over the designer-architect for the plans came from Spain. However, these were modified in Mexico by Gómez de Mora. Further modifications were made by Pedro García Ferrer who designed and constructed the great dome. *Visiting hours:* Open all day except from noon to 3 P.M.

The *Municipal Palace,* across the plaza from the

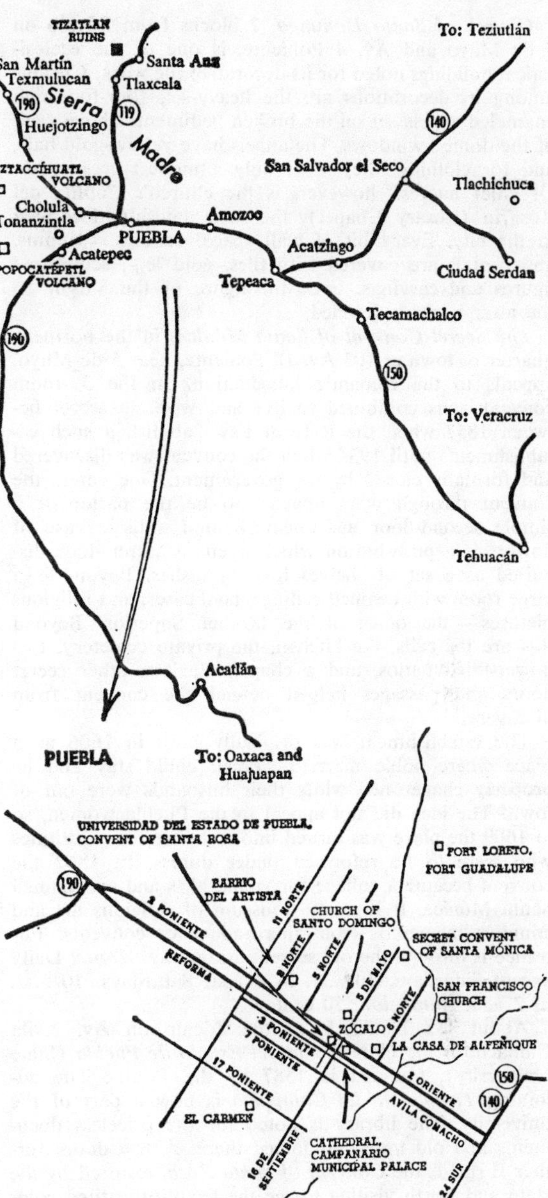

Cathedral is of interest for its modern Spanish Renaissance architecture.

La Casa de Alfeñique, Av. 4 Oriente and Calle 6 Norte, houses the *Puebla Regional Museum* — archaeological and historical exhibits on the 1st floor, colonial furnishing on the 2nd floor. This unique building is a prominent example of the architecture once peculiar to the city. The word *alfeñique* is Spanish for almond-cake, and the house received the name for its combination of florid ornamentation with elaborate tile work. The surface pattern is formed by blue and white glazed tiles set in a ground of plain red ones.[17] The mansion was once used as a residence for visiting dignitaries.

[17] *Puebla tiles.* Puebla is the home of Mexican polychrom tile. It was the first city to manufacture the product, and its citizens have used it in countless ways to add brilliance to their churches, private and public buildings and patios. They applied the vivid tiles lavishly on the domes of churches, on the façades of houses, in kitchens, on the risers of stairways, as the surface for patio fountains.

Church of Santo Domingo, 2 blocks from Zócalo on 5 de Mayo and Av. 4 Poniente, is one of the ecclesiastical buildings noted for its decorative tile work. Curious among its decorations are the heavy-set, four-foot-high enameled angels set on the broken pediments above each of the dome's windows. The angels have yellow-gold hair, and for clothing, they wear only a modest green sash. Of chief interest, however, is the church's Capilla del Rosario (Rosary Chapel), the most lavishly decorated in the city. Every bit of wall space, ceilings, columns, and portals are covered with tiles, gold leaf, sculptured figures and carvings. Even the figure of the Virgin on the altar is richly jeweled.

The Secret Convent of Santa Mónica, in the northern quarter of town at 103 Av. 18 Poniente, near 5 de Mayo, appeals to the romantic imagination. In the 39-room convent nuns continued to live and work in secret between 1857 when the Reform Laws abolished such establishments until 1934 when the convent was discovered and formally closed by the government. One enters the convent through what appears to be the parlor of a simple second-floor apartment. Behind a large vase of flowers is a push-button which opens a secret door disguised as a set of shelves holding dishes. Beyond is a large room with beamed ceilings, bookcases, and religious pictures — the office of the Mother Superior. Beyond this are the cells, the kitchen, the private cemetery, two flower-filled patios, and a chapel. Various other secret doors and passages helped defend the convent from discovery.

The establishment was originally built in 1606 as a place where noble married women could stay and be properly chaperoned while their husbands were out of town. The idea did not appeal to the Puebla women, so in 1609 the place was turned into a shelter for prostitutes who were to be reformed under duress. In 1862 the convent became a college for young girls and was named Santa Mónica. It is now a museum of religious art and contains mementos from this and other convents. Entrance is through the old secret passageway. *Hours:* Daily except Saturdays, 10 A.M. to 4 P.M. Saturdays, 10 A.M. to 2 P.M. *Admission:* 50 centavos.

About 1½ blocks E of the Zócalo on Av. Avila Camacho is the *Universidad del Estado de Puebla* (State University), founded in 1587 by the Jesuits. The adjoining *Templo de La Compañia* is now a part of the university. The library is noted for the priceless documents and old tomes contained there. A few doors further E stands the *Convent of Santa Rosa,* restored by the state and worth visiting to see the beautifully tiled colonial kitchen. Two blocks to the N, on Calle 8 Norte (not far from the Casa de Afeñique) is the *Barrio del Artista,* a group of some 20 shops remodeled by artists into studios. Visitors welcome.

Nearby is the Palafox Library, noted for its collection of rare colonial books and documents.

The *Forts Loreto and Guadalupe,* 2 m. NE of the plaza are interesting historical memorials of the bitter battle when the French were defeated here on May 5, 1862. From the battlements there are excellent views of the city and the volcanoes. Fort Loreto contains a museum. Fort Guadalupe lies ¼ m. beyond. Both forts may be visited during daylight hours.

Admirers of Talavera tile and Puebla's fanciful way of utilizing it, will find endless examples in the 60 or more churches in the city. In addition to those already described, of architectural or artistic importance are the churches of *San Francisco* (E quarter of town, across the river), noted for its red brick and lime façade; the former monastery of *El Carmen,* the *Church of Nuestra Señora de la Paz,* the little church of *Nuestra Señora de Guadalupe,* the *Church of San Marcos* and that of *Santa Catalina.*

In contrast to the colonial the *Centro Escolar Niños Heroes de Chapultepec,* on Calle 8 Sur, about ten blocks from the Zócalo, offers the visitor an interesting picture of what modern Puebla is doing in both education and architecture. The school is set in spacious, landscaped grounds, has its cafeteria, nursery, kindergarten, small hospital, and recreational facilities. May be visited during daylight hours.

While in Puebla most visitors make a stop at one of the factories producing the Talavera tiles or the carved "onyx" souvenirs. Unless you can wait for a shipment of dishware or tiles it is best to find what you can in one of the shops on Calle 18 Poniente (near the Santa Mónica Convent) or at *Ceramica Uriarte,* 4 Poniente 911.[18]

EXCURSIONS SOUTH AND SOUTHEAST OF PUEBLA: A most interesting excursion not far from the city of Puebla is to Tonanzintla, site of one of the most unique artistic treasures in the region. A circuit tour including Acatepec, Tonanzintla, and Cholula can be done comfortably in a half-day. Take CN-190, highway toward Oaxaca. About 8 m. from Puebla at *Acatepec* there is a turn-off, 1 m. NW to Tonanzintla. Paved.

While still on the highway it is worthwhile to visit the parish church of *San Francisco Acatepec,* considered by art historians as the most elaborate and richest of all tiled churches in the region. The façade, made of multicolored tiles and elaborate Churrigueresque embellishments, is like a dazzling jewel. The mass of color and detail were once repeated in the interior, now badly damaged by fire.

Tonanzintla, Pue. Pop. 1590. A tiny off-the-highway village noted for one of the marvels of Mexican popular art — the *Church of Santa María Tonanzintla* (toe-nan-ZINT-la). The exterior of this doll-like church is quite insignificant, giving no hint of the treasure within. The simple façade is relieved by bright Puebla tiles, some white gesso adornments like sugar-coating on a

The *Puebla majolica* — pottery with a tin-enamel glaze — got its start in Mexico soon after the conquest when Toledan potters were brought to Puebla where nearby suitable clays and silicate deposits were available. The potters brought with them the techniques of manufacturing Spain's celebrated Talavera ware (made at Talavera de la Reina, near Toledo). Although other centers — Guadalajara and Dolores Hidalgo, Gto. — produce a similar ware, Puebla remains pre-eminent in the field. The colors of the glaze made in Puebla are applied thickly and are slightly raised above the white ground, giving the surface a wavy appearance. Blues and yellows predominate, sometimes combined with a contrasting green, orange, brick-red, or dark brown. Designs are usually geometric patterns, conventionalized flowers, birds and animals.

[18] The State of Puebla is one of the largest and richest of the Central States. It covers 13,280 sq. miles and has a population upward of 1,988,600. It is bounded on the N and E by the State of Veracruz, on the S by Oaxaca and Guerrero, on the W and NW by Morelos, Mexico, Tlaxcala, and Hidalgo. Topographically it is a mountain state, including the Sierra Madre ranges, the snow-capped volcanoes Iztaccíhuatl and Popocatépetl, as well as the lower slopes of the gigantic Orizaba peak. There are notable *barrancas* in the state, chief among them *Zacatlán* where one finds the products of the Temperate Zone and Torrid Zone growing almost side by side. The *barranca* in the district of Huachinango (see Index), through which the Necaxa River flows and forms several fine cascades, is particularly noteworthy. Some of the falls on this river are over 500 ft. high.

Agriculture is the chief industry of the state — corn, wheat, maguey, sugar, fruits, and rice being raised in abundance. There is some mining, especially in the area around *Teziutlán.* The onyx and marble quarries in the state are celebrated.

cake, and a plain tower. Once you step inside you are dazzled by color — the brilliant Indian crimsons, azure blues, metallic greens, and bright yellows. The place fairly boils with vivid tones and imaginative sculpture. The favorite decorative motif is the cherub, usually surrounded by Baroque bunches of grapes, Salomonic columns, flowers, and angels dressed in short skirts. This fanciful work was carried out by the Indian villagers who raised the money for the project among themselves and also devised the amazing embellishments. The church may be visited during daylight hours.

Just outside of the village is the *Observatorio Nacional de Tonanzintla,* one of the most important astronomical observatories in Latin America. The plant houses a new-type 27-31 inch Schmidt telescope that is almost the twin of the Jewett Memorial telescope at the Harvard Observatory. It is said that 90 per cent of the Milky Way is visible here. In 1942 more than 40 distinguished astronomers and physicists gathered here to celebrate the dedication of the observatory.

Continuing on the road to Oaxaca, the only town of touristic interest is *Acatlán, Pue.,* near the Oaxaca state line. Acatlán, a Zapotec Indian town, is noted for the very imaginative ceramic figures and black-slipped pottery made there. *Hotel Romano,* Reforma 4 (emergency only). *For car repairs,* Servicio Vega, Independencia 16. Sunday is market day. Acatlán celebrates several colorful fiestas: October 4, noted for its regional dances; on March 25, the Fiesta of San Gabriel; St. John's Day, June 24.

To the SE of Puebla, following CN-150, route to Tehuacán and Veracruz —

Amozoc, Pue. Pop. 5410. About 10 m. E of Puebla, a picturesque Indian village which has been famous since colonial times for its miniature clay figures and for one of the rarer of Mexican crafts — the silver-chasing of spurs, bridles, guns, and knives. There are several shops along the highway.

Tepeaca, Pue. Pop. 5000. About 20 m. E of Puebla on CN-150. One of the first Spanish towns founded in Mexico. It was for years an important stagecoach stop. In the sleepy village are ruins of an imposing sixteenth-century Franciscan monastery, one of the first four fortified convents built in the country (1530). Of interest also is the house in which the Viceroys used to stay when traveling between Mexico City and Veracruz. In the center of the plaza is a curious Moorish tower called *El Rollo* which was ordered built by Cortés.

Thirteen miles beyond Tepeaca the highway passes through *Tecamachalco,* another picturesque Indian village dominated by another great and deserted Franciscan church-monastery.

Tehuacán, Pue. Pop. 23,300. Alt. 5500. A popular resort area noted for its mineral springs and dry exhilarating air. Tehuacán (teh-wa-KAHN) water is said to be similar in composition to the Carlsbad waters in Europe, and efficacious in kidney and liver disorders. Tehuacán is one of the most widely distributed bottle-waters in Mexico. The springs, of which there are a great number, are scattered over the adjacent country. The best known are: *El Riego, San Lorenzo, Peñafiel, Altepateutlali,* and *Axoxopan.*

HOW TO GET THERE: *Via car* — CN-150 east from Puebla, about 72 miles. *Via bus* — A.D.O. Line from Mexico City or Puebla. Autobuses Flecha Roja (second class). *Via railway* — National Railways of Mexico. Two trains daily on the Mexico City-Puebla-Oaxaca line. Best is the Pullman leaving Mexico City at 4 P.M. (Puebla at 9:58 P.M.), arriving in Tehuacán at 7:15 A.M.

HOTELS AND RESTAURANTS: *Gran Hotel Spa Peñafiel,* 1½ m. NW of town, just off highway. A 200-room resort hotel on nicely landscaped grounds. The place is a little dated, but is well kept and the food served is quite good. Cocktail lounge and bar, golf course, pool, tennis, frontón, gym, Turkish baths. Music every evening. Rates: AP $200 MN dble. Tel. 190. *Hotel Mexico,* in center of town, Av. Camacho and Libertad. A comfortable and friendly colonial-style hotel. 80 rooms, good dining room, illuminated mineral water pools, cocktail bar and lounge, roof garden and gardens. Free parking. Rates: AP from $90 MN to $120 MN dble. Tel. 19.

DIRECTORY: *Banks* — Banco Méxicano, Av. Independencia 105; Banco Mercantil de Puebla, Av. Independencia 101. *Bus lines* — A.D.O. Buses, Av. Libertad 100. Tel. 96. Flecha Roja, Independencia 302. Tel. 1-87. *Car repairs* — Perez de Tehuacán, Avila Camacho and Calle 4 Pte.

Motorists in an exploratory mood can take a new, still unpaved, road that slices SW, through interesting virgin country, finally connecting with the Oaxaca highway at *Huajuapan de León,* 71 difficult miles, no gas stations.

AREAS EAST AND NORTHEAST OF PUEBLA: For the casual motorist or bus traveler there is very little of interest directly to the E of Puebla, nor in the mountainous, almost roadless vastness of the northern part of the state. Along the highways — CN-140, going from Puebla via Jalapa to Veracruz, and CN-136 branching north to *Teziutlán* — the scenery is quite beautiful. In the northern part of the State of Puebla there are networks of new, sketchy roads (not recommended for fancy cars) leading into fascinating country filled with primitive, tucked-away Indian villages, magnificent *barrancas,* and tropic valleys. It is country for the off-trail traveler. The more important towns on the traveled routes are —

Acatzingo, Pue. Pop. 5390. On CN-140, about 29 m. E of Puebla. An old Indian colonial town noteworthy for its fortress-like Franciscan mission-church. Across the plaza from it is a newer, typically Mexican church containing paintings by Zendejas.

A half-hours' drive farther, at tiny *San Salvador el Seco* is the turn-off, SE, via rough road to *Ciudad Serdan* and to *Tlachichuca* — bases for alpinists climbing Orizaba.

Teziutlán, Pue. Pop. 15,000. On CN-136, a short distance from the Veracruz state line. An interesting old colonial city with a fine plaza, massive colonial buildings. Sunday market day is unusually colorful.

Hotel Virreinal, Av. Hidalgo 78. Modest rates. Fair dining room. Colonial-style and best available. *Car repairs* — Vehículos de Teziutlán (Ford), Juárez 98.

EXCURSIONS WEST AND NORTH OF PUEBLA: All the major points of interest in this area are within an hour to an hour and a half drive from the city of Puebla. Automobile, bus, or hired cab are almost the only feasible means of communication in this area. Taking the Mexico City-Puebla Highway, CN-190, W from Puebla —

Cholula, Pue. Pop. 11,616. Alt. 7000 ft. Just off the highway, 9 m. W of Puebla. Once the Holy City of the Aztec Confederation, and also the center of the Toltec culture (when the Toltecs had fled Tula), Cholula (cho-LOO-lah) was estimated to have had 100,000 inhabitants at the time of its destruction by Cortés. In Indian times it was said to have had over 400 shrines and temples. Even today it is famed for its number of Christian churches. Legend has it that there is one for every day of the year, though factually, this is not quite correct.

During the Spanish conquest of Mexico Cholula figured in a bloody massacre when Cortés, having come up from the coast at the invitation of ambassadors from Cholula, and while being housed in the sacred city, learned of a conspiracy instigated by Moctezuma to attack the Spaniards as they marched out of the city. Cortés' answer was a wholesale massacre in which an estimated three to six thousand natives were slaughtered during one night.

WHAT TO SEE: Cholula's chief attraction is the *Tepanapa Pyramid* and the little *Sanctuario de los Remedios* which tops it. The pyramid is a few blocks E of the town plaza. The *teocalli* appears like a great hill covered with vegetation. In size it was the greatest of all Mexican pyramids, and in terms of volume (not height) it is larger than the Pyramid of Cheops in Egypt. When Cortés saw it, it appeared as a great array of platforms with a temple on top. The Spaniards, and since then, weather have rendered it beyond reconstruction. Some 5 m. of tunnels have been opened within the structure, and these are electrically illuminated for the benefit of visitors. A museum at the entrance contains temple artifacts. HOURS: daily from 9 A.M. to 1 P.M., and from 2 P.M. to 4 P.M. ADMISSION: 2 pesos.

Atop the pyramid there are spectacular views of Cholula, its countless churches, and the wheeling plain dotted with hamlets and church towers. The little Baroque church which the Spaniards built on the crown of the *teocalli* when they tore down the pagan temple here is dedicated to *Nuestra Señora de los Remedios*. The building has been so radically restored that it is without architectural interest. It remains however one of the chief shrines to this potent Virgin, and each year thousands of pilgrims come from all parts of the country to pay homage to the Virgin of Remedios.[19]

Franciscan Church of San Gabriel (E side of plaza) is by far the finest of the churches to be seen from atop the great pyramid. This Gothic structure was begun in 1549. It is noted for its broad atrium, Plateresque entrance, massive doors and the exceptionally fine rib-vaulting in the nave. Adjoining San Gabriel is the *Capilla Real,* undoubtedly inspired by the great Mosque of Cordova, Spain. The chapel has 49 domes supported by a forest of columns forming seven aisles.

FIESTAS: Traditionally a holy city in both pagan and Christian times, Cholula is noted for its many fiestas. The following are among the most interesting.

February 2. Fiestas de la Candelaria during which there are religious processions and the figures of the Virgin are adorned with collars of bread made in the shape of animals, stars, dolls.

July 25. *Church of Santiago Tzocuila,* the dance of the Moors and Christians is performed.

August 15. Religious fiesta honoring the Assumption of the Virgin.

September 6–9. The big fiesta dedicated to the Virgin of Los Remedios. Brilliant Indian dancers, etc.

November 2. Day of the Dead. Before many houses, from the street to the door of the house, a cross is laid. The foot of cross often extends into the house to an altar where offering for the dead are set out. The road-cross indicated the path the dead spirits should follow.

Huejotzingo, Pue. Pop. 6374. Alt. 7000 ft. An unusually interesting market-town on CN-190 (66 m. E of Mexico City, 19 m. W of Puebla). Huejotzingo (way-hote-SEEN-go) is in the center of a highly cultivated, fruit-growing area and is noted for its cider (some made up as a spurious sort of champagne). For years the place was famed for its serape weavers. There are numerous serape and souvenir stands flanking the road. It is wise to be cautious of the bargains. Huejotzingo serapes are now often of very inferior quality.

Market day is on Thursday and Saturday. The colors of the myriad displays set under white tentlike umbrellas, and the rich green of the huge trees in the square and the distant white peak of Iztaccíhuatl make the market one of the most vivid in Mexico, especially if visited on a clear, sunny day.

Most tourists visiting the market are oblivious of the fact that just across the highway, up a broad flight of stairs and through a three-arched gateway, is one of the oldest monuments in Mexico's architectural history, and one of the finest examples of Gothic-style churches on the continent. The church and monastery, *San Francisco de Huejotzingo,* was begun in 1525 under the direction of Fray Juan de Alameda, and completed some 40 years later. The church has an extensive atrium with two interesting peaked-roof shrines. The interior has a Gothic rib-vaulted ceiling that is one of the finest in Mexico. The church is now a museum. HOURS: daily, 9 A.M. to 1 P.M., 3 P.M. to 5 P.M. ADMISSION: 50 centavos, free on Monday.

A short, unimproved road leads south from Huejotzingo to *Calpan, Pue.,* a tiny village containing another notable sixteenth-century monastery.

San Martín Texmelucan, Pue. Pop. 11,500. Alt. 7100 ft. On CN-190 (57 m. E of Mexico City, 28 m. from Puebla). An important weaving center (serapes and woolen fabrics) and road junction. One of the roads to nearby Tlaxcala, CN-188 branches off here.

Like all the towns in this area, San Martín has its sixteenth-century church and monastery. Of greater interest is the Indian market held Tuesday mornings. La Albertina on Av. Libertad 45 (highway) is a large and unusually good shop handling the best of the woven goods from here and Tlaxcala, as well as tasteful popular arts and crafts from other parts of the country.

[19] Our Lady of the Remedies. There are numerous other shrines dedicated to Nuestra Señora de los Remedios. (See Index: Shrine of Los Remedios, and Sacromonte.) All the shrines are dedicated to a very tiny image of the Virgin said to have been carried by one of Cortés' followers. According to legend this wooden figure was taken, a few days before the disastrous La Noche Triste retreat from Tenochtitlán, and hidden near Naucálpam, beneath a giant maguey. Twenty years later it was found by a former Indian noble who carried it to his home, made an altar for it. During the night it vanished, and the next day the man found it again under the maguey. The Indian took the figure home again, put it in a chest and slept on the lid. Next morning it was gone again, only to be found once more beneath the maguey. The events were reported to a priest who announced that a miracle had been performed.

A shrine was built on the hill where the figure was found, and the tiny wooden doll was dressed in satins and pearls. Her powers of warding off epidemics and droughts were so great a larger shrine was soon built. She was so revered, she was solemnly received by viceroys and bishops, and lavish gifts were thrust upon her. At the time of the War of Independence the Spanish royalists made her their protectoress (in opposition to the dark Virgin of Guadalupe who led the Mexican troops to ultimate victory), and she was made a General of the Royal Army. According to tales, when the Virgen de los Remedios was captured during a battle, she was stripped of her uniform by a Mexican general, and she was ordered deported from Mexico. She was allowed to remain on, only when it was promised that she would stay out of politics.

The town's most important fiesta, honoring St. Martín, extends from November 3 to 12. Regional dances, bullfights, etc.

Tlaxcala, Tlax. Pop. 6000. Alt. 7500 ft. Capital of the tiny State of Tlaxcala (tlax-CAH-hah)[20] and the center of one of the most noted wool-weaving regions of Mexico.

HOW TO GET THERE: Tlaxcala lies 19 m. due N of Puebla. From Puebla one can drive either directly to Tlaxcala via unnumbered paved road, or via CN-190 and turn off at San Martín Texmelucan. From Mexico City the CN-190 route can be taken, or one can go via CE-136 (the Mexico City-Texcoco-Jalapa-Veracruz Route) and turn off to Tlaxcala at Apizaco, Tlax. *Via bus*—(second class) Auto Transportes Tlaxcala-Apizaco y Humantla, leaves from 8 Poniente 320 in Puebla.

HOTELS AND RESTAURANTS: Tlaxcala had no recommendable tourist accommodations. In emergencies, *Hotel Tlaxcala,* Morelos 9. It's badly run-down.

THE TOWN AND ENVIRONS: Though once an important Indian capital, Tlaxcala is now just a sleepy, somewhat melancholy town grown up around the inevitable, but rather nice plaza. Facing the plaza is the interesting *Palacio Municipal* which has unusually heavy, almost Romanesque piers supporting molded segmental arches.

[20] State of Tlaxcala, is the smallest of all the Mexican states, with a population of around 200,000 inhabitants and an area of 4132 sq. kilometers, covering a territory corresponding almost exactly to that of the ancient Tlaxcalan kingdom or nation. It is bounded on the N, E, and S by the State of Puebla, on the W by Mexico. The mean altitude of the state is 6600 ft., with the magnificent volcanic peak of Malinche *(Malintzi)* rising to 13,690 ft. The region is quite mountainous and has some excellent forest land. Several of the valleys are broad and very fertile, especially the Valle de Humantla and the famed Llanos de Apam (Plains of Apam), the latter for centuries noted as Mexico's great *pulque* producing region.

HISTORY: The character, institutions and the history of the Tlaxcalan people are among the most fascinating in Mexico. The Tlaxcalans were a branch of the Chichimecas. They had originally settled near Lake Texcoco, but eventually withdrew across the mountains to the security of the Tlaxcala country. Alliance with the Otomís, then fierce warriors, allowed them opportunity to develop as a powerful small nation that evolved into a kind of republic. Their region was divided into four dominions, each autonomous in its system of government, but in case of war the four rulers elected one supreme head.

The Tlaxcalans' bitterest enemies were the Aztecs, to whom they never submitted. They were at constant war with the Aztec tributaries: the Cholulans, the Totonacs, who cut off their route to the sea, and the residents of Cempoala. When Cortés appeared and offered them freedom from their enemies (after a few rugged battles with the Spaniards) they joined him in the conquest of Tenochtitlán. Without the Tlaxcalans Cortés might never have conquered Mexico. Three quarters or more of his force was made up of Tlaxcalans. Following his first expulsion from the Aztec capital, Cortés returned to Tlaxcala, spent a year in recuperating his forces and in building a fleet of brigantines with which to attack the island-city, Tenochtitlán. The fleet was pre-fabricated in Tlaxcala, tested in the river there, then carried over the mountains to Lake Texcoco by Tlaxcalans.

In return for their loyalty Tlaxcala was made a most noble city by order of the King of Spain, and the people were exempted from paying taxes. Tlaxcala became the cradle of Christianity in America. The first sermon was preached here, the first Christian wedding celebrated. Here the four chieftains of the Tlaxcalan republic were baptized by Don Luis Díaz, chaplain of the Spanish force, with Cortés and Alvarado as godfathers.

The arches over the second-floor windows are richly decorated with Mudéjar-Indian ornamentation.

In the town itself, by far the most interesting church building is *La Iglesia de San Francisco* (½ m. S of plaza, on road to Puebla). Claims are made that it is the oldest church in the Americas. Interesting are the highly carved cedar beams of the ceiling, as well as the exquisite, inlaid woodwork under the organ loft (the finest existant example of Mudéjar *laceria* ornament in Mexico). In the adjacent *Chapel of the Tercer Orden* stands the old fount where the king, Xicoténcatl, was baptized. On the old pulpit is an inscription which reads: "*Aquí tubo principio al Santo Evangelio en este nuevo mundo*" ("Here the Holy Evangel had its beginning in this new world.") The church may be visited during daylight hours.

The *Sanctuary of Ocotlán.* This celebrated shrine, one of Mexico's national treasures, is set upon a hill ½ m. from town. The façade of the Santuario is of gleaming white plaster deeply carved into intricate and weird Churrigueresque forms flanked by towers with bases covered with vermilion tiles and upper stories of plaster carving as ornate as the façade. The interior is as fancifully decorated with woodcarving and with gilded and polychrome figures. The Indian sculptor, Francisco Miguel, devoted 25 years to the execution of the work.

According to legend the sanctuary commemorated the appearance of the Virgin in 1521, who, in answer to the prayers of a pious Indian, made water flow from the spot during a period of severe drought.

Although Tlaxcala is noted throughout the country as a weaving center, especially for fine bolt-textiles and Indian tweeds, most of the weaving is done in nearby villages, chief among them, *Santa Ana* (1½ m. to E paved). On the main street of Santa Ana there are numerous shops offering bolt goods and serapes.

RUINS OF TIZATLÁN (archaeological zone). Two m. N of Tlaxcala, via country trail, lies the village of *San Esteban Tizatlán,* once the center of the third Tlaxcalan dominion. Some years ago, according to the story told in the village, one of the townsmen dreamt that the spirit of King Xicoténcatl appeared to him and revealed the site of a treasure hidden in a mound near the churchyard. The man and his friends attacked the mound at night, working as secretly as possible. Instead of finding the kind of treasure they hoped for, they uncovered the ruins of a temple. At this point the government stepped in to save the important archaeological structure and, incidentally, unearth some of the finest examples of ancient frescoes found in Mexico. The frescoes are on large rectangular slabs arranged on a platform which may have supported a shrine. The frescoes are vividly colored depictions of the ancient gods. Especially interesting is that of Camaxtli, the war god, wearing a smoking mirror on his head, so he could see all that went on among the people of the earth.

Nearby, in contrast, is a sixteenth-century open-chapel with an interesting Moorish roof. The chapel contains a painting of the Baptism of Xicoténcatl, attributed to Rodrigo de Cifuentes.

THE MEXICO-MORELOS RING

This section of the Central Region of Mexico lies closest to and girdles the Federal District and Mexico City, the political, economic, and touristic heart of the republic. It includes the rambling State of Mexico (which all but surrounds the Federal District), and the small State of Morelos. Embracing the truly beautiful valleys of Mexico, Toluca, Texcoco, and Morelos, with their surrounding mountains, the natural attractions are endless. Everywhere there are remnants of pre-Cortesian grandeur, colonial monuments, and magnificent resort areas.

There is no need to list the means of communication to and through the area. Standing as a ring around Mexico City toward which all the major airlines, chief bus lines, trains, and most highways lead, the region is served by them. For the visitor and sightseer, the most comfortable and central base from which to take tours in the surrounding area is Mexico City where hotel accommodations are ample and varied enough to fit every taste and budget. For descriptions of Mexico City accommodations see Index.

SIGHTSEEING AND VACATION HIGHLIGHTS: There are endless, fascinating places in the ring surrounding Mexico City. A visitor making his or her first dip into the area ought to visit: 1) the *Pyramids of Teotihuacán,* 2) the garden-resort city of *Cuernavaca,* 3) the agricultural college at *Chapingo* (Rivera's greatest murals) and nearby *Texcoco* and the *Molino de las Flores,* 4) the colonial sanctuaries of *Acolmán* and *Tepotzotlán,* 5) *Tepoztlán, Mor.,* and 6) the *Nevado de Toluca* and *Valle de Bravo* area.

EXCURSIONS NORTH OF MEXICO CITY: **Tepotzotlán, Mex.** Pop. 1626. 27 m. NW of Mexico City via CN-57. The town is 1 m. W of the highway. Turnoff just before the toll station.

Tepotzotlán (teh-pote-so-TLAHN) is the site of one of Mexico's national monuments, the Jesuit built *Seminario de San Martín,* one of the most notable examples of Churrigueresque architecture in the hemisphere. The seminary was founded in 1584 but the present building dates from the middle of the eighteenth century. Thanks to its isolation the edifice escaped the destructive touch of overzealous restorers. The building is finely proportioned and has a magnificent façade and tower covered with exceedingly rich carved decorations.

The interior with its masses of gilded carvings and polychrome figures is a perfect expression of opulent Churrigueresque exuberance that is breath-taking. Of the several chapels, the Camarín of the Loreto Chapel is the most richly decorated. The room was specially built as a sacred boudoir for the vestments of the image of the Virgin of Loreto. Its walls are a blaze of rich colors, paintings, and polychromed sculpted Indian figures. As one art historian expressed it, the whole effect is one of oriental barbaric splendor. The seminary is now a government museum. *Hours:* 9 A.M. to 6 P.M. *Admission:* $2 MN.

The town of Tepotzotlán has little else to offer except a nondescript plaza. It should not be confused with Tepoztlán, Mor., a picturesque village noted for its Dominican church and archaeological ruins.

Pyramids of Teotihuacán (archaeological zone). One of Mexico's greatest pre-Hispanic centers, 1¼ m. from the village of San Juan Teotihuacán (sahn hwan teh-o-tee-wah-CAHN).

HOW TO GET THERE: The best way to reach Teotihuacán is by car. A new super-highway linking Teotihuacán to Mexico City is scheduled to be completed by 1965. The distance from the capital is about 31 m. Take the Laredo highway, CN-85 and branch off to r. at *Venta de Carpio.* For bus travelers there is a half-hourly bus service leaving from 19 Calle Alarcón, in Mexico City. It is possible to go by train; both the Méxicano and Interoceánico lines connect Teotihuacán with the capital. The railway trip is not recommended unless you are awfully fond of this type of locomotion and have plenty of time. Most of the tourist agencies in the capital run comfortable daily tours to the pyramids. If you do not have your own car these are by far the most reasonable and enjoyable ways to make the trip.

AUTO ROUTE: Leave the capital via Insurgentes Nte. CN-85. About 13 m. from the city, after passing a number of industrial plants, you come to a settlement called *San Cristóbal Ecatepec.* On the l. is a colonial building and museum, the *House of the Viceroys,* where in colonial times the outgoing viceroy received his successor. Here, also, the great champion of Mexican Independence, Morelos, was executed in 1815. Just beyond, the road crosses the Gran Canal del Desagüe (the drainage canal for Mexico City and the valley). The highway continues along an earthen and stone causeway built by the colonial Spaniards to lessen the annual flooding of the city. At the north end of the dyke is Venta de Carpio. Here at the road-fork bear to the right toward Teotihuacán. At km. 32 (20½ m. from city) a short lane to the left leads to a new prehistorical museum — *Museo de Tepexpan.* In it are the remains of mammoths and the skeleton of the Tepexpan Man, an elephant hunter who roamed the valley sometime between 8000 and 12,000 years ago. *Hours:* 9 A.M. to 1 P.M., 3 to 6 P.M. *Admission:* 2 pesos. A few miles beyond (24 m. from city) the road skirts *Acolmán,* noted for its Augustinian monastery (see Index). The route continues on through *San Juan Teotihuacán.* The archaeological zone lies little more than a mile beyond the village.

The zone is open daily from 8 A.M. to 6 P.M. The local museum is open 10 A.M. to 4 P.M. Admission, $4 MN, payable at the admission booth near the entrance of the zone. There is no charge on Sunday. Guides are available at the booth (bargain hard with them), or less expensive, the *Official Guide to Teotihuacán* booklet sold at the booth. $7 MN. The highlights of the zone can be seen in one hour. A more thorough tour takes about 3 hours. There is a free parking space in the heart of the zone, next to the Pyramid of the Sun.

THE RUINS: The zone is a parklike area covering more than 7 sq. m. dotted with majestic pyramids, temples, and courts. The center of this broad expanse, the sacred city, was once entirely paved with volcanic stones and the building plastered with lime and mortar.

The most impressive and probably oldest structure is the *Pyramid of the Sun.*[21] It has a rubble core faced with volcanic rock, originally covered with stucco. In height the pyramid soars to over 210 ft. At the base it measures 735 ft. and covers an area of 540,000 sq. ft. Unlike the great pyramid at Giza, in Egypt, instead of functioning as tombs the Teotihuacán structures served as the bases for temples which crowned their level tops. The pyramid is formed of five symmetrical terraces with a stairway

[21] The history of Teotihuacán (meaning, The Place of the Gods) is not at all precise for no written records were left concerning it. The first builders, (a culture called Teotihuacana) were rooted in the archaic cultures of Mexico that existed many years before the time of Christ. Undoubtedly the Pyramid of the Sun was begun by them. The Teotihuacanos were affected and influenced by other native civilizations, among them the Toltecs whose influence is most evident among the ruins. Teotihuacán flourished until the eighth or ninth centuries of our era when it was destroyed by conquest, by fire, and abandoned. For centuries even the Aztecs knew little about it except through certain myths they held regarding it, namely, that it had once been a place inhabited by the gods.

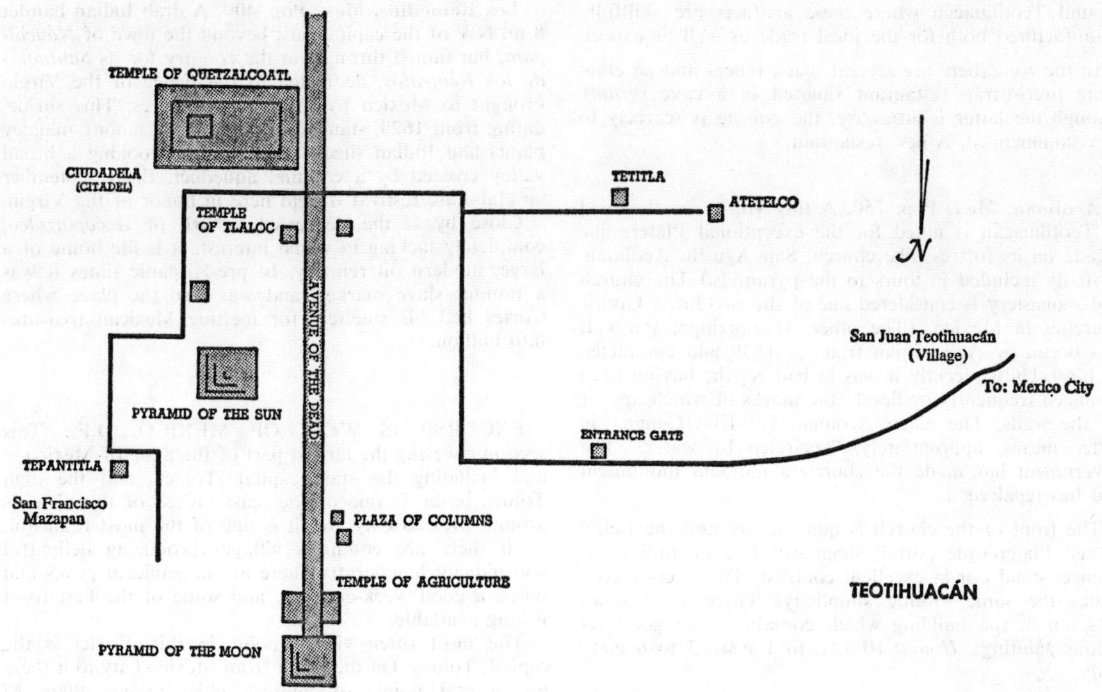

on the W side offering access to each terrace and the top temple platform where the ancient rites and human sacrifices were offered. The stones which project from the face were simply brackets or supports inserted by the builders to hold the thick stucco surface which has now disappeared.

The *Avenue of the Dead* which begins at the foot of the *Pyramid of the Moon* and runs south in a straight line for over a mile serves as the axis for the entire ceremonial area. It derives its name from the Aztecs who imagined that the mounds flanking it were tombs. In actuality they were small pyramids which served as substructures for temples. The *Pyramid of the Moon,* though smaller than the Pyramid of the Sun, rises to the same level, having been constructed on higher ground. It remains unrestored. In height it is over 135 ft.; its base which is rectangular measures 490 by 390 ft.

The *Temple of Agriculture,* standing between the two huge pyramids, owes its name to the murals which decorated it at the time of its discovery. The murals depicted personages making food offerings to the gods. Unfortunately, the frescoes were painted on unbaked clay, and have perished.

The "Viking" Group, a series of newly excavated structures S of the pyramids. The group owes its name to the fact that funds for the excavation were provided by the Viking Fund. Noteworthy here are floors made of mica and lime, unique in the area. *The Plaza of Columns,* just S of the Temple of Agriculture, is still largely unexplored and remains in mound-state. *Temple of Tlaloc,* a small building a bit S of the Viking Group that may have been dedicated to the Rain God.

The *Ciudadela* (Citadel) and *Temple of Quetzalcoatl.* Following the Pyramid of the Sun, this is the most impressive complex of structures at Teotihuacán. It stands at the southern end of the zone, facing the Avenue. It is an enormous quadrangle, about ¼ m. per side, and fortress-like in appearance. On the W a broad stairway leads up to the quadrangle.

The area was undoubtedly reserved for important ceremonies, possibly that of the New Fire which was celebrated every 52 years honoring the survival of the sun. According to the Aztecs, the sun's death, greatly feared, had occurred on four different occasions. Several facts indicate that such ceremonies were held here. In the quadrangle is a small pyramid with stairs on each of its four sides, and each stairway has 13 steps, totaling 52. In addition, the center of the rectangle is exactly in line with the center of the great rectangle surrounding the Pyramid of the Sun. Both these in turn are aligned with the peak of a hill called Cerro Gordo which serves as a backdrop for the Sun Pyramid when seen from the Citadel. Archaeologists feel that when the New Fire was kindled in the Citadel the ceremony could be seen from a temple on Cerro Gordo, and a sacred fire was lit there in turn to signal the whole region that the world would not be destroyed.

Most elaborate of the temples in the quadrangle (at rear) is the Temple of Quetzalcoatl (kate-sahl-COH-ahtl), the Feathered Serpent, the Toltec God of the Air. This edifice is a four-bodied, stepped pyramid, still faced with a thick coat of plaster. While making excavations it was discovered that this structure hid another structure covered with some of the most marvelous carvings in the New World. There is a stairway and on both sides, stone panels in several tiers filled with sculpture — serpents' heads with collars like flower petals, masks of Tlaloc, all done on a large scale in bold relief. The sculpture is Toltec. It is powerful and dramatic.

About ¼ mile E of the Pyramid of the Sun, in the village of *San Francisco Mazapan,* is an archaeological site called *Tepantitla,* noted for the remains of a mural painting which represents the paradise of the Teotihuacanos.

In and around the pyramid zone travelers are often approached by children and adults offering clay, stone and obsidian figurines claimed to be pre-Hispanic in origin. It should be noted that there are seven villages around Teotihuacán where these artifacts are skillfully manufactured both for the local trade as well as export.

In the zone there are several snack places and an elaborate tourist-trap restaurant situated in a cave *(gruta)*. Though the latter is attractive, the cuisine is scarcely to be recommended. A new restaurant,

Acolman, Mex. Pop. 750. A tiny village on the road to Teotihuacán is noted for the exceptional Plateresque façade on its fortress-like church, San Agustín Acolman. (Usually included in tours to the pyramids.) The church and monastery is considered one of the two finest Gothic churches in Mexico. (The other, Huejotzingo, Pue.) It was begun by Augustinian friars in 1539 and completed in 1560. Until recently it was in bad repair, having been damaged frequently by floods, the marks of which appear on the walls. The name Acolman (ah-KOHL-man) in Aztec means, appropriately, "encircled by water." The government has made the church a national monument and has repaired it.

The front of the church is quite severe and the richly carved Plateresque portal, singularly free of Indian influence, stand out in excellent contrast. The interior continues the same Gothic simplicity. There is a small museum in the building which contains some good religious paintings. *Hours:* 10 A.M. to 1 P.M., 3 to 6 P.M., daily.

Tlalnepantla, Mex. Pop. 10,330. An industrial suburb on the edge of the Federal District, 9 m. from the capital. Tlalnepantla (tlahl-neh-PAHN-tlah)[22] is noted for its pottery, and for the nearby *Tenayuca Pyramid* and archaeological zone. To get there either take CN-57 northward 9 m. from the capital, then turn E 2 m. to Tlalnepantla; or, follow Insurgentes Nte. to the Monumento de la Raza, then turn NW along the Tlalnepantla Road. The Tenayuca Pyramid is 2 m. E of the town.

The *Pyramid of Tenayuca* (teh-nah-YUH-kah), Aztec for "Place Where They Erected Walls," is all that remains of a large city that was part of the Chichimeca Empire in the twelfth century, and was occupied by the Acolhuas and Tepanecs. It is probably the best example of Aztec architecture that has survived in the Central Region, largely because the Aztecs themselves covered it to hide it from the Spanish.

The pyramid, often called "the *Building of the Serpents,*" is 140 ft. square and about 50 ft. high. Its walls rise steeply in a series of terraces to a flat platform. On three sides are low narrow platforms along the edge of which are stone serpents, 52 on each side. The sculpture is very severe, showing none of the lavishness of Toltec sculpture seen at Tenochtitlán. Tunneling has shown that the mass was rebuilt five times, an indication of its age and history, for the Aztecs rebuilt or enlarged their pyramids each 52 years, their century or cycle. The last reconstruction occurred in 1507, the last known celebration of the New Fires and the 52 year cycle.

[22] In an early edition of *Terry's Guide to Mexico* there occurs the following note concerning Tlalnepantla. "The Parochial Church contains a number of pre-Columbia relics in the form of chiselled stones, monoliths and whatnot of considerable interest to archaeologists. An old cylindrical vase, in the *bautiserio,* and a font *(cuauhxicalli)* in the body of the church are particularly interesting. The earthquake of March 1908 opened a subterranean cavern beneath the town and disclosed idols and relics which lead archaeologists to believe that the present town rests on the ruins of a Toltec city antedating the discovery of America." When this note was written Tenayuca had not yet come to public attention.

Los Remedios, Mex. Pop. 400. A drab Indian hamlet 8 m. NW of the capital, just beyond the town of *Naucálpam,* but famed throughout the country for its *Santuario de los Remedios,* dedicated to the image of the Virgin brought to Mexico by the Conquistadores. This shrine, dating from 1629, stands rather forlornly among maguey plants and Indian shacks on a hill overlooking a broad valley crossed by a colonial aqueduct. Each September an elaborate festival is held here in honor of the Virgin.

Close by is the depressed suburb of *Azcapotzalco,* completely lacking in visual interest. It is the home of a large, modern oil refinery. In pre-Hispanic times it was a famous slave market, and was also the place where Cortés had his smelters for melting Mexican treasures into bullion.

EXCURSIONS WEST OF MEXICO, D.F.: This section covering the largest part of the State of Mexico,[23] and including the state capital, Toluca, and the high Toluca basin, is one of the least visited of the districts around Mexico City, yet it is one of the most beautiful. In it there are countless villages producing delightful and piquant handicrafts, there are magnificent peaks and lakes, a good week-end spa, and some of the best trout fishing available.

The most often visited point in this district is the capital, Toluca. On the route from Mexico City to it there are several points of interest, chief among them *El Zarco,* a pretty park and home of one of the Federal Trout Hatcheries. It lies on the right-hand side of the road, CN-15 (Nogales to Mexico City), at the km. 29 marker. Visitors are welcome. It is a favored picnic area. The surrounding pine-clad heights have been made a National Park *(Parque Nacional de Hidalgo).* There is a monument to Father Hidalgo on the site of the Battle of Las Cruces, (the point where Hidalgo routed the Spanish forces and might have taken Mexico City, but for some unaccountable reason, withdrew his forces). The pass where the monument stands is 10,381 ft. above sea level.

About 31 m. from Mexico City, is *Lerma, Mex.,* a small roadside village founded in 1613. The town is noted for its reed weaving and tropical furniture industry. The Lerma River passes nearby.

Toluca, Mex. Pop. 60,000. Alt. 7500 ft. Capital of the State of Mexico, an important commercial city and

[23] *State of Mexico,* one of the smaller Mexican states — population, 1,654,592, and an area of 8365 sq. miles — yet it rambles almost haphazardly around the Federal District. It is bounded on the N by the State of Hidalgo, on the E by Tlaxcala and Puebla, on the S by Morelos, the Federal District and Guerrero, and on the W by Michoacán and a corner of Querétaro. During the Spanish dominion it was called the Intendencia de México and included a much wider area. Its capital was then Mexico City. Since the founding of the republic and the formation of the Federal District, the state capital was removed to Toluca.

Nature has divided it into two well-defined regions; the E a plain, the W a mountainous region. Between the various ridges which characterize the latter are fine valleys, some dotted with lakes and salt marshes. Certain regions are grandly rugged. The state shares the slopes and snow-capped peaks of Popocatépetl and Iztaccíhuatl with neighboring Puebla, while in the western area the countryside is dominated by the handsome, often snow-capped Nevado de Toluca. The Lerma, one of the most important and longer rivers in the republic rises in the state. The mountain regions are rich in mineral deposits, while the agricultural products range from bananas to wheat. Many of the large industrial plants serving the country are located in the state, mostly near Mexico City.

road junction. Toluca is famed for its Friday Indian Market.

HOW TO GET THERE: *Via road* — Toluca lies 41 m. W of Mexico City, route CN-15. Motorists coming from Nogales follow CN-15. Motorists entering Mexico through El Paso, or coming down CN-57 from Texas, can take in Toluca by following CN-71 from San Juan del Río, Qro. *Via bus from Mexico City* — the Turismos line runs frequent service to Toluca from Antonio Caso 187, Mexico City, Tel. 16-40-41. Fare: about $5 MN. Also, Transportes Corona Roja (hourly) from Plaza Vizcaínas 17 A, Mexico City. *Via railway* — two trains daily, Ferrocarriles Nacionales de México (Uruapan line), leaving Mexico City at 7 A.M. and at 9:30 P.M. Trip, about 2 hours 15 minutes. Fare: $3.90 MN.

HOTELS AND RESTAURANTS: The Toluca hotels are by and large *viajero*-style, fairly comfortable but not especially geared for vacation or tourist trade. Best available: *Hotel San Carlos,* Portal Madero 34, 100 rooms, bar, fair dining room. Rates: EP $40 MN dble. Tel. 20-17. *Hotel Rex,* Av. Morelos 31. 46 rooms, restaurant and bar. Rates: EP from $40 MN dble. *Restaurant El Rey,* Portal 20 de Noviembre 111 (near the market). Spotless, good food, reasonable.

DIRECTORY: *Bank* — Banco Nacional de México, Morelos 37. *Car repairs* — Automotriz Méxicana, Av. Hidalgo 76 (GM); Cia. Automotriz de Toluca (Ford), Av. Hidalgo and Humboldt. Hernandez & Hno (general repairs), Degollado 30. *Bus lines* — Autobuses Toluca-Mexico (Turismos), Constitución 3 C, Tel. 20-49. Auto Transportes de Occidente, 5 de Febrero 11-bis. Tel. 32-44. Auto Transportes Mexico-Valle de Bravo, Lerdo 25, Tel. 28-12.

THE CITY AND ENVIRONS: Toluca (toe-LOO-cah) from *Tollocan* — where there are tules (reeds), is officially known as Toluca de Lerdo in honor of the Mexican statesman, Sebastián Lerdo de Tejada. The Spanish settlement was founded in 1533 upon the site of an older Indian settlement.

Although Toluca is an unusually clean city, with straight, well-laid-out streets, some attractive parks and old buildings, it remains somehow a city that is a bit chilly in atmosphere and unappealing to travelers. The cold breezes that often blow through the city and the unusually bitter winters contribute to this. The principal tourist attraction in the town is the *Municipal Market* which, on Friday mornings, becomes one of the largest and most colorful regional markets in the country. It covers several blocks, an endless series of stalls and displays of produce, handicrafts from nearby villages as well as from the distant corners of the state. The market is just off Av. Juárez, 2 blocks N of Av. Independencia.

The *Plaza Principal* (also, *Jardín* or *Zócalo*) is the focal center of the city and the prettiest plaza. Just to the S of the plaza is a long block of *Portales,* one of the longest arcades in Mexico. It is filled with shops and is the favorite promenade in the city. On the W side of the plaza stands the *Palacio del Gobierno* (Governor's Palace), built in 1872 on the site of the old *Casa Consistorial* (Guild Hall) which was occupied for many years by Cortés' son, Martín.

Museum of Archaeology, the state museum, 1 block N of the plaza on Calle Cura Merlin, contains a number of important artifacts from the nearby archaeological zone of *Calixtlahuaca.* Noteworthy is the ancient God of Wind figure. Across the street from the archaeological museum is the *Museum of Fine Arts,* containing some excellent colonial paintings and an interesting visual exhibit of the history of Mexican equestrian art.

The city's most delightful museum is the *Museo del Arte Popular* (arts and crafts) situated on the highway at the E edge of the city. The museum is open daily, except Monday, 9 A.M. to 1 P.M.

Toluca's best attractions lie outside of the city, some within 5 to 20 miles, such as certain of the handicraft villages, the archaeological zone of Calixtlahuaca and the lakes atop the Nevado de Toluca, others more distant, such as El Oro and Valle de Bravo. Most can be reached by car or cab. TAXI RATES, authorized by the city and state governments are: $2 MN for any trip within the city; $3 MN where call is made to a cab-stand and the taxi goes to pick you up; $10 MN per hour on hourly basis. Beyond the city limits fares must be agreed upon in advance, but as a guide, the average is 50 centavos per kilometer (about 7 U.S. cents per mile) plus a time charge of $15 MN per hour.

Calixtlahuaca, Mex. (Archaeological zone). About 5 m. N of Toluca off CN-71. Calixtlahuaca (ka-lees-tla-WAH-ka), meaning "Place in the Prairie," is one of the most recently studied, and not yet fully explored, ancient sites covering an area of at least 12 miles. Experts believe it will doubtless prove to have been one of the great cities of pre-Hispanic America.

Little is known yet concerning the original builders, the Matlatzinca culture, or where these people originally came from. There are indications of Toltec relations, of Otomí links as well as influences from the Tarascan culture in Michoacán. It is also apparent that in later times, the Aztecs controlled or occupied the area.

Excavations up to this moment have revealed great paved terraces on which pyramids were built, forming a series of public buildings. Of the many mounds, only five have been uncovered. The first to be seen by visitors is the *Calmecac,* or seminary for priests. Only the lower walls of this labyrinth are still standing. Nearby is the *Ball Court.* Part way up the hillside stands the *Temple of Quetzalcoatl,* an unusual structure consisting of cylindrical drums getting progressively smaller. Farther up the hill are the *Pyramid of Tlaloc* and the more interesting *Tzompantli* (House of Skulls), decorated with carved skulls.

The Nevado de Toluca, an exinct volcano towering over Toluca offers an interesting dry-weather excursion. The peak, rising 14,900 ft. above sea level, is Mexico's fourth highest mountain, and the only volcano you can drive right up into the crater. The Indian name for the imposing cone is *Xinantecatl,* "The Naked Man."

The route to the peak, approximately 27 m. is via the *Toluca-Temascaltepec* road, at km. 13 turn off on the old road to *Sultepec.* Following a short distance there is another turn-off called *Raíces* which leads up the peak. The road is dirt, but passable in good weather.

There are two lakes in the crater, the *Laguna del Sol* (largest) and *Laguna de la Luna* (Lakes of the Sun and the Moon). The changing color of the lakes, especially the larger, is spectacular, ranging through tones of opal and emerald to that of steel. A transparent type of fish inhabit the waters of both lakes. The views from the volcano's rim are breath-taking. At the moment there is a modest lodge (really a hut) maintained by the state tourist department. There are no tourist accommodations, though plans are afoot to make a resort of the area, to build a hotel, to pave the road and install a lift.

Metepec, Mex. Pop. 5379. A picturesque pottery-making village 4½ miles from Toluca, just off the highway to Ixtapan de la Sal. The Monday morning market is very colorful. The piquant polychrome pottery figures made here are rarely seen in the market however. You must go to the shops and homes of the potters for these.

Note: In the hills around Toluca, and especially in this area SE of the city there are numerous villages noted for their handicrafts and local markets, among them: *Tianguistenco* (serapes), *Almoloya* (embroidered tablecloths), and *Villa Victoria* (embroidery). A traveler interested in visiting them should consult with the director of the Popular Arts Museum in Toluca for detailed information regarding market days, road conditions, etc.

Valle de Bravo, Mex. Pop. 4600. Alt. 6281 ft. A charming, infrequently visited little mining town in a beautiful mountain valley, and situated on the edge of a large artificial lake, one of a chain of such lakes that are a part of a vast federal hydroelectric project. Boating, fishing, and swimming. Tourist accommodations are somewhat inadequate. Best available hotels: *Refugio del Salto,* 3½ m. from town. 21 rooms, dining room, bar, nice location. Rates: AP $200 MN dble. Not too well maintained. *Avandaro Courts,* Paseo Fontana.

To get to Valle de Bravo, follow CN-15 W out of Toluca. 6 m. beyond the city there is a turn-off, left, paved road (CE-56), about 42 m. The paved road continues on some 35 m. traversing magnificent mountain, canyon and tropical country and passing through the villages of *Colorines* and *Nuevo Santo Tomás de los Platanos* (St. Thomas of the Bananas), the latter spectacularly perched on a high cliff like an Alice-in-Wonderland village.

Real del Oro, Mex. Pop. 4283. Alt. 9200 ft. An interesting and once celebrated mining town which has almost become a ghost town. The town came into prominence late in the eighteenth century when the Spaniards discovered the enormously rich Descubridora vein. For years miners and prospectors from all over the world were attracted by the gold in the area and for a while the town had an estimated 50,000 inhabitants.

In a lovely wooded region some 20 minutes' drive beyond El Oro there is a good trout lake and some fine trout streams.

To reach El Oro (as it is called locally) go N from Toluca on CN-71 to *Atlocamulco.* From the center of the town a paved road branches W. 19½ m. to El Oro. The town is on the Uruapan-Toluca line of the National Railways and there is one slow train per day between Mexico-Toluca and El Oro. There are no accommodations in the town. Even the hardiest camper shudders at the thought of staying in El Oro's picturesque hotel.

Ixtapan de la Sal, Mex. Also called *Nueva Ixtapan.* Pop. 2571. On CN-55, about 40 m. S of Toluca, 92 m. from Mexico City (see route log below).

Ixtapan (ix-TAH-pan) is an attractive village with attached resort and radioactive mineral water spas. The place is very popular with Mexico City vacationers. In the village there remains an interesting sixteenth-century façade on the parochial church.

HOTELS: *Hotel Ixtapan.* 82 rooms and bungalows on beautifully landscaped grounds. Good dining room, cocktail lounge, swimming pools, thermal mineral baths. 9 hole golf course (green fees, $25 MN per day. Caddy fees, $6 MN for 9 holes, $10 MN for 18 holes). A good restful place, this is the only hotel with its own thermal baths. Rates: AP from $250 MN to $300 MN dble. Tel. 2. *Hotel Kiss,* 22 rooms, very good dining room, cocktail lounge. A very new and nice hotel, but so chromed up it is like a jeweler's window. You hate to disturb anything and enjoy yourself. Rates: AP from $200 MN to $240 MN. *Posada Don Manuel,* a smaller, modest inn. Reasonable rates. Likewise *Restaurant-Bungalows Lolita.*

A short distance south of Ixtapan at the village of *Tonatico* (a coming resort spot) there are thermal baths and a new, small pension hotel.

THE TOLUCA-IXTAPAN-TAXCO ROUTE: This highway, newly paved and extended makes it possible for the traveler to enjoy a circuit tour beginning at Mexico City, taking in Toluca, then going south through Ixtapan to Taxco, and return via Cuernavaca or Amecameca. It is one of the most beautiful drives in the State of Mexico. The route is posted, CN-55.

MILES FROM TOLUCA	ROUTE LOG
0	Toluca.
4	Turn-off l. to Metepec. (½ m.)
12	Tenango de Aristo. Sideroad to l. goes to Almoloya del Río and Tianguistenco. Road is poor.
31	Tenancingo. A town noted for its *rebozo* weaving and its tropical palm-weave furniture. A side road (in poor condition) leads E 7½ m. to Malinalco and 16 m. to Chalma (see Index).
37	Villa Guerrero.
40	IXTAPAN DE LA SAL (Nueva Ixtapan)
44.5	Tonatico.
62	State line between Mexico and Guerrero.
74	Turn-off, ¼ m. to Cacahuamilpa Caves (see Index).
79	Junction with CN-95 (Mexico City-Acapulco Route). To r. goes to Taxco; to l. leads to Cuernavaca.

Malinalco, Mex. Pop. 2947. An isolated town 16 m. E of Tenancingo over poor road. Nearby is one of Central Mexico's important archaeological zones with a complex of temples hewn into living rock, and which are as fascinating as the famous Egyptian rock tombs of Abu-Simel.

Malinalco (mah-leen-AHL-ko) was inhabited by the Malinalcas, a cultural branch of the Nahoa people. They were related to the Matlanzincas. The constructions date from around 1476 when the Aztecs conquered the area. The Spanish conquistador Andrés de Tapia overthrew the Malinalco population.

THE RUINS are set upon platforms and terraces cut into various levels of the hillside. Most interesting, and one of the finest pre-Hispanic edifices existing, is the *Temple of the Warriors,* so called for the sculptured tigers and eagles on it. In the archaeological museum at Toluca there is a carved, wooden war drum which was found here.

In the village of Malinalco there is an interesting early sixteenth-century Augustinian monastery, memorable for its primitive simplicity.

Chalma, Mex. Pop. 304. This tiny, mountain-locked, one-street village, about 100 m. from Mexico City, is the mecca for some of the greatest religious pilgrimages in the country. During religious fiestas as many as fifteen to twenty thousand people gather here, honoring a miraculous, life-size Christ on a cross — *El Señor de Chalma.*[24]

The great Chalma pilgrimages and fiestas are staggered throughout the year. Years ago it became the custom to assign villages their fixed annual pilgrimage dates and this is still continued. January 6 is for Otomí and Aztec villages from the central region; February 2, for the Zapotecs from the Oaxaca region; the first Friday in Lent for people from Morelos, Guerrero, Tlaxcala, and Puebla. In addition there are smaller fiestas honoring San Miguel, San Agustín, and during Christmas. During the fiestas there are religious exercises, Indian dancers, thousands of people camping in the open. Lacking sanitary facilities there is indeed a need for the purifying bath, a part of the festivities which occurs in a sacred pool near the shrine. The purifying bath was also a custom at Chalma before the apparition of the Señor.

HOW TO GET THERE: The two easiest routes are by car via Toluca and Tenancingo to Malinalco; or from *Ajusco* on the old Mexico City-Cuernavaca highway, a road branches westward to Chalma. The most beautiful route, but difficult, is from Mexico City to Tianguistenco to *Ocuilán* (third-class buses go this far). From Ocuilán you follow the pilgrim route on foot, a trail with mountains on one side, and on the other, a gorge with the river tumbling through it.

EXCURSIONS EAST OF THE FEDERAL DISTRICT: One of the most popular tour areas east of Mexico City is to the storied city of Texcoco and the surrounding country. The easiest way to get there from Mexico City, by car, is to follow Av. Fray Servando Teresa de Mier to CN-190 (Puebla Route). At the Los Reyes road junction take CE-136 to the left and this leads past Chapingo (National Agricultural College) to Texcoco. Buses leave Calle Emiliano Zapata 92-A, Mexico City, every hour for Texcoco.

Texcoco, Mex. Pop. 8000. Alt. 7391 ft. An important textile center about 29 m. E of Mexico City. The present-day town is rather squalid, completely lacking in architectural charm, good restaurants, or hotels. It is noted for its Sunday market (very good cooking pottery), its woollen *serapes* (the best woven in the nearby town of *San Miguel Chiconcuac*), and for its historical associations.[25]

At the entrance of the town there is a tablet marking the spot where Cortés assembled and launched his brigantines used in the siege of Tenochtitlán. At that time Lake Texcoco came to the edge of the city. The lake is now dry.

The attractions of Texcoco are almost entirely situated outside of the city, and are:

Molino de Las Flores, an unusually picturesque deserted hacienda, a fair walk from the town. A road leads to it, but is poor. The hacienda, a tiny city in itself, with its gardens, waterfalls, and Baroque chapels, was founded shortly after the conquest by a Spaniard named Cervantes. Until the turn of this century the property had been held by the same family. The *molino* is now part of a national park. It is a delightful place for picnics.

Texcotzingo (archaeological zone). 5 m. E of Texcoco. A national park in which are a few remains of the summer palace of the Texcocoan poet-king, Netzahualcóyotl. There remain little more than evidences of the long stairway, the royal baths and the aqueduct which fed the pools, and cascades. According to records the place was once a New World Versailles with beautifully landscaped gardens, temples, statuary, and waterfalls. The *Cerro de Texcotzingo* is now quite barren.

Chapingo, Mex. About 8 m. E of Texcoco, on CE-136 (road to Mexico). Chapingo (cha-PEEN-go) is the *National Agricultural College.* Touristically, it is chiefly noted for the murals painted by the late Diego Rivera in the school's main building and chapel. Art critics consider these the finest and most powerful Rivera murals in the country, and Chapingo chapel is often

[24] El Señor de Chalma appeared in 1533 as a kind of Augustinian competitor to the Franciscan Virgin of Guadalupe (see Index). According to religious records Friars Nicholas Perea and Sebastian Tolentino, while working among the natives near Ocuilán, were faced with the fact that the people preferred to worship a stone idol in a cave above the present sanctuary. Their efforts were aided by the mysterious destruction of the idol, while in its place in the cave was found the crucifix of the Lord of Chalma. In addition, the place was miraculously filled with flowers and holy fragrance. The news of this miracle, and of others, brought about wholesale conversions in the region, and since then the popularity of El Señor de Chalma, especially among the Indian population of the entire country, has vied with that of the Virgin of Guadalupe.

One of the early pilgrims to the shrine was a Jalapa, Ver., shoemaker who became a monk and remained in the service of the Señor de Chalma for the rest of his life. This Fray Bartolomé de Jesús María became the head of the order and built the first sanctuary, the convent with its cells and cloisters for pilgrims. In 1683 when the present larger church was dedicated the figure of Christ was placed on the altar in a gilded glass case.

[25] Long before the Spanish conquest Texcoco was a rich and populous city, second only to Tenochtitlán in importance, and the seat of the Tezcucan kings. Situated on one side of Lake Texcoco, the city was at first much more powerful than the Aztec city across the lake. Even later, when Tenochtitlán became the military and commercial center of the plateau, and the two cities formed an alliance, Texcoco remained the Athens of the pre-Hispanic world — pre-eminent in the arts, intellectual pursuits, and sciences. It was noted for its fine temples, palaces, gardens, music, and poetry. Here the erudite Netzahualcóyotl (Hungry Coyote), the greatest of the Texcocoan monarchs, ruled and wrote his enduring poetry.

Cortés defeated the Texcocoans and made the city his lakeside base from which to mount his final attacks that brought about the destruction of the Aztec capital. The Texcocoans had apparently not been very strong in their resistance to the Spanish because relations with their Aztec allies had become strained, due in part to the fact that Moctezuma's sister had married the Texcocoan chief, but having been a bit too free with her favors to the young men of the court, had been put to death.

referred to as the Sistine Chapel of the Revolution. *Hours:* 9 A.M. to 1 P.M., 3 P.M. to 5 P.M. *Admission: Free.*

Huexotla, Mex. A few miles to the E of Chapingo, near the village of Huexotla (hway-HOT-tla) is an archaeological zone with the ruins of what was once an important pre-Hispanic town. There are ruins of massive walls and traces of temples, most of them yet to be excavated.

Somewhat to the SE, though considered part of the same zone, is the site where the great Monolith of Coatlinchan was discovered lying in a brush-covered ravine. This 165-ton statue of the Rain God, Tlaloc, was one of the mysterious relics of the Texcocoan kingdom. It was found by the Spaniards on the summit of the *Cerro de Tlaloc,* several miles away. It is said the Spaniards removed the figure from there and tossed it into the valley below — a remarkable feat because in 1964 it took Mexican engineers considerable effort, using heavy-duty modern equipment, to move the figure to the new Museum of Anthropology in Mexico City.

To the SE of Mexico City, along the vast slopes of the volcanoes Iztaccíhuatl and Popocatépetl, there are a number of interesting villages, and for the motorist, the drive over highway CN-115 is one of the loveliest in the valley. A circle tour can be made by following CN-115 to Cuautla, Mor., and returning to the capital via Cuernavaca.

Chalco, Mex. Pop. 5222. Alt. 7442 ft. On CE-115. A picturesque old town, once the capital of the Chalcas, a Nahoa tribe. Chalco (CHAHL-co), meaning Many Months, is connected with Xochimilco by a system of canals. In the village there is an interesting sixteenth-century Franciscan church.

Tlalmanalco, Mex. Pop. 4000. A picturesque village at the foot of the volcano, Izta. Tlalmanalco (Azt On a Plain) pronounced tlal-mahn-AL-coe, has a noted Franciscan convent containing frescoed cloisters and an open chapel, the columns of which are profusely decorated with Renaissance details carried out with Indian touches. This is considered one of the best of the open chapels in the region.[26]

Amecameca, Mex. Pop. 9700. Alt. 8101 ft. On CN-115, about 37 m. from Mexico City.

Amecameca (ah-meh-ka-MEH-kah), meaning (Azt.) "Many Water Holes," stands on the site of an old Aztec town at the foot of the volcanoes Iztaccíhuatl and Popocatépetl. It is the base for climbing the two peaks (see Volcanoes, below). A road branches from the highway, S edge of town, going a short distance up the mountainside to *Izta-Popo Park,* a national park between the famed volcanoes.

The town of Amecameca is a sprawling site with a vast, barren plaza, with arched gateways and churches spreading out over the landscape. The old Dominican church, *La Parroquia,* is an interesting sixteenth-century edifice containing a good Plateresque altar. The *Shrine of Sacromonte* (Sacred Hill) above the town is one of Mexico's famed pilgrimage shrines. Dedicated to a venerable image of Christ (the Santo Entierro), it is almost as popular as the meccas at Los Remedios (see Index) and at Cholula. A zigzag cobbled walk leads up to the sacred hill which rises about 500 ft. above the town. The way is lined with stately old trees and Stations of the Cross. Often pilgrims traverse the entire way on their knees. There is a small church built around a cave where Fray Martín de Valencia, one of the 12 Mexican apostles,[27] took up his abode and eventually died. According to legend, when some muleteers were transporting images to be sold in Amecameca, a mule broke away and went up to the cave already made holy by the good friar. The animal refused to budge, and when his load was taken off it was found to be a life-size figure of Christ made of some material so light it could be lifted by a child. This was taken as a divine sign, so a shrine was built to house the figure.

Farther up, on the crest of Sacromonte there is another chapel dedicated to the Virgin of Guadalupe. Originally an Indian Temple of Teteoinán was located here. The principal Sacromonte fiestas are: Ash Wednesday (huge market and hundreds of Indian dancers), and during September.

The Volcanoes — Popo and Izta. These two imposing, snow-clad sentinels are among the highest peaks in North America. Although there seems to be little agreement among experts regarding their exact heights, Popocatépetl (Azt. Smoking Mountain) soars approximately 17,887 ft. Iztaccíhuatl (meaning, Sleeping Woman) rises 17,343 ft. The latter is a "ruined" or dead volcano while the former still smokes. The last eruption of Popo occurred in 1802. In 1921 there were violent outbursts of smoke and gases, but since then it has smoked quietly, exhaling sulphuric vapors from the many breathing holes *(solfateras)* in the crater.

Since the conquest the crater of Popo has been a gigantic brimstone factory whence many thousands of tons of sulphur have been extracted. The soldiers of Cortés were the first to dig out the mineral in order to manufacture gunpowder to carry on their campaign against the owners of the mountain.

ASCENT OF POPO AND IZTA: Both peaks are relatively easy objectives for experienced alpinists. For the inexperienced they can be deadly, especially Iztaccíhuatl which takes a toll of lives each year. The best and safest climbing season is from October to March. There are two routes up Popo — the rest is a mass of shifting volcanic ash. The best route is from Amecameca, driving to *Tlamacas* (12,788 ft.), a few miles past the monument in the Pass of Cortés. Spend the night at the fine shelter here. Beginning the climb at around 2 A.M., one can reach La Cruz by dawn, and the remainder of the journey in another four to five hours, allowing the afternoon for the descent. The other route up Popo is by way of El

[26] Open chapels were a purely American feature of the Franciscan, Augustinian and Dominican convent-church edifices in Mexico. These are chapels, either connected with or set apart from the church itself, actually a kind of shell or cover for the altar. They were brought about by the necessity of saying Mass for huge crowds of Indians who could not be accommodated in the churches, and who were also accustomed to worshiping out of doors.

[27] The Franciscan Order, the first to work in Mexico, was introduced by 12 friars (popularly known as the 12 Apostles of Mexico) from the Franciscan Province of San Gabriel, Spain. Their leader was the superior of the province, Fray Martín de Valencia. The group arrived in Mexico (San Juan de Ulua, Ver.) May 23, 1524. In their heavy homespun robes and open-sandals they walked the long distance from Veracruz to Mexico City. At Texcoco they had been joined by Fray Pedro de Gante who had already been in Mexico a year. On June 23, 1524, the thirteen arrived in the capital, weary, dusty, and footsore. Cortés and his lieutenants went out to meet them and, to the amazement of the Indians, their conquerer dismounted, knelt and paid obvious homage to the monks. It was a gesture and event that created a tremendous impression on the Indians and enhanced the influence of the friars.

Ventorillo, a flue-like crack up the eastern side. It is steep, tricky, but more direct.

The climb up Iztaccíhuatl is considered one of the hardest of Mexican climbs, offering a number of alpine situations and a test of ropemanship.

Guides for the climbs are available in Amecameca. For alpine equipment, some can be rented in Amecameca, or purchased at Deportes Marti, V. Carranza 19, Mexico City. The Club de Exploraciones de México at Calle J. A. Mateos 146. Tel. 19-52-46 offers information regarding mountain climbing throughout Mexico.

Ozumba, Mex. Pop. 403. Just off highway CN-115, and at the foot of Popocatépetl. Nearby are the pretty waterfalls, *Salto de Chimal* and the *Chimalhuacan Gardens.* In the village there is a sixteenth-century Franciscan church, unfortunately poorly refurbished a century later. The murals in the church likewise have been retouched. One of them depicts the Franciscans being received by Cortés.

14 m. S of Ozumba and to the E of the highway is the hamlet of *Nepantla,* of historical interest only — as the birthplace of Mexico's famed nun-poetess, Sor Juana Inés de la Cruz. On one of the walls of the *hacienda* where she was born there are some tiles bearing some of her best poems.

EXCURSIONS SOUTH OF MEXICO CITY: Long before Cortés and his heirs, the modern tourists, had decided that the State of Morelos (just south of Mexico City) was an ideal weekend resort area, the Aztecs had hit on the same notion. The traveler bound for Cuernavaca and its environs should be warned that this area which has been a "tourist belt" for hundreds of years is fairly sophisticated. It is quite different from the rest of the republic, yet it has siren charms, some of the best vacation accommodations anywhere and, perhaps, the most idyllic climate in all Mexico.

THE STATE OF MORELOS: named in honor of the revolutionary patriot José María Morelos, covers about 1939 sq. miles and has a population upward of 388,929 inhabitants. It is bounded on the N by the Federal District, on the west, northwest, and northeast by the State of Mexico, on the E and SE by Puebla, on the S and SW by Guerrero. The little state has a great range of altitude, from the very high mountains in the N to the low Amacuzac River Valley to the south. Temperatures range from cool to tropical. The Ajusco range in the N divides the state from the Federal District and is visible both from Cuernavaca and Mexico City. The most important industry is agriculture (and the tourist business). Rice, coffee, sugar, vegetables, and a cornucopia of tropical fruits are the principal products. The state capital and favorite resort is —

Cuernavaca, Mor. Pop. 35,000. Alt. 5000 ft. A gay and balmy semitropical city less than an hours' drive from Mexico City. An ideal vacation spot for visitors to Mexico who have little time to explore the more distant regions.

HOW TO GET THERE: The only comfortable means of going to Cuernavaca is by automobile or bus. From Mexico City, via Av. Insurgentes Sur, one connects with the old Cuernavaca highway, CN-95, or the faster, parallel toll road, 95 CP. (see Index: Highway Routes — Mexico City — Acapulco). Motorists may also make a circle tour by skirting beneath the volcanoes, Popo and Izta, CN-115, to Cuautla, then across to Cuernavaca and back to Mexico City via CN-95 CP. For those who admire railway travel, an ancient, wooden-benched train makes a leisurely daily trip to Cuernavaca.

HOTELS: Cuernavaca's big season is winter. For accommodations during it reservations are advised. The same is true for weekends throughout the entire year.

Posada Arcadia, Leyva 37, 1 block S of Cortés Palace. A new, small, outstanding downtown inn with only 13 rooms and a city block of attractive gardens. Pool, cocktail terrace, golf privileges. Very friendly atmosphere and excellent service. Good dining room. Rates: $150 MN dble, incl. breakfast. Tel. 2-02-20. *Posada Jacarandas,* Av. Chapultepec, 1½ m. E on Cuautla road. Perhaps the swankest inn around. 49 very attractive units, pool, good dining room, cocktail bar and terrace, frontón, tennis, beautiful landscaped grounds. Excellent service. Rates: from $125 MN to $300 dble, EP. Tel. 2-21-59. *Las Mañanitas,* Calle Apulche 14, near center. Excellent small inn. 10 rooms, pool, pretty garden, magnificent restaurant (see below). Rates: $150 MN dble, incl. breakfast. *Casa de Piedra,* downtown near Cathedral. Small and exclusive. 10 rooms, beautifully furnished, in a lovely old stone mansion. Excellent dining room. Rates: EP $200 MN dble. *Casino de la Selva,* on old Cuautla road. 150 rooms, bungalows, pools, nice grounds, fair dining room. Rates: AP $205 MN dble. *Arocena Holiday,* pleasant new motel, pool, good dining room, bar. Rates: reasonable.

The following hotels are rated from fair to good. Prices range from $60 MN to $125 MN dble, some include breakfast. Most have pools, gardens, cocktail facilities. *Casa Arocena,* Av. Hidalgo 15. Tel. 2-03-08 (9 rooms). *Hotel Capri,* Obregón 104. Tel. 2-16-88 (34 rooms). *Bella Vista,* on the plaza (50 rooms). *Del Parque,* Jardín Juárez 2 (29 rooms). *Miller's El Buen Retiro,* just beyond Casino de la Selva (an excellent 31-room inn).

Some passably comfortable, budget-style hotels: *Savoy,* on Av. Morelos. *Asturias Hotel,* downtown. *Iberia Hotel,* downtown. *El Papagayo,* Motolinia 12 (81 rooms). *Ja Joya Motel,* on CN-95, 2½ m. N.

RESTAURANTS: (in addition to those indicated in hotels above). *Las Mañanitas,* Calle Apulche 14, near center, this has for some years been one of the really fine restaurants in Mexico. It is operated by Bob Krause, a man with epicurean leanings. Lunch is especially colorful, served on the garden lawn with peacocks strolling about. Specialties: vichyssoise, curries, and rich desserts. Quite good. *Terraza Majestic,* N end of town, just west of CN-95. Pleasant surroundings, good food. *Casa Cárdenas,* facing Jardín Pacheco, Mexican style food.

DIRECTORY: *Banks* — Banco Nacional de México, Calles Arteaga and Matamoros; Banco Mercantil del Sur, Jardín Juárez and Lerdo de Tejada. *Auto repairs* — Cuernavaca Motors (GM), Av. Juárez 30. Motores de Morelos (Ford), Av. Morelos Sur and Calle Tepatitlán. Automotriz Morelense (Dodge), Morelos 1. *Bus lines* — Linea Mexico-Cuernavaca-Zacatepec-Jojutla, Jardín Morelos 7, Sur; Autos Pullman Mexico-Cuernavaca, Galeana 9; Estrella de Oro, Morelos and Tepatitlán (office in Mexico City, Fray Teresa de Mier 72); Turismo Triangulo Azul (Mexico, Cuernavaca and the Caves route), Netzahualcóyotl and Abasolo (Mexico City terminal, Netzalhualcóyotl 184-C. First-class service each 15 minutes to Cuernavaca. Rate: $6 MN). *Real estate rental agent* — Albert Abkarian, office in Hotel Marik Plaza. *American books and magazines* — Pablo's Marik Plaza Bookshop. *Doctors* — Dr. José Kirchner, Abasola 35-4, Tel. 2-28-58; Dr. Francisco Vazquez Gómez (ear, eye, nose and throat), Degollado 24, Tel. 2-01-63; Dr. Enrique Borbolla (pediatrics), Morelos 307-H, Tel. 2-00-71. *Churches* (English language services) — St. Michael and All Angels (Episcopal), Guerrero and Degollado, Sundays, 10:30 A.M.

THE CITY AND ENVIRONS: Cuernavaca (kwekr-nah-VAH-cah) was originally the capital of the Tlahuicas, a Nahoa tribe who wandered down from the north ahead of the Aztecs. They called their town Cuauhnahuac (Near the Woods), a name which the Spanish struggled with and turned into Cuernavaca (meaning in Spanish, Cow's Horn).

During the period of Aztec occupation the place became a favorite retreat for the nobles. It was one of the cities granted to Cortés by the king of Spain and, likewise, became his favored place of residence. Since those early days the balmy climate, the gaily tinted houses with their red-tiled roofs and the luxuriant vegetation has attracted a constant stream of visitors ranging from Maximilian and Carlotta, ambassadors and presidents to pure and simple one-day tourists. Living within its flower-exuberant confines today is probably the largest retired foreign colony of any Mexican city.

Due to over-crowding and garish new constructions the town's once lovely plazas, (Juárez and Plaza de la Constitución), now resemble Coney Island. The residential areas remain attractive. Cuernavaca's chief architectural points of interest are:

The *Palacio de Cortés,* flanking one side of the plaza, was begun in 1530 by the Conquistador. It was his favorite residence in Mexico. The building has been considerably altered since his time, and is now used as the seat of the state legislature. The fine *loggias* on the second floor afford a good view of the valley and the volcanoes Popocatépetl and Iztaccíhuatl rising in the distance. The strikingly vivid murals on the walls of the gallery, showing scenes from the conquest of Mexico, the exploitation of the Indians by the Spaniards and their later redemption by Mexican patriots, were painted by Diego Rivera. The murals were a gift to the city, presented by Dwight W. Morrow when he was U.S. Ambassador to Mexico.

The Cathedral, at Hidalgo and Morelos, was begun in 1529 at the request of Cortés. It was originally established as a Franciscan monastery and was raised to cathedral rank in 1891. It is massive and severe, an attractive old relic possessing more historic than artistic value. To the rear of the cathedral is the *Chapel of the Third Order,* of a later period, and noteworthy for its half-dome on the side facing the cathedral.

The Borda Gardens (Jardín de la Borda), opposite the Cathedral, was the former home and gardens of José de la Borda (Joseph le Borde), a Frenchman who came to Mexico in 1716 and amassed a fortune in silver mines at Zacatecas and Taxco. It is said he spent over a million gold pesos on the gardens alone. Though the gardens have not been kept up, they remain a charming, nostalgic spot. It was a frequent retreat of Maximilian and Carlotta during their short rule in Mexico. Adjoining the gardens is the *Church of Guadalupe,* built by Borda's son and used as a family chapel. *Admission to the gardens:* 1 peso.

Pyramid of Teopanzolco, near the railway station. An archaeologically interesting, but not spectacular pyramid, discovered by accident during the Revolution of 1910 when a mound used as an artillery emplacement for bombarding the city shook apart, revealing the construction below. Upon excavation it was discovered that the pyramid had an unusual double stairway on the western side, and that an inner (older) pyramid had a similar double stairway.

Salto de San Antonio, a scenic waterfall 1 m. W of the edge of town. The pottery-making village of San Antonio clings to the heights above the falls.

EXCURSIONS OUT OF CUERNAVACA: **Tetpoztlán, Mor.** Pop. 3900. An unusually beautifully situated, picturesque village, amazingly unspoiled though it is less than a half hours' drive to the NE of Cuernavaca via paved road. To get there turn E off of CN-95 at N edge of city, or from the toll road, turn E 0.8 of a mile below the toll station. From here it is 10½ m. to Tepoztlán (teh-pos-TLAHN).

Tepoztlán is a charming, sleepy village dotted with lovely trees and surrounded by towering cliffs. The villagers, for the most part, still speak Náhuatl (Aztec) rather than Spanish, and they jealously preserve many of their old traditions. One of the most unique pre-Hispanic temples, of the many in the area, is the *Shrine of Tepozteco* which stands on a pinnacle some 1200 feet above the valley and village. The ancient shrine was dedicated to Tepoztecatl, the Aztec Bacchus, and God of Pulque. A step path leads up to the pinnacle and the temple is reached by a small stairway on the western side of a pyramidal base. Three entrances lead into an inner shrine where one may see carved, bold-relief hieroglyphics.

Originally an image of the god stood within the shrine but at the time of the conquest, Spanish friars caused it to be thrown over the cliff to prove it was not divine. Teetotalers and Christians claim the figure was smashed to bits and these were used to construct the foundations of the parochial church. Admirers of the God of Pulque (the bulk of the village population) claim that the god landed intact and had to be broken up by hand. Whichever occurred, and despite the church in town, Tepoztecatl won out. He remains the patron god of the district and each year, September 8, a brilliant fiesta with colorful Indian dances and an ancient theatrical production in Náhuatl, is held in his honor.

Convent of Tepoztlán, below the plaza, was begun in 1559 by the Dominican friar Francisco de Becerra. The church and monastery stand deep within an unusually large and pleasant atrium. Noteworthy are the huge buttresses rising the full height of the structure, and the fanciful Indian decorative motifs over the doorway — a sun and a moon, along with stars, animals, and other Indian symbols. Though architecturally nothing about the edifice really hangs together, it remains singularly imaginative and a pleasing composition.

FIESTAS: In addition to the September 8 festival honoring the God of Pulque, another unusual festival is held during the three days before Ash Wednesday. During this carnival period the famous *Chinelas* and *Brinco* dances are performed. Men and boys dressed in vivid, long, domino-like costumes, wearing Conquistador-beards and curiously embroidered, lampshade-like hats, red wigs, etc., do a tireless, old, jumping dance (*Brinco* is derived from the Sp. *brincar,* to jump or hop).

On May 8, in the Ixtacatepec section of the village, a 7-day fair begins, featuring market, religious processions and the dances of *"los pastores"* the *"apaches"* and the *"moros."*

Lagunas de Zempoala, Mex. Though just over the Morelos border and in the State of Mexico, the only approach to these lovely mountain lakes is from the Morelos side. A perfect picnic spot, popular on Sundays. During the weekdays there is an atmosphere of brooding melancholy and quiet in the pine woods. To get there turn off CN-95, toward E at *Tres Cumbres*[28] (just north of Cuernavaca). A 7 m. paved road leads to the lakes.

Xochicalco, Mor. (archaeological zone). About 24 m. SW of Cuernavaca. To get there take CN-95 south (16 m.) to *Alpuyeca,* turn W 5¼ m. A sign points toward Xochicalco (N) one mile.

Xochicalco (so-chee-CAHL-co), Náhuatl for "House of Flowers," is spread out on a hill that is bleak and unappealing. Although the mounds cover an area of some 6 sq. miles, only one pyramid has been uncovered and restored. The building is rectangular, with steep sides. What remains of the walls reveal elaborate carving — bands of snakes between whose undulating coils are placed squatting human figures wearing plumed headdresses. The ruins are honeycombed with underground passages, some showing remains of cement floors. The zone is not particularly intriguing except for the archaeological puzzles suggested. No one knows exactly who built Xochicalco. Elements in the structures and decorations suggest the Toltecs, while other clues indicate Zapotec or even Maya influence.

Grutas de Cacahuamilpa (Caves of Cacahuamilpa). On the same road to Xochicalco, but about 21 miles further W on the border between the states of Morelos and Guerrero. These caverns, the largest yet discovered in Central Mexico vie with those at Carlsbad in size, complexity and wealth of formations. Some of the caverns are over 200 ft. in length, 150 ft. high, and as wide as they are long. The opening portal is 70 ft. high, 150 ft. wide, and with rocks so symmetrically disposed the whole resembles the work of a builder of titanic arches. The caves were discovered in 1835, but even to date they have not been fully explored. Since early times they have attracted countless visitors, among them Empress Carlota, in 1866, who wrote on one of the walls: *"María Carlota reached this point."* Eight years later President Lerdo de Tejada, an opponent of monarchies and pro-tem successor of Juárez, visited the caves and scribbled on the same wall the significant phrase: *"Sebastián Lerdo de Tejada pasó adelante"* (went beyond).

There is a first-class *turismo* service, "Triangulo Azul" making trips from Mexico City, through Cuernavaca to the caves. Buses or coaches leave Mexico City every 15 minutes from the terminal at Netzahualcóyotl 163. Terminal in Cuernavaca at Rayón 5. Rates: Round trip from Mexico City, $24 MN.

The Cacahuamilpa (cah-cah-wah-MEEL-pah) caves are open daily. Regular conducted tours through the illuminated caverns start at 11 A.M., 1 and 3 P.M. Admission, one peso. Guides are available for taking private parties through at other hours. Rate, $10 MN. There is a one peso parking charge for cars.

Hacienda Vista Hermosa, Mor. A fabulous retreat-hotel 21 m. S of Cuernavaca, near Lake Tequesquitengo. The elaborate *hacienda* was built by the Spaniards in 1529, later became a monastery, a sugar mill, and a ranch headquarters. It was restored and modernized in 1945. 104 delightfully colonial-style rooms and suites. Unique dining room, good food. Cocktails served. Music at luncheon and supper. Dancing. Pool, miniature golf course, bowling, airstrip. Beautiful grounds. Rates: AP from $170 MN to $250 MN dble. Tel. Tequesquitengo 10-012.

To get there from Cuernavaca, take CN-95 or the toll road S to *Alpuyeca* turn-off. Left on CN-138 to *Xoxocotla* (3½ m.), then right (S) 3 m. to the *hacienda.*

Lake Tequesquitengo, Mor. About 22 m. S and E of Cuernavaca (see above, route to Hacienda Vista Hermosa). A small natural lake which has become an increasingly popular resort with Mexico City water-sport fans. A curious thing about the lake is that it covers the site of an Indian village which had to be abandoned when the ground roundabout the town began to subside and the place was gradually engulfed. The people moved to the present village, Tequesquitengo (tay-kays-kee-TEN-go) in 1820.

[28] Tres Cumbres used to be a stagecoach stop on the old Cuernavaca highway, CN-95. This beautiful and winding road was laid out by Cortés upon an Indian trail. Before it was paved and graded it took two days or more to make the trip from Mexico City to Cuernavaca, rather than two hours. Maximilian frequently traveled it in a specially built carriage having lockers for provisions, a desk and writing materials. His coach was drawn by 12 white mules harnessed in turquoise-colored leather. The grooms and coachmen wore *charro* costumes — tight-fitting mouse-colored chamois suits embroidered with silver, and huge white felt hats.

HOTELS: *Hacienda Vista Hermosa,* 2 m. from lake (described above). *Oasis Club and Hotel,* E side of lake. An informal, Mexican style resort hotel that is fairly comfortable. 23 rooms, terrace, dining room, fair food, cocktail bar and lounge, free canoes, pool and lake swimming, water skiing facilities. Rates: AP from $225 MN to $280 MN dble. It isn't one of the best vacation buys in Mexico by far. *Hotel Tequesquitengo* — this popular, lakeside hotel closed for several years, has now reopened.

Cuautla, Mor. Pop. 9800. Alt. 4200. A thermal springs resort town about 30 m. E of Cuernavaca by paved road CN-138. It can also be reached from Mexico City via CN-115 which passes through Amecameca.

Cuautla (coo-WOW-tlah), quaint and semitropical, was known to the Aztecs who made long pilgrimages to bathe in the sulphurous waters which are said to be efficacious in rheumatic complaints. In 1605 the Spanish founded a settlement and it became a fashionable Spanish spa. The baths, called, *Agua Hedionda,* are a series of connected hot sulphur pools about 2 m. S of the town. Facilities include an outdoor swimming pool, a pavilion, and baths. On Sundays they are apt to be crowded and untidy.

The town, divided by the river, is tranquil and blessed by a benign climate. The newer section containing modern homes and villas is on the north side of the river. The southern part, called San José, has a colorful Sunday market.

With Cuautla are connected the names of two Mexican revolutionary heroes, Morelos and Zapata. During the War of Independence (1810–20) José María Morelos y Pavón, with only 3000 men held Cuautla against a besieging Spanish force of 20,000. Following three months of bitter struggle Morelos managed to extricate his force. Tradition has it that upon being informed of this and other Morelos feats, Napoleon observed, "With five Morelos, I could conquer the world." A century later Emiliano Zapata, agrarian leader of the 1910 Revolution, also held Cuautla. He was assassinated on a *hacienda* in the region.

DIRECTORY: None of the Cuautla hotels can be rated as first class. Several are modest and comfortable. *Hotel Vasco,* Reforma 40. 90 rooms, passable restaurant, bar, pool, golf facilities and nice gardens. Rates: EP from $50 MN dble. Tel. 2-42. *Quinta Erica,* Calle Virginia Hernández 117. 11 rooms, dining room, nice gardens. Rates: AP from $85 MN dble. Tel. 2-79. Other hotels (listed but not recommended): *Hotel Colonial, Hotel Reforma, Quinta Amelia.*

Restaurant — We found the best food at *La Tia,* Av. Reforma 171 (highway). Excellent broiled chickens from the restaurant's own farm. The owner is Turkish and produces Armenian-Turkish dishes including shishkabab *(Alambres de filete)* and Turkish coffee *(café turko).*

Bank — Banco Nacional de México, Galeana 31. *Bus line* — Autos Pullman, 2 de Mayo, no number (first class to Mexico City). *Auto repairs* — Motores de Morelos (Ford), 2 de Mayo 85.

FIESTAS: September 30, commemorating the birthday of Morelos, and the lifting of the siege of Cuautla.

ENVIRONS OF CUAUTLA: There are a number of interesting villages within 15 to 30 minutes drive or bus trip from Cuautla, among them: *Oaxtepec, Mor.* (on road to Cuernavaca), a favorite garden spot of the Aztecs and retreat used by Moctezuma. There are several springs, picturesque streams and a sixteenth-century Dominican convent. *Yautepec, Mor.* (Pop. 8138), a quaint village on the banks of the Yautepec River. Another sixteenth-century monastery and open chapel as well as some partially explored pre-Hispanic ruins. The town is on the Cuernavaca highway. A short distance to the NE of Cuautla are: *Tepalcingo, Mor.,* having a noteworthy sanctuary with a finely carved façade dating from 1780. *Yecapixtla, Mor.,* containing one of the finest Augustinian convents in this region. The edifice, begun in 1540, has a remarkable Plateresque façade.

50. Mexico City and the Federal District

Nestled in a high valley surrounded by spectacular mountains, Mexico City is one of the world's most beautiful and fascinating capital cities. In size the metropolis ranks among the five largest cities in the Western Hemisphere, and is the tenth largest in the world. It has a population of about 4,300,000 and an altitude of 7349 ft. It is the cultural, political, economic, and social hub of the nation, and the one place practically all travelers to the country visit.

Once a city of flat roofs and squat colonial buildings, much of it has changed in less than a decade, becoming a sophisticated center marked by magnificent avenues and stunning modern skyscrapers. It has become noted for its handsome hotels, fine restaurants, and glittering shops.

Situated but 19 degrees N of the equator it is well within the Tropical Zone and despite its altitude it is blessed with a year-round favorable climate. Residents of the city wear wool suits throughout most of the year and there is little need of top coats or furs except possibly during a few weeks of snappy weather during December or January. The rainy season begins in mid-May, extending through September. Usually the rains occur late in the afternoon and clear up rapidly, though in the words of Charles Flandrau, *"No hay reglas fijas"* ("There are no fixed rules"). In

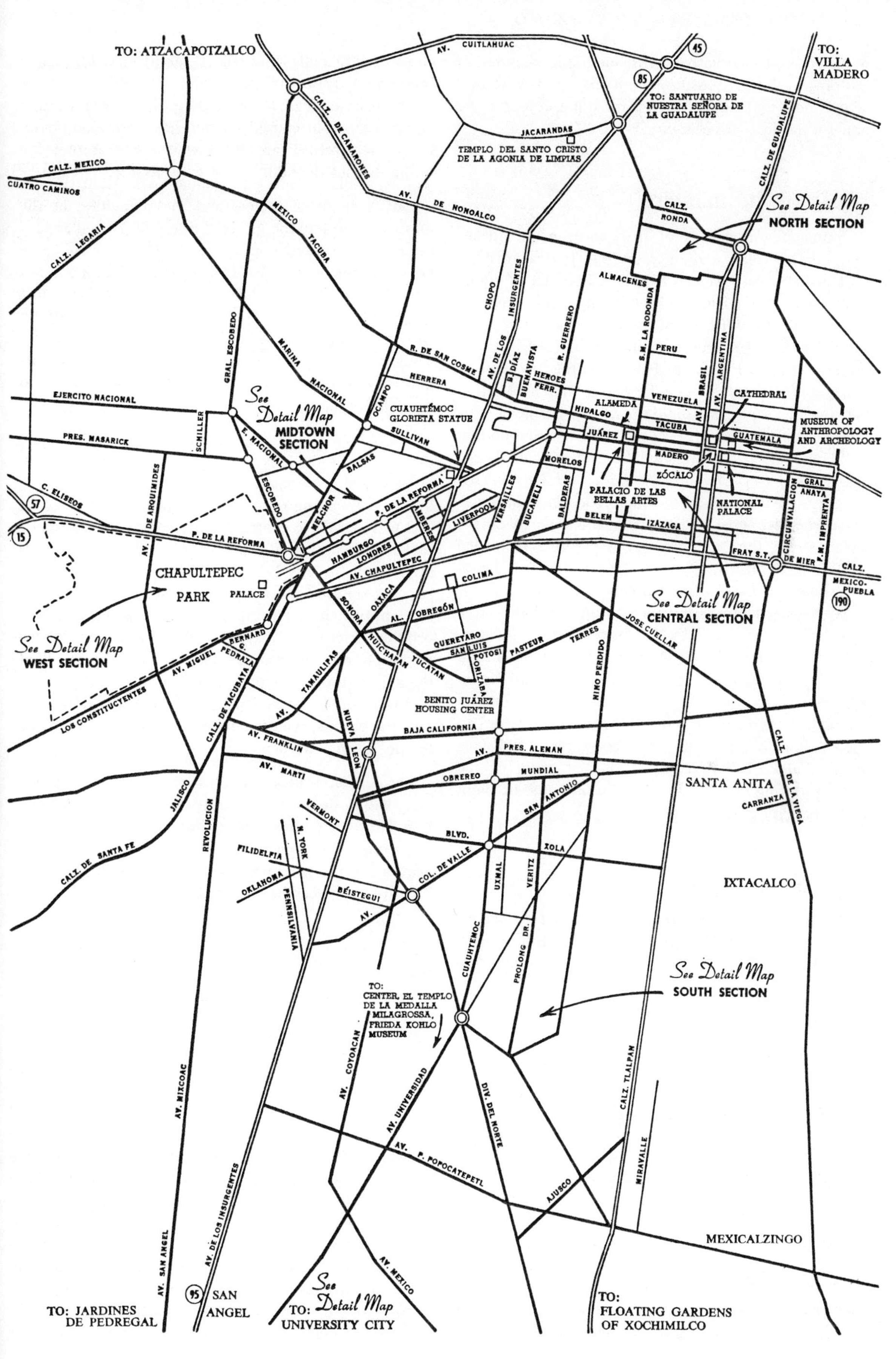

TO: ATZACAPOTZALCO
AV. CUITLAHUAC
45
85
TO: VILLA MADERO
TO: SANTUARIO DE NUESTRA SEÑORA DE LA GUADALUPE
CALZ. DE CAMARONES
JACARANDAS
TEMPLO DEL SANTO CRISTO DE LA AGONIA DE LIMPIAS
CALZ. DE GUADALUPE
CALZ. MEXICO
CUATRO CAMINOS
AV. DE NONOALCO
CALZ. RONDA
See Detail Map
NORTH SECTION
MEXICO TACUBA
CALZ. LEGARIA
ALMACENES
CHOPO
AV. DE LOS INSURGENTES
R. GUERRERO
S. M. LA RODONDA
GRAL. ESCOBEDO
MARINA NACIONAL
R. DE SAN COSME
PERU
BRASIL
AV. ARGENTINA
HERRERA
B. DÍAZ
BUENAVISTA
HEROES
FERR.
EJERCITO NACIONAL
See Detail Map
MIDTOWN SECTION
OCAMPO
CUAUHTÉMOC GLORIETA STATUE
ALAMEDA
HIDALGO
VENEZUELA
CATHEDRAL
SCHILLER
E. NACIONAL
SULLIVAN
JUÁREZ
TACUBA
GUATEMALA
MUSEUM OF ANTHROPOLOGY AND ARCHEOLOGY
PRES. MASARICK
BALSAS
MORELOS
MADERO
ZÓCALO
AV. DE ARQUIMIDES
ESCOBEDO
MELCHOR
P. DE LA REFORMA
VERSALLES
BUCARELI
BALDERAS
PALACIO DE LAS BELLAS ARTES
NATIONAL PALACE
C. ELISEOS
57
15
P. DE LA REFORMA
AMBERES
LIVERPOOL
BELEM
IZÁZAGA
CIRCUNVALACION
GRAL ANAYA
F. M. IMPRENTA
HAMBURGO
LONDRES
FRAY S.T. DE MIER
CHAPULTEPEC PARK
PALACE
AV. CHAPULTEPEC
COLIMA
CALZ. MEXICO-PUEBLA
190
OAXACA
SONORA
AL. OBREGÓN
See Detail Map
CENTRAL SECTION
See Detail Map
WEST SECTION
BERNARD
G. PEDRAZA
AV. MIGUEL
QUERETARO
SAN LUIS POTOSI
PASTEUR
TERRES
JOSE CUELLAR
HUICHAPAN
TUCATAN
ORIZABA
NIÑO PERDIDO
LOS CONSTITUCYENTES
CALZ. DE TACUBAYA
AV. TAMAULIPAS
BENITO JUÁREZ HOUSING CENTER
AV. FRANKLIN
BAJA CALIFORNIA
NUEVA LEON
AV. PRES. ALEMAN
CALZ. DE LA VIEGA
AV. MARTI
OBREREO MUNDIAL
SAN ANTONIO
SANTA ANITA
JALISCO
REVOLUCION
VERMONT
CARRANZA
N. YORK
BLVD.
XOLA
FILIDELFIA
UXMAL
VERITZ
CALZ. DE SANTA FE
OKLAHOMA
PENNSILVANIA
BÉISTEGUI
AV. COL. DE VALLE
IXTACALCO
CUAUHTEMOC
PROLONG DR.
See Detail Map
SOUTH SECTION
TO: CENTER, EL TEMPLO DE LA MEDALLA MILAGROSSA, FRIEDA KOHLO MUSEUM
AV. COYOACAN
AV. UNIVERSIDAD
DIV. DEL NORTE
CALZ. TLALPAN
AV. MIXCOAC
MIRAVALLE
AV. P. POPOCATEPETL
AV. DE LOS INSURGENTES
AJUSCO
MEXICALZINGO
AV. SAN ANGEL
AV. MEXICO
95
SAN ANGEL
TO: JARDINES DE PEDREGAL
TO: See Detail Map UNIVERSITY CITY
TO: FLOATING GARDENS OF XOCHIMILCO

Mexico City conservative dress, including neckties, is customary. It is a cosmopolitan city, not a resort. The middle and upper classes are quite conservative and formal in their behavior.

VACATION HIGHLIGHTS

Among the hundreds of truly worthwhile attractions in the city and surrounding federal district (D.F. — *Distrito Federal*) here is a bouquet of sights a traveler should definitely take in: (1) *Avenida Juárez* and its continuation, the *Paseo de la Reforma,* the most beautiful avenue in the world (even including the Champs Elysées in Paris), (2) the *Museum of Anthropology and Archaeology* (see Index: Mexico City) with its priceless exhibits of pre-Hispanic artifacts, (3) the impressive *Zócalo* and its surrounding buildings, the *Cathedral* and the *National Palace* (see Index), (4) *Chapultepec Park and Palace* (see Index), a few hours at (5) the *"Floating Gardens" of Xochimilco* (see Index), (6) the *Palacio de las Bellas Artes*, the National Opera House which also includes exhibits of Mexico's great modern artists (see Index), (7) *Ciudad Universitaria* (see Index), Mexico's spectacular university complex built on a lava bed, plus the nearby *Jardínes de Pedregal* residential district (see Index), (8) a tour of suburban *San Angel* (see Index) and the nearby *Frieda Kahlo Museum* (see Index), if you are entertainment minded, (9) a Sunday afternoon bullfight or an afternoon at Mexico City's handsome race track (see Index), and (10) a pause at one or more of the city's glittering cocktail lounges, restaurants, or night clubs (see Index).

ROUTES TO MEXICO CITY

Almost all the major trunk highways (see Index: Highway Routes) lead to the capital. Information regarding airlines, buses and railways serving the capital (*see* Transportation section).

GUIDES AND TRAVEL AGENTS

Information concerning guides, official guide fees, a list of travel and tour agencies, etc., see Index. Travelers arriving via air, and without hotel reservations will find an information and reservation booth at the airport. The clerk can make immediate reservations for you.

TAXIS, BUSES, AND STREETCARS

For several years the city has been suffering a transportation crisis. There are only 150,000 private cars, 15,000 taxis (not all in service), 6600 public buses and 1300 streetcars and trolley-buses — nowhere near enough to serve the public. Exasperating delays are often caused by this situation. Frequently taxi drivers refuse fares because it may require going into a district they don't care to go to, etc.

City taxis have meters and the regulation at the moment is to pay the metered rate plus 50 centavos if the cab has picked you up on the street, or add one peso if it has been called from a stand. Tipping is not done except for special services such as carrying baggage, etc. The hourly cab rate is $15 MN. Certain cabs, stationed around big hotels, are called *turismos.* They come equipped with English-speaking chauffeur-guides. Arrangements as to fees must be made with them beforehand.

Taxis fees to the airport are about $6 MN from the center of the city. The airport has special cabs, however, to take passengers into the city. The rate is higher, depending on the area you go to. It is about $12 to $15 MN to central hotels. At present an odious racket is being practiced on tourists (and Mexicans) arriving in the city by train. The metered cabs in the parking stand at the station attempt to run fares to a destination without using their meter, and charge exorbitant prices. They are governed by the city transportation regulations and should only charge what the meter reads, plus one peso. The fare to the center of town should be around $3.50 MN to $4.50 MN, plus the peso. Deviations from this should be reported to the Tourist Bureau.

On certain routes (Av. Insurgentes to downtown, and Paseo de la Reforma to downtown) so-called *peso-cabs* pick up and drop fares and the charge is one peso. The driver usually goes along holding his arm out of the window, indicating with upheld fingers how many spaces he has in the cab.

Bus lines and some streetcars run to all parts of the city. There is no transfer system. First-class buses (marked with a sign on the sides, *primera clase or 1ª clase*) are fairly comfortable and are supposed to carry only as many passengers as can be seated. Fares on first-class bus: 30 to 40 centavos. Streetcars, 25 centavos. See list of city bus route, Index.

City bus and streetcar routes

Mexico City has over 6000 buses and streetcars in operation, some first-, some second-class, and many that evade classification. The following is a list of the better lines and where they go. Routes cannot be definitely guaranteed for the author has too often been taken astray by bus drivers who momentarily wander from their routes to pick up a girl friend or pass their homes to pick up lunch. Most lines stop operating around midnight.

BUS LINE	DOWNTOWN PICKUP	GOING TO
Lomas-Chapultepec-Hipódromo	5 de Mayo	Hipódromo de las Américas via Ejército Nacional
Lomas-Chapultepec-Virreyes	5 de Mayo	Lomas de Chapultepec via Reforma
Insurgentes Tepayac-Lindavista	W side Bellas Artes Palace	Basílica de Guadalupe
Madero Glorieta-Clasa	Carranza and 20 de Noviembre	Churubusco
Mexico-Tacuba-Normal	Back of the Bellas Artes	Normal School via Calz. Mexico-Tacuba
Insurgentes-Villa Obregón (Ciudad Universitaria)	Uruguay and San Juan Létran	University City
Xochimilco-Milpa Alta	Carranza and 20 de Noviembre	Xochimilco
Colonia del Valle-Coyoacán	Gante and 16 de Septiembre	Coyoacán
Roma Piedad via Eugenia	E of the Bellas Artes	Ball park
STREETCARS		
La Villa	Zócolo, E side	Basílica de Guadalupe
Xochimilco	Zócalo	Xochimilco via Calz. Tlalpan
Obregón	Uruguay and San Juan Létran	San Angel, Obregón Monument

HOTELS

During the height of the tourist seasons — June, July, August, and December, January, February — it is advisable to make reservations in advance, with confirmation in writing stating the cost of the room. There are more than 60 good hotels in the city ranging from luxury establishment, through first-class hotels and many small modern hotels down to a myriad of low-cost little hotels. In addition to a handful of hotels, both expensive and modest, meriting special comment, there is included below a general list in the categories of (1) De luxe (2) First Class (3) Small Inexpensive (4) Motels (5) Furnished Apartments (6) Pensions.

All rates quoted are for European Plan, lowest double room price in pesos. Locations are indicated by the following key, in parentheses, following the address. Key: (D) Downtown, (M) Midtown, Reforma-Genova area, (S) South, mostly south on Av. Insurgentes, (O) Outlying.

Tecali, Mariano Escobedo 736 (M). New and super-swank. Suites only, incl. 2 bedrooms, living room, dressing rooms, bar, kitchen, 2 baths, some balconies, TV and hi-fi sets. Hotel also has rooftop dining room, cocktail lounge, free parking. Rates: $400 to $850 incl. breakfast. Tel. 11-96-20. 26 suites.

Del Paseo, Paseo de la Reforma 208 (M). New and distinctive. 115 tastefully appointed rooms. Pool. Lovely rooftop dining room, dancing. Garage. One of the very nice, not too garish hotels in the city. Rates: $130 to $190. Tel. 25-76-00.

Reforma, Reforma and Paris (M). 253 units, an old, comfortable well-operated de luxe hotel. Excellent dining room, grill, coffee shop, bar and cocktail lounge. Garage service. Rates: $160 to $200. Tel. 46-96-80.

El Presidente, Hamburgo 135 (M). New, super-de luxe 150 unit employing an army of servants who sometimes get in each other's way at the cost of guest-comfort. However, very fashionable. Poolside cocktail lounge lovely. Rates: $160 to $200. Tel. 25-00-00.

Continental-Hilton, Reforma 166 (M) 408 units, the usual high standards of the Hilton chain. Decorative schemes somewhat overimaginative. The rooftop Belvedere Room, dancing, offers a wonderful night view of the city. Rates: $125 to $200. Tel. 18-07-00.

Hotel Bamer, Juárez 52 (D). One of the de luxe hotels, 111 rooms very chic, but marred by too many bellhops holding out their hands, palms up. Rates: $130 to $230.

Alffer, on Revillagigedo and Independencia (D). Fine, de luxe, completely air conditioned, good service. Drive-in garage. Rates: $120 to $180. Tel. 18-09-20.

De Cortés, Av. Hidalgo 85 (D). A very popular colonial-style hotel with patio and colonial-style entertainment (Saturdays). No longer quite as attractive as in former years. 40 rooms. Dining room only fair. Cocktail service. Rates: $90. Tel. 10-15-05.

Suites El Sol, Av. Insurgentes Sur 15 (formerly Calle Guzman) (M). Excellent small hotel noted for its friendly service and moderate rates.

Hotel Alameda, Av. Juárez (D). Largest, new, downtown de luxe hotel. 400 units, pool, superb restaurants, garage. Rates: EP, $150 MN up, dble. Tel. 12-66-16.

Hotel Maria Isabel, Paseo de la Reforma 325 (M). New, plush, Balsas-chain hotel. EP, $150 MN to $240 MN dble. Suites are higher. Four dining rooms and coffee shop, 2 bars, swimming pool, roof-garden, garage. Tel. 25-51-39.

GENERAL HOTEL LIST

NAME, NO. OF ROOMS ADDRESS & TELEPHONE	RATE PER DOUBLE	OBSERVATION
De luxe and expensive		
Alffer		See notes above
Ambassador — 200 Humboldt 38 (D) 18-01-10	$125 up	Ultramodern, air conditioned.
Bamer		See notes above
Continental-Hilton		See notes above
Del Paseo		See notes above
Del Prado — 411 Juárez 70 (D) 18-00-40	$100 up	Tops and central.
Plaza Vista Hermosa — 110 Sullivan and Insurgentes S. (M) 46-45-40	$160 up	Ultramodern, inconvenient corner.
Monte Cassino — 129 Genova 56 (M) 25-15-80	$90 up	Fair accommodations
Reforma		See notes above
Emperador Suites — 70 suites Av. Cuauhtémoc 614 (S) 19-55-90	$130 up	New and handsome, just opened.
Londres Hotel Residencial — 28 suites Londres 101 (M) 11-96-47	$145 up EP	No restaurant. New and de luxe.
First class — medium expensive		
Cristóbal Colón — 120 Colón 27 (D) 18-03-00	$125 up	New and glossy.
Diplomatico — 120 Insurgentes Sur 1105 43-36-60	$90	
Gin — 28 Eufrates 3 (M) 35-16-13	$125	New, nice, morning coffee served.
Premier — 100 Milán 11 (M) 35-30-60	$125	New, air conditioned, very nice.
Prince — 160 Luis Moya 12 (D) 21-96-80	$70 up	Unusually good and central.
San Francisco Luis Moya 77 (D)	$70 up	Newly opened.
Beverly — 73 Nueva York 301 (S) 23-60-65	$80 up	Attractive suburban, has pool.
De Cortés		See notes above
Francis — 76 Reforma 64 (M) 35-80-60	$80 up	Older but nicely kept and central.
Frimont — 72 Jesús Terán 35 (M) 46-25-80	$70	New, fairly comfortable.
Geneve — 450 Londres 130 (M) 25-15-00	$60 up	New parts good, old rooms somewhat shabby.
Insurgentes — 42 Av. Insurgentes Sur 1168 (S) 43-09-27	$95 up	Suburban, a bit overpriced for what you get.
Luma — 150 Orizaba 16 (S) 11-97-20	$85 up	Modern, quiet.
Guadalupe — 75 Revillagigedo 36 (D) 18-52-40	$75	Not recommended unless services perk up.
Majestic — 85 Madero 73 (D) 21-86-00	$55 up	Colonial, rooftop restaurant overlooking Zócalo. Friendly.
Hotel Montejo — 58 Reforma 240 (M) 11-98-40	$75 up	Old but pleasant.
Pennsylvania — 40 Pennsylvania 280 (S) 23-61-14	$120 up	Nice apartment hotel near bullring.
Meurice — 42 Marsalla 28 35-80-95	$75	Small, well managed, good service.
Polanco — 45 Edgar Allan Poe 8 (O) 20-60-40	$60 up	Fair. In nice suburban district.
Regis — 400 Juárez 77 (D) 18-08-00	$60 to $100	*Viajero-type* but good.

NAME, NO. OF ROOMS ADDRESS & TELEPHONE	RATE PER DOUBLE	OBSERVATION
Ritz — 41 Madero 30 (D) 18-13-40	$60 up	Old but redecorated.
Romfel — 75 Revillagigedo 35 (D) 10-45-30	$60 up	Modern. Friendly atmosphere.
St. Moritz — 24 Paris 11 (M) 46-99-55	$55 up	
Vasco de Quiroga — 56 Londres 15 (M) 46-26-14	$65 up	Good management.
Versailles — 55 Gral. Prim at Versailles (M) 46-93-00	$60 up	Pleasant. Very well operated.
Smaller economy class hotels		
María Cristina — 77 Lerma 31 (M) 46-98-80	$50 up	Colonial. Nice garden. Pleasant atmosphere.
Virreyes — 152 José María Izazaga 8 (D) 35-31-70	$50 up	Poor district, but good values.
Del Bosque — 85 Melchor Ocampo 323 (O) 25-15-20	$50 up	
L'Escargot Filadelfia & Oklahoma (S) 23-61-47	$60	Nice gardens. Hotel a bit tacky.
Emporio — 69 Reforma 124 (M) 46-99-08	$60 up	Old, central, friendly atmosphere.
Vermont Vermont 29 (S) 23-49-43	$50	
Lincoln — 40 Revillagigedo 24 (D) 18-12-28	$45 up	Good food.
Charleston Querétaro 209 (S) 25-76-80	$50 up	New, small.
Calvin — 29 Azueta 35 (D) 10-15-35	$45 up	
Diligencias — 100 B. Dominguez 6 (D) 26-58-40	$38 up	New, fairly nice.
Guardiola — 60 Madero 5 (D) 21-85-80	$50 up	Old, central.
Carlton — 50 Ignacio Mariscal 32 (D) 35-49-64	$45 up	
Oxford Ignacio Mariscal 67 35-17-20	$50 up	Old but fair.
Mancera V. Carranza 49 18-04-89	$35	Small, clean, modest.

NAME, NO. OF ROOMS ADDRESS & TELEPHONE	RATE PER DOUBLE	OBSERVATION
Gran Hotel Texas — 40 Mariscal 129 (D) 46-46-26	$35	Central, clean, friendly.
Motels		
Dawn Motor Hotel — 42 CN-57, 7 m. N City 27-65-50	$100 up	Modernistic, nice, but in depressed area.
Jardín Amazonas — 20 Río Amazonas 73 (M) 11-87-47	$85 up	New, nice grounds, pool.
Park Villa — 32 Gómez Pedraza 68 (O) 15-52-45	$56 up	Old but fair.
Shirley Courts — 67 Sullivan 166 (M) 46-92-80	$80	Well run, excellent coffee shop.
Villas Eldorado — 14 Belmont 2 (near race track) 20-91-75	$100 up	Nice, but overpriced.
Atlauco Gral. Anaya 52 (S) 10-53-68	$90 up	New.
Furnished apartments		
Vendome Balsas 37 (M)	$100 up	Luxury.
Calri — 88 Ejercito Nacional 32b (O) 11-86-86	$550 weekly	Popular, well kept.
Convair — 18 Mariano Escobeda 501 (O) 25-46-76	$130 up	Pleasant.

Note. Both the National University and Mexico City College maintain recommended lists of rooming houses for student-visitors enrolled in those institutions.

RESTAURANTS AND SUPPER CLUBS

Mexico City has a number of good restaurants, many featuring Continental cuisine, a few devoted to regional specialties — Chinese, Spanish, Arabian, or Yucatecan. The better restaurants serve only *à la carte.* The entrée usually includes a vegetable and potatoes, but appetizers, soup, salad, dessert, coffee, and beverages are extra. In the more expensive restaurants you can figure that the trimmings may add an extra ⅔'s to the total of your bill. If your entrée costs $20 MN, and you surround it with a cocktail or two, an appetizer, salad, dessert, and coffee your tab may run up to $60 or $80 MN. Some restaurants also add a small cover charge *(cubierto)* for linen, rolls, etc.

One can get a good dinner in Mexico City for $10 MN (80 cents U.S.) up to $200 MN ($16 U.S.). From the hundreds of restaurants and supper-clubs in the city which we have sampled over many years we have selected a small group for special comment, either because of their excellency of cuisine, or cuisine and atmosphere, or in some instances, because of the values offered. In addition we add a general list of restaurants with brief comments.

JENA (pronounced, HAY-nah), Morelos 110 (M). A luxury restaurant, perhaps the finest in town. Excellent Continental cuisine surrounded by fine service and décor. Specialties: Moro crabs on cracked ice, roast duck *à la orange*. Entrées run from $20 to $45 MN. Reservations suggested. Tel. 10-27-40. 1 P.M. to 1 A.M.

RIVOLI, Hamburgo 123 (M). Italian-Continental cuisine, very nice décor and service, quiet piano or violin music. Expensive but good. Entrées run $35 to $45 MN. Tel. 25-68-62. 1 P.M. to 1 A.M.

SAN ANGEL INN, in San Angel (S). De luxe dining in a charming colonial setting. Unusual showplace.

DELMONICO'S, Londres 87 (M). One of the best luxury restaurants in town. The flaming sword signature is somewhat overdone. Delmonico's cocktail lounge is well worth a visit, refined atmosphere, wonderful cheese appetizers and superb martinis — just a touch of vermouth blown in with an atomizer. Entrées, $26 to $45 MN, salad included. Tel. 25-53-00. 1 A.M. to 1 P.M.

MURALTO, atop the Torre Latinoamericana. Fancy bar and grill. Spectacular view over the city. Music. Tel. 21-77-51.

PERIGORD, Yucatán 33 (S). A small Parisian style place, not fancy at all, but has the best French cuisine in the city. Entrées from $14 to $30 MN. 1 P.M. to 11 P.M.

PRENDES, 16 de Septiembre 10 (D). One of Mexico's oldest restaurants. Plain, turn-of-the-century style. Serves the best seafood in town. Entrées from $10 to $25 MN. Best time to go is for midday dinner.

CIRCULO SURESTE, Lucerna 12 (D). Consistently one of the best Mexican restaurants. Modest place. Specialty is Yucatecan food. Inexpensive. Noon to 11 P.M.

FOCOLARE, Hamburgo 87 (M). An excellent luxury restaurant specializing in Continental and Italian dishes. Lovely garden-restaurant, cocktail lounge, orchestra (except Sundays). Entrées from $22 to $35 MN. Tel. 11-26-79. 1 P.M. to 1 A.M.

YI-YEN, Hamburgo 140 (M). Mexico's best small Chinese restaurant. Cantonese cuisine, cocktail service. Dinners from $18 MN. Noon to midnight.

GENERAL RESTAURANT LIST

NAME & ADDRESS	TYPE	NOTES
De luxe — full dinner from $60 MN up		
Ambassadeurs Reforma 12	French	Old and fine. Nice bar.
La Cava Insurgentes 37	French	Air conditioned, music, excellent cuisine.
La Normandia Lopez 15	French	Unusually good.
La Normandia Niza and Reforma	French	Supper-club, dancing until 4 A.M. Excellent food.
Chipp's Génova 59	Cont.	Very swank. Music.
Derby Reforma 400	Amer.	Hollywood's Brown Derby on the Reforma. Good.
Mauna Loa Hamburgo 172	Chinese	Beachcomber style.
La Ronda Génova 39	Cont.	Good.
Rincon de Goya Toledo 4	Spanish	Night spot. Entertainment good, food only fair.
Seignorial Hamburgo 188 Morelos	Cont.	Night club show.
Belvedere Room Continental-Hilton Hotel	Cont.	Rooftop view, dining and dancing. Tops.
Quid Puebla 154	Cont.	Smart and good.
El Parador Niza 17	Spanish	Good paella and gaspacho.
Cardini Internacional Av. Morelos 98 Tel. 55-50-88	Italian	Excellent.
Can Can Génova 44	"	Hours 10 P.M. to 3 A.M.
Jacaranda Génova 46	"	Hours 10 P.M. to 3 A.M.
Terraza Casino Insurgentes Sur, 953	"	Good nightclub with international entertainment.
Medium priced — dinner from $30 to $50 MN		
Cardini's Madrid 21	Italian	Quite good.
Kineret Génova 14	Kosher	Best available.
Chalet Suizo Niza 37	Swiss	Popular.
Embassy In San Angel	Italian	Garden dining, fair.
Del Prado Grill & Dining Room Hotel del Prado	Cont.	Fine.
La Gran Tasca Morelos 77	Spanish	Night spot, simple entertainment. Food so-so.
La Lorraine San Luis Potosí 32	French	Not impressive.
Lincoln Grill Lincoln Hotel	Cont.	Good, reasonable.

NAME & ADDRESS	TYPE	NOTES
Majestic Hotel Roof, Majestic Hotel	Cont.	Good view of Zócalo. Inexpensive
Passy, Ambéres 10	French	Very good.
Tampico Club, Balderas 33	Mexican	Veracruz dishes.
Bamer Dining Room, Bamer Hotel	American	
Jardín, Hotel Reforma	American	Very good.
El Patio, Aténas 9	Cont.	Night club. Some of the best entertainment in town.
Sanborns, Madero 4, Reforma 45, Juárez 70	American	Favorite American center. The food is no longer exceptional.
Pam Pam, Reforma 45	American	Good.

Economy range — dinners from $12 to $30 MN

NAME & ADDRESS	TYPE	NOTES
El Faisán, San Jeronimo 201 (San Angel Inn)	Mexican	The best Yucatecan food in the city.
Bellinghausen, Londres 95	German	Old, substantial, and good.
Cafe Tacuba, Tacuba 28	Mexican	Excellent regional food.
El Casino, Oaxaca 42	German	Fair but a bit high.
El Refugio, Liverpool 166	Mexican	Very good.
Flor de Lis, Huichapan 21	Mexican	Good and very clean.
Hostería de Sto. Domingo, Santa María Mina Ote. 916	Mexican	Regional dishes well done.
Konditori, Génova 61	Danish	Wonderful pastries and coffee.
Las Cazuelas, Colombia 69-A	Mexican	Interesting and old, best Sunday afternoons.
Tibet Hamz, Juárez 64	Chinese	Skip unless you're starving
Leblón, Hamburgo 117	Inter.	Tasty lunches.
Vienna, P. Popocatépetl 33	German	Good Viennese food and pastries.
Shirley Courts, Sullivan 166	American	Excellent home-style American food.
Sep's, Insurgentes and Paris, also Sonora 46	American	Plain, good, and very reasonable.
Danubio, Uruguay 4, Azueta and Independencia	Seafood	Unusually inexpensive.
Casino Español, Isabela la Católica 23	Spanish	The Spaniards flock here.
Centro Asturiano, Orizaba 24	Spanish	Spanish Asturian food.
Centro Vasco, Madero 6 (upstairs)	Spanish	Real Spanish food, Basque style. Good.
Pabellon Suizo, P. de Miravalle 17	Swiss	Good and reasonable.
Luao, Niza 38	Chinese	Good Cantonese food.
Yi-Yen, Hamburgo 140	Chinese	Best Cantonese cuisine in town.
Chapultepec, Reforma 509	Hungarian	Good.

MEXICO CITY DIRECTORY

U. S. Embassy and Consulate, Paseo de la Reforma & Danubio. Protection officer on duty day and night. Mail received and held for travelers at downstairs desk.

Banks — Banco Nacional de México (main offices), Isabel la Católica 44. Also numerous branches throughout the city. National City Bank of New York, Isabel la Católica and Uruguay (branch at Plaza de la República 9).

Auto repairs — Armadora Méxicana (Nash), Reforma and Niza 6; Automotriz O'Farrill (Chevrolet, Cadillac), Alfonso Herrera 67; Bush (Ford), Jalisco 127; Automotriz Pegaso (Dodge), Sullivan 25; Automóviles Metropolitanos (De Soto), Insurgentes Sur 724; Mariscal Motors (Buick), Insurgentes and Havre 43.

Auto rentals — Alquiladora de Autómoviles (Hertz System), Versailles 6, Tel. 46-76-58 and 46-76-53; Aviz de México (Avis Rent-a-Car System), Del Prado Hotel Arcade, Tel. 18-65-85 and 12-06-59.

Travel Agents (see Index). TOURIST INFORMATION: Departmento Autónomo Federal de Turismo (Federal Tourist Bureau), Reforma 35; Pemex Tourist Bureau, Juárez 89 (free road maps); Mexican Tourist Association (Asociación Méxicana de Turismo), Balderas 36. AUTO CLUBS: Asociación Méxicana Automovilística (National Automobile Association), Av. de Chapultepec 276; Asociación Automovilística (National Automobile Association) Miguel Schultz 140.

Airline Offices (see list index). RAILWAY: *Ferrocarriles Nacional de México* (Mexican National Railways), tickets and main terminal, Estacion Central de Buenavista, Plaza de Buenavista. Downtown ticket office at Bolivar and 5 de Mayo. **Bus lines:** *A.D.O. Autotransportes del Oriente,* Buenavista 9, Tel. 35-16-00 (to Veracruz, Campeche, etc.); *Transportes del Norte,* Insurgentes 137 Sur, Tel. 35-50-84 (to Saltillo, Monterrey, Laredo, Durango, Mazatlán); *Transportes Fronteras,* Buenavista 7, Tel. 47-42-61; *Servicio Unidos Autobuses Blanco "Flecha Roja,"* Héroes Ferrocarrileros 45, Tel. 35-68-02 (to Laredo via Pan American Highway); *Transportes Chihuahuenses,* Bernal Díaz and Puente de Alvarado 5, Tel. 47-38-58 (to El Paso); *Autobuses "Anáhuac,"* Bernal Díaz 8, Tel. 21-42-20 (to Eagle Pass, via Querétaro, Saltillo); *Autotransportes del Sureste Cristóbal Colón,* Calzada Mexico-Puebla 38, Tel. 22-57-63 (to Puebla, Oaxaca, Chiapas, and Guatemala border); *Lineas Unídas de Primera Clase "Autobuses Rojos,"* Columbia 21, Tel. 29-16-41 (to Pachuca, Villa Juárez, Tecolutla,

Tampico, etc.); *Sociedad Cooperative de Transportes México-Cuernavaca-Grutas "Turismos Triangulo Azul,"* Netzahualcóyotl 163, Tel. 12-76-03 (to Cuernavaca and Caves); *Estrella de Oro,* Fray S. Teresa de Mier 72 and 74, Tel. 12-72-68 (to Ixtapan de la Sal, Acapulco, Taxco, Zihuatanejo); *Autotransportes Tres Estrellas de Oro,* Niño Perdido 19, Tel. 12-84-88 (to Morelia, Guadalajara, Mazatlán Guaymas, Nogales, Tijuana). NOTE: *There is a central bus-travel agency at Paseo de la Reforma 34, Tel. 46-67-99, that makes reservations, sells tickets and arranges trips via all bus lines.*

Telephone Services and Numbers: *Long Distance* — within Mexico, dial 02; international calls, dial 09. The telephone company maintains a long-distance phone station where calls may be made from at Calle del Parque and Río Amoy (midtown), also, on Paseo de la Reforma, next to the Hotel Reforma. For information, dial 04. *Fire* — 22-15-20. *Police* — 18-06-40. *Police Radio Patrol (Radio Patrulla)* — 18-06-06. *Telegraph* — (local) 10-44-00; (international) 19-59-20. TELEGRAPH OFFICES — Tacuba 15 (D), Concepción Béistegui 803 (S), Dolores 3 (D), Homero 610 (W), Juárez 1 (San Angel), Sierra Nevada 415 A (W).

Taxi Stands *(Sitios)* — Cuauhtémoc district (M), Tel. 46-13-46; Lomas (W), 20-42-50 and 20-00-18; Condesa (W), 25-10-33; Colonia del Valle (S), 23-02-70 and 23-02-91; Polanco (W), 20-35-64; San Angel (S), 14-70-92.

Emergencies: AMBULANCES: (Red Cross) Tel. 14-56-18; (Green Cross), Tel. 47-96-59.

HOSPITAL: American British Cowdray, Av. Victor Hugo 79 (W), Tel. 11-49-00.

DOCTORS: *(Cardiologists),* Dr. Sigfrido Becker, Río de la Plata 56-102 (M), Office Tel. 25-30-10, Residence, 43-02-88; Dr. Ignacio Chavez, Reforma 211 (M), Office and Res. Tel. 46-52-59. *(Internal Medicine and General Practitioners),* Dr. David Brucilowski, Hegel 228-1, Tel. 45-84-88, 45-84-47, Res. 20-78-80; Dr. Ernesto Chavez, Reforma 510, Office Tel. 14-23-23, Res. 11-92-35; Dr. Hubert DeKanter, Calle Arquimedes 131, Tel. 45-97-61. Dr. José Gutiérrez Suárez, Génova 16 (M), Office Tel. 11-07-35, Res. 11-40-18. *(Gynecologists),* Dr. Hubert DeKanter, (see above); Dr. Miguel Vales, Atoyac 110, Office Tel. 11-21-43, Res. 20-09-53. *(Pediatricians),* Dr. Julia Baker, Campos Elíseos, 15 (S), Office and Res. Tel. 45-52-38. *(Dentists),* Dr. C. H. Kuhlmann, Reforma 510, Office Tel. 11-31-80, Res. 20-85-36. *(Dermatologist),* Dr. Jorge Millan G. Alvaro, Obregón 242. Office Tel. 11-60-71, Res. 23-98-97.

ATTORNEYS: Hardin, Hess & Suárez, Lopez 1, Tel. 46-27-45. Goodrich, Dalton, Little & Riquelme, Balderas 36.

Church Services: *Beth Israel Community Center,* Virreyes 1140, Pres. Joseph Cohn. Friday evening services. Tel. 20-85-15; *Capital-City Baptist Church, Christ Church Episcopal,* Artículo 123 #134. Canon, Rev. Gordon T. Charlton, Jr. Tel. 12-74-47; *First Church of Christ Scientist,* Dante 21, Tel. 14-66-03; *Holy Trinity Methodist Church,* Gante 5. *La Votiva* (Catholic), Reforma 290, Fr. Enrique Torroella, S.J. Tel. 25-88-60; *Lutheran Church of the Good Shepherd,* Palmas 1910, Tel. 20-33-43; *Mormon Church,* Monte Libano 520, Tel. 20-05-29; *St. Patrick's Church* (Catholic — English-speaking priests), Calle Bondojito, Tel. 15-19-93; *Union Evangelical Church* (interdenominational), Reforma 1870, Tel. 20-04-36; *Unitarian Fellowship,* % American Society, Lucerna 71, Tel. 46-46-20.

Cultural and Social Organizations: *American Benevolent Society,* Copenhagen 21, Tel. 14-54-65; *American Chamber of Commerce,* Plaza Santos Degollado 10, Tel. 13-47-22; *Cornell Club,* Melchor Ocampo 171 (Cornell alumni); *Harvard Club,* Sierra Paracaima 275, Tel. 20-52-67; *Mexican-American Cultural Institute,* Hamburgo 115, Tel. 25-16-54 (lectures, art exhibits, English and Spanish classes); *M.I.T. Club of Mexico,* Margaritas 139, Tel. 24-83-18 (for alumni of Massachusetts Institute of Technology); *Pan-American Round Table,* Colima 230, Tel. 34-47-26 (for women interested in promoting Pan-American understanding through cultural activities); *University Club,* Reforma 150, Tel. 35-14-50; *Yale Club,* Lopez 1, Tel. 18-19-00; *American Society,* Lucerna 71, Tel. 46-46-20 (the central community agency of the American colony residing in the capital).

Cinema and Theaters: (Cinemas): *Alameda,* Juárez 34; *Arcadia,* Balderas 39; *Chapultepec,* Reforma 505; *Las Americas,* Insurgentes and Baja California; *Metropólitan,* Independencia 90; *Paris,* Reforma 92; *Paseo,* Reforma 35; *Roble,* Reforma 133; *Variedades,* Juárez 58. (Legitimate Theaters): *De Los Insurgentes,* Av. Insurgentes Sur 1587; *Palacio de las Bellas Artes,* Juárez and Serdán; *Del Bosque,* in Chapultepec Park, behind the National Auditorium; *Fabregas,* Donceles 24-A; *Esperanza Iris,* Donceles 36.

Spectacles, Shows, Sporting Events: *Arena Coliseo,* Perú 77 (boxing, basketball, etc.); *Auditorio Nacional,* in Chapultepec Park, near Reforma and Molina del Rey (international exhibits, ballet, basketball, etc.); *Estadio de la Ciudad Universitaria,* University City (football and international soccer matches); *Estadio Olimpico,* Ciudad de los Deportes, off of Insurgentes Sur near Diagonal San Antonio (football, soccer); *Plaza de Toros México,* Cd. de los Deportes, same as above (bullfights); *Plaza de Toros El Toreo,* Cuatro Caminos, at entrance to city on CN-57 (bullfights); *Plaza de Gallos,* same area (cockfights); *Rancho del Charro,* Ejército Nacional and Schiller (Mexican-style rodeo and horsemanship); *Rancho la Tapatía,* Los Pinos (the same); *Frontón México,* Plaza de la República (jai alai); *Fronton Colón,* Ramírez and Cerrada de Vallarta (jai alai with women players); *Parque del Seguro Social,* Av. Cuauhtémoc and Obrero Mundial (professional baseball). *Hipódromo de las Americas,* Lomas San Jacinto (horse racing).

Museums: *Museum of Anthropology and Archaeology,* Chapultepec Park; *National Museum of History,* in Chapultepec Palace; *Churubusco Historical Museum* (in Convent at Churubusco); *Museum of Religious Art,* Guatemala 17; *Colonial Museum of El Carmen,* at El Carmen Convent in San Angel; *Geology Museum,* Cipres 176; *Museum of Natural History,* Chopo 10; *National Museum of Flora and Fauna,* Chapultepec Park (zoo and botanical gardens); *Palace of Fine Arts Museum,* Palacio de las Bellas Artes, E of the Alameda; *Museo Nacional de Industrias y Artes Populares,* Juárez 44 (Mexican arts and crafts); *Museo Frida Kahlo,* Londres 127, in Coyoacan. *Museo Memorial Clemente Orozco,* Hamburgo 113; *Galeria de San Carlos* (Colonial paintings), Academia 22; *Museo Postal,* in central post office, third floor (historical stamp collections); *El Anahuacali Diego Rivera Museum of Pre-Columbian Art,* in San Pablo Tepetlapa, north off of Calzada Tlalpam, just behind the Clasa Movie Studios.

Art Galleries: *Artistas Méxicanos Unidos,* Hamburgo 36; *Galería de Arte Contemporáneo,* Ambéres 12; *Galería de Arte Méxicana,* Milán 18; *Galería José Clemente Orozco,* Hamburgo 111; *Galería Proteo,* Génova 39-2; *Galería Romano,* J. Marroquia 5; *Salón de la Plástica Méxicana,* Puebla 154; *Taller de Gráfica Popular,* Netzahualcóyotl 9; *Galería Misraeli,* Génova 20.

Libraries: Benjamin Franklin Library, Niza 53.[1]

SITUATION, HISTORY, AND CHARACTER OF THE CITY

The city lies in the Valley of Mexico (Vale of Anáhuac) which is almost entirely surrounded by volcanic mountains. Prior to the conquest the valley was dotted with numerous lakes which provided great waterways between the important Indian cities of the valley. Azcapotzalco, Coyoacan, Chapultepec, Texcoco once stood on the borders of Lake Texcoco *(Tezcuco),* the largest of the lakes. These are now almost dry, partly the result of the national desiccation which seems to affect most of Mexico's shallow lakes, and as a result of several drainage projects begun in colonial time and continued over the centuries to protect Mexico City from serious annual floods.

The city is perhaps the oldest continuously occupied city in the Americas. It was founded in 1235 on several islands of what was then Lake Texcoco, by a tribe of the Aztecs, the Mexicas (see Index). The city was called Tenochtitlán *(te,* in; *nochtli,* tuna or fruit of the Nopal cactus, and *tlán,* place). In time the city grew in power and wealth, dominating a great confederation of allied or subject nations. When the Spaniards arrived the city was impressive, indeed. It covered a wide area, its center being approximately the same as the present center of town, where was located a great *teocalli* or temple, the palace of the nobles, huge markets, etc. The Aztec city probably had a population of 300,000, substantial buildings of stone and cement, broad avenues, and a Venice-like network of canals. The island metropolis was connected to the mainland by several causeways built of lime and stone, defended by drawbridges, and apparently broad enough for 12 horsemen to ride upon them abreast.

Hernán Cortés, the first European to enter Tenochtitlán, arrived November 8, 1519. He had with him a force of less than 400 Spaniards, and a great army of Indian allies. He was welcomed by Moctezuma II. The Spaniards remained there until Moctezuma was killed in an uprising of the people. On June 30, 1520, the Spanish were driven from the city — the memorable and disastrous retreat called the *noche triste* (sad night). It was not until August 13, 1521, following a long and bitter siege, that Cortés again entered the city. With the fall of the city and the destruction of Aztec power, the Spanish set about leveling what remained, and began building a new city. Ecclesiastical zealots broke up the Indian idols and temples. The canals were filled in with the debris.

[1] Library facilities in Mexico City, especially for scholars doing research in Latin American affairs, history, and archaeology, are very ample, but little known. Recently a *Directory of Mexico City Libraries,* compiled by Mary D. Parsons and Roberto A. Gordillo (Mexico City College Press), has for the first time brought together invaluable material concerning the numerous private, public and institutional libraries in the city, including hours, character of the collections, special or important manuscripts, etc.

The city remained a squalid, swampy, unhealthy place until Juan Vicente de Güemez Pacheco de Padilla, the Conde de Revillagigedo, was sent from Spain as Viceroy (1789–94). He initiated civic improvements which caused him to be regarded as the real founder of the modern city. Other civic improvements were initiated, or at least suggested by Maximilian, and more were carried through as a result of the Reform Laws drawn up by Juárez.

As the seat of government, the history of the city is closely tied to the history of the nation. Though revolutions began in the provinces, they always culminated in the capital (see Index: *History of Mexico*).

At present the city is growing at an incredible rate. The center sprouts imaginative modern office buildings and hotels, the residential districts (colonias) are strung with beautiful homes and parkways. Mexico City is truly a place of flowers and fountains. Each spring the parkways of the principal boulevards are planted with millions of vivid flowers. The city has 109 handsome fountains and is rapidly catching up to Rome with her 150 fountains.

Behind the growth of this remarkable city is a perpetual problem of water — too much and too little. Built on a spongy foundation, a bed of subsoil water *(colchón de agua),* the city remained fairly stable as long as houses remained low and were constructed of the lightweight volcanic *tezontle* rock. However, to prevent disastrous inundations, the valley was drained and the water-cushion vanished, resulting in a very unstable subsoil. Parts of the city are sinking at an alarming rate while in places, where buildings are on firmer foundation, they remain fixed, but appear to be rising in relationship to others around them. Frequently it will cause a building to tip alarmingly or split open. The Palacio de las Bellas Artes has sunk some 13 feet so that its ground floor is now basement. During the past 20 years the rate of sinking has increased considerably — approximately 7 meters.

The layout of the city is fairly regular. Most of the streets running E to W are designated as avenues *(avenidas),* while the N and S streets are called *calles* (streets). The heart of the city extends from the *Zócalo* to the W end of the *Alameda.* Along Av. Madero, which becomes Juárez, are many of the principal shops, restaurants, and hotels. Another favorite shopping, restaurant, and hotel district lies just S of the Paseo de la Reforma and W of Av. Insurgentes Sur.

The highway hub of the city is the Monument to Cuauhtémoc Glorieta (circle) at the junction of Av. Insurgentes and Paseo de la Reforma. Here, if you dare let your eyes stray from the traffic, are posted the directional signs for seven principal highways — CN-15, 45, 85, 95, 140 and 190.

CENTRAL SECTION OF THE CITY

THINGS TO SEE: Plaza de la Constitución (the Zócalo), Palacio Nacional, Cathedral, Municipal Palace, National Museum, San Carlos Gallery, Plaza de Santo Domingo, Hospital de Jesús Nazareno, National Pawnshop, Iturbide Palace, Church of San Francisco, House of Tiles, Torre Latino-Americana, Palace of Fine Arts, Post Office, the Alameda.

ZÓCALO: (SO-cah-lo), also known as the Plaza de la Constitución or Plaza Mayor, was the geographic center of the old Aztec city. Here the wandering Mexicas (Aztecs) first saw their symbolic eagle and snake, here they built their great *teocalli* or temple, and here Moctezuma had his palace and gardens. It has been the mirror of almost all of Mexico's history, battles,

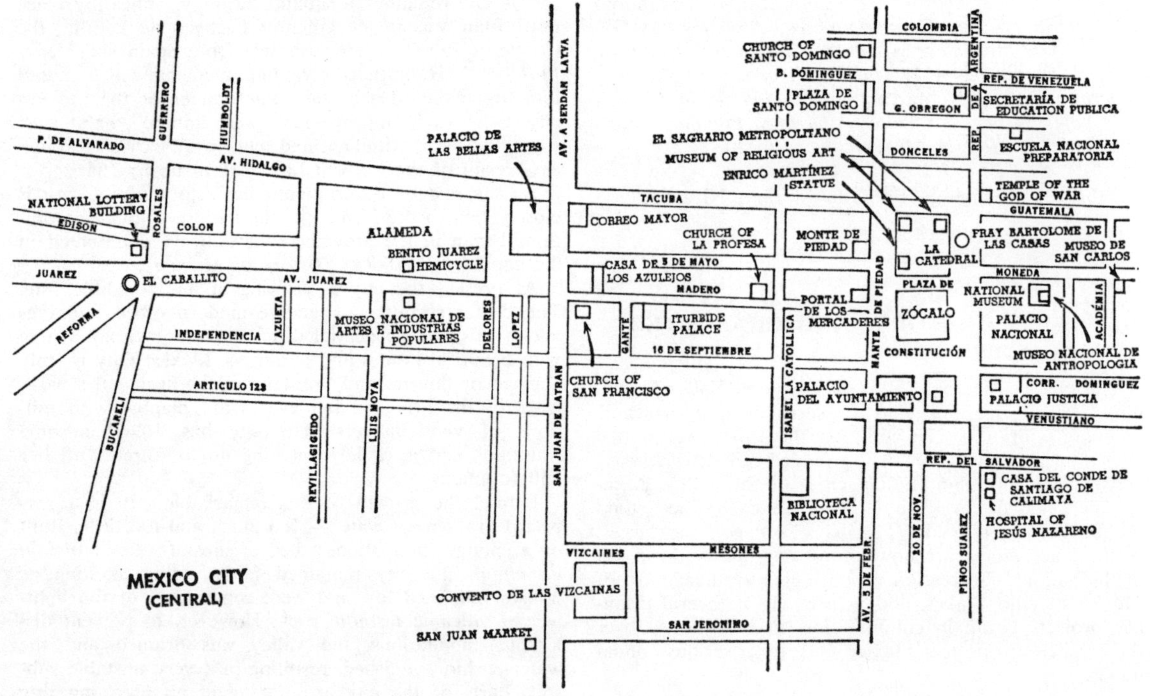

great fiestas, coronations of home-grown emperors, scene of the first bullfight in Mexico, market place. Until about 100 years ago it served as a market and was called the *parian*. The southern half of the plaza was crowded with nondescript wooden shacks which were destroyed in 1865 by a fire which began in a Chinese barber shop. The fire was fought in an eminently characteristic manner. The fire brigade consisted of clergymen headed by the archbishop, and the fire-fighting apparatus was a formidable array of holy relics held up in sight of the flames. The method was not successful.

From the time of Maximilian to fairly recent times the Zócalo was filled with tall trees. When the trees blocked the aim of revolutionists bombarding the National Palace, they were removed. The plaza is now a bleak, broad expanse, the largest plaza in Mexico. It is seen at its best during the night, especially Saturdays, Sundays, and national holidays when the surounding buildings are magnificently illuminated.

THE PALACIO NACIONAL: covering an entire city block, flanks the E side of the Zócalo, with a frontage of 675 ft. It is a massive, unattractive building that now houses several government offices, the Office of the President, and on one side, the *National Museum*. The façade is pierced by three imposing entrances. The r. (S) door is called the Puerta de Honor, because the President and diplomats enter here. Above the Central Doorway is the famed liberty bell (Campana de la Independencia) rung by the patriot Miguel Hidalgo in the Dolores Church. From the balcony at this point each September 15, the President voices the celebrated Grito de Dolores. The lines of small turrets *(almenas)* along the upper cornice of the building, following the principles of heraldry, indicate that the edifice is inhabited by a war lord with vassals.[2]

The interior of the massive building is a labyrinth of *salóns* and great patios. Outstanding among these are: the Salón del Estado Mayor (State Reception Room), a most regal chamber with massive furniture, fine Japanese vases, beautifully inlaid chairs; the Comedor or Banquet Hall with its notable ceiling and walls of carved paneling; the impressive ballroom. One of the most popular attractions in the building is the group of murals within the central entrance, executed by Diego Rivera. *Hours:* daily except Monday, 9 A.M. to 1 P.M. Guide available.

At the SE corner of the Zócalo stands the Palacio de Justicia (Supreme Court Building), a colonial style, but modern edifice completed in 1943. Of interest in it are frescoes by Orozco. Flanking the entire S side of the plaza is the Palacio del Ayuntamiento (City Hall) which suffered the same fate as the National Palace in that it was originally purchased from the Cortés family by the city, and was destroyed by mobs during the riots of 1692. The present structure dates from 1720–24, with a later, 1909, remodeling. The building houses the offices of the Federal District administration. The *Archives (archivos)* contain immensely valuable collections of old books and city records including those of the first council meeting held in the Spanish city. *Hours:* 9 A.M. to 2:30 P.M., 4 to 6 P.M.

THE PORTAL DE LOS MERCADERAS: (Arcade of Shopkeepers) flanking the W side of the Plaza formerly was a very crowded market area jammed with stands and tiny shops. The stalls have now been cleared away for the sake of civic beauty.

[2] The site upon which the palace was built had been occupied by Moctezuma's "new" palace, destroyed by the Spaniards. Cortés started a fortress-like residence and office on the spot, but it was mostly destroyed during riots in 1562 and again in 1692. The beginning of the present building dates from 1692–99. The building has since been altered many times, the third story of pink *tezontle,* added as recently as 1927, and the second floor entirely refaced.

THE MONTE DE PIEDAD: (National Pawnshop). At the NW corner of the Plaza and Av. 5 de Mayo. The palace, of rather severe Baroque architecture (much remodeled), stands on the site of Moctezuma's "old house" where Cortés was first entertained by the Aztec ruler, and where the latter met his death. Cortés built a vice-regal palace here. The property later came into the possession of José Romero de Terreros, Conde de Regla, owner of the fabulously rich mines of Real del Monte (see Index) who founded the pawnshop in 1775. Established for the public benefit, the pawnshop (with many branches throughout the city and country) makes low-interest loans on personal property. Almost anything, except livestock, is accepted — jewels, heirlooms, pianos, beds, cars, cameras, etc.

When an article is offered as a pledge, an expert valuator fixes the price and a certain percentage of its supposed cost is loaned. If the article remains unclaimed and cannot be sold the valuator must take it and pay for it. The pledge is held for its owner as long as interest is paid regularly. Should this cease it is marked at a price considerably in excess of the sum loaned, and placed on sale. If sold at this price the house deducts the interest due and gives the difference to the owner, if he can be found. Each month for five months a lower price is marked on unsold articles. The lowest price represents the amount loaned, plus interest. If it cannot be sold for this base price the borrower is asked to redeem it, or the valuator must buy it. Frequently there are auctions *(remates)*. Unless one has a great deal of patience and can follow the slow monthly decline in the price of an article, you will find very little in the Monte de Piedad that you cannot get cheaper in a regular market or department store. *Hours:* Weekdays 10 A.M. to 2 P.M., 5 to 7 P.M.; Saturdays, 10 A.M. to 2 P.M.

A rather curious monument (SW corner of the Cathedral) is that dedicated to *Enrico Martínez,* the Portuguese cosmographer who sought to drain the valley of Mexico by constructing the Nochistongo Cut.[3] This monument, of a woman depositing a laurel upon the tomb of the hydrographer, has inscriptions on its base offering all sorts of odd and now useless data — the exact geographic position of the monument, its magnetic declination, the water levels of the Lakes at Xochimilco, Texcoco, Zumpango, and Zaltocan, the average tidal measurements at Veracruz and a comparison between the English yard, the meter, and the Mexican *vara.*

THE CATHEDRAL *(La Catedral):* on the N side of the Zócalo, is the largest and most imposing church edifice in the country, and although it scarcely hangs together architecturally, its massiveness and individual features allow it to dominate the Zócalo with a lordly grandeur. It is built on the site of an earlier Christian church which was removed in 1573. The impressive work was ordered by Philip II of Spain, and the original plans were drawn by the Royal Master of Architecture Alonzo Pérez de Castañeda. While the work was in progress modifications of the original plans were made by Juan Gómez de Mora. It took almost one hundred years before the building was completed (1667), without towers; and it was not until 1797 until the final features were finished. It is believed that the foundations are composed almost entirely of sculptured Indian images, and the remains of what once formed the body of the great Aztec *teocalli* that stood near.[4]

The cathedral building is a gigantic cruciform of basalt and gray sandstone, with an interior nave and two aisles which gradually decrease in height from the middle toward the outer walls. Excluding the thick walls, the interior measures 387 ft. in length, 177 ft. in width, and an interior height of 179 ft. Its tall, well-proportioned twin towers rise 203 ft. above the atrium. The façade, reflecting the changes of style in the seven generations that it took to build the cathedral, is a blending of several orders — Ionic, Doric, and Corinthian — some of it richly ornamented. The massive dome and lantern, designed by Tolsa, is as unrelated to the rest of the structure in size and proportion as other individual parts of the building.

The interior of the cathedral is a museum of styles — Gothic, Churrigueresque, and neoclassic. Continual renovations have extinguished any unity it might have had. Of the numerous chapels the finest is the Capilla de los Reyes, occupying the apse directly behind the main altar, (built for the use of the Spanish king who was always expected, but never came). The Capilla with its marvelous maze of woodcarving, hosts of gilded and painted angels, is one of the most resplendent in Mexico. It was executed by the Seville artist, Gerónimo Balbas, famed for his King's Altar in the Cathedral at Seville, Spain. The paintings here are by José Rodríguez Juárez, and the canvas just above the altar *(The Adoration of the Kings)* is considered his masterpiece.

The *choir (coro),* a huge quadrilateral structure occupying the S end of the nave mars greatly the interior view of the church. The choir is a museum of richly carved stone and wood. The *sillería* (carved seats) is a notable work of intricate and richly carved wood. Separated from the choir by a heavy wall of masonry (facing the cathedral's front doors) is the Capilla del Perdon, one of the finer chapels in the building.

There are two Murillo paintings, one hanging above the bishop's chair in the choir (there is some doubt regarding the authenticity of this one), the other, a painting of *The Virgin of Bethlehem* which is kept in a small chapel called the Capilla del Cabildo. This small canvas is considered the gem of the cathedral and one of the most valuable paintings in all the Republic.

EL SAGRARIO METROPOLITANO: facing on the plaza, and adjoining the cathedral. This separate church which served as a depository for consecrated objects related to the Episcopal see, has undoubtedly the finest Churrigueresque façades in the city. The building was designed by Lorenzo Rodríguez and begun in 1749. The high-relief sculpture, an exuberance of figures and adornments,

[3] The *Tajo de Nochistongo,* a 4-mile long, gigantic trench constructed with a view to drain the Valley of Mexico. It was begun November 28, 1607. The orginal idea was to cut a tunnel through the mountains at Nochistongo (N of the city), thus allowing the free passage of water from the valley. Some 15,000 Indians were forced to do the work, which was considered complete 11 months after its inception. The first water was admitted into the tunnel (21,650 ft. long, 10 ft. wide, and 15 ft. deep) in the presence of the viceroy and the archbishop. The result was disappointing. Only Lake Zumpango drained out, leaving Lakes Texcoco and Chalco unaffected. During the following years there was much bitter controversy between Martínez and the colonial authorities. It culminated with the exceptional heavy rains of 1629. Fearful of the destruction of the tunnel, Martínez ordered the entrance walled up. The immediate effect was a vast inundation of Mexico City which lasted from 1629–34. The unhappy engineer was imprisoned, then released upon promising to convert the tunnel into an open ditch. It took almost two hundred years more to complete the ditch satisfactorily.

[4] The great Aztec Calender Stone, now in the National Museum, is believed to have been thrown down from the Temple of the Sun by Cortés' soldiers. It was discovered in 1560 and hastily reburied by order of the archbishop who feared it might cause the Indians to revert to paganism. Rediscovered in 1790, it was fixed into the wall of the Cathedral until it was removed to the museum.

are uncommonly fine, beautifully proportioned, and graceful. The interior of the church is built in the form of a Greek cross, with the dome above the center. Unfortunately, the church was repaired and redecorated in 1908, and in the unhappy rage for restoration it was despoiled of most of its best adornments.

Facing the east side of the Sagrario is a striking monument and fountain dedicated to Fray Bartolomé de las Casas, a famed protector of the Indians following the conquest. At the rear of the cathedral on Guatemala Street is the MUSEUM OF RELIGIOUS ART, containing numerous treasures — sacred vessels, jeweled crowns, chalices, tapestries, gold-brocaded vestments — valued at over $15,000,000. *Hours:* Weekdays 10 A.M. to 7 P.M.; Sundays, 10 A.M. to 3 P.M. *Admission:* 50 centavos.

Just NE of the cathedral, corner of Guatemala and Seminario (also Argentina) are some archaeological excavations which reveal a corner of the great *teocalli* of the Aztec city, the *Temple of the God of War*. The ruins consist of a portion of a flight of steps, at the bottom of which is a carved serpent's head. This was evidently part of one of the earlier structures, buried within the larger pyramid long before the Spaniards arrived.

MUSEO NACIONAL DE ANTROPOLOGÍA (National Museum of Anthropology and Archaeology); in Chapultepec Park, N side of Av. de la Reforma.

Until September 1964 this marvelous archaeological collection was housed in the former National Mint building at Calle Moneda 12. The museum was founded as a general museum by decree of Mexico's first president, Don Guadalupe Victoria. It was first established in the old university until Archduke Maximilian ordered it transferred to the Mint building where, July 1886, he and Carlotta dedicated it. Under President Lázaro Cárdenas the role of the museum was fixed as representing pre-conquest exhibits. All other natural history exhibits were moved to other sites. The rapid expansion of interest in archaeological studies in recent years has dictated the need of a large site to house the collection.

The new museum, one of the finest in the world, has some remarkable features. There is a large Summary Room offering visitors a quick, dramatic picture of the various historic processes and diverse theories concerning the development of mankind in America up to the time of the conquest. From this room one can branch off into various rooms and sections, each devoted to a particular culture or anthropological development: the Pre-Classic Rooms, the Northern Cultures, the Eastern Cultures, the Teotihuacan, Toltec, the Mexique, Oaxacan, Gulf Coast and Mayas. These rooms are so arranged that they include garden or exterior areas in order to exhibit archaeological objects in their natural setting.

In addition to the regular exhibit rooms, fanning out from a central portico, the museum also houses a small children's museum, a restaurant, a large conference room and the 25,000 volume National Anthropological Library. The museum is also the home of the National School of Anthropology with a 500 pupil capacity.

The building is entirely air conditioned and equipped with the latest lighting and sound facilities for high-lighting the exhibits.

Among the exhibits is the world's most priceless collection of codices (pre-Columbian picture writing). Other noteworthy show pieces include: the *Colossus of Tula*, a gigantic Toltec sculpture; the *Piedra del Sol* or Aztec Stone of the Sun or Calendar Stone. This extraordinary work, measuring 12 feet in diameter and weighing 24 tons, is carved from a single piece of basalt. It is a representation of the sun's face (the Sun God, Tonatiuh), as well as a calendar representation of the Aztec year and a record of the various creations and destructions of the world. It is believed the stone was carved around 1479, during the reign of Axayacatl, Moctezuma's father.

Another great monolith, the *Stone of Tizoc* (mis-called the Sacrificial Stone by misguided guides), is a massive disk of hard andesite with carvings recording the victories of the chieftain Tizoc during his various wars. The stone measures some nine feet in diameter and three feet high. It was found in Mexico City. The punitive Tizoc is represented in the fifteen groups of figures decorating the rim of the stone. He is garbed as Huitzilopochtli, the War God, and he holds a captive by a lock of hair.

The most awesome of the monolithic statues is the huge, barbaric representation of Coatlique — Lady of the Serpent Skirt. In Aztec cosmology she was the important Mother of Gods, of the Sun, the Moon and the Stars. Her head is formed of two serpents' heads meeting face to face; she wears a necklace of human hands and hearts with a skull pendant from this; her hands are the heads of snakes; her skirt is a writing mass of intertwined snakes fastened by a snake belt — truly a monstrous figure. In the words of the Mexican savant, Alfonso Caso, "The figure does not represent a being, but an idea."

In addition to the fabulous exhibits from the old museum, important private collections have been acquired for the new museum, making it one of the great treasure houses of the world. In 1964 the famed *Monolith of Coatlinchan*, the largest single-piece archaeological item known in Mexico, was moved to the patio of the museum. This figure, believed to be of the Rain God, Tlaloc, stands over 22 feet high, and is over 9 by 12 feet in girth. It weighs approximately 165 tons. For years it lay in a gully near Texcoco, too ponderous to be removed. Bringing it to the museum was an unusual engineering feat. It is one of the most important archaeological objects to have been moved by man since the transfer of the Egyptian obelisk to the Vatican Plaza.

Hours: regular exhibits, Weekdays 9:30 A.M. to 7 P.M.; Sundays, 10 A.M. to 3 P.M. No admission charge on Sundays. On weekday evenings there are also special lectures and exhibits with lights and sounds.

MUSEO DE SAN CARLOS: also called, Académia Nacional de San Carlos. One block E of the National Palace at Académia 22. Founded in 1788 by order of Charles III as an art and architectural school, the San Carlos came to be known as the National Picture Gallery for in it was assembled one of the most valuable collections of European masters and Mexican painters in the New World. As a result of recent changes canvases of the Early Mexican school and of modern artists have been removed, and the gallery is devoted to the European Schools. There are eight exhibition rooms containing works of Murillo, Zurbarán, Titian, Ruben, Heironymus Bosch, El Greco, Van Dyck, Brueghel, and other masters. *Hours:* 10 A.M. to 2 P.M. *Admission:* $2 MN.

Three blocks N of the Zócalo at San Ildefonso 43 is a fine Baroque building, the former Colegio de San Ildefonso, built in 1749 to house several Jesuit seminaries. The building now is the ESCUELA NACIONAL PREPARATORIA (National Preparatory School). In the Salón El Generalito (Council Room) are the former choir stalls of the old San Agustín Church, dating from 1692, and probably the finest examples of woodcarving in all Mexico. These portray biblical scenes in bold relief. When the San Agustín Church was dismantled in 1861 to be converted eventually into the National Library, these carved masterpieces were stored in the lumber room of the National Museum for some thirty years before they were rescued and installed in their present location. In the Anfiteatro Bolívar (Bolívar Amphitheatre) there are frescos by Diego Rivera and Fernando Leal. *Hours:* 9 A.M. to 2 P.M.

Nearby is the impressive SECRETARÍA DE EDUCACIÓN PUBLICA building (Ministry of Education). On Av. Argentina, 3½ blocks N of Zócalo. Though modern, this colonial-style building has great three-story courtyards. It is much visited for the Diego Rivera murals depicting the struggle of the Indians from slavery to freedom. *Hours:* weekdays, 9 A.M. to 6 P.M.

PLAZA DE SANTO DOMINGO: 3 blocks N of the Zócalo on Av. República del Brazil. This is one of the most fascinating of the colonial *plazuelas* remaining in Mexico City. On the west side are picturesque *portales* or arcades where *evangelistas* (professional letter writers) have their stalls and gaudy nickel-plated typewriters. For generations these public scribes have served the illiterate, turning out streams of passionate love letters, business notes, and what-not. The CHURCH OF SANTO DOMINGO, all that remains of the one time great monastery and central church headquarters of the Dominican Order in Mexico, stands at the N end of the Plaza. The present building, erected in 1736, is an interesting example of Baroque architecture and Churrigueresque interior.

A step from the *plazuela* (NW corner of Brazil and Venezuela) is a huge colonial building that recently housed the School of Medicine (now moved to Ciudad Universitaria). This edifice was formerly the Tribunal del Santo Oficio (Holy Office of the Inquisition).[5]

Just 3 blocks S of the Zócalo near the corner of Calle República del Salvador and Pino Suárez (the latter street noted for centuries as a leather center) are two of Mexico's most famed old buildings. At Pino Suárez 30, the CASA DEL CONDE DE SANTIAGO DE CALIMAYA, originally built in 1528 by a relative of Cortés, and still in possession of descendants of the original owner. The façade, especially around the portal, is notable for its beautiful carved decorations. HOSPITAL DE JESÚS NAZARENO (Hospital of Jesus of Nazareth), around the corner at Salvador 117, now administered by the Sisters of Charity, is the oldest functioning hospital in the Americas. It was founded by Cortés in 1527 on the spot where it is said his first meeting took place with Moctezuma. The exterior of the building is nondescript, but the interior is a delight — lovely patios and gardens, unexpected architectural features. In the council or reception room, said to have been used by Cortés (and containing his personal files), there are lavishly carved panels and beamed ceilings which make this historic spot well worth a visit.

Going S from the Zócalo, the most interesting street is the 7-block-long Av. Francisco I. Madero. At San Juan Letrán it becomes Avenida Juárez, and later, the Paseo de la Reforma. Along it are glittering shops and several important landmarks. Two blocks S of the plaza at Calle Isabel la Catolica is the CHURCH OF LA PROFESA, an excellent example of Baroque architecture, though the tower is decidedly out of plumb. In the tribune there is a good example of Mudéjar *laceria* (carved wood screen).

The several blocks to the S along Isabel la Catolica is the center of Mexico's banking world. The main offices of the Banco Nacional de México, the National City Bank of New York, Credito Bursatil (a leading brokerage house with New York affiliations), and other financial houses are located here. Directly across the street from the National City Bank is a small plaza and the BIBLIOTECA NACIONAL (National Library), corner Rep. del Salvador and Isabel la Catolica. The library is rather poorly housed in a former Augustinian church.[6] It is a treasure house of rare and old books. *Hours:* weekdays 9 A.M. to 10 P.M., Sundays, 10 A.M. to 2 P.M.

One block S of Isabel la Catolica (Bolivar and Madero) is a building that was formerly the town house of the celebrated silver baron, José de la Borda. Within the patio is the Borda restaurant, specializing in German food. About 3 blocks S on Bolívar is the *Tupinamba Café,* for years a favorite hangout of bullfighters and *aficionados* of the spectacle. On Av. Madero, a few doors W of Calle Bolívar is the imposing ITURBIDE PALACE, the best preserved Baroque seignorial mansion in the capital. Built in the eighteenth century, it was occupied from 1821–23 by Agustín de Iturbide, the first Mexican Emperor after the War of Independence. The building was for a long time, a hotel, and is now used for shops and offices. Its four-story façade of red *tezontle* trimmed with handsomely carved stone is almost Florentine in detail. Visitors can enter the patio to observe the wealth of detail, the balconies and fretwork therein.

A block farther W at the corner of Madero and Condesa is the celebrated CASA DE LOS AZULEJOS (House of Tiles) occupied by the Sanborns establishment — restaurant, drugstore, shops. Before it was crowded in by larger buildings it was one of the handsomest and most interesting manorial houses in Mexico, and remains one of the finest examples of Mudéjar architecture in the country. The entire face of the building, even to the corner shrine, is covered with blue and white Puebla tiles. The interior, with its great carriage entrance on Madero and the vast patio with its fountain (now the restaurant) are handsomely decorated with stonecarving and tile facings. Even the rather subdued Orozco mural on the grand stairway blends in with the atmosphere of the place.

The history of the House of Tiles is unusually fascinating. Originally built in 1596, the house (untiled then) passed through numerous hands until, through marriage, it joined the properties of Don Luís de Vivero, the second Conde del Valle de Orizaba. About 150 years later a son of one of the Condes developed such extravagant tastes, and a distaste for serious work, that his disgusted father remarked to him, "My son, you'll never achieve a house of tiles" *("Tu nunca harás casa de azulejos")* —

[5] The Inquisition, a Spanish institution founded about 1480 by Tomás de Torquemada (first Inquisitor General). According to some authorities this "Holy Office" burned 34,612 persons, imprisoned 288,109, and burned in effigy another 18,048 persons, between 1481 and 1808. The last person to have suffered under the Inquisition in Spain was a woman charged with having laid an egg.

The Dominicans founded the Holy Office in Mexico City in 1571, and Pedro Moya de Contreras was the first Inquisitor General of New Spain, Guatemala, and the Philippine Islands. The Indians were exempted from the jurisdiction of the *Santo Oficio,* whose tremendous powers were exercised against all unbelievers. The principal crimes punishable were heresy, sorcery, polygamy, seduction, and imposture. Where the crime was of a mild nature the victim was often strangled before being burned. The first auto-da-fé was celebrated in Mexico City in 1574 and Fray Baltasar de Medina mentioned the event with much satisfaction, writing, "there perished 21 pestilent Lutherans." The last Mexican tried by the Inquisition was the revolutionary patriot General José María Morelos who was tried as an "unconfessed heretic, an abetter of heretics, a disturber of the ecclesiastical hierarchy and a profaner of the holy sacraments, a traitor to God, the King, and the Pope."

[6] The new central library at Ciudad Universitaria (see Index) was designed to house the National Library, but politics has somehow prevented this useful change from being effected.

in those days, the equivalent of saying, "You'll always be a wastrel." Apparently piqued by this the lad set to work diligently, married a wealthy woman, and when the property became his he had the entire mansion covered with tiles. Later, the house was acquired by Don Diego Suárez de Peredo (a descendant of Doña Catalina Suárez, first wife of Hernán Cortés) who was murdered on the grand stairway of the house by a young army officer who had been paying unwanted attention to Don Diego's daughter. The house passed through various other hands until, during the Díaz regime it was the home of the celebrated Jockey Club.

CHURCH OF SAN FRANCISCO: directly across the street from the Madero entrance of Sanborns' House of Tiles. Founded in 1524 with money granted by Cortés, it was the headquarters of the Franciscan Order and a power in New Spain. The building materials were taken from the great Aztec *teocalli* demolished by the invaders, and the site was that of Moctezuma's zoological garden. Here Cortés was accustomed to hearing Mass, here his bones were buried for a while, here the first *Te Deum* was sung for the Independence of Mexico. When the church and its conventual establishment was finally completed in 1716 it comprised of the church, 11 chapels, 9 dormitories with 200 cells. The whole embraced almost two entire city blocks. Today it is a mere shadow of its former greatness; clipped by commerce, officialdom, greed, and progress, only a tiny bit of garden and the magnificent Churrigueresque façade are visible from the street.

One half block E of the House of Tiles (corner of Madero and San Juan Letrán) is the TORRE-LATINO AMERICANA, the tallest building in Latin America. Soaring 44 stories, this slim, ultramodern building is an engineering wonder. Due to the spongy subsoil of the city the building is set upon deep, floating piers. During the city's severest earthquake (1957) which shook buildings all around, it rode through it without a pane of glass being cracked. Atop the building there is an observatory affording a breath-takingly beautiful panorama of the city. Open from 10 A.M. to 10 P.M. Tickets for the observatory sold downstairs, $6 MN.

PALACIO DE LAS BELLAS ARTES: (Palace of Fine Arts) stands catty-cornered from the Torre Latino Americana, and at the E end of the Alameda. This immense structure, bitterly criticized and beloved, is truly the hub of the city. It houses among other things: the National Theater, famed murals, the nation's great collection of modern art, exhibition rooms, and a multitude of small *salas* where wonderful concerts are held.

The building is an imposing structure of shimmering marble, precious woods, beautiful bronzes, stained glass, and minor enrichments — the dream of Porfirio Díaz. Although it was begun in 1905, it was not dedicated until 1935. The original architect was an Italian, Adamo Boari, designer of the nearby Central Post Office. The exterior of the building is not really handsome; there are touches of too many styles — Maya, Aztec and Zapotec motifs, plus the formalism of Europe. The interior, on the other hand, is opulent. For years the most talked of treasure in the building has been the huge Tiffany-made stained-glass curtain separating the stage from the luxurious theater. The curtain consists of yard-square sections of glass in a steel frame, weighing altogether about 2204 pounds. It is a gigantic painting of the Valley of Mexico, dominated by the twin volcanoes Popocatépetl and Iztaccíhuatl. The painting was done by Dr. Atl (Gerardo Murillo). During a short (20 minute) program held each Sunday morning, the curtain is illuminated from behind by an ingenious system of lights to create the illusion of dawn breaking behind the volcanoes and the daylight gradually increasing. The program, with music, is given at 9:15 and 9:45 A.M. (in season), and at 9:30 A.M. during the remainder of the year. *Admission:* $4 MN.

More important than the glass-curtain novelty is the collection of modern art housed in the Bellas Artes until a planned modern art museum is constructed in Chapultepec Park. On the balconies above the lobby (before going into the theater) is a stunning assembly of Mexico's best muralists; works by Tamayo, Rivera, Orozco, Siquieros, and others. On all four floors of the building there are gallery rooms devoted to exhibits, not only of Mexican artists, but of painters, sculptors, and designers from abroad. In that there is no permanent exhibit (except the murals) and shows are continually revolving, there is no permanent catalogue. When you go in simply ask one of the guards on duty for El Museo de Arte Moderno. *Admission:* $2 MN on weekdays, free on Sundays. *Hours:* daily (except Monday), 10 A.M. to 5 P.M.

CORREO MAYOR: (Central Post Office) at the corner of Tacuba and Serdán. Although of modern vintage (1904) the post office is one of the city's best examples of colonial Plateresque style. The original plans were by Boari. Of interest is the fact that the decorative stone sculpture was done on the building after the stones were fitted into place. The magnificent bronze fitments in the interior came from Italy. Upstairs there is a museum of philately, with an important collection of historic stamps. *Hours:* 9 A.M. to 1 P.M.

About 6 blocks S of the Bellas Artes, down San Juan Letrán and ½ block to the E on Calle Vizcaínas, is the CONVENTO DE LAS VIZCAÍNAS (Vizcaínas Convent). This magnificent Baroque building which housed the Colegio de San Ignacio, later called Colegio de la Paz, was founded by three Biscayan businessmen as a vocational school for girls. The building dates from 1734. Although the building has deteriorated from lack of care and the neighborhood is most depressing, the place is most impressive. The entire building is faced with *tezontle.* The façade, almost 500 ft. long, has an impressive double row of great windows. The paved, arcaded central patio is one of the largest in Mexico.

Two blocks S and 1 block W at Arcós de Belém and Valenzuela is the handicraft building of the SAN JUAN MARKET. Tons of baskets and colorful reedwork, woodcarving, etc. Skillful bargaining is called for.

THE ALAMEDA: (poplar grove, from *alamo,* poplar). The city's beautiful central park, paralleling Av. Juárez and just W of the Palacio de la Bellas Artes. The park is noted for its noble trees (ash, elm, etc.) some of them two or three centuries old, and for the finely laid out walks, fountains and statuary. Located on the Juárez side is the BENITO JUÁREZ HEMICYCLE, one of the handsomest monuments in the Republic. It was dedicated in 1910 to commemorate the one hundredth anniversary of Mexican Independence.

During the Aztec era the Alameda was the Indian *tianguis* or great marketplace. With the advent (in 1571) of the Dominicans with their baneful Inquisition, the W half of the then park was converted into what was long called the Plaza del Quemadero (Burning Place) because of a large stone platform where victims of the Holy Office were burned or strangled. In 1791 the Viceroy, Juan Vicente Pacheco, converted it into a fashionable promenade. There are band concerts in the park on Sundays, currently at midday.

Directly across from the hemicycle, Juárez 44, is the MUSEO NACIONAL DE ARTES E INDUSTRIAS POPULARES (National Museum of Popular Arts and Crafts). Exhibitions of the cream of native handicrafts. There is a sales room on the street floor. *Hours:* daily, except Sundays and holidays, 10 A.M. to 6 P.M.

EL CABALLITO: (Little Horse) the bronze equestrian statue of Charles IV which stands in the busy *glorieta* (circle) where Av. Juárez turns and joins the splendid Paseo de la Reforma. The huge statue, in addition to being the first important statue in bronze to be cast in the New World, is one of the great equestrian statues in the world. Humboldt rated it as second only to the statue of Marcus Aurelius in Rome. The work was brilliantly conceived by Tolsa (see Index). The figure stands 15 ft. 9 inches in height and weighs nearly 30 tons. The casting was done by Don Salvador de la Vega. The molds and furnaces were constructed in the Garden of San Gregorio, and it took two days to fuse the metal into a single piece.

The Little Horse was first erected in the Zócalo in 1803 and remained there until 1822. During the War of Independence the feeling against things Spanish was so bitter, to preserve the monument from destruction, it was enclosed in a huge wooden globe, painted blue. This proved insufficient and the statue was removed to a corner of the cloister of the old university, where it remained, half-forgotten, until 1852, when it was set on its present base. It is said the figure is tolerated primarily because of the beauty of the horse. No one ever refers to the figure of the ignoble monarch depicted.

The tall building on the N side of the circle, looking down upon El Caballito, is the NATIONAL LOTTERY BUILDING. Here on certain evenings of the week, in the *gran sala,* one can watch the winners of the lottery being picked. This building was the first modern skyscraper construction in the city. It has a floating foundation.

MIDTOWN SECTION OF THE CITY

This section of Mexico City, directly west of the central section, was until a decade or so ago considered the western residential outskirts of the capital. It has become, along with Av. Juárez, the most fashionable, popular shopping, hotel, restaurant and business district of the city. It extends more or less along the Paseo de la Reforma, from the Caballito to the entrance of Chapultepec Park, and includes the neighborhoods just to the N and S of the Reforma.

PASEO DE LA REFORMA: one of the most beautiful boulevards in the world, extending from the Caballito, 8 m. up into the fashionable western suburbs of the city. The 2 m. stretch from the Little Horse to Chapultepec Park is wide, tree-lined, has lateral parking streets and is dotted with statues of prominent men. Originally the street was called Paseo de Hombres Illustres (Illustrious Men) but following the removal of Maximilian and Carlotta (who were largely responsible for the beautiful avenue) it was named after the Reform Laws of 1861. In the stretch to Chapultepec there are 6 *glorietas* or circles, each about 400 ft. in diameter (though some have been badly cut up to ease traffic), adorned with monuments and flowers.

Going westward along the Paseo one sees the following landmarks and points of interest: U. S. EMBASSY, Reforma and La Fragua, in a modernistic skyscraper. It is the U. S. Government's second largest embassy abroad. On the ground floor of the building is the largest of the many Sanborns establishments in the city (drugstore, soda fountain, bar, restaurant, shops). The mural decorations in this Sanborns are by Rufino Tamayo. Just beyond (W) is the *Glorieta Colón* (Columbus Circle) with its imposing statue of Columbus done by French sculptor Charles Cordier. The four heroic-size seated figures below the Navigator are: Padre Juan Perez de Marchena, protégé of Columbus on his expedition to the New World; Fray Diego Dehesa, Confessor of King Ferdinand and supporter of Columbus; Fray Pedro de Gante, pioneer missionary, and Fray Bartolomé de las Casas, called the Defender of the Indians. A block beyond (on r.) are the Hotel Reforma and the Teatro Roble, the city's largest, swankest movie palace.

The next circle, where Reforma intersects with Av. Insurgentes (the city's main north and south boulevard), is called *Glorieta Cuauhtémoc.* The monument and statue here is dedicated to the last of the Aztec kings, who was imprisoned, tortured and killed by the Spaniards. This impressive work was sculpted by Miguel Noreña and was dedicated in 1887. A tablet in the base depicts the story of Cuauhtémoc.[7] At various times during the year, but

[7] Cuauhtémoc or Cuauhtémotzin (Eagle Which Descended) was the heroic nephew of Moctezuma who opposed the latter's friendly or quisling attitude toward the Spanish *Conquistadores.* After Moctezuma was killed he assumed the leadership of the Aztecs and bitterly fought the Spaniards until captured. Believing he knew the hiding place of the Aztec treasures the Spanish tortured him repeatly. According to legend he bore the pain with amazing fortitude. On one occasion when a companion was also being tortured and the latter begged Cuauhtémoc to reveal the location of the gold, the Aztec prince rebuked him, saying, *"Estoy yo acaso en algun deleite ó baño?"* ("Am I taking my pleasure in my

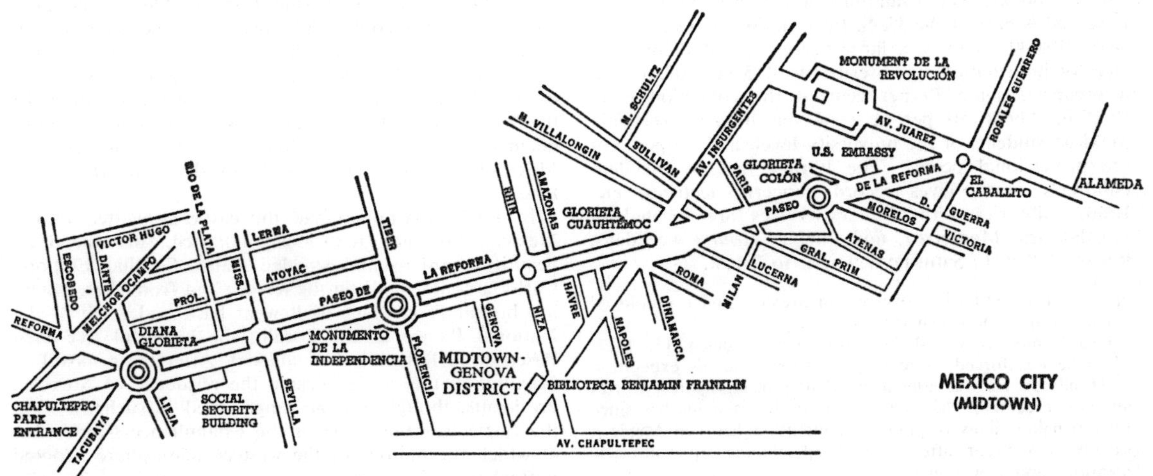

especially August 21, the anniversary of Cuauhtémoc's torture, Indian dancers in full regalia perform at the base of the monument. The 15-story Continental Hilton Hotel stands at the SE corner of the circle.

Continuing along the Reforma, two circles farther (intersection of Calle Tiber), is the nation's most honored monument, the MONUMENTO DE LA INDEPENDENCIA (Independence Shaft), popularly called "The Angel" or "Little Angel." The handsome 150-foot-high cylindrical shaft surrounded by sculpted figures and surmounted by a golden, winged-woman (the Winged Victory) was designed by architect Antonio Rivas Mercado and was dedicated in 1910. The central figure at the base is that of Hidalgo; others are of Guerrero, Mina and Nicholas Bravo, all in Carrara marble. The other bronze, seated figures represent Peace, Law, Justice, and War. During the earthquake of 1957 the golden figure toppled to the ground. This caused more national consternation than all other damage combined and the government had to issue special reassurances to the public that their beloved "Angel" would be immediately replaced — a difficult accomplishment for she measures 19 feet and weighs over 15,000 pounds.

A few blocks farther W (1.) is the handsome 13-story, glass-front SOCIAL SECURITY BUILDING *(Seguro Social)*. There are interesting murals in the lobby. Just beyond is the DIANA GLORIETA, one of the city's loveliest fountains surmounted by a bronze statue of Diana the Huntress. Beyond is the entrance to Chapultepec Park (see Western Section of the City).

MONUMENTO A LA REVOLUCIÓN: (Monument to the Revolution), 2 blocks N of the Columbus Circle or U. S. Embassy, on Plaza de la Revolución. A tall marble, steel- and copper-roofed monument commemorating the success of the last revolution. It measures 205 ft. high by 110 ft. on each side. Sometimes referred to as the elephant, it is the ugliest and least successful of monumental structures in the city.

THE MIDTOWN-GENOVA DISTRICT: A compact wedge-shaped area just S of Paseo de la Reforma (bounded by the Reforma to N Av. Insurgentes Sur to E Av. Chapultepec on S and Calle Florencia to W) which has become in the last few years the glittering shopping and tourist center of the city. It is jammed with fine hotels, de luxe shops, art galleries, night clubs, and a larding of some of the handsomest restaurants. Also in this district is the BIBLIOTECA BENJAMIN FRANKLIN (Benjamin Franklin Library) at Niza 53 (corner of Insurgentes Sur), a unique and useful library, one of the few in Mexico that circulates its books. The Franklin Library was founded in 1942 and is part of the U. S. Information Service. It has about 30,000 volumes, a large percentage of them technical or informational; subscribes to 415 periodicals and newspapers. Some 79 per cent of the collection is in English. About 50 per cent of the library users are Mexican students of the university level, and 28 per cent are professional people. The library has an excellent children's room, gives record concerts, lectures, etc. Branch libraries with similar services are located in Guadalajara, Monterrey, and Puebla. *Hours:* weekdays, 9 A.M. to 8 P.M., Saturdays, 9 A.M. to 2 P.M.

bath?"). This dictim is proverbial in Mexico, and is employed when one has one's own troubles.

Cuauhtémoc remained in prison until August 15, 1521, when he was forced to accompany Cortés on his expedition to Honduras. He was later accused of plotting against Cortés and was executed. The whereabouts of his remains has since then remained a lively point of contention between Mexican savants who, year after year, keep coming up with new locations and new bones.

WEST SECTION OF THE CITY

SIGHTS: Chapultepec Park and Palace, Zoo, the Presidential Residence, Rivera Murals at the Lerma Waterworks, Lomas de Chapultepec residential area, Hipódromo de las Américas race track, Panteón de Dolores, Noche Triste Tree, etc.

PARQUE DE CHAPULTEPEC: (shah-PULL-tay-peck—from Aztec, *chapulin,* grasshopper, *tepetl,* hill). The park itself flanks both sides of Paseo de la Reforma, beginning at the Diana Glorieta. At the E end there is a hill about 200 ft. high, Grasshopper Hill, on which (during Aztec times) there was a pagan temple and fortress. When Tenochtitlán became an important city the fortress was converted into a summer residence for the rulers who used to boat across Lake Texcoco to this westernmost shore. The adjacent forest (now the park) was the resort of ocelots, eagles, and wild fowls and other pampered symbols of the Aztec divinities.

The present-day park or forest *(bosque)* is a beautiful stream- and lake-dotted woodland intersected by well-kept walks and drives that stretch beneath giant trees as large and perhaps as old as the giant redwoods of Yosemite. It is to Mexico City what the Bois de Boulogne is to Paris, but undoubtedly more beautiful. It is especially nice on Sunday mornings when the bridle paths are resplendent with horsemen wearing their silver embroidered *charro* outfits, the lagoons are filled with boaters and the amusement sections are crowded with brightly dressed Mexican children.

Entering the main gate of the park (Diana Glorieta) one comes upon a striking hemicycle monument with five dominant columns, EL MONUMENTO A LOS NIÑOS HEROES (Monument to the Boy Heroes), dedicated to the young Mexican cadets who lost their lives in defending Chapultepec Castle against U.S. soldiers in the War of 1847. The hillside drive up to the palace or castle is just beyond the monument. There are generally two soldiers on guard at this gate.

CHAPULTEPEC PALACE (usually called El Castillo — castle) stands on the top of the wooded hill commanding a magnificent view of the park, Paseo de la Reforma and all the city. The present castle was begun in 1783 by Viceroy Gálvez, a man with notions of having a summer palace, magnificently fortified, with subterranean vaults capable of holding provisions sufficient to feed an army, where he and his wife (the first notable blonde ever seen in Mexico) could while away the time. The viceroy never completed his fortified summer palace and for years the place lay idle, until the 1840s when a branch of the Military School was installed in the building. In the War of 1847 Chapultepec was the final strong point taken by General Gideon Pillow's American forces. The Mexican cadets defended it heroically and with great loss.

In 1866 Maximilian had the castle converted into a Mexican Miramar, luxuriously outfitted, surrounded by beautiful gardens and wooded walks. So that Empress Carlotta could stand on the terrace and from there watch her husband's carriage as it went back and forth to the National Palace at the Zócalo, the beautiful tree-lined Paseo de la Reforma was laid out. After the removal of Maximilian the castle became the residence of Mexican presidents, though it is no longer used as such. In 1945 the castle was the scene of the Chapultepec Conference at which the nations of the western hemisphere adopted mutual security measures.

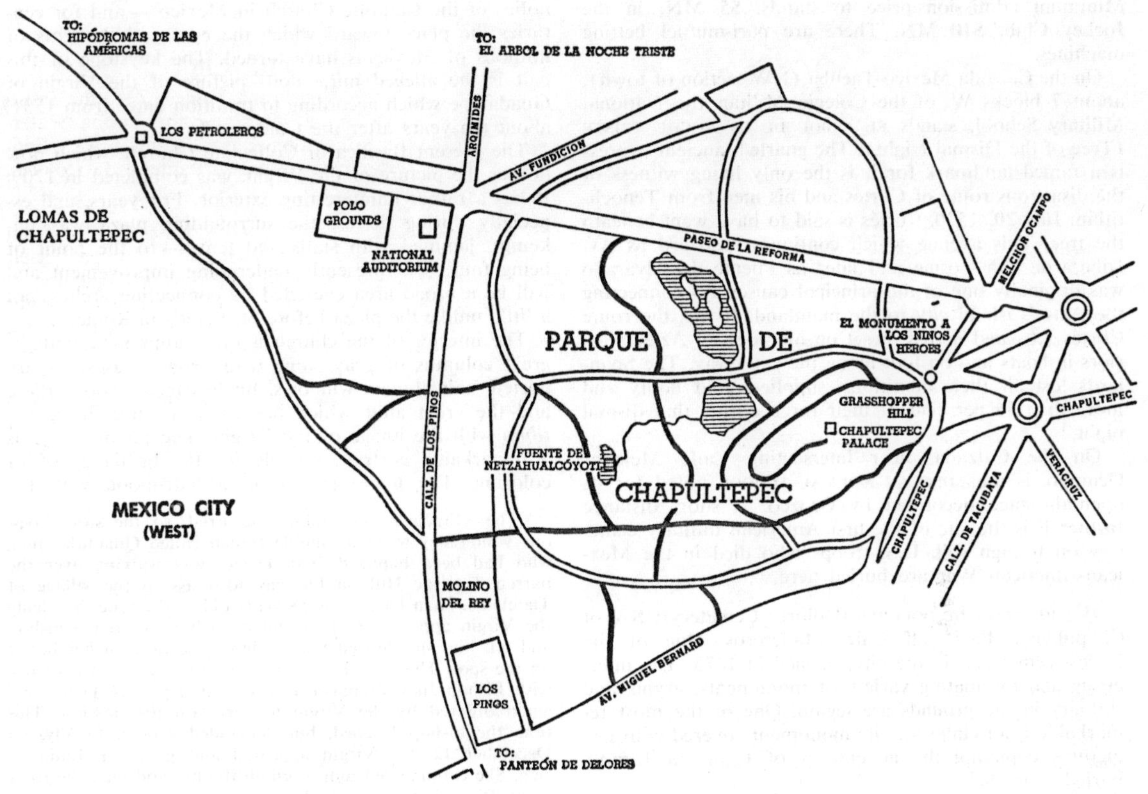

The castle has now become the NATIONAL MUSEUM OF HISTORY (Museo Nacional de la Historia). Of interest among the exhibits are the many relics of Maximilian and Carlotta, colonial heirlooms, jewels, decorations, and historical documents. Many of the rooms in the castle are notable for their fine woodwork, Gobelin tapestries, and other decorations. In 1960, to commemorate the 150th and the 50th anniversaries of Mexico's independence and the revolution, two handsome new rooms were dedicated. The Sala de la Independencia contains the newly executed, and one of the best, murals of Juan O'Gorman, author of the huge mosaic mural on the Ciudad Universitaria library.

A modernistic annex, just W of the palace, (to house additional historical exhibits), will open in 1962.

Chapultepec Castle and Museum hours: 9 A.M. to 5:30 P.M., weekdays; 10 A.M. to 2 P.M., Sundays. *Admission:* $2 MN. Free on Sundays. On Sundays there are often concerts on the castle terrace.

At the foot of Chapultepec Hill, near the Monument to the Boy Heroes is the *Arbol de Moctezuma* (Moctezuma's Tree), one of the hoary giants of the Chapultepec forest. It stands over 200 ft. high and its trunk measures 44 ft. in circumference. Following the principal drive through the park, just W of the castle are the picturesque lagoons. Here during the Spring Festivals bewitching ballet performances and concerts are staged in a floating platform. The ZOO and BOTANICAL GARDENS lie just W of the lagoons.

To the N of the lagoons the park is bisected by Av. Molino del Rey (N and S). Toward the S corner of the park and this avenue stands MOLINO DEL REY, a pinkish-red old mill, the scene of one of the most bitter skirmishes of the Mexican-American War. Just south of it stands LOS PINOS, the residence of the Mexican presidents since the term of Lázaro Cárdenas. Behind the presidential establishment (in the park) is one of the city's finest fountains, the unusual FUENTE DE NETZAHUALCÓYOTL. A short distance north of Los Pinos is the LERMA WATER DISTRIBUTION TERMINAL, main pumping station for the city's water system. Of interest here are some relief-murals executed by Diego Rivera. The famed underwater murals he did in the reservoir tanks have largely washed away — they were literally drunk by Mexico City.

To the north, along Paseo de la Reforma, a new civic entertainment and cultural center is growing in the park. Here, near the old Polo Grounds, stands the modernistic and somewhat repulsive NATIONAL AUDITORIUM. Behind this is the lively experimental theater, TEATRO DEL BOSQUE, and also a Children's Theater. The fountain and glorieta on Paseo de la Reforma, marking the western end of the park is called *Los Petroleros,* and is dedicated to the nation's petroleum workers. West of this the Reforma winds through the gently sloping, handsome Lomas de Chapultepec residential district.

HIPÓDROMO DE LAS AMÉRICAS (race track): North of the Lomas de Chapultepec, near the Hospital Militar (Military Hospital) and the El Toreo bullring. The hippodrome is one of the most beautiful race tracks in the world and has a seating capacity of over 60,000. Worth a visit is the Jockey Club, above the stands. There is an excellent dining room where you can lunch and watch the races. Races Tuesday, Thursday, Saturday, and Sunday afternoons. The first parade to post is at 2 P.M. Minimum admission price to stands, $5 MN; in the Jockey Club, $10 MN. There are pari-mutuel betting machines.

On the Calzada Mexico-Tacuba (NW section of town), about 7 blocks W. of the Colegio Militar, the National Military School, stands EL ARBOL DE LA NOCHE TRISTE (Tree of the Dismal Night). The gnarled, ancient cypress is a famed landmark for it is the only living witness of the disastrous route of Cortés and his men from Tenochtitlán, July 20, 1520. Cortés is said to have wept beneath the tree. This avenue which continues eastward as Av. Ribera de San Cosme and later as Puente de Alvarado was originally one of the principal causeways connecting the Aztec's island city to the mainland. It was the route Cortés retreated across, beset on all sides by Aztec warriors in boats and on foot along the causeway. The Spaniards lost all their munitions, supplies, gold booty and more than 50 per cent of their force during that dismal night.

On the Calzada, near intersecting Calle Melchor Ocampo, is the MEXICAN NORMAL SCHOOL noted for its open-air stage decorated by Orozco. A short distance farther E is the site of the first American military cemetery on foreign soil. U.S. troops who died in the Mexican-American War are buried here.

THE PANTÉON DE DOLORES (Dolores Cemetery): SW of Chapultepec Park, off Calz. Madereros. One of the largest cemeteries in the city, opened in 1875. The interesting and fascinating variety of monuments, crypts and statuary in the grounds are legion. One of the most remarkable is an elaborate tile monument covered with gay pictures depicting the adventures of Conchita Jurado, buried beneath.[8]

NORTH SECTION OF THE CITY

The northern sections of the city are for the most part unattractive, reserved for industry, warehouses, rundown neighborhoods. The few points of interest in this area are the Shrine of Guadalupe, Plaza Santiago, the Lagunilla Market, the new railway station.

LA BASÍLICA DE LA VIRGEN DE GUADALUPE (Shrine of Our Lady of Guadalupe): NE edge of town in the suburb now called Villa Madero. To get there by car take Av. Insurgentes Norte, CN-85, northward. After passing the *Monumento de la Raza* (a pyramid-like monument to the race), continue N to the third glorieta, turn right on Montevideo St. It leads to the shrine. The suburban town and shrine lie at the base of the Cerrito de Tepeyac (Tepeyac Hill). According to some authorities the early village was called Quautlalapan which the Spaniards corrupted into Guadalupe.

The spot is the focus of the most fervent and powerful religious cult in the Mexican Republic — the holy of holies of the Catholic Church in Mexico — and for centuries the place toward which the eyes and thoughts of millions of Mexicans have turned. The keystone of this cult is the alleged miraculous picture of the Virgin of Guadalupe which according to tradition dates from 1531, about ten years after the Conquest.[9]

The present Basílica or Collegiate Church, which now houses the picture of the Virgin, was completed in 1709. It has a rather uninteresting exterior. For years, and especially during fiestas, the surrounding plaza was unkempt, jammed with stalls and tents — to the point of being foul. It is presently undergoing improvement and will be a broad area encircled by connecting arches, not a little unlike the plaza before St. Peter's in Rome.

The interior of the church is quite impressive with its great columns of gray stone with bronze bases, its imported stained-glass windows, finely carved wood *sillera* and the great altar which has as its central figure the *tilma* with the image of the Virgin. The picture itself is a remarkable portrait, notable for the brilliancy of its coloring. The figure stands on a half-moon with the

[8] Conchita Jurado was a penniless, gray-haired, bespectacled schoolteacher who, during her 67 years led a fabulous double-life that kept Mexico's high society spinning. Masquerading as the elegant Don Carlos Balmori, the wealthiest living Spaniard, famed duelist, big-game hunter, owner of railways and castles in Spain, Conchita began her career by disguising herself as a young suitor and appearing before her own father to ask for her hand. As Don Carlos she was the center of a mysterious and exclusive society known as Los Balmori whose members were those who had been duped by Don Carlos. The club membership fostered the Don Carlos reputation by passing out $100 bills and $1000 checks. Each year now the memory of Don Carlos is revived (in December) with a pilgrimage to Conchita's grave.

[9] The Miracle of Guadalupe occurred, so the story goes, one winter day when a humble Indian called Quauhtlatohua, who had been baptized Juan Diego, was walking over the barren Tepeyac Hill on his way to Mass in the village of Tlatelalco. Juan Diego was 58 years old at the time. Suddenly the Virgin appeared to him and bade him go to the bishop and tell him she desired that a church be built in her honor on the spot. The poor Indian was unable to gain an audience with Bishop Juan Zumárraga. The next day Juan Diego was again ordered by the Virgin to carry on the mission. This time the bishop listened, but demanded proofs. Finally, on December 12, the Virgin appeared and gave the Indian a sign. She commanded him to climb the hill and pick the roses there (though no roses had ever been known to grow upon the barren slope). Juan obeyed, and to his amazement he found the hill covered with flowers. These he brought to the Virgin, who filled his *tilma* (mantle) with them and told him to return to the bishop. When Juan Diego finally unfolded his *tilma* before the bishop, instead of roses falling out, upon the cloth there appeared a beautiful painted image of the Virgin. This time the bishop accepted the fact that a miracle had occurred. The painted figure was placed in the cathedral until a small shrine to the Virgin was built at the site that she had indicated, then the holy image was brought there (1532).

Steps were taken to secure Papal recognition of the apparition, which was finally accorded by Papal Bull, May 25, 1754. The Virgin became the Patroness of Mexico and her cult has steadily grown. At the onset of the War for Independence the patriot priest, Padre Hidalgo, took a picture of the Virgin from the Sanctuary at Atotonilco and made it the standard of the revolutionary army. The word "Guadalupe" became their war cry.

It is interesting to note that this shrine to the Virgin Mother was built at the foot of the hill where the Aztecs previously worshipped the goddess Tonantzin, which in Aztec means, fittingly enough, "the Mother of God." One cannot but admire the positive genius of Bishop Zumárraga in deftly planning that the Virgin appear in Mexico not as the carved figure, nor yet in the likeness of a Spanish woman, but rather in the guise of an Indian princess, dark of visage, with some resemblance to the revered goddess Tonantzin, thus striking the Indian population at the most vulnerable point. It is interesting, too, that the apparition occurred during the incumbency of Bishop Zumárraga who committed the unpardonable offense of burning the priceless manuscripts of the Texcocoan library, destroying irreplaceable records concerning the early history of the American peoples.

As a by-product of the apparition, there was the effect of stimulating jealous friars in other regions with the result that in due course another Juan Diego came into prominence in Tlaxcala, discovering a spring and a miraculous picture of Nuestra Señora de Ocotlán. Others were found in swift succession, and soon Mexico was knee-deep in *santos* and *santas* "miraculously" disclosed to humble Indian neophytes.

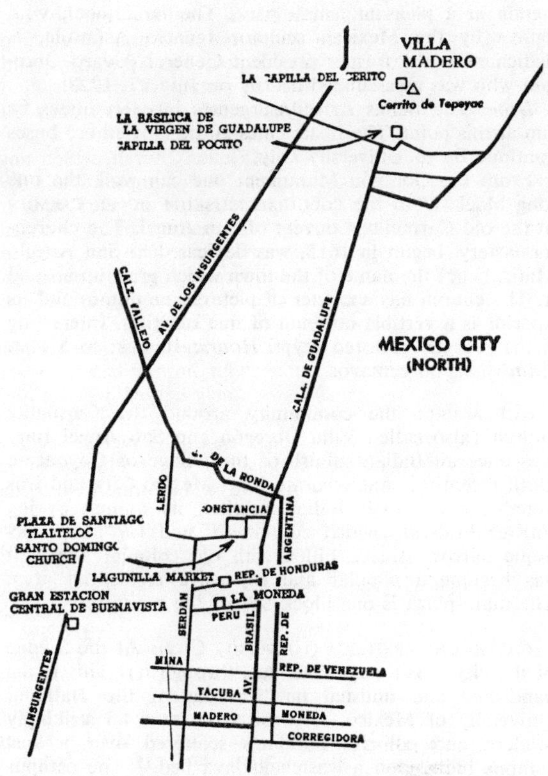

points upward. There is a background of golden rays of light. The Virgin's head and hands are finely proportioned, her garments extremely well executed, indicating that there is nothing primitive or amateur about the representation as is so often the case with other revered figures and paintings in Mexico.

The Virgin's crown, brought out for special occasions, is a gorgeous affair, kept in a steel safe in the sacristy. It is Parisian made and is said to have cost $30,000. It weighs 30 pounds and is a maze of jewels, silver and gold angels, ecclesiastical symbols, state shields, etc. There are, incidentally, two such crowns on hand. One is a copy, and this latter is often shown to visitors.

CAPILLA DEL POCITO (Chapel of the Well): This curious little shrine, a few hundred yards from the church, is of far greater architectural interest than the basílica itself. Built between 1779 and 1791 by Francisco Antonio Guerrero y Torre who designed the Iturbide Palace, it is a lovely example of exuberant architecture that stands out in its tawdry surroundings like a piece of Florentine jewelry. It covers a bubbling spring, the waters of which the devout believe to be miraculous. According to tradition the spring burst forth when the Virgin commanded Juan Diego to pick flowers.

Further up on Tepeyac Hill is La Capilla del Cerito (Hill Chapel) built upon the site where Juan Diego gathered the miraculous flowers.

NOTE: Most of the conducted tours from Mexico City to Acolmán and the Pyramids include Guadalupe as one of the stops.

GRAN ESTACION CENTRAL DE BUENAVISTA: The central railway station of the Mexican National Railways (Ferrocarriles Nacionales de Mexico) facing Plaza Buenavista, N on Av. Insurgentes. The huge modern building and terminal, completed in 1959, is one of the handsomest railways stations in the world.

PLAZA DE SANTIAGO TLATELALCO, at N edge of city: An important and opulent market in the heyday of the Aztec capital. After the Spaniards began building the new city, Tlatelalco became the center of the Indian community. The area is now rundown and slummy but is of interest for the restored Santo Domingo Church, one of the first built in Mexico to serve the Indians. Just beyond the church atrium are the ruins of an Aztec pyramid.

LAGUNILLA MARKET: (Mercado Municipal de Lagunilla) at República de Chile and Perú. Once the so-called "thieves market," the Lagunilla has been largely packed up in tidy new buildings and much of the old atmosphere of the Persian bazaar is gone. There is still, however, an open-air, street section devoted to secondhand goods, books, antiques, and what-nots. Best time is Sunday between 10 A.M. and midafternoon.

LA MONEDA: (The National Mint) on Calle de Perú is situated in an ancient monastic building with high Gothic vaulted ceilings and a tiled fountain in its entry court. The entire operation of the mint, from the foundry located in the church part of the building to the testing methods, appear completely medieval. Each day some 11 tons of metal — brass, bronze, and silver — are processed, producing Mexico's coins and the precious metals for the silver and gold artisans of the country. A visitor's permit is required to visit here.

SOUTH SECTION OF THE CITY

THINGS TO SEE: CIUDAD UNIVERSITARIA (University City), Jardines de Pedregal residential zone, San Angel and the El Carmen Convent, Coyoacan and the Frieda Kahlo Museum, Churubusco Historical Museum and Convent, Churubusco Country Club — and at the farther outskirts of the city — the "Floating Gardens" of Xochimilco, the Pyramid of Cuicuilco, the Desierto de los Leones.

CIUDAD DE LOS DEPORTES (Sports City), about 4 m. from the center, near Insurgentes Sur and Diagonal San Antonio. The sports center includes a 65,000 capacity football stadium and, behind it, *Plaza México,* the world's largest bullring. Capacity, 50,000. Both stadiums are set partially below ground so that spectators entering from the street find themselves near the top of the structure.

TEATRO DE LOS INSURGENTES, Av. Insurgentes Sur 1587: The capital's most ultramodern legitimate theater, with a strikingly decorated interior, a revolving stage with moving belt and central platform lift as well as intricate lighting effects. The theater has a capacity of 1200. The colorful exterior mosaic mural running the length of the façade was done by Diego Rivera. It relates an allegorical history of the Mexican theater from pre-Hispanic times to the present. The large central figure is that of Cantinflas, Mexico's Charlie Chaplin. While the mural was being sketched upon the building Rivera shocked the city by painting the Virgin of Guadalupe on the comedian's cape. It was covered over later.

MIXCOAC (about 7 blocks N of Insurgentes Sur): Once a picturesque village, and now part of the city. There

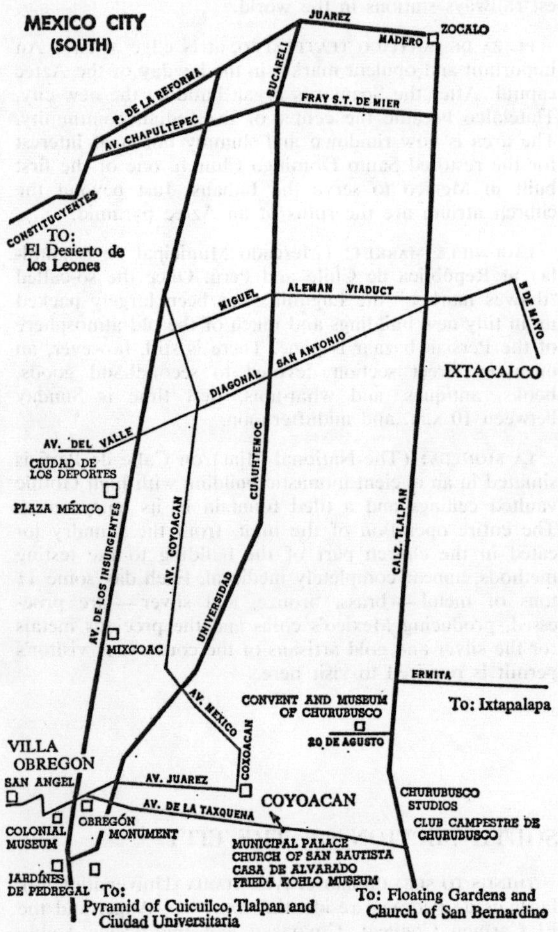

remains a tiny, colorful *plazuela* where occurred one of the strangest chapters in U. S. History — the mass hanging of 46 deserters from the U. S. Army during the war with Mexico.[10]

OBREGÓN MONUMENT: facing Insurgentes Sur at intersection with Tasqueña. The severe, cubistic monument stands in a pleasant, small park. The monument, with figures by the Mexican sculptor Ignacio Asúnsola, is dedicated to the former president General Alvaro Obregón who was assassinated nearby on July 17, 1928.

Note: The Bellas Artes-Insurgentes bus terminates its run at this point. The Insurgentes-20 de Noviembre buses continue on to University City.

From the Obregón Monument one can walk the one long block W to the COLONIAL MUSEUM OF EL CARMEN in the old Carmelite Convent of San Angel. The church-monastery, begun in 1615, was dedicated to San Angelo Mátir, hence the name of the town which grew up around it. The church has a cluster of picturesque domes and its interior is a vertible museum of fine old tiles. Interesting is the recently restored crypt. *Hours:* 10 A.M. to 5 P.M. *Admission:* 50 centavos.

SAN ANGEL: the community around the Carmelite church (also called Villa Obregón and San Angel Inn) was once an Indian suburb of the village of Coyoacan. Until recently it was separate from Mexico City and was noted for its small Indian market, its annual Spring Flower Festival (which continues), and for its picturesque narrow streets. Filled with old colonial homes it has become a popular and expensive residential area. The main plaza is one block SW of the monastery.

CIUDAD UNIVERSITARIA (University City): At the S edge of the city (Insurgentes Sur cuts through it). This is the handsome and unusual new campus of the National University of Mexico. It consists of some 80 strikingly modern and colorful buildings scattered over a vast campus built upon a wasteland lava bed.[11] The campus complex includes a 15-story science building, a vast liberal arts building, a stadium seating 100,000, a unique central library, a cosmic ray laboratory, and the world's largest olympic swimming pool.

The best route to University City is S on Av. Insurgentes Sur, via taxi, bus or car (about 15 minutes from Paseo de la Reforma). Av. Insurgentes once promised to be a handsome boulevard, and it is pleasant in parts, but has been largely defaced by mushrooming commercial establishments, hot-dog stands, and what-not.

The new campus was begun during the administration of President Miguel Alemán, but was not ready for occupancy until 1955. The planning was directed by architect Carlos Lazo and a team of 140 architects, plus the country's leading painters, sculptors, and designers. Previously, the university was scattered through the downtown section of the city in its many venerable colonial buildings. One of the oldest and scholastically finest of

---

[10] The Saint Patrick's Battalion. In 1846 when General Zachary Taylor's troops were massing on the Mexican border a third of his men were Irish Catholic immigrants. Mexican priests, with an ahead-of-their-times grasp of psychological warfare persuaded more than two hundred of the Irish into deserting to the Mexican side where they became the first and only U.S. deserters in history to form a battalion and fight for the enemy. Their San Patricio Battalion fought brilliantly at Buena Vista in the north, but in defending a vital bridge at Churubusco, outskirts of Mexico City, they carved a niche in history for themselves. Flying their banner, a green flag with the figure of Saint Patrick, a harp, and a shamrock on it, they fought off six U.S. regiments for five hours.

Of the 260 Irish, 87 were captured. A handful were pardoned, some were punished with 50 lashings of a bullwhip and branded on the cheek with a "D." The rest were hanged. The first 16, their necks in ropes, stood on the tailgates of lined-up carts in the Mixcoac plaza and were excuted rapidly. The largest group, (thirty), suffered a more agonizing fate three days later. They stood on an elevated gallows, watching in the distance the storming of Chapultepec Castle. They were told they would die the moment the Stars and Stripes rose over the castle. For two hours, with their necks in nooses, they watched the terrible battle until U.S. troops led by Robert E. Lee and Ulysses S. Grant triumphed.

In the plaza before the Church of San Jacinto in San Angel there is a plaque bearing such names as Hogan, O'Connor, Sheehan, and Flaherty, with an inscription reading, *"In memory of the soldiers of the heroic San Patricio Battalion, martyrs who gave their lives for Mexico during the unjust American invasion of 1847."*

[11] The Pedregal Lava Beds upon which the university campus is built is a basaltic lava stream some 2½ m. wide, 6 m. long and from 20 to 50 ft. thick. It is supposed to have poured from the crater of Ajusco (SW end of the Valley of Mexico) or from the more recently active Xitli (NE of Ajusco) some 2000 years ago. For years the motionless stream, eloquent evidence of the once tremendous activity of the mountains around the valley, were the one-time haunt of brigands who hid out in the lava caves.

A good idea of the Pedregal can be had visiting the recent archaeological excavations of Copilco, near San Angel. Here beneath a 20 ft. thick lava overlay the bones and pottery of an ancient archaic Indian people have been found. Their date is estimated to be some 1500 years before Christ.

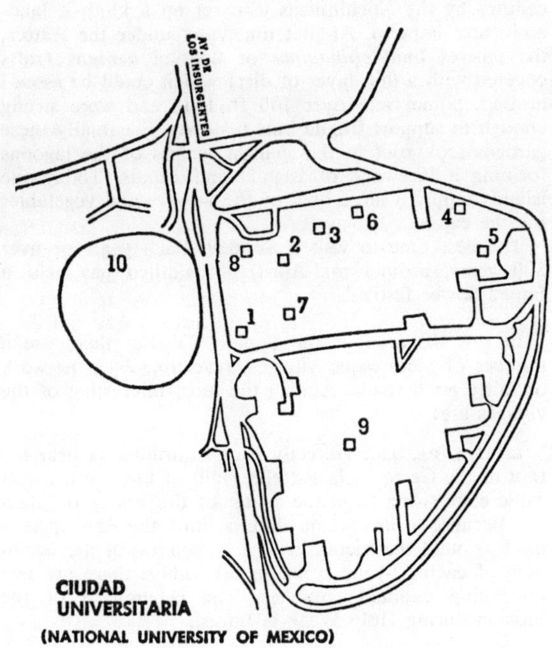

CIUDAD UNIVERSITARIA
(NATIONAL UNIVERSITY OF MEXICO)

universities in the New World, it also occupies the most modern campus. For a visitor the most striking feature of the campus is the assembly of vivid outsize murals on the many buildings.

The principal buildings are: (see numbered diagram) (1) *Administration Building (Rectoría)* W side of main quadrangle. The murals on this building are by David Alfaro Siqueiros. That on the south wall depicts students returning to the motherland the fruits of their learning; the mural on the N side is a typical Siqueiros motif, a questioning as to when will occur the next revolution. (2) *Biblioteca Central* (Central Library), a 12-story building, the upper ten windowless, and completely wrapped around with a huge stone mosaic mural that measures over an acre of art. The pictorial themes are a blending of the old and new; on the S wall a symbolic history of culture and education in Mexico; on the N wall, a picturization of the cosmology of the pre-Hispanic cultures. The narrower E and W walls treat with aspects of modern education, science, and athletics. The work was conceived and executed by painter-architect Juan O'Gorman, who also was one of the two architects designing the building. The upper section of the building is air conditioned and reserved for stacks to house 1,200,000 volumes. The lower two floors are reading rooms. One should note that the translucent material on the upper half of the reading room windows, rather than being tinted glass, is thinly sliced slabs of onyx.

(3) *Humanities,* including the Faculties of Philosophy, Literature, History, Law, Commerce, etc. This group of buildings is nearly ¼ m. long. Each of the Schools or Faculties has its own extensive library in addition to the Central Library. The individual buildings also have their own caféterias, auditoriums, etc. (4) *School of Dentistry.* On the inside of this second quadrangle which the Dentistry building faces is a small square metal building housing a nuclear physics lab and a Van der Graaff atom accelerator. The nearby shell-shaped edifice is a cosmic ray laboratory. (5) *Medical School,* an impressive group of connected buildings at the E end of the campus. (6) ***Science and Chemistry* buildings.** Note the interesting louvering of the windows and the serrated arrangement of the lecture halls. The mosaic mural on the S wall of the Science building is by Chavez Morado, and depicts man moving from darkness toward light and learning. (7) The *Schools of Engineering, Architecture.* (8) The *University Theater,* and adjacent building housing bookstores, bank, post office, art gallery. (9) *Sports Area* — soccer, football, and baseball fields, olympic swimming pool, tennis courts. Interesting are the *frontón* courts built of lava rock and designed to look like pre-Hispanic pyramids. (10) The Olympic Stadium, N across Av. Insurgentes. It is one of the most beautifully designed stadiums in the world, its form seemingly taken from the shape of the hills that furnish a backdrop for the campus. The rather weird high-relief colored mosaic forms decorating the outer wall were done by Diego Rivera.

A very interesting aspect of the university is a department called *Dirección General de Difusión Cultural* (Cultural Dissemination) which organizes concerts, ballets, lectures, and other cultural projects for the public benefit. On Sundays organized trips are made to nearby archaeological zones, places of historical interest, etc. — each conducted by a professor knowing his field. The public is invited. Information regarding such activities can be gotten from the office of *Difusión Cultural* at the university.

PYRAMID OF CUICUILCO: (Archaeological zone), about 1 m. S of the university on Insurgentes, then to l. ⅛ m. This circular pyramidal structure is believed to be the oldest man-made construction on the American continent. It was partially covered by the lava flow that formed the *Pedregal.* Visually it is not nearly as impressive as the thought of how long man has been building things on our continent.

COYOACÁN, D.F.: A suburban village on the S edge of the city, now more or less surrounded by the spreading capital. Coyoacán (co-yo-ah-CAHN — from the Aztec, *coyotl,* wolf, and *huacan,* place of) antedates Mexico City in European occupancy. For the final assault that reduced Tenochtitlán, Cortés made the place his headquarters. The town once stood on the edge of Lake Texcoco and was a favorite Aztec suburb. The first seat of the Spanish Government in New Spain was established at Coyoacán in August 1521. On the main square stands the modest MUNICIPAL PALACE, claimed to have been built by Cortés, and the place where Cuauhtémoc, the Aztec prince, was tortured. Here also Cortés was said to have poisoned his first wife, Doña Catalina. In actuality the Municipal palace was built by descendants of Cortés. The original Palacio de Cortés stood back of the church which faces the plaza. No vestige of it remains.

Directly across the lovely treed plaza is the CHURCH OF SAN BAUTISTA, built by the Dominicans in 1583, and the badly kept adjacent monastery (1530). The church is an excellent example of early colonial architecture, especially the massive tower and belfry, and the side gate, the latter being an important example of Indian influence on ornamentation.

Of interest also is the so-called CASA DE ALVARADO, popularly but wrongly believed to have been built by Cortés' lieutenant. (W on Av. Juárez). An interesting shrine and figurine adorn the entranceway. The building is now occupied by the Panamanian Embassy. Perhaps the most fascinating point of interest in Coyoacán is the MUSEO FRIEDA KAHLO at Londres 127, Coyoacán. This for many years was one of the homes occupied by painter Frieda Kahlo and her husband Diego Rivera. It is now a national museum, filled with unusual native furniture, priceless examples of popular arts, pre-Hispanic artifacts and a great number of the curious and dreamlike paintings of this talented woman. *Hours:* 10 A.M. to 5 P.M. weekdays, 10 A.M. to 1 P.M., Sundays. *Admission:* 1 peso. (Closed Mondays.)

JARDÍNES DE PEDREGAL, on the Pedregal lava beds, just W of Ciudad Universitaria. Entrance on Calle San Gerónimo, at the shocking pink gates. This, the Gardens of Pedregal, is the newest and most imaginative of Mexico's residential districts, a veritable fairyland of beautiful landscaping, daring architecture and lovely backgrounds. It is like a world's fair put to private use; and much more tastefully planned than the vast pseudo-swank Ciudad Satélite (Satellite City) at the NW edge of the city on CN-57.

CONVENT AND MUSEUM OF CHURUBUSCO (choo-roo-BOOS-co). In pre-Columbian days Churubusco was an important Aztec town called Huitzilipocho after the god of war, Huitzilopochtli. The Spaniards mismanaged the name into its present form. (It lies about 6 m. S of the Zócalo, just off Calzada Tlalpan.) Because of its temple and special pagan import the Spaniards seized the area and promptly built a church and convent (Santa María de Los Angeles) on the site. When this was destroyed in 1660 the Franciscans built the present structure, the CONVENTO DE SAN MATÍAS and the tiny chapel of SAN ANTONIO ABAD, both lovely colonial monuments well worth a visit. The buildings were used as a fortress during the Battle of Churubusco, August 20, 1847, when U.S. troops under General Winfield Scott fought General Anaya's men who were forced to surrender for lack of equipment. Neglected for a long time, the buildings have been restored and designated as the CHURUBUSCO HISTORICAL MUSEUM. *Hours:* weekdays, 10 A.M. to 7 P.M.; Sundays, 10 A.M. to 3 P.M. *Admission:* 50 centavos.

Nearby, E side of Calzada Tlalpan are the *Churubusco Studios,* the largest motion picture studios in Mexico, and owned in part by RKO. A colonial chronicler, Baltazar Medina, wrote of Churubusco: "This was the dwelling and diabolical habitation of infernal spirits that with fearful noises and howling disturbed all the regions round about where the Idol had usurped the worship of the true God." To anyone who has seen a Mexican-made movie it is obvious that the studios are doing an effective job of keeping up this old tradition.

A bit south of the studios, on the left, is the *Club Campestre de Churubusco* (Churubusco Country Club) the oldest and one of the finest golf clubs in the district.

THE "FLOATING GARDENS" OF XOCHIMILCO (so-chee-MEAL-co — from the Aztec, *xochitl,* flower; *milli* and *co,* flower-bed or place where flowers grow). It lies about 14 m. SE of the Zócalo. Follow Calzada Tlalpan southward, past Churubusco, past the Clasa Film Studios (on r.) and XEW radio transmitting tower (on l.) until you come to a Y (gas station in the center of Y). Turn left and follow the winding road. On reaching the town of *Xochimilco,* drive through, passing the open market and the handsome *Church of San Bernardino* with its great flying buttress resting against the bell tower; beyond the town you pass ½ m. of pine woods and come to a split in the road. Either the paved or dirt road will bring you shortly to the canals and gardens. If you get lost ask for the *Amapola Restaurant.* The vividly flower-decorated launches are here. The flat-bottomed boats *(trajineras)* are poled through the canals, Venice-style, by boatmen. The official hire prices *per boat, not per person* are: Yellow *franja* (fringed or border marking) boats holding 2 to 8 passengers — $15 MN per hour; Red *franja* boats, 8 to 12 passengers — $20 MN per hour; Green *franja,* 12 to 25 passengers — $30 MN per hour. These rates are government set.

Xochimilco was once a Chichimeca Indian stronghold, but they were driven out of the area in the thirteenth century by the Xochimilcas who set up a kind of land-and-water imperio. At that time, and under the Aztecs, the natives built *chinampas* or floating gardens (rafts covered with a thin layer of dirt) which could be moved around. Some were over 100 ft. long and were strong enough to support fragile huts *(chozas).* Eventually these gardens took root in the shallow waters of the lagoons forming a lacework of islands and canals. Today the islands supply a large bulk of the flowers and vegetables for the capital.

The best time to visit is Sunday. Each year for over 500 years, around mid-April, Xochimilco has held a famed flower festival.

In this SE area of the Federal District there are a number of picturesque villages, reachable by a network of fairly good roads. Among the most interesting of the villages are:

IXTAPALAPA, D.F.: (directly E of Churubusco) near the foot of the Cerro de la Estrella (Hill of the Star), a volcanic cone rising from the center of the Valley of Mexico. Because of its commanding position the Aztec priests used to build the sacred fire on its summit at the beginning of each 52-year cycle. In the village there are two interesting colonial churches. The celebration of the Passion during Holy Week is famed.

IXTACALCO, D.F.: In the nearby parish of Santa Anita a colorful Fiesta of the Doves is celebrated on Good Friday each year. It is followed by a fair and folk dancing.

TLALPAN, D.F.: (TLAHL-pahm) About 10 m. S of the city via the road to Cuernavaca. Tlalpan is a pleasant suburban town on the slopes of Mount Ajusco. It was a favorite residence of several of the early viceroys. During the early part of the nineteenth century it acquired an evil reputation because of the great gambling fete held about Whitsunday of each year. From 1827 to 1830 the town was the capital of the State of Mexico. Of historical and architectural interest is the parish church, SAN AGUSTÍN DE LAS CUEVAS (on the plaza), built in 1532.

EL DESIERTO DE LOS LEONES: (Desert of the Lions) an utterly charming picnic spot and fascinating former ecclesiastical hideout SW of the city. To get there you have a choice of two routes. (1) Take CN-15 (Paseo de la Reforma) west toward Toluca. About 7 m. from town there is a turn-off left (paved) leading 3 m. to the Desierto. (2) From San Angel take the Camino del Desierto through lovely winding hills and forests 15 m. to the Desierto.

The center of this lovely retreat is the elaborate ruins of a vast Carmelite monastery, built in 1602 and dedicated to Our Lady of Mount Carmel. The present curious name is a cluster of misnomers. There is no desert nor lions involved. The ruins are surrounded by a brooding pine forest which, it is said, once belonged to a family named Leones. The place is now a national monument and park. Open 7 A.M. to 6 P.M.

Some of the walls, domes, cloisters, and patios are still standing. The gardens, hemmed in by giant whispering trees, give one a glimpse of what a Hesperidian garden of roses, jasmine, sweet cicely and incense this place must have once been. However, the barefooted Carmelites who went there as hermits, to judge from reports, did not always go to commune exclusively with God and nature. The shrewd old English monk, Thomas Gage (1596–1656), who joined the Dominicans in Spain and was a missionary in Mexico and Guatemala, had a caustic word to say about such retreats, El Desierto in particular. He wrote of the merry life of some of the alleged hermits, of their love of leisure and repose, their feats of the trencher, their furtive interest in the swish of a silken kirtle and their devotion to the "purple goddess beloved by Bacchus."

To see El Desierto at its best, avoid a Sunday visit when picnic parties overcrowd the area.

THINGS TO DO IN MEXICO CITY

In addition to plain sightseeing there are countless ways of entertaining oneself or being entertained in the Mexican capital. Here are a few suggestions:

SHOPPING: One of the favorite tourist sports in Mexico is sampling the vivid shops of the city for jewelry, silver, unique native crafts, leather goods, and eye-catching souvenirs. The best shopping districts for such are along Av. Juárez and Madero, and the Midtown district around Genova and Londres. For more detailed directions consult *In Mexico,* the shopping guide by James Norman. If you are interested in handmade glass a visit to the oldest and most famed glass factory, Avalos Brothers at Carretones 5, is both fascinating and worthwhile. For native basketry the huge central market, LA MERCED, several blocks E of the Zócalo and 2 blocks S. Or, the basket market building of the San Juan district market at Arcos de Belém and Lopez.

SPORTS: (1) Spectator sports. *Football* on Sunday mornings at either the Ciudad de los Deportes stadium or at the University City stadium (this is, *futbol,* i.e. soccer). *Bullfights,* Sunday afternoons at 4 P.M. at either El Toro or at Plaza México. *Baseball* (night games usually) at Parque de Seguro Social. For all the above one should check with one's hotel information service or the English language newspaper, *The News,* for programs and hours. *Jai alai* or *frontón* is played at the Frontón México every day except Monday. Afternoon and evenings. *Boxing and wrestling,* fairly good semiprofessional bouts at the Arena México (Saturdays, 9 P.M. and at Arena Coliseo (Wednesdays, 9 P.M.) *Polo* at the Casino Militar polo field in Chapultepec Park, on Sundays, in season. *Charreadas,* Mexican style horsemanship and rodeos, Sunday mornings at the Rancho del Charro and the Rancho La Tapatía.

(2) Participation sports. *Golf.* There are three first-class clubs: Churubusco, on the Tlalpan road S of the city; Chapultepec, on N side of the city, 2 m. beyond the race track; Club México, S on the Tlalpan road. (See Index regarding entrance and green fees.) *Tennis.* There are excellent courts at the Club Deportivo Chapultepec on Calzada Mariano Escobeda and Victor Hugo. *Riding.* The best bridle paths are in Chapultepec Park. Good stables are Pensión Madrid at Calzada Tacubaya; Pensión Welton on Calle Agararismo and Pensión Victoria at Calzada Morales 361. *Bowling.* The best alleys are the Casablanca, Insurgentes 640; Boliche Polanco, Goldsmith 40; and Hispano-Méxicano, Santa Bárbara 23; and Bolerama, in the Ciudad de los Deportes.

THEATER, BALLET, OPERA: The year-around programs at the Palacio de Bellas Artes sponsored by the government's National Institute of Fine Arts (INBA) are tops in cultural entertainment. These include opera, with stars from abroad, local and international ballet companies, theatrical productions, concerts, etc. Ticket office opens daily between 11 A.M. and 2 P.M., and 4 P.M. to curtain time.

A spectacular "must" for visitors in Mexico is to see the famed *Ballet Folklorico de Mexico* (National Folk Ballet) directed by Amalia Hernandez, and presented several times each week at the National Opera house (Bellas Artes).

Mexico City lacks a Broadway, but there are a half-dozen fair Spanish-speaking theaters. Check the daily papers for programs. Addresses listed in directory, see Index.

The city has several lively *Music Halls* (vaudeville and follies). The best is *Teatro Lírico,* Calle de Cuba 46, noted for its top-rank entertainers. Others are: *Teatro Margo,* Aquiles Serdán and Mina; *Teatro Follies,* Gabriel Leyva 41; *Teatro Iris,* Donceles 36. Orchestra seats range from $5 MN to $10 MN.

NIGHT SPOTS: The better supper clubs have been indicated in the restaurant directory, see Index. The capital, however, has very few night clubs offering the lavish entertainment or high quality shows one is accustomed to in Las Vegas, Hollywood, New York, or Paris. Perhaps the best purely Mexican night club is *El Patio,* Aténas 5. It is a big, old-fashioned, Spanish-style place noted for its two excellent orchestras, top Spanish and Mexican entertainers, and its reasonable prices.

Less impeccable are the dozens of night spots that welcome gentlemen without women. According to recent statistics $3,500,000 MN are spent daily in the city's bars, *cantinas* and night spots *(cabaretuchos)* of which there are over 3400 of the latter alone. The Mexican press states that a million and a half citizens are involved in *la parroquia negra* (the night or black parish). For visiting sailors the following are suggested, not recommended: *Mil y Una Noches,* Uruguay 14 — lively floor show and high prices. *Pigalle,* Santa María la Redonda 90. *Río Rosa,* Oaxaca 99, big, old and sometimes rough. Has good orchestras.

Colorful and suitable for a mixed party is a nighttime visit to the *Tenampa* in Plaza Garabaldi, a tawdry but at times fascinating hangout for the *charro* outfitted *mariachi* musicians who wait around to be hired and taken off to parties.

THE NEW LOOK

The Mexican since pre-Columbian times has been noted for his preoccupation with the monumental, and often for his daring architectural ideas. Visitors in the city will be struck by various new edifices, a number of them churches, which combine either one or both of these qualities. Some of the newer buildings not mentioned previously are well worth seeking out. Among the monumental are:

BENITO JUÁREZ HOUSING CENTER: Calle Anza and Orizaba, a vast colorful low-cost federal housing project containing more than a thousand apartments, shops and surrounding park.

MINISTRY OF COMMUNICATIONS CENTER: S on Av. Universidad. This monumental building complex is the headquarters of the Secretaría de Comunicaciones and Secretaría de Obras Públicas, the government ministries in charge of communications, public highways, etc. The 9-story-high mosaic murals decorating the buildings are by Juan O'Gorman and Chavez Morado.

More exciting however are the daring, imaginative, and curvilinear churches being erected in the city. The most important and audacious of the modern works is EL TEMPLO DE LA MEDALLA MILAGROSA (Church of the Miraculous Medal) designed by the brilliant Spanish-Mexican modern architect-engineer Félix Candela. The SANTUARIO DE NUESTRA SEÑORA DE LA PIEDAD (Our Lady of Pity) on Obrero Mundial near Monterrey, combines both soaring monumentality with a web-like concrete tracery. The temple DEL SANTO CRISTO DE LA AGONIA DE LIMPIAS on Av. Jacarandas, the work of architect Nicolás Mariscal Barroso, is a unique semisphere covered with blue Venetian mosaic tiles.

51. *Central Western Mexico*

This region covering 82,719 sq. miles of unusually mountainous country includes the Central West Coast states of Jalisco, Colima, Michoacán, and Guerrero. Although the physical features of each state will be touched upon separately it is worthy of note that this region has the most beautiful of Mexico's fine beach resorts, undoubtedly the best year-round climate (along the coast); it has some of the most forbidding and least explored terrain in the republic, and, especially in Michoacán, many of the most picturesque Indian communities in the land.

The communications picture of the region is likewise unique. The Pacific shoreline is spectacularly beautiful being dotted with fine ports and charming, tucked-away tropical villages, yet there is no coastal highway. One can travel all along the coast by jeep, but the proposed ocean-view highway so frequently announced in tourist literature remains a distant dream. The region is served by two trunk highways — CN-15 coming down from Nogales on the U.S. border, through Guadalajara to Mexico City, and by CN-95 linking the capital to Acapulco. The Guadalajara-Mexico City stretch meanders along the inside or northern edge of the region. From it a few roads make tentative gestures at reaching down toward the coastal villages.

Vacation accommodations along the trunk highways and at the playground ports are from good to excellent in that much of the region is just beginning to open to tourism and everything is new.

TRAVEL HIGHLIGHTS: The outstanding points of interest in the region are many. Among them: *Guadalajara,* Mexico's second largest city, noted for its easygoing life and wonderful year-round climate. *Lake Chapala,* largest natural lake in the republic, and a popular resort area. The beautiful pine-clad mountain country and Tarascan Indian towns around *Lake Pátzcuaro*. *Morelia,* Mexico's regal colonial city. *San José Purua,* an outstanding thermal spa. Colonial *Taxco* where every vista is a memorable picture and where silverware and jewelry pours out of every alleyway. And, of course, the fishing and beach resorts: *Acapulco,* with its unbelievably beautiful bay and glittering hotels; *Puerto Vallarta* and *Zihuatanejo,* still somewhat tucked away; *Manzanillo* and any number of nearby off-trail paradises.

AREAS OF MAXIMUM INTEREST	BASE
Jalisco-Colima Country	Guadalajara and Manzanillo
Michoacán Country	Morelia or Pátzcuaro
The Guerrero Country	Taxco and Acapulco

JALISCO-COLIMA COUNTRY

The Jalisco-Colima section embraces one of the largest and the smallest of the western states — Jalisco, with an area of 31,517 sq. miles, and population of over 2,443,261; Colima, covering 2009 sq. miles with a population of 153,622. The latter is almost surrounded by Jalisco except for a short border with Michoacán on the SE and its Pacific Ocean frontage. Jalisco, on the other hand is a sprawling state stretching from the Pacific Ocean, eastward over the Sierra Madre Occidental and extending well into the central tableland. It has borders on the N with the states of Nayarit, Zacatecas, Aguascalientes, to the E with Guanajuato, and to the S with Michoacán. Between Jalisco's high central plateau and the low tropical west coast the mountains are so rugged, slashed by *barrancas* as deep as 2000 ft., this area has practically defied penetration. In this rugged land are two striking volcanoes, El Nevado de Colima and Volcán de Colima. El Nevado (14,235 ft. above sea level) is one of Mexico's stateliest peaks. The rivers — Pingito, Túxpan, Ayuquila, Tomatlán, and Tuito — all flow into the Río Lerma (called El Río Grande de Santiago, by the Indians) which empties into the Pacific. One of the great natural sights in the Jalisco country is the Falls of Juanacatlán, the Niagara of Mexico.

FLORA AND FAUNA: The coastal lands of both Colima and Jalisco are noted for their extensive reserves of

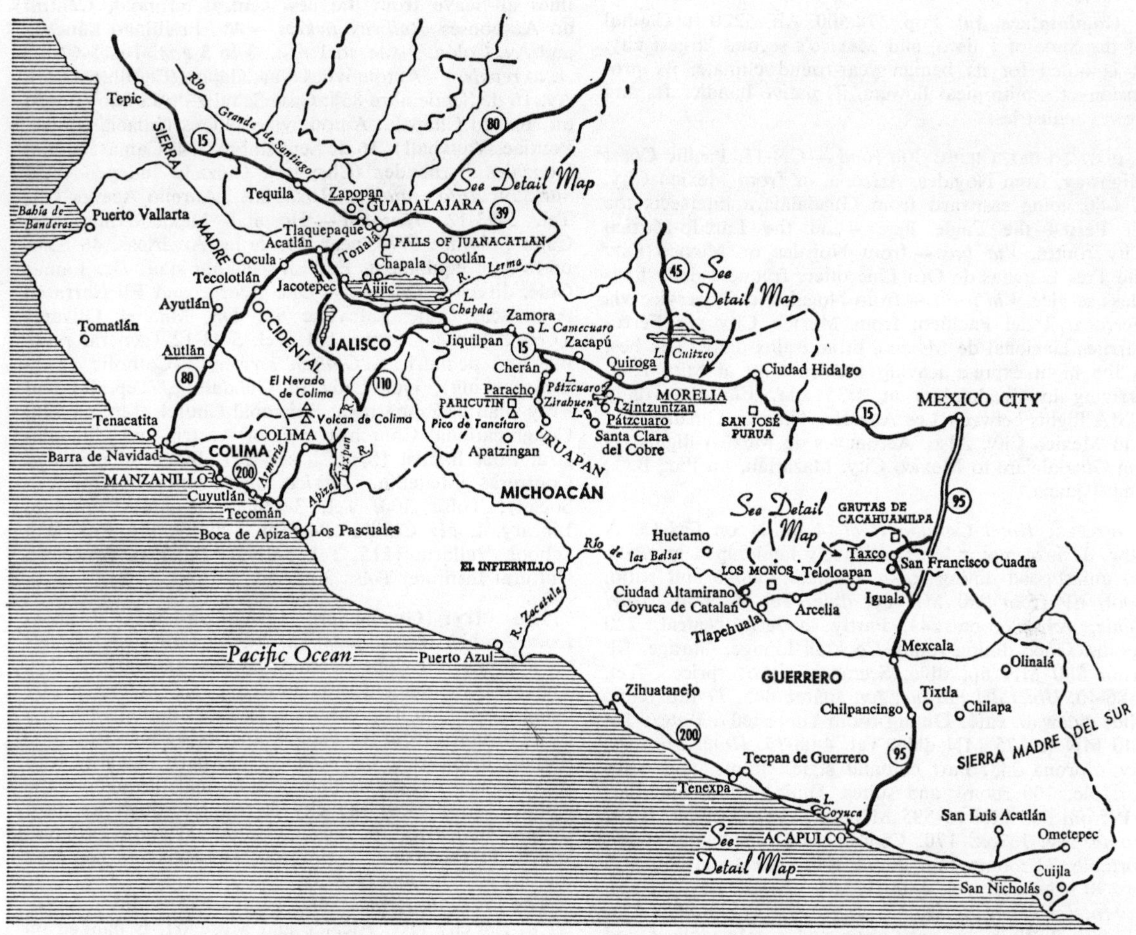

tropical forests, huge coconut palm haciendas, and banana plantations. It is a dazzling green world of banyan trees, palms, ebonies, rosewoods adorned with rare blooms. The forests and *barrancas* fairly teem with gorgeous tropical birds: flamingos, herons, parrots and parakeets, ducks and wild turkeys. Hunting for bigger game is notable, especially for deer, mountain lion, jaguarondi. In the jungle-walled rivers, the hidden lagoons and in the open sea the whale, porpoise and manta ray are still common, and game-fish are bountiful, particularly the great sailfish, marlin, barracuda, and Spanish mackerel.

HISTORY: Before the conquest the Jalisco-Colima area was inhabited by various tribes, some who had developed their own unique cultural forms, others who were a part of the Aztec Confederation. Among these various tribes were the Huicholes (see Index); the Tarascans, whose home base was in Michoacán, but who had spread over parts of Jalisco and Colima; the Coras and a tribe calling themselves the Colimas. The latter were situated around the Bay of Manzanillo and there is evidence to indicate that for centuries before the coming of the Spaniards they carried on a trade with the Orient through either Chinese or Malayan traders who visited the Mexican west coast.

Within a few years after the fall of Tenochtitlán Cortés sent expeditions under Nuño de Guzmán, Captain Juan de Oñate and Pedro de Alvarado to add the Michoacán and Jalisco countries to the Spanish crown. By 1528 several settlements were established and Guzmán was appointed their governor. During one of the later expeditions Alvarado was grievously wounded during a skirmish with Indians near Manzanillo. He died in Guadalajara, July 4, 1541. After Jalisco and Colima came under Spanish rule, Manzanillo became an important shipbuilding port. It was there that Miguel López de Legaspi constructed an armada to gain control of the Philippine Islands discovered in 1521 by Magellan.

THE PEOPLE TODAY: Apart from the more retiring ethnic groups — Huicholes and Tarascans — it might be said that Jalisco and Colima are much more Mexican than Indian. Along the coast one finds the people pleasant and easygoing and a bit cosmopolitan as a result of the liberal sprinkling of Chinese and Negro blood in the coastal stock. On the plateau, especially around Guadalajara, the Spanish influence is stronger. The people of Jalisco speak of themselves as *Tapatíos* (derived perhaps from the heavy tasseled *tápalos,* embroidered shawls or mantles the colonial Spaniards wore). The Jaliscans have come to regard their state as a place noted for its brave and *macho* (manly) men and beautiful women — *estado de los hombres valientes y las mujeres bonitas.* This romantic glamorization of themselves is piquantly reflected in their expression of the Jarabe Tapatío, a colorful *jota*-like dance which has become the "national folk dance" of Mexico. (See Index: Folk Dances.)

Guadalajara, Jal. Pop. 378,500. Alt. 5220 ft. Capital of the State of Jalisco, and Mexico's second largest city. It is noted for its benign year-round climate, its profusion of semitropical flowers, its native handicrafts and newer industries.

HOW TO GET THERE: *Via road* — CN-15, Pacific Coast Highway, from Nogales, Arizona, or from Mexico City. CN-80 going eastward from Guadalajara intersects the El Paso — the Eagle Pass — and the Laredo-Mexico City routes. *Via bus* — from Nogales or Mexico City the Tres Estrellas de Oro Line offers frequent daily first-class service. *Via train* — from Nogales, daily service via Ferrocarril del Pacifico; from Mexico City via Ferrocarriles Nacional de México, three trains daily. The best is the night express leaving Mexico City at 8:20 P.M., arriving in Guadalajara at 8:35 A.M. *Via air* — daily CMA flights between Los Angeles, Tijuana, Guadalajara, and Mexico City. Also, Aeronaves de México flights tying Guadalajara to Mexico City, Mazatlán, La Paz, B.C., and Tijuana.

HOTELS: *Hotel Camino Real,* 4 m. N on CN-15. A new, de luxe motor hotel on lovely landscaped grounds. 50 units, good dining room, cocktail lounge and patio, pool. EP from $90 MN up, dble. Tel. 4-29-30. *Hotel Fénix,* Av. Corona 243. Partly modern, central, 220 rooms. Good dining room. Cocktail lounge. Garage. EP from $80 MN up, dble. Seems a bit overpriced. Tel. 4-86-40. *Hotel del Parque,* Av. Juárez 845. 77 fair units. Nice sidewalk café. Dining room (untested). Rates: EP $40 MN to $75 MN dble. Tel. 4-08-75. *Hotel Morales,* Av. Corona 243. Part colonial style, simple, and comfortable. 100 rooms and suites. Dining room and bar. EP from $45 MN to $95 MN dble. Tel. 3-29-69. *Hotel Roma.* Av. Juárez 170. Central, *viajero*-style but comfortable. 72 rooms. Fair dining room. EP from $50 MN to $90 MN dble. Tel. 4-08-10.

Motel Campo Bello, Av. Ingenieros 1599 (CN-15). Modest, 28 unit inn, very clean and comfortable. Good restaurant. EP $50 MN dble. Tel. 5-95-17. *Motel Chapalita,* Av. Ingenieros 1617. Modern, 81 unit, cocktail lounge, dining room, pool. EP from $65 MN to $80 MN. Tel. 5-08-76. *El Cortijo,* 4¼ m. S on CN-15. 18 unit motel on nice grounds. Restaurant. EP from $40 MN. Tel 5-96-66. *Motel Malibu,* 3 m. N on CN-15. Brand new. 40 units. Rates: EP from $50 MN up. *Motel Tropicana,* 6½ m. N on CN-15. New, nicely furnished 26 unit motel on pleasant grounds. Dining room, bar. Two pools. EP $75 MN dble. *Hotel Frances,* Maestranza 35. A modernized, former monastery, lovely patio, comfortable rooms, reasonable. Good dining room.

RESTAURANTS: *Campo Bello Motel Restaurant,* address above. Excellent U.S. style cuisine. *Zamponi,* Av. Lafayette 13, good Italian style. Bar. Hours: noon to midnight. Closed Sundays. Tel. 5-96-48. *La Copa de Leche,* Juárez 414. Attractive, air conditioned, so-called international cuisine. Seems not up to what it used to be. Hours: 8 A.M. to midnight. *El Parador Germano,* Lopez Cotilla. German style. *Los Otates,* Av. Union 28. Fair regional dishes. *Cadillac,* Juárez 492. Good steaks. The new, swank and fine, La Calandria restaurant, on Lafayette, one block S of Vallarta. Evenings. International cuisine.

DIRECTORY: *U. S. Consulate,* Av. 16 de Septiembre 489. Tel. 3-29-98. *Banks* — Banco Nacional de México, Av. Juárez and Corona; Banco de Jalisco, Madero 395. *Airline offices* — CMA, Corona and P. Sanchez. Aeronaves de México, Corona and Madero. *Bus lines* — Autotransportes Tres Estrellas de Oro, and various other lines all leave from the new central terminal, Central do Autobuses. *Railway tickets* — Av. Priciliano Sánchéz and Av. Colón. 9 A.M. to 1 P.M.; 3 to 5 P.M. Tel. 3-62-87. *Auto repairs* — Automóviles Guadalajara (Cadillac, Opel), Av. 16 de Septiembre 858; Casa Schultz de Jalisco (Ford), on road to Chapala; Automóviles Nueva Galacia (Buick, Pontiac, Vauxhall), 16 de Septiembre 574; Camarena and Gonzales Fernandez (Chrysler), Calzada Independencía Sur 559. *Auto rentals* — Roxa, S.A., Aurelio Aceves 171, Tel. 5-93-12. *Hospital* — Hospital México-Americano, Calle Colomos 1776, near Av. de las Américas. 46 beds, up-to-date equipment. English-speaking staff. Dr. Lamar Cole, director. *Doctors* — Drs. George and Eli Carrasco Amavisca, Calle Lafayette 98; Dr. Manuel Olivares Torres, Aurelio Aceves 171. Tel. 5-93-12 (general practice and pediatrics). *Church services* — Catholic (English-speaking), Our Lady of Guadalupe, Tepeyac and Fray Juan de Zumárraga; Episcopal Church, Molina 126; Congregational Church, corner of Austria and Guadalajara; First Baptist (Spanish service), Independencía and Contreras Medellín. *Service organizations:* American Society, Tolsa 300. Tel. 3-62-64; Benjamin Franklin Library, Lopéz Cotilla 594, Tel. 3-49-99; the American School, Vallarta 1515, Tel. 5-01-31; Mexican American Cultural Institute, Tolsa 300. Tel. 3-62-64.

THE CITY: Guadalajara (gwah-dah-lah-HAH-rah — from Arabic, *Wad-al-jadjarah,* rock-strewn river) stands on a gentle hill slope overlooking the *Atemajac Valley.* The early settlement was moved twice before finally being fixed upon its present site in 1542. Perhaps because of its distance from the capital, and its western isolation, the city history and development has been less shot with violence and upheavals than was normal throughout the country. At present the city is going through its most intense upheaval — a gigantic modernization program which, in the name of progress, is sacrificing some of the city's traditional charms.

The *Plaza de Armas,* once garden-like traditional center of the city (Av. Alcalde and Moreno), is flanked on one side by the imposing *Palace de Gobierno* and the picturesque *Portales* or cloister-like colonnades, and on an adjacent side by the *Cathedral.*

The *Cathedral,* begun in 1571, seems to have been started as a Gothic pile, but during various reconstructions the builders became enamored with, or learned something about, Tuscan, Mudéjar, Byzantine, Corinthian, Doric, and other enrichments so that nothing was left out. The exterior has suffered severely from both earthquakes which destroyed the façade and towers and at the hands of architects. The present twin towers, pyramidal Byzantine, rise some 200 ft. above the street, are outfitted with incandescent lights and lightning rods. To repeat the scholarly Sylvester Baxter, in his 10-volume cathedral to architecture, "The chief example of ecclesiastical architecture [in Guadalajara], the cathedral, is so absolutely bad as to be unworthy a place in this volume."

However, within the garish interior of the church there is a treasure that makes up for all other faults. It is the Assumption of the Virgin by Murillo, without a doubt one of the finest works of the master. It can be found in the sacristy.

Palacio de Gobierno (W side of Plaza), dating from 1643, is of architectural interest as one of the best examples in Mexico of the Churrigueresque blended with the rococo and applied to a secular building. The building also contains some of Orozco's earlier murals depicting Man and His Philosophies and Progress in a Spiritual and Material World. Historically the Palace is

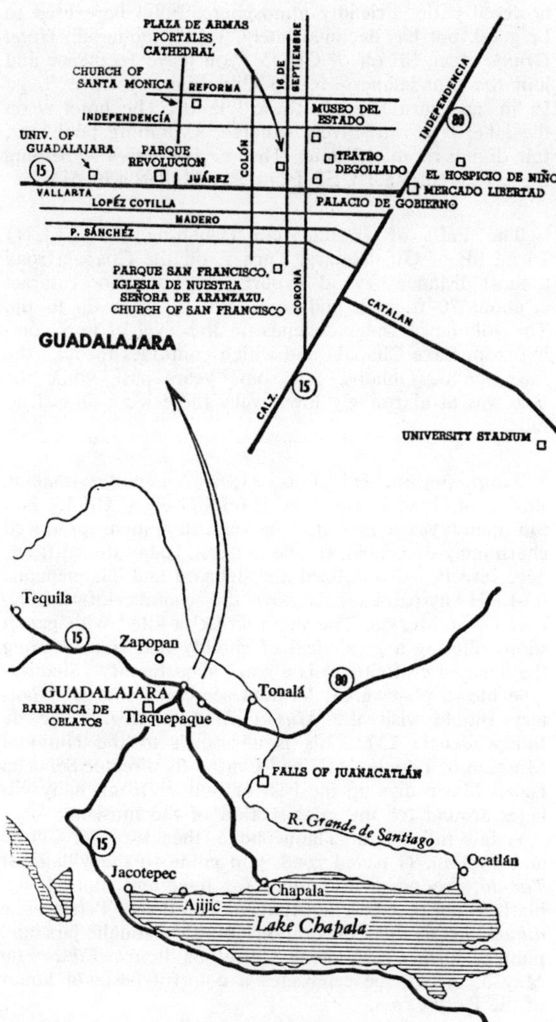

remembered as the site where Padre Hidalgo (1810) decreed the abolishment of slavery in Mexico.

A block N of the plaza is *Museo del Estado* (State Museum), on Av. Corona. The museum is housed in a fine old colonial one-time seminary which has a noble patio. There are exhibits of outstanding Spanish and Colonial paintings, some archaeological artifacts, and an excellent collection of old costumes and regional arts and crafts. One serious lack in the museum is that nothing is identified. It is almost as if the curators themselves don't know what they possess or are inarticulate about it. *Hours:* daily, 10 A.M. to 1 P.M.

Church of Santa Monica, 6 blocks W and N of the Plaza, is the finest Baroque church in the city and one of the nation's architectural gems. It is extraordinarily rich in fanciful carved decorations, twisted columns in the form of vines, leaves and fruit, heraldic devices, lions, and eagles.

Universidad de Guadalajara (University of Guadalajara) 2 blocks W of Parque de la Revolucion, on Av. Juárez (continuation of Vallarta). The university was founded in 1791 and ranks as one of the finest educational institutions in Latin America. Housed in a former Jesuit monastery and church, the school attracts a constant stream of visitors for its famed murals by José Clemente Orozco (in Lecture Hall of main building). The themes on the dome interior and 450 sq. ft. painted surface are: Man the Creator and Investigator; Science and Human Problems; the Development of Arts, and minor subjects. In addition to the Orozco murals there are some excellent murals done by Siqueiros and Cuevas in the chapel. For information about the university's summer sessions for foreigners, see Index.

Another group of Orozco murals, among his most powerful and famed, may be seen in the chapel of *El Hospicio de Niños* or *Hospicio Cabañas,* a progressive orphanage founded in 1803 by Bishop Ruiz de Cabañas. The murals *(pinturas murales)* by the Jaliscan artist (see Index) fill the chapel of the orphanage. Their themes are: The Elements (fire, water, air, earth), the Arts and Sciences; the Conquest of Mexico, with portraits of the leading personages of that era; the powerful and savage Four Horsemen of the Apocalypse.

The orphanage building itself is worth wandering through. Supposedly designed by Tolsa, it is a vast parallelogram 610 ft. long by 500 ft. wide. There is a maze of 26 flower-filled patios linked by tiled corridors. The *Hospicio* is located at Calle Hospicio and Av. Cabañas, near the bullring.

Mercado Libertad, 2 blocks SW of the orphanage, at juncture of Av. Juárez and Calzada Independencia. The city's huge and colorful central market. *Parque San Francisco,* 2 blocks S of Av. Juárez at Corona. A picturesque plaza once surrounded by four churches. Of the two remaining churches, *San Francisco* and *Iglesia de Nuestra Señora de Aranzazu,* the latter is noted for its beautiful Churrigueresque altar.

Teatro Degollado, corner of Morelos and Degollado, 2 blocks from the Plaza de Armas. A handsome old theater (opened 1866), now the home of the Guadalajara Symphony Orchestra. A newer point of pilgrimage in the city is to *El Museo Taller Orozco* (Museum Workshop of José Clemente Orozco), Calle Aurelio Aceves 27, W edge of city ½ block from the Arch that straddles Av. Vallarta. This was the studio of perhaps the greatest of Mexico's Big Four muralists. There are 92 of his paintings on exhibition. *Hours:* daily (except Monday), 10 A.M. to 2 P.M., 4 to 8 P.M. *Admission:* one peso.

ENTERTAINMENT AND ACTIVITIES: (Also, see below, *Excursions out of Guadalajara:*

Night life — Guadalajara is a bit too staid to go in for Acapulco-style night spots. The gaiety is left to Ajijic. The nonathletic can enjoy themselves sightseeing, visiting the markets, shopping for the mountains of craft goods that enter the city from nearby villages.

SPORT AND SPECTACLES: *Football* (soccer) is one of Guadalajara's big sports. The city has three professional teams. Games are played in the University Stadium. *Baseball games,* Central Mexican League, may also be seen at the Stadium. *Bullfights* (the *corridas formales*) from November to May. Sunday afternoons. *Boxing,* Saturday nights at the Arena Coliseo. *Wrestling,* Sunday nights, same place. *Cockfights* (better than in Mexico City) are held Thursday and Saturday night at the Plaza de Gallos on CN-80. Snacks are served, there is *mariachi* music, and the proceeds go to the underprivileged children's fund. *Golfers* can arrange to tee-off at the Guadalajara Country Club which has a splendid 18 hole course. *Swimming and yachting* at Lake Chapala, see below.

EXCURSIONS OUT OF GUADALAJARA: **Lake Chapala** (el Lago de Chapala — chah-PAH-la — from the Aztec onomatopoetic *chapalal,* splashing of waves),

Mexico's largest natural lake (70 m. long, 20 m. wide; covers 270 sq. miles and is 5159 ft. above sea level) straddles the boundary line between Jalisco and Michoacán states. The lake lies 32 m. SE of Guadalajara and is linked to the city by several good roads. Surrounded by low-lying mountains the lake area has one of the most ideal climates imaginable — never too hot in the summer, placidly temperate in the winter. Boating on the lake is a popular sport, as is swimming in the warm fresh water. The most prized fish are *bagre,* a species of catfish; *mojarra,* a sunfish; *blanco,* a delicious native white fish or lake herring with a taste like lemon sole. The region around the lake is one of the most populous bird havens in the republic, a veritable ornithologist's paradise. There are a number of picturesque or interesting fishing and resort villages around the lake — Chapala, Ajijic, Ocotlán, Jocotepec.

Chapala, Jal. Pop. 6000. The most popular and semi-sophisticated resort town on the N shore of Lake Chapala.

To get there from Guadalajara take CE-35. Taxis from the city charge between $6 and $7. The bus line, Cooperativa Guadalajara-Chapala makes frequent daily trips.

The village makes no attempt to be a splendiferous resort. Its principal appeal is the mild climate and charming primitive surroundings which have enticed an unusual number of Americans, Canadians, and Britishers of advanced age to retire there. Chapala offers some quiet forms of social activity: the Club Campestre Chapala (Country Club) maintains a club house and golf course overlooking the lake, and the Yacht *(Yates)* Club is building a new $50,000 club center on the lake shore.

HOTELS AND RESTAURANTS: *Hotel Villa Monte Carlo,* W of town, on lake shore, 24 rooms and bungalow units. Thermal spring-water pool. Cocktail bar. Rates: AP $140 MN to $175 MN dble. Reservations suggested. *Country Club Arms Hotel,* Niños Heroes 59. 14 units. EP $50 MN to $65 MN dble. *Chapala Motel,* on CN-35. A nicely run, small, new motel. Rates from $50 MN dble, up. *Chulavista Motel,* W on road to Ajijic. *Paradise Inn* (restaurant), across from the Chulavista, is American-operated and specializes in hamburgers, pies as well as complete meals. *Restaurant La Viuda* overlooks the lake and is pleasant.

Ajijic, Jal. Pop. 2400. About 4½ m. W of Chapala via gravel road. Ajijic (ah-he-HEEK) is a sometimes somnolent fishing village on the edge of the lake that has become a popular artist colony and sun-drenched bohemia. The women of the village do very fine embroidery. A local craft center, Ajijic Looms, produces excellent hand-loomed cotton and woollen fabrics.

HOTEL AND RESTAURANT: *Posada Rancho Santa Isabel,* E edge of village. Pleasant, informal, cottage-type establishment with 10 units. Fair dining room. Cocktail service. Rates: AP $120 MN dble.

From Ajijic one can continue westward on the gravel road (CE-94) about 11 m. to *Jocotepec, Jal.* Pop. 6500. A fishing village at W end of the lake. Founded in 1528, it has taken on a patina of age and a pleasant quaintness that makes it one of the more interesting of the lake villages. Heavy, rather good hand-loomed serapes are one of the important crafts of the town. Market day is Sunday. The village celebrates a pretty fiesta, Feria de los Dulces Nombres (Sweet Names) on January 14–15.

HOTELS: In town, *La Quinta.* A small, 10 room inn established in an ancient colonial building. Quaint, lovely flowered patio. Friendly atmosphere. Food here used to be good, but has declined lately. Rates, moderate. *Hotel Granja Azul,* SE off of CN-15 (you leave Jocotepec and join the Guadalajara-Mexico City highway, turn S, go ½ m. and turn E again toward lake). The hotel is on the lake. It is attractively situated, swimming pool, bar, fair dining room. 15 units. The service leaves something to be desired. Rates: EP from $48 MN to $70 MN.

The Falls of Juanacatlán (whan-nah-chat-LAHN) 16 m. SE of Guadalajara. Turn E off the Chapala road a short distance beyond airport. The horseshoe cataract is about 70 ft. high and some 500 ft. from tip to tip. The volume of water depends on the level of flow coming from Lake Chapala and which continues through the Barranca de Oblatos. For some years past, while the lake was at alarmingly low levels, there were almost no falls.

Tlaquepaque, Jal. Pop. 21,000. A pottery-making suburb of Guadalajara, 5 m. E off CN-80 or CE-35. Not too many years ago this one-industry town produced charmingly decorated, fragile pottery. Today the craft has been largely industrialized and debased and Tlaquepaque (ta-LAH-kay-pah-kay) is now the chamber-of-ceramic-horrors of Mexico. The main street is filled with garish shops offering a great deal of shoddy materials. Among the debased crafts there is a good glass factory (Spanish-type blown glassware). Visitors searching for good pottery should visit the *Museo de Cerámica,* Calle de Independencia 237. This is a branch of the National Museum of Popular Arts and Crafts. Its director Señorita Isabel Marín digs up the best of pottery from many villages around for the sales section of the museum.

A few miles E of Tlaquepaque, then turn off CN-80 and go 1 m. N paved road, you come to the village of *Tonalá,* producers of pottery far finer and more imaginative than that of Tlaquepaque. The famed Persian-like *dibujo de petatillo* decorations on the Tonalá jars and platters have made them collector's items. *Fiesta:* on May 3, the village celebrates a colorful fiesta in honor of the Holy Cross.

Barranca de Oblatos (Monk's Canyon), a deep (2000 ft.) gorge about 5 m. SW of the city. The great rift was formed by the Río Grande de Santiago (Lerma River). Beyond this there is still a deeper gorge reached through the village of Zapopan.

Zapopan, Jal. Formerly an Indian village NW of the city, now one of its suburbs. Zapopan has a great seventeenth-century Baroque Franciscan church with a Mudéjar tiled dome and an elaborate Plateresque façade. The church and community are famed throughout the country for the exceptional fiesta of the Virgen de Zapopan, the tutelary saint of Guadalajara; brought to Jalisco by a Franciscan friar in the sixteenth century. For several months during each year the brightly appareled figurine, accompanied by devotées and Indian dancers, visits the leading Guadalajara churches, and on October 4 (the day of the fiesta) is returned to her Zapopan sanctuary with great ceremony and festivities.

In the nearby community of *Atemajac del Valle* there are unique trimmings added to the August 15 Feast of the Assumption. A play-dance is staged (entitled *The Conquest*), in which Malinche, Cortés, and Moctezuma are the leading characters. The old sixteenth-century bronze bell in the village church rings a continuous 24 hours, so you hear none of the play.

Tequila, Jal. Pop. 5936. Alt. 4000. On CN-15, 39 m. NW of Guadalajara. Tequila (teh-KEY-lah — from a Nahoa word meaning drink made from Mescal) is a small upland town in the midst of huge maguey plantations. Hereabouts the corrosive in quality, of lethal potency, and fiery distillate of the maguey — the drink called tequila — is made. Tours through the tequila distilleries are available.

THE JALISCO-COLIMA COASTS: Guadalajara is usually the take-off point for trips to the delightful beach resorts of Puerto Vallarta, Manzanillo, and numerous other tucked-away Tahiti-like coastal villages. At the present moment the only way to reach Puerto Vallarta is by plane. There is regular first-class service. Although a road is sketched upon maps, only some ungainly, open-air, high-wheeled buses make the trip. It takes them about 2 days to make the 200 m. trip.

To the Manzanillo area there are two road routes in addition to good communications by air and train. The first and best road to Manzanillo is to take CN-15 to Jiquilpan, Mich., and from there follow CN-110 down to the coast. (See Index: Highway Routes — Nogales-Mexico City.) A shorter and more direct route from Guadalajara toward Manzanillo is opened, but the road does not offer comfortable driving yet. Sections are still battered and unpaved. The log for this route, CE-80, follows:

MILES
000 GUADALAJARA. Leave capital via CN-15 going south.
22 Turn-off, W on new road.
25 Acatlán.
37 Cocula. According to tradition, this Indian village is the original home of the *mariachis* — wandering troubadors.
— Tecolotlán.
90 Ayutlán. Here on the road deteriorates.
121 Autlán. **G.** Sections of the road west of here are being worked upon and paved.
186 Barra de Navidad. A new, developing resort area. (See Index.) From here a motorist can continue N via sketchy road (CE-200) to Tenacatita (see Index), or turn SW along CE-200 to,
206 MANZANILLO.

Manzanillo, Col. Pop. 14,000. Alt. 20 ft. A picturesque and yet busy Pacific seaport and resort area with fair vacation accommodations.

HOW TO GET THERE: *Via highway* — both highway routes described above. *Via bus* — Autotransportes Tres Estrellas de Oro (from Mexico City or Guadalajara, first class). *Via railway* — Ferrocarriles Nacionales de México, Guadalajara-Manzanillo line. Express leaves Guadalajara Tuesday, Thursday, and Saturday at 11:25 P.M., arrives Manzanillo at 8:40 A.M. A daily passenger train leaves at 10 A.M., arriving at 7:25 P.M.

HOTELS AND RESTAURANTS: *Posada,* Playa Azul ½ m. NW of town. Small, popular, nicely informal, and friendly inn. Cocktail service. No dining room. Reservations advisable. *Colonial Hotel,* Av. México and Gonzáles (central), 40 rooms, fair dining room, bar. A pleasant, old-fashioned colonial-style hotel. Rates: AP $100 MN dble.

Bungalows La Audiencia, Playa de la Audiencia, Santiago Peninsula, 6 m. NW of town. 5 bungalows. EP $100 MN dble. *Bungalows Clara,* Playa Azul, 4 units, EP $120 MN dble.

The following hotels, motels and furnished apartments vary greatly in quality of service, furnishings and other vacation niceties. Some, such as the Pez Vela Hotel, though new, big, and glossy-looking from a distance, suffer from that ailment so common in Mexican hotels — Spartan furnishing, indifference toward their customers, etc.

Anita Hotel, Playa de Santiago, 112 rooms, AP $125 MN dble. *Foreign Club,* Morelos and 21 de Marzo (on Plaza). 40 rooms. Pleasant open-air café-restaurant downstairs. Rates: EP from $38 MN dble. *Pez Vela Hotel,* Playa San Pedrito. 36 rooms, poor restaurant, EP from $75 MN dble. *Apartments Olas Altas,* Bahía Santiago, 12 units, EP from $100 to $200 MN daily. *Manzanillo Courts,* Playa Azul, 9 units, EP $70 MN dble. *Jaragua Apartments,* Playa Azul, EP $500 MN per week. *Bayardo Hotel,* Playa de Santiago, 15 rooms, AP $53 MN dble.

Manzanillo is the place for sea food — fresh oysters and shrimp at sidewalk stands, fish dinners at the *Colonial Hotel Restaurant,* and others.

DIRECTORY: *Bank* — Banco Nacional de México, corner of Mexico and Ingenieros. *Car repairs* — Automóviles de Colima, Carillo Puerto 250. *Bus lines* — Tres Estrellas de Oro, Av. Mexico 1.

THE CITY AND ENVIRONS: Manzanillo (mahn-zah-KNEE-yo — from Manchineel; *malum mahianum* "poison tree"), the main Pacific port for Guadalajara, Michoacán, and Mexico City is a turn-of-the-century holdover, skipped over by main highways, tourists, airlines, and tourist agents. The town is squeezed on a slender spine of land that separates two bays. It is a place full of atmosphere; narrow streets, picturesque houses, and shacks climbing up several hillsides, a spacious and clean waterfront made for evening strolls. The beaches — Playa San Pedrito, Playa Azul — stretch around the broad curve of bay toward the Peninsula of Santiago, a beautiful point with its own fine coves, beaches, and residential sections. To the north and south of the city there are magnificent coconut forests, huge coconut and banana plantations edging down to the sea.

According to tradition, Manzanillo was the ancient capital of the Coliman people who apparently had some contact with the Orient, through Chinese and Malaccan traders, perhaps in the twelfth century or earlier. At the time of the first Spanish expeditions into the area the Indians called the town Tzalahua (place where cloth is stretched and dried). The Spanish twisted this into Salagua (salt water), a name which didn't stick. When Cortés first visited the settlement in 1526, he initiated the shipbuilding industry. These primitive beach-shipyards are still interesting to visit, though only fishing boats are shaped of the fine tropical hardwoods from the hinterland.

For the vacationer the chief attractions are the swimming (best beaches are at the far end of the bay around Santiago Peninsula — Playa de Santiago, Playa Audiencia. Coco, and Las Ventanas beaches have heavier surf); deep-sea fishing and skin-diving (fishing boats for rent or charter at the Yacht Club. Across the street from the club there is a supply shop that sells or rents both fishing and skin-diving equipment. Sailfish, manta ray, red snapper, marlin, and bonita are in abundance. Best fishing is from November through March, with sailfish *(pez vela)* running heaviest during November and December.

Best vacation season is between November and May. July and August are excessively hot.

EXCURSIONS FROM MANZANILLO: Going SE from Manzanillo on CN-110 there is a stretch of 27 m. along the ocean and *Laguna de Cuyutlán* that is one of the most beautiful jungle and coconut forest drives in the world.[1] At the S end of the long lagoon (turn r. off highway) is *Cuyutlán* (4 m. from highway), a tiny, hidden-away beach resort noted for its Spring Festival, March 15 to May 1. There are a number of very modest, poorly furnished hotels — the *Marina*, the *San Rafael, Colima,* and others, all facing on the beach.

About 27 m. from Manzanillo, where the highway turns inland there is a paved turn-off, S leading 3 m. to *Tecoman,* a scarcely visited town of about 8000 inhabitants. Colimans use it as a kind of base for vacationing in this flower-garden area. There are three rather run-down hotels — *El Ceballo, El Gayatan,* and the *Costeño.* Budget vacationers can have fun here. About 6½ m. (paved road) is *Los Pascuales,* a paradise-like beach village at the mouth of the Armeria River. Excellent swimming. 14 m. farther south of Tecoman via part paved, part dirt road, lies another bathing and fishing haven, *Boca de Apiza,* at the mouth of the Río Apiza which divides Colima from Michoacán.

Colima, Col. Pop. 28,658. Alt. 1538 ft. Capital of the State of Colima (koh-LEE-mah), on the slope of a fertile valley amply watered by the Colima and Manrique Rivers. The town, it is said, was founded in the eleventh century and was called Cajitlán (Aztec for, place where pottery is made). The town is noteworthy for its large number of simple, nonecclesiastical colonial buildings; its quiet atmosphere and its exuberant gardens. Towering above the city, forming a striking contrast with the pretty plaza and the sub-tropical gardens are the snow-capped volcanoes, Colima and El Nevado. Of minor interest are the antique Palacio de Gobierno, facing the plaza, and the Cathedral with its twin towers and fine dome surmounted by a lantern pierced by wheel-windows.

DIRECTORY: No hotel recommended, but in an emergency, *Hotel Casino,* Portal Medellín 7 (it is pure old-fashioned *viajero*-style). The same applies to the restaurants around the plaza. Better is the *Motel Costeño,* on Jiquilpan road. 13 units, fair restaurant, bar. Rates: EP $50 MN up, dble. *Bank* — Banco Nacional de México, Av. Hidalgo 90. *Auto repairs* — Automotriz Colimense (Chrysler), Medellín 68; Automóviles de Colima (Ford), Hidalgo 67. *Bus line* — Tres Estrellas de Oro, Juárez 78 bis. Tel. 4-48.

Along the coast, about 38 m. NW of Manzanillo lies *Barra de Navidad, Jal.,* on Bahía Navidad. The place is tropically picturesque, has magnificent stretches of golden beach and is just beginning to develop as a tourist haven. A good new road reaches it from Manzanillo. *Hotel: Melaque Hotel,* at N end of the bay. New and pleasant, 55 rooms, bar, dining room, pool. Rates: AP $160 MN, dble.

On tiny Cuastecomate Bay, 5 m. N of Barra de Navidad, there is a pleasant hide-away — *Motel El Dorado,* new, 12 units, bar, dining, excellent fishing. Rates: AP $160 MN, dble. For reservations, telephone, Guadalajara — 4-44-21.

Much more delightful is TENACATITA, JAL. 18 m. NW of Barra de Navidad. This is one of those off-beat South Sea paradises. A magnificent curve of yellow beach at the head of sparkling Tenacatita Bay. There is no town, but an enterprising soul has put up Polynesian thatched huts which serve as cottages (screened-off baths open to the sky), no running water, but you have inner-spring beds standing on sand floors. Bring your own food.

Eventually the proposed coast road will continue on, up to TOMATLÁN, the Aztec village that originated our tomato, and it will continue on to Puerto Vallarta.

Puerto Vallarta, Jal. A remote, charming fishing village on Bahía de Banderas, one of the west coast's most beautiful bays. The town, climbing up the slopes of mountains that surround the bay is Mexico's nearest equivalent to a quiet Mediterranean village, even to the tourists who are beginning to discover it.

HOW TO GET THERE: Daily flights via CMA's DC-3s from Guadalajara, or by mail plane from Tepic. There is no railway, first-class bus or good road communication.

HOTELS AND RESTAURANTS: *Hotel Oceano.* Small, 10 room, but very nicely run hotel. The most satisfactory in town. Good dining room, delightful cocktail hour. Rates: AP $130 MN dble. *Hotel Tropicana,* across the river on Los Muertos Beach (the swimming beach). Good food, nicely run. Rates about the same as above. *Hotel Rosita,* the largest hotel and most poorly designed. It is perhaps unique in being one of the few hotels in Mexico where you can shave, take a shower and perform other morning necessities, all at the same time — and without moving an inch once you get into the bathrooms. Incidentally, the service is also poor. Rates: from $80 MN up. EP.

There are several fair to good restaurants. For breakfasts, try the *Flamingo,* on the beach near Hotel Tropicana. Food is quite good. In town, the American-run *Delmar* is the best. It also has a nice bar. *El Patio Restaurant,* Canadian managed, very good.

There are a number of apartments for rent in town. They range in price from $125 to $150 per month, including maid, utilities, etc.

[1] In 1959 much of this section of the coast was struck by a freakish and disastrous typhoon that sheered away vast sections of the forest land. Manzanillo and other beach towns were badly mauled, suffering great loss of life and property. The towns are rebuilding rapidly, but it may be some years before the arching palms that graced the roadsides return to their full glory.

THE VILLAGE AND ENVIRONS: From the *Malecón* or seaside promenade one can look westward over the bay and the Pacific Ocean, or eastward where the town with its red tiled-roof houses and cobbled streets cling to the hillsides. There are numerous fine sandy beaches, the best being to the N and S of the town. A favorite is *Los Muertos,* 1 m. S and across the river. There are bathhouses, dressing rooms, beach umbrellas for rent. The beach also comes equipped with boys who run along selling cooked fish on sticks.

Some fishing boats are available for deep-sea fishing. A new sport-fishing fleet of de luxe, 32-foot, 22-knot per hour cruisers, equipped with ship to shore radio, has recently begun operation. The fleet is run by a firm called Flota Bahía Banderas. Rates are $625 MN per day, including tackle and bait for a party up to 6 persons. Sailfish and marlin are caught the year-round. Tuna and rooster fish run during the dry season.

There is excellent hunting — quail, duck, deer, and some mountain cats — in the country behind the port.

Among the few excursions one can make from Puerto Vallarta is the boat trip to *Yelapa, Jal.,* a tiny Indian village along the coast that is Mexico's nearest approximation to the storied Manga Reva in the South Sea Islands. Enroute one passes Los Arcos, some unusual water-eroded rock formations in Banderas Bay. Yelapa is an escapist's dream — a white tropical beach, palm-thatched village, a vivid jungle backdrop, and the sound of the sea. It even has a small thoroughly enjoyable rustic hotel, *Hotel Lagunita.* You live in grass huts with sand floors (there are good inner-spring beds), and there is a big central, thatched-roof, open-air dining room right by the sea. Rates: $60 MN single, AP. The food, fresh from the sea, is excellent. Nearby are some interesting waterfalls.

THE MICHOACÁN COUNTRY

If one were limited to visiting only one state in Mexico, and one wanted to say he had seen the country's most beautiful civil and ecclesiastical colonial architecture, the most beautiful countryside, the most fascinating regional dances, the best native crafts, the most fabulous Indian market, one of the finest of hotel spas, then one would choose the State of Michoacán.[2] It has the most of everything that is natural and wonderful, concentrated in the smallest space.

The most fascinating part of the state is the remarkably beautiful area extending from the city of Morelia, through Pátzuaro to Uruapan, much of it flanking the West Coast Highway, CN-15. It is called "the Mexican Switzerland," a land of forest-covered mountains, of intimate lakes and endlessly picturesque villages. This is the heart land of the Tarascan Indians. Living in a world of their own, of isolated lakes and brooding mountains, they were never completely dominated by either the Aztecs, the Spanish, or the influences of our modern civilization. The Tarascans are still an Indian people, many of them living and working today much as they must have lived hundreds of years ago. For a short or a long visit in their country the best accommodations are to be found in Morelia.

Morelia, Mich. Pop. 62,648. Alt. 6235. Capital of the State of Michoacán and the republic's most regal city.

HOW TO GET THERE: *Highways* — Morelia is on the West Coast Highway, CN-15, about 194 m. NW of Mexico City. From the Central Highway, CN-45, Morelia may be reached via the Salamanca-Morelia road (see Index). *Via bus* — Tres Estrellas de Oro (from Nogales, Guadalajara or Mexico City); or, Corsarios del Bajío (from San Luis Potosí or Mexico City). *Via railway* — Ferrocarriles Nacionales de México (Mexico City-Uruapan line). Two express trains daily, the Pullman leaving Mexico City at 9:30 P.M., arriving at 6:15 A.M.; the day express leaving at 7 A.M., arriving at 4:45 P.M. Aerovías del Sur flies DC-3 between Morelia and Mexico City. Office in Mexico City at Luis Moya 115-A, Tel. 21-24-69. In Morelia at Hotel Alameda.

HOTELS AND RESTAURANTS: *Villa Montaña,* 2 m. S of center in the *Santa María Hills* overlooking city. A small, de luxe garden retreat (14 suites), beautifully situated. It is the best small hotel in the entire country, comparable to some of the fine villas and country hotels in Europe. Excellent cuisine, cocktail service, bungalow suites, a pool-with-a-view. The owner, Sr. Raymond Cote, is a skilled chef, a cultured raconteur and Morelia-fan who makes you feel like an old, favored friend. Rates: $225 MN dble., AP, lower rates when you remain more than one day. Well worth it. Reservations advised; write % Villa Montaña, Apartado 233, Morelia, Mich.

Hotel de La Soledad, 1 block N of the plaza at Zaragoza and Melchor Ocampo. A new and most tastefully decorated hotel in an historic colonial building. Magnificent patio and cloisters, 30 comfortable rooms, excellent and very friendly service and atmosphere. Rates: EP from $50 MN to $90 MN dble. Tel. 18-88. 30 rooms. *Hotel Virrey de Mendoza,* center, on Plaza. An older, colonial-style hotel. Fair dining room, bar. 54 units. There is a very lovely *mirador* offering a fine view of the plaza and cathedral. Rates: EP $45 MN to $90 MN, dble. Tel. 633. *Hotel Alameda,* across the street from the *Virrey* and owned by the same chain. 30 units, café serving breakfast and lunch. Rates: EP $70 MN dble. Tel. 23. *Villa San José,* in the Santa María Hills, opposite the *Villa Montaña.* Attractive gardens and cottage units (15). Cocktail service. Dining room with lovely view of city. Rates: AP $140 to $190 MN dble.

DIRECTORY: *Banks* — Banco Nacional de México, Portal Aldama 157; Banco de Comercio de Michoacán, Allende 29. *Car repairs* — Morelia Automotriz (Ford), Madero Ote. 766; Motores de Morelia (GM), Madero Pte. 994; Michoacán Motors (Chrysler), Galeana 171.

[2] State of Michoacán, with a population of 1,851,876, and an area of 23,474 sq. miles, is bounded on the north and west by the States of Colima and Jalisco, to the N by Guanajuato, to the E by the State of Mexico, and on the S and SW by Guerrero and the Pacific Ocean. The general character of the state is mountainous, with plains and valleys immensely rich in vegetation. The Sierra Madre Occidental range traverses the region from SE to NW while lateral ranges break the territory in almost every direction. The highest mountain is the Pico de Tancítaro (12,653 ft.) between the cities of Uruapan and Zamora. In this area, also, is the famed new volcano, Paricutín, now quiescent. Oddly, though Michoacán has a beautiful coastline, there are almost no communications with it and no developed seaside resorts.

The climate follows the same pattern as the other Central Western States — cool to cold in the mountains, temperate on the plains and hot in the southern tropic portions.

The Río Lerma and Río de las Balsas are the chief features of the river systems. The state is famed for its beautiful lakes, the most important being Chapala (shared with Jalisco), Lake Pátzcuaro, Lake Zinapécuaro, Lake Zirahuen, and Lake Cuitzeo.

The flora and fauna are similar to those of the Jalisco-Colima areas, with perhaps a more bountiful spread of highland pine forests. The state is primarily agricultural — staple cereals, tomatoes, melons, tropical fruits, coffee, and cattle. Next in importance is lumbering, and some mining.

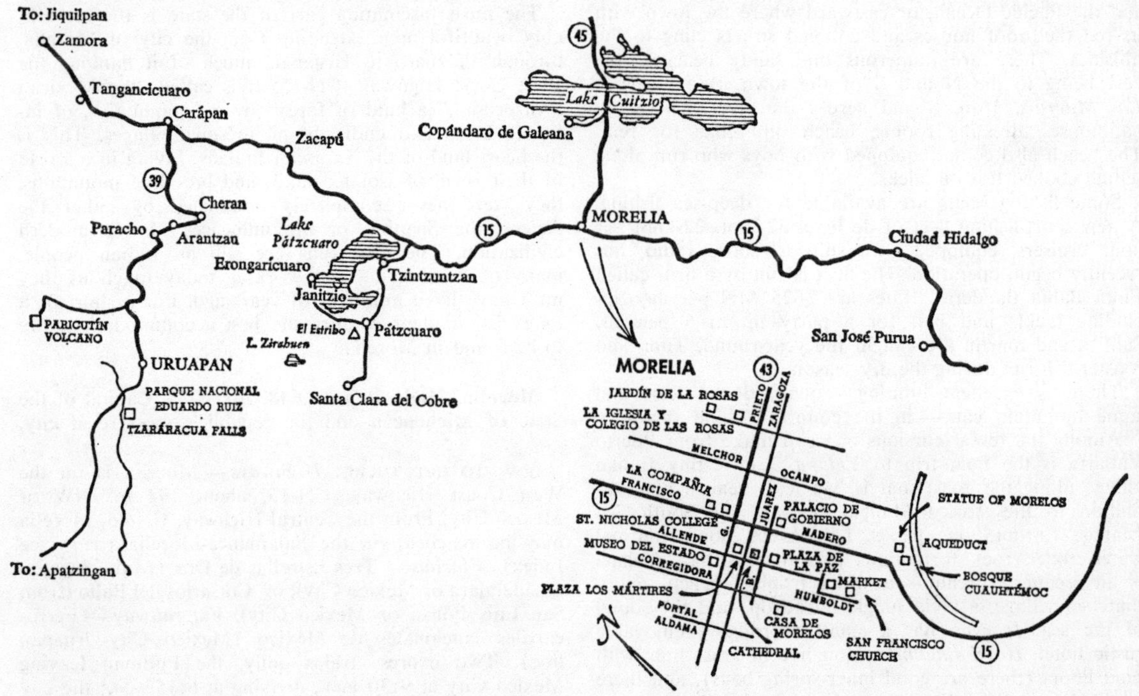

Bus lines — Tres Estrellas de Oro, Zaragoza 79, Tel. 11-86. *Railway tickets* — offices at the station. *Airline* — Lineas Aereas Picho (a bush line flying from Morelia to Uruapan and Puerta Azul). *Doctors and Hospital* — Sanitario de la Luz (Presbyterian). E side of town. Tel. 25. Dr. Ross is the director. *Instituto Cultural Mexican-norteamericano de Michoacán* (Cultural), Guillermo Prieto 86. *Taxis* — Taxicab rates in the city are $4 MN anywhere in town or to the aqueducts; $8 MN to Santa María Hills; $12 MN per hour.

THE CITY AND ENVIRONS: Morelia (moh-REH-lyah), situated in the view-rich *Valley of Guayangaro,* was founded in 1541 by Spain's first viceroy in Mexico, Don Antonio de Mendoza, who named it Valladolid after his home town in Spain. The city is celebrated as the birthplace of the revolutionary patriot, José María Morelos y Pavon, in whose memory a legislative decree of September 12, 1828, gave the place its present name.

Morelia has maintained its enviable position over the centuries as the most aristocratic of all Mexican cities. Its history is as vivid as a rich Gobelin tapestry; its physiognomy, as intriguing as a small Paris. Every approach offers bewitching views. The entrance from the E is along a great eighteenth-century masonry aqueduct of more than 250 superb arches. The approach from the N is remindful of such Spanish cities as Toledo and Granada. The entire city has a delightful Old World patina, and to maintain these charms ordinances require that all new constructions conform to the colonial style.

Plaza de los Mártires, the center of the city, is a splendid tree-shaded square with a handsome bandstand where an unusually good concert band plays on Sunday evenings and holidays. Most of the city's architecturally fine public and educational buildings are within a few blocks radius of the plaza. Flanking the plaza on the south, west, and north are splendid portales. On the E is the *Cathedral,* the queen of Morelia's many treasures, and considered the most beautiful of all the cathedrals of Mexico. Although it took over a century to build (1640–1744) it has a singular unity of style, and was not in the least affected by the severe High Renaissance nor the busy Baroque touching other cathedrals. It is pure Plateresque. It is constructed of a warm pinkish-brown trachyte. Its proportions, particularly of the towers, are magnificent, expressing power and majesty, yet showing a striking delicacy of line — low-relief ornament concentrated in the customary Spanish manner between the broad and massive tower bases, about the transept portals and upon the exquisitely graceful towers. A stone-flagged atrium extends across the front and along two sides of the building, enclosed by a latter-date iron fence.

The once celebrated massive silver communion railing and other valuable ornaments were confiscated in 1858 when the church refused to pay a war contribution of $100,000. Though the interior was redecorated in 1899 in a comparatively modern style, the design remained harmonious and simple, combining soft colors of brown and gold. Unlike most Mexican cathedrals, the nave is uninterrupted and filled with seats, permitting an uninterrupted view of the magnificent proportions within. Noteworthy is the finely carved wood organ case, with gilded pipes, above the main entrance. Over the *coro* and in the sacristy there are a number of interesting paintings, some by J. Rodríguez Juárez, Ibarra, and Cabrera.

To the E of the cathedral is a smaller plaza called the Plaza de la Paz. Across the palm-lined boulevard (Av. Madero) from the park and cathedral is the *Palacio de Gobierno* (State Capitol), a handsome example of early colonial architecture. In the entranceway is a plaque quaintly proclaiming the altitude of Morelia, and the temperature as of May 1902. Entering the patio one finds murals decorating the right stairway walls. These are by Alfred Zalche, a native Morelense and one of Mexico's top-ranking artists.

Museo del Estado (State Museum) on Calle Allende

a few steps from the SW corner of the main plaza. The museum is housed in a lovely eighteenth-century palace. The central stairway (facing entrance) has a mural by Zalche, while on the opposite balcony (second floor) is an interesting mural by Cantú of the Four Horsemen of the Apocalypse. The street floor of the museum has several rooms containing excellently displayed and important archaeological treasures from the Michoacán region as well as other parts of the country. There is also an art gallery on this floor. Upstairs there are exhibits of colonial religious paintings, colonial furniture, a gallery of nineteenth-century painting and a Salon de Armas (Museum of Weapons). *Hours:* 9 A.M. to 1 P.M.; 4 to 6 P.M. *Admission:* 2 pesos.

Casa de Morelos, (home of the patriot, Morelos) at corner of Iturbide and Morelos. The building was purchased by Morelos after he achieved prominence. It is an interesting example of domestic colonial architecture. Now a museum, it contains many of Morelos' personal effects, old manuscripts, the eye blindfold he wore when executed, a camp bed used by Allende. In the courtyard are two interesting carriages (formerly in the state museum). One, popularly called "the stove" was used to carry the Holy Host on sick calls. The other belonged to a Morelense gay blade, Francisco Velarde, who had his carriage elaborately furnished and decorated with solid-gold-headed tacks. *Hours:* 9 A.M. to 1 P.M.; 4 to 6 P.M. *Admission:* 2 pesos.[3]

A block W of the plaza and just N of Av. Madero is an imposing and historically important group of buildings. One is the *Colegio Primitivo y Nacional de San Nicholás de Hidalgo* (St. Nicholas College) founded originally in Pátzcuaro in 1540 by Bishop Vasco de Quiroga. It is the oldest collegiate relic in Mexico. The only earlier educational institution was that of Santa Cruz Tlatelalco, founded in Mexico City by Bishop Zumárraga in 1537, for the higher education of the sons of Aztec nobles. San Nicholás was moved to Morelia in 1580. The patriot-priest Miguel Hidalgo y Costilla studied and taught philosophy there, and José María Morelos was one of his pupils. Agustín de Iturbide likewise studied there. The present-day Universidad de Michoacán is an outgrowth of San Nicholás, and occupies some of the original building.

Across the street, occupying what was formerly a Jesuit church and monastery, *La Compañia* (of which only the original tower remains) is the imposing *State Library* and *Industrial School.* This massive and imposing structure dates from 1681. Two blocks to the N, facing the picturesque Jardín de las Rosas, a favorite spot where the university students study, is *La Iglesia y Colegio de las Rosas* (Church and College of the Roses). The church has a double entrance with particularly fine Plateresque stone carving over the portal. To the right there are handsome second-floor *loggias.* Las Rosas is the oldest music school on the continent. Originally it was founded to teach liturgical music. At present its Escuela de Musica Sagrada de las Rosas (School of Sacred Music) is the home of the internationally famed Children's Choir of Morelia (Niños Cantores de Morelia) who have sung in Rome, as well as at Carnegie Hall. Their present director is Sr. Luis Verver. Visitors in Morelia can often hear their concerts and attend rehearsals at Las Rosas.

Morelia's *Municipal Market,* in the neighborhood of the *San Francisco Church* (one of the three oldest in Mexico), is a pleasant market to browse through. Thursdays and Sundays are the best days. At the E end of Av. Madero there is a small plaza with a horrible monument (Indians and fruit). Just beyond is the magnificent aqueduct that was begun in 1785 to bring potable water into the town. The vast construction extends more than a mile and many of the arches stand about 30 ft. high. Going through the massive arches, at right-angle to Madero, one enters the *Calzada de Guadalupe,* a stone causeway 400 ft. long by about 40 ft. wide. This shaded promenade is a sort of Poet's Walk leading to the *Santuario de Guadalupe,* a curious church, almost Arabic in style, and seems to be all gold-leaf gingerbread. The façade is classical with semi-Moorish minarets. On the cupola of the tower there are interesting Indian rubbings. In the side chapel there is an unusually large collection of retablos and ex-voto figures. On the N side of the church is the tiny *Parque Azteca* containing some old Indian monoliths. Nearby is the *Escuela Simon Bolívar,* an impressive up-to-date grammar school. In the park-promenade fronting the church, and to S there stands a fine bronze equestrian *Statue of Morelos.* S of the statue, on the other side of the aqueduct, is an extensive parklike woods called the *Bosque Cuauhtémoc,* a restful retreat and favorite Sunday promenade for the Morelense families.

Santa María de Guido. A tiny picturesque village on the heights (Santa María Hills) just S of the city. It is about ½ mile up the hill, paved road, from the hotel Villa Montaña. The views from here are magnificent. The village is widely noted for its fine woodcarving center; the workshops are worth visiting. The water supply for the city now comes from this area rather than via the aqueducts.

FIESTAS AND ART CRAFTS: In Morelia there are several good shops selling the delicate embroidery, the hand-loomed *rebozos,* the woodcarving, pottery, and lacquerware for which the Michoacán region is famed. Woodcarving, pottery, and serapes can also be found in the market. The city is also celebrated for a fruit candy called *ates,* made locally and sold in the shops and stands under the *portales.*

The principal city fiestas are: May 18, celebrating the founding of the city. There is a fair, dances, fireworks. On August 15 there is a very picturesque celebration *(Romería)* in Santa María. The most important fiesta date is September 30, anniversary of the birth of Morelos.

EXCURSIONS TO EAST OF MORELIA: Along the highway (CN-15) going toward Mexico City one views some of the most magnificent scenery in the country. At *Ciudad Hidalgo, Mich.* Pop. 10,000. Alt. 8175 (63 m. from Morelia) there is an interesting sixteenth-century Franciscan church with a notable sculptured arched doorway. The church has a huge monolithic font covered with Tarascan relief carving. It was used in pagan religious rites when the town was an important Tarascan city, known as Tajimaroa. The font is now used for Christian baptisms.

San José Purua, Mich. (sahn hoe-SEH poo-ROO-ah) One of the two or three most celebrated mineral water spas in Mexico. About 81 m. E of Morelia; 113 m. from Mexico City. The hot springs are ¼ mile of CN-15. Transportation to San José Purua: Tres Estrella de Oro

[3] Misinformed guides frequently tell that Morelos was born in this house. The liberator was actually born under rather inconvenient and sudden circumstances, in the entranceway of a house his mother happened to be passing. The house is near the San Agustín Church, and there is an appropriate plaque on the wall.

The city is filled with illustrious birthplaces as well as residences once occupied by the famous. There is a house on Calle Iturbide where Agustín de Iturbide, liberator and onetime Emperor of Mexico, was born in 1783; the house where patriot Melchor Ocampo lived, another where Padre Hidalgo lived, and the residence of Archduke Maximilian, corner of Aldama and Matamoros.

buses, private car, or transportation service maintained from Mexico City by the *Hotel Balneario San José Purua.* The hotel, 193 units, is beautifully poised on the brink of a canyon, has elaborate gardens, several large pools, thermal baths, a handsome-view dining room with good food, night club, billiards, bowling, horseback riding. Tel. Mexico City 46-50-48. Rates: AP $260 MN dble. It is a very pleasant, restful place.

OTHER HOTELS: Agua Caliente, 25 rooms, fair, and less expensive. *Rancho Agua Blanco,* on the highway, just west of the San José turn-off. 20 rooms, nice surroundings. Modest rates.

AREA WEST OF MORELIA — PÁTZCUARO-URUAPAN SECTIONS: This region is one of the most beautiful in Mexico. Its picturesque lakes need only a red pagoda, a Shinto shrine, or its accompanying *torii* reflected in their pellucid waters to remind one of hill-girt Chuzenji, the charmingly poetic Lake Biwa, or the lovely lake around Fujisan in Japan. Even the houses in villages such as Pátzcuaro, with their low tiled roofs and widely projecting eaves are exotically Oriental in appearance.

Formerly the center of the Tarascan Indian empire, it still remains one of the most Indian of Mexico's regions, the descendants of the early Tarascans preserving many of the old traditions, arts and folklore.

THE PEOPLE AND THEIR HISTORY: The origin of the Tarascos (Tarascans, Purapecha Indians) is still shrouded in mystery. It is believed that they were descendants of an archaic civilization (see Index). At the time of the conquest they were an isolated, but highly cultured people, with their capital at Tzintzuntzan on the edge of Lake Pátzcuaro. According to their own legends they were ordered by hummingbirds to erect their city at this spot. The birds, of course, were spokesmen for the gods.[4]

When the Tarascans learned that Tenochtitlán had fallen, they sent ambassadors to the Spaniards (perhaps considering them allies since they too had continually fought off thc Aztecs). Cortés immediately dispatched Cristóbal de Olid to the Michoacán country. The expedition was ruthless in its destruction of Tarascan temples, idols, and in the plundering of the villages. (It is said, against Cortés' orders.) A group of Franciscan missionaries followed, and strove with difficulty to right the wrongs committed on the people. They almost succeeded when Nuño de Guzmán, recently deposed as president of the first *Audiencia,* and in search of further conquests, invaded the Michoacán area, doing even greater damage than Olid. He tortured the Tarascan chief, Calzontzin, and had him burned to death over a slow fire. Terrified by the barbarousness of the Spaniards the Indians fled to their mountains, and to this day have never regained complete trust in foreigners. Their eventual, though still distrustful, conversion to Christianity was the work of a most remarkable man, Don Vasco de Quiroga, whose name and memory is intimately woven in the fabric of Tarascan life.

Don Vasco, an eminent lawyer in New Spain, had opposed the rapaciousness of his countrymen, and had attracted the attention of Charles V, who selected him to redeem as far as possible the cruelties inflicted upon the Tarascans. Because the Church had extraordinary powers, Don Vasco took Holy Orders (rather late in life) and was quickly raised through successive grades to that of bishop. In 1538, at the age of 68, he made the difficult journey to his bishopric, the church of San Francisco at Tzintzuntzan. His limitless patience and devotion and his somewhat liberal communal ideas gained the confidence of the Indians to such an extent that the memory of *Tata* (our father) Vasco is still fresh in the hearts of the people today.

[4] The tiny scintilating hummingbirds, plentiful in this region, have played a fascinating role in Tarascan life. There is a Tarascan tradition that Tezpi (their Noah), escaped from the great flood in a boat filled with various kinds of animals and birds. After some time, a vulture was sent out, but remained feeding on the dead bodies of giants who had then inhabited the earth. A little later a hummingbird *(huitzitzilin)* was sent out to see if the flood waters had subsided. It returned with a symbolic twig in its beak. The coincidence with the Hebrew and Chaldean narratives is obvious.

Conspicuous and unique, also, was the Tarascan art of making beautiful pictures and ceremonial robes by cunningly attaching the resplendent plummage of hummingbirds to a fabric made of maguey fiber (see Index). According to Prescott, "The *Conquistadores* were amazed to find that many of these pictures represented a supernatural Virgin, to which the Purapecha legends refer."

Even today, in the village of *Paracho* (see Index), the women weave a fringe on their rebozos, made of silk or rayon, overlayed in short, vivid strands, so as to appear like hummingbird feathers.

Pátzcuaro, Mich. Pop. 12,000. Alt. 7180. One of Mexico's most picturesque towns, typically sixteenth century in atmosphere and architecture. Home of one of the republic's two most famed and colorful outdoor Indian markets. 41 m. SW of Morelia.

HOW TO GET THERE: *Highway* — turn S off the West Coast Highway, CN-15, at *Quiroga.* Paved, CN-41 leads 14 m. to Pátzcuaro, passing Tzintzuntzan and other picturesque villages on the way. *Via bus* — Autobuses Tres Estrellas de Oro (from Mexico City, Morelia or Guadalajara). *Via railway* — the Mexico City-Uruapan line of the Ferrocarriles Nacionales de México.

HOTELS AND RESTAURANTS: In various ways the hotels of Pátzcuaro leave something to be desired. Best available is the *Posada de Don Vasco,* 1¼ m. N on Av. de las Américas (CN-41). Old, colonial-style inn, 55 large, comfortably furnished rooms, fair dining room, casino, bowling, billiards, poor cocktail lounge arrangements. Well established and nicely located, this could be an excellent hotel. Rates: AP $125 to $170 MN dble. Tel. 27. Reservations suggested Thursdays and Fridays. *Motel Albergue Toliman,* across the road from the *Don Vasco* and under the same management. 19 units. Rates: EP from $70 MN dble. *Hotel Posada la Basilica,* Arciga 6 (in town). Nicely situated on a picturesque plaza. Lovely view of town and lake from the patio. 10 rooms, fair, but not too well kept. In sunny, warm weather the hotel can be quite pleasant; in cold wet weather it is dreary. Rates: EP $35 MN and up, dble. Tel. 108. *Hotel Dolatri,* Plaza Gertrudis Bocanegra 6. A *viajero*-style hotel, very modest. Inside rooms too cramped. Rates: EP $35 MN up dble. Tel. 1-43. *Restaurant El Gordo,* 1 block below railway station on road to boat docks. Very rustic, but serves excellent Pátzcuaro whitefish. Hours: 9 A.M. to 9 P.M.

DIRECTORY: *Bus line* — Tres Estrellas de Oro terminal, Hotel Doltari. *Railway tickets* — at station, 1½ m. N. *Arts and crafts shops* — the two best shops handling regional crafts, especially Tarascan weaving, embroidery, lacquerwork, jewelry, etc., are: *Vicki,* on Av. de las Americas (no number); and, *Casa Cerda,* Dr. Coss 15.

THE TOWN: Pátzcuaro (PAHTZ-kwah-ro — from Tarascan, "Place of Delights") was built in the early sixteenth century on the site of an ancient Tarascan city. It is located on the slopes of a small range of hills which overlook the lake of the same name. The narrow cobbled streets, the houses with their curious projecting roofs and carved beams makes the town one of the quaintest and most venerable appearing in all Mexico. The heart of the town is its two plazas — the *Plaza Chica* (tiny plaza) seen first on entering the village, and a block away, the *Plaza Grande* or *Plaza Principal.* Each of the plazas is surrounded by hoary *portales. La Biblioteca Publica* (Public Library) housed in a former Augustinian church, N end of *Plaza Chica,* is noteworthy for its large interior mural executed by artist-architect Juan O'Gorman. It is one of the artist's best works. The thematic material is the history of the region.

Plaza Grande, 1 block S. This gigantic square, covering almost two city blocks, filled with towering century-old ash trees and surrounded by crouched-down public buildings (jail, city hall) and arched *portales,* is one of the loveliest plazas in the country. On a bright day it is spattered with shade and speckled sunlight, it is touched by a melancholic atmosphere reflecting a culture encircled by forests. On Friday mornings this and the smaller plaza become the center of one of the greatest and most colorful Indian open-air markets *(tianguis)* in the Western world. Early in the morning Indians from the hill and lake villages stream toward the town, their burros and canoes piled high with produce and craft goods which are spread out beneath the trees of the plaza. Here you rub shoulders with a completely Indian world — Tarascan women wearing their traditional costume, a curious twenty-pound skirt made of yards and yards of rich homespun wool; it has so many pleats gathered up in the back and draped over a woven belt, fanwise, it resembles a huge, soft accordion. The women wear their distinctive jewelry, a hand-hammered or filigree silver cross suspended from a rosary necklace fashioned of hollow silver balls and red European beads. From morning to midafternoon both the large plaza and the smaller (pottery and woodcarving) vibrate with gentle movements, the hum of soft, liquid Tarascan voices and the harsher tones of commerce.

Museum of Popular Arts and Crafts (Museo del Arte Popular) 1 block E of the large plaza. Housed in the venerable building where Bishop Quiroga originally founded the famous College of San Nicholás, later moved to Morelia, this tiny museum is utterly charming. It contains exquisite examples of the all-but-vanished excellent crafts of the region, a colonial kitchen and dining room, a lovely patio. *Hours:* 9 A.M. to 1 P.M., 3 to 5 P.M. *Admission:* 2 pesos.

About 1½ blocks above (E) of the Plaza Chica is a vast and picturesque plaza in which stands the most historical and interesting of Pátzcuaro's ancient buildings — the *Colegiata.* In 1540 a Papal bull sanctioned the erection of a cathedral in Pátzcuaro to accommodate the bishopric moved from Tzintzuntzan. The structure was conceived along colossal lines, including a tremendous dome, never built. Only part of the nave was erected. A severe earthquake damaged this, and fearing recurrence, the bishopric was again moved, this time to Valladolid (Morelia). The brownstone façade with its huge wheel-window and niches containing life-size figures of the apostles is comparatively recent. The unfinished tower imparts a crippled and odd appearance. On the main altar is a much venerated image of Nuestra Señora de la Salud (Our Lady of Health), believed to have been found floating in a canoe on the lake. The image is the magnet attracting many pilgrimages, for it is believed to be miraculous. The Indians claim the Virgin is "not like a virgin at all; she is dark, like a real person, and perspires." Due to the homely Virgin the church was raised to the category of a *Colegiata* by Papal edict in 1907.

A short walk to the S is the old *Church of La Compañia de Jesús,* built by Quiroga in 1546. In a small chapel behind the main altar is an urn locked in a modern steel safe, with Bishop Quiroga's name on it. It contains his ashes.

El Estribo (Stirrup Peak) 2 m. SW of plaza. A pleasant picnic spot offering magnificent views of the town, the lake and surrounding villages. The road to it is cobbled.

C.R.E.F.A.L. North, just off of Av. de las Américas, opposite the railway station. An interesting UNESCO-sponsored center for training Latin American rural educators. Pronounced, cray-FAL, the center is housed in the former residence of ex-President Cárdenas, who donated the property to the project. Visitors welcomed.

THE LAKE AND LAKE VILLAGES: **Lake Pátzcuaro,** 6717 ft. above sea level, is an irregular shaped body of fresh water about 13 m. long from N to E and about 30 m. in circumference. The shores are studded with Tarascan villages, 15 or more standing directly on the beaches. There are a number of small islands, chief among them are Janitzio, Jaracuaro, Pacanda and Tecuen. The inhabitants of these exaggerated cameos on a grayish-green sea live much to themselves, disliking and mistrusting their neighbors. Many of them live today as they did hundreds of years ago. They paddle about the lake in dugouts, propelling them with paddles that look like large lollipops, and they fish with peculiar, graceful "butterfly" nets native to the area. When hunting for ducks they still use the *atlatl,* a triple-pointed throwing stick or lance and a launching sheath which has two holes for the fingers and a grove for the spear shaft. In preparation for the important Day of the Dead Fiesta there is held a huge ceremonial duck hunt, the *kuirisi-ataku,* in which as many as 50 to 100 dugouts with three to four hunters in each is involved. It is an incredible sight to witness this early-morning, primitive spearing of ducks.

The principal product of the lake is a delicious, small, almost transparent white fish *(pescado blanco).*

There are regular passenger launches and hire-launches for making trips to the islands and nearby lake villages. The official boat rates set by the government are: Round trip to Janitzio Island, large launches with fixed motors (1 hour stop on island), $25 MN per launch. Extra large launch, to Janitzio, $30 MN, round trip. For the same, but with a stop to see and photograph the "butterfly net" fishermen, $5 MN extra. (The fishermen are waiting. They expect a tip, from $5 to $15 MN, depending on number of passengers ogling them, and photos taken.) Launches with fixed motors, $12 MN per hour (minimum hire, 2 hours). Larger launches $15 per hour. There are 35 "fixed motor" boats, and 5 outboard motorboats available on the lake for recreational purposes. If you have problems over fees, etc., contact Sr. Felíx Guerra Lara, Captain of the Port.

Janitzio, Mich., on the Isla de Janitzio, the most important of the lake islands. The village is picturesquely Mediterranean, fishnets drying in the sun, quaint tiled-roof houses climbing up the steep hillside. On the crest of the island (footpath up to it) is the gigantic statue of Morelos designed by Guillermo Ruíz. The concrete-covered-with-stone figure, taller than the Statue of Liberty, is heavy, squat, and ugly.[5] Within the statue there is an arduous winding stairway leading up to the head where

[5] One architectural authority, commenting on the colossal statue and its lack of artistic merit, said; "Due to the location of the colossal monument, at the top of a steep hill, on a small island in the middle of the lake, its construction presented many difficulties. Unfortunately, they were not insurmountable."

one is afforded a fine view of lake region. The stairway walls contain 50 murals portraying the life of Father Morelos. In the head of the statue is a death mask of the patriot priest. *Hours:* daylight hours. *Admission:* 50 centavos.

Janitzio is the site of one of Mexico's most unusual and impressive semipagan, Christian fiestas, the Day of the Dead ceremonies held November 2, in the village graveyard. Called *"animecha-kejtsitaku"* in Tarascan, this impressive fete involves the entire town. Toward midnight the villagers, garbed in their best, gather in the cemetery where tablecloths and napkins and masses of flowers are spread upon the graves and specially prepared repasts for the dead are set forth. There are countless candles flickering — so many that the place is fantastically lighted, as a stage. Around each grave there are also small crosses, figures molded of sugar, angels, and sugar skulls. There is an amazing quiet and solemnity about the place as the families of men, women, and children sit waiting for the dead to reappear and eat. Throughout the night a bell tolls mutedly. In addition to the offerings on the individual graves there is a large arch fashioned of flowers, corn, and the fruit from the region. This is dedicated to those departed souls who no longer have living families to make offerings to them. Songs, the marvelously melodic and melancholy music of the Tarascans, are also heard.

Erongarícuaro, Mich. A tiny, unusually pretty Tarascan village on the far side of the lake. Reachable by a rough gravel and rock road. Erongarícuaro (air-on-gah-REE-qua-roh) has a large, grass-grown, tree-shaded plaza surrounded by one-story buildings lined on the front with colonnades of wooden posts with carved post caps. Sunday market is fascinating. There is a fine old Augustinian church set in a spacious, melancholy, treed atrium surrounded by a high wall. Within is a beautiful wrought-iron cross (of modern design) in the atrium, and in the side open chapel or baptistry an unusual mural, Medieval French in design, and totally strange in Mexico. The work was done by Michel Cardoret, a former resident in the town, and was financed by the French colony in Mexico City and some Houston, Texas, art patrons. Erongarícuaro is the center of some of the finest cambric *(cambaya)* hand-loomed fabrics in Mexico, and also exceptional native embroidery. These are produced by the Elena Gordon looms, and by the Vicki Shop.

Tzintzuntzan, Mich. Pop. 1336. The lake region's most historic town, situated at the N end of the lake, on CN-41. Tzintzuntzan (tsin-SOON-sahn, meaning "hummingbird" in Tarascan) was the ancient Tarascan capital until the conquest, and once had a population estimated at 40,000. There is an archaeological site ½ m. above the town: five T-shaped, truncated pyramidal structures called *yacatas,* running from E to W on the crest of a low ridge. Many years ago an unusual pre-Columbian sculptured figure called Jhuatzio, resembling the Toltec and Mayan Chac-Mools, was taken from here. The so-called museum at the *yacatas* may be skipped. It has nothing and is simply a racket run by the caretaker to sell *ídolos.*

Worth seeing is the picturesque parish church in the town. It was Bishop Quiroga's original headquarters. The church has a splendid Plateresque entrance, and it faces on a huge atrium filled with gnarled olive trees planted by Don Vasco. A recent fire in the church, fortunately or unfortunately, destroyed a celebrated painting attributed to Titian, Cabrera, or Ibarra, thus effectively ending an art controversy that had gone on bitterly for many years.

Tzintzuntzan is noted for its primitively decorated pottery, a limited amount of hand-loomed fabrics, reed weaving, and tropical-type furniture produced by the villagers.

FIESTAS: Tzintzuntzan celebrates several important and unusual fiestas. From February 1 to 7, Fiesta de Cristo Rey, also called Señor del Rescate. Fair, regional dances, etc. On February 22, a pottery fair, including folk dances, "Los Viejitos" (see Index). During Holy Week the church and atrium become the setting for one of the country's most interesting Passion Plays.

Santa Clara del Cobre, Mich. Pop. 3000. Alt. 7100 (also called *Villa Escalante*). About 20 minutes drive S of Pátzcuaro on CE-120, paved. A quaint Tarascan upland village where a large part of the population is involved in producing hand-hammered copperware. The craft was introduced by Bishop Quiroga in the sixteenth century.

Lake Zirahuen, Mich. A jeep trail goes the 14 m. from Santa Clara to within a short distance of the lake. May also be reached from Pátzcuaro via the Mexico City-Uruapan line of the National Railways. Flag stop near the lake is *Copándaro de Galeana.* The lake, with its surface colorings almost like opals and sapphires, has been hailed by travel writers as the most beautiful in the world, another Lake Como or Japanese Chuzenji. Unfortunately these opinions were based on glimpses of the lake from a train window. The lake is pretty, a lovely place to camp by, but there being no tourist accommodations anywhere, it does not warrant breaking one's neck to reach.

Uruapan, Mich. Pop. 35,000. Alt. 5500 ft. One of Mexico's loveliest and least visited semitropical cities, situated in beautiful wooded country, noted for its lacquerware crafts.

HOW TO GET THERE: *Highway* — turn off West Coast Highway, CN-15, at Carápan, follow CN-39, the 49 m. S to Uruapan. This is a beautiful drive. *Via bus* — Autotransportes Tres Estrellas de Oro from Mexico City, Morelia, or Guadalajara. *Via railway* — Mexico City-Uruapan line of the Ferrocarriles Nacionales de México. Night Pullman leaves Mexico City 9:30 P.M., arrives at 10:10 A.M. Day express leaves at 7 A.M., arrives 8:20 P.M.

HOTELS AND RESTAURANTS: Being off the beaten tourist routes Uruapan never developed elaborate vacation accommodations. There are several, modest, comfortable hotels, *Casa Maravillas,* Morelos 7, 1 block from plaza. A family-run colonial inn, very pleasant atmosphere, extremely clean. Dining room serves quite good food. 8 rooms. Rates, EP $40 MN dble. Tel. 218. *Hotel Mi Solar,* 22 rooms, fairly nice, dining room variable. Rates: $40 MN dble. Tel. 323.

DIRECTORY: *Bank* — Banco Nacional de México, Av. Cupatitzio 17. *Car repairs* — Jiménez (Ford), Av. Juárez and Cupatitzio; Automóviles y Camiones de Uruapan (GM), Cupatitzio (no number). *Bus lines* — Tres Estrellas de Oro, Hotel Progreso, 5 de Febrero 15. Tel. 110; Autobuses Galeana, Obregón 10 (Route: Lombardía, Nueva Italia, Apatzingán, etc).

THE CITY AND ENVIRONS: Uruapan (oo-roo-AH-pan, from the Tarascan *uraní*, gourd, or *urupán*, where flowers bloom), was founded in 1540 by the Franciscan friar Juan de San Miguel who named the settlement San Francisco Uruapan. Though the town has almost no exceptional architecture and little that is picturesque, nevertheless it is a beguiling place, noted for its beautiful parks, its paradise-like gardens and flower-flaming patios.

The city has three plazas strung in a row. The most attractive is the Jardín de los Martíres, at W with its monument commemorating military heroes. The middle square is the Plaza Principal; that at the E the Plaza Fray San Miguel.

La Guatapera, formerly a hospital and chapel, facing on the Plaza, is now one of the finest of Mexico's regional museums of popular arts and crafts. The building, with its lovely patio, is a gem of sixteenth-century architecture. Especially noteworthy is the lacelike carved front of the chapel.

A block behind the Guatapera are the streets which, on Sunday, become the city's meandering market. The pottery sections are unusually colorful and very extensive. At the N edge of town, off of Calzada la Quinta is the *Parque Nacional Eduardo Ruiz* (National Park), an extensive and unusually beautiful municipal woodland filled with tropical plants, bubbling and rushing streams, rustic bridges and pretty walks. At the entrance of the park there is a small Municipal Museum displaying and selling woodcarving, ceramics and the lacquerware for which Uruapan is celebrated.

Tzaráracua Falls, about 6 m. from town, paved road. The falls (tzah-RAH-rah-cwah) are among the most beautiful in Mexico, the waters gushing from a number of fissures around a natural stone amphitheatre, forming a kind of bridal-veil of water that drops some 90 ft. into a pool. It is a lovely picnic area.

Paracho, Mich. Pop. 5000. Alt. 6100 ft. On CN-39, about 35 minutes drive N of Uruapan. Paracho (pah-RAH-cho, Tarascan for "home of instrument makers"), lies at the foot of the extinct volcano *Cerro de Paracho.* The village is unique in that its men are largely occupied with woodcarving and guitar-making; they produce a large percentage of all the guitars, violins, and other stringed instruments sold in Mexico. The women weave handsome rebozos.

On August 8 the town celebrates a curious fiesta which seems to have no religious root. Girls in *China Poblana* costumes parade through the streets leading a bull fancily decorated with the ingredients for a special regional dish, *shuripo* — consisting of meat, several types of chili peppers, onions, and spices. There is dancing, then the animal is killed and becomes the main ingredient of the festive fare.

Parícutin (pah-REE-coo-teen — from the Tarascan meaning, "across the gorge") is a now somnolent volcano which came into history on Saturday, February 20, 1943, in the cornfield of an Indian named Dionisio Pulido. During its short and very explosive life Páricutin destroyed several villages and forced more than 5000 people to abandon their homes. Today much of the surrounding region is still blackened, but farmers are returning to rework the land. The volcano's base (more than a mile in diameter) sits squarely in the center of Don Dionisio's *ranchito.*

To get there drive N from Uruapan about 9 m. on CN-49, turn W off the highway. The volcano area is 15 m. farther on the branch road.

Along the highway N of Uruapan there are a number of interesting Tarascan villages, many of them noted for their regional crafts, and in some instances, their sixteenth-century churches. Among them: *Arantzan,* where rebozos are woven; *Cheran,* a well-preserved sixteenth-century church. On the West Coast Highway, CN-15, near the town of *Zacapú* (pop. 15,000), stand ruins of pre-Hispanic temples said to have been built by the Tecos Indians, who antedated the Tarascans. The parochial church in the town was begun by the Franciscans in 1540 and it has an exceptionally fine Plateresque arched entrance.

El Infiernillo, a new giant dam and enormous lake deep in the Balsas River basin, 110 m. S of Uruapan. This project, undertaken by the Mexican Electrification Commission in a region which less than a decade ago was unexplored and forbidding, includes the largest hydroelectric dam in Latin America (175 meters high), and will create the largest artificial lake in Mexico, (over 65 m. long). A new, gravel road, S from Uruapan through Nueva Italia, runs through spectacular country. Due to heavy traffic (equipment and provisions supplying the project) on the road, travelers must obtain special permits to visit the area. In 1965 this virgin region will be opened to tourism.

Lake Camecuaro, just N of *Tangancicuaro, Mich.,* off CN-15. Lake Camécuaro (kah-MAY-qwah-ro) is picturesquely surrounded by century-old, huge cypress trees. It is a charming picnic spot.

Zamora, Mich. Pop. 25,000. Alt. 5281. A busy commercial center on CN-14, about 132 m. SE of Guadalajara. Centered in a once important Chichimeca Indian region, the town was built as a Spanish stronghold. As a tourist stop it offers little of interest. There is a fair hotel, *Hotel Mendoza,* Morelos and Ocampo. Rates: EP $20 to $30 MN dble. The hotel café is also fair.

Jiquilpan, Mich., on CN-15, about 36 m. NW of Zamora. The turn-off for the Manzanillo Highway, *Jiquilpan* (hee-KEEL-pahn) has a picturesque plaza, was the birthplace of former president Lázaro Cárdenas. The library *(biblioteca),* in center of town, has some interesting murals by Orozco.

Puerto Azul, Mich. This is Michoacán's only Pacific Coast resort. As yet it is completely primitive and difficult to reach. Lineas Aereas Picho, a small state airline, flies there from Morelia and Uruapan. There is a rough road (not recommended) going south about 150 m. from Uruapan. The road is paved from Uruapan to Apatzingan (a rich agricultural center), some 51 m. Puerto Azul (also called Playa Azul) is situated along a striking coast of sea-cliffs and mountain ridges. The small village has several inns with rustic accommodations. There are fine beaches.

THE GUERRERO COUNTRY

Guerrero, southernmost of the central western group, has the singular honor of being one of the least explored and most poorly mapped of Mexican states, and yet is one of those few that is host to the bulk of foreign vacationers coming into the country. Though there is some mining and agriculture, the state's principal revenue comes from two tourist meccas — colonial Taxco, in the northern part of the state, and sophisticated Acapulco, in the south. Except for the superhighway joining these two centers, there are almost no roads or other towns worthy of mention. Large sections of the state, especially to the W of the highway, and to the SE are literally unexplored.

The state, with a population of over 1,186,716 and an area of 25,719 sq. miles is bounded on the N by Michoacán and the state of Mexico, on the NE Morelos, on the E by Puebla, to the E and SE by Oaxaca. To the S and W lies the Pacific Ocean. The physical country consists mainly of mountains and narrow valleys. The climate varies from tropical heat and torrents of summer rains to frosts in the higher northern and eastern altitudes. The largest river draining the region is the Balsas, meandering across the state from E to W and emptying into the Pacific near Zacatula.

The state is named after the insurgent patriot, General Vicente Guerrero.

Taxco, Gro. Pop. 14,000. Alt. 5500. The best known of Mexico's "colonial monument" towns. It is celebrated for its picturesque streets, its silver crafts, and as a popular tourist resort. It can be comfortably visited in a one-day round-trip tour from Mexico City. Driving time, about 3 hours each way.

HOW TO GET THERE: *Via highway* — the Mexico City-Acapulco Route, CN-95 (see Index: Highway Routes). *Via bus* — Estrella de Oro line (first-class, de luxe service, Cuernavaca, Taxco, Acapulco). Terminal in Mexico City at Fray S. Teresa de Mier 72 and 74. Tel. 12-72-68; Linea Los Galgos, at Fray Teresa de Mier 148, Tel. 10-20-25 offers 8 passenger limousine service daily. *Tours* — the larger tourist agencies in Mexico City conduct regular limousine tours to Taxco. There are no rail nor air communications with Taxco.

HOTELS AND RESTAURANTS: *Hotel Victoria,* in town. 75 comfortable rooms and suites. Nice views from balconies. Very good dining room, cocktail bar, music and dancing nightly. Good parking. Management helpful and friendly. Rates: AP from $160 to $200 MN dble. Tel. 10. *Hacienda El Chorrilla,* N edge of town, just off highway. A delightful old hacienda modernized. Tiny (9 units), atmospheric, good food, cocktail service, small pool. Very friendly atmosphere. Reservations suggested. Rates: AP $170 MN dble. *Posada de la Misión,* N edge of town, on highway. First-class colonial-style hotel, 39 rooms and suites, good dining room, tropical bar and cocktail lounge, heated pool. Music and dancing (except Sundays). Rates: AP $180 MN dble. Tel. 63.

Hotel de la Borda, N edge of town on highway. 150 rooms, first class to average accommodations, service uneven. Fair dining room, bar and cocktail lounge. Dancing nightly by pool. Nice grounds. Rates: AP from $140 to $300 MN. Tel. 25. *Hotel Rancho Telva,* in town, Soto de la Marina 5. Attractive, colonial-style, on hill overlooking town (next to the Victoria). Operated by Wells Fargo-American Express Co. 52 rooms and suites, nicely kept. Fair dining room, cocktail bar, lounge, dancing nightly. Free parking. Rates: AP $180 MN dble. Tel. 4. *Casa Humboldt,* the plaza. A pleasant guest house, modest accommodations, good food. Rates: AP $125 MN dble. *Motel Loma Linda,* on highway, S edge of town. An excellent new motor inn, 25 units. Pool. Rates: EP $80 MN dble, or AP $150 MN dble.

Hotel Santa Prisca, Cena Obscuras 1, block from plaza. An older, neatly kept hotel with an attractive patio. 22 rooms, fair dining room, bar. Free parking. Rates: AP $155 MN dble. Tel. 80. *Hotel Real de Taxco,* in town, San Agustín 2. A pleasant, American-operated older hotel. 25 rooms. Good dining room. Cocktail service. Rates: AP $125 to $150 MN dble. *Hotel Los Arcos,* Alarcón 2, 27 rooms. Old but neat. Rates: AP $150 MN dble. *Hotel Meléndez,* San Agustín 4. Older, but recently refurbished. 30 rooms. Rates: EP $50 to $65 MN dble.

Definitely *viajero*-style (minimum comforts, budget prices) are: *Casa Grande,* near plaza. 20 rooms. *Hotel Colonial,* on highway near bus station. *Hotel Roselim,* in town.

NOTE: The very colorful *Hacienda San Francisco Cuadra* is commented on separately, see Index.

Except for the hotels, Taxco has no independent restaurants worthy of note. *Doña Berta's Bar,* on plaza, facing the church, is a favorite rendezvous of the bohemians and serious tipplers.

DIRECTORY: *Bank* — Banco del Sur, Calle de la Muerte (no number). *Bus lines* — Autobuses Estrella de Oro, Cruz Blanca 22 (on highway) Tel. 48; Linea Los Galgos, Melendez. Tel. 80. *Car repairs* — Antonio Meija, Santa Ana 23.

THE TOWN AND ENVIRONS: Taxco (TAHS-co — either from *Tasco,* Tarascan, or from the Aztec term for "ball court") was a populous Indian village long before Columbus was born, and was even then a source of silver. The original settlement was about 7 m. SE of the present town. When Cortés explored the area in 1522, so much silver was found, a regular town was established near the mines. In 1528 the old Taxco moved over, joining with the new. The town's real development dates from the time of José de la Borda who came in 1716 and soon amassed a fabulous fortune from the mines he located and operated.

The town has changed little since Borda's time. It is a place of interesting tiny plazas, twisting cobbled streets and lanes, of houses perched picturesquely on sheer hillsides. Seen from a distance the red-tiled roofs are like a cascade of warm colors spilling down a mountainside. Because of its quaintness, unusual colonial architecture and traditions, it has been designated by the government as a National Colonial Monument, thus the building of modern-style structures is prohibited. Visually, it is a magnificent place for an artist or photographer; every vista, nook and lane is like a stage set, stirring the imagination.

The *Central Plaza,* tiny, pleasantly shaded by Indian laurels (which successfully block a comprehensive view of the parochial church) is one of the prettiest in Mexico. Facing on the plaza is the notable *Iglesia de San Sebastían y Santa Prisca,* the parochial church often erroneously called a cathedral. Dwarfing everything else in the town, it is one of Mexico's almost perfect gems of ultra-Baroque architecture. It was begun in 1751 by Diego Durán and Juan Caballero, and was completed in 1758 at a cost said to have exceeded 8,000,000 pesos. Practically everything about the church indicates that its patron had only one purpose, that was to excel everything previous done in Mexico and to spare no expense in achieving this.[6] As a result it is perhaps the most complete example of ecclesiastical art that the period produced anywhere in this hemisphere.

The exterior of the edifice, especially the ornamentation of the façade is more rococo (late Baroque) than Churrigueresque, repleat with vigorous and boldly han-

[6] It is said that José de la Borda, the patron who financed the church and built much of Taxco as well as the famed Borda Gardens in Cuernavaca (see Index), had many ups and downs before stumbling on the mines that changed his fortunes. He had chosen for a motto, "God gives to Borda and Borda gives to God," which took physical form in the parochial church of Taxco.

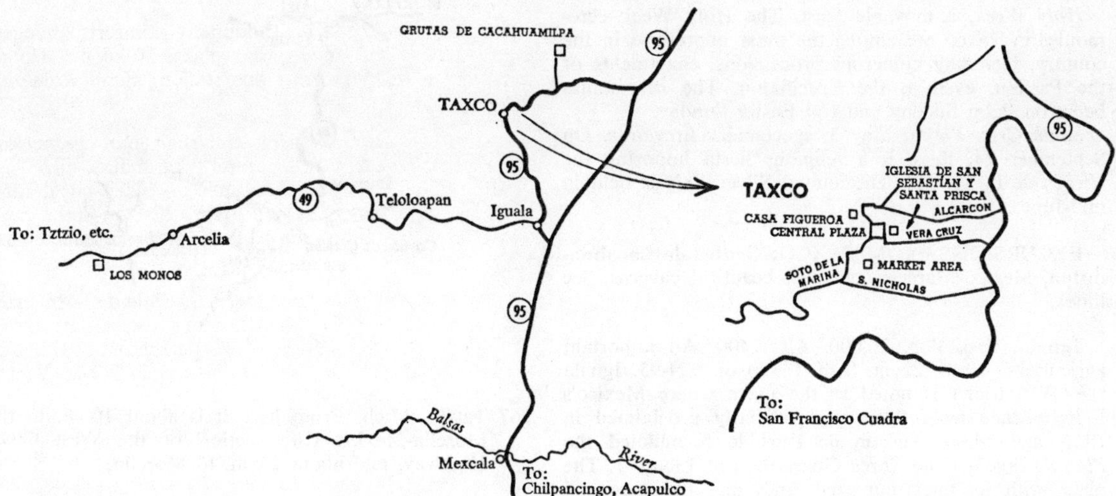

dled carvings. The twin towers rise above rather simple brownstone bases, while the towers themselves are a mass of imaginative carvings. Architecturally the towers with their mass of decorations appear somewhat top-heavy in relation to the plain and narrower bases. The great dome, built upon a high octagonal drum, is covered with glazed tiles to portray in bright colors the inscription on the frieze of the drum, *"Gloria a Dios en las alturas"* ("Glory be to God on the highest").

The interior stonework is a natural beautiful pink in color. It well sets off the wealth of Churrigueresque altars, the elaborate and richly carved, gilded and colored *retablos* which are among the most beautiful and best preserved in the country. The decorative paintings throughout are by Miguel Cabrera, one of the great mural painters of Colonial Mexico (see Index). His *The Nativity* and the *Ascension of the Virgin*, both in the sacristy, are among his finest works.

Silver Shops. On the Plaza itself, and along the various streets and lanes fanning out from it, climbing above it, or spilling down ravines below it, are the myriad shops and workshops *(tallers)* of Taxco's countless silversmiths. Though very little silver is mined around Taxco now, it is Mexico's silver center — thanks in part to the American artist and writer, William Spratling.[7] The showrooms and *tallers* of the Castillo brothers, Sigi, Antonio Pineda and brothers, Salvadore, Margot of Taxco and of Spratling (now out of town on the road to Iguala) are sparkling silver circuses well worth a visit.

Casa Figueroa at Guadalupe 2 (near plaza) is a curious old mansion built in 1767 by the Conde de Cadena, the magistrate of Taxco. The original building contained 26 rooms and a total of only two windows, both barred and opening on an inner patio. The Indians called this house the Casa de las Lágrimas (House of Tears) because the count forced them to work off their fines in labor upon the building. The Mexican artist Fidel Figueroa purchased and partially modernized the house in 1943 for use as a studio. The public is admitted from 10 A.M. to 1 P.M.; 3 to 7 P.M. *Fee:* 1 peso.

Another house of interest, for its rich Moorish façade, is the *Casa Humboldt* which is now a guest house. During the tourist season (January to March, June to August) there are guided tours of some of the outstanding Taxco homes and of artists' studios. The tours are on Tuesday and Friday at 4 P.M. *Charge* — $20 MN including refreshments. Tickets are available at the hotels.

The Market (mercado) is downhill and just S of the plaza. Market day is on Sunday. The display of produce, vivid tropical fruits, handicrafts, etc., is very colorful.

San Francisco Cuadra, an enchanting colonial *hacienda* founded in 1540 by Doña Juana de la Cuadro, and now converted into a charming resort-hotel. The *hacienda* is a tiny village in itself, with cobbled streets, a doll-size church, rustic pool and walks, baronial halls. Whether you stay there or not, a visit to the *hacienda* is an unusual treat. Unlike so many historic places converted to modern use, this one has not been ruined by improvements. There are 28 guest rooms furnished in a Spanish rustic-colonial style, good dining room, bar service, pool, horseback riding. Transportation furnished to and from Taxco. *Rates:* $180 MN and up, dble. AP. Tel. 1-99. For reservations write, Apartado Postal 37, Taxco, Gro.

To get there drive 3 m. S from Taxco on CN-95, turn r. off highway. A spectacular all-weather gravel road leads 2 m. to the *hacienda.*

FIESTAS: Both the religious and civil fiestas of Taxco are unusually brilliant as well as numerous. The more important and colorful are:

Fiesta de Santa Prisca, January 18. Brilliant fireworks, fair atmosphere, regional dances including the dances of *Los Moros,* the *Tecomates* and the *Pastores.*

Fiesta de la Candelaria, February 2. Religious festival, including a blessing of the animals.

[7] After the turn of the century, and following the Revolution, Taxco's importance as a mining center declined. The bottom dropped out of the world silver market, and the once busy village became a somnolent place. There was a few tin- and silversmiths in the town who produced unimaginative, somewhat crude work, only on order.

To revive the minor arts of the town William Spratling gathered the smiths together and founded the Taller de las Delicias, a primitive workshop that began to turn out quality jewelry. Many of the most important designers and craftsmen, some of them now among Taxco's successful and wealthy businessmen, started as barefoot apprentices in the Taller de las Delicias. From that single workshop Taxco's head-spinning new silver boom has sprouted.

Fiesta del Crucifijo de la Vera Cruz (the Crucifix of the True Cross), March 4. Of interest is a curious dance performed by children, ages five to eight, who dress like roosters and perform a dance in imitation of a cockfight.

Holy Week, a movable feast. The Holy Week ceremonies in Taxco are among the most impressive in the country, including numerous processions, enactments of the Passion, even to the Crucifixion. The ceremonies begin on Palm Sunday and end Easter Sunday.

Santa Cruz Fiesta, May 3, spectacular fireworks. On September 24, there is a religious fiesta honoring the Virgen de la Merced. The annual Silver Fair is held in mid-June.

EXCURSIONS FROM TAXCO: **Grutas de Cacahuamilpa,** Mexico's largest and most beautiful caverns. See Index.

Iguala, Gro. Pop. 20,000. Alt. 2400. An important agricultural center 22 m. S of Taxco on CN-95. Iguala (ee-GWAH-lah) is noted as the place where Mexico's Independence from Spain was officially proclaimed in 1821, and where Agustín de Iturbide formulated the *Plan de Iguala* (The Three Guarantees of Liberty). The plaza with its thick tamarind trees and the parochial church are of interest. The Friday market has good basketry and pottery. Occasionally amethysts, for which the state is celebrated, can be bought here.

For the off-trail traveler, equipped with a rugged vehicle or able to rough it on second- and third-class buses, there is a road (listed part way as CE-140, and in part as CE-49) going westward down into the tropical Balsas River valley. A brief sketch of the route:

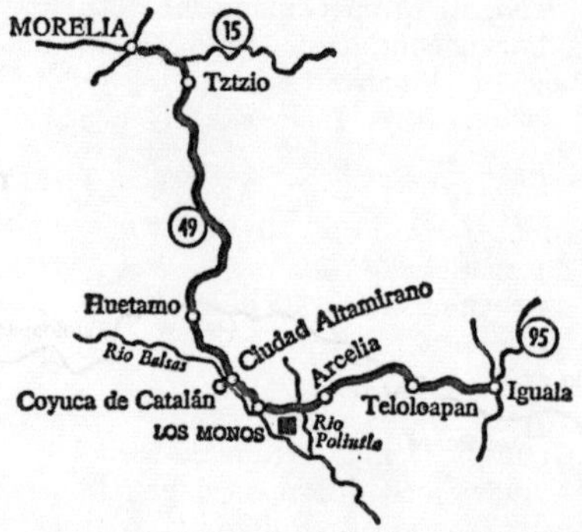

MILES — POINTS OF INTEREST

0 Iguala, Gro.

36 Teloloapan, Gro. **G.** Pop. 8297.

86 Arcelia, Gro. About 9 m. beyond the town, after crossing the Río Poliutla, and just to the S of the road, is an extensive archaeological zone known as Los Monos. The ruins, extensive pyramids, ball courts and temple groups have still to be systematically explored. The constructions date from the seventh century. To get there it is advisable to secure horses and guides in Arcelia. The trip takes about ½ day. The country is quite mountainous and beautiful. There are many mines in the area.

105 Tlapehuala, Gro. Pop. 3500. The road comes to the broad Balsas River and continues along its bank to,

119 Ciudad Altamirano, Gro. Pop. 6000. **GHR.** An interesting, relatively sophisticated tropical town. Considering its isolation, the accommodations are fair. From here one can continue the few miles to the interesting river town of Coyuca de Catalán, crossing the river by bridge just before the town. Or, from Altamirano the road (very poor) crosses into the State of Michoacán to,

155 Huetamo, Mich. Pop. 6200. **GHR.** There are two nameless hotels, one on the plaza, the other ½ block N of the plaza. The latter is best. Huetamo is hot and tropical. It is interesting for its tiny Sunday market where a half-dozen goldsmiths sell their elaborate and fine gold filigree jewelry. In this area one also comes upon blue-eyed, blond Indians. During the French intervention in Mexico a Napoleonic regiment was pushed down into the jungle where it surrendered. Some of the soldiers stayed.

From Huetamo the (semblances of a) road passes through magnificent mountainous country northward to,

267 Tztzio, Mich. From here it is about 10 m. to the Morelia-Mexico City section of the West Coast Highway, and about 25 m. to Morelia.

From Iguala, southward to Acapulco, save for the interesting and excellent mountain drive, there are scarcely any points of touristic interest (see Index: Highway Routes). At *Mexcala,* on CN-95, the road crosses the Balsas River. Here one can indulge in an exhilarating and delightful sport of rafting down the Balsas. There are boatmen who shoot the numerous rapids and shallow falls in flat-bottomed barges made of *parota* wood. You can go as far as Coyuca de Catalán and from there take a bus back to Iguala.[8]

About midway between Iguala and Acapulco is the capital of the State of Guerrero.

Chilpancingo, Gro. Pop. 14,000. Alt. 3800. Capital of Guerrero, Chilpancingo (cheel-pahn-SEEN-go) is also called Ciudad Bravo in memory of the revolutionary heroes Nicolás, Leonardo, and Miguel Bravo. The town is mentioned as one of the sources whence Moctezuma drew some of the gold that so dazzled the Conquistadores. To the NW of the town is an extensive, but still unexplored archaeological site. The first Mexican Congress was held at Chilpancingo in 1813.

The town at present is a typical agricultural center, somewhat sprawling and untidy. Of moderate interest are the Palacio de Gobierno and the House of the 1st Revolutionary Congress.

DIRECTORY: *Bank* — Banco Nacional de México, Jardín Cuéller 6. *Auto repairs* — Chilpancingo Ford, Guerrero 5; Automotriz del Sur, Av. Pres. Alemán 10. *Bus lines* — Estrella de Oro, tickets and stop at Posada Meléndez (Mexico City-Taxco-Acapulco); Auto Transportes Vicente Guerrero, Morelos and Victoria (to Tixtla and Chilapa).

HOTEL: *La Posada Meléndez,* Prolongación Av. Juárez. Small, but quite satisfactory in an emergency. Reasonable. Dining room fair.

From Chilpancingo a graveled road, CE-150, goes E into the mountains 12 m. to Tixtla, the birthplace of

[8] To date only two men, Albert Fagerberg and Sten Bergman, former students at Mexico City College, have ridden the Balsas to its mouth at the Pacific Ocean. They made the perilous journey in a lightweight American canoe during the summer of 1952, conquering the treacherous El Infiernillo (Little Hell) canyon and waterfalls (between the village of Churumuco and the sea) which had stopped better equipped, previous expeditions.

Vicente Guerrero, and 22 m. to Chilapa, an interesting town, noted for its hand-loomed, beautifully embroidered woollen *rebozos.* From Chilapa the adventurous traveler can, via horse, continue on into the mountains to the tiny village of Olinalá, the home of the unique *rayado* type of lacquerware. It is made nowhere else in the country.[9]

Acapulco, Gro. Pop. 30,000. Alt. 20 ft. Mexico's plush, internationally famous seaside resort situated around one of the world's finest and most beautiful natural harbors.

HOW TO GET THERE: *Via highway* — CN-95 south, see Index: Highway Routes. Acapulco is about 283 m. S of Mexico City; 6 to 8 hours' driving time. *Via bus* — Estrella de Oro line schedules 14 first-class departures throughout the day from its Mexico City terminal at Fray Teresa de Mier 72 and 74. Tel. 12-72-68. Five of the runs are *de lujo* (de luxe) and include free cold drinks, stewardess service, etc. Autobuses de Acapulco (ADA), Fray S. Teresa de Mier 36, Tel. 21-10-14 offers first-class Pullman service. Linea Los Galgos, Fray S. Teresa de Mier 148, Tel. 10-20-25 offers limousine service to Acapulco. *Via air* — CMA and Aeronaves de México. *Via boat* — Each December the Matson company's de luxe *Lurline* makes a luxury cruise from San Francisco and Los Angeles to Acapulco. See your travel agent. The Grace Line runs passenger-carrying freighters from San Francisco and Los Angeles to Acapulco about twice a month. Naviera Turistica Mexicana's swanky cruise ship, the S.S. Acapulco makes regular runs between Los Angeles, California and Acapulco. Office in Mexico City, Paseo de la Reforma 46.

HOTELS: There are more than 86 hotels belonging to the Acapulco Hotel Association. These and numerous small *pensiones* offer a broad range of accommodations from modest and budget-appealing to luxurious and expensive layouts that would open the eyes of an oriental potentate. Most of the hotels are on the American Plan, though some are beginning to offer European Plan. The rates in our list are the "in-season" prices. During the "off-seasons" (end of March to end of November) most of the hotels offer lower rates. In our listing below special comments are made regarding the better, more popular or unusual hotels. The remaining hotels are catalogued according to general types and location.

Hotel Pierre Marqués, 11 m. SE on far side of bay near Revolcadero Beach. The most de luxe and finest hotel on the coast, run by the Hotel Pierre of New York. Here former President Dwight D. Eisenhower stayed during his historic visit in 1959 with Mexico's President Lopez Mateos. 101 rooms, suites and bungalows in a ranch-style setting. Magnificently landscaped grounds. Dining room has excellent cuisine. Bar, cocktail lounge, and terrace. Open-air dining room. Nightly dancing. Tennis courts, pools, lawn games. Hotel air conditioned throughout. Free bus service to and from town. Rates: MA[10] from $475 to $575 MN dble. Lower rates April 15 to December 15. Tel. 2-96.

Hotel Las Brisas Hilton, 7 m. SE on drive to Puerto Marquez. A fabulous hotel of 158 bungalow units on beautifully landscaped, terraced grounds that make you think of the hanging gardens of Babylon. The bungalows are nicely appointed, each with its stocked refrigerator and terrace, and 38 have their own pools. Large saltwater pool. There is a terrace dining room for breakfast and dinner; a beach club for supper. Terrace cocktail bar and lounge. Dancing. Hotel has its own rental boats, water skiing, and fishing equipment, and a fleet of gay, pink and white candy-striped rental jeeps for its guests. CP from $250 to $400 MN dble. Tel. 4-01-75.

Hotel El Presidente, 3½ m. E on Calzada Costera Miguel Alemán. 11-story. 200-room and -suite ultramodern hotel completely a/c, on its own beach. Rooms tastefully furnished, have circulating purified ice water, radios, and hi-fi music. Good dining room; poolside luncheon service. Night club in-season. The hotel is run by the same chain operating El Presidente, the Alffer, and Del Prado in Mexico City. Rates: MA from $375 to $425 MN dble. Tel. 40-0-10.

GENERAL HOTEL LIST

HOTEL & NO. ROOMS ADDRESS & PHONE	RATES PER DOUBLE MN	OBSERVATIONS
Large, first class, and expensive		
El Mirador — 76 La Quebrada Tel. 88	AP $270 to $420	On cliff. Some a/c. Very pleasant.
El Elcano — 120 on Alemán Tel. 40-05-50	AP $360 to $420	New, own beach, a/c, pool, fancy.
Caleta — 300 Caleta Beach Tel. 2-85	AP $330	Very good, has everything.
Club de Pesca — 122 on Alemán Tel. 17-91	AP $340 to $380	On bay, a/c, hotel and bungalows. Has everything.
Hotel Boca Chica — 40 Caletilla Beach Tel. 16-25	CP $180 to $250	Very pleasant. Nice swimming cove.
Prado Americas — 117 Cerro de los Canones	AP from $325	Older, high up, has cable car to beach.
Palacio Tropical — 133 Cerro de la Pinzona Tel. 5-00	AP $300 to $385	High above the bay, exotic, rooms only fair. Dancing, etc.
Hotel Costera — 35 on Alemán Tel. 4-01-31	AP $250 to $475	On bay, very nice.
Hotel Maris — 80 on Alemán Tel. 18-00	AP $250 to $300	New, attractive, on beach.
Majestic — 122 Pozo del Rey 73 Tel. 5-11	AP $300	Nice view, poorly furnished rooms. Some a/c. Nice terraces.

[9] There are three types of lacquer work done in a few Mexican villages and towns. *Encrustado,* in which a design is cut into the surface of a lacquered piece, the layer lifted out and a contrasting color lacquer is laid in. This is the technique used in Pátzcuaro and Uruapan. The *rayado* technique calls for two thick layers of lacquer in contrasting colors. Designs are cut out of the top layer revealing, cameolike, the contrasting under layer. This is the specialty of the Olinalá craftsmen. A third technique, called *aplicado,* is simply the painting or appliquéing of designs on a lacquered vessel or surface. Such work is done in Mexico City and Quiroga, Mich., largely for tourists who don't know the difference.

[10] *Code for Acapulco Hotels:* AP — American Plan (with meals). EP — European Plan (without meals). MA — Modified American Plan (two meals). CP — Continental Plan (breakfast included, but no other meals). a/c — air conditioned.

HOTEL & NO. ROOMS ADDRESS & PHONE	RATES PER DOUBLE MN	OBSERVATIONS
Noa Noa — 78 on Alemán Tel. 15-55	EP $90 to $140	Modernistic, across from beach.
Playa de Hornos on Alemán		New.
Los Flamingos — 43 Gran Vía Tropical	AP $250 up	High on hill. Only fair.
Hotel Del Monte — 92 Cerro de las Pinzona Tel. 72	AP $250 to $350	Pleasant. Some a/c rooms. View. Nightly dancing.
Less pretentious — medium to low price		
Hotel el Pozo del Rey — 21 Av. Pozo del Rey Tel. 12-03	AP $225	Lovely grounds, pleasant atmosphere, pool.
Hotel Santa Clara — 15 Costa Grande 320 Tel. 10-23	AP $125 to $150	Nicely run. No hot water. German-American food. Good.
Hotel Los Siete Mares — 21 Av. Pozo del Rey Tel. 6-55	AP $150	Modest. Very satisfactory. EP available.
El Cano — 108 on Alemán	AP $150	Fair.
La Riviera — 40 on Alemán	AP $200	Good.
Colonial 15 Plaza Alvarez 3	AP $120	
Coral — 15 Quebrada 56	AP $80	
Charleston — 17 Dragos 70	AP $190	
De la Playa — 60 Playa Caleta	AP $185	Good. Some a/c.
Del Pacifico — 137 Playa Caleta	AP $145	Good for the price.
Villa España — 16 CN-95	AP $120	13 bungalows. Pleasant.
El Oasis — 11 Av. Oasis	EP $50	Has 7 suites.
Florencia — 35 Alemán 87	EP $50	
Jardín — 22 Quebrada 46	AP $70	Up high.
Las Anclas — 36 CN-95	AP $190	Fair.
Las Hamacas — 93 on Alemán	AP $260	Fairly nice.
Leighton — 19 Suiza 23	AP $200	New and nice.
Lindavista — 20 Playa Caleta	AP $100	
Monserrat — 24 Caleta district	AP $110	
Monterrey — 9 Hidalgo 13	AP $100	
Napoles — 20 Diablo 28	AP $70	
Paris — 18 Gran Vía Tropical	AP $120	
Papagayo — 300 on Alemán	AP $100 up	On beach, pool, popular with Mexican middle-class. Good buy. EP available.
Puerto Arturo — 38 Las Playas	AP $130	High up. Fair.
Quinta María — 35 Playa de Hornos	AP $80	Pleasant. Opposite beach.
Casa Ramon — 35 Felipe Valles 7	AP $55	

Beachcomber prices	SINGLES	
Casa Juanita Progreso 13	AP $50	
Casa Alicia Arteaga 9	AP $50	
Casa Romano Dominguillo 7	AP $35	
Pension Granada Quebrada 38	AP $35	
Casa Huita Arteaga 12	AP $50	
Casa Bazan Carranza 2	AP $50	
Casa Esther Juárez 14	AP $50	
Casa Esparza Hidalgo 28	AP $50	
Casa Mireya Quebrada 40	AP $35	
Pension Santa Isabel Arteaga 14	AP $40	
El Catalefo Playa la Condesa	AP $25	Hammocks, 2 meals/day plus beachcomber fun

Motels		
Bali Hai Motel		New, de luxe, moderate rates.
Motel Monaco — 37 E. on Alemán Tel. 4-01-25	EP $100 to $120	Very modern and comfortable. Pool, dining room, bar.
Motel Acapulco — 61 E. on Alemán Tel. 4-02-00	EP $80 to $135	Modern. Some a/c. Pool, dining terrace, cocktail lounge.
Motel Tampa — 60 E. on Alemán Tel. 4-00-71	EP $100 to $120	Nice. Pool, dining, cocktail lounge.
Motel el Toro Alemán 77	EP $50 and up	

RESTAURANTS AND NIGHT SPOTS: In comparison to French and Italian Mediterranean resorts even smaller than Acapulco, the latter is poverty-stricken when it comes to good independent restaurants. A fastidious gourmet could starve in Acapulco. There is a great deal of glitter, obviously expected to replace good chefmanship. The American Plan, with its captive audience, has often made hotel chefs overconfident and discouraged the independent restaurants.

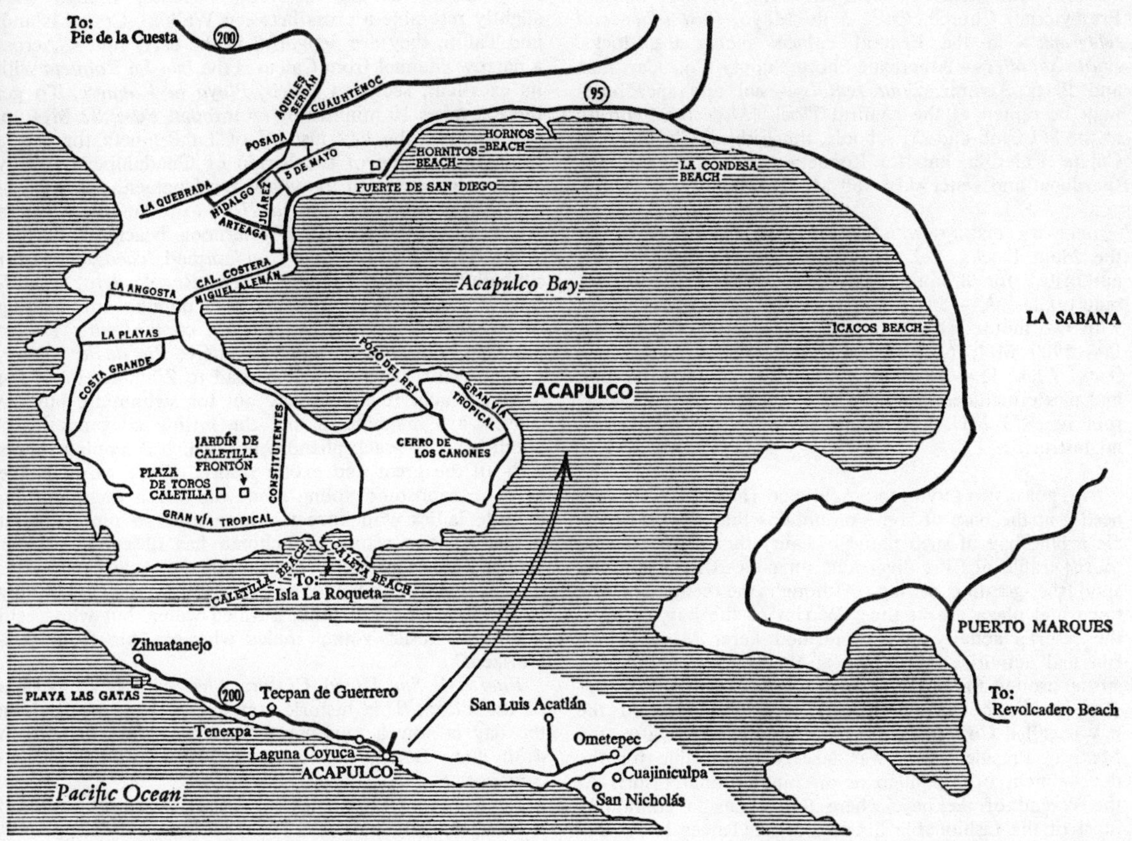

The very best of international cuisine is found at the *Hotel Pierre Marqués,* expensive and a long distance to go to eat. Swank, glossy plus fair cuisine come out expensively at the *Focalore* and the *Belair.* Interesting is *Armando's* at Quebrada 7, also the *Cantamar,* and, for Italian food, *Dino's.* The *Aku-Tiki Restaurant* at Calzado Miguel Alemán 407 has delightful décor and the finest Cantonese dining in Mexico. The *Sao Paolo,* Miguel Alemán 44, has excellent charcoal broiled steaks. The *Lido Restaurant,* Miguel Alemán 400 has Italian cuisine and music. The *El Rebosa* is at Miguel Alemán next to the Hotel Presidente. It is a supper club with entertainment. In the lower price bracket (and not particularly good) are the *Tirol,* just off the plaza (German food), *Hungry Herman's* (open all night — but why?), *Pipos,* just off the main fishing dock, for excellent *ceviche* (fish cocktail). *Si Como No,* on Costera Alemán, 2 blocks from the plaza is quite fancy and just satisfactory.

Acapulco's night spots offer unique atmosphere, sometimes a good show, and more important, a romantic setting. There is nothing like dancing on a tropical night with a view of the Pacific below. The *Jacaranda Room* in the El Presidente Hotel, operated by the same group who have the Jacaranda in Mexico City, is Acapulco's most expensive and elegant. The décor and mural are by Salvador Dali. NOTE: in almost all the night spots there is a minimum or cover charge ranging from $25 to $50 MN.

The *Cantamar,* mentioned above, is quite charming. It is situated on the water's edge and you reach it via cable car from the Hotel Prado Américas. You can also boat right in to your table. *La Perla* at the El Mirador Hotel overlooks the sea; there is dancing (the floor is too small) and the same show year in, year out — the spectacular high-dive from the Quebrada cliffs. The dives take place shortly after 10 P.M. and midnight. You can also see it from the hotel terraces. The *Club de Esquies* offers dining and a nightly aquatic review at 10:30 P.M. *Cabaret Rio Rita* and the *Nylon Club* are sailor-slanted, the latter featuring strip teases, as if you hadn't seen enough on the beaches during the day.

DIRECTORY: *Bank* — Banco Nacional de México, corner of Alemán and Juárez. *Auto repairs* — Acapulco Ford, Malaspina and Av. Cuauhtémoc; Motores de Acapulco (GM), Diego Hurtado de Mendoza 13; Servicio Cano, Dominguillo 19. *Bus lines* — Estrella de Oro, Alemán 179, Tel. 1-52; Linea los Galgos, Juárez 2, Tel. 6-84; Autobuses de Acapulco (ADA), Alemán 161, Tel. 2-25-22. *Airlines* — Aeronaves de México, Costera Miguel Alemán 252, Tel. 2-13-13 (scheduled flights to Mexico City); Aerolineas Vega, Costera Miguel Alemán 108, Tel. 2-13-25 (scheduled flights to Oaxaca City and Puebla). Direct flights to Oaxaca daily. Flights with stops at Ometepec, Cacahuatopic, Pinotepa Nacional, Jamiltepec, on Tuesday, Thursday, and Saturday. Mexicana de Aviación (CMA) Costera Miguel Alemán, Tel. 2-41-43. *Sea travel* — Agencia Maritimas del Pacifico, on Alemán next to the Aduana warehouse. Freighters to Los Angeles and San Francisco; Servicio Maritimo de México, next door to the above. Mexican mail boats to coastal ports. *Auto rentals* — Hertz de Acapulco, Annex 5, Hotel Presidente, Tel. 4-05-66; Arrendadora de Jeeps (jeep rentals), Progreso 2, Tel. 12-40. *Travel agents* — Agencia de Viajes Pacifico, Lobby Hotel El Cano, Tel. 4-04-04; Wells Fargo (American Express), Hotel Presidente, Annex 3, Alemán 187. *Church services*—(Catholic) La Soledad, downtown at Jardín Alvarez; Sagrado Corazon, in the Costa Azul section near the Naval Base; (Protestant) Evangelical Church, at Calle Aquiles Serdán; Presbyterian Church, Calle 5 de Mayo. *Post office and telegraph*—in the Federal Palace, facing the docks. *Photo supplies*—American Photo Supply Co., Carranza and Plaza Alvarez. *Boat rentals*—sail and speedboats may be rented at the Central Dock *(Malecón Central)*, at the Ski Club and ski schools, the Fishing Club, and at Caleta, Caletilla, and La Roqueta Beaches. Charge for speedboat and water skis, $60 MN per hour.

DEEP-SEA FISHING AND SKIN-DIVING: Charter boats at the Main Docks, Tel. 2-10-99. Rates (set by the port authority) for 8 hours are: Boat with one motor (2 seats), Class A—$420 MN; Class B—$365 MN. Boats with two motors (4 seats), Class A—$1000 MN; Class B—$900 MN; (3 seats) Class C—$800 MN; (two seats) Class D—$630 MN; Class E—$550 MN. Bait and tackle included. Skin-diving equipment (Aqua Lungs) rent for $75 MN. This charge includes the services of an instructor.

THE PORT AND ENVIRONS: Acapulco (ah-cah-POOL-ko) nestles at the base of some mountains that all but encircle a blue bay of such natural beauty that neither heavy tourist traffic nor the diversions introduced for them can spoil the gemlike setting. Although the center of the town and plaza are at the NW rim of the bay, little of the resort's activity is concentrated here. Most of the fun and activities take place at the beaches and hotels strung around the bay like an exotic necklace. The handsome scenic boulevard skirting completely around the bay is called Costera President Miguel Alemán, after the Mexican President who was largely responsible for the development of Acapulco as an international resort. At the W end of the bay, where the peninsula containing most of the fashionable hotels and residences hooks out into the blue waters, the scenic drive becomes the Gran Vía Tropical.

Though Acapulco has had a colorful history,[11] there are almost no mementos of the past—no picturesque colonial streets, houses or great architectural monuments. The principal attractions are the brilliant cocoanut palm fringed beaches. *Playa Caleta* and its twin beach, *Caletilla,* known as the Morning Beaches, though they slightly resemble a cross between Waikiki, Coney Island, and Tahiti, they are delightful in the early hours. Across a narrow channel from Caleta is the *Isla La Roqueta* with its excellent, secluded beach, *Playa la Roqueta*. To get there it takes 10 minutes by motorboat. *Fare:* $2 MN up, one way. In the bay just off of La Roqueta there is a submerged statue of the Virgin of Guadalupe, the only underwater shrine in the world for frogmen.

Playa Hornos and *Playa Hornitos,* flanking Costera Alemán, are the so-called "afternoon beaches." Farther along E and SE are *Playa Condesa* and *Icacos,* more for sunbathing than swimming. *Playa Revolcadero,* a half-mile beyond *Puerto Marquez,* is a popular surf-bathing beach for swimmers capable of coping with savage breakers. There is an undertow here. *Pie de la Cuesta,* 7 m. NW of the port on the road to Zihuatanejo, is the Sunset Beach. It is definitely not for swimming, but the sunsets are magnificent and the setting is romantically South Seas. A beach phenomenon which Acapulco shares with all the great and exotic resorts of the world is the tribe of handsome young men who for a consideration console ladies who have too long suffered repression at home. As one astute Frenchman has observed: "Their bronze skin, fine teeth, languorous eyes and bullfighter figures have a rejuvenating effect on women who may insist on pasteurized milk, purified water, but who seem unable to resist young males who are far from pasteurized."

Fuerte de San Diego, Costera Alemán, a few blocks E of the Plaza. This historic star-shaped fort overlooking the bay is now a museum. *Hours:* weekdays, 9 A.M. to 4:30 P.M.; Sundays, 9 A.M. to 3 P.M. *Admission:* 50 centavos.

La Sabana (Archaeological Zone), a newly explored site not far from the city. There are mounds dating from about 2000 years ago. Artifacts found here indicate pre-Hispanic contact with Asia—figures reflecting pre-Hellenic Hittite forms, others like the Easter Island figures, and some showing Teotihuacán influences.

ENTERTAINMENT IN ACAPULCO: In addition to swimming and sunbathing at the beaches Acapulco offers amusements to suit almost every taste:

Fishing—The local waters are renowned for sailfish, black marlin, bonito, tuna, barracuda, dolphin, pompano, red snapper, giant manta rays, and turtle. An international sailfish rodeo is held each April. The sailfish average about 90 pounds, more than twice the average size of the catch off Florida. See directory, for charter-boat rates.

Hunting—Excellent duck shooting in the lagoons around Acapulco. In the back-country there are wildcat, deer, wild pig *(jabalí)*, and other game.

Golf—There is a fine country club, 18 holes. Special green fees to hotel guests.

Water skiing—Several ski clubs rent speedboats, skis, and offer instruction. Club Sirroco de Ski, on Alemán, and Club de Esquies at Alemán 100. Also, Escuela Morlet, and Escuela Batani. Rates are $60 to $75 MN per hour, including boat, skis and instruction.

Cruises and Bay Tours. Glass-bottom boats leave from Caleta Beach. They are called *fonde de cristales*. In addition to these there are several large schooners making sailing tours around the bay in the afternoon, and also an evening moonlight cruise. Trips usually last three hours. There is music and dancing. The cruise boats are: *Sea Cloud, Ave de Tahiti, Barca de Oro,* and the *Monserrat.* Check with your hotel for reservations and tickets.

[11] *History*—Shortly after the conquest of Tenochtitlán Cortés began exploring to the west and came upon the Bay of Acapulco. A settlement was founded in the early 1530s, principally to build ships for exploring expeditions. The first two such ships, the *San Miguel* and the *San Marcos,* were launched in 1532 and used by an expedition headed by Diego Hurado de Mendoza, a lieutenant of Cortés. In the following years ships sailed from Acapulco to Peru and also northward to the Colorado River in search of the fabled golden city of Cibola. Following Magellan's discovery of the China coast and the Philippine Islands, and the seafaring monk Fray Andrés de Urdaneta's famed pioneering voyage from the Philippines to Acapulco (1565), the port became a lively link in the China trade route. Spanish, Chinese, and Japanese ships brought riches from the Orient, the goods being transported overland from Acapulco to Veracruz for transshipment to Spain. A famed fair came to be held in the port with the arrival of the China ships.

The rich trade naturally attracted pirates, among them Sir Francis Drake. To defend the port a fortress called El Castillo de San Diego was built in 1616. It was destroyed by an earthquake in 1776, and was replaced by the star-shaped Fuerte de San Diego on Costera Alemán. During the War of Independence the fort was attacked by Morelos. After a four-month siege he forced the Spanish to capitulate. Following the War of Independence the China trade practically ended. The mule route to Mexico City fell into disuse and was overgrown by jungle. Acapulco became an almost forgotten port. In 1927 a road was again pushed through to the port. In 1938 the first resort-hotel was built. Finally, in 1955 the superhighway was opened.

Rates are from $40 to $50 MN, depending on the size of the boat. This includes free beer and soft drinks.

Bullfights. On Sunday afternoon, in season, at the Plaza de Toros Caletilla. Tel. 15-83.

Jai alai. First-class jai alai games every night at the Jardín de Caletilla Frontón, near bullring. 9 P.M. Closed June to October.

Boxing and Wrestling. Saturday nights at Arena Coliseo, Calle Terraplén 7.

THE COAST NORTHWEST OF ACAPULCO: The coast both NW and SE of Acapulco, known as the Costa Brava (Great Coast) and Costa Chica (Little Coast) are literally unknown, untraveled, having been hidden for centuries behind the massive barrier of the Sierra Madre del Sur. They offer a dazzling diversity of vivid green life, violent colors, palm forests, and mysterious lagoons. The great *coquito* palms stand behind crescent coves alive with flamboyant fish. The great *roble* trees make a gorgeous show, bursting into flower with clusters of rose-pink blossoms while the tree is leafless. Here *cuijas,* insect eating lizards, smack their lips with a sound that is like a kiss, hence are called *"besadores."* Here along river-banks are Bali-like scenes — nearly nude women bathing and washing, their brown skin glistening, children splashing around them. The areas wait for visitors seeking the new and mysterious. Roads however remain mere projections, passable in dry weather, and in most cases only by jeep or truck.

Going NW from Acapulco along the coast, CN-200, there is a stretch of about 100 miles that is paved but battered. It skirts the long Laguna Coyuca, a veritable bird paradise, passes through Tecpan de Guerrero. From Tecpan a short road leads down to the fishing village of Tenexpa (Pop. 2012). The last section of the road leading on to Zihuatanejo is unimproved and passable only in dry weather. There are several river fords.

Zihuatanejo, Gro. A delightful, tiny, hideaway resort, still isolated and undeveloped. Population about 1500.

HOW TO GET THERE: *Via road* — 147 m. NW of Acapulco, CN-200. Road condition described above. *Via air* — Aeronaves de México runs scheduled flights. Round-trip fare costs approximately $10 from Acapulco, $18 from Mexico City. *Via bus* — The first-class Mexico City-Acapulco buses now make a daily run to Zihuatanejo.

HOTELS: There are about 60 tourist units in Zihuatanejo, scattered among six or seven small hotels, cottages and one up-to-date hotel. Reservations (needed only during the winter season) can be made by telegraph, there being no telephones in the village. Felipe Valles', *Hotel Belmar,* has the most comfortable habitations in the village. Rooms, food, and service can be typified as pleasantly rustic. Rates: $65 to $85 MN, AP per single. *Hotel Catalina,* on a hillside overlooking the bay, but a few kilometers out of town, is the up-to-date hotel. You descend to the beach by funicular, go back and forth to town by chauffeured jeep. Rates: AP $100 MN single.

THE VILLAGE AND SURROUNDINGS: Zihuatanejo (zee-huah-tah-NAY-ho, from the Aztec *zihuatl nejotl,* meaning dark woman) was established about 100 years ago as a fishing village and port for a large nearby cocoanut and banana *hacienda.* The village is on the inside of a nearly landlocked bay surrounded by mountains. There are a number of lovely beaches separated from each other by cliffs and outcroppings of rocks. One of the best is *Playa Las Gatas,* almost directly across the bay from the village. Local boatmen perform a taxiing service running visitors from one beach to another.

As yet Zihuatanejo makes no serious attempt to entertain tourists. There are a few boats capable of deep-sea fishing. There are no night clubs, fancy restaurants or other means of amusement. The town gets its electricity from a small diesel plant that operates from sunset to around 11 P.M. After that, everything folds up. The charm of the place is its fine bay, its idyllic South Sea atmosphere and good sea food. Best months to visit are October to June.

SOUTHEAST OF ACAPULCO — THE COSTA CHICA: S of Acapulco's *Playa Revolcadero,* the rugged, jungle-like Great Coast gives way to the Costa Chica, a country of low hills, flatlands, and sparsely treed areas that are sometimes remindful of the African veldt. Inland from the coast, along the skirts of the Sierra Madre there are half-ruined cities that were once famous gold mining centers, among them *San Luis Acatlán* and *Ometepec.*

Ometepec, Gro. Pop. 5200. About 136 m. E of Acapulco via very rough road, unpaved. The town (oh-MAY-tay-peck) is fascinating because of its appearance of grand decay. Planes from the Aerolineas Vega line (Acapulco-Oaxaca) make scheduled stops here. Several medical missionaries from the Southern Presbyterian Church (U.S.) operate a small mission hospital here, the Hospital de la Amistad.

Of interest to anthropologists and folklorists are several unusual villages, toward the coast and directly south of Ometepec. These villages — *San Nicolás* and *Cuijla* (the almost forgotten official name of the latter is *Cuajiniculpa*) — represent a touch of Africa in Mexico. These are settlements of Negroes, the descendants of escaped African Bantu tribesmen who escaped from slave ships[12] bringing them to Acapulco in colonial times. To a large extent the Negro fugitives were scattered, maintaining themselves precariously until the latter part of the nineteenth century when they were brought together in settlements by a German-American born in Pittsburgh, Pennsylvania, Johann A. Schmidt (in Mexico he called himself Don Juan A. Smith), who ruled the region as a tyrant until the Revolution of 1910.

Today in largely Negro Cuijla and San Nicolás there remain strong evidences of the peoples' African roots. In Cuijla the huts are made of wattle, have thatch roofs and are round as are African huts. In San Nicolás the wattle walls are a brilliant orange-red. As in Africa, the people are accustomed to carrying water jars and loads on their heads. Likewise, as in Africa, the women carry their babies on one hip, the children's legs straddling the mother's waist. Everywhere else in Mexico infants are carried wrapped or slung in a *rebozo.* A curious marriage custom among the villagers is that generally the girls are kidnaped (sometimes by arrangement of all parties) by the suitor and his friends. If the girl proves not to be suitable, or is not a virgin, she is returned to her family. If she is kept, the civil or religious ceremony is held some weeks or even months after the kidnaping.

[12] Of the 78,000 people who were annually kidnapped from Africa during the slave-trade days Mexico received about one hundredth of these each year. Baron von Humboldt calculated that just before Mexico achieved its independence (in which slavery was abolished) there were about 10,000 Negro Mexicans. Although Veracuz was the only port authorized by the Spanish crown to receive slave shipments, there existed a good deal of contraband slaving through Acapulco.

52. *Eastern Mexico*

This region, combining the States of Veracruz and Tabasco, lying along the Gulf of Mexico coast, is, historically, Mexico's oldest travel region. The first visitors to be impressed by its sights were the Spanish explorers, Grijalva and Cortés.

It is a region of dramatic contrasts: the green, tree-choked mountains of the Eastern Sierra Madres, the flower-surrounded cane, coffee and orange plantations of the lower slopes and the humid jungle lowlands where rivers and mangrove swamps are lined with lush tropical growth and choked with water hyacinths. It possesses some of the oldest pre-Columbian and Spanish cities in the republic, as well as some of the youngest, brawlingest, and slickest new cities.

Along the lowlands the best season for vacationing is fall, winter, and early spring, while on the Gulf slopes spring is almost eternal and rarely too hot. In many areas tourist accommodations are fair to excellent. An amazing network of roads allow for all sorts of fascinating circle trips and side junkets.

The most interesting highway circle trips are the following: (1) *The Vanilla Route*, via Pachuca, Túxpan, Jalapa, Veracruz to Mexico City. (2) Mexico City via Puebla, Jalapa to Veracruz, and return by way of Orizaba and Cordoba. (3) Mexico City to Veracruz, Alvarado, Lake Catemaco, thence across the Isthmus of Tehuantepec and back to Mexico City via Oaxaca. Route descriptions: see Index: Highway Routes.

TRAVEL HIGHLIGHTS: Cities — Veracruz and Jalapa; a river trip up the Río Papaloapan (River of Butterflies) to the town of Tlacotalpan; the sacred city of the Totonac Indians, El Tajín, and a visit to Papantla, especially for the fiesta of Corpus Christi; a pause at the Swiss-like Lake Catemaco, and a trip to the Maya ruins at Palenque. For the very active — mountain-climbing up the 18,851 ft. snow-capped Orizaba, or for the less active, a restful stay at the de luxe spa, Fortín de las Flores. There is also good hunting and fish along the coast and in the jungles of Tabasco.

AREAS OF MAXIMUM INTEREST	BASE
Veracruz-Jalapa-Orizaba country	Veracruz
Papantla country	Papantla or Tecolutla
Tabasco country	Villahermosa

THE REGION: The two states making up this coastal region are an unusual contrast. Veracruz, possessing both mountains and coastal plain, is well developed industrially and agriculturally. It encompasses an area of 28,084 sq. miles and has a population of over 2,727,899. Tabasco, lying in almost flat country, covered by steaming jungles, swamps and innumerable rivers, with an area of 9897 sq. miles, has a population of about 496,340. Veracruz has been crossed by networks of roads since early colonial times; Tabasco has had hardly 100 miles of roads, and no railroad, until a decade or so ago. Veracruz is one of the richest of Mexican states, growing nearly half the coffee crop of Mexico, excellent tobacco, ⅓ of the nation's sugar crop. It supplies the world with fine vanilla, is the country's chief petroleum producer and possesses the nation's major port. Tabasco, though rich in hardwoods, rubber trees, cacao, and having extremely fertile land, due to lack of communications, has been unable to develop its wealth.

FLORA AND FAUNA: A listing of the trees and plants that flourish in this region would be endless. The areas seem to be explosive with flowers and verdure: countless variety of wild orchids, including the vanilla plant, tropical hardwoods, chicle (*zapote* tree), bananas, papayas, oranges, and other fruit trees, coffee, coconut and sugar cane. The area especially around Cordoba, Fortín, and Jalapa are the unforgettably lovely flower gardens of Mexico.

The lagoons of the region are the breeding grounds for northern ducks who fly in each fall by the countless thousands. The lagoons, rivers, and swamplands, especially in Tabasco, teem with alligators and other reptiles. Tabasco, like neighboring Campeche, is virgin big-game country, noted for its abundance of deer, jaguar, puma, ant bear, wild boar, monkey, tapir, and every variety of tropical bird.

HISTORY: The region is almost the birthplace of both pre-Hispanic and post-Hispanic history. The hot lands of Veracruz and Tabasco were the home of the ancient Olmecs who may have been the first spreaders of culture in Mexico. Along with them, parts of the region were occupied by the Totonac and Huasteca Indian cultures, sons, kins, or cousins to the Olmecs and Mayas. Both the Totonac and Huasteca spoke a Maya tongue, or one somewhat similar, though relationships are still somewhat vague. As one observer, Trent Stanford, has stated it, "the Gulf Coast region offers a wealth of ancestral possibilities." (See monographs on history, and on architecture, Index.)

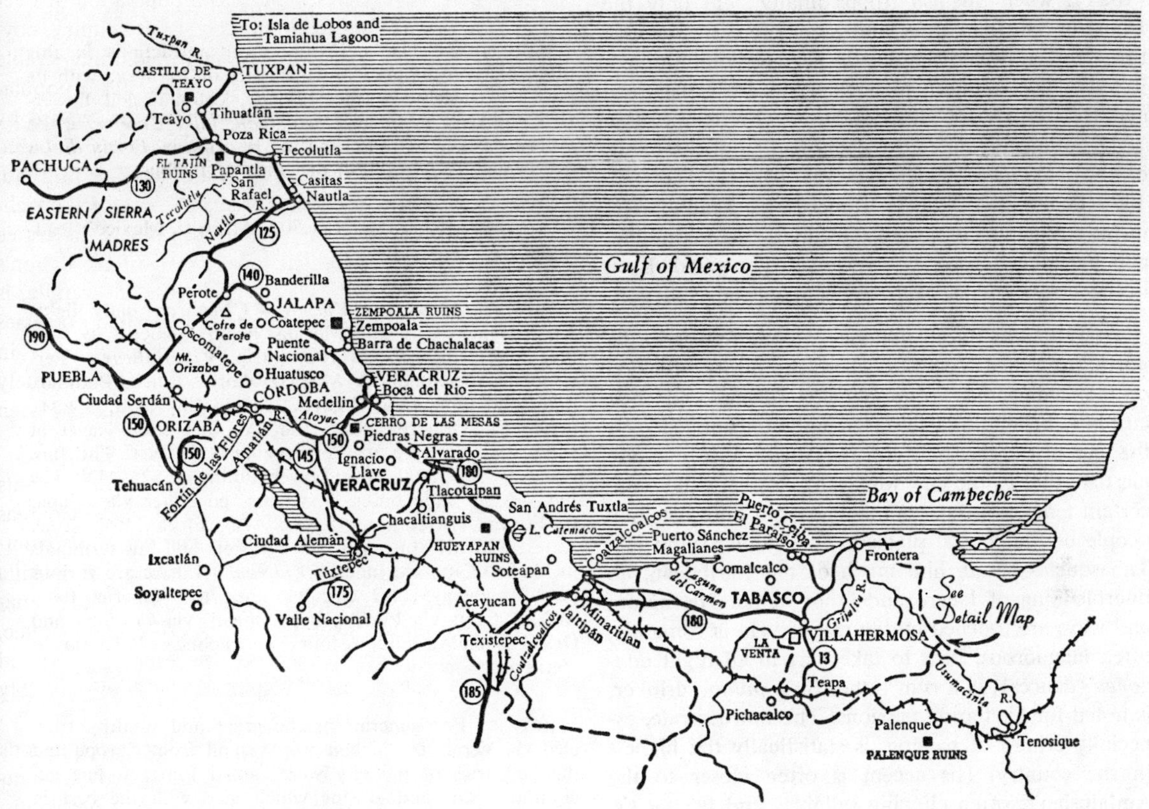

When the early adventurers, like Juan de Grijalva in 1518, sailed around the bend of Yucatán, they began to make Mexico's modern history. On his way to his date with the Aztec lord, Moctezuma, Cortés paused to sail up the Grijalva River in Tabasco where, at the Indian town of Tabasco, two skirmishes occurred with the natives. Cortés conquered and the Spanish built a settlement there called Villa Victoria, which became the capital of the province.[1]

Cortés continued on, down the coast to a spot near the island of *San Juan de Ulúa* where the year before Grijalva had found the mainland rich and intriguing. On April 21, 1519, he anchored there, erecting a settlement near the Indian village of Chalchiuhouecan. (See Index: *A Digest of Mexican History.*) The town site was found to be unhealthy, and another settlement was built in a hilly area about a mile from the Indian village Quizhuiztla (the present-day Antigua). From there he marched to the Totonac city of Zempoala; where, with considerable perfidy, and not a little cruelty, he secured the adhesion of the Totonac people as allies in his future battles with the Aztecs.

By 1599 Gaspar de Zuñiga, the viceroy, ordered the town re-established on the original site. Most of the region had been subjugated by this time and other settlements, especially along the road to Mexico City, were established. In 1746 a massive wall was erected around the port of Veracruz to protect the port from pirates. The wall had seven gates (one solely for the use of the viceroy). For some three centuries the city suffered heartbreaking trials. It was repeatedly sacked by buccaneers, bombarded by foreign fleets, the region scourged by cholera and yellow fever, torn by internecine strife and buffeted by hurricanes. In 1683 the city and environs was captured and badly mauled by pirates.[2]

[1] Villa Victoria was found to be an unhealthy site so in 1598 the capital was moved and renamed San Juan Bautista or the present Villahermosa.

[2] As early as 1568 pirates took their toll of the region. In 1568 the English corsair, John Hawkins, aided by Francis Drake, plundered the coast. On May 17, 1683, the notorious Lorencillo (Laurent de Gaff), a much-feared Captain Kidd, with 200 of the 800 pirates aboard his ships, disembarked in pirogues, fell upon the sleeping town of Veracuz and captured it. Houses were sacked and burned, men murdered, and a large part of the inhabitants were herded into the parochial church. Here some 1500 unfortunates were held for four days, dying of suffocation and hunger, while the pirates calmly searched their houses for loot. The pirates carried away 4,000,000 pesos in silver as well as all the jewels and valuables. When a thing is lost in Veracruz it is still the custom to say, "*Lorencillo lo ha tomado*" ("Lorencillo has taken it"). Later the pirate Nicholás de Agramonte robbed the city of 7,000,000 pesos in silver and transported 300 citizens to the nearby Isla de Sacrificios, where they were left to perish of starvation.

Nor were pirates the only destructive element. At the close of the Mexican War of Independence (1821), when Spanish troops finally held only the Island of San Juan Ulúa, and were forced to evacuate this, they subjected the city to such a bombardment it was almost reduced to powder. In 1838 the town and fort both were attacked by the French, and in 1847 both again suffered a cannonading at the hands of the Americans under General Winfield Scott. In 1859 Benito Juárez made Veracruz his headquarters in his struggle to drive out the forces of Maximilian, and here the Reform Laws were promulgated. Even in this century U. S. Marines occupied the Gulf port.

THE PEOPLE: Except for the Totonac forests in the northern part of Veracruz where the purity of blood of this indigenous group remains strong, and their customs, beliefs, and fiestas remain unchanged over the centuries, the bulk of the region's people are mestizo, that is, the new Mexican. However there are certain tempering factors making them different than people of the central plateau. The Veracruzano and Tabasqueño has in him much of the Caribbean, an interblending of Negro and other blood. His nature and ways are touched by the tropics. He is romantic, often languorous, likes to take part in all night *danzones* (dances), is a rum rather than *pulque* drinker, is noted for his flaring passions. The murder rate, especially crimes of passion, is statistically the highest in the country. His accent is often closer to the Andalusian's, often clipping syllables and lisping s's. His music leans heavily on Afro-Caribbean rhythms, (*see* Index: *Mexican Folk Dances*).

VERACRUZ-JALAPA-ORIZABA COUNTRY

This is the heart region of the State of Veracruz, and it includes the port city, the capital (Jalapa), the flower-garlanded resorts around Orizaba and Fortín, Mexico's magnificent snow-capped Orizaba Peak, and some of the best beaches in the region.

The climate of the Veracruz area and, of course, Tabasco, is moist and during the summer season (May to September) is unbearably hot. From late August until April *nortes* (northern winds) blow. These *nortes* are the monsoons of the Western Hemisphere, bringing fogs, heavy rains, and lower temperatures to the entire Gulf region. *Nortes Fuertes* (heavy northerners) are also known as *hueso colorado* (red core). They blow fiercely for several days or more and are followed by delightful weather. A *norte* that blows up with a rising tide is called *norte chocolotero* (chocolate colored), and sometimes last a fortnight, assuming the character of a gale, halting shipping, closing down the ferry boats at all river mouths. During *nortes* the dense masses of rain-charged clouds skim over the coastal plain and travel toward the Sierras of Orizaba and Perote, massing there until sunset. Usually the land breeze which blows seaward during the night sends the clouds back to the coast where they precipitate their moisture. The prevailing southern winds begin about May, bringing heat, and at times destructive hurricanes.

HIGHLIGHTS: The most important attractions in this often picturesque area are the cities of *Veracruz* with its port and nearby beaches; *Jalapa,* colonial and flower-rich; the river town of *Tlacotalpan; Lake Catemaco;* the volcanic peak, *Orizaba,* and the resort-spas, *Fortín de las Flores* and *Tehuacán* (in the State of Puebla).

Veracruz, Ver. Pop. 101,500. Alt. 6 ft. Mexico's leading port.

HOW TO GET THERE: *Via air* — CMA runs daily flights from Mexico City and Mérida. From Mexico City, 1½ hrs. Fare: around $30 round trip. *Via railway* — Ferrocarriles Nacional de México, daily service, Pullman, diner and lounge car. Leaves Mexico City at 8:25 P.M., arrives in Veracruz, 8:15 A.M. Another train leaves at 9:05 A.M., arriving in Veracruz at 8:50 P.M. The fare one way is $25.60 MN. Lower Pullman, $25 MN. *Via bus* —ADO Line buses, first class, go either via Jalapa, or Fortín. Travel time: 8 hrs. Also, Flecha Roja Line. Rates: $25 MN one way. (For tickets and bus terminals in Mexico City, see Index.) *Via road* — there are various paved highways and circuit routes to Veracruz from Mexico City: via Puebla, bypassing it, via Cordoba and Orizaba, and a circuit tour via Pachuca, Papantla to Veracruz.

HOTELS: For generations the great and wealthy traveled via Veracruz on their way to and from Europe and the hostelries of the city were famed for their fine accommodations and cuisine which vied with the best in Europe. Since the decline of sea travel from Veracruz in favor of auto, train, and plane, accommodations in the city have become ordinary. Although some of the hotels are first class, we describe none as outstanding.

Hotel Mocambo, 6 m. S on road to Alvarado, and on the only beach with charm anywhere near the city, 95 rooms, 2 pools, cocktail bar, dining room and terrace. The whole is somewhat shabbily run, yet the best place if you want seaside atmosphere. Rates: AP $150 MN dble, and up. *Hotel Veracruz,* 1 block from the Plaza Principal. 175 rooms, dining room, bar. An attractive, ultramodern plant. *Diligencias Hotel,* on the Plaza Principal. 100 rooms. A good, old-fashioned hotel, right in the center of things. Rates: EP $50 MN dble, and up. *Emporio Hotel,* on Paseo Malecón, facing waterfront, 150 rooms, garage, swimming pool, dining room, bar, night club. Brand-new, with some air-conditioned rooms, the general atmosphere is chrome-plated and not especially attractive or friendly. Rates: EP $45 to $80 MN, dble. *Colonial Hotel,* on Plaza Principal, 75 rooms. A well-run, modest hotel excellent for those who travel inexpensively. Rates: EP $40 MN, dble. *Villa del Mar,* Boulevard, Avila Camacho, facing the ocean, 60 rooms, tennis, dining, bar, bungalows. Fair but somewhat sadly run. Rates: EP $50 MN, and up, dble. *Prendes Hotel,* on Plaza Principal, 34 rooms, good dining room. Old-fashioned and somewhat shabby. Rates: EP $50 MN and up, dble. *Hotel Florida,* Boulevard Avila Camacho and Cordova, 40 rooms. Barren accommodations, but it faces the ocean. Rates: $40 MN, dble, EP. In case you go to Veracruz for the famed Carnival when rooms are short, here is an added list of better-than-nothing lodgings:

Hotel Villa Rica, Boulevard Avila Camacho 1; *Hotel Castelan,* Boulevard Avila Camacho; *Hotel Imperial,* Lerdo 53.

RESTAURANTS: The sea food for which Veracruz is famed, once attracting people from far and wide, is good — but not *that* good any longer. Closest to being satisfactory is *Prendes,* in the hotel on the Plaza. *La Dilgencia* on the Plaza is also fair. Our favorite sidewalk café is *La Parroquia* on the Calles Independencia and Zamorra corner of the Plaza. Sitting there, sipping a *café con leche,* and watching the people go by is one of the pleasures of Veracruz.

For sea food in the rough, see *Mandinga,* listed below under Boca del Río excursion.

DIRECTORY: *Banks* — Banco Nacional de México, S.A. corner Madero and Rayón; Banco Veracruzano S.A., 5 de Mayo and Madero. *Federal tourist office* — Municipal Palace, facing on the Plaza. *Bus lines* — ADO (Autobuses de Oriente), Calles Doblado y Prim. Tel. 39-00. *Transportes del Istmo,* 20 de Noviembre y Calle Nueva. *Flecha Roja Line,* Calle Zaragoza 4 (buses to Mexico City via Jalapa) and 20 de Noviembre 5 (terminal for buses to Mexico City via Cordova). *Airlines* — CMA ticket office, Independencia 86, Tel. 22-42. *Railway* — Ferrocarriles Nacional de México, and Ferrocarril Méxicano, tickets at railway station. *American Consulate* — Corner of Arista and Malecón. *Doctors* — Dr. Guillermo Deschamps, (specialist in internal medicine and tropical diseases), Lucas Deschamp (surgeon), both bilingual and U.S.-trained; Office at Independencia 105. *Garages and car repairs* — Distribuidora de Autos, (General Motors), Díaz Mirón 231; Manuel Nieto (Ford), Rayón 79; Motores del Golfo (Chrysler, Plymouth), 10 de Mayo 324; Veracruz Motors, S.A. (Dodge) Víctimas del 25 de Junio 98. *Church Services* (Catholic) — La Parroquía Church, Sundays from 6 A.M. to 1 P.M.

THE CITY: Veracruz is the most Spanish of the Mexican ports, a corner of the Old World on the Gulf, with an atmosphere that has earned it the nickname of "Little Havana." It is gay, cosmopolitan, noisy. Its citizens and visitors delight in lolling around the Plaza in the late afternoon, sipping beer or soft drinks and playing dominoes, listening to wandering musicians as well as the town band. The city has no great museums or architectural wonders — its art is simply the art of living.

A stroll through almost any part of the city is sufficient to make a lasting impression on one. The buildings are of stucco or wood, painted mellow colors, and having long overhanging balconies. In the picturesque *barrios* tiny houses of clapboard and tiled roofs are painted unusual shades of pale pink, ochre, salmon, and blue, with red or emerald green doors and wooden *rejas* (iron grilles rust). They are set in the midst of small gardens crowded with almond trees, oleander, bougainvillaeas, and acacias.

The focal and social center of the city is the *Plaza Principal (Plaza de Armas, Plaza de la Constitución),* an animated spot flanked by the arched *portales* of the Municipal Palace (E side), of hotels (N and W side) and the parochial church (W side). A bandstand, tall coconut palms, and tropical flowers lend a gay touch to the plaza.

The Parochial Church (La Parroquia), on Avenida de la Independencia, facing the Plaza, is the most picturesque building in the city, and occupies the site of the church erected by the Spaniards soon after they founded the town. It was dedicated June 13, 1734, to Nuestra Señora de la Asunción. The interior is neither attractive, nor contains treasures of interest. The exterior, stained by time and salt winds, and lashed by hurricanes, has a patina of antiquity that is far more attractive than the interior.

Church of Christ of the Safe Voyage (La Parroquia de Santo Cristo del Buen Viaje), said to be the oldest church on this continent, facing Plaza Gutiérrez Zamora, (6 blocks from the Plaza on Ave. Independencia).

Several blocks E of the Plaza lie the harbor, docks and customs offices of the port. A walk down the Paseo del Malecón in the area of the lighthouses is interesting. At the end of the Malecón one can continue along Boulevard Avila Camacho which flanks the sea, for a promenade of several miles along the bay.[3]

Open-air trolley cars run between the center of town and the beach area and the Villa del Mar Hotel.

The Fortress of San Juan de Ulúa (Castillo de San Juan) is the city's prime local monument. Though historically important it is not particularly attractive. It lies in the harbor on Gallega Reef and can be reached either by boat from the lighthouse (hour trip, 2 persons, about $35 MN), or you can get there by car or cab in 10 min., going to the *Aduana* (Customshouse) on the waterfront two blocks from the Plaza, there crossing over the bridge to the causeway that leads past the docks and out to the fortress.

The Fortress, composed of arsenal, chapel, drydock, marine signal station plus prison dungeons, was begun in 1528 on the spot where Grijalva landed 10 years before. The foundations and ramparts of the fortress are unusually massive, having withstood the pounding of the sea and fierce naval bombardments over four centuries. Between 1746 and 1771 the fortress had a fortune poured into it, equipping it with arms and defenses — 100 brass cannons, some 170 other pieces of ordnance and mortars. So much was spent on Ulúa, over 40 millions of pesos, that according to one story, Charles V of Spain once stood on the balcony of his palace in Madrid and stared out to the west. When a courtier asked what he was looking for, the king replied, "I am looking for San Juan de Ulúa. It has cost me enough to be seen across the sea."

The site was used more as a prison than fortress, and a sentence to this *presidio* was the equivalent of sure death. During the Spanish regime unfortunates sent there were thrust into dungeon holes which were half-flooded at high tide. Some of the dungeons were too small to admit the bulk of a man in any but a crouching position, and the walls were vermin-infested and slimy with the filth of centuries. When the tide came in the unhappy prisoner sat immersed to his chin in salt water. Food was lowered to him through a manhole in the upper pavement. Much of this atmosphere is still evident.

From the fortress one has fine views of the city and, farther out to sea the Isla de los Sacrificios (Isle of Sacrifices) which was so named because the Spaniards first witnessed or saw evidences of human sacrifices there. The island can be visited via boat excursion. (Boats leave the main wharf.)

FIESTAS: Veracruz is famed for its Carnival or Mardi Gras. The week before Lent almost all business in the city comes to a stop for the gay festivities, the street dancing, floats, and costumed merrymakers. For days no one sleeps and the streets are a vivid labyrinth of Veracruzanos dancing their *huapangos* and *bambas,* strumming harps and guitars and singing happily.

EXCURSIONS OUT OF VERACRUZ: BOCA DEL RÍO area: Pop. 2048. A fishing village at the mouth of the Río Atoyac (CN-180), 7 m. S of Veracruz. River fish-

[3] The bay and harbor, formed by the coast and the Gallega reef has an area of over 550 acres and an average depth of over 30 ft. The sea wall, with a coping of Scandanavian granite, was constructed after the turn of the century. The breakwaters *(rompeolas),* constructed of 35-ton concrete blocks, form some of the favorite promenades.

ing, water skiing at the Club Boca del Río. Once the cluster of fishing shacks making up the village were a favorite Veracruzano eating place, but their popularity has been superceded by a village called *Mandinga.* To get there, cross the bridge at Boca del Río, turn left on the side road that leads to the Naval Academy. Go 4 m. then turn right to Mandinga. There is a cluster of fishing shacks and two lagoons, one which is fished for shrimp, the other for clams. Waterfront-style feasts of fried fish, squid *(pulpos),* clams and shrimp plus refreshments are available.

An ideal picnic spot in this vicinity can be reached by turning left after crossing the Boca del Río bridge, then instead of continuing on the Mandinga road, turn left again a short distance from the highway and go as far as you can go. Here and to the left there are sand dunes, wooded areas, lovely beaches. Beware, however, of sharks.

FROM VERACRUZ TO TLACOTALPAN: One should allow two days for this pleasant excursion up the Papaloapan River. Although one can reach the river town by newly opened roads branching off from the Veracruz-Orizaba highway, the most delightful way is to go by boat from Alvarado.

Alvarado, Ver. Pop. 8850. On CN-180, about 40 miles S of Veracruz. Daily bus and train service from Veracruz to Alvarado. *Hotel: Puerto de Alvardo,* very primitive and not recommended except in an emergency. A ferry, $5 MN, takes cars across the Papaloapan River where the highway continues to Coatzacoalcos.

The town is a somewhat picturesque fishing port at the mouth of the Papaloapan River. It stands on a peninsula formed by the sea and river. A line of sand dunes rises directly back of the port. In the village a time-stained church bears the date 1779. The townspeople have a reputation throughout Mexico as being the bawdiest, toughest-talking people in the country, and birthplace of some of the best sea-food cooks. The men are indeed tough — in 1914 when the Americans seized Veracruz, Alvarado was occupied by forces under a Lieutenant Hunter of the U.S.S. *Scourge,* and the town was the scene of several sanguinary battles.

For trips up the river to *Tlacotalpan* and *Tuxtepec* there is a daily mail-line boat that carries passengers. Directly behind the boat dock is a garage where you can safely leave your car. The river trip (to Tlacotalpan) takes about two hours.

FROM ALVARADO TO TLACOLTALPAN TO TUXTEPEC: Shortly after leaving Alvarado the river channel narrows. The scenery is tropical and fascinating; on each side of the river are small ranches devoted to cane and coconut culture. The banks are dotted with palm-thatched huts from which a path invariably leads to the river edge where a log canoe is usually moored. Tall coconut trees shade each diminutive native home and furnish many articles necessary to the native economy.[4]

As the boat ascends the river the coconut groves thin out, replaced by banana plantations and ranching country.

Tlacotalpan, Ver. Pop. 5900. The first large town on right-hand side of the river (N bank). This is one of the most completely charming towns in Mexico. It is, as a French visitor observed, "a kingdom of confectionary colors." The town, known as La Perla de la Costa (Pearl of the Coast) is almost like a make-believe theater set — flower-embowered homes, the two pink and blue churches on the plaza, the river front with its arching palms, and the streets which are wide, and covered from curb to curb with intense green lawn. Until recently no automobiles were able to enter the town.

The place has some fine houses, often filled with wonderful old furniture, for the town was a kind of winter home for the wealthy of Veracruz. Being upriver it served as an important port and trading center, for it was sheltered from pirates. On the river, opposite the town, a white line of foam marks the junction of the waters of the San Juan and the Papaloapan Rivers. River fishing here is excellent.

HOTELS: *Hotel Central* (facing the boat landing) and two others in town have deteriorated sadly. Your best bet is have one of the boys who meet you at the dock take you to the private home of one of the several families who take in visitors.

The fiesta honoring the Virgin of Candelaria, around February 2, is celebrated with wonderful intensity in Tlacotalpan. It is one of the most colorful in the country and includes regional dances, serenades, fireworks, and some of the most exciting *bamba* dancing and regional *sones* this writer has witnessed in Mexico. Sometimes there are *embalses,* the bringing of fighting bulls across the river and letting them loose in the streets so everyone can fight them, much as in the street bullfights in Pamplona, Spain, during the feast of San Fermín.

Normally smaller launches can continue up the river to *Tuxtepec,* formerly a shipping town of some importance. Due to changes being made in the river itinerary (the Hydraulic Works Ministry is presently harnessing the river) one must sometimes transfer to smaller boats at *Chacaltianguis.* Above *Tlacotalpan* vast banana plantations line the riverbank, and farther up, huge sugar and tobacco plantations. One estate, *San Cristóbal,* had its own small railway, employed over 600 workers to produce some 2000 barrels of sugar and 120 barrels of rum per day. The entire region, the Papaloapan Basin, is currently undergoing rapid changes.[5]

[4] The original home of the coconut tree *(Cocos nucifera)* is the East Indies, although it is now common in tropical America. On the many crescent-shaped beaches along the Gulf and Pacific shores, these noble trees may be seen in all their beauty and productiveness. The rough cylindrical trunks, sometimes 2 ft. thick, soar 50 ft. or more above the ground, bearing thick clusters of valuable fruit amid their crowning tufts of feathery leaves. What the cactus is to the Mexican highland, the coconut is to the people of the tropical littoral — its fruit furnishes food and drink, its leaves are used to thatch their cottages, to make floor matting, and for clothing; for baskets and bags, fans, etc. The unripe coconut milk supplies a very refreshing (but slightly laxative) drink. For this the nut is taken when quite green, the cap is cut off the small end by a quick blow of a machete, and the sweetish milk is drunk clear, or mixed with rum. In resorts along both coasts this drink is popularly called *"coco loco"* (crazy coconut).

When the nut is half-matured a small white lump (the ovule), like the stalk of a young mushroom, can be discerned amid the creamy, half-formed mass. This ovule is always opposite the soft eye (the two remaining are filled with hard shell) and as the nut lies in the sand, exposed to heat, rain, and dew, the lump develops into a baby finger which seeks the vulnerable exit. Once in the sunlight the finger curves upward, while fibrous nerves draw sustenance from the albuminous cream which lines the inside of the shell. As the roots grow downward the green embryonic trunk starts upward. In seven years it matures and the tree bears fruit during its 60 years or more of life.

[5] Papaloapan Basin is the site of one of the Mexican Government's vast TVA-type electrification, irrigation, and reclamation projects. The basin includes nine major river and smaller tributaries contributing to the Papaloapan River which itself is about 130 m. long and navigable half its length. The basin takes in part of three states — Oaxaca, Puebla, and Veracruz (½ its area is in the Gulf side of Oaxaca; 38 per

VERACRUZ TO LAKE CATEMACO AND COATZACOALCOS: Although this excursion can be done in one day, it is well worthwhile to pause overnight or longer at Lake Catemaco.

Take Gulf Coast Highway south to Alvarado (CN-180, see Index). Cross the Papaloapan River and continue south. To the south of the highway, deep in the jungle are the difficult-to-reach Olmec archaeological sites of *Tres Zapotes* and *Hueyapan* where the baffling, colossal carved stone heads with the "football player's" helmets were found. The first head was found at Tres Zapotes during the middle of the last century by farmers who thought the head (buried) was the bottom of a huge inverted kettle. It was not until 1938, however, that complete excavation of the head was made by a National Geographic Society and Smithsonian Institution expedition headed by Matthew W. Stirling. Tourists may see some of these colossal heads at the interesting outdoor archaeological museums in Jalapa and Villahermosa.

San Andrés Tuxtla, Ver. Pop. 15,200 (140 m. from Veracruz on CN-180). Alt. 1332 ft. The town is in a picturesque kettle-shaped valley formed by volcanoes; a pretty place with white houses, tiled roofs, and overflowing with tropical flowers.

HOTEL AND RESTAURANT: *Hotel Colonial,* Pino Suárez and Belisario Domínguez. *Viajero-type.* A better, or at least newer restaurant, is situated in the ADO bus-line station on the highway at the entrance of the town.

A short distance from the town is a small crater lake, *Laguna Encantada* (Enchanted Lake), 1½ m. in circumference, believed to be bewitched because the water level rises during the dry season and sinks in the rainy season.

San Andrés is also noted for an important archaeological discovery made by a native working in a tobacco field near the town. The man uncovered a pale green jadeite figurine, beautifully carved and polished. The 8-inch high figure represented a fat bald-headed priest with a jolly face and duck's bill mouth. On its stomach were Maya dot and bar characters indicating a date (98 B.C.) which made it one of the most important archaeological finds in America. The figure caused a good deal of controversy since the nearest known Maya outpost was at Comalcalco. Tab., 150 miles' distant. Since then, of course, more has been learned about the Olmecs and their relationship with the Mayas. Also, in 1939 Stirling at Tres Zapotes (20 miles from Tuxtla), discovered a stone slab with a jaguar mask on one side and a glyph date on the opposite, corresponding to 291 B.C.

The jade "Tuxtla Statuette" is now in the National Museum, Washington, D.C.

Lake Catemaco. On the highway, 8 m. from San Andrés Tuxtla. The lakeside village (1 m. from highway) is called Catemaco. Pop. 6000. Alt. 1254 ft.

HOW TO GET THERE: *Via railway* — Ferrocarriles Nacional de México, Veracruz to San Andrés Tuxtla, thence by bus or taxi to the lake. *Via bus* — ADO line from Veracruz.

HOTELS: The only suitable hotel is the somewhat chrome-plated style *Hotel Playa Azul,* at Playa Azul beach. 41 rooms, dining room only fair, bar, beach, and boats. Rates: EP $40 MN dble, and up. *Hotel Julita,* in Catemaco, facing lake. Rather third class.

RESTAURANTS: There are several open-air eating places on the lake front — *Julita, Carmucha,* and *La Luna* — specializing in locally caught *mojarra* (sunfish) and regional cuisine. *La Luna* serves good fish and the best hot *tortillas* this writer has tasted anywhere in Mexico.

THE VILLAGE AND LAKE AREA: The village is lazy and picturesque. The market is held on Sunday mornings. A popular mineral water "Coyame" is bottled here. The lake, surrounded by volcanic mountains and magnificent jungle verdure, is one of the most beautiful natural lakes in the country, reminding one of some of the Bavarian lakes. Its attractiveness has not yet been spoiled by the clutter of speedboats and so-called fashionable resort hotels that crowd other Mexican lakes. Boat trips to Playa Azul and other lake villages make pleasant outings. Rates from $3 MN to $25 MN, depending on the distance. Hunting and fishing in the area excellent. One can also take pleasant short outings to the villages of *Arroyo Agrio* and *Cuetzalapa;* the *Teoteapan Waterfalls* (½ m.). *The local fiestas:* Candelaria (February 2) and Virgen del Carmen (July 16) are most colorful.

The region east of Lake Catemaco, to the Gulf shore, is an anthropologist's heaven. It is an isolated area of rugged mountains — the San Martín volcano reaches about 6165 ft. — and tiny, lost villages reachable only by jeep or horseback. There are abandoned coffee *fincas* and villages of Popoluca Indians *(Ocozotepec, Soteápan, Mecayápan,* and *Piedra Labrada)* which are Popoluca linguistic isles scattered among surrounding Náhuatl speaking people. Among these villages Mecayápan is especially interesting for the local customs, crafts and folklore which are yet untouched by the twentieth-century highway passing not far away. The village is rather pretty, has an enormous thatch-roofed church and a separate thatch tower or steeple on stilts, much resembling an overgrown mushroom. The women handweave

cent in Veracruz, and 12 per cent in Puebla). About 53 per cent of the area is mountainous. The government work of opening this area and bringing it into the stream of national development has been unusually difficult because of the nature of the terrain and the isolation of the people in it. Some one million and a half people inhabit the area. Due to lack of communications, even language barriers, many of the Indian groups had no concept of what Mexico was, what the government was trying to do. Often the tribes within the area were utter strangers to each other.

Among the peoples in this amazingly isolated, beautiful region we find the *Jarochos,* living on the lower plain, a sickly people afflicted for many generations by malaria and parasitic diseases. To the south the *Popolucas,* an extremely primitive group, wearing archaic dress, the women going nude from the waist up, and the people eating mud to appease their nutritional poverty. West of them are the *Chinatecos,* occupying one of the most fertile areas of the basin, and raising the highly prized cigar-leaf tobacco known as *Valle Nacional.* Some 20,000 *Mazatecos* lived in the area which the government set aside for a dam-lake. Two of their towns, *Soyaltepec* and *Ixcatlán* now are islands in the lake. The latter town was one of the region's most important witchcraft centers; its men talk to one another across great distances in whistle codes. In addition to these there are the *Zapotecs, Chochos* and *Mixes* of the upper basin (see *People of Oaxaca,* Index). In one isolated pocket there is even one primitive Negro village.

Today the region is fairly accessible to travelers. In addition to river routes, a network of roads now crisscrosses the area. From Veracruz it is now possible to drive in via the Córdoba-Veracruz Highway, turning off at *Las Tinajas,* toward *Ciudad Alemán* (45 m.). The Ciudad Alemán road is paved. From there less comfortable roads reach to Cosamalopan (where there is a small, new hotel) and to Tlacotalpan. There is also a very rough road up through the sierra from Ciudad Alemán, through *Túxtepec, Valle Nacional* to *Oaxaca City.*

Ciudad Alemán is the administrative center of the project, a modern settlement with functional houses, a small hotel, restaurant and clubroom (mostly for engineers). The climate and the location makes it almost uninhabitable.

their own marvelously colored striped skirts, and Bali-like, they wear nothing else.

Still farther is the Gulf section of the Isthmus of Tehuantepec, tied to this century by the Trans-Isthmus branch of the National Railways and the new Gulf Coast Highway. This area has little to recommend it touristically, except that you can breakfast near one ocean and drive across the continent and have lunch at the shores of the Pacific. The district back of Coatzalcoalcos, however, is of increasing importance to Mexico for its subterranean wealth — oil and sulphur.

In the past ten years a boom fever as intoxicating as the local rum has swept the towns of Coatzacoalcos, Minatitlán, and Jaltipán. The discovery of vast, undreamed-of sulphur deposits have poured new wealth into the area. Refrigerators and air-conditioning units are being bought by Mexicans with bulging bankrolls; slapdash buildings are mushrooming in the towns, honky-tonk bars sprout overnight.

The Isthmus deposits are estimated to be the world's richest. In a matter of less than a few years Mexican production of sulphur leaped from almost zero to over 2,500,000 tons annually, more than half the U.S. production and 40 per cent of the world total — and production is only beginning.[6]

Jaltipán, Ver. (on the Gulf Coast and Trans-Isthmus Highways). Locale of the vast Jaltipán Sulphur Dome. Hernán Cortés' mistress, Malinche, was supposed to have been born here, and is said to have come back once.

Minatitlán, Ver. (½ mile from highway, about 10 m. E of Jaltipán). Pop. estimated over 23,000 and growing. The town is something like a wild West boom town, being an important sulphur and oil center.

HOTELS: *Hotel Del Tropico,* Hidalgo and Iturbide. 59 rooms. EP, $40 MN, dble. *Viajero*-type. *Auto services* — Juan Osorio Lopez (Ford), Calle Hidalgo; Salvador Bustani y Cia. (Nash), Calle Iturbide. *Banks* — Banco Nacional de México, S.A., Calles Hidalgo and Iturbide.

Coatzacoalcos, Ver. Pop. 25,000. (On CN-180 and also CN-185; about 178 m. SE of Veracruz). A busy, smelly, noisy port, formerly called Puerto México. It is the Gulf terminus of the Trans-Isthmus branch of the National Railways and of the Trans-Isthmus Highway, and an important shipping center for petroleum, sulphur, tropical fruits, and hardwoods.

The town is situated at the mouth of the Coatzacoalcos River which here forms a deep, horse-shaped, almost landlocked bay. There are high sand dunes facing the gulf. The huge portworks, jetties, etc., were built by the British in 1900 when the Isthmus Railway was expected to compete successfully with the Panama Canal. Failing, the port declined and its equipment rotted and has only begun to be refurbished as a result of the sulphur boom. Though the city is hot and drab, nearby villages — Cosoleacaque, Oluta, and Texitepec — are noteworthy for their tropical beauty.

HOTELS: *Hotel Lemarroy,* Zaragoza 15. Best of the not very attractive hotels in town; *Hotel Oliden,* Boulevard Avila Camacho 3, and *Hotel Cortazar,* Colón 36, will both do in a severe pinch. The only two restaurants we visited were: *Restaurante del Casino Puerto,* Hidalgo and Corrigedora; *Merendero* on Venustiano Carranza. Good sea food in both, otherwise, so-so fare.

DIRECTORY: *Car repairs* — J. Roque Lemarroy (GM), Calles Zaragoza and Corrigedora; Juan Osorio Lopez (Ford), Calle Juárez 4; Amelia Candanedo (Dodge), Malpica 32. *Bank* — Banco Nacional de México, S.A., Avenida Juárez and Corrigedora. *Airline* — CMA, Zaragoza 31-A. Tel. 12. *Railway* — Mexican National Railways, tickets at depot. The terminal for the Sureste Railway is across the river at Allende. The ferry crossing the river charges $5 MN per car.

EXCURSIONS SOUTHWEST AND WEST OF VERACRUZ: Medellín is a favorite Veracruzano picnic and river bathing spot about a half hour drive from the port (12 m.). Local buses go regularly and the Veracruz to Alvarado line of the railroad stops there. Motorists can drive from the port via the Jalapa-Mexico City Highway (CN-140). About 4½ m. from the port, turn left on the paved road to Medellín (6½ m.).

Medellín, Ver. Pop. 590. At the junction of the Atoyac and Jamapa Rivers. The site was occupied by an Indian town of some importance before the conquest. The ruins of a prehistoric town, *Xicalanco,* lie in the forest nearby. The Spaniards destroyed the old town and Cortés, who had a predilection for the spot, founded the new town and named it after his native city in Spain. Here he returned after his disastrous expedition to Honduras in 1526. During the siege of Veracruz by the Imperial troops under General Miramon (executed with Maximilian) this spot was the headquarters of the army.

An excursion to Cordoba, Fortín de las Flores, and Orizaba (Mexico City, Puebla, Cordoba, Veracruz Highway, CN-150) is about 200 miles round-trip from Veracruz and is one of the most spectacular drives in the country. Some of the more interesting points and side trips include:

Cerro de Las Mesas, Ver. (Archaeological Zone). About 58 m. from Veracruz. Take CN-150 and about 6 m. W of Mecayucan there is a turn off, left (S) toward Piedras Negras and Ignacio Llave (pronounced YAH-vay). Cerro de las Mesas is the center of a vast

[6] The men largely responsible for this fabulous development are the three Louisiana-born Brady brothers — Ashton, Lawrence, and William. They first picked up the scent of Mexican sulphur in 1940 when Ashton, while browsing through a 1904 Shell Oil Company exploration report, noted a mention of salt-dome formations in Tehuantepec. The brothers figured there might be sulphur in the domes and, working as a team, began prospecting and exploring in the steaming jungle. Their operations were slowed down by the war, lack of sufficient funds, by torrential rains which turn the region into a quagmire six months of the year.

Following two unsuccessful tries they brought in a well at San Cristóbal, 35 m. inland from Coatzacoalcos. By 1947, with 3,000,000 tons proven out, they moved on, 20 m. west to Jaltipán where they discovered the great Jaltipán Dome, now considered the greatest sulphur dome yet found, surpassing even Texas' famed Boling Dome. From there they moved on to score again by locating the Mezquital Dome.

What makes Mexico's sulphur so important is the fact that the deposits are located in domes which can be mined by the Frasch process — superheated water is pumped into the ground, liquefying the sulphur which is pumped to the surface. The Frasch process is as low as one tenth the cost of other methods which must be used where difficult-to-find domes do not exist.

A large percentage of the companies now involved in the Isthmus sulphur boom are U.S. or foreign, their having been the only ones to risk capital in the venture. Since Mexican law classifies sulphur production as mining, there have been few restrictions on foreign activity in this field. The companies, Pan American and Gulf Sulphur Corporations, work under an agreement with the Mexican government in which they pay a sliding scale of production royalties of between 4 per cent to 15 per cent, plus an export tax ranging up to 8 per cent.

archaeological zone that runs along the Río Blanco in the jungle and grassland between the villages of Piedras Negras and Ignacio Llave.

This area, translated as "Hill of Altars," is of fairly recent discovery and has not been completely investigated. It is Olmec Culture. There are hundreds of mounds (probably tombs) and small pyramids separated by wide plazas and courts. The area was undoubtedly occupied from a period before the time of Christ to the period of the conquest. A stele uncovered by Dr. Spinden, bears a date corresponding to 206 A.D. Of unusual interest are some carved monolithic altars with life-size figures sitting on them, cross-legged, in a kind of arched niche; and a great monolithic altar in the form of a colossal head which has a hole starting at one ear and emerging at the mouth, a remarkable prehistoric Henry Moore sculpture, which may have been used as a Western Hemisphere Oracle of Delphi.

A short time ago a sensational discovery was made at Cerro de las Mesas when Matthew W. Stirling and a group of archaeologists unearthed one of the most magnificent caches of jade ever found in America — over 700 objects, including jade skulls, jewelry, carved figures, and an eight-inch boat with the Olmec jaguar-baby face decorating each end.

Córdoba, Ver. Pop. 32,733. Alt. 2625. CN-150 (88 m. from Veracruz). A picturesque, tropical town, center of an important tobacco, coffee and fruit region.

HOTELS: None of the hotels in town are attractive enough to recommend, being of the *viajero-type*. If you do not mind minimum comforts — *Hotel Zevallos,* Av. 1 11; *Hotel Mansur,* Av. 7. and Calle 3.

BANK: Banco Nacional de México, S.A., Av. 3a #140.

AUTO SERVICE: Gonzales S.A. (GM), Av. 3 and Calle 5; Sustaeta S.A., Av. 3 and Calle 2 (Ford).

RAILWAY: Ferrocarril Méxicano, service from Mexico City to Veracruz. A very scenic route but the service and equipment do not recommend themselves for comfortable touring.

THE TOWN AND ENVIRONS: Córdoba (also spelled Córdova, from the Arabic, *Karta-tuba* — important city) was founded April 18, 1618, by order of the Spanish Viceroy Don Diego de Fernandez de Córdoba. Though the climate is warm and moist, rain falling frequently during 9 months of the year, and despite the mud of the market and the medieval sanitary arrangements of the city, Córdoba with its grass-grown streets, its tropical gardens and the jungles beyond, has a great deal of charm.

About 50 years ago T. Philip Terry described Córdoba thus: "Some of the houses, erected when the town was founded, are very ancient and time-stained. Antique Spanish-Moorish windows *(ventanas),* heavily barred with iron, quaint wooden balconies, massive colonial doors with huge iron knockers *(llamadores)* and studded with broad-headed hand-wrought copper nails, are characteristic features. Most of the houses are low and are roofed with red tiles *(tejas)* which form a pleasing contrast to the luxuriant green of the tropical vegetation. The roofs are the favorite promenades of splendid peacocks. Somnolent *zopilotes* (buzzards) constitute the street-cleaning department. The inhabitants are ostensibly very religious; clanging bells awaken the sleeper at five A.M. and for a time thereafter the streets are filled with towns-people going to early Mass. . . . Four fine palms and some handsome gardenias are the chief features of the dreary plaza, which is flanked on one side by a new municipal building; on the others by the church and some ancient *portales.* Many of the old residents assemble here and take the rest-cure throughout the drizzling days. To the sound of squawking parrots they sit around metal tables and smoke cigarettes, criticizing the doings of the *metropolitanos* at the capital, swap discarded political ideas, play dominoes, re-clothe jokes that came over with Cortés and sip claret diluted with seltz-water squirted from blue-glass syphons encased in wire network. The general atmosphere of this region is hazy and lazy. Facing the plaza is a house where the unfortunate Archduke Maximilian is said to have slept. Another house is pointed out as the spot where the treaty that recognized the Independence of Mexico was signed (August 24, 1821) by General Augustín de Iturbide and the last Spanish representative under vice-regal rule, Don Juan de O'Donoju.[7] The *Church of San Antonio* was founded in 1688 by the Franciscans: the present building (uninteresting) was completed in 1725. The *Church and Convento de San Hipólito* (also uninteresting) were founded in 1793. Córdoba recalls to mind the querulous traveller who complained that " 'there was nothing to see and they wouldn't let him see it!' "

If Mr. Terry could revisit Córdoba today he would find nothing changed, nothing missing but the seltz-water and claret. The peacocks are still there, the exuberant flowers, the uninteresting churches and the domino players. There is nothing to see in Córdoba. Its charm is in its persistence at remaining unchanged.

About 4 m. from the city, via unimproved road, lies the interesting Indian village of *Amatlán,* said to be inhabited by people of Maya stock. The villagers market fruit and bamboo carvings. May 1 to 4 there is a colorful fiesta honoring El Señor del Santuario.

Fifteen miles from the city, via good roads, lies *Atoyac,* an interesting tropical village and the nearby *Gruta de Atoyac* (Atoyac Caves) in which were found pre-Columbian skeletons, pottery, and other artifacts. The railway line crosses a section of the caves and the rumble of the trains overhead sounds like reverberating thunder.

Fortín de las Flores, Ver. Pop. 4565 (on the highway, 4 m. W of Córdoba). Fortín, meaning "fortress" was so named because it was a Spanish outpost during the colonial period. It is now famed as a resort village. Gardenias, orchids, azaleas, and other tropical flowers grow here in profusion. From the village there are excellent views of Orizaba Peak.

HOTELS: *Hotel Ruiz Galindo.* 150 rooms, fair dining room, gardenia-filled swimming pool, cocktail bar, bowling, 9-hole golf course. Rates: AP $200 MN to $235 MN, dble. EP also available. A popular tourist spot attempting to be de luxe. *Posada Loma Motel,* (½ m. E on CN-150), a pleasant and comfortable motor court with 8 units set in a beautiful tropical garden. Swimming pool. Rates: AP $138 MN to $150 MN, dble. EP available. *Hotel Yola,* Calle 7 Norte and Av. 1 Poniente. 20 rooms, modest rates, suggested only in a pinch.

TOWN AND SURROUNDINGS: Market day, Sundays. Fruit and flowers brought in from the surrounding region are eyefilling — fine Manila mangoes (introduced by Juan Antonio Gomez in 1770), excellent oranges, pineapple, papaya, and short, fat, yellow bananas *(Dominicos),* deliciously sweet. The latter are very perishable and are difficult to obtain in Central Mexico.

Well worthwhile is a stroll through the delightful Las Animas Gardens (belonging to the Ruiz Galindo Hotel)

[7] The treaty, known as the Pact of Córdoba, was signed in the building now occupied by the Hotel Zevallo.

and 2 m. beyond to Hacienda Mata Larga, an immense plantation growing oranges and limes and where, each day, the truckloads of gardenias are gathered for the hotel swimming pool.

From April 15 to 17 the town has a flower fair, and on August 3, a gay fiesta commemorating the founding of the village.

Huatusco (Archaeological Zone). On CN-15 which junctions with CN-150 at Fortín. About 26 m. N. Near the village of Huatusco, Pop. 6561, is an exceptionally well-conserved Aztec pyramid with temple similar to those that were destroyed in the Aztec capital, Tenochtitlán.

In the village of *Coscomatepec* (halfway between Fortín and Huatusco), on December 12, there is an especially interesting fiesta honoring the Virgin of Guadalupe in which the people of the village enact tableaux of the four appearances of the Virgin.

COFFEE ZONE: The area between Córdoba, Fortín and Orizaba is the heart of Mexico's richest coffee country and the highest grade native coffee is produced here, especially the valued *café caracolillo* (pea-bean coffee).[8]

Orizaba, Ver. Pop. 55,600. Alt. 4029 ft. On CN-150, about 93 m. from Veracruz.

The city is an important manufacturing center, having some of the largest cotton mills in the country, the famed Moctezuma Brewery, cement plants, a movie studio and nearby marble quarries. Noted for its pleasant climate it attracts winter visitors from the central plateau and summer visitors from the coastal regions.

HOTELS: *Gran Hotel de France,* Oriente 6, 21. Has 74 rooms (60 with bath). Budget-style *viajero.* Vacationists go on to Fortín.

DIRECTORY: *Auto repairs* — Automotores de Orizaba (GM), Poniente 7, 69; Automotriz de Córdoba, Poniente 7. *Bus lines* — Flecha Roja; Autobuses ADO. *Banks* — Banco Nacional de México, S.A., Madero and Oriente 2; Banco Veracruzano, Oriente 2 and Sur 3.

THE CITY AND ENVIRONS: Set in the lush vegetation of the tropical Maltrata Valley, Orizaba enjoys a year-around mild climate and almost year-around gentle rains. It occupies the site of a pre-Columbian Indian village which the Aztecs conquered in 1447 and which they renamed Ahuaializapan (Joyful Waters) for the many streams in the area.

Although industry had changed Orizaba, the city still retains touches of its colonial, tropical past. There are lovely quiet streets, white-walled, tiled-roof houses and flower-filled patios. The Plaza Principal with its bandstand, parterres of flowers, palms, roses, azaleas, and cacti is an attractive spot. *La Parroquia* (the Parochial Church) dominates the plaza, and is of some interest because of its unusual number of domes and its other colonial architectural features including an ungainly square tower that seems to have been an afterthought.

On the outskirts of the city is the Tuxpango Waterfalls and the powerplant that supplies the region with electricity. In the immediate area there are numerous picnic spots.

From the hills N of town excellent views are to be had of the Peak of Orizaba.

Pico de Orizaba (Orizaba Peak), also called Citlaltépetl — Mountain of the Star. Elevation, 18,851 ft.; the highest peak in Mexico. The perfect volcanic cone, snow-capped throughout the year, dominates the entire region and can be seen from as far as Veracruz and Puebla. According to Aztec legend, when Quetzalcoatl (God of the Air) died, his body was brought to the peak of Orizaba, where it was consumed by divine fire. His spirit took flight heavenward in the guise of a peacock. They believed his spirit would return to Mexico, and to the present-day Indian the mountain remains sacred.

Orizaba Peak is one of the prime targets of modern-day alpinists. The first recorded climb was made by a party of American officers of General Winfield Scott's army in 1848, and shortly afterward by a Frenchman, Alexander Doignon (1851). An iron crucifix now surmounts the peak. The usual climb-route is from *Ciudad Serdán, Pue.* A new route leaves from *Tlalchichuaca, Pue.*, to Villa Hidalgo (10 m. very rough road), and includes an overnight stop at *Piedra Grande* at 14,476 ft.[9]

EXCURSIONS FROM VERACRUZ TO CHACHALACAS, ZEMPOALA, JALAPA: Halfday or longer trips immediately N of the port to the beach area, Chachalacas, to the ancient Totonac city of Zempoala, and W to the state capital Jalapa, can be done easily by car. There are also rail and first-class bus connections with Jalapa. The highway route is CN-140 (Veracruz, Jalapa to Mexico City) — and to the beach area, an all-weather road that will eventually be part of the Gulf Coast Highway.

Boca de Chachalacas, Ver. Pop. 455. Turn off the highway, r. at Tamarindo (37 m. from Veracruz or 2 m. N of Puente Nacional). Chachalacas is a tiny fishing village at the mouth of the river of the same name. The beach is lovely and lonely. Accommodations are very primitive, about as they were when Cortés trudged along this beach. The local folks whip up some delicious sea food, especially freshly dug, small, sweet clams.

Zempoala, Ver. (Archaeological Zone). About 5½ m. N of Chachalacas, or 13 m. from the highway. The sixteenth-century Totonac capital famed for the role it played in the Spanish Conquest of Mexico. The city once had some 30,000 inhabitants. When Cortés landed on the Veracruz coast he proceeded to this Indian capital which the Spaniards called Cempoala. As the Spaniards made their way along the streets of the city they were struck with the beauty of the buildings, the vivid gardens, and by the joyous welcome the inhabitants gave them. The Totonacs and the famed "fat chieftain" of the place became Cortés' first allies.

Zempoala is the most extensive group of ruins of the

[8] Coffee, an Arab beverage, introduced into Europe during the mid-1600s, was perhaps brought to the New World through a single plant which a French naval officer carried to Martinique, in the West Indies, in 1720. The offspring from this plant has since been crossed and subdivided until there are now over 16 kinds produced in the Americas. It is Mexico's second-ranking agricultural export commodity, and the State of Veracruz grows 50 per cent of the total production.

The best beans grow at an altitude of 1000 to 3000 ft. Warmth, moisture, shade, and proper altitude are indespensable requisites for its successful culture. Coffee bushes are planted between rows of banana trees sufficient in number to shade the young plants which grow quickly and produce a marketable bean in two or three years. The leaves of the bush are broad, and glossy green, sometimes concealing the berries which cluster along the slender twigs and branches. The blossoms are very pretty — a handsome white flower resembling small tuberoses. The berry is shaped like a small bean enclosed in a pulp covered by an outer skin; forming a double berry about the size of a cherry. When the berries turn a bright red they are harvested, dried in the sun on level floors of stone and cement, separated, hulled, and stored.

[9] Before undertaking any Mexican climb, amateur alpinists should contact Sr. Mancilla or other members of the Club de Exploraciones de México, for the latest climbing data and routes. Address: J. A. Mateos 146, Mexico D.F. Tel. 19-52-46.

Aztec period to be found in the country. There are a number of pyramids built around a great courtyard, the largest being the Pyramid of the Temple of the Sun. It is built on the same platform that holds the Great Temple — the two constructions being separated by a terrace. The pyramid itself has six levels. Scattered over a wide area beyond the main courtyard are other temples. Most interesting is the Caritas (Temple of Little Faces) which has a series of niches with clay faces set in them.

When the Spaniards visited the city the stone walls were covered with white stucco that so glistened in the sun, at first sight, they imagined the walls to be of silver.

Jalapa, Ver. Pop. 51,200. Alt. 4540. Capital of the State of Veracruz, often called "The City of Flowers" and one of Mexico's most charming small cities.

HOW TO GET THERE: *Via railway* — daily trains from Mexico City and Veracruz. A de luxe Pullman (night) goes from Mexico City to Jalapa. Mexican National Railways. *Via road* — Mexico City, Texcoco, Veracruz Highway (see Index) and Mexico City, Puebla, Jalapa, Veracruz Highway (see Index). *Via bus* — first-class ADO buses and Flecha Roja buses from Veracruz or Mexico City.

HOTELS: *Hotel Salmones,* Av. Zaragoza and Pablo Sidar. The largest and most acceptable hotel in town. Old-fashioned, clean, friendly atmosphere. Good dining room. Garage. *Hotel Mexico,* Dr. Lucio 2, *viajero*-type. Low rates.

RESTAURANTS: *Restaurante Salmones,* in Hotel Salmones, good service and food. *Restaurante Don Quixote,* in Hotel Mexico at the back of the patio. Very good Spanish food. *Restaurant Emir,* Enríquez 15, a coffee shop and snack place within the *pasaje* of the building. Excellent coffee. *Papaloapan* has fair sea food.

DIRECTORY: *Auto repairs* — Jalapa Motors S.A. (GM), Calle Ursulo Galván 114. Super Autos Jalapa S.A. (Ford), Av. del Maestro 16. Mercantil Motors S.A. (Dodge), Avila Camacho 4. *Banks* — Banco Nacional de México S.A., Calles Lerdo and Carillo Puerto. Banco Veracruzano S.A., Calle Enríquez 10. *Bus lines* — Autobuses de Oriente ADO, Zaragoza and Bravo. Tel. 39-83. Autobuses Flecha Roja, Av. Revolución 115. Tel. 35-57. *Railway* — Mexican National Railways, ticket office at station. *Doctors* — Dr. José Fernandez, Talma 13 (bilingual and has studied in the U.S.).

MUSEUM: *Museo Arqueologia,* on the Highway to Mexico City about 2 m. from center of town. A beautiful and interesting museum and garden-museum containing priceless Olmec, Totonac, and other exhibits. Well worth a visit. *Hours:* 9 A.M. to 6 P.M. Free.

THE CITY: Jalapa, also spelled Xalapa (as X and J are convertible consonants in Spanish) and pronounced, ha-LA-pah, was a thriving Indian village when Cortés and his band of hardy adventurers marched through it on their memorable journey to the Aztec capital. The town's name is derived from the Indian word *xalli* (sand) and *apan* (river). The name of a popular hero, *Enríquez,* has been added to the Indian name, though it is seldom used.

The city, like Rome, is built on seven hills, situated in a valley flaming with tropical flowers, and guarded by imposing peaks — the distant Orizaba, and nearby Cofre de Perote (13,552 ft.), the latter so named because the topmost point resembles a chest. The Indian name for the Cofre was Nauchampatépetl (Square Mountain). Jalapa itself is a veritable Eden. The houses are pink, blue, and yellow, and the gardens are a riot of color. Many of the homes and public buildings are relics of vice-regal days — a blend of Spanish-Moorish architecture with massive walls and prisonlike windows flush with the pavement and protected by heavy iron bars. The overhanging balconies are usually laden with flowers; the tiles with which most of the quaint dwellings are roofed impart an air of great antiquity. In the early mornings the narrow, cobbled paved streets are thronged with donkeys bearing panniers of fruit and flowers for the local markets.

Soon after the fall of Tenochitlán the Spaniards settled in Jalapa. It became both a stronghold, a convenient stagecoach stop and a market center. During colonial times it was noted for its great annual fair held here to dispose of the merchandise brought back from Spain by the "silver fleet." In recent years a commemorative fair or fiesta (March 30 to April 20) has been initiated, but with the emphasis more on culture than on commerce.

Jalapa has become one of the most important cultural and educational centers in the country. Its school system is the most advanced in the nation; its small but fine university is staffed by a remarkably able group of teachers and intellectuals. The university has its own publishing house, experimental theater, art gallery, etc. The Xalapa Symphony is one of the two top symphony orchestras in Mexico.

One of the charms of the city is its student body, and the girls of Jalapa who are celebrated throughout the country for their loveliness. The proverb *Las Jalapeñas son halagüeñas* (The Jalapa girls are bewitching) is current in the vernacular.

Almost the only shortcoming of this city which is so remindful of parts of Naples — the twisting hilly streets and narrow delightful ways — is the frequent drizzle called *chipichipi,* caused when the clouds from the Gulf bank against the mountains behind the city and condense under the influence of cool air.

The city has no great architectural monuments or other treasures (excepting the museum of archaeology), but it needs none. The city is vivid and exhilarating itself. There are pleasing promenades and sights on every side. Jalapa has no true central plaza, its place being made up for by the handsome Parque Juárez (also called Jardín Morelos) with its beautiful promenades and its view of the city and valley. The Palacio de Gobierno, a relatively new (colonial style) building faces upon this park. The *Municipal Palace,* a new and similar style building in on the W facing the park. A few steps to the N directly across the main avenue from the Government Palace is the *Cathedral,* a late eighteenth-century edifice. The Cathedral is massive, with an ill-fitting pseudo-Gothic façade. It is one of the few churches in Mexico outfitted with stained-glass windows. It is built upon a steep slope and even the interior floor is more like a toboggan slide than an ordinary floor; the tiles making the stretch from the door to the altar even more slippery than would ordinarily be the case. It would be relatively easy for one to backslide in this church.

Via short taxi drive from the center of the city are the following attractions (within the city limits taxis charge $5 MN per trip, $15 MN per hour):

Macuiltepec (one of the seven hills). On the crest there is a *mirador* (lookout) offering enchanting panoramas of the region. On a clear day you can see the Gulf . . . *Parque Hidalgo* also called *Los Berros* (E edge of town) a picturesque promenade, a favorite study spot for the university students . . . A few blocks E of *Los Berros* is the new "Olympic" stadium and the handsome *Zona Universitaria* (University Campus). The University conducts an excellent summer school for foreign students (see Index). *Instituto de Antropología de la Universidad* (Museum of Archaeology) SW edge of town, flanking the highway to Puebla. Several of the colossal Olmec heads grace the museum garden. Although the museum has several buildings yet to complete, it is one of the best laid-out small museums in Mexico.

When local guides are nonplussed to find something more to interest the visitor they will point out the house in which Mexican President Lerdo de Tejada was born; the one occupied by Marshal Bazaine when with his French troops he retreated from the capital and left Maximilian to his fate; and the spot where American soldiers under Scott and Worth played baseball (1847) with the wooden leg[10] captured from General Santa Anna.

EXCURSIONS FROM JALAPA: NW of Jalapa, 4 m. on the road to Puebla, at *Banderilla* there is an extensive tropical garden, the Jardín Lecuona, famed for its over 200 varieties of orchids as well as azaleas, camellias, and other flowers.

Coatepec (12 m. S of Jalapa, via paved road). A quaint, attractive Indian village in jungle country filled with exquisite flowers and interesting walks . . . Las Animas coffee *finca* (a few miles from Jalapa on highway toward Veracruz) where you can tour a working coffee plantation and sip the final product . . . On the Puebla highway 33 m. N of Jalapa, and following a climb to 7800 ft., *Perote,* a nondescript roadside village. Nearby is the massive eighteenth-century fortress of San Carlos de Perote, scene of several sanguinary engagements between Mexican and French forces, and site also occupied by General Worth in 1847. From here, magnificent views of the Cofre de Perote.

THE PAPANTLA COUNTRY

This area, the northern portion of the State of Veracruz is most attractive, partially because it has remained somewhat isolated from the port city and the rest of the republic. It is a charming region noted for its excellent beaches, deep-sea fishing, its fascinating orchid jungles and one of the most unusual archaeological ruins in the country — El Tajín.

[10] Santa Anna's famed wooden leg, captured by the 4th Illinois Regiment, has resided for years in Memorial Hall at Springfield, Illinois. The leg purchased and worn later by the discomfited general is in the Morelia Museum.

The scrimmage in which the bombastic and irascible Santa Anna lost his real leg smacks of burlesque. The ten-year War of Independence keyed the Mexicans to such a fighting pitch that civil wars seemed almost a necessity in order to drain their martial enthusiasm. In one of these family disagreements (sacking the Parian at Mexico City in 1828) certain French subjects got between the firing lines, and France preferred a claim of $600,000 against the Mexican government. One item of the claim was demanded by a French pastry cook for pies and cakes alleged to have been stolen and eaten by the revolutionaries. This claim became known derisively as the *reclamación de los pasteles* — the pie claim. The French ultimatum of March 21, 1838, was followed (in October) by the appearance of a French squadron which captured the fortress of San Juan de Ulúa and occupied Veracruz on December 5. A landing party attacked the city early one morning while Santa Anna, its defender, slept. As the sailors entered their boats after a repulse, the drowsy general rushed them, and in the squabble was shot in the leg — which was amputated in a crude way, and was later removed from its resting place at Manga de Clavo and deposited under a fine monument at Mexico City. The real leg was later torn from its tomb in Mexico City (1863) and dragged with a cord through the streets, midst insults, albeit it was later secured and buried.

Several good highways enter the area: the Gulf Coast Highway (see Index) and the so-called Vanilla Route — Mexico City, Pachuca to Tuxpan (see Index). From Veracruz and Jalapa there are bus and highway connections. The base city, for extended exploration of the area, is Papantla (or Tecolutla), a few hours' drive from Jalapa.

Papantla, Ver. Pop. 11,361 (on CN-180). Alt. 983 ft. Important vanilla center and present-day focal center of the Totonac Indians.

HOTELS: *Tajín,* Calle Dr. J. Nuñez 12. Tel. 121. 42 rooms. Small, old-fashioned, clean and pleasant. Rates: $25 MN per dble. EP. *San Antonio,* Enríquez 3. Tel. 80. 24 rooms. Very modest, *viajero-type.* Rates, same as the Tajín. *Reservations should be made long in advance for Papantla's famed Corpus Christi fiesta, both in the town and at nearby Poza Rica and Tecolutla.*

RESTAURANTS: Nothing fancy here, but a regional dish can sometimes be incomparable. *Restaurante Tajín* in the Tajín hotel. *Pastrana,* Artes 2. *Isabel,* Enríquez 3.

DIRECTORY: *Bank* — Banco Nacional de México, Calles Enríquez and Piño Suárez. *Car repairs* — Lopez and Cia, Portal Madero 1. *Bus lines* — Linea Estrella, Av. Serdán (direct route to Mexico City). Transportes Papantla, Av. Serdán, (regional service). *Airlines* — there is no direct air service to Papantla. Lineas Aereas Unidas, S.A. (LAUSA) runs daily flights to nearby Poza Rica (within taxi distance of Papantla), plus extra flights on Fridays, Saturdays, Sundays, Mondays, and holidays. Round-trip rate to Poza Rica: $124 MN. Office in Mexico City, Izazaga 8-E. Tel. 18-68-41.

PAPANTLA AND THE TOTONAC INDIANS: Papantla (pah-PAHN-tlah), meaning, "land of papanes" a tropical bird, is one of the Gulf Coast's loveliest towns, cupped in an area of rolling hills covered with vivid green jungle. The town is the New World's principal vanilla-producing center and the heady odor of this valuable bean permeates much of the area. Throughout most of the year Papantla is pleasantly somnolent, coming to life on holidays and Sundays when the Totonac Indians of the region gather in the plaza and lend the place a dreamlike quality.

The Totonacs, descendants of the pre-Hispanic Totonac civilization (see Index, *Digest of Mexican History*), are one of the most interesting of Mexico's present-day indigenous groups. They are the wealthiest, thanks to their vanilla industry, and they have preserved their customs and cultural heritage more completely than almost anywhere else. Thought to be distant cousins of the Maya, they are (along with the contemporary Mayas of Yucatán) the most spotless and clean community in the country; their clothes shine in their whiteness, and their persons seem to radiate cleanliness. Their dress, both everyday garments and fiesta dress, is one of the fascinating sights in Papantla. Both men and women dress in white. The men wear a kind of voluminous white trouser, tied at the ankles, and resembling the harem pantaloons of dancing girls of the Near East. They wear a loose, long-sleeved white jacket with pleated yoke and open sport collar. A touch of elegance is added by a colored scarf, the *luxón,* worn rolled and knotted at the neck. Altogether they remind one of immaculate Pierrots. The women wear what resembles a bridal dress; skirt *(kan)* of transparent cotton with a colored petticoat beneath. Over their shoulders they wear a mantle of pre-Hispanic origin — the *quexquemetl* (Totonac, *quesquén*) — of white material with lacy edges, and beautifully machine-embroidered. Everyone goes barefoot.

FIESTAS: One of the most spectacular of all Mexican festivals is Corpus Christi in Papantla, with its famed "flying pole" or Voladores dance. The feast, a movable Catholic holiday occurring sometime between the middle of May and the middle of June, lasts ten days. As one writer has noted, the Christian celebration is incidental and "serves the Totonacs as an excuse, rather than a reason, for the annual festival. So far as the Indians are concerned this is the annual Vanilla Festival, celebrating the harvest — and the sale of the crop — with the age-old pagan dances that belong by tradition, to the season."[11]

The Voladores spectacle of Papantla is especially interesting for the involved folklore and customs attached to it. In her *Treasury of Mexican Folkways,* Frances Toor describes the background and event thus:

"The Totonacs of Papantla have only four flyers and a musician, who is also captain. The flyers are generally young, unmarried youths, who promise to fly for seven years in return for some favor already, or yet to be, received through the intercession of a saint. The boys are not supposed to have sweethearts, thus to keep their thoughts pure and their bodies strong for the offering. . . . They perform every year during the fiesta, and each time a new pole is set up. A week or so before the fiesta a large group of men go with the flyers to look for the pole, cutting their way through the jungle forest with their *machetes,* indifferent to the dangers of reptiles, heat and fatigue. When they reach their destination, they select a meeting place and disperse to look for the tallest, straightest, slenderest and most beautiful tree that is farthest away from where women live. Sometimes they find it quickly, because before leaving they have consulted a sorcerer . . .

"After finding the tree the group dance around it, begging its pardon for cutting it down. Then before cutting the branches off, the men give it a drink of *tepache* and spill a little on the ground after the first twenty blows to make it forget its pain. The cutting off of branches, the felling and transporting of the trunk is done with greatest care so there will be no scars on the tree when it is put up. Whenever it is necessary to stop to rest on the way in, then men sprinkle the trunk with brandy, in the middle and at the ends.

"A messenger informs the people at home when the party is to arrive, and many men go outside of the town to meet them at a place called La Garita. When they reach the plaza, more people are there to welcome them. Church bells ring, rockets burst, and the band plays. The flyers are given a feast, but before this they go to church to pray. Afterwards the tree is also fed, for the hole in which it is to stand is blessed with holy water and in it is placed an offering of food, drinks and smokes so that it may be content and not claim the life of a flyer.

"On the morning of Corpus Christi, the flyers, who are called *tocotines,* arrive in the plaza, dancing in single file, with their captain playing and dancing at their head. They wear red suits, short trousers and tight jackets, and pointed hats with a bunch of feathers on top and ribbons hanging down behind. From there they dance all the way to the pole, without breaking their line. At the pole the musician dances away from his companions, who form couples, facing each other. They then weave a dancing chain, one going to the right backwards, the other, left forwards, but always taking care not to turn their backs on the pole. Each movement is repeated three times and the entire dance, seven times around the pole. After this dance is finished the flyers climb the pole to their places on the frame at the top. The captain climbs up last and sits on a tiny drum platform.

"First the musician greets the east with his tune, which he repeats as he bends his body back until it forms an arc, playing all the time with greater intensity until he returns to a sitting posture. After he renders the same homage to the west, north and south, he hands his cap to one of the flyers who rubs the cap on the musical instruments as a sign of approbation. When he has it on his head again, he stands up facing the east, and makes seven turns on the minute platform. As he turns, he marks synchronously with both feet in jumps about ten inches high the rhythm of the melody he is playing. Sometimes, while standing on one foot, he makes ballet steps with the other in the air.

"When the musician is again seated, he hands his flute to the same flyer at his right, who receives it as if it were sacred, and expresses veneration for it by rubbing it against the frame and ropes as far as he is able to reach. After returning the flute, all prepare to fly. Upon hearing the first note of the melody, they let their bodies fall gently backwards. The ropes fastened to them begin to unwind. With head down, arms extended, they fly around the pole in circles.

"The captain remains on top, playing. One of the flyers, also with drum and flute, plays the same melody as he flies." The flyers make thirteen revolutions around the pole, representing the ancient Indian life-cycle of 52 years, divided into four epochs of 13 each.

In addition to the Voladores, the Totonacs have three other colorful dance groups performing at this fiesta, and at other times during the year. These are the Quetzales, the Negritos, and the Moros. Because of the well-to-do situation of the Totonacs, their dance and fiesta costumes are among the most vivid and expensive in the country.

THE VANILLA JUNGLE: The principal industry and source of wealth for the Totonac people is the raising of vanilla, the ice-cream orchid *(Vanilla planifolia),* the flower from which comes the finest vanilla extract. In pre-conquest times, the *Vanilla planifolia* used to grow wild in the jungle, but by the time that Cortés came to Mexico the Indians around Papantla were cultivating the climbing vine and carrying on a brisk vanilla trade with the Aztecs who used it as a medicinal charm and a flavoring for their chocolate. The Spanish carried vines from Mexico to the Philippine Islands, and from there it spread to other islands of the East, and to Madagascar (now the principal world producer).

According to Totonac legend, vanilla got its start in those dim, long-ago years when gods often spent their time among men. The Totonacs say that Xanat, lovely daughter of the Fertility Goddess, fell in love with a handsome Totonac boy, but being immortal, she could not marry him. Grieved by this, she turned herself into a flowering plant which, like love, would bear a fruit that brought only happiness. In this manner she would belong to her Totonac lover. Thus she became the orchid plant which twines lovingly around trees in the Totonac forest — bringing happiness and well-being to the Totonac people. Even today the Indian name for the lovely white flower that turns into the heavy-scented vanilla bean is called *Xanat.*

Today 90 per cent of Mexico high-quality vanilla is grown by the Totonacs. In the spring when sprays of this ivory orchid appear and are fully opened, they are pollinated by hand. Entire families of Totonacs go into their forest before daybreak to spend the morning carefully fertilizing the individual flowers and tending the plants. In late spring the vanilla bean begins to form from the flower, developing slender green pods somewhat like a string bean. By fall they are ready for harvest. The government has established the official harvest date

[11] *Made in Mexico,* Patricia Fent Ross. Knopf.

as November 15. Following the harvest the Indians nowadays bring their green beans into town and offer them for sale to the curers, descendants of the French and Italian settlers who came to Mexico in the 1860s and colonized this coast.

For the next five to seven months the beans undergo a constant process of sweating and drying, both in the sun and in steam ovens, so that the final product remains rich in extract, yet is so moisture free as not to mold. The cured bean turns to a rich chocolate brown. Although the bulk of the crop goes to plants where the vanillin is extracted and bottled, a small amount is sold in bean form for those cooks who like to make their own fresh extract which has a more exotic flavor than the processed extract.

EXCURSIONS FROM PAPANTLA: A number of interesting trips can be made in the Papantla area, none taking more than an hour to two hours. In order of interest or importance the high spots are El Tajín, Tecolutla, Tuxpan, described below. Though there is a road from Papantla to El Tajín (and most travel books and maps indicate it as the only one) it is suitable only for a jeep, and then is difficult. A paved road leads from Poza Rica to El Tajín, and is recommended.

AREA NORTH OF PAPANTLA: **Poza Rica, Ver.** Pop. 15,000. (12 m. from Papantla, near junction of the Gulf Highway CN-180 and the Pachuca-Tuxpan Highway, CN-130).

Poza Rica (POH-sah REE-kah) is Mexico's chief petroleum producing center. The countryside around is dotted with oil wells and is eerily lighted at night by the flaming gas wells. The town has in less than a decade been turned from a thatch-hut village into a bustling city with wide boulevards, tasteless modern buildings, and other indications of progress. The odor that permeates the air here is one of sulphur and oil.

HOTELS: The several hotels are all new, but strictly *viajero*-style. Rates range from $25 MN to $45 MN per dble, EP. The hotels are: *Hotel Poza Rica,* (best available), Av. 2 Norte. 60 rooms, some air conditioned. *Hotel Topatico,* Av. Central Norte 131. *Hotel San Roman,* across from the football stadium.

DIRECTORY: *Bank* — Banco Nacional de México, Av. 8 Norte and David Cano 3. *Auto service* — Automotriz Huasteca S.A., Av. Central Norte 1. *Bus lines* — Transportes Lázaro Cárdenas, Av. 2 Norte. *Airlines* — LAUSA (Lineas Aereas Unidas, S.A.) runs daily flights between Mexico City, Poza Rica and Tampico.

A paved road (11 m.) leads from Poza Rica to El Tajín. Ruins are a mile off the road, to l. (dirt road). The turn-off is not too well marked.

El Tajín: (Archaeological Zone). Hours sunrise to sunset. Admission, $2 MN. Tajín, meaning place of smoke (possibly incense), was the sacred city of the Totonacs, though some authorities state that the original builders were Olmecs. The ruins are set among beautiful verdure-covered hills which impart an air of pleasant melancholy and make Tajín one of the most attractive "ruined cities" on the continent. The area covered by the ruins is considerable, but as yet only a small portion has been explored and only a few buildings have been tastefully restored. The most important, and one of the spectacular buildings of ancient Mexico is The Pyramid of the Niches, a seven-story structure (showing Toltec influence) made of volcanic rock and adobe, covered with a whitish basalt, and unusual because of the windowlike niches (366 of them) which may have had something to do, in an occult way, with the Toltec calendar.

Notable also are the bas-reliefs and sculpture and columns found among the other buildings, and especially near the 100-yard-long Ball Court.

Castillo de Teayo: (Archaeological site). A late Toltec pyramid, about 21 m. N of Poza Rica. Interesting to archaeologists because it is one of the few such structures outside of the Maya region in which the original roofing of the temple is preserved. Ordinary vacationists skip it. To get there take CN-130 toward Tuxpan. Turn left at Tihuatlán and follow unimproved road to Teayo. The pyramid stands in the center of the plaza of the village that sprang up around it during the last century.

Tuxpan, Ver. Pop. 15,700. Alt. 10 ft. An old, somewhat downgraded seaport on the Río Tuxpan (also often written, Tuxpam). Seaside terminal of the Pachuca-Tuxpan Highway, CN-130, and also on the new Gulf Coast Highway, CN-180 (from Tampico to Yucatán).

Except for fishing and bathing, Tuxpan lacks worthwhile tourist attractions. The ocean and beach lie about 9 m. E of the city at La Barra Norte. This is a magnificent beach, wide and clean, stretching along the coast some 25 miles. You can drive along much of it — no road, just hard sand. Unfortunately there are no first-class resort accommodations. A few places offer food and primitive accommodations.

HOTELS: The local hotels, in the city or on the river (none at the beach) are poorly kept. Best available: *Los Mangos Motel,* Av. Independencia, on the river. 30 rooms, dining room, pier and boat service. AP, $140 MN to $155 MN per dble. EP, $60 to $75 MN. *Hotel Florida,* Av. Juárez 23. 62 rooms. Rates about the same as above.

RESTAURANTS: In town, the *Sobera,* Av. Juárez and Correo Viejo. Somewhat edible fare. On the beach at Barra Norte, *Florentino Ruiz* and also *Chita's Place.* Sea food without imagination.

DIRECTORY: *Bus lines* — Autobuses Estrella & Tres Estrellas, Av. Garizurieta and Berriozábal (first class to Tampico, Mexico City, Tecolutla, Nautla). Autobuses Lázaro Cárdenas, Av. Berriozábal 8 (Mexico City-Tampico). *Airlines* — CMA (daily flights to Mexico), Av. Morelos 11. *Bank* — Banco de Tuxpan, S.A., Av. Juárez and Garizurieta. *Auto repairs* — Automotriz de Tuxpan, Av. Juárez 1.

EXCURSIONS FROM TUXPAN: It is reported that the best fishing and skin-diving areas lie some 35 to 40 miles N along the coast at Isla de Lobos (Wolf Island) and in the *Tamiahua Lagoon.* They are reached by boat from Tuxpan. When completed, the coastal section of the Gulf Highway will skirt Laguna Tamiahua.

AREA EAST AND SOUTHEAST OF PAPANTLA: **Tecolutla, Ver.** Pop. 740. Alt. 5 ft. (On the Gulf Coast Highway, 26 m. E. of Papantla.) A quiet, somewhat shabby bathing and fishing resort on the Gulf and mouth of the Tecolutla River. Despite its barren accommodations there is a certain atmosphere about the place that makes you think of a still handsome woman, a bit past the bloom of youth, who just doesn't care about putting her hair up any longer. The palm-fringed beach is one of the nicest along the coast.

HOTELS: Best place, with good dining room, bar, and on the beach, is the one-time luxury hostel *Hotel Balneario Tecolutla.* It is about as passé as a 1930 Hollywood musical film. Badly maintained. Rates: AP, $125 MN and up. *Hotel Marsol,* on the beach, 50 rooms, chrome-plated style, and rundown. Rates are modest. AP, $90 MN and up, dble.

Nautla, Ver. and *Barra de Nautla.* Pop. 1450. (1 mile off the Gulf Coast Highway; 55 m. E at Papantla.) Nautla and neighboring *Casitas,* both attractive beach villages, though undeveloped touristically. Nautla is a river-delta town that has a wide arm of sand protecting the town from the ocean and forming a calm cove.

Eight miles inland (on the highway) and on the Nautla River is *San Rafael.* Pop. 2000. Like Nautla and other villages along this part of the coast, the town's inhabitants are largely of French descent. Just as you enter the town there is a tiny restaurant, *Tio Foncho,* where, if you give them time, you can get an excellent French meal. Owner Alfonzo Couturier and his family also have a modest hotel in town.[12]

THE TABASCO COUNTRY

The third section of the Central East Coast region is the State of Tabasco, a place of dense jungles, big-game areas, sparse population and inadequate communications. The name Tabasco (tah-BAHS-coe), meaning "damp earth," is an understatement, for from the air great sections of the state seem to be vast swampland, meandering river deltas and lagoons. The principal means of communication are the many beautiful rivers, the two largest — the Usumacinta and Grijalva — are navigable for considerable distances. The climate is generally hot, the rainfall, heavy in areas.

TRAVEL HIGHLIGHTS: Compared to other states, Tabasco has little to offer touristically. It is a place you cross through on your way to the fascinating Yucatán Peninsula, or to get to Palenque, one of the great Maya ruined cities in the adjoining State of Chiapas. Properly, it is a country for the off-trail explorer: hunting trips up the rivers and in the dense jungle, or discovering undeveloped Eden-like beaches along the coast, or even the adventure of riding through steaming jungles on the Sureste Railway.

The principal city, and our base for excursions, is Villahermosa.

Villahermosa, Tab. Pop. 40,000. Capital of State of Tabasco. Alt. 165 ft.

HOW TO GET THERE: *Road* — from Mexico City, Veracruz, and Coatzacoalcos via the new, paved Gulf Coast Highway, CN-180. *Via bus* — from Mexico City or Veracruz on the ADO Line (Autotransportes del Oriente). *Via air* — CMA runs daily scheduled flights from Mexico City to Veracruz, Villahermosa, and Mérida. *Via railway* — Sureste Railway stops at Teapa (nearest station to Villahermosa) and there is a train-bus service to the State capital. *Description of the railway route and schedules, see Index.*

HOTELS: Since tourism is brand-new to Villahermosa there are almost no happy accommodations. Most hotels are of the *viajero*-class. Best available are: *Hotel San Rafael,* Av. Constitutión 24 (backing on the river). 32 rooms (5 air conditioned). No dining room. Information service for hunting and fishing. Rates: $35 MN to $70 MN, dble, EP. *Hotel Manzur,* Madero 11. With a new 5-story, air-conditioned annex. 40 rooms. OTHER HOTELS: *Hotel San Diego,* Juárez and 27th de Febrero. For budget travelers there are several new, clean, and very modest hotels on Calle Lerdo between Av. Madero and Juárez — *Hotel Gallardo, Hotel Caballero, Hotel Palenque.* Rates: $60 MN, dble, EP., a/c rooms higher.

RESTAURANTS: There are no de luxe restaurants, but the eating is good to fair in the following: *Astoria,* corner of Reforma and Aldama; *Lourdes,* Juárez 62; *Restaurante Juárez,* Av. Juárez 63.

MUSEUM: *Museum of Archaeology,* on the main plaza. An absolute must for anyone going through Villahermosa. Likewise *El Parque Arqueozoológico* at the edge of town. See below.

DIRECTORY: Banks — Banco Nacional de México, corner of Juárez and Reforma. *Auto service* — Automotriz de Tabasco (Dodge), Madero 10; Casa Manrique (Ford), Juárez 26; Leandro Vidal (GM), 27th de Febrero 13; Moises Hernandez (Nash), Piño Suárez and Zaragoza. *Airlines* — CMA, Av. Hidalgo and 27th de Febrero. Tel. 11-69. TASA (Cia. Tabasqueña de Aviación S.A., for local flights in Tabasco and charter flights to Palenque, Bonampak, etc.), Independencia and Hidalgo. Tel. 10-55. *Railway* — Ferrocarril del Sureste office, Zaragoza and Aldama. *Buses* — ADO Line, Terminal Teapa, block east of the plaza; Transportes Teapa, Paseo Pasteur 2 (Villahermosa to Teapa); Transportes La Chontalpa (second class, route to Comalcalco, etc.). *Post office and telegraph:* corner of Aldama and Lerdo.

THE CITY: For years Villahermosa was described as a steamy, backward, flyspecked town, almost medieval in outlook. Today, due to new roads and links with the outside, it is anything but this. Instead there is an atmosphere of a borderland boom town. As yet the city isn't attractive; its blocks and streets are being torn up to make way for a new sanitary system, new buildings, and modern avenues. It is noisy, dusty, and often muddy.

The city lies on the bank of the majestic Grijalva River down which a great deal of produce from the region is shipped. The riverside docks are the take-off point for lanuch trips up or down the river. Until recently large side-wheelers and stern-wheelers, brought up from the Mississippi, cruised both the Grijalva and the Usumacinta River. The last of these fabulous vessels was wrecked in 1959.

Despite its air of chaos and growing pains, Villahermosa has several charming spots and important attractions. One need pay no attention to the architectural hodgepodges that are the *Palacio de Gobierno* and the *Palacio Municipal,* at the N and S ends of the *Plaza de Armas* (Principal Plaza). However, the *Museo de Tabasco* (Museum of Archaeology) at the SE corner of the Plaza, should definitely not be missed. It is by far the best-organized, presented, and equipped museum outside of Mexico City. Housed in a massive old building, once a prison and a school, the museum is tastefully decorated and contains a priceless collection of La Venta (Olmec), Maya, Aztec, and other sculpture and artifacts.

The *salas* (exhibition rooms) of the museum are as follows: 1 and 2 — (downstairs) Olmec culture, includ-

[12] This area, S of Tecolutla, was once almost solidly French. The colony was started in 1832 by a man from Dijon named Guénot who purchased sizable tracts along the coast then talked countless homefolk into settling here. Additional settlers came at Maximilian's invitation and became involved and powerful in the vanilla industry. For many years they had their own schools (French) and were permitted double citizenship. Many served in both the French and Mexican armies.

ing a magnificent colossal head of a smiling youth; 3 — Teotihuacán culture; 4 — México (Aztec) civilization; 5 — Excellent copies of the pre-Hispanic codices; 6 — West Coast cultures (Colima and Nayarit); 7 — Totonac culture. The exhibit is one of the finest in the country; 8 — Examples of the Mixtec and Zapotec civilization; 9, 10, 11, 12 — Exhibits devoted to the Maya civilizations. In the last room there are fine, actual-size copies of the celebrated Bonampak murals (see Index).

The museum, presenting an imaginative and valuable picture of the development of pre-Hispanic cultures and their interlacings, owes its existence and imaginative form to Carlos Pellicer, one of Mexico's most distinguished anthropologists and present director of the museum and, also to the various state officials who supported this unusual project. *Museum hours:* 10 A.M. to 2 P.M., 4 P.M. to 6 P.M. *Admission:* $2 MN. The museum is air conditioned (the only one in the country that is).

A little over 2 m. from the center of the city, on the road to Coatzacoalcos, situated next to the attractive city park *Parque Tabasco* and its idyllic Laguna de las Illusiones (Lake of Illusions), is the unique open-air *Museo de La Venta* (La Venta Museum and Zoological Park). This, another of Dr. Pellicer's imaginative projects, is an unusual and highly successful attempt to transfer an important, yet inaccessible archaeological zone to a place where people can see and appreciate it. A few years ago the colossal Olmec heads, altars — indeed, a whole archaeological zone — were moved from La Venta (65 m. away) to Villahermosa.[13]

The outdoor Museum of La Venta at Villahermosa is an attempt to re-create the old La Venta within reach of the city. Hollows and lanes have been cut out of the

[13] *La Venta,* one of the most recently uncovered Olmec sites, lies in an almost unapproachable swamp near the Tancochapan River, on the Tabasco side of the Veracruz-Tabasco state line. Some archaeologists feel that La Venta, occupied over more than 3000 years, was the site of the mother culture of all Mexican ancient civilizations. The area was first discovered by an expedition led by Franz Blom in 1925. Though the group found a number of the colossal monoliths no excavation was done. It remained for M. Stirling to do a thorough initial exploration of the site in 1940. Stirling uncovered many of the huge Olmec heads and other figures. Some measured more than 8 ft. in diameter, were of basaltic rock, weighing 15 tons in one piece. Another, a monolithic altar covered with a carving of a jaguar skin weighed more than 30 tons. These were dragged to the area through swamp and jungle from the nearest quarry, perhaps 100 m. away. In addition to these monumental carvings, tombs yielded smaller artifacts — beautiful jade carvings and some of the finest and most beautiful ceramic sculpture produced in the New World.

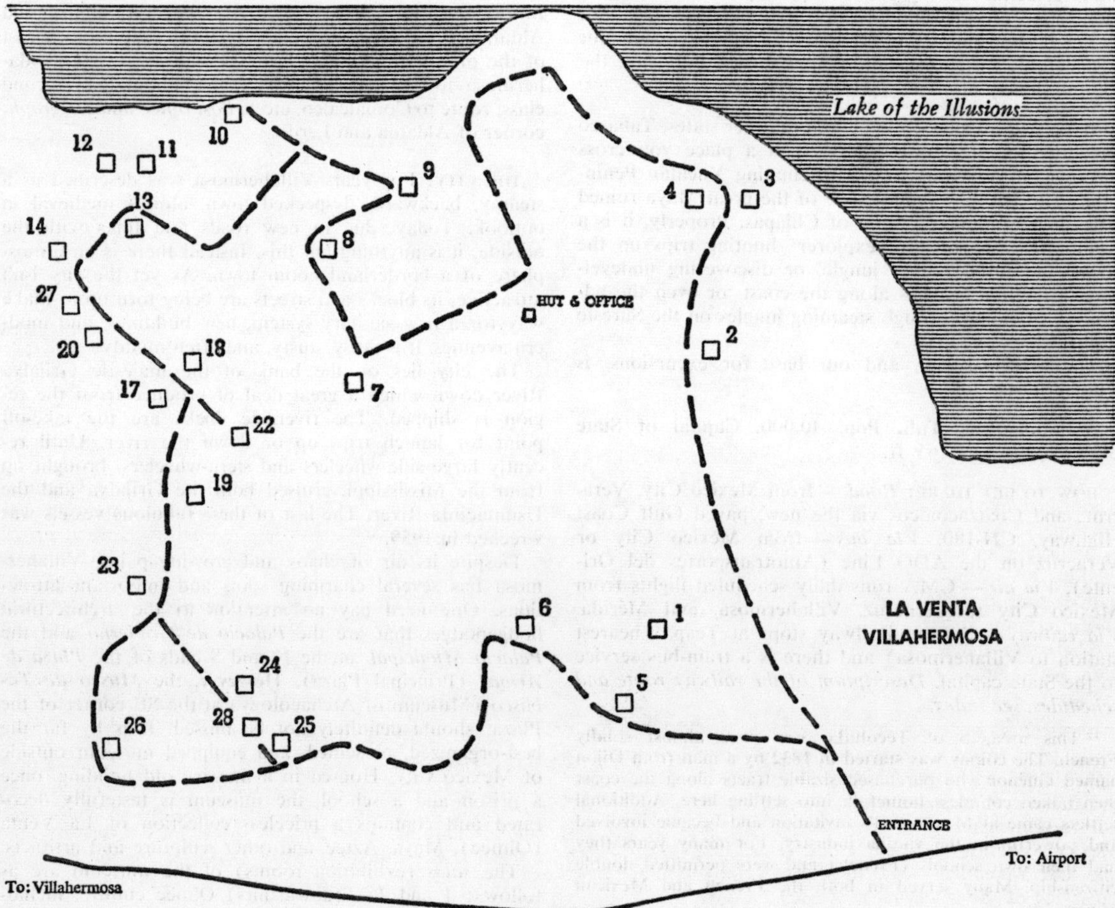

jungle verdure beside the Laguna de las Illusiones, and the monumental figures have been set there. The effect is magnificent, for the illusion of the orginal La Venta is captured.

Since there are no signs, no railings, or other indications that this is not real and isolated jungle (only a small number pegged in the ground near the exhibits), a list of the contents of this unique museum is included here: (see diagram) 1) Great altar with carved face of monkey in front. This object weighs 30 tons. 2) Columnar carving of monkey ascending to heaven. 3) Small basalt jaguar (all the La Venta figures are of basalt). 4) Large fish or shark adorned with inscriptions. 5) Altar decorated with owlheads. A bearded figure is seen coming from a niche at the front of the piece. 6) Olmec Madonna, monument representing a mother holding a child. They are set in a sculptured niche and the mother bends over the child tenderly. Around the sides are handsome bas-reliefs of men and women holding children with jaguar faces or masks. 7) The largest and finest of the monuments — sculptured figure of a nude, corpulent figure before a niche. The figure has a feathered headdress, a serpent necklace and pectoral which may have once contained a jade inset. Above the figure and a part of the same massive stone is a huge jaguar-face which also represents the sun. 8) A floor mosaic of a hard green stone resembling serpentine, and representing a tiger or jaguar face. 9) Stele of a king surrounded by warriors. Weighs 20 tons. 10) Colossal head. It is believed the La Venta heads are of Olmec notables. The massive sculpture is remarkable for Negroid features and magnificent modeling. This head weighs 20 tons. 11) Semidestroyed altar decorated with a seated carved figure and on the left lateral a remarkable bas-relief carving of two people heatedly arguing. 12) Stone with bar-and-dot carvings, numerals indicating a date. 13) Defaced altar with sculptured figure before the classic La Venta niche. 14) Sculpture of a young god (?). One of the oldest in the park. 15 and 16) Basalt columns used by the Olmecs to fence off ceremonial area and important tombs. 17) Mosaic similar to 8. 18) Stele of a bearded man (which has disturbed archaeologists for the figure has an angular face and aquiline nose, totally unlike other La Venta sculpture. It wasn't dropped at La Venta by accident for it weighs 19 tons). 19) Reconstructed royal tomb. In it Stirling discovered a treasure of jade objects, now on exhibit in the National Museum of Anthropology in Mexico City. 20) Figure making an offering. 21) Tomb. 22) A cylindrical sculpture of a figure half-nude. 23) Head of a youth. 24) Copy of the head in the museum in town. 25) Colossal head of an old man. The largest and one of the best sculpted of all the giant heads. 26) Oldest and smallest of all the La Venta altars. 27) Grand throne with inscriptions. 28) Unfinished head. *Museum hours:* 9 A.M. to 6 P.M. *Admission:* $2 MN. In wet weather or following a rain, it is advisable to wear sturdy shoes. The paths become muddy. An insect repellent will help keep off the mosquitoes and tropical insects during early morning and late afternoon visits.

There are plans to add a zoological section to the park, with animals and reptiles native to the jungle region.

EXCURSIONS FROM VILLAHERMOSA: The two most worthwhile trips from Villahermosa are to Palenque and to Yaxchilán deep in the Chiapas forest (see Index: *Southern Mexico, Chiapas Country*). Like Franz Blom, it is our feeling that if one were allowed to see only two of Mexico's countless ancient cities, these would be Palenque and Yaxchilán — the most beautiful, dramatic, and satisfying of the Maya masterpieces.

The easiest way to reach Palenque is to fly directly there via TASA airline. The planes are charter Cessnas and the round-trip costs about $400 MN ($35) for the plane which has place for two passengers. Budget-travelers can reach Palenque via the Sureste Railway. Buses or cabs go to the train station, *Teapa,* in 1½ hrs. from Villahermosa. The train leaves Teapa at 8:30 P.M., Monday, Wednesday, and Friday, arrives in Palenque shortly after midnight. Motorists can drive to Teapa over a good paved road and leave their cars at the San Lorenzo Hotel. Return trains pass through Palenque, Monday, Wednesday, and Friday at midnight, arrive in Teapa at 4 A.M. The ruins are about 7 m. from the Palenque station. Vehicles from the local hotel meet the train.

The trip to Yaxchilán requires more time, endurance and a spirit of adventure. You can either fly to *Tenosique,* Tabasco, via the scheduled TASA flights, or take the same Sureste train to Tenosique (arrival time 1:10 A.M.) From there you can either go by boat up the Usumacinta River to an abandoned logging camp, *Agua Azul,* and continue on by outboard-powered dugout to Yaxchilán. Or from Tenosique arrangements can be made to fly to Agua Azul in Don Paco Villanueva's Cessna. Rate for the flight, round trip, $128 MN.

Tenosique, Tab. Pop. 7000. Alt. 205 ft. A very picturesque tropic river town (on the Río Usumacinta), remote from the state capital and almost on the Guatemalan border. Founded by the Spanish in 1540. Birthplace of martyred Vice-President Piño Suárez who was assassinated along with President Madero in 1913. A new graveled road now links Villahermosa to Tenosique.

Teapa, Tab. Pop. 2793. (On CE-13, 37 m. S of Villahermosa.) The state capital's link on the Sureste Railway. A somewhat picturesque town in the foothills of the sierras, and favorite resort of the Tabasqueños because of its cooler climate. Nearby are the interesting Caves of Coconá *(Grutas del Coconá)* and the thermal baths *El Azufre* (The Sulphur).

HOTELS: *San Lorenzo* (1 block below plaza). 30 rooms, *viajero*-style, but clean and well run. Dining room. Rates: EP, $18 MN and up, dble. The San Lorenzo has a big enclosed garden where motorists can garage their cars while going to Palenque.

A spectacular new road is being built across the sierras into Chiapas to connect with the Pan-American Highway CN-190, near *Chiapa de Corso.* (Index: Escopetazo, Chis.) At present the route is a jeep road, passable only in dry weather. From Teapa the fair, all-weather stretch to *Pichucalco* is an interesting drive.

EXCURSIONS TOWARD TABASCO'S GULF COAST: This area is just beginning to open, new roads connecting the capital with some extraordinarily beautiful beach areas.

Tabasco's most beautiful "undiscovered" beach area is *Puerto Sánchez Magallanes,* a tiny fishing village not far from the Tabasco-Veracruz state line. Lovely white sands shaded by coconut palms, the sea on one side and the *Laguna del Carmen* on the other. As yet, accommodations are where you can hang your hammock. A new road leads to it from the Gulf Coast Highway.

Comacalco, Tab. Pop. 4300. A nice village in the Tabasco flatlands, noted for its Maya ruins (the farthest northward outpost of the Maya culture. The ruins, not far from the village, are surrounded by luxuriant vegetation. The site has still not been fully explored, but many of the buildings have a certain resemblance to Palenque — severe architecture with simple molding and friezes.

The site was first visited by the French explorer, Desiré Charnay in 1880. In 1925 Franz Blom and Oliver La Farge discovered there an important tomb on the W slope of the Palacio (Temple 1). A chamber in it was embellished with stucco relief figures painted red. The modeling of the faces and figures is remarkably expressive.

Comacalco may be reached via TASA airline, charter planes from Villahermosa, 15 minute flight. By auto, follow Highway CN-180 toward Coatzacoalcos, at Cárdenas (31 m. from Villahermosa) turn right (N). Fair road, 25 m. to Comacalco. The Transportes La Chontalpa bus line (second class) goes from Villahermosa to Comacalco.

On May 15 there is a colorful fiesta in the town, honoring San Isidro.

Due N of Comacalco, 13 m. farther on the same road are the fishing villages of *El Paraíso,* and 2 m. beyond, *Puerto Ceiba.* The latter, with its South Sea island-look and a population of 15, moved one well-traveled local poet to call it the "Hawaii Tabasqueño," and he wasn't in error — during the winter months it's like heaven. Two miles farther is the isolated and beautiful *El Limón Beach.* Accommodations are as broad as the beach. In *El Paraíso,* pop. 2804, there is a small hotel, primitive.

Frontera. Pop. 8449. Alt. 15 ft. Tabasco's principal port, at the mouth of joined Grijalva and Usumacinta Rivers, 85 m. from Villahermosa (on Gulf Coast Highway, CN-180). Cars ferry across the river to the town. Ferries cross every 2 hours. Rate, $15 MN.

The town is usually shabby and has little to offer touristically. Accommodations are very poor. Best available hotel is *San Agustín,* on the plaza, corner of Av. Juárez and Piño Suárez.

THE SURESTE RAILWAY ROUTE

Trains of the Ferrocarril del Sureste make the 434 m. trip from Coatzacoalcos, across the interior of Tabasco, with dips into Chiapas, to its terminal, Campeche, on the Yucatán Peninsula, in about 22 to 25 hrs. (The slow trains, *Mixto,* 25 to 36 hrs.) Connections at Coatzacoalcos with the National Railway to Mexico City; and at Campeche, with the Yucatecan Line to Mérida. There is now thru Pullman train service between Mexico City and Mérida, eliminating the numerous changes tourists had to make. Trains leave Mexico City Sundays, Tuesdays, and Thursdays at 7:25 A.M., arriving in Mérida approximately 26 hours later. Return trains leave Mérida on Wednesday, Friday, and Saturday. The route is via Veracruz and Coatzacoalcos.

Until the opening of the new Gulf Highway motorists often shipped their cars from Coatzacoalcos to Campeche, and this is still advisable during the rainy season. *Rates:* $431.35 MN to Campeche or back. Add about $35 to $50 MN for cost of rope to secure the vehicle on the flatcar and for tipping the laborers.

The Sureste, as the line is popularly called, is one of Mexico's fabulous railway lines. Until it was completed in the early 1950s there was no land communication between Tabasco, the Peninsula of Yucatán, and the rest of Mexico. Though it was the ambition of several administrations to complete this link, it took more than 30 years of Herculean effort to finish the line which was pushed foot by foot through vast malarial mangrove swamps, dense, jaguar-filled jungle, and across broad rivers.

In part, the route closely follows the path traced by Hernán Cortés in his fabulous journey toward Hibueras (Honduras). Cortés left Mexico City, October 1524, and along the way, surveyed the route followed by the train as far as Pichucalco. From there, with his force of 140 men, he plunged southward into Guatemala.

Leaving Allende station the train travels SE traversing swamp and jungle land until it reaches the Tancochapa River where it crosses from Veracruz into Tabasco. At Chontalpa there are bus connections to Comacalco and the beach area at El Paraíso. A short distance beyond, the line crosses the Mezcalapa River and crosses a section of the State of Chiapas. The most interesting town on this section of the line is Pichucalco. Chiapas, a picturesque village in the foothills, surrounded by intense green, and with a curious plaza — every building is painted a bright red. Leaving Chiapas the train soon reaches Teapa (bus connections to Villahermosa). The line passes through rich country to Tacotalpa, which after the conquest was the estate of chronicler Bernal Díaz del Castillo. At kilometer 337, Palenque station, gateway to the famed Maya ruins. The line continues across a foothill section of Chiapas, then enters Tabasco again, crossing the Río Usumacinta. At Tenosique, kilometer 404, the route turns northward through dense jungle forests, crossing into the State of Campeche. At kilometer 506 the train crosses the Candelaria River. Candelaria is a take-off point for hunting trips up the river. Escárcega (kilometer 568) is a railroad and lumber-mill town within easy reach of the fabulous Laguna de Silvituc hunting region (see Index). The train continues through Campeche forest country to the port city, Campeche.

Although the Sureste line boasts of modern equipment — diesel trains made by the Linke Hofmann Busch plant in Germany — the unforgettable journey demands a certain amount of hardiness and adventurousness on the part of the traveler. Riding the Sureste is like trying to stick on a bucking bronco. The roadbed is extremely rough; often you can see water squish up between the railway ties as the train passes over them. Occasionally a car jumps the tracks, but it is a minor matter. Jacks are carried to set it back on the rail, and everyone gets out to lend a hand. The trip through the jungle amply makes up for the discomforts.

The whining call of catbirds, the squawking of strident-voiced parrots and the deep monotonous sound of countless insects leads one into a mysterious world. The tropical vegetation grows with such vigor in this sun and moisture-drenched region that chemicals are employed to destroy the creepers that constantly hedge in on the tracks. The chemical compound is thrown in a hot, liquid form from a heated tank car, sprayed by means of a steam-heated atomizer. Although the application kills all nearby plant life, others arise to replace it so rapidly that the battle against the encroaching jungle must be almost continuous. In some areas jungle plants flap wet feelers against the cars which move forward through a veritable tunnel of luxuriant foliage. The flora of the region through which the train passes is a perpetual delight. Most of the forest trees bear some kind of beautiful flower, and the splendid orchidaceous and other epiphytic plants that cling to them present unusually beautiful masses of color.

The forest trees are hung with brilliant flowering vines; some are covered with huge ant nests and swinging bird nests. Many of the trees bear curiously shaped pods, some of which the natives gather and use as a pocket receptacle for coins. The bird and animal life in the trees and rustling jungle command constant attention. One may note splendid specimens of the Mexican goshawk, goatsuckers, and Mexican caciques — the beautiful yellow and black orioles of the tropics. Their swinging nests hang 3 to 4 ft. from the tips of branches, swaying in the slightest breeze. The birds are usually black, with long crests and bright yellow shoulders, lower back and tail, save the two inner feathers. The Mexicans know them as calandrias. Long-tailed crested blue jays are very numerous and are among the most beautiful birds seen in the tropic lowlands. Their brilliant blue and white forms are graceful in every motion, and they resemble the macaws or some of the handsome long-tailed parrots for which the region is noted. A notable feature of the landscape is the parrot fruit tree *(Pileu conica)*. This odd-shaped fruit, resembling okra, is four-sided, green in color, and grows on a tree entirely void of leaves. It is juicy, sticky, and in form resembles a green parakeet. Evidently mindful of this useful camouflage, the parakeets dash to the tree when frightened, and stand upright and motionless. So nearly alike are they to the fruit that a predatory hawk will sometimes fly past a tree on which a score or more of these saucy sprites are standing, apparently unaware of their presence.

53. *Southern Mexico*

The southern region of Mexico is a huge area covering almost 66,000 sq. miles and encompasses two of the republic's largest and most interesting states, Oaxaca and Chiapas. The region is bounded on the N by the States of Veracruz and Tabasco, on the W by Guerrero, on the S by the Pacific Ocean and, on the E by the Republic of Guatemala. Along with the Yucatán Peninsula, the southern region has perhaps the largest native or indigenous populations in the country. In some areas the people have scarcely been touched or influenced by the 400 years of Western or modern civilization introduced by the Spaniards.

The climate follows the usual Mexican pattern — along the coast and the low Isthmus of Tehuantepec the winters are marvelously mild. The summers, May through September, steaming hot and wet. In the highland areas winters are mild and pleasant, with the exception of Chiapas' lovely San Cristóbal Valley which, although it is almost as far south as you can go in Mexico, is biting cold. The summers in the highland sections are quite warm, but not too uncomfortable for travel.

The principal highway route linking the elongated region is the southern extension of the Pan-American Highway, CN-190, which threads together the chief cities — Oaxaca City, Tehuantepec, Tuxtla Gutiérrez, San Cristóbal de las Casas — and then reaches to the Guatemalan frontier. There is very good bus transportation the entire length of the route. CMA runs daily scheduled flights to Oaxaca City, Tuxtla Gutiérrez, and Tapachula, from Mexico City. Aerolineas Vega has regular scheduled flights linking Oaxaca City with Acapulco and Puebla. Railway communications between Mexico City and Oaxaca are good; between the national capital and Chiapas they are round-about, tedious and extremely uncomfortable.

Tourist facilities and accommodations vary greatly; in Oaxaca City, excellent; in the Isthmus of Tehuantepec cities, there are accommodations but they are poor; in Chiapas' Tuxtla, and San Cristóbal they are fair to good.

TRAVEL HIGHLIGHTS: The Southern Region has something to please almost any traveler who has a special interest in Mexico, be it photography, sketching, shopping for native goods, archaeology, local customs, or visiting churches. In the order of their accessibility rather than importance here are the outstanding things of interest: (1) Oaxaca City with its several examples of marvelous architectural gems; its opulent Indian market day (Saturday); its picturesque nearby handicraft villages of Teotitlán del Valle, Coyotepec, and Tlacolula; and its two great Zapotec-Mixtec archaeological ruins, Monte Albán and Mitla. (2) Tehuantepec, noted for its hefty beauties and romantic traditions. Try to get there for a wedding or fiesta. (3) San Cristóbal de las Casas and surrounding villages for the remarkable Indian population and their colorful costumes and crafts. (4) These only for the off-trail explorer — (in Chiapas) the Montebello Lakes, the most vivid and beautiful in Mexico; the world-famed Mayan ruins at Palenque, Bonampak, and Yaxchilán. (5) the unique Sierra de Oaxaca villages such as Yalalag and Alta Villa.

PHYSIOGRAPHY OF THE REGION: Oaxaca and Chiapas combined have an exceptionally long and varied Pacific coastline, but due to the parallel intervention of the rugged Sierra Madre del Sur the coastal regions are effectively cut off from the populous central ridge except at the Isthmus of Tehuantepec, Mexico's narrowest and lowest passageway between the Atlantic and Pacific. Both states are extremely mountainous, but each has fine and rich valley areas. Oaxaca's highest peak is *Zempoaltepec* (11,965 ft.). Atop this towering giant one may enjoy the unusual experience of looking clear across the continent; the Gulf of

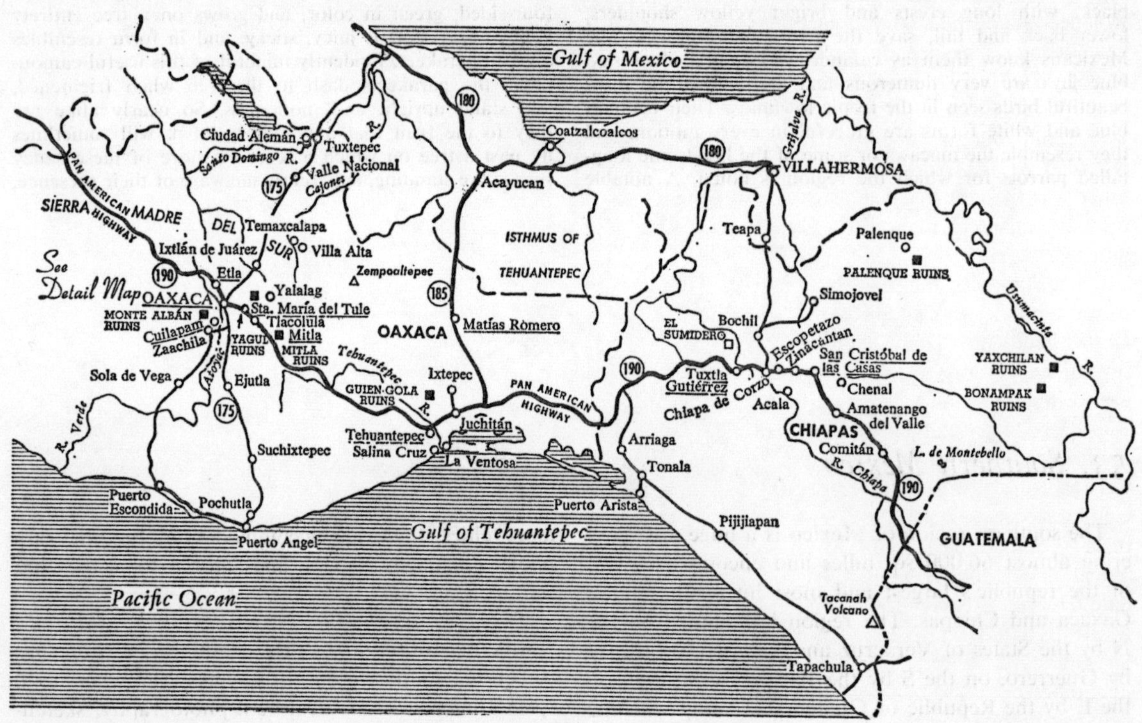

Mexico is visible on the E and the Pacific Ocean on the W. The highest peak in Chiapas is the majestic volcano *Taconah* (11,970 ft.); the dividing line which separates Mexico from Guatemala passes across its summit.

The highlands of Oaxaca are the source of several important rivers — the Santo Domingo, the Cajones — draining into the rich Gulf Coast Papaloapan Basin; while the Río Atoyac (Verde) and Tehuantepec drain into the Pacific. Chiapas has the more splendid rivers of which two — the Chiapa (Grijalva) and Usumacinta — are navigable great distances.

FLORA AND FAUNA: The region possesses a large variety of trees, flowers, medicinal plants, and crop plants such as vanilla, cacao, pineapple, coffee, tobacco, sugar cane, sesame, tropical cabinet woods (70 varieties), timber (50 types). The Comitán area of Chiapas is Mexico's finest orchid country. Chiapas has extensive jungles and forests of mahogany and other valuable woods.

The fauna covers a wide range making the region, particularly Chiapas, one of the great untapped game reserves of the republic. There are over 60 species of mammals, 100 birds, 40 fishes, and countless insects. The beautiful quetzal (the Aztec bird of paradise) makes its home in the dense unexplored forests, which are also the resort of wild turkey, wood pigeons, pheasants, while the beautiful American egret *(Herodias egretta)* is found on the coast of Chiapas near Tonalá and Soconusco. The lakes and rivers swarm with fish and reptiles. Mexican ocelots, jaguars, wildcats, tapir, wild pig, deer, monkeys, and a variety of smaller animals abound in the mountains and forests.

HISTORY OF THE REGION: The pre-Spanish history is principally that of three of Mexico's great Indian cultures; the Maya in Chiapas (see Index: *History*), the Zapoteca, and the Mixteca cultures in the Oaxaca region. Man first appeared in the great Valley of Oaxaca (once an immense lake) sometime between 700 and 300 B.C. There is some belief that these early settlers may have come from the so-called Olmec region to the E or have been influenced by them. Other people entered the valley toward 300 B.C., probably coming from Guatemala (with Maya cultural traits, possibly) and these fused to form the Zapotec culture which dominated the Oaxaca region until about the fourteenth century A.D. when the Mixteca culture appeared and shared the valley, sometimes struggling with the Zapotecs, at times uniting with them against the Aztecs who penetrated their country toward the end of the fifteenth century and established some garrisons.

In 1521 the Spaniards invaded the region under Diego de Ordaz, a lieutenant of Cortés. For some years there was considerable guerrilla warfare between the Mixteca and the Spanish. In 1529 by royal edict Cortés was made Marquis of the Valley of Oaxaca and granted immense tracts of land. During the War of Independence, Oaxaca remained royalist and had to be subdued by General José María Morelos. The history of Oaxaca has often been marked by unusual violence, bloodshed, and colorful events; its people have been and are proudly independent and not easily cowed. Two of Mexico's most famous presidents came from Oaxaca. Most outstanding and beloved was Benito Juárez, a pure Zapotec Indian, who is regarded as the Abraham Lincoln of Mexico. The other was the controversial figure of Porfirio Díaz — fearless patriot in his youth, durable dictator in his latter years.

Chiapas, one of the most isolated and remote areas of the republic, was added to the Spanish crown by a Cortés lieutenant, Don Diego de Mazariego, who led several expeditions into the region which met with astonishing resistance on the part of the natives. Mazariego eventually prevailed and in March 1528 he founded a royal town, the present site of San Cristóbal de las Casas. In 1542 the Audiencia de los Confines was created (Captaincy General of Guatemala — embracing Honduras, Guatemala, Nicaragua, Yucatán, Campeche, and Chiapas), and from that date Chiapas was considered a Guatemalan province. In 1821 Chiapas declared its independence from Spain and its adherence to the new Mexican republic. Somewhat later, having no voice in its own affairs, Chiapas withdrew from the republic, but again rejoined it. In 1857 it was elevated to the rank of a free and sovereign state of the *Federación Mexicana.*

THE PEOPLE TODAY: Travelers will find that in Oaxaca and Chiapas, but especially the former, their stay will usually be made more pleasant by contact with the friendly, independent, and relatively prosperous local people. In this region the Indian as well as the Mexican strike a nice balance between too much and too little interest in tourists. The people of Oaxaca seem less troubled by the psychological tensions that affect and influence the Mexican in so many other regions. The Zapotec people, for example, are lively, keen, outgoing; they have great personal pride and seem to know their worth without having to prove it constantly. Their mood and temper is just the opposite of the Tarascans of Michoacán, who are melancholy, withdrawn, and suspicious. In Chiapas, partly due to the continued isolation of the region, the more Indianist sections of the population remain withdrawn and are difficult to make contact with.

Both these states have unusually large Indian or ethnic populations, groups who maintain their ancient Indian outlook, customs, and traditions to such an extent that they are endlessly interesting to the folklorist, anthropologist, or traveler sensitive to unique regional customs. In Oaxaca there are some 15 or more Indian tribes, mostly of Zapotec or Zoque stock. These are: the Zapotecs, the Mixtecos, Chontals, Cuicatecos, Chatinos, Mijes, Netzichos, Pinomes, Mazatecos, Choconas, Papolucas, Tepozcolulas, etc. In Chiapas there are as many distinct Indian people, each with their own language, unique outlook, religion, and customs. Travel writers have a tendency to bunch them all, and call them "Chamulas." Though most are of Maya stock, their languages and ways are distinct. Among the more important or interesting ethnic groups there are: the Chamulas, Tzeltales, Zinacantecans, Tzotziles, the Lacandones, Zoques, Mamé, Chiché, etc.

THE OAXACA COUNTRY

The Oaxaca country (State of Oaxaca — population 1,727,266, area 36,801 sq. miles) is broken into three distinct areas of which the Valley of Oaxaca, closest to Mexico City, is of unusual travel interest. It is the cultural, economic, and social, as well as historical, center of the region. The other two sections — Isthmus of Tehuantepec and the coastal section S of Oaxaca City are of limited appeal. The base city for trips through the region is Oaxaca City, simply called "Oaxaca" in Mexico.

Oaxaca (city), Oax. Pop. 50,000. Alt. 5068. The most important city in southern Mexico, capital of the state of the same name.

HOW TO GET THERE: *Via highway* — Pan-American Highway, CN-190, from Mexico City. About 342 m. (see Index: Highway Routes). *Via bus* — ADO y Auto Pullman line, Mexico City terminal, Buenavista 9, Tel. 35-16-00; Transportes del Sureste Cristóbal Colón, Calzada México-Puebla 38, Mexico, D.F. Tel. 22-37-72; Autobuses del Sureste, same as above. *Via air* — CMA offers one flight a day from the capital. Aerolineas Vega offers daily flights from Puebla and Acapulco to Oaxaca. *By railway* — Ferrocarriles Nacional de México, night Pullman (express), daily. Leaves Mexico D.F. at 4 P.M., arrives at 7:15 A.M. A daylight train leaves at 7:15 A.M., arrives in Puebla at 1:30 P.M., but here you must transfer to the Oaxaca Pullman at 9:58 P.M.

HOTELS AND RESTAURANTS: *Hotel Victoria,* on CN-190 at km. 545. A new, extremely nice hotel and bungalows on heights overlooking the city and valley. 64 roomy and tastefully furnished units on pleasant grounds. Good dining room, cocktail lounge and bar. Swimming pool. Friendly atmosphere and excellent service. Though the prices may seem high for the southern region, you get something for your money. Rates: EP $80 MN and up, dble. Also AP if wanted. Tel. 32-19. *Oaxaca Courts,* Calzada Porfirio Díaz 1, ½ block from km. 546.2 of CN-190. A very pleasant bungalow court on spacious, lovely grounds. American owned and operated. 28 units, cocktail lounge, pool, dining room. The food is close to the best in town, if not the best. EP $50 MN and up, dble. AP available. Tel. 22-40.

Hotel Principal, 2a 5 de Mayo 16. Small (18 rooms) and central. At the moment the best inexpensive hotel in town. Friendly atmosphere, good service, modest and neat accommodations. Rate: from $20 MN dble. EP. *Motel Margarita,* Calzada Madero 100, N end of town. 27 neat, comfortably furnished units, cocktail service, fair dining room. Rates: AP $110 MN dble. EP available. Tel. 30-85. *Hotel Marques del Valle,* on central plaza. Once the best hotel in town. At present it is overpriced

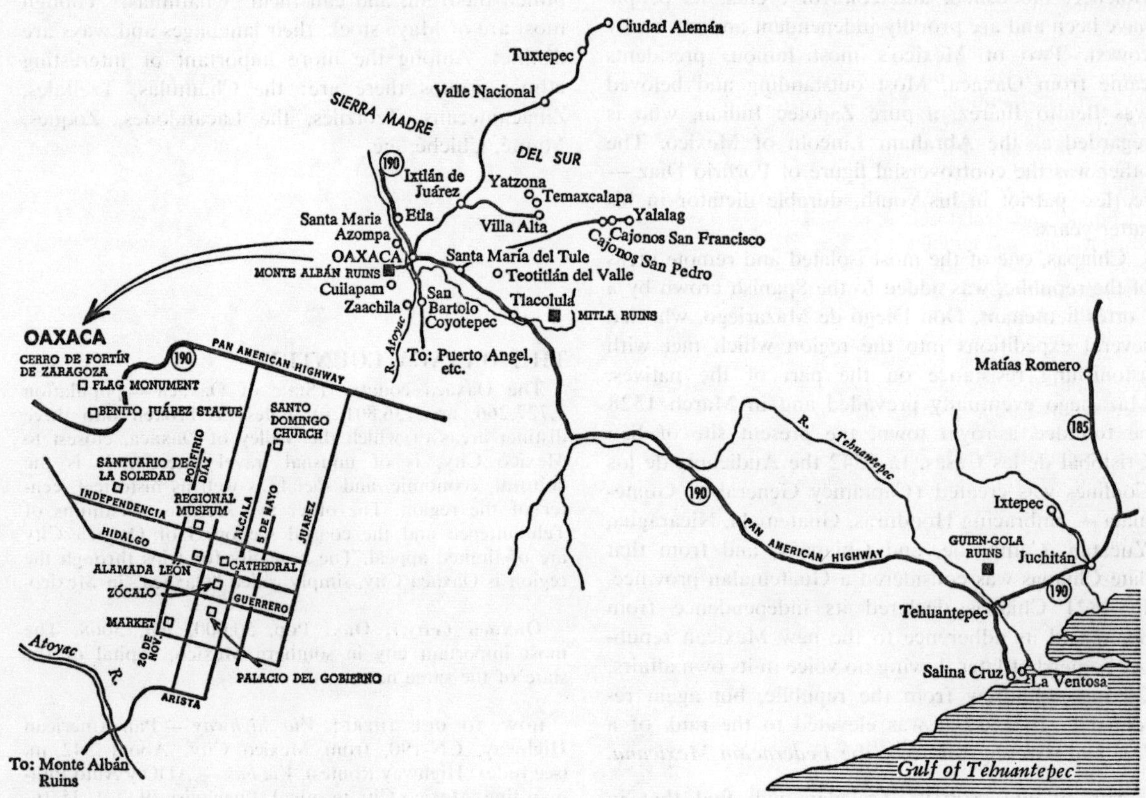

for services and comforts rendered. 100 rooms, not always tidy, bar service, restaurant. Rates: EP from $70 MN up, dble. *Monte Albán,* corner Hidalgo and León. Formerly the Bishop's Palace. The hotel is a fine old place gone to pot. About 38 rooms out of the original 50 are available, the restaurant has been decommissioned and the help has largely vanished. Gypsy rates: EP $40 MN dble. *Hotel Francia,* 20 de Noviembre 10. Small *viajero*-style, near market. Rooms are large and clean, friendly atmosphere, food fair. Rates: EP $35 MN dble. *Pension Suiza,* Calzada Madero 7. Pleasant, good food, inexpensive. EP $30 MN dble.

Hotel Rancho San Felipe, about 2 m. from town, E in suburb of San Felipe, Av. Hidalgo. 20 very plain rooms, beautiful secluded grounds, almost like a Mediterranean villa. Hotel is fairly short on efficient service.

Oaxaca has no recommendable eating-out restaurants. One can snack comfortably at the sidewalk café under the *portales* of the *Hotel Marques del Valle,* also at the *Merendero de Tule,* second floor, N side of the plaza. *La Pidia,* the dining room in a *Casa de Huespedes* at Miguel Cabrera 7 (W of the market) offers very inexpensive Mexican cuisine that occasionally is quite good. For nicely served, not always exciting meals, stick to the hotels. See *Oaxaca Courts,* above.

DIRECTORY: *Banks* — Banco Nacional de México, Armenta y Lopez 4; Banco de Comercio de Oaxaca, Armenta y Lopez 4. *Auto repairs* — Hamilton Service (Ford), Independencia 72; Automotriz de Oaxaca (Chevrolet), Hidalgo 64, *Bus lines* — Autotransportes del Sureste Cristóbal Colón, 20 de Noviembre 4; Autos Pullman, Independencia 47. *Airlines* — CMA, Portal del Marques (on plaza), Tel. 27-96; Aerolineas Vega, Hidalgo 58, Tel. 32-65. Aerovias Rojas, 5 de Mayo and Morelos (Cessna flights to Puerto Angel, Puerto Escondido, etc.). *Railway tickets* — at station, N on Av. Madero. *Post office* — Av. Independencia, behind the Cathedral. *Telephone Office* — Armenta y Lopez 2. *Federal and State Tourist Bureau* — Independencia 60-A.

THE CITY AND ENVIRONS: Oaxaca (wa-HA-kah — a Spanish corruption of the Indian *Huaxyacac,* meaning "place covered with trees") is one of those rare cities where, once you have been there and perhaps lingered over a coffee in one of the cafés around the plaza, you are reluctant to leave. The city's peculiar charm does not come from its location, as is true of Taxco or Acapulco, but rather from within — from its magnificent plaza, from the buildings with their air of sturdy age, and from the people. The city is a happy blending of old and new. Perhaps because of the construction required due to earthquakes (houses are thick-walled and massive), or because much of the building material is soft, ageless looking, pale green stone, there seem to be few garish "sore-thumb" contrasts in the city. Towering Sierra Madre peaks surround the semitropical Valley of Oaxaca in which the city is situated.

Although the valley was for centuries the heart of the Zapotec-Mixtec civilizations, the city itself was not founded until about 1486 when soldiers of the Aztec lord Ahuizotl established a fort on the banks of the Atoyac River. When the Spaniards came through in 1521 they established their own stronghold on the site, calling it Antequera for an old Roman town in Spain. On July 6,

1529, it was raised to the status of a city by royal edict and its name changed to Oaxaca. In 1872 its official name was made Oaxaca de Juárez. The first convent was established in 1529 and, according to an old chronicle, dated 1532, Oaxaca had "five hundred Castilian families of pure blood without an African, a Jew or a Turk among them."[1] Even though the city got its start with 500 Castilian families, Oaxaca today is really a Zapotec city in a Zapotec country. One need only attend the Saturday market and hear the volume of Zapotec spoken to be convinced.

The Zócalo (Central Plaza or Plaza de Armas) the geographic and social center of the city, is one of the most pleasing and enticing plazas in the whole country. There is a fine bandstand, magnificent trees making speckled patterns of lazy shade upon the walks, and around the plaza, arched *portales* equaled only by those in Mérida. The sidewalk cafés vie with any Acapulco terrace as Mexico's most satisfying place to just sit and loll. Throughout the day a small army of hucksters, public letter writers *(evangelistas),* rug peddlers from Teotitlán, *rebozo* weavers and souvenir hawkers pursue their vocations beneath the shade of the arcades.

Palacio de Gobierno (State House) is the impressive colonial-style building flanking the entire S side of the plaza. Catty-cornered from the NW end of the Zócalo is another smaller tree-shaded square, the *Alameda León.* Facing it on the S is one of Oaxaca's two great ecclesiastical monuments, the *Cathedral.* The building is of interest largely for its beautifully carved façade, the work of an unknown seventeenth-century artist. The church itself was begun in 1553, but took almost 200 years to complete. The interior has been thoughtlessly ruined by restoration, and the entire building has, at various times, been the unfortunate target of both bombardments and earthquakes. An oddity is the huge clock on the S side. It was presented to the church by one of the kings of Spain. Its works are made entirely of wood.

In the City of Oaxaca there are three things a visitor must see above all else — the *Zócalo, Santo Domingo Church,* and the *Regional Museum.* This last, *El Museo Regional de Oaxaca,* a step from the cathedral, on Av. Independencia, facing the N end of the Alameda León, is one of the best small museums in the country. It contains many interesting and well-arranged exhibits of archaeological artifacts from Oaxaca's many ancient ruins, a fascinating exhibit of regional arts, crafts, and costumes. Most important is the famed and priceless jewelry excavated from tomb 7 at Monte Albán (see Index) — hundreds of fabulous pieces, ornaments of gold, fine jade carvings, beautiful alabaster vessels, and intricate bone carvings. *Hours:* Tuesday through Saturday, 9 A.M. to 1 P.M. and 4 to 6 P.M. (closed Monday); Sunday and holidays, 9 A.M. to 1 P.M. *Admission:* 2 pesos.

Santo Domingo Church, 5 blocks N of Zócalo at M. Alcala and Gurrion, is without a doubt one of the most beautiful Baroque structures in the country, and its interior is certainly the most superb example of such decoration in the Western Hemisphere. Whether one is Catholic, Protestant, or nonbeliever, whether one is attracted by architecture or not, Santo Domingo is one of those unique places where once you have seen it, you keep returning to be utterly amazed by the breath-taking splendor.

The building itself is one of the largest conventual establishments in Mexico. The largely despoiled adjoining monastery is now used as a military headquarters. The church together with the convent occupies a space of well over 500 feet on a side. Its walls, constructed to resist earthquakes measure up to 6 yards thick in places. These have withstood various quakes as well as violent sieges and bombardments. Santo Domingo was founded in 1575 and completed a century later. It is related that when the church was begun there was available only 2½ pesos to start the work with. On completion it had cost a sum of 12 million.

Its exterior has an elaborately carved Baroque façade with innumerable niches occupied by carved figures. The massive towers, somewhat battered, are capped with glazed tiles in a checkerboard pattern. The interior of the church, however, is its glory. The walls and great barrel-arched ceiling are covered in every part with heavily gilded ornament and polychrome sculpture in high relief, against a background of white, creating an effect of indescribable richness. Particularly noteworthy is the curious genealogical tree of the Virgin on the low-vaulted ceiling beneath the balcony (choir loft) just inside the entrance. This great tree with branches and leaves of gold extending in all directions has some 34 figures growing from the branches. In the ceiling of the loft which is dome-shaped there are niches with busts of saints diminishing in size as the apex is reached. Flanking the single tile-paved nave are eleven lateral chapels, enclosed within screens of wrought iron, but connected by an interior passage. The largest and finest of the chapels is the Chapel of the Virgen del Rosario (Virgin of the Rosary), on the right as you enter the church. It is a spacious temple in itself, having its own choir, sacristy, and even its own towers. In splendor its interior vies with the main church.

The original high altar of the main church, an elaborate affair of carved and gilded wood, was made in Mexico City, and transported at enormous expense over the almost impassable trail to Oaxaca where it was installed in 1612. This and a later altar were destroyed by French troops during the French Intervention. Much of the church's rich decoration, and especially in the monastery, was vandalized when the buildings were converted into barracks at the time of the Reform Laws.

Santuario de la Soledad: This massive church standing about 4 blocks W of the Museum, built in 1682–90, has an interesting carved Baroque façade and masses of columns in a variety of orders. The place is of interest not so much because of its architecture but due to the celebrated image of the Virgin of Solitude housed there. She is the patron of the city and the state, and to her are attributed the usual miraculous healing powers. The figure stands in a glass and gold enclosure. She wears a robe of black velvet solidly embroidered in gold and studded with precious stones. She also possesses the jewels and wardrobe of a queen. There is an exceptionally large pearl placed in her forehead. The sculptured face is quite beautiful, a bit brooding, remote and austere.

According to legend this regal *santa* made her appearance when one day a muleteer driving his caravan of 12 mules suddenly noticed that a thirteenth pack animal had joined the group. On arriving at the spot where the church now stands this animal fell dead. Fearful that he would be accused of having stolen the mule, the driver hastened to notify the town authorities who came to inspect the box the animal was carrying. On opening it

[1] Curiously, though Oaxaca has produced many of Mexico's great revolutionaries and patriots, among them the liberal and humanitarian Juárez, the city has always been eminently conservative and intensely Catholic. When Miguel Hidalgo (1810) declared for Independence, he was violently denounced by the Bishop of Oaxaca as an instrument of Satan. The bishop so inflamed the public imagination that when two of Hidalgo's aides (Señores Armenta and Lopez) entered the city disguised as peddlers in order to measure the trend of events, they were seized and beheaded, their heads exposed publicly on the street where they were captured. The present Calle de Armenta y Lopez is a relic of that ghastly occurrence.

they found the image of the Virgin and a note identifying her as "Our Lady of Solitude at the Foot of the Cross." Inevitably, a shrine was built on the site.[2]

Beginning on December 18 there is a 3-day fiesta honoring the Virgin of Soledad, with some overtones of those ageless rites performed at the winter solstice. There is a solemn ceremony of lights, fireworks, and regional dances.

Cerro del Fortín de Zaragoza, a hill standing some 350 ft. higher than the city, and just off CN-190 (near Hotel Victoria). On the lower level there is an esplanade and a gigantic bronze statue of Benito Juárez. The figure was sculpted by A. Cencetti and was cast in Rome in 1891. A short road winds upward to the crest of the hill where stands a pyramidal monument to the Mexican Flag. The panoramas of the city and valley are splendid. The tall hill directly to the S is Monte Albán. The river which winds around its E base is the Atoyac.

The Market. The central market building lies 1 block W and 1 block S of the Zócalo. The most interesting sections, however, are the surrounding streets (1 block farther S) where there are vast and vivid displays of regional pottery, baskets, and other handicrafts. The Oaxaca market day is Saturday — a fabulous gathering of Indians from countless valley and Sierra villages forming a brilliant mosaic of colorful costumes, sounds, and sparkling impressions.[3]

FIESTAS: Oaxaca's fiestas are among the most brilliant and quaint; many of them draw visitors from all over the republic. The most important are:

Lunes del Cerro (Mondays of the Hill). A curious celebration commemorating both the Aztec corn goddess, Centeotl, and the Christian, Virgen del Carmen (Our Lady of Mount Carmel). Each of the state's seven regions presents its indigenous dances with authentic costumes and traditional music — the famed Danza de las Plumas (Feather Dance), the Jarabe de Yalalag, Jarabe del Valle, Jarabe Mixteco, and the Zandunga. The festivities are held on the first and second Mondays after the Feast of Carmen, July 16. Ceremonies occur on the *Cerro del Fortín* (see above) and in the city.

Fiesta of San Ramón, August 31, Day of the Animal Blessing in Oaxaca.

Fiesta of San Francisco, October 2–4. Religious processions *(calendas),* and on the closing day, Dance of the Aztecas.

Fiesta of San Rafael, October 22–24, held at the San Juan de Dios church behind the market. This is the Indians' favorite church. It is worth visiting to view its bizarre paintings.

Fiesta for the Virgen de la Soledad, December 16–18. This also begins the round of Christmas festivities, the *posadas* and processions. On December 23 is Radish Night (Noche de Rábanos) held in the Zócolo and Alameda where stands are set up and extraordinary shaped or carved radishes are exhibited and sold. On this same night the traditional *buñuelos* (a light, crisp, flaky, deep-fried pancake) are sold on special plates. After you've eaten them the plate is supposed to be tossed in the air and broken — then you make a wish for good luck. The custom is obviously related to the Aztecs' ceremonial pottery smashing at the end of their 52-year cycles.

EXCURSIONS AROUND OAXACA CITY: **Monte Albán** (Archaeological Zone), ancient Zapotec holy city and Mixtec burial ground; it is one of Mexico's most important pre-Hispanic ruins.

TO GET THERE: Monte Albán lies a short distance SW of the city. From the Zócalo follow Calle Carlos María de Bustamente S to Calle Arista. Turn r. on Arista, then l. on Calle 20 de Noviembre which takes you to the bridge crossing the Río Atoyac. Beyond the bridge there is a fork. Follow the road on your right. It leads up a winding, paved road directly to the archaeological area. Taxis from the city (Sitio Alameda, across from the Cathedral) charge $40 MN for the round trip, with an hour stop at the ruins.

[2] This legend is strangely identical to the story of the appearance of the Cristo de la Capilla, Saltillo, Coah. Mexico has a curious penchant for immortal mules who carry holy statues.

[3] Market days in the Oaxaca area are staggered. The picturesque market at *Ocotlán* is held on Fridays; in Oaxaca City, Saturdays; at *Tlacolula,* Sundays; at *Zaachila,* Mondays, and in *Etla,* Wednesdays.

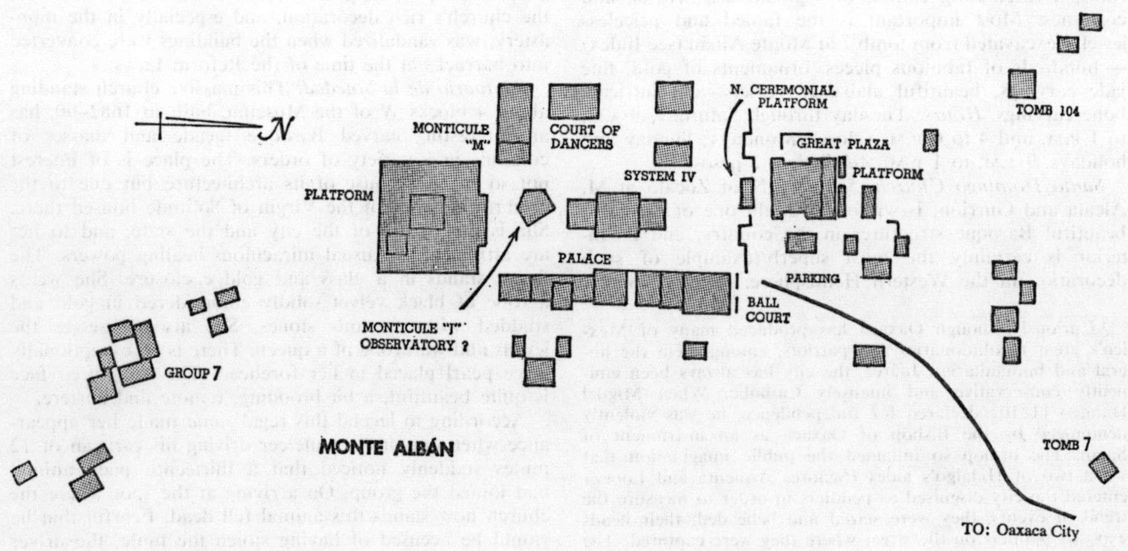

THE RUINS: stand upon the summit of a hill that had its crest artificially leveled to accommodate the enormous group of buildings. The main area which has been explored and partially restored covers but a small part of the ancient city which once spread over several nearby hills. The most interesting area is around the *Great Plaza,* one of the most remarkable monumental complexes in America. The rectangular plaza, measuring some 300 meters long by 200 meters, is bounded by four large ceremonial platforms. The principal structures around the Great Plaza are: the *Ball Court* (E side); next to it and on the same side, platforms which were evidently used for dwellings or possibly a palace; at the S end is a great platform which has not been excavated yet, only the stairs rising from the plaza have been restored. Along the W side of the plaza are several platforms and temple buildings, the most interesting being The *Building of the Dancers,* the name having been given because of the great number of low-relief sculptured figures in attitudes of the dance. These date back to about the fifth century B.C., and are accompanied by glyphs and numerical calendar signs. At the N end of the plaza is a great platform with its magnificent broad stairway.

Archaeologists have indicated that there were primitive buildings on Monte Albán as early as perhaps 700 B.C. The constructions were continually being changed and enlarged upon. The ruins one sees now are called Monte Albán III B, and date from about the year 1000 A.D. Owing to a phenomenon as yet unexplained, at the end of this period (about tenth century A.D.) Monte Albán was abandoned, or rather no new buildings were put up and the place became a necropolis where numberless individuals were buried. The Zapotec, and later Mixtec, political centers were moved to the valley towns of Etla, Zaachila, and Mitla. Thus far some 250 ancient sites have been discovered, indicating that the region was densely populated.

To the right of the road, before reaching the top of the Monte Albán, is the site of Tomb 7 where one of Mexico's most famed treasures was found. In January 1932 the noted Mexican archaeologists Dr. Alfonso Caso, Juan Valenzuela, and Martin Bazán opened the Mixtecan vault and found a dazzling array of gold jewelry, masks, gold pectorals, some executed by the intricate lost-wax process. There were pearls as large as duck's eggs, beautifully carved jades, turquoise mosaics, ornaments, and vessels of pure crystal and alabaster. It took seven sleepless nights and days for the investigators to photograph and catalog all the objects in the vault. A few of the marvelous pieces are in the National Museum in Mexico City, but the bulk of the treasure may now be seen in the museum in Oaxaca City.

It is ironic that despite his keen nose for gold, Cortés passed within gunshot distance of Monte Albán and never knew it existed. The ancient city remained well hidden from the conquerors. Curiously, it was never mentioned in any of the early codices. The Indian (Mixtec) name for the holy city was *Yucu-Cui.* Its present name comes from the Spanish, monte de alba (white mountain).

Hours: the zone is opened during daylight hours. *Admission:* 2 pesos.

Cuilapam, Oax. A tiny Indian village S of Oaxaca, noted for its historic ruined monastery and for its cochineal industry.[4] The massive monastery is a derelict sight, standing alone on a low hill. Within the basilica-type church, still used, are the tombs of perhaps the last of the Zapotec and Mixtec royalty — the Mixtec Prince of Tilantongo and his spouse, the daughter of the Tehuantepec king, Cosijopi. To get to the village take the Monte Albán route out of Oaxaca. After crossing the Río Atoyac bridge and reaching the road fork, take the left-hand road. It is an all-weather gravel road. Cuilapam (kwee-lah-PAHM) is about a 20-minute drive. From Cuilapam one can drive E a short distance to *Zaachila,* former Zapotec capital, now a bucolic and lovely village, and from here return to the Monte Albán fork.

In Zaachila the village saint's day fiesta occurs around June 31. In Cuilapam there is a traditional fair on January 25, and for the fiesta honoring Santiago, July 25, there are regional dances — Dance of the Jardineros and the Feather Dance.

Santa María del Tule, Oax. On CN-190, about 4 m. SE of Oaxaca. In the center of the valley of the same name (TWO-lay), the village is celebrated for its delicious mangos, and as the home of the largest tree in Mexico. The big tree stands in the yard of the parochial church. Judged to be more than 2000 years old, with a height of about 140 ft. and a circumference of 160 feet at the base (exceeding the largest of the California redwoods), the tree is truly impressive. When Cortés passed through the valley he rested beneath the massive *ahuehuete* (species of cypress). A second large tree, beside the church, is said to be the *hijo* (son) of the monarch.

Teotitlán del Valle, Oax. About 8 m. SE of Oaxaca and off CN-190. Dirt road from highway to the town. Teotitlán (tay-o-teet-LAHN), once an important Zapotec capital, is now a charming, somnolent village noted for its serape weaving.

Yagul, Oax. About 19 m. SE of Oaxaca, and just off CN-190. A newly opened archaeological site now being investigated and restored by students and professors of

[4] Cochineal, an important dye long ago discovered by the Zapotecs or Mixtecs. It is derived from the dried bodies of the female cochineal *(Coccus cacti)* and provides a rich and lasting scarlet for serapes and other fabrics. These tiny lice or mites feed on the *Opuntia Cocchinillifera* cactus, remaining attached to the spot on the pad where they were hatched, their bodies growing rapidly as they absorbed the juice of the cacti, until legs, antenna and proboscis (hardly visible to the naked eye) are fully developed. They are so small that 70,000 or more, in a dried state, weigh but a single pound. The females, which alone produce the dye, contain the greatest amount of coloring matter immediately prior to the escape of the young from the egg. They either fall or are detached from the plant and are killed by being placed in boiling water or in hot ovens. Afterward they are sun-dried and marketed in packages of from an ounce to a pound.

During the colonial period the Spanish crown had a monopoly on cochineal and great *haciendas* were built around the industry in Oaxaca and in the Canary Islands. The magenta red dye was the rage in Europe. The resplendent uniforms of the British redcoats whom the American colonists fought in 1776 were cochineal colored. The monopoly began to break when a Frenchman, Thierry de Menonville defied the Spanish death-sentence-edict forbidding the export of the cactus plant. He smuggled some plants from "Juaxaca" as he called it, to Haiti. His first shipment of dye material went to Paris and was used to render the "liberty red" in the first tri-color flag of the new French Republic.

Until 1703 it was believed that the cochineal was a seed or bloom of the plant. Then the scientist Anton van Leeuwenhoek, having just invented the microscope, discovered the *Coccus cacti* moved! During the period of French Intervention in Mexico, a German at Maximilian's court sent samples of the mite to a chemist in Berlin. The chemist, Herr Karl Liebermann, shortly thereafter, developed *alizarina,* a synthetic cochineal color. From then on Germany took hegemony of the dye industry. Today, the synthetics have replaced cochineal even in Mexico, though some villagers still use the dye taken from the mite.

Mexico City College's Department of Anthropology and Archaeology. Some of the constructions are similar to the temples at Mitla. Nearby (other side of CN-190) is *Tlacolula, Oax.,* Pop. 6000. Alt. 4000 ft. This town, dating from the middle of the thirteenth century, is noted for its Sunday market which in many ways is more picturesque and interesting than the Oaxaca market. The sixteenth-century parochial church is noteworthy for its fine wrought-iron work and its elaborate polychrome interior decorations which are similar to those at the Santo Domingo Church in Oaxaca. On the second Sunday in October there is a fiesta with regional dancers.

Mitla, Oax. Pop. 2865. About 24 m. SE of Oaxaca and 3 m. E off CN-190 (all paved). A rather dusty, cactus-fenced village noted for its *rebozo* weaving, a unique New Year ceremony, and for its famed nearby archaeological zone. In the village, just off the plaza you will find,

Museo de Arte Zapoteca, originally a private museum of interesting Zapotec and Mixtec artifacts collected by the late E. R. Frissell, which has now been taken over by Mexico City College's Centro de Estudios Regionales. Admission, 1 peso.

Posada La Sorpresa, a rustic, 6-room inn connected with the above museum, and run by Mrs. Gertrude Frissell. Pleasant atmosphere. Rates: $80 MN dble., AP. The patio is a restful place to stop in for a snack or cool drink after a visit through the ruins.

The *Archaeological Zone* lies ½ m. N of town via dirt road. Mitla (from the Aztec, *Mictlán,* Place of the Dead — the Zapotec name was *Lyobaa,* meaning Tomb) was a Zapotec religious center and burial place which was in use even after the Spanish conquest of Mexico. There are 5 groups of buildings, some which have not been completely explored or restored. The most important of the groups is that to the N near the church which was built upon one of the ancient temple foundations, utilizing its stones.

The Hall of Monoliths is one of the most remarkable of the restored buildings. The great hall, 125 ft. long by 23 ft. wide has a center row of tall columns of porphyry about 14 ft. high and some 3 ft. in diameter. Connected with the hall via a narrow passage is a handsome enclosed court. Throughout this building and the other temples making up the group there is a wealth of intricate fretwork in stone. This peculiar geometric ornamentation, resembling Greek frets, makes the temples of Mitla unique among ancient American buildings. Unlike the temples and pyramids at Chichén Itzá, Teotihuacán, Palenque or even at Monte Albán, no human figures or mythological symbols were portrayed in sculpture. All of the stone decoration is geometric, almost resembling frozen lace.

The Patio de los Cruceros (The Patio of the Crosses) is part of the north group, and is of interest for its subterranean cruciform vaults, again decorated with elaborate fretwork. Although visually (excepting the fretwork) Mitla is scarcely as interesting as many other archaeological ruins, one is amazed by the engineering skill involved here in the raising of the enormous monoliths, in setting in place the entranceway lintels, some of which are nearly 20 ft. long and weigh as much as 15 tons. *Hours:* 9 A.M. to 5 P.M. *Admission:* 2 pesos.

The Zapotecs of Mitla celebrate an unusual and colorful New Year's Eve fiesta at the Cruz de los Pedimientos (Cross of Petitions) which stands outside of the town on a stone base, or also at the Cruz de Matatlán (a village a short distance SE). The people spend the entire night at the cross, first praying, lighting candles, and blowing incense in the four directions in the sign of the cross. They make fanciful miniature reproductions of things they petition or wish for and set up these unique constructions around the cross.

In addition to the above described towns immediately around Oaxaca City, there are countless fascinating hamlets, some noted for their interesting customs and traditions, others for special folk arts or handicrafts. Chief among these are: *San Bartolo Coyotepec,* on CN-175, noted for its black smudged pottery and animal figures; *Santa María Atzompa,* NW of Oaxaca, also noted for its unique green glazed and unglazed ceramic animal figures and cooking pottery; *Etla,* 12 m. NW on CN-190, famed for its ribbonlike Oaxaca cheese and its Wednesday market, and a vivid fair and market day, April 1.

To the NE of the city both in the foothills of the sierras and beyond there are a number of unusual towns that are an anthropologist's delight for their old ways and fascinating customs. A few can be reached by bus or jeep, or even some of the smaller European cars. A new road is being pushed across the sierras, linking Oaxaca with the Papaloapan River Basin and the Gulf Coast. This road, CE-175, still little more than an enlarged pack-trail is for dry-weather travel only. The road winds upward, passing from range to range, passing the *Natividad Mining Settlement* (the mines have been in operation almost continuously since the conquest) to *San Pablo Guelato,* birthplace of Benito Juárez, a pretty, white town with small bronze statue of the Mexican Lincoln in its plaza. As far as *Ixtlán de Juárez,* about 29 m. the road is fair back-country travel. Ixtlán is a charming old town with nice plazas rimmed by fine old stone buildings, a jewel of an eighteenth-century Churrigueresque church, its decorations aflame with the gold from the Natividad mines.

From Ixtlán the road is newly hacked from the mountains. It twists and turns the 80 m. to *Ciudad Alemán, Ver.* On the way it passes through *Valle Nacional,* an important fine-leaf tobacco-growing center, and *Tuxtepec,* birthplace of Porfirio Díaz. About 9 m. from Tuxtepec it crosses the Papaloapan River into the State of Veracruz. From here a paved road lances NW connecting with the Mexico City-Orizaba-Veracruz Highway.

In the sierras E and SE of Ixtlán, is a necklace of villages, the majority in their own cuplike little valleys. Their names — *Yatzona, Texmaxcalapa, Villa Alta, Zoogocho, Yalalag,* and others — excite the imagination for they are among the few remaining reservoirs of truly indigenous Mexican handicrafts, old traditions, and costumes.

Yalalag is the most noted, partly because of the picturesqueness of its houses and the costume of its women. To get there from Oaxaca the best route is the road through *Teotitlán del Valle,* up through Cuajimaloyas to the two Cajones (San Pedro and San Francisco). A bus or jeep can get this far. From Cajones a horse can take you the rest of the way in a half-day.

Yalalag (yah-LA-la) is situated on a mountain slope rather than the usual valley. The houses are remarkably substantial for so isolated a place. Most have decorative murals and prayers, geometric designs, flowers or fruit painted on their façades. There are huge ceramic crosses placed over the door or on the ridgepole of the houses. Curiously, the crosses are almost Gothic in design. The women wear long *huipiles* of a hand-loomed, homespun cotton, which are as shapeless as old-fashioned nightgowns, yet are attractive because of their draping, and for the tassels of colored silk fixed to them. Noteworthy are the *rebozos* they weave of homespun cotton and of silk which is spun in the area, and also the curious heavy silver Yalalag Cross traditional in the town.

EXCURSIONS TO THE OAXACA PACIFIC COAST: The country lying directly S of Oaxaca is largely roadless and the few small ports — idyllic in their setting, and potential resorts — have been scarcely developed. Of interest to off-trail travelers are the tiny exotic ports known as Puerto Angel and Puerto Escondido.

Puerto Angel, Oax. Pop. 700. Alt. 10 ft. On CN-175 about 157 m. S of Oaxaca (route log below). A tiny Pacific coast port built to serve the coffee plantations dotting the highlands behind the coast. Until very recently it could only be reached by boat, or by plane from Acapulco or Oaxaca. At present second-class buses make the trip, and there are flights from Oaxaca (see Oaxaca City Directory). There are no hotels in the port village, but several families rent out rooms. The best, though rustic accommodations are in nearby *Pochutla* at a small hotel, the *Casa Salinas*. The best Puerto Angel beach for swimming as well as camping is just beyond the cemetery. Winter is the only recommended season for a visit here.

Route Log to Puerto Angel

MILES FROM OAXACA	LOG
0	Oaxaca. From Zócalo follow Calle Bustamente S CN-175.
7.5	San Bartolo Coyotepec. Noted for its lovely, satin-like black pottery.
20	Ocotlán de Morelos. Pop. 4900. Interesting Indian market on Fridays. On May 11, Spring Festival with Plume Dancers.
38	Ejutla. Pop. 4290. Fiesta on September 8.
61	Miahuatlan. Pop. 6000. Gas. Road up to this point paved. The remainder being worked on. The route traverses magnificent mountain country.
93	Suchixtepec. Pop. 1417.
115	Pochutla. **GHR.** Pop. 4000. The best available accommodations here. A pleasant town.
122.5	Puerto Angel.

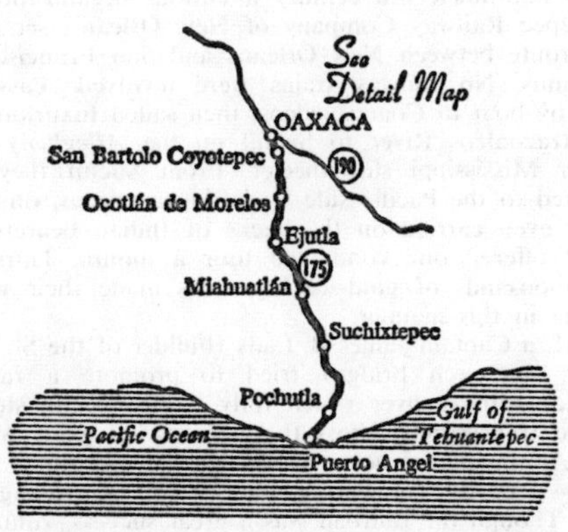

Puerto Escondida, Oax., (Hidden Port). About 170 m. S of Oaxaca, and on the coast W of Puerto Angel. Much more beautiful than Puerto Angel, less cluttered with commercial shipping. Fine beaches. No hotel accommodations, but rooms are available with local families. At present writing the only way to get there comfortably is by plane from Oaxaca. There is a jeep-passable road, CE-131, that turns off CN-175 a little beyond *San Bartolo Coyotepec*. It is fair up to *Solar de Vega*.

SOUTHEAST OF OAXACA CITY — ISTHMUS OF TEHUANTEPEC: The Isthmus of Tehuantepec, where Oaxaca's west coast curves NE to form Mexico's narrow waist, is one of the nation's more storied regions. Although bereft of the beautiful colonial towns, picturebook valleys and magnificent mountains found elsewhere in Mexico, and though plagued by a steaming climate, burning winds and sand, the Isthmus nevertheless has a certain off-beat charm. On the west coast or Oaxaca side of the narrow waist of land there are several interesting towns and a handful of easy-to-reach beaches.

Tehuantepec, Oax. Pop. 12,000. Alt. 328 ft. One of the two principal cities on the Pacific side of the Isthmus. 17 m. from the Port of Salina Cruz; 158 m. SW of Oaxaca City on CN-190. The town is noted for its tropical atmosphere, gold jewelry and picturesque costumes of its women.

HOW TO GET THERE: *Via road* — the Pan-American Highway, CN-190 from Mexico City. From Veracruz, CN-180 to *Acayucan*, thence CN-185, the Trans-Isthmus Highway. *Via bus* — Autobuses Del Sureste and Autotransportes del Sureste Cristóbal Colón (from Mexico City via Oaxaca). *Via railway* — the rail trip for Mexico City is impossibly round about (Puebla, Jalapa, Veracruz, then down to make connections with the Trans-Isthmus line).

HOTELS AND RESTAURANTS: *Hotel Tehuantepec,* on the highway 1 m. from center. The best available in the area, and rather sad. 48 rooms poorly maintained, no hot water. Pool, fair dining room, bar. Rates: EP $40 MN dble. *Hotel Perla,* center, 1 block from plaza. Small, primitive, very reasonable. Restaurant.

DIRECTORY: *Bank* — Banco Agricola y Ganadero, Calle Benito Juárez. *Auto repairs* — Distribuidores del Istmo (GM), Carretera Transistmica 4; Hugo Guasti, Entronque Carretera Panamericana (Ford); Istmo Motors (Dodge), 5 de Mayo 5.

THE TOWN AND ENVIRONS: Tehuantepec (tay-wan-tay-PECK) is situated in a wide gorge bounded by rather low hills and by a wide bend of the Tehuantepec River. It is humid, exuberant with flowers and tropical growths, dusty in dry weather, and is one of those towns a traveler can hate quickly, or fall in love with in an enduring way. The town is best seen during the winter months, either in the evening or in the very early morning.

A broad shaded plaza occupies the center of the town, and facing it is the Palacio Municipal, a white building with many supporting columns. In the plaza is a poor bronze statue, probably the only public monument in this hemisphere to a lady of easy virtue. It is of Doña Juana Romero, a local heroine said to have been as beautiful as Cleopatra. She became the mistress of Porfirio Díaz while he was stationed in Tehuantepec during the war against the French, and this arrangement lasted until their deaths, even though both were married. The peasant girl's connections with the dictator resulted in her being rewarded with wealth and position. Notable among the houses in the town is the two-story, ornate, incredibly tasteless house where Doña Cata, as she was called, resided and entertained the President when he visited in Tehuantepec. The tracks of the Trans-Isthmus railroad pass before the house, routed there by order of Don Porfirio because his lady liked to watch trains go by.

Although Tehuantepec and its long-time chief charm, its women, have somewhat gone to seed, enough remains for a traveler to occasionally catch a glimpse of its former glory — especially during fiestas. The women of the Isthmus have been noted for their beauty, striking carriage and poise, to say nothing of their fierce independence. A striking characteristic is their sharpness and commercial enterprise. They run the markets in the various towns, do most of the commercial trading, even take part in government, while their men work in the fields. For fiestas and religious holidays they wear a costume that is almost Oriental in its brilliance. This *vestido de olán* (dress of lace or ruffles) consists of a matching skirt of rich purple or vermilion velvet, the *huipil* (blouse) thickly and elaborately embroidered with floral designs. Around the hem of the skirt there is a wide fluted ruffle of starched lace. This is matched by a lacy headdress, one of the most baffling articles of feminine vanity ever devised. It is actually a stiffly starched child's blouse which has tiny arms, sleeves, collar, and an abundance of lace. At formal fiestas it is worn so that the collar frames the girl's face, almost like an overlarge Elizabethan ruff. For informal affairs this *bida:niró* (Zapotec) is thrown back over the head and is worn in the manner of a Sioux Indian's war bonnet.

According to an early edition of *Terry's Guide*, certain additional observations regarding the Tehuanas — these queens of the tropics — were made which this reviser has been unable to verify, namely: "the Tehuanas bathe often and are clean. Many of the women smoke and some of the children are almost weaned on tobacco fumes. Like certain other native mothers, they nurse their youngsters until they are three or four years old, and it is no uncommon sight to see a child descend from its mother's knee, after a lacteal repast, repair to an easy chair, light a cigarette and enjoy an after-dinner smoke. Children are sometimes seen smoking a cigar as fat as their own little legs."

FIESTAS: There are numerous fiestas in Tehuantepec during the month of May. Others of interest are: August 15, festival in Santa María Barrio; August 16, fiesta in the San Jacinto Barrio; August 22, fiesta in the San Sebastián Barrio; September 8, Virgen de la Natividad fiesta; December 10–12, Virgen de Guadalupe — the Tehuanas pay homage to the Virgin in their gala costumes.

Guien-Gola, Oax. (Archaeological Zone) situated about 10 m. NE of Tehuantepec (dirt road). One of the important ancient Zapotec fortress cities situated on Guien-Gola Mountain. Here the Zapotec king, Cosijoeza, successfully resisted the siege of the invading Aztecs. The ruins stand ⅓ the way up the mountain (about 1300 ft.) and extend to the top where Chontal Indians now raise corn.

Halfway up are the remains of a wall, 10 ft. high, 6 ft. thick, which once surrounded the entire mountain. There are two more walls, evidently inner lines of defense, then a short flight of stairs leads into the great plaza surrounded by pyramidal ruins, temple platforms, etc. A ball court lies to the S of the plaza.

Although limited exploration and almost no reconstruction has been done here, the site is an interesting one to visit, especially if one includes a picnic lunch and a swim in the Tehuantepec River that winds around the base of the mountain.

Salina Cruz, Oax. Pacific Coast port and terminal of the Trans-Isthmus Highway (CN-185) and railway.[5] About 17 m. S of Tehuantepec.

The town is shabby and can be bleak and sand-scoured when the wind blows, yet interesting if the weather is nice. There are excellent beaches (see also, *Ventosa*). Best available hotel in town is the modest and very reasonable *Hotel Guasti*. Sea food served here is very good. Also, *Restaurant Pinguenos* for sea food.

La Ventosa, Oax. A tiny fishing village about 2½ m. SE of Salina Cruz (via dirt road). Situated on the shore of La Ventosa Bay, the place has become a popular beachcombing site and swimming resort. The beaches are excellent. No accommodations except grass huts.

Juchitán, Oax. Pop. 15,000. Alt. 125. Sister city and principal rival of Tehuantepec. About 16 m. E of the latter, and ¼ m. S off CN-190 and 185.

Juchitán (who-chee-TAHN), although less picturesquely situated, has largely overtaken Tehuantepec both as the economic and cultural center of the Tehuantepeceños. Her women appear to be less slovenly and more appealing, her fiestas more elaborate. Especially lively is the 10-day Spring Festival in mid-May, when the traditional dance of the region, the Zandunga, may be seen at its best.

---

[5] *Isthmus of Tehuantepec and the Trans-Isthmus routes* — the Isthmus *(Istmo)*, in the humid tropic zone of southern Mexico stretches across the states of Oaxaca and Veracruz, stands 7000 ft. below the great Mexican tableland. Being the narrowest, and one of the lowest parts of the republic, it represents one of the shortest transcontinental routes in America. The story of the 400-year struggle to span the Isthmus by road, railroad, and canal is one of the most intriguing in Mexican annals.

Hernán Cortés was the first to realize the enormous strategic importance of rapid communications between the Atlantic and Pacific Oceans. He talked the Spanish crown into granting him land and water rights across the narrow waist of land, but he did nothing further. In 1774, Bucareli, the Spanish Viceroy in Mexico, ordered a survey and proposed building a canal between Coatzacoalcos (briefly called, Puerto Mexico) and Salina Cruz. Similar projects were elaborated upon by Humboldt and scores of British and American engineers, but action upon them were usually impeded by local politics or civil wars.

In the mid-nineteenth century a curious organization, the Tehuantepec Railway Company of New Orleans, set out to open a route between New Orleans and San Francisco, via the Isthmus. No railway trains were involved. Passengers traveled by boat to Coatzacoalcos, then sailed luxuriously up the Coatzacoalcos River to Suchil on the *Allegheny Belle*, a former Mississippi side-wheeler. From Suchil they were transported to the Pacific side by jolting carriages, on horseback, or even carried on the backs of Indian bearers. The company offered one conducted tour a month. During its heyday thousands of gold-seeking 49ers made their way to California in this manner.

In 1881, a Captain James B. Eads (builder of the St. Louis, Missouri, steel-arch bridge) tried to promote a fantastic triple-track railway over which fully loaded ocean steamers would be transported across the Isthmus on giant wheeled cradles. Although that never materialized, the Isthmus got its railway — a costly Toonerville affair which was inaugurated in 1907. Though the railroad was a great success, running as many as 20 trains a day from ocean to ocean, seven years later the opening of the Panama Canal undermined its value. Now about one train makes the trip each day, when it can sum up the effort.

The recently built Trans-Isthmus Highway, termed "the asphalt canal" by people in the region, is a high-speed road, 186 miles long, linking Salina Cruz and Coatzacoalcos. Using it, a motorist can enjoy the unique experience of bathing in the Pacific before breakfast and taking a dip in the Gulf of Mexico after lunch.

The town market day is Sunday, and likewise is more colorful than in the sister city.

Juchitán is celebrated as the home of a beautiful flower called by the Aztecs, *Tlapalizqui-xochitl* (*Cheirostemon planifolium, Bombaceas*). The tree is supposed to be medicinal and venerated by the Indians. It bears a curious and beautiful red flower, the center of which is in the form of a hand, the fingers bent inward a little. Foreigners know it as the *Arbol de las Manitas* (Tree of Little Hands). The flower is said to have once caused a savage war between Moctezuma II and the Mixteca lord, Malínal. Moctezuma, struck by the beauty of the flower, ordered a shipment. The refusal provoked a war which resulted in disaster to the Mixteca.

HOTELS: Juchitán's hotels leave a lot to be desired. They are *viajero* in style and quite inexpensive. *Hotel Gonzales,* Jardín Juárez, and *Posada San Vicente*. The latter is also the terminal for the Autotransportes del Sureste Cristóbal Colón buses.

Ixtapec, Oax. Pop. 12,300. About 11 m. NW of CN-190. A railway center and nearest scheduled airline stop (CMA) for the Tehuantepec region. It is one of the points from which automobiles can be rail-shipped to Tapachula and Guatemala. Motorists bound for Guatemala in this manner should make shipping reservations in Mexico City at the Industrial Agent's office of the Mexican National Railways, Calle República de Chile 8. Rates (subject to change) are approximately $450 MN, including loading and unloading charges. It is advisable to stay with your car (on the flatcar) for security purposes.

HOTELS: *Hotel Panamericano,* 16 de Septiembre and Ferrocarril (best available). 40 rooms, clean, large (no recent report on rates).

Matías Romero, Oax. Pop. 7200. On CN-185, about 27 m. N of the CN-185 and 190 junction. A rather quaint railroad town, slightly above the tropic humidity. It is noted for its exuberant annual fair, February 22–26. *Hotel Mary* is the best available.

THE CHIAPAS COUNTRY

One of the most remote, least visited parts of Mexico, Chiapas remains to be "discovered" by travelers. It is without question one of the most scenic states, the most fascinating from the point of view of folklore studies, also, one of the finest hunting regions in the republic. Until the opening of the Chiapas stretch of the Pan-American Highway in 1950, in order to reach the capital of the state one had to go four days on horseback from Arriaga, the nearest railhead. To reach San Cristóbal de las Casas, the picturesque, ancient Spanish colonial capital, it took another 2½ days on horseback. Now these points can be reached from Tehuantepec in an easy day's drive.

Tuxtla Gutiérrez, Chis. Pop. 30,000. Alt. 1775 ft. Capital of the State of Chiapas.

HOW TO GET THERE: *Via highway* — CN-190, the Pan-American Route (also called "Carretera Cristóbal Colón"); Tuxtla is 160 m. from Tehuantepec, 345 m. from Oaxaca City. *Via bus* — Autotransportes del Sureste Cristóbal Colón (first class from Mexico City). *Air* — CMA, daily scheduled flights from Mexico City.

HOTELS: *Hotel Bonampak,* W edge of town on CN-190. Has 105 rooms, suites, and bungalows. In the new hotel section 41 of the 60 rooms are air conditioned. Nicely furnished. The 45 older units need refurbishing. Nice gardens, pleasant dining room, coffee shop, swimming pool and wading pool, *frontón* and billiards. A good hotel for this region. Rates: EP from $60 to $125 MN dble. Tel. 20.

The following hotels are small, *viajero-type* but new and relatively tidy. *Hotel Serrano,* Av. Central 24. No restaurant. Rates: EP $35 MN dble. *Hotel Esperanza,* Av. Norte and Central. Same as above. *San Francisco Motel,* at airport, is satisfactory. Has pool.

DIRECTORY: *Auto repairs* — Anza (Ford), Av. Central 72; Automotriz Farrera (Chevrolet), Av. Central 238; Pastrana de Pedrero and Cia. (Dodge), Av. 13a Pte. and Av. Central. *Banks* — Banco Nacional de México, Av. Central 18; Banco Mercantil de Chiapas, Av. Central and Calle 2 Pte. *Bus lines* — Autotransportes del Sureste Cristóbal Colón, corner of 1 Nte. and 1 Ote. *Airlines* — CMA, Av. Central and 2 Ote.; Compañia Inpulsora de Aviacion. (Local and charter flights to Villahermosa, Tab., to the archaeological ruins at Bonampak, Palenque, Yaxchilán, and Lacandón forest.) Inquire at airport or through hotel managers.

THE CITY AND ENVIRONS: Tuxtla Gutiérrez is a modern commercial town without any appeal. Its wide double plaza is uncommonly barren. The one relieving facet is that flowers bloom wildly in its tropical air. The few points of interest within the town are:

Botanical Gardens and Zoo, at E edge of town, noted for its wide variety of animals native to the region, and some unusual tropical flowers, plus an interesting collection of precious woods.

Museo del Estado, on Av. 1 Norte, 11 Oriente (near Bonampak Hotel). Nicely arranged exhibits of artifacts, sculpture and stelae from the famed Mayan ruins in the state. In the same building, but from an entrance on opposite side, in the *State Tourist Bureau;* there are excellent displays of regional handicrafts and indigenous costumes. *Hours:* 8:30 A.M. to 2:30 P.M., 4 to 6 P.M. *Admission:* free.

The Market: At times there are interesting pickings — Indian weaving, boxes of inlaid wood, *rebozos,* and some native gold filigree jewelry. Each April 21 to 26 Tuxtla celebrates a fiesta and a commercial fair featuring regional handicrafts. Native dances including the local specialty — marimba music.

EXCURSION TO EL SUMIDERO: A scenic canyon about 12 m. NE of the city (rough road). The canyon is one of the most formidable gashes in the republic, running some 26 m. in length, with sheer walls rising 6000 ft. above the channel of the Río Grijalva. Until 1960 the canyon resisted exploration. The best time of the year to view the canyon is in summer when its walls are covered with a sheath of vivid green verdure.

Chiapa de Corso, Chis. Pop. 7000. On CN-190, about 9 m. E of Tuxtla Gutiérrez. A pictorial colonial village on a bluff overlooking the Río Grijalva (also called the Río Chiapa in this state). The town was founded on the site of an Indian settlement by the conquistador, Diego de Mazariego (1528). Worth stopping for is the unusual Moorish fountain in the plaza. The imposing octagonal structure is shaped like the crown of the Catholic Kings of Spain, is made of *ladrillo* (an Arabic type brick). This strange and rather beautiful work was built in 1565.

Facing on the plaza is a small museum (connected with the National Museum of Popular Arts and Crafts) devoted to exhibits of the lacquered *jicaras* (gourds) which the Indians in this area have made since before the conquest.

A block from the plaza is the *Convent and Church of Santo Domingo,* an interesting sixteenth-century structure. The architecture is Gothic. In the tower there is a huge bell made of silver, gold, and copper.

As you leave the town, near the old cemetery, there is an important new archaeological zone with pyramidal platforms that are quite high and are believed to be Maya in origin. The current work of investigation and restoration is being done by the New World Archaeological Foundation (Orinda, Calif.).

From Chiapa de Corso one can take a launch trip part way into the El Sumidero canyon, or go by boat the other way to *Acala,* and from there take a battered bus to the picturesque Indian village of *San Bartolomé de los Llanos* (also called *Venustiano Carranza*). One seldom sees the villagers from San Bartolomé in the highway towns. If they visited too far afield, they'd arouse too much envy for they wear one of the most unusual and attractive costumes in the country. The women wear blouses of a lacelike material, and dark blue skirts embellished with stitched, colored embroidery. Their men wear curious white cotton jodhpur trousers, flaring from hip to knee and narrow from knee to ankle. The trousers are embroidered with tiny red figures, and this design is also carried to their shirts which are of a lacelike weave. Both men and women go about exposing a bare midriff.

San Cristóbal de las Casas, Chis. Pop. 17,450. Alt. 7454. The oldest Spanish city in Chiapas, formerly the capital. It is perhaps the most genuine colonial town in Mexico, with an unspoiled charm many of the tourist spots have lost.

HOW TO GET THERE: *Via highway* — CN-190, E from Tuxtla Gutiérrez, 51 m. From Oaxaca City, 396 m. *Via bus* — Autotransportes del Sureste Cristóbal Colón. (First class from Mexico City or Oaxaca). *Via air* — CMA scheduled flights from Mexico City or Veracruz to Tuxtla Gutiérrez, then by bus or charter plane to San Cristóbal de las Casas.

HOTELS: *Hotel Español,* 2 blocks from plaza at 1º de Marzo 5. A neat, very clean, colonial-type hotel. 20 rooms, some with fireplaces. Dining room serves very well prepared food. Cocktail service. Though this hotel is quite modest, the pleasant atmosphere and friendliness of the management make it superior to anything in Chiapas. Rates: AP, from $75 to $100 MN dble. Tel. Long Distance, 5. *La Posada de San Cristóbal,* Gen. Utrilla 11. 20 rooms, fairly new, restaurant. EP, $20 MN and up, dble. *Autel Colón,* on highway as you enter town. Roomy, but not recommended until the service improves.

DIRECTORY: *Bank* — Banco Nacional de México (agency), Mazariegos and C. Rosas. *Car repairs* — Refaccionaria San Cristóbal, Plaza 31 de Marzo. *Bus lines* — Autotransportes del Sureste Cristóbal Colón, Juárez 21.

THE TOWN AND ENVIRONS: San Cristóbal de las Casas (sahn chris-TOE-bahl day lahs KAH-sas)[6] is situated in the small, beautiful, mountain and tree surrounded Valley of Hueyzacatlán, an area that arouses nostalgic reminders of picturesque valleys in the Austrian Tyrol and the Kyoto region of Japan. The charm of Las Casas is its setting and its inhabitants, not its architecture. Like most Mexican colonial towns, Las Casas spreads out from a central plaza that is broad, has a lacy ironwork bandstand surrounded by fountains and flowers. Most of the houses in town are one-story, many colored, and roofed with red tiles. At either end of the town rises a hill topped with a church; to the W the small *Church of San Cristóbal,* to the E the *Church of Guadalupe.* Neither are interesting, but the vistas from the hilltops are lovely. Worth seeing, however, are the *Cathedral,* flanking the plaza, and the *Church of Santo Domingo,* toward the edge of town on Av. 31 de Marzo. The Cathedral is notable for its Baroque retablos and its magnificent gold encrusted pulpit. *Santo Domingo,* begun in 1547, has a fine Baroque façade and an interior covered with unusual retablos.

Photographers and artists are also attracted by the handsome façade on the *Casa de Mazariegos,* the Plateresque decorated "palace" of Don Diego Mazariegos, founder of the city. Also by the *Carmen Church* which has a street running through the base of its tower. Other points of interest are the *Instituto Nacional Indigenista* at the end of Av. 31 de Mayo Nte. This is a training school run by the Department of Indian Affairs, having as its objective the incorporating of the Indian communities into Mexican national life through raising their standards of education, community sanitation and well being.

Not far from the center is a handsome, sprawling colonial estate which has been converted into a kind of cultural clearinghouse for archaeological and indigenous studies by the late explorer-anthropologist Franz Blom. There is an excellent library related to Mexican archaeology and anthropology, a small museum. Rooms are available for visitors doing work in related fields.

THE MARKET AND SHOPS: The Las Casas market, daily except Sunday, is one of the most interesting in the republic because it is purely Indian. People come in by the hundreds from surrounding hamlets to trade. The native costumes are vivid, and there is almost no Spanish spoken. On Sundays the Indians hold market in their home villages. On the Calle Real de Guadalupe there are rows of tiny shops where the Indians also trade. One such shop, the *Segovia,* on Guadalupe Victoria 2, is a veritable gold mine of brilliant Indian handicrafts.

By far the most colorful of sights in Las Casas are the costumes of Indians from surrounding villages. The Zinacatecans are best distinguished by their flat, handwoven straw hats adorned with varicolored ribbons, a short cotton tunic, cotton shorts, and sandals. The rib-

[6] San Cristóbal de las Casas is frequently referred to as San Cristóbal, or more often, simply as Las Casas. The town was named for its patron saint (St. Christopher), and its famous bishop (Bartolomé de Las Casas). The Indians of the region have their own name for the town — Jovél, meaning "grassy plain."

In 1524 Cortés' captain, Luis Marín, and the famous soldier-historian, Bernal Díaz del Castillo, entered the valley and found that the Chamula Indians had fortified themselves on a mountaintop from which they resisted the Spaniards with vigor. Although the invaders eventually won this strongpoint (the Indians evacuated one night, leaving lances along the parapets and a small band of warriors to beat drums, to give the impression the place was still held), it took the Spanish some years to control the area.

Las Casas itself was founded by Diego Mazariego in 1528. Though Mazariego was a humane person with advanced ideas, the good works that he initiated were soon destroyed when the *Audiencia de México* appointed Juan Enrique de Guzmán to supersede him. Guzman's hatred of his predecessor was such he even renamed the town Villaviciosa (vicious town). In 1545 Bishop Bartolomé de Las Casas arrived with a group of more than 35 Dominican friars. The bishop, like Don Vasco de Quiroga in Michoacán, fought vigorously in behalf of the Indians, earning himself the title of "protector of the Indians."

bons are simply to attract the attention of girls. (*Note to women tourists:* Buy all the gay ribboned hats you want, but don't wear them on the streets of Las Casas. They are men's hats. Some of the Indians resent women wearing them.)

The Chamula men wear black or white tunics, but seldom sport ribbons on their hats. If one wears a black tunic and ribbons it indicates that he has or is holding a post in the Indian Government. The men from the village of San Juan Chamula have white sleeves on their tunics; those from San Andrés Chamula, red sleeves; those from Santiago, brown sleeves; those from Santa Marta and Magdalenas, blue sleeves. Men from the village of Huistán wear curious "diaper pants," actually long baggy trousers tucked up and under. They wear their small red hats adorned with red ribbons at a rakish angle. Their shirts are handloomed, and have pale blue ornamental stitching around the neck. The curious high heel-guards the Indians throughout the area wear on their sandals are a relic of Mayan days. On Maya monuments one sees the same heel-guards elaborately decorated.

FIESTAS: April 1 to 7, fair commemorating the founding of the city. July 31, fiesta honoring the town's patron saint, San Cristóbal. August 24, fiesta honoring Bartolomé de Las Casas. November 1 to 3, Day of the Dead ceremonies.

In the region around Las Casas there are numerous villages where the various Indian groups celebrate festivals and rites having their roots in the pre-Columbian past. In many instances the Spanish influences hardly touch them and they remain fascinatingly barbaric and beautiful. The two most accessible villages are Zinacantan and San Juan Chamula (noted for its interesting weaving and Sunday market). Both towns are less than 8 m. from Las Casas and can be reached by car. Taxis from Las Casas charge $85 MN round-trip. One can also rent horses in Las Casas for about $10 MN per day.

PARTIAL LIST OF FIESTAS IN LAS CASAS AREA

December 31 and into January: Interesting pre-Hispanic-flavored ceremonies celebrating the installation of Indian authorities for the coming year. *San Juan Chamula, San Andrés Chamula, Zinacantan,* etc.

Pre-Lenten Carnival: (movable). At various villages. The most colorful and spectacular is held at *San Juan Chamula* where avenues of dry grass are set fire to and Indians dance in it barefooted.

April 29: *Amatenango del Valle.*

May 30: *Zinacantan.*

June 5–6: *Chenalo,* fiesta of San Antonio.

June 13: *Simojovél,* village fair.

June 24: Two important fiestas honoring San Pedro at *San Juan Chamula* and at *Chenalo.*

August 24: *San Bartolomé de los Llanos,* large fiesta.

Comitán, Chis. Pop. 1175. Alt. 5236. On CN-190 about 55 m. from the Mexico-Guatemala border. Comitán (coh-mee-TAHN) is an uninteresting, hot, mountain town whose only relieving feature is the orchids that thrive in this area. The *plaza principal* is filled with them. The town is the chief market center for the Tzeltales Indians. Their name for the place is Balum Canán (New Star).

HOTELS: *Hotel de los Lagos,* edge of town as you enter. Recently refurbished, best available. 50 rooms, dining room, bar. Garden said to be filled with 2,500 orchids. Offers guide service and transportation to Montebello Lakes. Hotel Rates: EP from $35 MN dble. *Hotel Montebello,* in center, shabby *viajero-type.*

Lagos de Montebello (Montebello Lakes): A two-day trip (overnight stay) SE of Comitán via very rough road trails. This chain of magnificent lakes set in forest and mountain country are unquestionably the most beautiful and isolated in Mexico. Each lake seems to glow with different colors of the rainbow. In February 1960 the Mexican Government made the Montebello Lakes and some 20,000 sq. km. of the surrounding Lacandón Forest into a National Park. At present there are no suitable vacation accommodations near the lakes. The nearby Finca San José del Arcos (a ranch) can put up 14 guests, but for any extended stay you must pack-in your own food.

Of unusual interest are the Lacandón Indians, an extremely reticent, dying Maya tribe inhabiting the vast, scarcely explored country to the N and NE. Utterly cut off from the world, these people never experienced the impact of the Spanish Conquest nor what followed it. As Franz Blom observed, "It is useless to speak to them of the Independence or the Revolution. They've never been subjugated; never known a boss, nor have they been in contact with one. They have no idea what the Mexican nation is, nor what the State of Chiapas is." They are so poor most of them use wooden knives, lack sufficient food and shelter. Many build fires near their hammocks because they have no blankets. Their beliefs reach back far into the Maya past. They believe in a supreme deity, Hachakyum, the creator of heaven and earth, who resides in the Mecca of the Lacandónes — the marvelous ruins of Yaxchilán on the banks of the Usumacinta River. One of their gods has the unusual mission of protecting the world from snakes, tigers and other animals; and since these people find it hard to visualize a world without women, all Lacandón gods have wives.

THE MAYA RUINS IN CHIAPAS: About one third of the State of Chiapas is roadless forest and jungle. In this hidden country there are hundreds of known archaeological sites, located, registered, yet still to be explored; in addition to these archaeologists are sure there are hundreds of other ruins still to be found. Some may be as elaborate and large in area as Uxmal or Palenque, but they are so well hidden and the jungle is so little explored that almost any day, someone might stumble upon an imagination-shaking lost city.[7] Of the more important Maya ruins in this secret world the most easily reached is Palenque, then with some difficulty, Yaxchilán, and with great difficulty, Bonampak. All are goals for the off-trail traveler.

Palenque, Chis. (archaeological zone). The *Ruinas de Palenque* (ruh-EE-nahs day pah-LEHN-kay) were the first to awaken attention to the existence of ancient and unknown cities in tropical America. In 1750 a party of Spaniards traveling in the interior came upon, in the midst of a vast solitude, the remains of a city, some 20 sq. m. in extent, known to the Indians as *Casas de Piedra* (stone houses). The existence of such a city was entirely unknown: there had been no mention of it in any books, and no tradition that it had ever been. To this day it is not known by what name it was called, and the only appellation given to it is that of Palenque, after the village near which the ruins stand.

[7] On January 1, 1960, two young Americans, John P. Milton and Gene Dursan, accompanied by a Lacandón Indian, Bor, stumbled upon such a "find." Their discovery, considered quite important, consisted of a group of Maya buildings in the Yatoch Ku zone SE of the Lacanhá de Bonampak. These ruins, lost over 11 centuries, contain important interior murals in reds and greens, showing figures of hummingbirds and aquatic lilies.

HOW TO GET THERE: The best entry to Palenque is from Villahermosa, Tab., by air or rail. From Tuxtla Gutiérrez in Oaxaca there are direct daily scheduled flights to Villahermosa. One may also do it the expensive way, via charter-flight from Tuxtla or San Cristóbal de Las Casas. An auto road linking Palenque to Villahermosa is scheduled to be completed by 1965.

In the village of Palenque (7 m. from the ruins via good road) there are several primitive hotels that furnish jeep transportation to and from the ruins, air strip, and railway station. *Hotel La Croix* (the best) has 6 rooms, a few baths and charges about $35 MN dble, EP. If the place is crowded and a few extra guests are tossed in your room there is no extra charge. No charge also for the zoo in the back yard with its wild boar, deer, and spider monkey. *Hotel Cruz de Palenque,* 5 rooms, is a bit less sophisticated. Rates: EP $25 MN dble.

At the ruins there are no hotels nor provisions for food and water. You must take these along.

THE RUINS in addition to being tremendously exciting archaeologically, have a pure visual quality that would be difficult to match anywhere. They are set in jungled hills like diamonds set in jade. The ruins are upon a kind of plateau surrounded by dense vegetation. Pyramid after pyramid is crowned by a temple. From the top of any of them you can look back and see the lowlands of Tabasco, an endless sweep of forest and savannas.

According to best guesses Palenque was, in the seventh century A.D., what Teotihuacán was in the north — a holy city, a city of priests and pilgrims. It was one of the centers of the First Maya Empire, and is thought to have been abandoned around the twelfth century. It is a most remarkable place for its refined architecture, its stelae with bas-reliefs, its splendid figures in stucco and its magnificent temples and palace group.

The Palace is a complex gallery of rooms and patios placed upon a trapezoidal platform. In one of the patios there is a curious square structure known as *The Tower.* It has several stories of decreasing size. The corners are reinforced by slightly projecting pillars. There are inner stairs and rectangular windows.

The Temples — of the Sun, of the Cross, of the Foliated Cross, and of the Conde — are all rather similar since they consist of stepped substructures with vertical paraments, two lateral galleries with a sanctuary placed at the back of one of these. Each of the temples is crowned by a magnificent comb (a structure of carved stone with a great deal of open-work, like lace). The *Temple of the Inscriptions* has acquired considerable fame since archaeologist Alberto Ruz discovered a crypt in the heart of the building containing a royal burial which was sealed by a splendid sculptured slab. The walls of the chamber are adorned with 9 beautiful figures in stucco. The crypt itself contained the remains of a royal personage, including funerary objects, various jewels worked in jade and covered with cinnabar. The discovery has qualified or upset the widely held notion that Mesoamerican substructures lacked interior tombs.

Palenque likewise looms large in the speculations regarding direct trans-Pacific links between Mexico's cultures and the Orient. One of the striking analogies with Asia is the sacred tree or cross found on the *Temple of the Foliated Cross.* It occurs in America only at Palenque, and yet its almost exact sculptured counterpart is to be found on a sculptured panel at Angkor Vat in Cambodia. Similarly, at Palenque there are sculpted figures of divinities holding a lotus stem or flower, and they bear a remarkable resemblance to those that adorn a Hindu-Buddhist image from Khasaparna, India.

Hours: The archaeological zone is opened during daylight hours. There is a small museum in the zone, opened from 10 to 11 A.M.; the tombs are open from 11 A.M. to noon. *Admission:* 2 pesos.

Bonampak, Chis. Deep in the Chiapas jungle, Bonampak (bone-AHM-pahk) was discovered in 1946 by Giles G. Healey,[8] and is noted particularly for its unusual murals, considered the finest pre-Conquest painting on this continent.

The archaeological site is on a hill which has a number of stepped artificial terraces supporting temples and other structures. There are a series of small temples, with tiny rooms, vaulted roofs, and façades covered with figures in stucco. Facing the main building there is a broad plaza with an interesting stele with a bas-relief of a person splendidly arrayed.

Temple of the Murals rises on the first platform, above the plaza. It has three narrow rooms covered with frescoes. The entranceways have delicately carved stone lintels. The murals in the first room represent the dressing of Ahau Balám, the presentation of a young warrior to the assembled nobles, and the prayers, dances, and processions petitioning victory. The second room contains a depiction of blood rites celebrated in order to obtain victory, plus a battle sequence. The third room shows triumphal dances celebrated on the steps of a pyramid.

Excellent reproduction of these famed murals may be seen in the National Museum in Mexico City, and in the fine archaeological museum in Villahermosa, Tab. At present, the actual frescoes at Bonampak are disappointing to look at. Large sections of them are covered by a thin calcareous coating which requires special treating to clear the deposits away.

TO GET THERE: A trip to Bonampak is usually difficult and is not recommended. It requires a thorough knowledge of jungle travel and living plus excellent preparations. From Tuxtla Gutiérrez or Villahermosa, Tab., one must go by charter plane to El Cedro, a chicle camp, and from there it takes a day by horseback to the ruins. If the airstrips are overgrown crews must be sent beforehand from Tenosique to clear them. It takes these at least a week to get to El Cedro.

Yaxchilán, Chis. One of the most fascinating and beautiful of Maya ruins, located on the banks of the Usumacinta River, just across from the Guatemala border. Yaxchilán (yah-chee-LAHN) was first studied by Teobert Maler from 1897 to 1900, and it was he who gave the buildings their names. The city is much larger than Palenque, and of the same period in Maya history or representing the close of the Old Empire. Noteworthy throughout the jungle-choked ruins is the abundance of low-relief sculpturing, the finest in all the Maya areas.

The ruins lie in a curve of the great Usumacinta. There is one group of isolated buildings upon a high terrace, then the *Great Acropolis* with its complex of temples and courts which seem to surge up out of the jungle, looking much as Angkor Vat and Angkor Thom must have looked like when they were discovered. To the W there are structures called the *Lesser Acropolis.* Th principal temples are: *Temple of the Four Carved Lintels, Temple of the Inscriptions, Red Temple and Palace of the Seven Chambers.* Most of the structures

[8] The official announcement of the discovery was made in May 1947. However, the ruins had been unofficially discovered a year earlier. According to some accounts a young American named Charles Frey made the discovery. The name Bonampak, meaning "Painted Walls," was given to this unique group of temples by the late Dr. Sylvanus Morley, authority on Maya culture. According to Dr. Morley, Bonampak pertains to the First or Old Mayan Empire (about 317 to 987 A.D.).

have plain façades, the friezes framed with plain moldings. There are niches with magnificent sculptures and, upon many of the temples, splendid roof-combs very geometric in form with the hollows resembling countless small windows. Most remarkable, however, are the altars, lintels, steles, and stairs carved in exquisite bas-relief or decorated with hieroglyphics. Most of the lintels depict luxuriously arrayed personages.

HOW TO GET THERE: One can fly or take the Sureste Railway to *Tenosique, Tab.* (see Index), and from there fly to Agua Azul, a lumber camp on the Usumacinta. Or from Tuxtla Gutiérrez or Las Casas fly directly to Agua Azul. From Agua Azul you take a dugout canoe downriver about 5 hours. The trip is like a Conradian experience, drifting through primeval silence, broken only by the chattering of monkeys, the bark of a jaguar and the cries of jungle birds. The dripping, glistening, rustling jungle intertwined with creeping convolvuluses command the attention as much as do the microscopic flies and *chiquistes* which bite all ungloved hands and can make life a torture.

At Yaxchilán one can put up at the hut of the caretaker, Miguel Cruz. There are no other facilities. You bring your own food, hammock, and mosquito netting. Miguel, without much urging, will demonstrate how he calls jaguars *(tigres)* within shotgun range by blowing into an old, battered blue coffeepot.

In this region, NE of San Cristóbal de Las Casas lies one of Mexico's least visited and best game paradises, the country around the town of *Ocosingo, Chis.* It is jeep and pack horse country, but Ocosingo could, and someday will undoubtedly make a beautiful tourist haven. The relatively sophisticated town lies in a lovely pine-mountain-surrounded valley with the San Martín Mountains making a curve at the end of the valley like a football stadium. The town itself has a white church, a fountain, a pleasant plaza, with all the houses around it having colonnades. There is a small, nameless hotel with a nice patio. The rooms themselves are rather poor, but the rats and mice do not seem to mind. Better accommodations are to be had toward the Santa Cruz river at the *Finca El Real,* a spacious *hacienda* owned by the Bulnez family. The region around here is packed with game — deer, jaguar, wild turkey, pheasants. At Finca El Real you can sleep in the room where some of the great men of the literary, political, and archaeological world were put up, namely: Alfredo Tozzer, the noted ethnologist; Bruno Traven, the mysterious author of *The Treasure of the Sierra Madre* and *Death Ship;* Jacques Soustelle, anthropologist and moving figure in de Gaullist French politics.

At *Escopetazo,* 11 m. E of *Chiapa de Corso,* a gravel road goes off to the left (N) toward *Rayón* and *Simojovél.* This road crosses some of the most spectacular mountain and jungle valley country in Chiapas, connecting the Pan-American (Cristóbal Colón) Highway and the Gulf Coast Highway at Villahermosa, Tab. At present the road is jeep-passable in dry weather. It is under heavy construction, being widened for regular traffic. The route log:

MILES	TRIP LOG
0	Escopetazo, turn-off from CN-190.
10	Bochil.
26	Jitotal. A road branches from here to right toward the lovely tropical valley town of *Simojovél.* Road to Tabasco bears to the left.
55	Pueblo Nuevo.
89	Solosuchiapa. Spectacular winding road following the tropical river route the Spanish expedition of Luis Marín and Bernal Díaz withdrew through toward Tabasco when the Indian resistance in the Chiapas highlands got too hot for them. The town is a charming bucolic spot with a broad grass-covered plaza.
99	Ixta Comitán.
108	Pichucalco, Chis. Pop. 3100. **GH.** A picturesque, busy town situated in lovely wooded country. Curiously, every house on the plaza is painted some shade of red. From here on, across the Tabasco state line, the road is gravel and good. *Hotel Mexico,* Zaragoza 39. Primitive yet nice. Rates: $25 MN, dble. EP.
126	Teapa, Tabs. **GHR** (see Index).
145	Villahermosa, Tab. Capital of State of Tabasco (see Index).

THE WEST COAST OF CHIAPAS: The extensive area along the Pacific Coast of Chiapas trending in a southerly and southeasterly direction is an unusually rich and practically undeveloped region characterized by dense forests, commanding mountains and plains almost as level as the Kansas prairie. From the forests come precious woods, rare orchids, gums, and dyewoods, while on the plains there are large henequén and sugar-cane *haciendas* and *potreros* (stock farms). Unfortunately the coastal highway does not extend much beyond Pijijiapan, and there are almost no lateral roads up to the center of the state. A narrow-gauge branch of the National Railways of Mexico extends along the coast to Tapachula and the Guatemala border. The principal towns are:

Arriaga, Chis. Pop. 8735. (ah-ree-AH-gah) a drab and hot farming community, one of the shipping points for tourist autos on the Isthmian Railway. (See Index.) No recommendable hotel, but if you can stand dingy emergency accommodations there is the *Hotel Panamericano,* Calle 4 Ote. and Callejón Independencia. *Car repairs* — Distribuidores de Autocamiones de Chiapas (Ford), Av. Central Ote. 7.

Tonalá, Chis. Pop. 11,500. The more popular shipping point for tourists shipping their cars to Tapachula and Guatemala. The town is rather dainty, though humid, and there is a pleasant shaded plaza. About 11 m. S is one of Chiapas' few beach resorts, Puerto Arista. The best automobile route to Guatemala begins here.

Tapachula, Chis. Pop. 30,200. Alt. 480 ft. This frontier city, isolated from the rest of the republic except for rail and air communications, lies at the foot of the Taconah volcano. The town is rather charming, having a plaza adorned with magnificent royal palms. It is the center of a rich coffee, cocoa, cotton, and banana-producing area. Ten miles SW via paved road is the small port town and bathing resort of Puerto Madero. From Tapachula a good paved road leads 11 m. to the Guatemala border.

HOTELS: *Gran Hotel Internacional,* Av. Central Sur 84. A fair, emergency stop. 21 rooms, dining room, cocktail service. No hot water in rooms. Rates: EP $50 MN dble. *Hotel Columbia,* 8a Av. Norte 16, fair dining room, rooms shabby. EP $45 MN dble. *Hotel Fénix,* 4a Av. Norte 47. Has nicer rooms than the Columbia, but food not as good. 42 units. Rates: $45 MN dble.

DIRECTORY: *Banks* — Banco Nacional de México, 42 Av. Norte 12; Banco Mercantil de Chiapas, Central Poniente and 2a Av. Norte. *Auto repairs* — Casa Monroy (Ford), 3a Poniente 6; Automotriz del Soconusco (Chevrolet), Calle Central Ote. 28; Chiapas Motors (Chrysler), 3a Ote. 5. *Airlines* — CMA, Central Norte 9, Tel. 2-36.

54. The Peninsula of Yucatán

The Peninsula of Yucatán, embracing the States of Campeche and Yucatán, and the Territory of Quintana Roo, and jutting out between the Caribbean Sea and the Gulf of Mexico, is one of the most fascinating and least known of Mexico's many picturesque regions. This age-old, sunswept, mysterious land, hiding magnificent ruined cities in its brooding jungles, its brilliant beaches unvisited, its Spanish-Moorish cities scarcely changing over the centuries, has until recently been effectively separated from the main body of the republic by impassable barriers of swamp, river and jungle. Even now it remains a captivating Middle American *imperium in imperio,* still relatively isolated; a sort of Antillean garden midway between the cool north and the languid, steaming equatorial regions. Its citizens still think of themselves as almost an independent nation. Instead of calling themselves Mexicans, they proudly refer to themselves as Yucatecos.

Reliable air travel, a decade of intensive railway and highway construction, has finally made almost all sections of the peninsula easily accessible to tourists. One can reach the peninsula via daily air service from Mexico City, New Orleans, New York and Miami, in a matter of hours (see Index, for airline schedules to Mérida). There are direct connections by railway and bus to Yucatán; and one can now spin down the new Gulf Coast Highway from the U.S. border to the Caribbean shore of the peninsula (see Index: Highway Routes).

TOURIST ATTRACTIONS: The outstanding attractions are: (1) the spectacular Mayan archaeological ruins, some within comfortable reach of Mérida — Chichén Itzá, Uxmal, Kabah, and Labná. Tulum on the Caribbean coast. (2) The Islands of Cozumel and Mujeres, with their vivid beaches, skin-diving and fishing facilities. (3) The picturesque cities: Mérida and Campeche. (4) The Island of Carmen with its interesting tropical fishing port. (5) The exceptional deep-sea and river fishing, especially in the waters around Isla Carmen, Cozumel, and Chetumal. (6) Sports hunting in the jungles of Quintana Roo and Campeche for deer, jaguar, wild turkey, and wild pig.

AREAS OF MAXIMUM INTEREST	BASE
The Yucatecan Country	Mérida, Yuc.
Campeche	Campeche, Camp.
Quintana Roo Coast	Isla Cozumel, or Isla Mujeres, or Chetumal, Q.R.

THE PENINSULA is a wide, flat limestone plain, a young coral peninsula somewhat like Florida. Starting from the seacoasts, it rises gently toward the interior and culminates (in the south) in a series of hills called *Uitzes,* about 200 ft. high. In the north and northwest the land is low, calcareous and rocky. With the exception of the Campeche area there are no rivers and but few lakes. The soil is a thin skin, almost sterile. The region covers about 54,806 sq. miles.

CLIMATE: Much of the interior of Quintana Roo, Yucatán, and especially Campeche are jungle-hot, particularly through the months of April to November. The remaining months are comfortably warm to hot. The coastal areas, touched by cooling breezes are pleasant, as is the northern half of Yucatán.

The dry season, marked by occasional heavy showers, lasts from late October to May. The rainy season is from May to September. In Yucatán and Quintana Roo the rains fall for several hours in the midafternoon, while in the more dense forested country of Campeche they may seem endless and heavy.

THE RIVER SYSTEM of Yucatán and Quintana Roo is subterranean and still unknown in extent. Most of the located streams flow in a northerly direction to the sea. In many places the rainfall and sea seepage

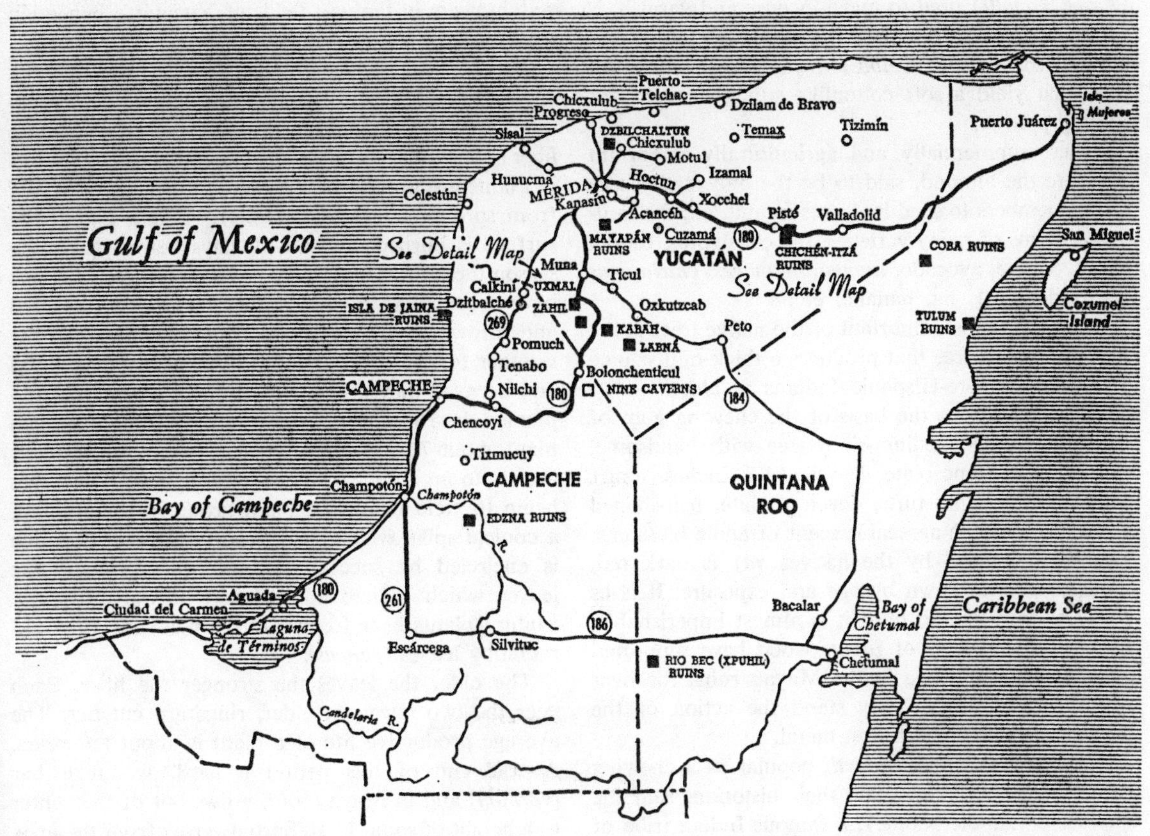

come to within 20 ft. of the surface, whence it is lifted by countless windmills for irrigation and other purposes. In Campeche, on the other hand, there are a number of very fine and beautiful tropical rivers, notably the Candelaria and the Champotón Rivers.

CAVERNS honeycomb the peninsula and sometimes are of great size and beauty. Most of these intricate labyrinths remain unexplored and unmapped — a speleologist's heaven. Certain of them, like the *Caves of Loltun* (stone flowers), the *Nine Caverns of Bolonchén* in Campeche possess magnificent galleries and grottoes whose walls are covered with petroglyphs and other prehistoric symbols. It is said that the ancient Mayas dwelt in cool spacious caverns protected from the blazing summer sun and amply supplied with chilled water. In pleasant weather they lived above ground, but if enemies appeared they retired to their subterranean retreats. These caverns were used as retreats and hideouts during the long, bitter War of the Castes — the people literally going underground. Legend has it that underground galleries connect the labyrinthine cave system of Yucatán with superb grottoes in subjacent Guatemala, the reputed home of the hero-deity *Itzamna* — whence the name *Itzas* (Mayas).

Cenotes or (Maya) *Dzonots,* that is, Water Caves, are among the most interesting natural curiosities of the peninsula. They are large or small pools of slightly saline water usually from 20 to 70 ft. below the surface of the ground. They form unique wells and bathing places, and supposedly are connected with the great system of underground rivers, since in some of them a slow current passes through. The Mayans built their ancient cities near such wells. The most famous of these *cenotes* is the sacred well used by a tribe called the Itzá, and who called their city, Chichén Itzá (Mouth of the Wells of the Itzá).

FLORA AND FAUNA: The forests of the peninsula, especially Campeche and parts of Quintana Roo, are luxuriant and dense jungle containing many fine and important commercial woods. Among the hardwoods are: richly tinted mahogany *(caoba),* cedar *(cedro),* the beautiful rosewood (Spanish, *palisandro;* Maya, *chechem*), a native ebony, and a wood called *amianto* (asbestos) because it will not burn. Campeche is noted for its logwood tree, the *palo de tinte,* or *de Campeche* (Maya, *ek* or *eek,* i.e., black thing), from which the valuable logwood dye was secured. Native trees used for building are the *jabin,* the *chac-té,* the *chulul* — whose iron-hard wood was used for making bows, arrows, and other objects. The resin *copal,* (Aztec, *copalli*) used to make incense and varnish, is extracted from a tree called *pom.* The kapok or silk cotton tree, *Bombax Ceiba* (Maya, *yaxché*) has seed pods that yield a soft cottonlike substance used for stuffing pillows.

Other commercially and agriculturally important trees are the almond, said to be the only native tree that remembers to shed its leaves in autumn; the mulberry, palms of many varieties, the eucalyptus, Indian laurel, orange, avocado, *mango, mameyes, chirimoyas* (custard-apple), fig, banana, etc.

One of the most important of the native trees is the *zapote,* a forest tree that produces a thick milky juice known to the pre-Hispanic Indians as *chictli* — the *chicle* which forms the basis of the chewing gum of commerce. This medium-sized tree with handsome, glossy, oval, lanceolate leaves (4-5 inches long) which grow in thin tufts, develop white, bell-shaped flowers having the agreeable scent of apple blossoms. The wood (called by the natives *ya*) is dark red, turns chocolate brown by age and exposure. It is as heavy as iron and so hard it is almost imperishable. It is said that beams of *zapote* wood have supported great weights of stone in the Mayan ruins for over two thousand years. They stand the action of the tropical elements better than metal.

The Spaniards found *chictli* popular as a chewing gum among the Aztecs, and their historians said the *Zapotecas* (zapote people), a famous Indian tribe of Southern Mexico were so called because of their extensive use of the *zapote* gum and fruit. Today, the gathering of *chicle* juice by *chicleros* is an important industry in Campeche and Quintana Roo.

The round, light-russet fruit (shaped like a cleftless peach) of the *zapote* has a rough, downy skin; a rich, sweetish juice and a smooth to granular pulp the color of seared rose. When eaten at the proper moment of ripeness they are somewhat like a pear, but slightly different and delicious. A black fruit *(zapote prieto),* with a skin resembling a green avocado that looks somewhat deflated, and with interior pulp like a smooth black tar, makes one of Mexico's most delectable desserts. The black pulp is whipped with a dash of lime juice and cognac, then chilled.

Henequén (eh-nay-KEN), a plant and fiber of the *Agave fourcroydes,* known also as sisal-hemp and sisal (because for many years it was exported through the old port of Sisal which, until 1871, was the chief port of entry of the peninsula). The plant is also remotely related to the Indian hemp, the *yucca* and *marijuana* as well as Mexico's ubiquitous *maguey.* The strong flexible fibers of the plant were known to the ancient Mayas who twisted it into ropes with which they hauled great stone blocks to the summits of their pyramids and temples. The name is believed to be derived from the Spanish *heno* (hay) and the Náuatl *nequén,* cloth or garment made of the fiber.

Because of its alcohol content, henequén burns as quickly and fiercely as sugar cane, hence the watchtowers in the vast fields of Yucatán's henequén *haciendas.*

Three wild varieties grow in Yucatán: the (Maya) *chelem, cahum,* and *citamci.* The cultivated variety are the *yaxci* (green fiber), and the *sacci* (white fiber). The latter produces the henequén of commerce.

Plants are produced from seeds, from cuttings and from sprouts called *hijos* (sons). A field is cut, the surface is burned, and 60–90 days before the rainy season the *hijos,* (usually 18 to 20 inches high) which have sprouted from the mother plant, are uprooted and thrown in a heap where they lie exposed to the weather for a month or more. When they look dried and decayed they are carried to the cleared field and planted in rows about four yards apart, and each plant about 7 ft. from its brother. About 1100 plants are set to an acre. Six years after planting the leaves begin to yield fiber. The plant grows in the form of a conical spike which springs from the center which is encircled by successive rings of long swordlike leaves which radiate upward and outward from it. Mature plants bear from 6 to 8 rings with 10 to 15 radiating leaves *(pencas).*

The older the leaves the stronger the fiber. Each year the two lower, or elder, rings are cut out. The average productive life of a plant is about ten years. At the end of this period a hard, woodlike bar *(varejón)* and in Maya *(bob),* grows out of the center to a height of some 15 ft. Sprouts grow from the apex of this bar, but they take from two to three years longer to develop than do the *hijos* cut away from the base of the plant. During harvest the leaves are cut out with the *corba* (a machetelike knife with a hooked end). They are hauled by ricks and tiny narrow-gauge railway to the scraping mill. A decorticator extracts the fiber from the pulp. The former is bleached, dried, pressed into bales and prepared for shipment.

The Spaniards early learned that ship cables made from the fiber were stronger and resisted dampness better than the Oriental hemp. Up through the First and Second World Wars the Peninsula of Yucatán was the world's chief supplier of high-grade sisal. Since then, due to the introduction of substitutes abroad, the market has steadily declined.

A great variety of pretty and useful articles are made of the fiber in addition to ropes and binding twine. Peninsula craftsmen are noted for their sisal weaving: hammocks, sandals, purses, bags, table mats, etc.

WILDLIFE: The *monte* (low, dense bush jungle) and the steaming forests of the peninsula — especially the Campeche country — remains one of Mexico's richest, most exciting, game-bountiful, virgin-hunting regions. When the Spanish first touched these shores the Mayas told them the names for their country were *U-Lumil-Ceh* and *U-Lumil-Kutz* (Land of the Turkey and of the Deer). The names still apply. After a week or two in the region the visitor cannot help but tire of the steady diet of venison and wild turkey served up in restaurants. When one strays from the city or main highway one comes upon men with antique guns and gamebags. Everyone seems to be hunting. You ride on a second-class bus and before long someone gets aboard with a deer or jaguar slung over his shoulders.

The principal game of this region includes: jaguar, the big, fierce spotted cat, harder to track and more prized by big-game hunters than the Indian tiger. The ocelot, mountain lion, wildcat, jaguarondi, etc. The big spotted jaguars are called *tigres* (tigers). The rare black jaguar is known in Maya as *Ek Balam* (Black Prince).

The forests abound with both spider and howler monkeys; with several variety of deer, the most prized by hunters being the brocket deer or red deer *(temazate)* which looks like a tiny antelope. Almost hunted-out now, and protected, is the sluggish tapir. Most plentiful are the wild turkey, javeli *(jabalíes)* or peccary; crested guan, pheasants, quail, jungle hen *(chachalacas)* and all variety of duck, including the Muscovy duck, a goose-size bird native to the region. There are some 300 or more varieties of avifauna — countless varieties of parrots and parakeets, and the venerated quetzal (trogon or Mexican bird of paradise) noted for its exquisite plumage. A host of other birds, doves, herons, flamingos, enliven the countryside.

Among the reptiles, some having commercial value, are: iguana or giant lizard; turtles, both the giant sea turtle and the valued tortoise-shell *(carey)* variety. Alligators *(largato),* the less often seen rattlesnake (Maya, *tza;* Spanish, *cascabel*), the coral snake, and a native poisonous viper called *uolpoch.* Big boa constrictors (Maya, *och-can* or *chaib*) which are harmless to men, are sometimes kept as housepets by villagers to rid their homes of rats and similar pests.

HISTORY: The discovery of the Yucatán Peninsula was an accident. In the early sixteenth century the Spanish had established themselves on Cuba and Hispanola, had crossed the Isthmus of Panama and had explored much of the northern coast of South America, but the great gulf and the lands west of Cuba remained unknown. In 1517, while sailing on a voyage of exploration, an expedition under Francisco Hernández de Córdoba encountered a violent storm and was blown off course and cast upon a strange shore. It was the Peninsula of Yucatán. There Córdoba found a hostile people who, compared to the natives of the Caribbean islands, seemed highly civilized. They wore cotton garments, ornaments of gold, and erected stone temples. Córdoba explored the coast as far as Campeche.

A year later another expedition under Juan de Grijalva returned to this coast and explored up into the Gulf of Mexico. Then, 1519, Hernándo Cortés landed at the Island of Cozumel, skirted along the peninsular coast, going on to what is now Veracruz and his fabulous adventure.

The people of the peninsula, found by these Spanish adventurers, were Mayas who had become a backward nomadic group, their ancient arts lost, their cities mostly buried, their numbers few. The final flowering of Mayan civilizations, the New Empire in Yucatán, had long ago disintegrated. (See *A Digest of Mexican History,* Index, and *The Arts of Mexico,* Index, for the story of the ancient Mayas).

The peninsula scarcely looked attractive and for a while the Spanish bypassed it. In 1526, Don Francisco de Montejo received a grant from the King of Spain for the exploitation of the peninsula. He landed with 400 men, horses and arms at Cozumel. He and co-conqueror Alonzo de Avila met with such resistance on the mainland that the project was abandoned for some years. In 1537 a renewed struggle for Yucatán was begun. Montejo turned over the task to his son (same name) and the latter was effectively aided by a cousin who also bore the same name.

In 1540 a decisive battle was fought at the Mayan town of Tiho (the present Mérida). Two years later Montejo officially founded the city of Mérida (Nuestra Señora de la Encarnación de Mérida) on the site. Two years before, the town of Campeche was founded. Even after the conquest of Yucatán had been accomplished a group of Itzás continued resistance for more than a century, fighting bitterly from the Quintana Roo and Petén area (Guatemala). They were not conquered until 1697.

The remaining history of the peninsula has been one of struggle against English pirates and recurrent separatist movements. From 1835 to 1836 and 1839 to 1843 Yucatán revolted and separated from Mexico, joining Guatemala briefly in an independent alliance. Following the Mexican-American War another serious peninsular insurrection occurred, the storied War of the Castes, an Indian revolt which again separated the peninsula from the republic. During this bitter struggle the whites were reduced to the strongholds of Mérida and the city of Campeche, and in 1846, were so desperate they offered the entire peninsula to the United States, to England and to Spain as a colony. Although the besieged were rescued in 1848 by the Federal Government, the rebellion continued until 1901, especially in the region of Quintana Roo.

Previous to the period of Porfirio Díaz (see Index) Yucatán and Quintana Roo were an entity. Díaz created an absurd geographic and economic situation which has persisted to the present, making the Quintana Roo area, (named after Andrés Quintana Roo, a writer and intellectual leader in the independence movement), a territory without autonomy and dependent on the Federal Government. The situation remains absurd because Yucatán with some 700,000 inhabitants and only 15,000 sq. miles of terrain, lacks mineral resources and forests, and is composed of rock and sterile soil. Quintana Roo, on the other hand, is rich in the natural resources Yucatán lacks, has almost 20,000 sq. miles of terrain and less than 50,169 inhabitants.

THE PEOPLE of the peninsula are descendants of the ancient Mayas, plus a sprinkling of people descended from the Spanish settlers. Unlike Central Mexico, the mixture of the two and the creation of the *mestizo* group has not been as widespread, except in a few urban areas such as around Mérida, Campeche, and Valladolid. The Mayan language is still spoken as a living language. The peninsula is one of the few areas in Mexico where all classes speak an Indian tongue. Naturally, in urban areas Spanish is also spoken.

In Mérida one still notes traces of a unique situation. It is said that practically all of the hundreds of old Castilian families in the metropolis are interrelated, many of them tracing their ancestry with unvarying directness to the early conquistadores. This preservation of lineage, due partially to the long isolation of the region, the Caste Wars and Yucatán's closer cultural contact with Europe than with Mexico, seemed to have brought one blessing. The girls and women of Mérida and Campeche are without a doubt among the loveliest in the country.

A most noticeable quality in the people of Mayaland is their extreme cleanliness. The dispiriting dress, the disorder in villages and apparent indifference to dirt that one finds in so much of Mexico is absent on the peninsula. The Mayans bathe several times a day and invariably wear immaculate white clothing. Their villages and homes, no matter how poor, are well ordered and kept.

Noteworthy also is the hospitality, openness, and genuine friendliness as well as a gentleness among the people of all classes and areas on the peninsula. The Yucatecan does not seem to be troubled by the psychological compulsions and conflicts that so disturb, and make difficult social contacts with the Mexican of other regions.

In the smaller towns and villages where the Spanish-Moorish building styles have not penetrated, the average Mayan house is usually square or oblong, with round ends and a hat of thatch. Furnishings are usually Spartan. Because of the climate beds are rare. Everyone sleeps in a hammock, and even hotel rooms have hammock hooks. It is estimated that upward of three-quarters of a million people on the peninsula use the hammocks as beds, are born and die in them. Hammock-making, said to be of Haitian origin, is a popular Yucatecan home pastime, like knitting or embroidery, and some of the home products are lace-like in texture, beautifully colored, soft and wide. The best are fashioned of fine linen thread, are washable and will last a lifetime. Hammocks are a customary feature of a bride's outfit. The *hamacas matrimoniales* (for married folks) are sometimes wide enough for a half-dozen persons to lie athwart them (the usual way) at a time.

The dress of the Yucatecan is almost a uniform, it is so universally worn and so unchanging. The male garments are prosaic — white loose trousers, sandals, and a loose, very comfortable pleated shirt-jacket of white cotton called a *guayaberra*. The woman's dress, though simple, is picturesque. It consists of a shapeless chemise-like garment, the *huipil* (pre-Hispanic in origin), that is cut of a single piece of white cotton. It extends to the calf, is sleeveless, the neck is cut square, and the startling whiteness is relieved by bands of colorful embroidery at the neck and the hem.

THE YUCATÁN COUNTRY

This area, covering the State of Yucatán and occupying most of the northern part of the peninsula, is the most interesting, historically, the best developed and the most progressive of the peninsular areas. The natural base for vacationing and exploring in it is Mérida.

HIGHLIGHTS: In the order of their importance, the principal things to see and do are: Two to three days visiting the famed Mayan archaeological zones of Chichén Itzá, Uxmal, Kabah. A day exploring Mérida, the plaza, museum, and market. If you have more time to go farther afield: a visit to the interesting Maya town of Ticul, and at the same time a peek at the important ruins of Sayil and Labná; a bus trip to the city of Campeche; a look at the in-progress reconstruction of Maya ruins at Dzibilchaltun, are all worthwhile. Of secondary interest: the churches and parks of Mérida, the henequén plantations, and the port of Progreso. Farther afield, though Mérida is the jumping-off point, flights to the Island of Carmen and the Island of Cozumel.

Mérida, Yuc. Capital of the State of Yucatán. Pop. 160,000. Alt. almost sea level.

HOW TO GET THERE: *By road* from the U.S. or Mexico City, drive to Veracruz or Coatzacoalcos, take the Gulf Coast Highway, CN-180 (see Index). *By air:* Pan American World Airways run 3 flights weekly from New Orleans, Saturday, Tuesday, Thursday. Time — 2½ hrs.; from Miami, Mondays, time — 3 hrs. 40 min.; from Mexico City (CMA — Compania Méxicana de Aviación), daily flights, time — 2½ hrs.; from Mexico City via Veracruz, Villahermosa, Isla Carmen, Campeche to Mérida, daily flights, time — 6 hrs. Round-trip fares from New Orleans, $110 first class; $92 tourist. Miami, $105 and $85. From Mexico City, $67 and $55. *Via railway:* take the Ferrocarriles Nacionales de México (Mexican National Railways). It is an interesting but wearing ride for the train (Sureste) is about as well ballasted as a bucking bronco. The Mexican National Railway runs thru Pullmans from Mexico City to Mérida three times a week. Passenger cars can be shipped from

Coatzacoalcos to Campeche or Mérida via rail. Rates — $431.35 MN to Campeche; $580 MN to Mérida. It is advisable to ride with your car during the trip, otherwise baggage or parts may be stolen. *To Mérida via bus.* The A.D.O. Line (first class) now runs a daily through trip from Mexico City to Mérida, time — 36 hours. *By sea:* passage to Progreso (Mérida's port) or to Campeche via boat is haphazard. From Veracruz the packet S.S. *Emancipación* makes regular trips. Rate approximately $180 MN. Booking office at Independencia 28, Veracruz. Another packet, *La Flecha* (more primitive) costs about $90 MN. Booking office at Av. Juárez 44, Veracruz. *Brovig freighters* from New Orleans. No set schedule. Query Smith & Johnson Inc., 909 National Bank Bldg., New Orleans 12, La.

HOTELS: *Hotel Mérida,* Calle 60 491, largest hotel in this region, 110 rooms, and one of the best operated. Service is good, the hot water is always hot. Pleasant dining room, air-conditioned bar, swimming pool and garden area. Some rooms air conditioned. Central. Rates — EP $55 to $90 MN; AP $159 to $194 MN. *Gran Hotel,* Calle 60 496, one block from main plaza and facing on pretty square, Parque Cepeda Peraza. Old, colonial-style but pleasant. No restaurant or bar. Rates — EP $30 to $50 MN, dble. *Hotel Colón,* Calle 62 483, comfortable and well run. Fair dining room, some air-conditioned rooms, excellent Turkish baths, garage. Colón travel agency connected with hotel. Rates — EP $75 to $90 MN. Also several suites. Near center. *Hotel Caribe,* Calle 59 500, block from center, and facing on Parque Cepeda Peraza. 36 rooms. Small but pleasant. So-so service. Rates — EP $35 to $60 MN. *Motel Yukalpeten,* on the outskirts of town, road toward Progreso, Calle 60 284. New, nice grounds, swimming pool, restaurant. 20 rooms. Rate — EP $60 MN and up. *Montejo Hotel,* Calle 57 507, 2 blocks from plaza. Friendly atmosphere, good dining room. Rates — EP $36 MN and up. *Hotel Tropical Maya,* edge of town on airport road, 33 rooms and suites, pool, bar, restaurant. New and pleasant. Rates: $80 MN dble and up, a/c. *Hotel Panamericana,* in town, new and comfortable. Reasonable rates.

OTHER HOTELS: *Flamingo, Posada Toledo, Casa Camara* (good pension, Paseo Montejo 495), *Hotel Princesa* (*viajero*-type).

RESTAURANTS: Mérida as well as most of the peninsula is lacking in good restaurants. Passable fare is obtainable at *El Mirador* in Hotel Mérida; *Los Tulipanes,* Calle 42 462a, at edge of city, a show place with pleasant garden, cenote where you can swim, dancing, specialty is barbecued chicken in banana leaves, and Papat Zules; *Cocina Yucateca Itzá,* Calle 58 495, serves excellent Moro Crabs (Cangrecos moros) and good venison; *Ciudad del Carmen,* Calles 59 and 62, sea food; *Club Bancario,* Bolos y Alberca, Paseo Montejo. *El Tirol* (good German food). *El Mesón del Castellano* (Spanish cuisine, good), Calle 62 468a.

TRAVEL AGENTS: *Barbachano's Travel Service,* Calle 60 480 and across street in Hotel Mérida. The largest and most efficient organization running tours on the peninsula. Rates are high but the service is excellent. *Yucatán Trails Travel Agency,* Calle 62 482, less expensive. *Colón Travel Bureau* in the Hotel Colón. All the hotels and tour agencies can get accredited guides for you. Some guides are capable, some do not know too much about the folklore and archaeology of their region. One of the best bilingual independent guides in the city is Benjamin Sanchez Bacelis, Calle 37 516-D. Tel. 31-44. He is a pleasant, very knowledgeable man.

TAXIS: Taxis are not metered. You must agree on rate beforehand for runs within the city. There are fixed rates for trips by cab to Chichén Itzá ($180 MN round trip) and to Uxmal ($114 MN round trip). *Calesas,* horse-drawn two-wheel surreys (also called *púlpitos,* from a fancied resemblance to pulpits), are for hire at their stand in Parque Cepeda Peraza. Rates: 3 pesos for a short one-way run, 5 to 10 pesos for longer circuits of the city.

BANKS: *Banco Nacional de México,* Calle 67 485. *Banco de Yucatán,* Calle 65 507. Banco del Sureste, Calles 60 and 65.

DIRECTORY: *Airlines* — CMA and PAA, corner Calles 58 and 61. Tel. 27-80 and 49-59. *Railways* — Ferrocarriles del Sureste, Calle 60 519. Ferrocarríl Unidos de Yucatán, Calles 55 and 48. *Bus lines* — Union de Camioneros de Yucatán, Calle 66 and 63. A.D.O. Line, Calles 68 and 69. *Garages* — Garage Internacional, Calle 64 537. Distribuidora de Automoviles (Ford), Olegario Montes (Chrysler), Calle 61 491, *U. S. Consulate,* 57 504, Tel. 45-53; Dr. R. H. Bolio Vales, Calle 57 523; Emergency Surgical and Medical Service, Calle 57 504, Tel. 45-53. *Church services* — (Catholic) Cathedral, on plaza principal, Sunday Mass at 5, 6, 7, 8:15, 10, 11 A.M., noon, 1, and 5 P.M. Santa Lucia, Calles 60 and 59, Mass at 7 and 9 A.M. — (Presbyterian) El Divino Salvador, Calle 66 518; Antioquia, Calle 74 468. Adventista, Calle 61, between Calles 68 y 70. *Photo service* — Foto-Color, Calle 57 501.

MUSEUMS: The Historic Museum and the Federal Museum of Archaeology are housed in the former State Mansion on Paseo de Montejo, near Calle 43.

THE CITY: Mérida (MAY-ree-dah), known as the White City (La Ciudad Blanca) because it is one of the cleanest cities in the Americas, was founded in 1542 by Don Francisco Montejo (the younger) on the site of the ancient Maya city of Tiho (Maya, *T'ho*). It was named after the Iberian-Roman city of Mérida *(Emerite Agusta),* long known as the Rome of Spain. Dazzled by the Indian palaces and temples of Tiho, the conquistadores likened it to, and named it after, the Old World city.

It is said that the one of the Maya pyramids, the great temple of H-chun-Caan, occupied the site of the present central plaza. The ancient stone blocks employed in their construction were later used by the Spanish to erect many of the present-day houses. The decisive battle which won the peninsula for the Castilians was fought in 1540 on the spot where the Cathedral now stands. April 30, 1605, King Philip III, in a royal edict, bestowed on Mérida the title of "Noble and Loyal City."

Today Mérida is a charming, cultured, easygoing city with a faint Continental atmosphere tempered by the patina of the tropics. It is noted especially for its clear, sparkling light and its Spanish-Moorish architectural styles enhanced by beautiful patios and gardens.

The city streets are numbered rather than named. Odd numbered streets run east and west *(oriente* and *poniente),* even numbers north *(norte)* and south *(sur).* The center of the city, the main square (Plaza Mayor, Plaza de Armas) is located at the intersection of Calle 60 and 61. Enameled plaques at street corners usually carry several numbers, for example: Calle 60 (60th Street), Cuartel

4 (4th Ward), Manzana la (Block 1). Originally the streets bore Spanish names, but since the untutored Indians had difficulties with the language, painted signs or sculptured figures were placed on buildings at street intersections. Thus the Calle del Flamingo was designated by a huge red flamingo painted on the corner houses. Today, the Calle del Elefante (Elephant Street) at the crossing of Calles 46 and 65, still bears the sculptured elephant figure on one of the buildings.

CENTRAL SECTION: *Plaza Mayor* (Plaza de Armas, Plaza Principal, Plaza de la Constitución, etc.) is approximately the geographic center of the city, is the social center, and in the area around it are located the principal businesses. The Plaza is flanked on the N by the Executive Palace; on E by the Cathedral; on the W by the Municipal Palace, and on the S by the Montejo mansion. The huge plaza, 193 ft. in length and width, is shaded by Indian laurels,[1] and is one of the most pleasing squares in Mexico; an excellent place to observe the life of the city.

The Cathedral, N side of plaza, occupies the site of an ancient Maya temple around which the decisive battle for control of the peninsula was fought. The edifice was begun in 1561 after the plans of architect Pedro de Aulestia, and was completed in 1598 by Juan Miguel de Agüero. The Cathedral is dedicated to San Idlefonso (a Gothic form of Alfonso or Alonso), a sacrosanct personage, one-time Archbishop of Toledo, and regarded as a saint of the first water.

The Cathedral is the largest and most impressive Christian temple on the Peninsula, measuring 231 ft. E and W, 110 N and S. The façade is 144 ft. wide and 153 ft. high. Artistically, the building has little to recommend it. Its once lavish interior, its altars, gold encrusted *retablos* and fanciful iron *rejas* have vanished. Of passing interest is a painting (over door, right-hand side) depicting the visit Mayan King Tu-tul-xiu made to conqueror Montejo. On the painting a glimpse of ancient Tiho, the Maya city replaced by Mérida.

To l. of main altar is the chapel of Cristo de las Ampollas (Christ of the Blisters). The image was sculpted in the Mayan town of Ichmul from the wood of a tree Indians reported several times having seen in flame during the night. Each time, at dawn, they could see no traces of fire damage. The image was venerated in Ichmul, drawing large peregrination of the faithful, until the village church was destroyed by fire. The fire-blackened image of Christ was discovered in the ruins — strangely, covered with blisters. In 1645 it was brought to the Cathedral. Each year, September 28 to October 13, a fiesta is held honoring Cristo de las Ampollas.

Archbishop's Palace, formerly occupied an entire block on the S side of the Cathedral and was joined to it by a long lofty arcade. Once a sumptuous building with vast gardens, it was confiscated in 1915, and separated from the Cathedral. A street was opened in between, the Pasaje de la Revolución (Passage of the Revolution). The building, now badly mauled, houses various federal offices and courts — Economy, Agriculture, Interior and the offices of the Military Zone.

Montejo Palace, actually the *Casa Solariega* (ancestral mansion) *de Don Francisco de Montejo, el adelantado* (bold leader). Built by Montejo the Younger in 1549, it originally occupied the entire south side of the Plaza Mayor, and was one of the first Spanish houses built in the old Maya city.[2]

The Montejo house is the only colonial building in Mérida that definitely warrants the attention of visitors — then, only its entrance. The entranceway is one of the finest examples of Plateresque decoration in Mexico. The façade bears the escutcheon of the Montejos and manifestly indicates their arrogant attitude as conquerors, for on either side of the entrance are carved figures of Spanish knights, each with a foot resting on the bowed head of a conquered Maya Indian! Sculpturally, the façade is a delight for its wealth of restrained detail, its rich Renaissance-like floral patterns, especially in the lower story around the main doorway.

Municipal Building, popularly called Los Portales (from the arched portals and passage fronting the building). This, the City Hall, is an unimpressive colonial-style structure that could look handsome and lend charm to the Plaza were its *portales* not so cluttered with nondescript candy, soft-drink, and *taco* stalls. The building fronts the W side of the Plaza. At the NE corner of the Plaza stands the severe, unimpressive nineteenth-century style *Palacio del Gobierno* (State House) containing the Governor's office and other state administrative departments.

In the block east of the plaza, on Calle 61, is a seventeenth-century colonial building, once a mental hospital supervised by the Juaninos Brothers, a religious order. Until recently the Museums of History and Archaeology were housed here. For some years to come you will still be directed to this location by hotel managers and guide maps. The museums are now on the Paseo de Montejo near Calle 43.

The Market, Mercado Municipal (mehr-CAH-doh mu-knee-SEE-pahl) four blocks SE of the plaza, near Calles 56 and 67, is a colorful provisioning center. Near the N entrance there are stalls selling regional craft goods, items of henequén, leather, etc. The *Central Telegraph and Post Office* are also near the N entrance of the market.

One block north of the Plaza Mayor (Calles 60 and 59) is the tiny tree-shaded square called *Parque Cepeda Peraza* (formerly known as Plaza de Jesús and Plaza Hidalgo), named after the Yucatecan patriot General Manuel Cepeda Peraza. The principal hotels are in the vicinity of the park. The *calesas* or surreys make their stand here. The *Café Expres,* a good place for snacks and breakfasts, faces the little plaza, as does the *Biblioteca Cepeda,* a public library (rare in Mexico) founded in 1867. It contains some 16,000 volumes, many old and valuable. Hours: daily, 8 A.M. to noon, 2 P.M. to 10 P.M.; Sundays, 8 A.M. to noon.

Flanking the park, facing 60th Street is the *Iglesia de Jesús,* a church founded in 1618 by the Jesuit Fathers, and still under their direction. Locally it is considered the most elegant church in Mérida and favored for fashionable weddings. To S of the church is a small park called *Morelos Park,* or popularly, Park of the Mother, from the statue in it called "Motherhood," a copy of the Francis Lenoir figure in the Luxemburg in Paris. Across the street, corner of Calle 60 and 57, is the *University of Yucatán (Universidad de Yucatán).* Originally it was a Jesuit school, founded in 1618. The pres-

[1] The laurels of Mexico, gracing plazas throughout the Republic were introduced from British India in the eighteenth century. The Mérida trees were originally brought from India to adorn the Prado in Havana. When the ship carrying them was wrecked off the Yucatán coast the trees were recovered and planted here.

[2] The Montejos, father and son, left an indelible imprint on the old Maya stronghold, which differs materially from every other city in Mexico. Montejo the Elder (1484–1550) was one of Grijalva's captains, and was an agent in Spain for Hernán Cortés from 1519 to 1522, and again in 1526. He was a picturesque figure in the New World, a man beloved by the king and hated by the Mayans for his arrogant and ruthless nature.

ent Moorish-style building was erected in 1938. During the summer months (July, August) summer courses on Mayan Culture are sponsored by the National School of Anthropology and Mexico City College.

One block N of the University, Calles 60 and 55, is a small, charming plaza partially surrounded by romantic colonial portales — *Plaza Santa Lucía.* During the coloniage it was the end of the line for coaches and horses of the travelers who came to the city. The small church on this plaza, Santa Lucía, was (between 1580 and 1620) the only church in which "mulattoes and people of color" were permitted to worship.

NORTHERN SECTION: The northern part of Mérida is largely residential, an area of beautiful tropical gardens and spacious homes. A pleasant drive through this garden-rich district is out along the handsome boulevard, Paseo de Montejo. Unfortunately the northern end of this charming street is marred by one of those grotesque civic monuments that seem endemic in Mexico. This one is called, as usual, *Monumento a la Patria.*

Museum of Archaeology and of History, Paseo de Montejo and Calles 43, (an imposing nineteenth-century mansion, formerly the Governor's Residence, and before that the "palace" of General Canton). At the time of this writing the two museums — the State Historical Museum with its excellent library, and the Federal Museum of Archaeology with its important collection of Maya treasures and artifacts — were being moved from downtown to this building, and the exhibits had not been completely installed. The announced hours in the new location are: 9 A.M. to 2 P.M., daily. There is a small admission charge, except Sundays.

EXCURSIONS FROM MÉRIDA: Many delightful trips, most of them short, are possible from the capital. They can be made by private car, cab, bus, or through the standard Mayan tours. The roads, though sometimes narrow, are generally paved and in good condition. The most important excursions are to the ruined cities: Chichén Itzá, Kabah, Uxmal, Mayapan, Sayil, Labná, and Dzibilchaltun.

FROM MÉRIDA TO CHICHÉN ITZÁ AND VALLADOLID: The principal attraction is the silent city of Chichén Itzá, 75 miles E of the capital. Although the round trip and visit at the ruins can be done in one day, because of the extensiveness of the ruins a 2- to 3-day excursion in this area is recommended.

Taxis from Mérida charge $180 MN for the round trip to Chichén (with several hours stopover). There are first- and second-class buses going as far as Chichén, or on to Valladolid. Most comfortable is the first-class Union de Camioneros de Yucatán bus departing from Mérida at 6:30 A.M. for Valladolid (Station on Calle 50, between Calles 65 and 67). *Fare:* about $19 MN.

Motorists leave Mérida via Calle 65, going E. This joins the Gulf Coast Highway, CN-180 (see Index: Highway Routes — Tampico to Yucatán).

On the outskirts of the city there are several huge plantations and henequén haciendas worth a brief visit. One of the largest is Hacienda San Pedro on the left-hand side, and 13 m. from the capital, Hacienda Ticopó.

Hoctún, Yuc. (22 m. from Mérida). A picturesque Maya village. Weekend of September 29 there is a regional fiesta honoring San Miguel. Colorful regional dances. *Junction* with fair sideroad leading 15 m. to Izamal.

Izamal, Yuc. Pop. 7084. You can also get here via Mérida-Izamal Line of the United Railways of Yucatán. An ancient Indian town noted for its archaeological site and also its most interesting conventual estate. The place is named thus because its ancient buildings were dedicated to the god Itzamná (Dew of Heaven). Most of the ancient structures are difficult to discern, being overgrown with weeds, and some having been torn apart to provide building material for the Convent of Izamal which was built over the so-called Maya Castle of the Kings, a pyramidal structure which had a base 200 yds. across.

The convent and church, with its vast colonnaded courtyard, is one of the oldest on the continent, dating from 1553. The building is of early Franciscan style and is attributed to Bishop Diego de Landa. A painted portrait of Landa adorns the *camarín,* along with a black *Cristo crucificado* — always an emblem of ecclesiastical appeal for tinted adherents to the faith. This remarkable church with its spectacular cloister, the somnolent village and the wide valley dotted with Indian mounds evokes a strange brooding atmosphere that is unique. From the roof of the church, to the right, a huge overgrown pyramid is visible in the distance.

In the village there is a lively regional fiesta for San Ildefonso each April 3, and an all-out fiesta honoring the Señora de Izamal around August 15.

Returning to the Highway, the route passes through the village of *Xocchel,* noted for its San Juan Fair, June 24.

Pisté, Yuc. (73 m. from Mérida), Pop. 820. The nearest town to Chichén Itzá (1½ m.) In Pisté there is a somewhat modern restaurant, the *Cunanchen.* It is advisable to stop there on your way to the archaeological zone to inform them that you will be lunching there.

Chichén Itzá, Yuc. (75 m. east from Mérida). Chichén is an archaeological zone, not a village.

HOTELS: *Mayaland Lodge.* 44 rooms and nicely appointed thatch-roofed Mayan cottages. Rates: dble, $200 MN and up, AP. The hotel is operated by the Barbachano Travel Service. Reservations should be made in Mérida. The hotel, set in charming gardens, with magnificent vistas of the nearby ruins, is friendly in atmosphere, one of the best-operated establishments in the country. Swimming pool, bar, good dining room, folk dancing, and entertainment. *Casa Victoria,* nearby, run by Doña Victoria. Extremely primitive. Not recommended.

THE RUINS: The archaeological zone borders both sides of the highway, covering an area of 2 m. from N to S and 1½ m. from E to W. Hundreds of buildings lie in the area, but only about 20 to 30 have been uncovered and may be seen by visitors. The zone is divided into two areas: New Chichén to the NE of the highway, Old Chichén on the SW, and S of the old Hacienda of Chichén Itzá. In reality the section called "Old Chichén" is no older than the former. Its buildings also represent the Classic and Toltec Period of Mayan history (see Index).

The main entrance to the zone is on the highway, ¼ m. N of the hotel. Hours: 6 A.M. to 6 P.M. Admission: $4 MN. Sundays, free. The interior of certain of the buildings are only open to the public at specific hours: Temple of the Warriors, 8 to 9 A.M. and 11 A.M. to noon. Temple of the Jaguars, 9 to 10 A.M. and noon to 1 P.M. El Castillo, 10 to 11 A.M. and 1 to 2 P.M. Official guide booklets to the ruins, published by the National Institute of Anthropology and History (in English or Spanish) can be purchased at the entrance. The booklet on Chichén costs $9 MN (in English), $7 MN (in Spanish).

According to the *Chilam Balam,* one of the sacred books of the Maya, written after the Spanish conquest in their native tongue, but using Latin letters, Chichén Itzá was founded approximately 435–455 A.D., was occupied for some 200 years, then abandoned. The Itzá tribe then lived in Chakanputún (Champotón, Campeche) until around 698 A.D., when they returned to Chichén and again extended their city. It was finally abandoned in 1204 A.D. During the latter period (tenth century, onward) the Maya culture at Chichén Itzá was no longer dominant. A foreign element, now established to be Toltec (from Central Mexico), influenced the architecture, the religious culture and life of the ancient city. The most spectacular structures date from this period.

In the first years after the Spanish Conquest Don Francisco Montejo established himself at Chichén Itzá. Though the area was abandoned, the Indians still considered it sacred and their hostility forced Montejo to abandon the site. During the first half of the nineteenth century the zone was visited by travelers and explorers, notably John L. Stephens whose books focused world interest on the ancient Maya civilization. In 1885 Edward Thompson from Worcester, Massachusetts, trader and U. S. Consul in Yucatán, purchased Chichén Itzá from a Spaniard for $75. For 39 years he was master of this opulent kingdom and lived like a feudal lord in the Chichén Hacienda, with temples for neighbors. He raised seven children there. Interested in proving or disproving De Landa's story that the Mayas tossed young virgins and treasures into the Sacred Cenote[3] at Chichén Itzá, Consul Thompson dredged and had divers probe the cenote. Skeletons, gold bells, medallions, and large quantities of carved jade were fetched up. Thompson dispatched his treasures to Boston via diplomatic pouch where they became a part of Harvard's Peabody Museum collection. For years Mexico has sued for the return of the Peabody trove. In December 1959 the Peabody authorities quietly returned a part of the treasure for permanent display in Mexico.

The principal building of the ruins (a misnomer for

[3] Fray Diego de Landa, first bishop of Yucatán, had learned the Maya dialect in order to convert the people to Christianity. He wrote an account of Maya life, plus such history as he could gather *(Relación de las Cosas de Yucatán).* The manuscript lay hidden in the Madrid archives until Brasseur de Bourbourg brought it to light in 1864, and gave it to the world as a recompense for De Landa's bigoted destruction of the rarest and most precious of the Maya writings and records. De Landa's work is still one of the anthropologists' main sources of information regarding the Maya.

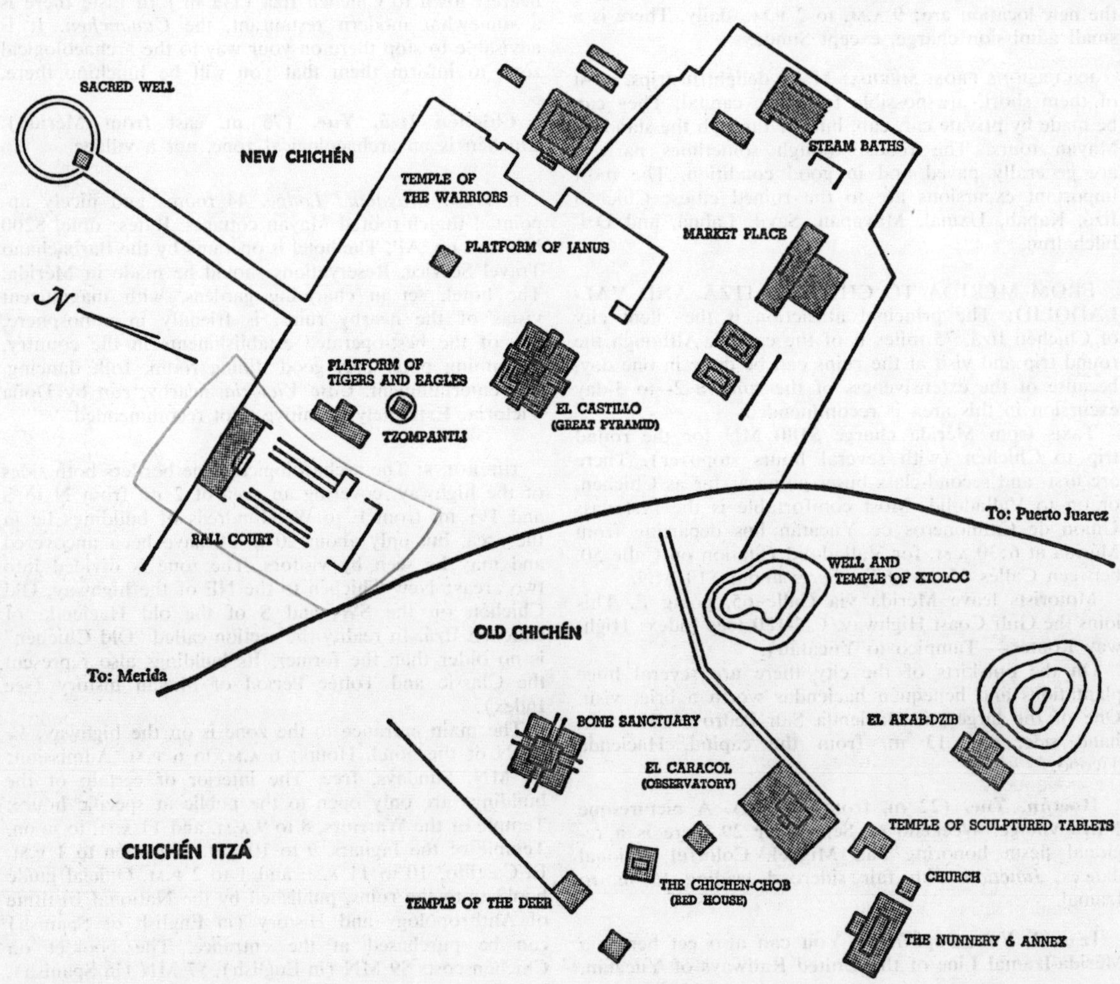

such an elegantly restored and curried park) are as follows:

El Castillo or Great Temple of Kukul-Kan, the largest and most imposing structure — a pyramid dedicated to the Feathered Serpent (Maya, *Kukul-Kan,* Aztec, Toltec, *Quetzalcoatl*). The pyramid is 25 yds. high, its sides 60 yds. long. There are 9 terraces and 45-degree stairways on each side leading up to the temple built on the top platform. The structure was built upon an older, inner pyramid. In an antechamber of the inner pyramid a remarkable chac-mool figure and a stone jaguar, painted red, and with eyes of magnificent jade, were found. These figures remain on view within the chamber.

The Sacred Well (Cenote) at the end of a 300 yd. Maya road running north from the central plaza of El Castillo. This huge waterhole or well, surrounded by jungle growth, called by the Maya, *Chen Ku* (Well of Sacrifice), is for tourists one of the most impressively romantic spots at Chichén Itzá. The *cenote* is more or less circular, about 65 yards in diameter, with vertical limestone sides that drop about 60 feet to still, jade-green waters.

The Mayas believed that the God of Rain *(Noh-Och Yum-Chac)* lived in the depths of the well. To him young virgins were sacrificed, being doped with copal incense and flung into the waters. According to De Landa, "although the victims were never seen again, it was not felt that they had died."

The Tzompantli (from Aztec, Wall of Skulls), near the Ball Court. A platform with carved representations of skulls placed upon poles. *The Platform of Tigers and Eagles,* nearby, is adorned with excellent relief sculptures of feathered serpents, tigers, and eagles holding human hearts in their claws.

The Temple of the Warriors (also called Group of the Thousand Columns), a vast architectural complex including pyramidal structures, colonnades, sunken courtyards, etc. Various sculptured pillars show warriors and other carvings identical to those found at *Tula* (see Index), the Toltec capital in Central Mexico.

In the southwest section (across the highway):

El Caracol (from its interior stairway which resembled a snail). This impressive building, circular in form, is believed to have served as an astronomical observatory. It stands about 75 ft. above the plain and is on a base consisting of two terraces, the lower one 223 ft. from N to S, and 150 ft. from E to W. Small openings in the walls pointed to cardinal directions and other important astronomical points.

The Chichan-Chob (Maya, meaning Small Holes, possibly from the lattice-work in the upper comb of the building). The edifice is also called "Red House" because of a red strip that was painted on the wall of the portico. A band of carved hieroglyphics, 37 ft. in length, adorns the interior of the chamber, and thus far has defied deciphering, as has most of the Maya writing. The sobriety of this building, the absence of Toltec elements places it as one of the few in the area to be purely Classic Maya (between seventh and tenth centuries).

The Nunnery and Annex, S across the plaza from the Caracol. One of the most beautiful of the ruins, thought by the Spanish to be a Maya convent. The decorations and architecture are typically Maya. The area covered by it is some 300 ft. long, 150 ft. wide.

There are numerous other buildings, some partially restored, others in their hidden or jungle-covered state, among them: The *House of Dark Writing (Akab-Dzib),* the *Church,* the *Temple of the Wall Panels,* the *House of the Dwarf,* and in the section called Old Chichén, the *Phallic Temple,* the *Temple of the Three Lintels,* etc.

Reconstruction work is still going on at Chichén Itzá, and even at this late date discoveries of importance still occur. Late in 1959 a tourist guide, Humberto Gomez spied a hole in the end of a cave called Balancanche, near Chichén. Widening it, he followed a 325-yard passage to a huge circular chamber full of incense holders, then found another secret room filled with stone braziers, plates, and other artifacts.

Valladolid, Yuc. Pop. 8200. (on CN-180, about 25 miles E of Chichén Itzá). A picturesque old city, second oldest in Yucatán. It is noted for its *cenotes.* At present it is the terminal of the first-class bus from Mérida. Travelers continuing by bus to Puerto Juárez and Isla Mujeres must transfer to crowded second-class vehicles. *Restaurant:* Nicte-Ha, at SE corner of the main plaza. Fair regional dishes.

A road leads from Valladolid, N 31 m. to TIZIMÍN where a lively traditional fiesta with Vaquerías Dances occurs each December 31, commemorating the construction of the Convent of Santos Reyes in 1660.

THE MAYAPÁN RUINS: A half-day excursion from Mérida, leaving the city via CN-180 toward Chichén Itzá. About 19 m. from the capital an unpaved road to r. leads to *Seye* and *Acanceh,* thence to Mayapán. A more direct, gravel road leads from Mérida, through *Kanasin* to *Acanceh.* Neither are very good.

Mayapán, Yuc. (archaeological zone). Called, "the Banner City of the Maya Lands." An important Maya city, especially during the "late" or "decadent" period. It was the citadel of many Maya chiefs during the Triple Alliance with Uxmal and Chichén Itzá. After Chichén was abandoned, Mayapán became the most important Maya city in Yucatán, and was occupied almost up to the Spanish Conquest.

At present the ruins, scattered over a wide area, are almost all overgrown with vegetation. The excavations conducted by the Carnegie Institution of Washington (the restorers of Chichén Itzá) have shown that Mayapán was surrounded by a wall, and that the various buildings, especially pyramidal structures in the area, are inferior in architecture to those of the great northern sites. Unfortunately, today one is unable to report, as did the earlier *Terry Guides* that the area is one of fallen columns, sculptured figures, and the haunt of jaguars. Mayapán is of secondary tourist interest.

SOUTHERN YUCATÁN — MUNA, UXMAL, TICUL, LABNÁ: There are two principal roads reaching into the not distant southern sections of Yucatán. Both routes leave Mérida via CN-180 toward Campeche (see Index: Highway Routes). Exit from the capital: north on Paseo de Montejo, left on Av. Colón to Av. de las Itzás which takes you past the Hospital O'Horan and the School of Medicine. Here you are on CN-180.

At Muna (about 38 m. from Mérida) there is a junction. The main highway continues toward Campeche, passing Uxmal, Kabáh, and the turn-off to Sayil and Labná. From Muna a paved road branches off SE to Ticul, one of the most interesting of Mayan villages, and continues on through jungle country to Chetumal, Q.R.

From Mérida one can take first-class buses that stop at Uxmal. Taxis will do the round trip for about $114 MN.

Uxmal, Yuc. (archaeological zone) 58 m. S of Mérida. Ruins begin some 200 yds. E of highway. *Hotel and Restaurant:* The only hotel is the de luxe *Hotel Hacienda Uxmal* operated by the Barbachano Travel Service. It is located on W side of the highway. There is also a separate cafeteria under the same management. *Rates:* AP $338 to $400 MN dble. 34 exceptionally nice rooms, dining room (cuisine excellent), bar, swimming pool, music. An expensive, yet exceptionally well-run and pleasant hotel. It lies a short walk from the ruins.

THE RUINS: Hours: 6 A.M. to 6 P.M. Admission: $4 MN. There is a parking space just outside the entrance of the ruins. If you park within the zone there is an extra charge.

Uxmal (Maya, *Oxmal,* meaning "Three Times Built") is more of a compact piece than Chichén Itzá. It covers an area ⅝ m. from N to S and some 700 yds. from E to W. The city was founded about 700 A.D. and went through several periods of development and abandonment until about 1000 A.D. when it was linked with the other Maya cities in a tribal federation. It was visited in the 1840s by John L. Stephens who wrote the first comprehensive study concerning it. In 1929 Franz Blom began a systematic exploration of Uxmal and completed the first authoritative plan of the site. Since 1938 the National Institute of Anthropology has been carrying on the work of restoration.

The majority of the buildings in the area represent the Classic Period of Maya history (seventh to eleventh

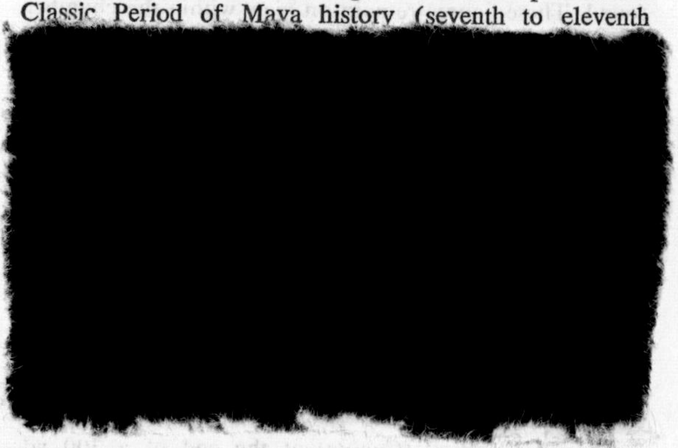

EAST GROUP
SOUTH TEMPLE
CEMETERY GROUP
CASA DE LOS PALOMAS
N
GREAT PYRAMID
COLUMN GROUP
ALTAR OF THE STELAS
CASA DE LAS TORTUGAS
HOUSE OF THE GOBERNADOR
BALL COURT
NORTH GROUP
CASA DE LA VIEJA
NUN'S QUADRANGLE
PIRÁMIDE DEL ADIVINO
To: Merida
HOTEL & RESTAURANT
To: Campeche

UXMAL

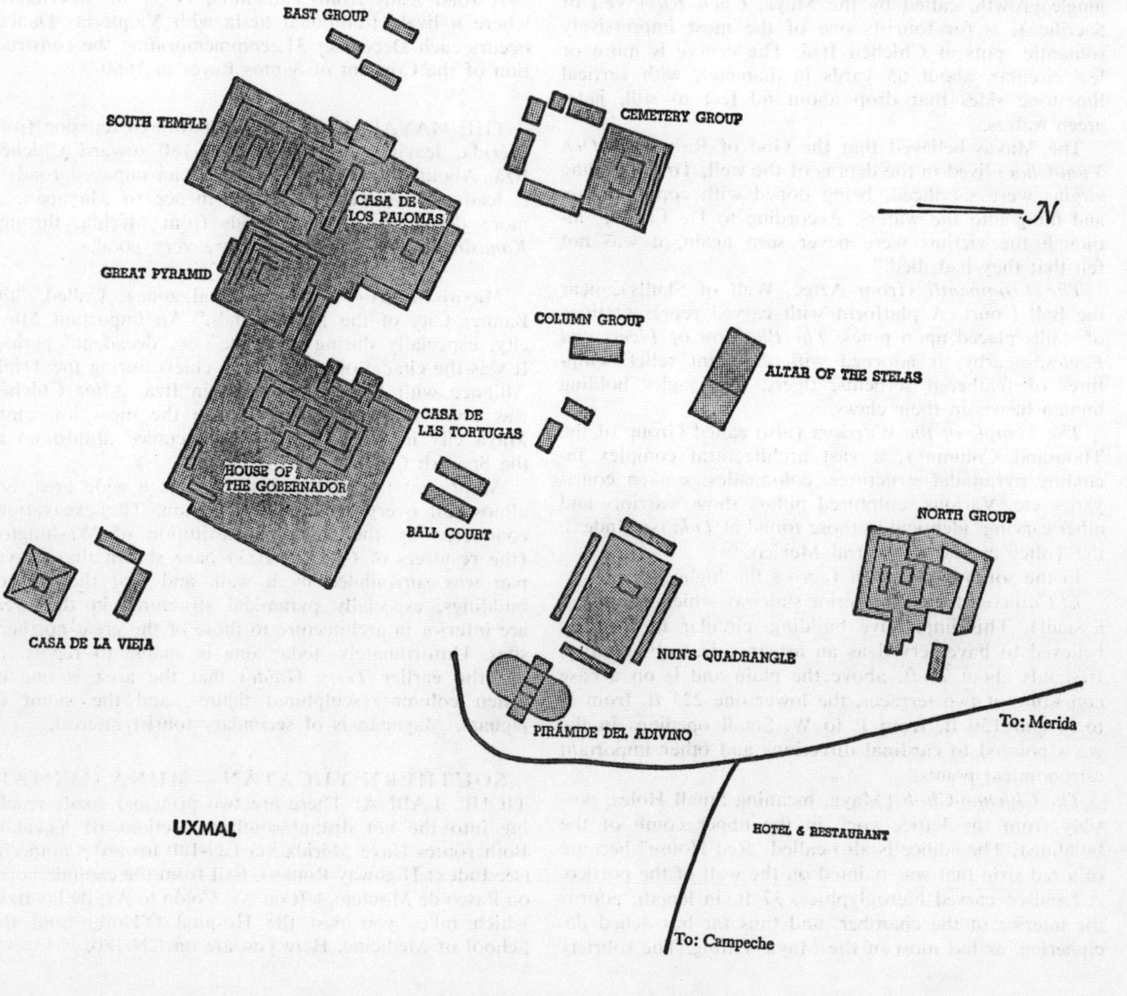

ent levels. It measures upward to 280 ft. long and is noteworthy for its strikingly beautiful architectural details. The triangular arched entrance to the patio is one of the most unusual features of the entire group of buildings.

House of the Gobernador (governor), one of the most impressive Maya structures in existence. The building itself, 322 ft. long, by 40 ft. broad, is set upon a vast platform or triple platform, the lower 630 ft. long by 450 ft., and the second platform, 485 ft. by 315 ft., and the third, 365 ft. by 200 ft. This notable mass, with its lateral buildings and vaulted passages decorated in classic *Puuc-Chenes* style (pure Maya forms), is a tremendous mosaic of carvings, grecques, interlaced stones suggesting an Apocalypse in stone, perhaps conceived by an Hieronymous Bosch.

Casa de las Tortugas, (House of the Turtles), at the NE corner of the lower platform of the House of the Governor. This is one of the simplest, most beautifully proportioned Mayan structures, elegantly austere in its decorations, having a simple frieze of half-columns and just below the cornices a band of widely spaced, small turtles.

Other buildings of interest are: Casa de las Palomas (Doves), Casa de la Vieja, House of the Dwarf, The Ball Court, Great Pyramid (still covered with verdure).

Kabáh (archaeological zone). On CN-180, 12 m. S of Uxmal, 62 m. from Mérida. The zone flanks both sides of the highway, but the principal area of interest is on the E side. *Hours:* 6 A.M. to 6 P.M. *Admission:* $2 MN.

The Ruins: cover a small area, the buildings rising on a series of artificial platforms. An archway to the southwest is held to mark the beginning of a wide, built-up road, or *sacbé,* connecting Kabáh to Uxmal.

The Codz-Pop (Coiled Mat) is the outstanding structure in the group, somewhat resembling a rolled-up mat. The building is some 45 meters long, with façades intricately decorated with carved masks of the rain god, Chac. The lack of restraint in the decorative motif gives the building a most impressive appearance.

Other buildings of importance are: the Teocalli, the Building of the Meanders, etc.

Sayil and **Labná** (archaeological zones). To reach both zones involves an off-trail excursion, which though somewhat bumpy and advisable only in dry weather, is well worthwhile. The turn-off to Sayil is at *Chac* (kilometer 105 on CN-180, about 18 m. S of Uxmal). A fair dirt road to the left, E, leads 3 m. to Sayil. From Sayil there is a very rough road, 10 m. to Labná.

RUINS OF SAYIL or Zayil, actually belong to both Yucatán and Campeche, the state line cutting across the zone. As yet, restoration has not progressed extensively and there are numerous mounds still among the brush. The buildings that stand preserved are remarkable. They represent the Classic Period *Puuc-Chene* style (Eastern Campeche and Southern Yucatán), i.e., substructures having sloping sides, buildings with open stretches divided by columns, frieze-like ornamental bands vertically placed, combs on the crests of buildings and carved masks as frequent decorative motifs.

The Palace, a most impressive three-story, stepped-back structure of excellent proportions. Its columns, friezes, and geometric restraint give almost the feeling of Roman kinship. It is the best preserved of the various buildings.

The Mirador Temple, set upon a large pyramid. It has a high central roof-comb with a series of rectangular openings, almost the only decoration. Its sobriety and architectural balance is distinctive, and very unlike so much of the Baroque Maya architecture found throughout the region. This and the Ball Court and the Palace are the only buildings thus far investigated.

RUINS OF LABNÁ: Set in slightly hilly jungle country, the ancient city now largely buried in vegetation, Labná was once an important Maya center. The two most remarkable buildings flank the central plaza, and both are unusual works of architecture. They are the Mirador and its famous Arch.

The Arch of Labná is remarkable for its size, its excellent state of preservation, and its intricate decorations. The Mirador, a pyramidal structure somewhat resembling the Adivino at Uxmal, has the remains of a temple on top with a roof-comb adorned with stucco figures. The Palace, in the NW part of the ruined city, is interesting for its combination of friezes, stone mosaics, Chac-masks and bundles of small columns.

Muna, Yuc. Pop. 4000. (CN-180, 37½ m. S of Mérida). There is an interesting late seventeenth-century Franciscan church and part of an old convent here. Junction here, CE-26 to Ticul, Santa Rosa and Chetumal, Q.R. (See Index: Bacalar, Q.R., for route description to Chetumal.)

Ticul, Yuc. Pop. 10,250. (On CE-26, 12½ m. from Muna.) A picturesque town noted for its straw hat weaving, pottery and its strong Mayan traditions. The people of Ticul still wear their traditional dress and the garments of the women are especially charming — long, lace trimmed, embroidered *huipiles,* the lace handmade. For fiestas a beautiful, gold-filigree rosary and cross is worn as a necklace. During Easter-week and around April 5, there are celebrated fiestas, La Pascua y Fería del Tabaco.

Oxkutzcab, Yuc. Pop. 6170. (on CE-26), has a colorful commercial fair and traditional dances from August 10 to 16.

NORTH OF MÉRIDA: The area N and NE of Mérida is the most populated section of Yucatán, crisscrossed with numerous paved or improved roads, and dotted with picturesque Mayan villages. In this region there are numerous lagoons, the principal winter haven and breeding ground for northern ducks. Several of the duck flyways coming down from Canada and the U.S. converge here, making it a sportsman's paradise.

Interesting excursions through this district include trips to the archaeological site at Dzbilchaltun, the port of Progreso, Sisal, Puerto Telchac Dzilam de Bravo, Motul.

Dzibilchaltun (archaeological zone). Less than a half-hour drive from Mérida. Leave the capital via Calle 60, the Mérida-Progreso highway, CE-9. Near Yaxché (Santa María), kilometer 15, about 9 m., turn right off highway (E).

The Ruins are undergoing excavation and restoration by experts attached to the University of Tulane and the National Geographic Society. According to E. Wyllis Andrews, Tulane archaeologist in charge of the project, the ceremonial center of Dzibilchaltun is of unusual importance because it predates other Yucatecan cities and has established that the peninsula was peopled from early pre-classical times, of which very little was known.

The area covers terrain nearly 1¼ miles in length. There are numerous buildings in ruinous condition, placed around great plazas. A large *cenote* in the center, explored by skin-divers, has produced a quantity of important artifacts. Aside from the actual viewing of excavation and restoration work, the only building that may as yet be of interest to visitors is the restored Temple of the Seven Dolls.

Progreso, Yuc. Pop. 13,340. 22 m. from Mérida via paved highway, CE-9. Daily railway and bus communication. The most important peninsular seaport, and port of call for steamers from New Orleans, New York, and Veracruz. The town has little interest.

A few miles to E of Progreso, along the well-kept beach drive is the village of *Chicxulub,* noted for its excellent beach and deep-sea sports fishing. *Hotel and Restaurant: Hotel Club Cocoteros.* Mexican style beach resort. Rates: AP, $137.50 MN dble. EP, $50 MN dble. Atmosphere chilly. *Hotel Tropical Riviera,* on beach, pool, good dining room, cocktails, a/c. New. Rates: moderate.

From Chicxulub there is an unimproved coastal road leading E to the village of *Puerto Telchac,* a tiny, picturesque beach village that celebrates a lively fiesta in honor of San Francisco, October 4. The road continues on to *Dzilam de Bravo,* another South Sea island village. Both these villages can be reached more easily via a fairly good road going from Mérida to Motul.

Motul, Yuc. Pop. 7789. CE-15, paved to Motul and Puerto Telchac. An interesting Mayan town, noted for its lively regional fiesta, July 8 to 16, honoring the Virgin of Carmen. There are so-called bullfights, a fair, and the picturesque *jarana* dances.

The region northwest of Mérida is dotted with good duck-hunting lagoons. There is a road out of the capital, paved as far as *Hunucmá* (Pop. 5533), to *Sisal* (Pop. 200), once the chief port of Yucatán, and now a quiet seaside village dominated by a lighthouse. From Sisal a passable trail-road follows the coast to *Celestun,* a pleasant grass-hut beach village. Here each December 8–12 there is a very primitive fiesta with dancing in honor of the Virgin. The celebration is fascinating because of its complete lack of pomp and the languid tropic surroundings it has for a setting.

Present-day Mayan village fiestas, customs, food: The present-day Mayan villagers in back-country towns are endlessly fascinating, especially regarding their customs, beliefs, and fiestas which have scarcely been touched by modern ways.

Many of the ceremonies and beliefs, a blending of ancient pagan ritual and Christian beliefs, are related to farming. Due to the sterile soil and the rocky nature of the land, the excessive heat and tropical downpours, the Mayan villager is unable to farm as in other parts of Mexico. The plow is practically unknown. A man clears a few dozen square yards of *monte* (jungle and brush), he seeks out cracks in the hard limestone surface when a little soil has gathered. With a pointed stick he pokes holes into the pockets of soil and drops in seeds, one by one. After a few years he and his village must move to another area of less exhausted soil. He prays to an assortment of gods to make the cornfields fertile, to control the rains and winds lest his sparse crop fail to come up.

His gods are called Yuntzilob (Lords or Patrons). Belief in them exists side by side with belief in the Christian God and the Saints — but it is the Yuntzilob who deal with the fields and rains. They come in three categories: *balams* who protect the fields, *kuil-kaaxs,* guarding forests, and the *chaacs* who bring rain. The latter, when ordered by Jesucristo (Christ) to make rain, ride through the skies on horses and sprinkle the earth with water from inexhaustible gourds. Sometimes they are accompanied by the Virgin Mary. The *balams,* protecting fields, are sometimes seen as little old men dressed in the native whites and wearing sombreros and sandals.

When the Mayan farmer prepares land for planting, he first sets up a small cross and places offerings of corn meal before it as an offering, and he calls upon the *balams* to accept the offering — a way of proving to them that the man who is using the land is a friend. Just before trees are felled and the *monte* is burned off, other offerings and prayers are made, asking Jesucristo and the *balams* to order a special wind to spiral over the area so the flames will burn properly. The wind is composed of souls who have committed sins of the flesh.

Among the Indians of Yucatán and Quintana Roo the Cross, a potent talisman also among the ancient Maya, is the most sacred of their religious symbols, a potent force against Kisin (Lucifer) who is believed to have an urge to steal a man's soul after death.[4]

A popular superstition, current throughout the peninsula (undoubtedly related to La Llorana and Malinche legend of Central Mexico, see Index), is the charming belief in Xtabay — an impossibly enchanting woman with hair so long it covers her entire nude body. She possesses the power to bewitch any man she finds abroad after midnight. She only appears when the moon is full, and is usually seated under a Ceiba tree (also magical), combing her beautiful hair.

FIESTAS AND DANCES: The Yucatecan fiestas and dances are usually less elaborate or sophisticated than those of Central Mexico, yet they are noted for their traditional charm. A visitor should, if possible, take part in a village fiesta (religious or secular) where the events and dances have a greater spontaneity than those he might see in Mérida.

One of the most interesting dances is the *Kub-pol,* or Offering of the Pig's Head, usually celebrated in conjunction with a Saint's Day. The dancers carry barbecued hogs' heads, with coins in the eye sockets and a cake in its mouth. The heads may also be decorated with colored paper flags and dolls, each with a little white bread in its mouth. Other dancers carry cylindrical frames covered with flowers and cut-out paper ornaments. The head is offered to the saint, along with cornhusks, bread, bottles of anís, candy, etc.

The folk dance of Yucatán is the *jarana.* The name is derived from the ukulele-like instrument which accompanies the dance. (The word *jarana,* itself, means *noisy diversion.*) The secular *jarana* calls for couples to dance, facing each other, the man with his hands clasped behind

[4] Frances Toor, in her informative book, *A Treasury of Mexican Folkways,* tells of a talking cross that appeared on a mahogany tree at Chan Santa Cruz, Q.R., the capital of the rebel Mayas in the War of the Castes against the whites. This cross, attributed to be the invention of a *mestizo* named Barrera, said to have employed a native ventriloquist to do the talking for the cross, became the focal center of an important shrine until federal troops destroyed the cross in 1851. Undismayed, Barrera and the Mayas encountered another miracle — three crosses, believed to be the daughters of the one destroyed. The crosses were enshrined, dressed in the *huipiles* of women, and not only talked, but wrote letters.

The crosses have since become the center of an important cult. Since 1931, following the invasion of the white man into Santa Cruz, much of the tribe has moved to X-Cacal, carrying with it one of the crosses and setting up a new shrine. The X-Cacal cross is considered the most potent of all. It is now called La Santísima (The Most Holy Cross). It is kept hidden in a wooden box behind a curtain on the altar of La Gloria in the shrine at X-Cacal, and armed guards watch it day and night. Neither it nor the sister crosses are ever taken out in processions; instead they are represented by a *fiadora,* or double, in all public rites.

his back, the girl raising her skirts slightly. They pass each other from time to time with arms curved upward, snapping their fingers, castanet-fashion. The village *jaranas* have a ritualistic aspect for they are danced during novenas (nine days of praying), as offerings to saints.

FIESTA FARE: Yucatecan traditional cuisine, once deservedly famous, has become a debased art. Occasionally at fiestas, family parties and very rarely in restaurants, one finds some of the excellent dishes that were served up almost everywhere a generation ago. Some of the more delicious dishes are:

Pavo en pebre, breast of turkey cooked with Sevilla (sour) oranges, almonds, onions, and tomato. The chef at Hacienda Uxmal can do it. With it he serves green limes stuffed with shredded coconut, and stewed until almost candied. *Chicken Pibil,* a chicken *tamale* wrapped in banana leaves, seasoned with saffron and barbecued. *Venado Pipian,* venison barbecued with a squash seed sauce.

THE CAMPECHE COUNTRY

The western section of the Yucatán Peninsula, the remote State of Campeche, is a sparcely populated mangrove and jungle area (about 160,000 inhabitants). Only in the last few years, with the completion of the Sureste Railway, the Gulf Coast Highway, and a thin network of interior roads, has this fabulous country begun to open up. Few travelers, least of all tourist agencies, are aware of Campeche's magnificent beach-girt coast, her unspoiled fishing villages and islands, and her teaming sport-fishing waters and hunting paradises.

The best base for a surface peek at Campeche's charms is her capital city, Campeche, one of the oldest most romantic cities in Mexico. For the serious fisherman or hunter the favored base is Ciudad del Carmen on the Island of Carmen.

HIGHLIGHTS: A day or more visit in the historic city of Campeche. A one-day trip to the archaeological ruins at Edzná. A visit at the Bolenchen Caverns. For the sportsman — hunting in the interior and tarpon fishing in the waters around Isla Carmen.

Campeche, Camp. Capital of the State of the same name. Pop. 32,000. Alt. 52 ft.

HOW TO GET THERE: Campeche is on the Gulf Coast Highway, CN-180, it is an important terminal for both the Sureste Railway and Ferrocarriles Union de Yucatán. Daily air flights from Mexico City, Veracruz and Mérida stop here.

HOTELS: *Hotel López,* Calle 12 189. 31 rooms. Rates from $48 MN, EP. Accommodations are first class for the area. The dining room is good. Some rooms are air conditioned. Bar, roof garden, garage. Very friendly atmosphere. The owner, Rodolfo López and family are most attentive and helpful. Other hotels: *Castelmar,* Calle 61 2, old, moderate rates. *Colonial,* new, small. *Hotel Baluartes,* central, facing sea, Campeche's newest hotel. Good dining room, bar, swimming. Rates $60 to $80 MN dble, EP. Tel. 28-94.

RESTAURANTS: *Miramar,* corner of Calles 8 and 16, (across from Hotel Castelmar), excellent sea food, especially shrimp caught that day, lobster and the succulent *Cangregos Moros* (Morro Crabs). Dining Room, *Hotel López,* see above.

DIRECTORY: *Travel Agents* — the Barbachano Travel Service, Yucatán Trails, etc., conduct guided tours to Campeche. See Index: Mérida. *Banks* — Banco Nacional de México, S.A., Calles 8 and 59. Banco de Campeche S.A., Calle 10 234. *Airline offices*—CMA, corner Calles 10 and 63, Tel. 24-10. TAMSA, Calle 59 19-A. Tel. 22-00. *Railway* — Ferrocarril del Sureste. Tickets at passenger depot. *Bus lines* — Union de Camioneros de Campeche, Calles 8 and 51 239 (service to Champotón, Aguada, Isla Carmen). *Drugstore* — La Paz, Calles 57 and 10 8, open until 10 P.M. *Garage and repairs* — General Motors parts and service, Calle 10 53. Ford, Calle 10 216, Olegario Montes S. A. (Dodge), Calle 12 125. *Church services* — (Catholic). The Cathedral. MUSEUMS: Museum of Arms in the San Carlos Fortress. The Museum of Archaeology, corner of 10 and 63rd Streets.

THE CITY: pronounced cahm-PAY-chay, a Spanish corruption of the original Maya name of the town, Kimpech (*kim,* serpent; *pech,* tick). The town is the point where Hernández de Córdoba first disembarked on the Mexican mainland, 1517, the year before Cortés' expedition. It was not, however, until 1540 that the present city was founded by Francisco Montejo and became the principal port of the peninsula during the years of the coloniage.

In atmosphere the city is one of the truly charming places in Mexico. Its ramparts facing the sea, designed to ward off English, French, and other buccaneers (chief among them the infamous Lorencillo) who repeatedly sacked the city in its early years, remind one of Spain's Cádiz. Part of these fortifications with their 8 ft. thick walls remain as relics of the early defenses. Many of the houses of the *Tenientes de Rey* (crown officials), with their massive iron-studded doors and Baroque entrances still survive.

The city is fairly compact and most of its points of interest can be visited on foot or by cab. The places of greatest interest are:

The *Fortress Walls* built as a protection against pirates, 1686 and 1704. At each end are the *Forts of San Carlos* and *Santiago,* with their great moats and bastions. The *Forts of San Miguel* and *San Luis,* situated on the Gulf Highway, SW edge of town; the first on a hill, the second at the edge of the ocean. The *Forts of San Matias* and *San José el Alto,* back of the railway station.

The *Cathedral,* in the center, is of historical interest simply because its construction is said to have begun the same day as the founding of the city, October 4, 1540. It is dedicated to the Virgin of the Conception. Of greater artistic interest is the simple and lovely *Convent of San Francisco,* built in 1546. The moist air has imparted a venerable patina to its walls. In one of its rooms was born Jerónimo Cortés, grandson of the Conqueror (October 31, 1562), and in a corner of the atrium (memorialized by a column) is the place where tradition has it that the first Mass was celebrated in Campeche.

The *Armory* (Museo de las Armas) contains interesting exhibits related to the colonial period and the city's constant battle with pirates. The *Museum of Archaeology* has some important Mayan artifacts from the ruins at Edzná, some magnificent figures from the Island of Jaina. *Hours:* 9 A.M. to 2 P.M.

The *Palacio Municipal* (City Hall), a time-stained monument built in 1600, still houses many of the municipal offices.

Not actually worth seeking out, yet of historical interest, is the *Well of the Conquest,* situated at the edge of the San Francisco River where Captain Hernández de

Cordoba's expedition stopped to replenish the party's watercasks in 1517. The site has enjoyed some latter-day notoriety due to a careless wording in a popular guidebook. Local guides, quoting from the work, are apt to innocently inform the visitor that, "here the Córdoba expedition made water."

The Market is interesting, especially during fiesta days when villagers from the back-country flock into the city to sell their regional craft goods. Notable among the articles are the Panama-type hats called *jipis,* made from *huano,* a very soft, reedlike plant. The best of such weaving comes from the village of *Jipis* and from *Becal.* Popular also are the combs, boxes, and articles of costume jewelry manufactured from tortoise shell *(carey),* the amusing and/or grotesque red-haired, blue-eyed masks carved from coconut husks, and objects fashioned from the extremely heavy logwood and other native hardwoods.[5]

FIESTAS: The city of Campeche is noted throughout Mexico for several very colorful fiestas. Gayest is the *Carnival* with parades, decorated floats, popular dances and general merrymaking during the weekend before the Lenten season. The next most important are: Fiesta de San Román, September 14–30, in honor of Christ of San Román, and celebrated especially at the sixteenth-century colonial church of San Román; Fiesta de San Francisco, October 4–13, at the Convent and Church of San Francisco; and, August 7, State Day.

EXCURSIONS FROM THE CITY OF CAMPECHE: For the traveler interested primarily in taking in "sights" and in finding only first-class accommodations, trips beyond the city are not recommended as yet. (Exception, the Island of Carmen, and for ruined city buffs, the archaeological zone at Edzná.)

The more adventurious traveler will find Campeche rich in off-trail places to explore, as well as a source of unusual experiences for the region is still pioneer country and its people exhibit many of the admirable and sturdy qualities so often found in a frontier society.

For the tourist with time and a knack for making the best of somewhat primitive travel fare, here are some Campeche high spots.

Edzná, Camp. (archaeological zone). About 50 m. SW of the capital via an improved road, dry weather only, to *Tixmucuy,* thence to the village of *Pichi.* The ruins are about 7 miles beyond Pichi. The zone is slightly over a half-mile in length and comprises a number of buildings in scattered groups. Very little restoration has been done and the site may disappoint people who have seen Palenque or the carefully manicured archaeological parks at Chichén Itzá and Uxmal.

The central group of ruins surround a large plaza, with the Great Acropolis to the E, the Lesser Acropolis to the S, the Ball Court to the N. The principal temple and most imposing structure, the Pyramid of Five Stories adjoins the central plaza. Its quadrangular base measures over 65 yards, and it stands 34 yards high. The first four stories consisted of rooms for housing the priests while the top structure was a shrine. The general architecture of all the buildings are remarkable for their simplicity. Stelea as well as pottery and some altars indicate that the site is of considerable age, dating perhaps to the Maya Old Empire.

Bolonchenticul, Camp. Pop. 1560. On CN-180, between Mérida and Campeche, about 81 m. S of Mérida or 74 m. from Campeche. Here one finds the famed Nine Wells (caverns) of Bolonchén, also called *La Gruta de Xtucumbi-Xunan,* (Hidden Woman), from a legend about a beautiful *mestiza* girl, victim of an unfortunate love affair, who resolved her problems by living as a hermit in this gloomy underground world.

The complex of underground *cenotes,* somewhat resembling the Bottomless Pit of the Mammoth Cave of Kentucky, are connected to the surface by a torturous stairway about 1400 ft. long. Some 500 feet below the entrance are seven wells or pools of still water. The first pool is called *Chacka,* in the Maya tongue — Red Water; the second pool, *Pucuelha* — reflux, because of a local superstition that the water is wavy like that of the sea, ebbing when the wind blows from the S, and making when it blows from the N. It is believed that this pool must be approached in absolute silence, else the over-sensitive waters will disappear. The third pool is called *Sallab* — waterfall; the fourth, *Akah-Há* — obscurity; the fifth, *Choco-Há* — hot water, because of its high temperature; the sixth, *Oichá* — for its milky-white color, and the seventh, *Chimaishá* — after a certain insect *(Chimais)* which swims around in it. Where the other two pools went (since *Bolonchén* signifies nine wells), remains a mystery to this author.

Ciudad del Carmen, Camp. Pop. 15,000. Alt. 10 ft. The picturesque fishing town on the Island of Carmen (Isla del Carmen). The Gulf Coast Highway, CN-180, traverses the island, cars and buses being ferried across from the mainland at the northern and southern tips. CMA runs daily flights to Carmen from Mexico City, Mérida, and Veracruz.

HOTELS: None of the hotels in Ciudad del Carmen even approach first-class standards in the way of equipment and outlay. By far the best is the small (14 room), comfortable *Hotel Fernández,* Calle 22 123. It is one of the few hotels along this entire coast where the plumbing works, there is always hot water and the premises are kept spotless. The owner, Sra. Josefina Fernández de Robidoux and her American husband, make up for the simplicity of the place with friendly attention and care. Rates: $25 MN to $40 MN, including breakfast. *Hotel Roma,* next best. Rates: $25 MN and up.

RESTAURANTS: The specialty of Ciudad del Carmen restaurants is sea food, particularly the unparalleled Campeche shrimp. The most acceptable restaurants are around the main plaza: *Café Mena,* the *Carmela,* across from the CMA office, and *La Parroquia,* near the church.

DIRECTORY: *Banks* — Banco Nacional de México, S.A., corner of Calles 25 and 22-B. *Bus line* — Union de Camioneros, Calle 20 89. *Airlines* — CMA, Calle 26 44, Tel. 89; TAMSA, Calle 27 4, Tel. 179. *Garage and repairs* — Luis Alfonso Montes, Calles 20 and 23; Carlos Herrera, Calle 35 187.

THE TOWN AND ISLAND: The island of Carmen is a lean shelf of shell, about 30 miles long and a few miles wide. Its northern coast faces the *Bay of Campeche* (a long graceful curve in the southernmost tip of the Gulf

[5] Logwood tree *(Hoematoxylon Campeachianum)* — for centuries Campeche was noted primarily for its dense forests of logwood, a heavy, red wood of firm texture containing a crystalline yellow substance called *hoematoxyline* — used extensively for dyeing and for coloring wines. An extract of the wood is employed as an astringent. The tree has a crooked, deformed stem (as if gripped by its own juice) and grows to a height of 25 ft. or more. The native name is *opiaxtle,* but it is known on the world market under the Spanish name of *palo de tinte* (dyewood). Until the advent of synthetic dyes on the world market, it was Campeche's chief export. At the turn of the century some 25,000,000 kilos were exported annually. Then, as today, many of the finest European wines owe their rich coloring to this tree.

of Mexico). The southern shore faces the *Laguna de Términos,* a vast, sweet-water lake (43 by 25 m.) fed by a multitude of streams. It is truly a small bay with the island blocking its mouth except for straits at the N and S tip of the island. The Laguna was discovered in 1518 by Antonio de Alminos, the pilot of the Grijalva expedition, who gave it its present name because he believed it was the terminus of what he thought was the Island of Yucatán. These waters are considered the finest tarpon-fishing areas in the world.

The island of Carmen itself is a small jewel, girded with beautiful beaches and shaded by forests of gold and emerald palm trees. The best beaches are the Bajamita and El Playon.

The town is somnolent and picturesque, many of its streets simply sandy *paseos* shaded by coconut palms. Such streets, the waterfront with its colorful fleet of shrimp boats, the drying fishnets and the brightly painted houses make the town a veritable painter's and photographer's paradise. One appropriately named and pretty street is that which leads to the cemetery; its palm-lined way is called El Ultimo Paseo (The Last Stroll). The discovery of fabulous beds of large pink shrimp in nearby waters has, during the last decade, made Carmen the shrimp-fishing center of Mexico and has brought the island a good deal of wealth.

There are two museums in the town, neither of great importance. The Museum of Archaeology, containing artifacts from the ruins, Guarixe and Xicalango, is situated directly behind the blue-trimmed, shrimp-pink church on the plaza. The Museo Carmelita (historical museum) is near the high school.

The most important and vivid local fiesta is held from July 15 to 31, honoring the island's patroness, the Virgin of Carmen, and to commemorate the final driving out of pirates from the island (July 16, 1717).

SPORT FISHING: There are numerous fishing boats for hire, for both deep-sea and lagoon fishing. The rates run from $200 MN to $300 MN per day. The finest sport-fishing cruiser belongs to Theodore Walker. Fishing arrangements can be made through the various hotels. Launches can be hired for fascinating trips up the Candelaria River which empties into the Laguna de Términos. For such junkets careful preparations should be made (see Index, *Outdoor Equipment*) since the Candelaria leads up into raw jungle country where the lagoons and streams are filled with alligators, the forest with jaguar and deer.

Aguada, Camp. A tiny Tahiti-like fishing village just across the straits from the W tip of Isla del Carmen (Puerto Real). Aguada is the ferry landing for CN-180, going toward Campeche and Mérida. The village is at the tip of a long, fingerlike peninsula attached to the Peninsula of Yucatán. It may have once been an island for it is still often referred to as Isla Aguada. *Hotel Tarpon Tropical,* a very clean, well-run fisherman's center. Unusually expensive. Write for reservations.

Fishermen willing to take potluck and hammocks, and hunters interested in low-cost expeditions into the Campeche interior should get in touch with Sr. Polo Rejón or his brother Torcuato who handle the ice and gasoline concession in the village, have their own boat, and camping locations in the back country. Address: Sr. Polo Rejón, Dirreción Conocido, Aguada, Campeche.

Champotón, Camp. Pop. 2860. Alt. 20 ft. On the Gulf Highway, CN-180, about 41 m. S of the city of Campeche. Bus connections from Campeche and Mérida.

An interesting fishing village at the mouth of the Champotón River and on the Bay of Campeche. *Hotel El Popular,* hammock accommodations. The hotel restaurant was once famous the length of the coast for its fine sea food and venison and wild duck. The cook, Doña Julia, was considered the best chef on the peninsula. Though she still runs the restaurant, the fare is now uneven. It is said she has been disappointed in love and her heart has gone out of her cooking. Nevertheless, the shrimp and crab are good, served in a flower-filled patio near cages filled with wild mallard, deer, and other denizens of Campeche forests.

Champotón, normally very sleepy, comes to life with a bang for the Fiesta of the Virgin of Candelaria which extends over more than a week, usually beginning January 28.

The town is also the turn-off point for hunting expeditions to the interior, and for a new road to Chetumal, Q.R., and British Honduras. Description below:

Champotón, Escárcega, Chetumal Road. (roads not posted, but to be numbered CN-261 from Champotón to Escárcega, and CE-186 from Escárcega to Chetumal). By 1965 this road, cutting through largely unexplored territory, will permit the motorist a circuit route from Champotón around to the Caribbean (Chetumal), thence back via Mérida. The first section to Escárcega and about 70 m. beyond is newly completed gravel and easily passable. At the moment, to go beyond requires a jeep and spare supplies of gasoline. The route log, with comments:

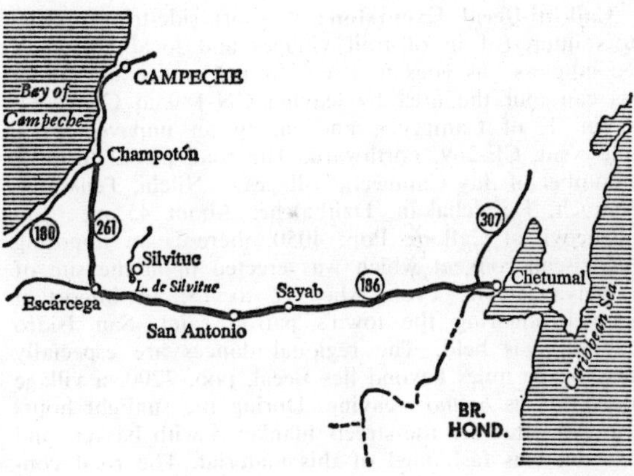

0 Champotón. New road leads directly S from the town.
13 Loreto.
19 Sacabchen. A fair size village.
Laguna de Chuyná, a pretty lake surrounded by big trees where an important Holy Week pilgrimage is held each year. The waters of the lake are purported to be curative and there is a small chapel (shrine) against a cliff at the lake-edge. During the 3-day festival thousands of people gather and the atmosphere is one of a huge picnic.
54 *Escárcega.* Pop. 2650. A pioneer-like town on the Sureste Railway line. *Hotel Rosemarie* (hammock style). Rate: EP $10 MN per day. Here you're fed jerked or fresh venison. The region immediately around is a thick tangle of jungle, filled with game. One of the best hunting guides in the

area is José (Pepe) C. Quintal R. Calle 25 12. He is a very reliable, personable young man, and charges about $1.50 per day, plus food, for his services.

An improved road, CE-186, continues to E about 70 miles to the region around Silvituc, a lumber camp where gasoline can sometimes be bought. Laguna de Silvituc, a nearby, large jungle-lake, a perfect site for hunters seeking duck, deer, wild turkey, wild pig, alligators, and jungle cats.

114 *Improved road ends.* From here on the road is under construction and at the time of this writing largely impassable. The total mileage from Escárcega to Chetumal, about 155 m. Along the route there are several lumber and chicle camps where water, some supplies and gas may sometimes be purchased — San Antonio, Sayab, Monos (just across the Quintana Roo border). A short distance beyond Monos the last 50 miles to Chetumal is improved road. 12½ miles from Chetumal the road joins CE-17 (see Index: Bacalar, Q.R.).

Isla de Jaina (archaeological zone). A tiny, mysterious island off the Campeche coast, less than 50 miles N of the capital. There are no spectacular ruins, but it is famed for the huge clay figures and abundance of other artifacts of Maya Old Empire provenance (sixth to tenth century) found there. The island is, indeed, such a treasure house of artifacts that unauthorized visits there are forbidden.

Calkiní-Becal Excursion: A short side-trip for visitors interested in off-trail villages and local crafts. A second-class bus goes to Becal from Campeche. Motorists can tour the area by leaving CN-180 at Chencoyi, 19 m. E of Campeche and taking an unpaved passable road, CE-269, northward. The road passes through a number of tiny Campeche villages — Nilchí, Tenambo, Pomuch, Hecelchakán, Dzitbalché. About 45 m. from Chencoyi, at Calkiní, Pop. 4050, there is an imposing Franciscan convent which was erected upon the site of a Maya temple. From May 12 to 15, an important festival honoring the town's patron saint, San Isidro Labrador, is held. The regional dances are especially nice. Seven miles beyond lies Becal, pop. 2200, a village noted for its *huano* weaving. During the sunlight hours you can often see the streets blanketed with baskets and Panama hats fashioned of this material. The road continues 50 m. to Mérida.

THE QUINTANA ROO COUNTRY

One of the two remaining federal territories of Mexico. Remote, isolated, it has the smallest population of any division of the republic, with most of its inhabitants descendants of the Maya Indians. This territory consisting of the eastern and southern sections of the Yucatán Peninsula covers some 19,861 sq. miles, has borders with British Honduras, Guatemala, the Mexican states of Campeche and Yucatán. The climate is hot and humid. The territory has great natural beauty, vivid tropical scenery and a coastline (the Caribbean Sea) dotted with Mayan ruins and old Spanish forts. Quintana Roo's principal wealth is derived from coconut ranching, fishing, fine hardwoods, henequén and chicle. The area was named after Andrés Quintana Roo (1787–1851), writer and intellectual leader in the independence movement.

HIGHLIGHTS: The most important areas of touristic attraction are: (1) the coastal region with its tropic islands, Cozumel and Isla Mujeres, the great seaside Maya ruins of Tulum; (2) Chetumal and the nearby Lake Bacalar area. The whole of Quintana Roo is dotted with archaeological ruins and lost cities, some known, others still to be found. Although most of them are difficult to reach, the most fascinating are Tulum, Cobá, Río Bec, and along the Caribbean coastline, El Meco, Nisucté, Playa del Carmen, Palmul, Acomal, Xelhá, Tancah, Chacmol, Tulum Playa, Xcaret, Cacakal, Punta Soliman, Canché Balam, and other sites in the Bay of Chetumal district.

To get the most enjoyment from this region — swimming, fishing, archaeological browsing — one should make the Island of Cozumel or Chetumal his vacation base and skip back and forth along the brilliant coast via fishing boats.

Cozumel Island, Q.R. Pop. 3000. The island (20 m. long, 8 m. wide) lies in the Caribbean Sea, about 12 m. E of the Yucatán Peninsula. The principal town, N end of the island, is called San Miguel. Cozumel signifies (in Maya), sea swallow or tern.

HOW TO GET THERE: From Mérida via plane. The fare is approximately $18. Occasionally boats from Progreso round the tip of the peninsula and call at Cozumel. Make arrangements through Barbachano Travel Service or Yucatán Trails in Mérida. Via private car or bus, one can get within boat-range of the island by either driving to Puerto Juárez (see Isla Mujeres, Index), and from there catching the more-or-less weekly boat to Cozumel; or by turning off of the Gulf Highway, CN-180 at Leona Vicario and taking a rather battered jungle road to Puerto Morelos, 25 m. from where a boat usually crosses the channel daily to Cozumel.

HOTELS: *Hotel Playa Cozumel* (28 rooms) run by Sr. Joaquin Ibarra. Rates: AP from $250 MN to $300 dble. *Hotel Las Cabanas del Caribe* on San Juan Beach. 30 lovely new bungalows, excellent dining, cocktails. Friendly and unusually fine service. Rates: AP, $300 MN, dble. Lower rates in off-season. *Caribe Islander,* in village. De luxe, air conditioned, furnished apartments. Rates: EP, from $175 MN per day, dble. For reservations at both the above, write — Barbachano Travel Service, 480 Calle 60, Mérida, Yuc. Newly opened, *Hotel Presidente Caribe*, de luxe, expensive.

OTHER LODGINGS: *Cabanas Cozumel,* modest, inexpensive. Or, if you are looking for budget accommodations, various families in San Miguel rent rooms (with or without board), among them the Rivero family, Lic. Vives, Sr. Maruffo, and Sr. Mendoza.

RESTAURANTS: The best dining by far is the *Cozumel Caribe* if its kitchen is on par with its affiliates on the mainland. Other restaurants, both very modest but often serving good sea food, are *La Candela* and *Casa de Denis,* also called *La Fonda Tropical.*

DIRECTORY: There is an affiliate of the Banco de Mexico in the village. *Church services* — the tiny San Miguel parish church is administered by the Maryknoll Fathers of the U.S.

THE ISLAND: Once a sacred Maya center, dotted with temples, the island was discovered by Juan de Grijalva in 1518, and the following year Hernán Cortés landed here while awaiting the arrival of two captive countrymen from the mainland, Jeronimo de Aguilar and Gonzales Guerrero, who had been shipwrecked off the coast and held captive for eight years by the Indians.

A century and more afterward the island became a general headquarters for the notorious pirates Henry Morgan, Jean Laffite, and "Pato de Palo." It was not until very recently that the island was "rediscovered" thanks to modern air transport and the Aqua Lung. Cozumel has rapidly become a vacation center, and especially a skin-diver's paradise. The surrounding waters, crystal-clear to a depth of fifty or more feet, are dotted with wrecked Spanish galleons, beautiful rock, and coral formations.

There are numerous vacation attractions: swimming, fishing, exploring the Maya ruins hidden in the forests of the island, and some shopping. Bicycles, boats, fishing, and diving equipment can be rented. Fully equipped charter boats rent for $25 per day.

PLACES OF INTEREST: *Playa San Juan,* Cozumel's finest swimming beach, a vivid expanse of golden sand backdropped by curving coconut palms. *Laguna Chankanab,* 5 m. from the village, (a small, jungle-rimmed natural lake of turquoise-colored water and filled with brilliant fish. The lake is a favorite picnic and swimming spot. Skin-diving is best at the northern and southern tips of the island, especially around the lighthouse, Faro de Puntas Molas, and *San Francisco Beach.* For tortoise hunting, *Laguna Ciega,* about six miles by boat from the village. There are Maya ruins at *El Real* (N end of island) and at San Benito, *El Cedral,* and *Celarain* (S part of the island).

EXCURSIONS FROM COZUMEL: Boat trips can be taken to *Isla Mujeres* (see Index), and to a number of fascinating fishing villages along the peninsula coast directly west of Cozumel. At several points — *Playa Carmen, Palmul, Acomal, Xelhá,* and *Tancah* — there are still unrestored Maya ruins. The most interesting excursion, however, is to *Tulum.* Charter boats charge $60, U.S., including meals and overnight stay.

Tulum (archaeological zone). About 25 m. southwest of Cozumel, on the Caribbean coast of Quintana Roo. Flights via chartered planes (TAMSA) can be made directly from Mérida, or from Cozumel by boat (about 5 hrs.). A trip there can be made in a day, allowing for several hours of sightseeing. Food and water should be brought along for there is no settlement at Tulum. Visitors interested in making a prolonged exploration can put up at the nearby coconut ranch, *Tancah.* Bring hammocks.

Tulum (Maya, walled fortress) is one of the most haunting Maya ruined cities. It is utterly alone in the Caribbean sun, standing guard on bluffs overlooking the sea and deserted beaches below. It is touched by wonderful isolation, no tourists and no souvenir peddlers.

The first mention of Tulum was made by explorer Juan de Grijalva who spied the spectacular sight from the sea while sailing along the coast in 1518. He wrote that "we saw a town so large that the city of Sevile could not appear larger or smaller." It was also, undoubtedly the city (Zamá) where the shipwrecked Spaniards Aguilar and Guerrero were held as slaves from 1511 to 1519. Following this early Spanish contact with Tulum, the place seemed to have been completely forgotten until the middle of the nineteenth century. No one knows how long it was inhabited after the conquest. During the War of the Castes, however, it was one of the principal revolutionary strongholds. In 1848 that remarkable explorer-writer, John Lloyd Stephens, and his companion, British artist Frederick Catherwood, came upon Tulum and brought it to the attention of the world. Later it was further explored by Howe and Morley, and from 1937 on the Mexican archaeologist Miguel Angel Fernández cleared the area and continued explorations.

Although there is a stele at Tulum dated about 564 A.D., the metropolis seems to have flourished in the fourteenth century, the marvelously preserved buildings showing Toltec influence as at Chichén Itzá.

Of the numerous constructions at Tulum the most interesting are: The Castle, a pyramid-type building topped by a two-room temple with simple columns at the entrance. The building is a magnificent sight from the sea. The Temple of the Descending God (N side of the central plaza), which has in-slanting walls making the roof-surface greater than that of the floor. Above its doorway is a remarkable carved figure (head down) of the Descending God, Kukulkán (Aztec, Quetzalcoatl), which is strangely remindful of carved deity figures at Ankor Vat in Cambodia and on some Bali temples in the Pacific. Temple of the Frescoes (center of city, direct E of the Plaza) is the most beautiful of Tulum's buildings. It is an exceptionally fine example of pre-conquest architecture; a two-story building decorated with exceptional frescoes and sculptured decorations of remarkable vigor and preserved colors.

In addition to these unusual buildings there are some 56 other structures within the walled metropolis, and several beyond the wall.

There is a jungle path leading several miles N along the coast to the Tancah coconut *hacienda.* Just beyond the plantation, gripped by tropical vines and brush, are the archaeological Ruins of Tancah. One building remains in good state of preservation.

Isla Mujeres, Q.R. Pop. approx. 1000. A tiny sand-spit isle on the Quintana Roo coast (6 miles from the mainland), about a one-day trip by boat from Cozumel, 200 miles E of Mérida.

HOW TO GET THERE: *Via air* — expensive charter flights from Mérida. *Sea* — occasional boats from Progreso, and haphazard service from Cozumel. *Road* — the Gulf Coast Highway, CN-180 goes from Mérida to Puerto Juárez. At Puerto Juárez you can leave your car in care of the customs official (no charge) and take the twice-daily, 30-ton freighter (it looks a bit like a Spanish galleon without sails) the *Carmita* across the 6-mile channel to the island. Fare on the *Carmita* is $3 MN each way. The boat leaves Puerto Juárez at 2:30 and 5 P.M. Sails from Isla Mujeres for the mainland at 7 A.M. and 1 P.M. You can also charter fishing boats for the crossing, but they are expensive, about $70 MN. From Mérida there is bus service to Puerto Juárez once a day. The first-class bus leaves Mérida at 6:30 A.M., arrives in Valladolid at 9 A.M. There you must transfer to second-class bus which arrives at Puerto Juárez at about 1:45 P.M. The Channel boat waits for the bus.

HOTELS: Tourist facilities on Isla Mujeres are very limited. *Hotel Tropical Caribe,* new, well managed. The two small hotels charge exorbitant prices, and can only be rated as but fair to primitive. *Hotel Poseda del Mar,* on the beach, 2 blocks from the landing, Playa del Norte. Small, well kept but without charm. Rates: AP, $225 MN dble, $140 MN per single. Dining room, fair. *Hotel Zazil-Há,* also known as *Casa de la Punta* and *Lima's Place,* 5 bungalows on the magnificent northern tip of the island. Although beautifully situated, with fairly nice bungalows, service, food, and accommodations are definitely substandard. Advertised hot water doesn't run hot, etc. Rates: AP, $225 MN, dble. Hotel has skin-diving equipment, compressors, boats for hire.

Other lodgings: A small new, nameless hotel (really furnished rooms, since service is not provided) on the beach. You must contact the owner, Don Pacheco, who runs the large grocery store in town. Rate: $25 MN dble. No dining or cooking facilities. Primarily furnished houses can be rented from Sr. Martinez for $20 to $40 per month.

RESTAURANTS: Best food is to be had at the *Hotel Posada del Mar.* There is also a restaurant, serving sea food, at the foot of the boat landing. Prices vary with the customer and moods of the owner. The cuisine is drab, though it is difficult to defeat a good freshly caught lobster.

THE ISLAND AND ENVIRONS: Isla Mujeres (Island of Women) derived its name from the numerous terracotta female figurines found in the Maya temples of the island by the Spanish conquerors.

The principal charm of Isla Mujeres is, first of all, its utter isolation. You are just about as far as you can get from the noisiness of Mexico. Though the beaches and rocky coast (windward side), and the coconut groves are as lovely as those of Acapulco, there are no night clubs, swank hotels, and promenades, and of course, few tourists. Facilities for fishing, swimming, clamming, and skin-diving are superb. The village itself, supported by a bit of fishing, coconut ranching, turtle-herding, and a government naval installation, is fairly interesting. There is a small government airfield suitable for private-plane landing.

THINGS TO DO AND EXCURSIONS: Except for aquatic sports, hunting on the mainland, there is little to do. Best swimming beaches are at the northern tip of the island. At the SE point there are ruins of a Maya sanctuary for the goddess Ix-Chel. An hour or more boat ride across the channel, just S of Puerto Juárez is the Island and Lagoon Cancuen. The first provides good fishing waters, the latter has an unexplored Maya ruin. The island has undoubtedly the whitest sands in the world. The fishermen of Isla Mujeres capture huge sea turtles which are kept in pens just south of the naval installation. Ships pick them up at regular intervals, taking them to Florida for delivery to the turtle-soup canneries.

Chetumal, Q.R. Pop. approx. 9000. Alt. 20 ft. Capital of the Territory of Quintana Roo.

HOW TO GET THERE: *Via air* — scheduled TAMSA flights from Mérida and Cozumel. *Sea* — occasional freighter and fishing vessel passage from Progreso, Yuc., and Cozumel. *Via road* — a new all-weather road (gravel) has been opened linking Mérida and Chetumal. At present there are few gas, garage, and eating facilities along the way. The drive, through brilliant jungle country, can be done in one day. The route and trip log are described below.

HOTELS: *Nuevo Hotel Los Cocos,* small, but has new bungalows, dining room, bar service. Rates: $60 MN per dble. A new, but somewhat simpler and equally comfortable hotel is *Hotel Jacaranda.* Rate: EP, $50 MN dble. No dining room.

RESTAURANT: Dining in Chetumal is catch-as-catch-can. However, a pleasant, very simple place to eat is *Restaurant Fina Musa,* Plaza Principal near the waterfront. It is open-air, run by a Lebanese woman who puts together some good sea food.

THE CITY AND ENVIRONS: For centuries Chetumal was the sinkhole of Mexico, isolated, forgotten, cut off even from the rest of the Yucatán Peninsula — without road, air, or railway connection with anywhere. The capital city was squalid, lacking in sanitary facilities, power, and other urban niceties. From the early 1920s to 1959 the territory was under the grip of a dictator-like governor (appointive) who controlled the region's rich hardwood lumber concessions, was connected with several of the foreign lumber companies, was involved in smuggling and other pastimes of normal Caribbean politicians. Partially due to scandals, and partly because a disastrous hurricane which completely destroyed the old, squalid Chetumal, the durable governor was removed and the city and territory received much-needed federal attention.

Chetumal is now rapidly rebuilding — turning into a spick-and-span, progressive port city with trim buildings, well-lighted streets and finely planned parks.

EXCURSIONS FROM CHETUMAL: The city is a natural base for fishing excursions in the Bay of Chetumal, and for deep-sea fishing among the keys and along the coast of British Honduras. Boat trips can also be arranged northward up the coast to visit the unexplored archaeological sites of Canche Balam, Chac Mol, Punta Soliman, and even Tulum. The hunting in this region — deer, peccary, and jaguar — is exceptionally good.

Bacalar, Q.R., about 30 m. NW of the capital, on the new road to Mérida. Near the present village of Bacalar there is the ruin of an interesting Spanish fort overlooking Lake Bacalar. The original Spanish settlement was founded in 1544, and was called Villa de Salamanca, though the Maya name Bakhalal (knoll of cane) has persisted. The Spanish settlement grew to contain 5053 inhabitants, all of them wiped out during the War of the Castes and in the final siege in 1858.

The Mérida to Chetumal Road Log:

0 Mérida, Yuc. Leave city, S via CN-180.

39 Muna. Junction, left, with CE-26, toward Ticul, Peto and Chetumal. Road is paved as far as Peto.

51 Ticul. **G.** See Index.

78 Oxkutzcab. See Index.

93 Tzucab. Here, according to existing maps, the road is supposed to go directly to Santa Rosa, bypassing Peto. *It doesn't.* It *goes* to Peto.

105 Peto. **G.** Pop. 5800. Terminal of the Mérida-Peto branch of the railroad, Peto is a fascinating town, periodically made uproarious by the tough, hard-drinking chicle gatherers who come into the village to celebrate after long work periods in the jungle. The village celebrates a lively week-long fiesta (December 26–31) honoring the Virgin of the Star.

120 Santa Rosa. The route has crossed into Quintana Roo.

139 Esmeralda. On some Mexican road maps the route is shown as continuing directly southward from this point. In actuality the road veers gently eastward to,

192 Felipe Carillo Puerto. Pop. 500. A *chichlero* and lumber village in the heart of the Quintana Roo forest. Gasoline may sometimes be found here. The town was once called Santa Cruz because of the ventriloquist who beguiled the Indians into believing that a certain cross could speak to them. In 1935 President Cárdenas ordered the town renamed Carillo Puerto after a socialist governor of Yucatán. There is a massive stone colonial church here, its interior unfinished. The road continues southward through chicle and lumbering settlements — Palmas, Cafetal, etc. — 63 miles to Bacalar.

267 Bacalar.

298 Chetumal.

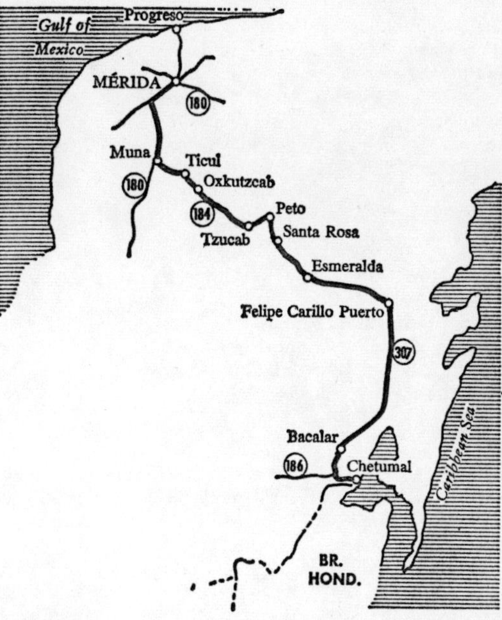

GLOSSARY

Glossary of Useful Spanish Words and Phrases

Although a knowledge of Spanish is not essential for an enjoyable trip to Mexico's more popular sightseeing and recreational areas, nevertheless a familiarity with some Spanish phrases and words are often helpful and may enrich the pleasures of a tour below the border.

Both the sound and spelling of Spanish are simple, the latter being almost phonetic. Most consonants have the same sound in Spanish as in English. The few exceptions are as follows:

- h — is always silent in Spanish.
- j — pronounced like English *h,* but from deeper in the throat.
- g — like the English *h* when followed by *i* or *e.* Otherwise it is like the *g* in "good."
- c — has a soft sound in Mexico, before *e* and *i,* otherwise it is pronounced like *k.* For example: *cinquenta* — seen-kwen-tah.
- ll — in Mexico is usually pronounced like a *y.* For example: *pollo* — po-yo.
- ñ — is a combination *n* and *y* and is pronounced as the *ni* in onion. For example: *niño* — nee-nyo.
- z — is pronounced like *s.*
- x — may be pronounced like *h* or like *s,* depending where it comes in a word. For example: *Xalapa* — ha-lah-pah, and, *extremo* — es-tray-mo.

Vowels are given their European values.

- a — pronounced as *a* in father.
- e — as the *e* in they.
- i — pronounced as *e* in "me."
- o — same as the English *o.*
- u — like the English *oo* in "boot."

The Spanish *r* is rolled slightly. The double *r* (rr) is handsomely rolled, just as a Scotsman would do it with the burr.

In Spanish, words ending in a vowel or *s* and *n* (used to form plurals) are always accented on the next-to-last syllable, while words ending in other consonants are stressed on the final syllable. The occasional exceptions to these rules carry an accent mark, such as in México. Indian words, especially Náhuatl words, receive their stress on the next-to-last syllable, no matter what the ending is.

USEFUL ADJECTIVES

bad	— malo	cheap	— barato
good	— bueno	clean	— limpio
dirty	— sucio	cold	— frio
hot	— caliente	hot (spicy)	— piquante
expensive	— caro	high	— alto
low	— bajo	quick	— pronto
small	— pequeño	large	— grande

Colors

color	— color	black	— negro
white	— blanco	red	— rojo
blue	— azul	brown	— cafe
green	— verde	yellow	— amarillo

NUMERALS

1. uno	12. doce	30. treinta
2. dos	13. trece	40. cuarenta
3. tres	14. catorce	50. cinquenta
4. cuatro	15. quince	60. sesenta
5. cinco	16. diez y seis	70. setenta
6. seis	17. diez y siete	80. ochenta
7. siete	18. diez y ocho	90. noventa
8. ocho	19. diez y nueve	100. cien
9. nueve	20. viente	200. doscientos
10. diez	21. viente y uno	500. quienientos
11. once		1000. mil

TIME

morning	— la mañana	today	— hoy
noon	— el mediodia	tomorrow	— mañana
afternoon	— la tarde	tonight	— esta tarde
night	— la noche	last night	— anoche
midnight	— la media noche	next week	— la semana próxima

Sunday	— el domingo	Thursday	— el jueves
Monday	— el lunes	Friday	— el viernes
Tuesday	— el martes	Saturday	— el sabado
Wednesday	— el miércoles		

What time is it?	¿Que hora es?
It is one o'clock.	Es la una.
It is two o'clock.	Son las dos.
It is three-twenty.	Son las tres y viente.
It is a quarter to six.	Son las quince para las seis.
It is nine-thirty.	Son las nueve y media.

DIRECTIONS

north	— el norte	street	— la calle
west	— el oeste	corner	— la esquina
south	— el sur	kilometer	— el kilometro
east	— el este	block	— la cuadra
right	— la derecha	highway	— la carratera
left	— la izquierda	boulevard	— el bulevar
straight ahead	— derecho	avenue	— la avenida
road	— el camino	address	— la dirreción

Where does this road go?	¿A dónde conduce este camino?
Show me the road to . . .	Enséñeme el camino para . . .
How far away is . . . ?	¿Qué tan lejos está . . . ?
How many kilometers is it to . . . ?	¿Cuántos kilometros hay a . . . ?
Is the road paved?	¿Está pavimientado el camino?
Is that road in good condition?	¿Está en bueno estado aquel camino?
What is the name of this city (village)?	¿Como se llama esta ciudad (pueblo)?
How many blocks to . . . ?	¿Cuantas cuadras a . . . ?
Where is the center of town?	¿Donde está el centro de la ciudad?

BUS AND RAILWAY

Where can I get a bus for . . . ?	¿Donde puedo tomar un autobus para . . . ?
Where is the bus terminal? The railway station?	¿Donde se queda la estación de los autobuses? ¿La estación del ferrocarril?
When does the bus (train) leave?	¿A qué hora sale el autobus (el tren)?
I want a first-class ticket to . . .	Quiero un boleto de primera clase a . . .
Round trip.	Viaje redondo (or) Ir y vuelta.
Please give me a Pullman reservation.	Por favor, hagame una reservacion por el Pullman.
I want an upper berth, lower berth, drawing room.	Prefiero una cama alta, cama baja, una alcoba.
Tell me where to get off.	Favor de decirme donde me bajo.

GARAGE AND CAR

Fill the gas tank.	Llene el tanque de gasolina.
Give me ten, twenty liters.	Deme diez, viente litros.
Check the oil.	Vea el aceite.
Change the oil, please.	Cambie Usted el aceite, por favor.
Grease the car, please.	Favor de engrasar (lubricar) el automóvil.
Check whether there is enough grease in the gear box.	Vea si hay bastante grasa en la caja de velocidades.
I have a puncture. Can you repair the tube?	Tengo un pinchazo. ¿Puede Usted componer la cámera?
Can you repair tubeless tires?	¿Puede Usted reparar llantas sin cámeras?
Please clean the spark plugs.	Favor de limpiar las bujias.
Put water in the battery.	Ponga agua en el acumulador.
The brakes (carburetor, distributor) needs adjusting.	Hay que ajustar los frenos (el carburador, el distribuidor).
The gas line is clogged.	La tubería de gasolina se ha atascado.
The fuel pump is out of order.	Está descompuesto la bomba de gasolina.
The clutch slips.	El embrague resbala.
The engine overheats.	Se calienta el motor.
The starter doesn't work.	El arranque automático no funciona.
I need a tow truck.	Necesito una grua remolque.
Is there a garage (gas station) near here?	¿Hay un garage (una estación de gasolina) cerca de aquí?
Please send a mechanic to repair my car.	Envie Usted un mecanico para reparar mi automóvil, por favor.

BANK

Where is there a bank?	Favor de decirme donde está un banco.
I wish to change some money.	Quiero cambiar dinero.
What is the rate of exchange?	¿A cómo está el cambio?
Can you change traveler's checks?	¿Podria Usted cambiar cheques de viajero?

HOTEL

hotel	— el hotel	boarding house	— casa de huéspedes
inn	— la posada	apartment house	— apartamentos
motel	— motel, campo turista	furnished room	— un cuarto amueblado
dining room	— el comedor	air conditioned	— aire acondicionado
room	— el cuarto	hot water	— agua caliente
bedroom	— la recámera	ice water	— agua con hielo
bathroom	— el cuarto de baño	elevator	— el elevador
towel	— la toalla	manager	— el gerente
washcloth	— la toalla chica	key	— la llave
soap	— el jabón	porter	— el mozo
		bellhop	— el botones

I want a single room, with bath.	Quiero un cuarto solo, con baño.
Double room, with twin beds.	Un cuarto para dos, con camas gemelas.
What is your price?	¿Cuál es el precio?
A front room, a rear room.	Un cuarto al frente, al fondo.
Will you send the baggage up? Down?	¿Favor de hacer subir el equipaje? ¿Favor de hacer bajar el equipaje?
We are leaving now, tomorrow.	Partimos ahora mismo, mañana.
Is there a garage?	¿Hay garage?
Is there laundry service?	¿Hay servicio de lavandería?
Dry cleaning.	Tintoría.
Where is the ladies' room, men's room?	¿Dónde esta el lavabo de damas, de señores?
Wake me at 7, please.	Favor de despertarme a las siete.
My bill, please.	Mi cuenta, por favor.

SHOPPING

Where can I buy . . . ?	¿Dónde puedo comprar . . . ?
What size is this?	¿Qué medida es esta?
Can I try it on?	¿Me permite probarlo?
How much is this?	¿Cuanto vale esto?
It is too expensive.	Es demasiado caro.
I'll take this.	Me llevo esto.
Do you have something cheaper?	¿Hay algo mas barato?
It is too small, large, tight.	Es demasiado chico, grande, ajustado.

American papers — periodicos americanos.

magazines	las revistas	clothing	la ropa
antiques	antiguëdades	hats	los sombreros
baskets	las canastas	jewelry	las alhajas
perfumes	perfumes	razor blades	hojas de rasurar
pictures	cuadras	silver	la plata
post cards	las tarjetas postales		

POST OFFICE

Where is the post office? — ¿Dónde está la oficina de correos?

airmail	correo aéreo	special delivery	entrega inmediata
register	certificar	general delivery	lista de correos
stamps	timbres	money orders	giros

RESTAURANT AND FOOD

Could you recommend a good restaurant?	¿Puede Usted recomendar un buen restaurante?
I wish to see the menu.	Quiero ver el menú, por favor.
Please serve us quickly.	Favor de servirmos pronto.
The bill, please.	La cuenta, por favor.
I like my meat medium rare (very rare, well done).	Quiero la carne tierna, (casi crudo, bien cocida).
Is it very hot (peppery)?	¿Está muy picante?
Hot sauce.	Salsa de la cocina.

breakfast	el desayuno	fork	el tenedor
lunch	el almuerzo	knife	el cuchillo
dinner	la comida	spoon	la cuchara
supper	la cena	glass	el vaso
the bill	la cuenta	cup	la taza
tip	la propina	plate	el plato
waiter	el mesero	napkin	la servietta
waitress	mesera (or) señorita		

Hors d'oeuvres — Entremeses

olives	las aceitunas	caviar	el caviar
anchovy	la anchoa	pickles	los encurtidos
salad	la ensalada		

Fowl and Game — Aves y Caza

rabbit	el conejo	pheasant	el faisán
hare	el liebre	duck	el pato
turkey	el pavo (or) el guajalote	roast turkey	pavo asado

turkey with special chili sauce — mole de guajalote

chicken	el pollo	stuffed turkey	pavo relleno
broiled chicken	pollo a la parilla.	breast of chicken	pechuga de pollo
		venison	venado

Fish and Shellfish — Pescado y Mariscos

trout	la trucha	clams	las almejas
tuna	atún, bonito	shrimps	los camarones
dried cod	bacalao	crab	el cangrejo
pickled fish	escabeche	lobster	la langosta
haddock	robalo	oysters	los ostiones
red snapper	huachinango		

Meats — Carnes

beef	carne de res	broiled	a la parilla
beef steak	biftec	roasted	asada
filet	filete	cold meat	carne fiambre
meatballs	albondigas	brains	sesos
ham	jamón	chops	chuletas
pork	carne de puerco	loin of...	lomo de...
mutton	carnero	Spanish sausages	chorizos
liver	higado	tongue	lengua
veal	tenera	bacon	tocino

Eggs — Huevos

fried — frito
soft boiled — pasado por agua
hard boiled — cocido duro
omelet — omlet
scrambled — revueltos
with chile sauce — huevos rancheros
poached — escalfados

Vegetables — Verduras

dried beans — frijoles
green beans — ejotes
corn — elote
lettuce — lechuga
tomato — jitomate
rice — arroz
celery — apio
squash — calabaza
spinach — espinacas
carrots — zanahorias
beets — betabeles
cabbage — col (or) repollo
onion — cebolla
peas — chicharos
sweet potato — camote
potatoes — papas
eggplant — berenjena
cauliflower — coliflor
mushrooms — hongos
artichokes — alcachofas

Fruits — Frutas

avocado — aguacate
apple — manzana
banana — plátano
figs — higos
guava — guayaba
strawberry — fresa
pineapple — piña
melon — melón
papaya — papaya
grapes — uvas
lemon — limón real
lime — limón
orange — naranja
custard apple — chirimoya
mango — mango de Manila
plum — ciruela
peach — durazno
watermelon — sandía
grapefruit — toronja

Bread — Pan

rolls — bollos
corn griddle-cake — tortilla
crackers — galletas
sweet roll — pan dulce
rye bread — pan de centeno
whole wheat — pan integral
toasted — tostada
cake — pastel

Beverages — Bebidas

coffee — cafe
milk — leche
wine — vino
tea — té
beer — cerveza
brandy — aguardiente
rum — rón
soft drinks — refrescos

Miscellaneous

soup — sopa
broth — caldo
sugar — azúcar
salt — sal
pepper — pimienta
butter — mantequilla
cheese — queso
ice cream — helado
custard — flan
honey — miel de abejas
meat stew — estofada
meat pie — empanada
boiled dinner — cocido
chicken and rice dish — paella valenciana
tortillas with meat, cheese and sauce — enchiladas
stew — guisado

GENERAL USEFUL EXPRESSIONS

Do you understand English?	¿Entiende Ud. el inglés?
I don't speak Spanish.	No hablo español.
Yes. No.	Sí. No.
Do you understand me?	¿Me entiende Ud?
What is this called in Spanish?	¿Cómo se llamo ésto en español?
What did you say?	¿Como se dice?
Please speak slowly.	Favor de hablar despacio.
I need.	Necesito.
I would like to telephone.	Quisiera telefonear.
I am sick.	Estoy enfermo.
Would you call a doctor?	¿Podría Ud. llamar a un medico?
Good morning, afternoon, evening.	Buenas días, buenas tardes, buenas noches.
Good-by.	Adios.
Thank you.	Gracias.
Excuse me.	Perdóneme.
I'm very sorry.	Lo siento mucho.
Don't mention it.	De nada.
May I speak to you for a moment?	¿Me permite Ud. una palabra?
Can you tell me . . . ?	¿Podría Ud. decirme . . . ?
With pleasure.	Con mucho gusto.
I don't know.	No lo sé.
Is it true that . . . ?	¿Es verdad que . . . ?
I don't know anything about it.	No estoy enterado.
Please be so kind as to . . .	Tenga Ud. la bondad de . . .
What do you mean?	¿Qué quiere Ud. decir?
How do you say that in Spanish?	¿Cómo se dice eso en español?
I'll try to explain it to you.	Intentaré explicárselo.
Can I count on you?	¿Puedo contar con Usted?
I'm sorry, but I've changed my mind.	Lo siento, pero he cambiado de idea.
Didn't you understand me?	¿No me ha entendido Usted?
Excuse me, but I didn't understand you.	Ud. dispense, pero no le he entendido.
It is not worth it.	No vale la pena.
You are very kind.	Ud. es muy amable.
It doesn't suit me (fit me, I don't like it).	No me queda bien.

INDEX

Note that in the index below, everything in and about Mexico City comes under that head, and this also applies to other principal cities. Where two or more towns have the same name, each is followed by its state abbreviation. When more than one page is listed, the chief mention or description of a town or place is set in bold-face numerals.

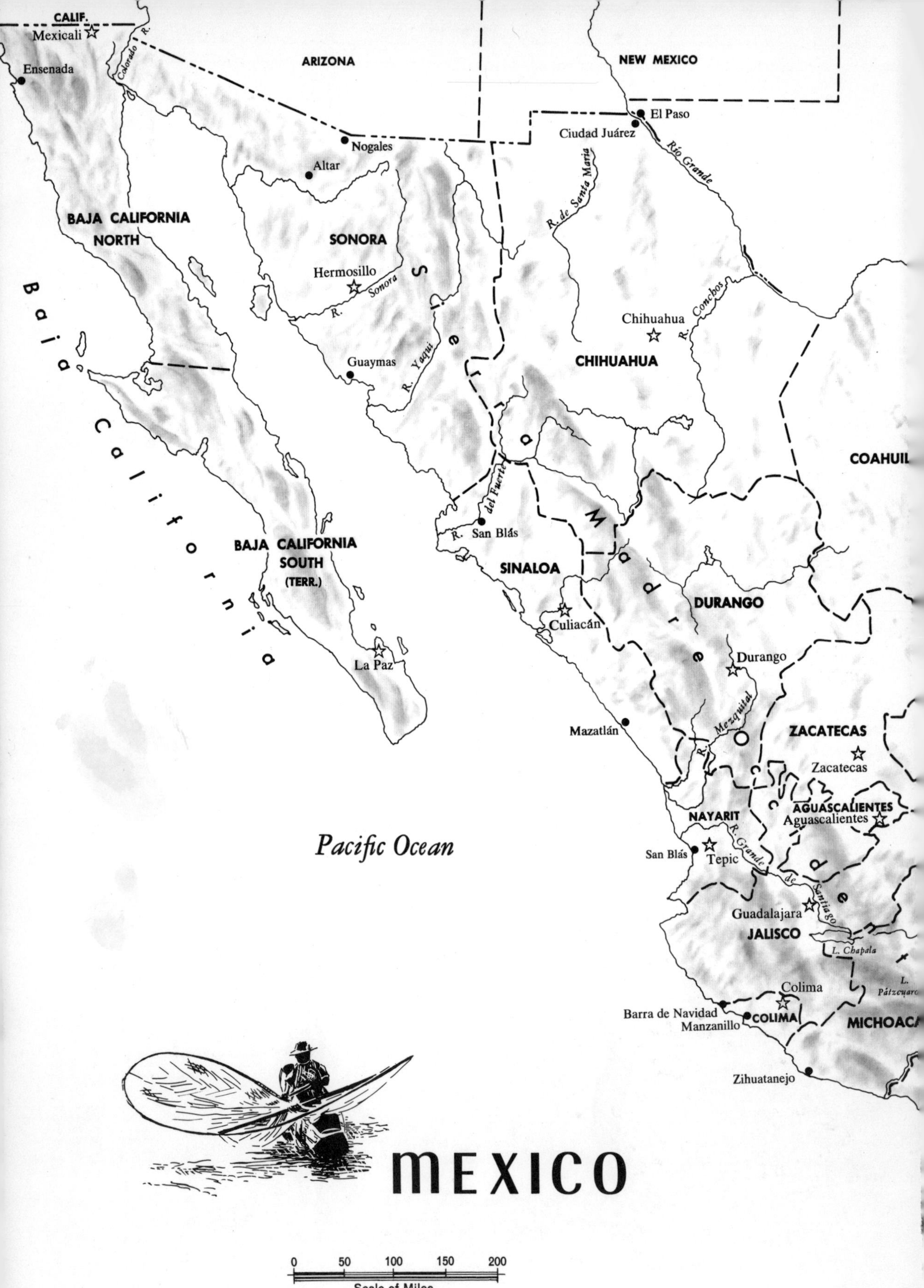

CALIF.
Mexicali
Ensenada
Colorado R.
ARIZONA
NEW MEXICO
El Paso
Ciudad Juárez
Río Grande
Nogales
Altar
R. de Santa Maria
BAJA CALIFORNIA
NORTH
SONORA
Hermosillo
R. Sonora
Baja California
Sierra Madre Occidental
R. Yaqui
Guaymas
Chihuahua
R. Conchos
CHIHUAHUA
COAHUIL
R. del Fuerte
R. San Blás
BAJA CALIFORNIA
SOUTH
(TERR.)
SINALOA
DURANGO
Culiacán
La Paz
Durango
R. Mezquital
Mazatlán
ZACATECAS
Zacatecas
AGUASCALIENTES
Aguascalientes
NAYARIT
R. Grande de Santiago
San Blás
Tepic
Pacific Ocean
Guadalajara
JALISCO
L. Chapala
L. Pátzcuaro
Colima
Barra de Navidad
Manzanillo
COLIMA
MICHOACA
Zihuatanejo
MEXICO
0
50
100
150
200
Scale of Miles